# ANNUAL REVIEW OF PSYCHOLOGY

# ANNUAL REVIEW OF PSYCHOLOGY

VOLUME 49, 1998

JANET T. SPENCE, *Editor*
University of Texas, Austin

JOHN M. DARLEY, *Associate Editor*
Princeton University

DONALD J. FOSS, *Associate Editor*
Florida State University

http://www.AnnualReviews.org     science@annurev.org     650-493-4400

ANNUAL REVIEWS     4139 EL CAMINO WAY     P.O. BOX 10139     PALO ALTO, CALIFORNIA 94303-0139

 ANNUAL REVIEWS
Palo Alto, California, USA

*International Standard Serial Number: 0066-4308*
*International Standard Book Number: 0-8243-0249-4*
*Library of Congress Catalog Card Number: 50-13143*

Annual Review and publication titles are registered trademarks of Annual Reviews.

The paper used in this publication meets the minimum requirements of American National Standards for Information Sciences—Permanence of Paper for Printed Library Materials, ANZI Z39.48-1992.

Annual Reviews and the Editors of its publications assume no responsibility for the statements expressed by the contributors to this *Annual Review.*

Typesetting by Ruth McCue Saavedra and the Annual Reviews Editorial Staff

PRINTED AND BOUND IN THE UNITED STATES OF AMERICA

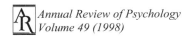

*Annual Review of Psychology*
*Volume 49 (1998)*

# CONTENTS

## INDEXES

SOME RELATED ARTICLES IN OTHER *ANNUAL REVIEWS*

From the *Annual Review of Anthropology,* Volume 26 (1997)

*Trafficking in Men: The Anthropology of Masculinity,*
Matthew C. Gutmann

From the *Annual Review of Neuroscience,* Volume 20 (1997)

*Sleep and Arousal: Thalamocortical Mechanisms,* David A. McCormick
and Thierry Bal
*Neurobiology of Speech Perception,* R. Holly Fitch, Steve Miller, and
Paula Tallal
*Genetics of Manic Depressive Illness,* Dean F. MacKinnon,
Kay Redfield Jamison, and J. Raymond DePaulo

From the *Annual Review of Public Health,* Volume 18 (1997)

*Searching for the Biological Pathways between Stress and Health,*
Shona Kelly, Clyde Hertzman, and Mark Daniels

From the *Annual Review of Sociology,* Volume 23 (1997)

*Culture and Cognition,* Paul DiMaggio
*Identity Construction: New Issues, New Directions,* Karen A. Cerulo

*Annu. Rev. Psychol. 1998. 49:1–24*

# SIBLING RELATIONSHIP QUALITY:
# Its Causes and Consequences

## Gene H. Brody

Department of Child and Family Development, Dawson Hall, University of Georgia, Athens, Georgia 30602; e-mail: gbrody@uga.cc.uga.edu

KEY WORDS: temperament, parent-child relationships, marital relationships, cognitive and psychosocial outcomes, differential treatment

## ABSTRACT

Current work on children's individual characteristics and family processes that contribute to variation in sibling relationship quality is reviewed. Findings from these studies are summarized in a heuristic model that specifies hypothesized links among family processes, intrapersonal characteristics, and variations in sibling relationship quality. The model is designed to provide researchers with a host of hypotheses to test and refine in future studies. The contributions that sibling relationships may make to cognitive and psychosocial development are then reviewed, with a suggestion that sibling relationships comprised of a balance of both prosocial and conflicted interactions create experiences that are most likely to nurture children's social, cognitive, and psychosocial development.

## CONTENTS

1

# INTRODUCTION

Research on siblings is almost as old as the science of psychology itself. The first studies were conducted over 100 years ago in the British laboratory of Charles Darwin's cousin, Sir Francis Galton, yet sibling research has just begun to address many issues that concern families. Earlier work focused on static variables such as the age spacing between siblings or the order of their birth, factors that proved to play a minor role in children's emotional and social development (Brody et al 1985, Buhrmester 1992, Dunn 1988, Minnett et al 1983, Teti et al 1989). In the past two decades, however, a growing interest in the family as an agent of change and the focus of preventative care has prompted researchers to investigate dynamic processes and problems in sibling relationships.

To parents and clinicians, and now, belatedly, to developmental researchers, the sibling relationship has great significance as a contributor to family harmony or disharmony and to the patterns that individual children's development takes within the family. Although in years past studies had identified sibling discord as one of the most common and persistent child-related problems that parents report (Clifford 1959, Kelly & Main 1979), few attempts had been made to understand why sibling conflict occurs. From a developmental perspective, this issue has special significance for several reasons. First, with an increasing number of parents employed full time, many siblings provide care for their younger brothers and sisters. Conflict in sibling relationships thus can make it less likely that younger siblings will receive prosocial and responsive care (McHale & Crouter 1996). Second, data suggest not only that the quality of the sibling relationship is stable from middle childhood into adolescence (Brody et al 1994b, Dunn 1996), but that rivalrous feelings originating between siblings in childhood persist well into adulthood and are associated with the closeness of adult sibling relationships (Ross & Milgram 1982). An understanding of the origins of sibling relationship quality is therefore important, given the degree to which siblings can serve as sources of mutual emotional support across the life span.

My goals in this chapter are (*a*) to review and synthesize the progress that has been made in identifying those characteristics of individual children and family processes that are linked with variations in sibling relationship quality, (*b*) to present a heuristic model of intrapersonal processes that mediate the links between family processes and variation in sibling relationship quality, and (*c*) to review critically the contributions of sibling relationships to different spheres of development.

## CONTRIBUTORS TO VARIATION IN SIBLING RELATIONSHIP QUALITY

The shift in focus from structural parameters to family processes in the study of sibling relationships can be partly attributed to the emergence of family systems theory as a guide for research (Minuchin 1988). According to this perspective, family members are part of an interactive, interdependent network in which behavior in one individual or subsystem affects the others. As applied to the study of sibling relationship quality, characteristics of individual family members or dynamics within family subsystems can contribute to siblings' attitudes toward and interactions with one another.

### *Contribution of Child Temperaments: Individual Temperaments and Sibling Relationship Quality*

Temperament refers to an individual's behavioral style as he or she relates to other persons and to the inanimate environment. It is generally considered to develop early in life; to persist, with some modification, across the life span; and to be at least partially rooted in the individual's genetic makeup (Buss & Plomin 1986, Lerner et al 1986, Matheny et al 1987). In the sibling relations studies reviewed below, the investigators have been particularly interested in children who display low persistence, high activity, and strong expression of emotions such as frustration and anger. These researchers hypothesized that such a temperament in any sibling would be associated with higher levels of conflict and lower levels of positivity in sibling relationships.

This hypothesis has received support from data indicating that temperament, measured using maternal reports, can contribute to sibling relationship quality from the relationship's beginning. Legg et al (1974), Thomas et al (1961), and Thomas & Chess (1977) reported that children with difficult, less adaptable temperaments displayed greater distress in response to the birth of a sibling than did easier, more adaptive children. Similarly, mothers participating in a study by Dunn et al (1981) reported that children who experienced more negative moods in general were more likely to withdraw and experience sleeping problems after the birth of a sibling than were children who scored below the median on negative mood. Children who were extremely emotionally intense and experienced frequent negative moods were "clingier" after the birth of a brother or sister than were children with easier temperaments. Children who were more withdrawn before the birth showed less positive interest in their new siblings than did more outgoing children.

Temperament continues to impact the sibling relationship as it develops. Brody et al (1996b) and Stocker et al (1989) found sibling temperaments to account for unique variance in explaining qualitative aspects of young children's sibling relationships, and Mash & Johnson (1983) found that children with highly active temperaments experienced four times as much sibling conflict than did less active children. Similarly, Brody et al (1987a,b) found that younger siblings directed more agonism toward highly active older siblings. They also found that, for girls, high activity, high emotional intensity, and low persistence were associated with greater sibling conflict; for boys, sibling conflict was predicted most reliably from these temperamental characteristics in younger brothers.

Although siblings share 50% of their genetic makeup, two children in the same family can have quite different personality characteristics and quite different temperaments (Plomin 1986, Rowe & Plomin 1981). Munn & Dunn (1989) conducted the first study directly addressing sibling temperament combinations. They computed absolute difference scores that reflected the degrees of similarity or difference in sibling temperament and found that preschool sibling dyads who were more temperamentally dissimilar experienced higher levels of conflict. Munn & Dunn concluded that the lack of fit between siblings with different temperaments put them at risk for conflict. Earlier, Brody et al (1987b) had developed an alternative hypothesis that Stoneman & Brody (1993) later tested in a study with school-aged children. Brody et al suggested that, when siblings' temperaments are dissimilar, positive temperamental characteristics in one sibling may function as a buffer to protect the sibling relationship from the detrimental effects of a difficult temperament in the other child. To test this hypothesis, Stoneman & Brody differentiated siblings with similarly placid temperaments from those whose temperaments were similarly high in activity and emotionality. Observational assessments revealed that the lowest levels of negativity and conflict occurred in sibling pairs in which both children were low in activity. Contrary to Munn & Dunn's similarity hypothesis, however, siblings who were both highly active experienced the most conflict. Contrary to the buffering hypothesis, sibling pairs in which the older child was highly active, but the younger child was not experienced high rates of negativity and conflict. The actual buffering component emerged only for highly active younger siblings with less active older siblings. Apparently the dominance of the older sibling during social exchanges creates an interactional context in which the older sibling's highly active temperament sets the tone for the interaction, overriding the calmer temperament of the younger brother or sister.

The aforementioned studies were conducted using contemporaneous research designs, in which assessments of child temperaments and sibling relationship quality were obtained at the same time. Brody et al (1994b) extended this work by obtaining temperament assessments during middle childhood and using them to forecast variations in sibling relationship quality four years later. Parents assessed their children's activity levels, emotional intensity, and ease of management, and siblings rated the positivity and negativity in their relationships. The children's temperament profiles were, in fact, linked with variations in both older and younger siblings' ratings of their relationships: Difficult temperament in the older sibling was linked with less positivity; in the younger sibling it was linked with more negativity.

These results are consistent with the presumption that temperamental difficulty has effects that, from earliest childhood, influence individual development and social relationships. Difficult temperament has been found to be detrimental to the development of self-regulation and prosocial orientations, both of which affect the quality of the sibling relationship. In their self-regulation model of temperament, however, Rothbart & Ahadi (1994) proposed that the expression of temperament is influenced over the course of development by the acquisition of more complex regulatory skills that develop over time as a function of maturation and experience. Thus, not all children with difficult temperaments necessarily continue to have conflicted sibling relationships. The ameliorative impact of other family relationships on children's difficult temperaments and their implications for sibling relationship quality will be discussed later.

## Contributions of Marital Processes and Parental Depression

Research has emphasized the interdependency among the marital relationship, the general emotional climate of the family, and sibling relationship quality. The link between marital quality and sibling relations is suggested by literature addressing children's responses to marital conflict, which has been conceptualized as an aversive event that creates distress in the child. Cummings's work (Cummings et al 1981, 1984) has demonstrated that expressions of unresolved anger are distressing to children who witness them. Whether assessed using parent diaries of children's reactions to parental conflict or laboratory analyses involving simulated fights between strangers (Cummings 1987), children as young as 12 months have been found to respond to episodes of anger that is not directed toward them with signs of distress, ranging from crying to an increase in aggression. Although many individual differences remain unexplained, both this series of studies and numerous field investigations (Emery 1982) indicate that anger directly causes negative emotional reactions in children, who often direct these affects toward others. Marital unhappiness, conflict, and less cohesive family emotional environments have been found to be associated with less positivity and more negativity in sibling relationships (Brody et al 1987b, 1992c, 1994a; Hetherington 1988; MacKinnon 1989). Although sibling relationships usually become more conflicted when children are exposed to bouts of anger (Cummings & Smith 1989, Hetherington 1988, MacKinnon 1989), some older siblings respond to anger among adults by increasing caregiving and prosocial behavior toward their younger brothers and sisters (Cummings & Smith 1989, Hetherington 1989, Jenkins et al 1989). Presumably this behavior is intended to buffer the younger children from the distress associated with adult conflict.

Researchers have also examined the contributions of parental negative affectivity, specifically depression and hostility, to variation in sibling relationship quality. Depressed and hostile parents have been found to be less involved with and affectionate toward their children, to feel more guilt and resentment, and to experience more general difficulty in managing and communicating with their children (Rutter 1990). Higher levels of parental negative affectivity have been found to be related to higher levels of negativity and lower levels of positivity in sibling relationships (Brody et al 1994a). The arousal generated by interacting with a depressed or hostile parent may disrupt or otherwise negatively affect children's capacities to regulate their emotions and behavior (Fabes & Eisenberg 1992), resulting in less supportive and more conflicted sibling interactions.

The effects of contextual variables such as marital conflict and parental negative affectivity on sibling relationships are mediated by their impact on parent-child relationships. The literature is consistent in demonstrating that the effects of marital processes and parental psychological adjustment on sibling relationships are mediated by the extent to which disruptions in these areas lead to hostile parenting. If parenting does not become hostile, marital distress and parental depression have no significant effect on sibling relationship quality (Brody et al 1994a,b, Hetherington 1988, MacKinnon 1989).

## Contributions of Parent-Child Relationships, Parental Differential Treatment, and Parental Conflict Management Strategies

Most research designed to account for variations in sibling relationship quality has concentrated on linkages with family processes. This focus is based on attachment theory (Sroufe & Fleeson 1986), which suggests that sibling relationships may be best understood as a function of the dynamic interplay between the current family relationship environment and each sibling's developmental history. Prior experiences in the family are not erased by current ones but are integrated into new relationship patterns and continue to influence the sibling relationship at subsequent points in time. Evidence consistent with this perspective indicates that knowledge of early family interactions improves one's ability to predict subsequent sibling relationship quality. In addition, longitudinal continuities or discontinuities in sibling relationships have been linked to changes in other family processes, particularly parent-child relationships (Brody et al 1994b, Dunn & Kendrick 1982, Stillwell & Dunn 1985, Volling & Belsky 1992).

Positive parent-child relationships are hypothesized to contribute to the development of prosocial orientations among siblings, in accordance with attachment (Sroufe & Fleeson 1986) and social learning (Parke et al 1988) theories. Attachment theorists propose that children develop internal representations of relationships from interactions with their primary caregivers, which they subsequently use in maintaining other relationships. Social learning theorists have shown that behavior patterns enacted during parent-child interactions are generalized to children's interactions with their siblings (Patterson 1984) and peers (Parke et al 1988). An impressive consensus of research findings (Brody et al 1986, 1987b, 1992a,c, 1994a,b, 1996b; Dunn & Kendrick 1982; Hetherington 1988; Howe 1986; Stewart et al 1987; Stocker et al 1989) indicates that higher levels of parent-child relationship positivity are linked with higher levels of positive affectivity and prosocial behavior in the sibling relationship. Similarly, negativity, intrusiveness, and overcontrol in the parent-child relationship are associated with aggressive, self-protective behavior in the sibling relationship.

Recently, researchers have sought to refine these associations by considering whether they are affected by children's temperaments, which, as previously noted, exert considerable influence on sibling relationships. Because child temperament is linked to parent-child relationships as well, it is possible that the associations between parent-child and sibling relationships diminish when variance from temperament assessments is taken into account. Brody and his colleagues (Brody et al 1994b, 1996b), however, found that both contemporaneous and longitudinal associations of mother-child and father-child relationships with sibling relationships remained robust when variance attributable to children's temperaments was removed.

Parents' differential treatment of siblings is also hypothesized to contribute to variations in sibling relationship quality. Discrepancies in parents' treatment of their children have been described in social learning (Bandura 1977), psychoanalytic (Freud 1949), self-esteem maintenance (Tesser 1980), and equity (Adams 1965, Walster et al 1973) theories, and are conjectured to create negativity in the sibling relationship by inducing feelings of rivalry and anger.

Data from several research programs support this hypothesis, revealing that sibling relationships are characterized by more negativity and less positivity when parents direct unequal amounts of intrusiveness, responsivity, positive affect, and negative affect toward their several children, as well as different amounts of control and discipline in response to similar child behaviors (Boer 1990; Brody et al 1987a, 1992a,b, 1994a,b; Bryant & Crockenberg 1980; Hetherington 1988; Koch 1960; McHale et al 1995; Stocker et al 1989; Volling & Belsky 1992).

Sensitive parenting, however, often requires that children in the same family be treated differently. Children of different ages require developmentally appropriate parenting, and children with different personalities and behavioral styles require parental responses suited to each child's inclinations. Differential treatment is hypothesized to compromise sibling relationships when children interpret their parents' differential behavior as an indication that their parents are less concerned about them or that they are less worthy of love (Kowal & Kramer 1997). Children are less likely to draw such conclusions when their relationships with their parents are attentive, responsive, and nurturing.

Differential treatment that forecasts compromised sibling relationships is often associated with marital difficulty. The emotional dysregulation that accompanies marital distress has been found to increase parents' differential treatment of their children, which in turn has been linked contemporaneously and longitudinally with elevated levels of sibling conflict (Brody et al 1992b, 1994b; McHale & Crouter 1996). Two hypotheses have been proposed to account for this link. The first posits that differential treatment of siblings may result from the formation of parent-child coalitions, which often arise in distressed families (Reiss 1993). The second proposes that parents' ability to regulate their emotions is compromised during periods of marital discord, altering family interaction patterns. During such periods parents may be less able to be vigilant in monitoring the ways in which they treat each of their children (Brody et al 1992b).

Parents' management of their children's disputes and quarrels is important in helping siblings to develop prosocial attitudes to guide their behavior toward one another. To date, research on this topic has been conducted primarily with preschool-aged siblings. Data from these studies indicate that parents intervene in their children's disputes, address issues that the children raise, take positions on those issues, and enforce rules for the children's treatment of one another. When parents do not intervene, older siblings are likely to dominate their younger siblings (Dunn & Munn 1986, 1987; Ross et al 1994). Mothers' discussions with siblings of preschool age about their younger siblings' needs and feelings have been found to be associated with sibling caregiving and friendliness. When mothers discussed these issues during routine daily activities, siblings engaged in friendlier and more sensitive interactions (Dunn et al 1991a,b; Howe & Ross 1990). Presumably, these naturally occurring conversations help children to develop empathic and perspective-taking competencies that enhance their sibling relationships.

Very little research addresses parents' management of disputes between siblings in middle childhood and adolescence. Although no studies have been conducted on parents' naturalistic responses to such conflicts, Christensen & Margolin (1988) and Ihinger (1975) have suggested that consistent enforcement of rules emphasizing norms of equity and fairness may help siblings in middle childhood and adolescence to develop mutual respect. Using a structured discussion task, Brody et al (1992c) examined the ways in which observed family interaction designed to resolve sibling problems predicted sibling conflict. Siblings in middle childhood whose mothers and fathers treated them impartially during the problem-solving discussions, and whose family interactions were harmonious even when discussing sibling problems, were more likely to develop less conflicted sibling relationships over a span of one year. Clearly, more research is needed to address the ways in which parents manage conflict in older sibling dyads and the impact of this socialization not only on the sibling relationship but also on each sibling's social and emotional development.

## Transactions Among Child Temperaments, Family Processes, and Sibling Relationship Quality

The research reviewed thus far examined the links of child temperament and family processes with variation in the quality of sibling relationships during childhood. From this review, one could be led to adopt a main effects model and conclude, for example, that sibling dyads that include a child with a difficult temperament will necessarily experience higher levels of conflict. The development of sibling relationships, however, defies such an easy explanation. Sibling relationships develop different qualities depending on the child-rearing contexts within which they are nested. In some families, the quality of parent-child relations will exacerbate siblings' risk for conflict, whereas in others the parent-child relationship will ameliorate this propensity. From this perspective, then, the quality of the sibling relationship is determined by no single factor. Rather, the fit between individual children's temperaments and the characteristics of the larger family context will influence their relationships with others in the family. The matches or mismatches that are created by the meshing of particular child characteristics with particular parent and family characteristics are significant. Approaches similar to this have been proposed by Sameroff & Chandler (1975), Thomas & Chess (1977), Lerner & Spanier (1978), and Werner & Smith (1992).

In families in which the quality of parent-child interactions is not determined primarily by the predispositions of children with difficult temperaments, parents may be able to smooth out the potential conflict-provoking effects of child temperament. A child with a difficult temperament who experiences affectively positive relationships with his or her parents will be likely to generalize positive interaction styles to the sibling relationship, develop prosocial orientations, and approach relationships expecting them to be supportive and responsive. Kochanska's (1993) research on child-rearing practices and internalization of compliance-related behaviors has heuristic value for this hypothesis. In a sample of young children with active-impulsive and emotionally intense temperaments, the types of disciplinary strategies that their mothers used (e.g. induction, power assertion) did not forecast subsequent internalization of behavioral prohibitions, but affectively warm mother-child relationships did. Such supportive parent-child relationships overrode the dispositions of children prone to noncompliance, resulting in internalization.

A study by Brody et al (1996b) supports this transactional hypothesis. They found evidence of moderating effects of mother-child and father-child relationship quality on the association between difficult child temperament and sibling relationships. A contemporaneous association emerged between parent-child and sibling relationship quality for older siblings with more difficult temperaments. When mothers and fathers were able to develop and maintain affectively positive relationships with temperamentally difficult older siblings, the parent-child relationship served as a protective factor to ameliorate the effect of difficult temperament on the sibling relationship. Further research is needed to determine whether the buffering effects of family relationship processes act upon interpersonal behavioral styles, mediators such as self-regulatory skills and prosocial orientations, or all of these.

## WHAT INTRAPERSONAL PROCESSES MEDIATE THE LINKS BETWEEN FAMILY PROCESSES AND SIBLING RELATIONSHIP QUALITY? A HEURISTIC MODEL

Parent-child relationship quality, differential treatment, and parental management of sibling conflict can be integrated into a theoretical framework for understanding variation in sibling relationship quality. According to this framework, presented in Figure 1, family processes (*left panel*), with which child temperaments continually interact, contribute to children's individual behavior patterns, skills involving emotion regulation and coping, attributions used in explaining sibling relationship events, and norms regarding aggression and fairness in sibling relationships (*middle panel*). The selection of these mediators for inclusion in the model was based on two criteria. First, each has been

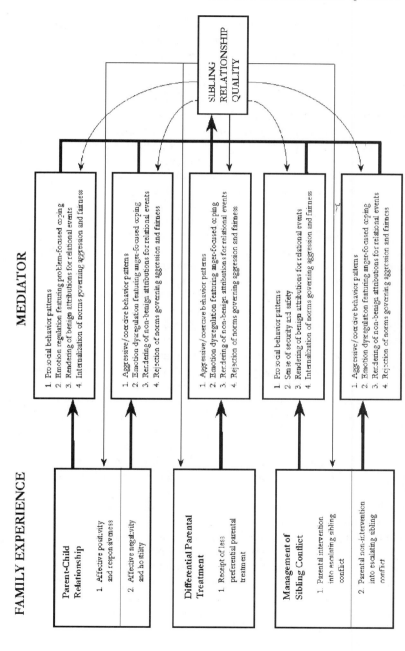

*Figure 1*   A heuristic model showing several proposed mediators between family experiences and sibling relationship quality.

shown to affect the quality of close personal relationships, and second, each has been linked both theoretically and empirically to family experiences. Events in the sibling relationship (*right panel*), in turn, feed back over time to influence parent-child relationships, differential treatment processes, and parental management of sibling conflict; they also feed back to influence the mediators.

The indirect link from parent-child relationship affectivity to sibling relationship quality via the proposed mediators may be theoretically explicable in terms of several mechanisms. Social cognitive theory (Bandura 1991) suggests that, as part of their affectively positive and responsive interactions with their children, parents demonstrate task-oriented problem-solving skills that children acquire through observation and modeling. This acquisition could occur directly during transactions between parent and child or indirectly as the child observes a parent interacting with a sibling or the other parent. Children's observation of supportive communications between family members can help them learn how to listen to siblings, to empathize with siblings' distress, and to engage in cooperative efforts to resolve disputes (Dubow & Tisak 1989, Fabes & Eisenberg 1992). To the extent that the children have repeated opportunities to see alternative solutions considered and problem-solving skills demonstrated, they may be more likely to approach sibling disputes expecting them to be solved through direct action and less likely to cope with problems through avoidance and anger.

Conversely, children whose relationships with their parents involve harsh parenting and unresolved anger are likely to develop behavioral styles, emotion regulation strategies, and cognitions that will feed sibling conflict. They are likely to approach sibling disputes with anger-focused coping strategies and aggressive, coercive behaviors. Each sibling is likely to render nonbenign attributions and to provoke the other to respond aggressively during objectively neutral encounters (Crick & Dodge 1994). Despite repeated parental pronouncements about the importance of not fighting and the sharing of resources, the children will reject those norms and continue a tradition of hostile responses, precipitating conflict and reciprocating hostility.

Receiving less preferential parental treatment is particularly significant to a child because of the potent implications it carries. Large discrepancies in the affective quality of the parent-child relationships that brothers and sisters experience are hypothesized to contribute to the children's development of behavior patterns and self-schemas that are incompatible with close, supportive sibling relationships. Children's recognition of the inequity in their relationships with their parents is hypothesized to occasion emotional dysregulation, leading to anger that is displaced onto the favored brother or sister. Repeated experiences of less preferential treatment are further hypothesized to influence the child's sense of self, leading the child to feel less worthy of love and contributing to the child's development of feelings of inferiority. Such feelings may decrease the likelihood that the less preferred sibling will enact prosocial behaviors during sibling interactions while increasing the likelihood that he or she will reject the parents' norms for sibling behavior.

Parental intervention in escalating conflict can reassure children that their parents are available to help and protect them when they are upset or in danger. This intervention can not only help children resolve their immediate conflict situations but also enhance overall parent-child attachment in ways that will benefit the sibling relationship in the long run. Attachment theory proposes that parents' appropriate responsiveness will increase the effectiveness of socialization processes, helping children to develop the ability to regulate their responses during times of emotional distress (Rothbart et al 1994) and enhancing their internalization of the parents' norms (Kochanska 1993).

Regarding children's enactment of prosocial or aggressive/coercive behavior patterns, Patterson (1984) has demonstrated that children in some families learn that certain prosocial behaviors, such as talking, laughing, or negotiating, are followed by the termination of conflict, whereas in other families children find that coercive behaviors such as yelling, fighting, and name-calling terminate conflict. This process is analogous to escape conditioning. When presented with the aversive stimulus of conflict with a parent or sibling, a child tries out different behaviors until he or she finds one that is successful in ending the conflict. The response that worked is strengthened, and the child becomes more likely to use that behavior on future occasions. The operation of these processes during parent-child interactions helps to determine whether a child will use prosocial or coercive behaviors during sibling interactions. Children whose family relational experiences train them to select coercive behaviors are doubly handicapped. Not only have they learned to be coercive, but they have not learned the prosocial skills required for supportive relationships with siblings or anyone else (Snyder & Patterson 1995).

The emotion regulation mediator, which involves problem- or anger-focused coping, is derived from attachment theory. An important proposition of attachment research is that caregiver responsiveness and sensitivity to a young child's affective signals provide an important context within which the child organizes affective experiences and regulates feelings of security (Sroufe & Fleeson 1986). Thus, if caregivers are available and responsive to the child's distress signals, the child learns to regulate distressed feelings by using strategies that involve seeking comfort and support. As children continue to develop throughout later childhood and adolescence, their expectation that the world will be responsive and supportive contributes to their ongoing development of active and problem-focused responses in coping with relational and daily-life stressors. In less optimal circumstances, caregivers may reject the child's attempts to gain comfort, be inconsistently available, or lack the knowledge and caregiving skills needed to comfort the child effectively. The child may come to associate instances of distress with negative outcomes and develop coping strategies in which anger is used as a self-protective mechanism. Eisenberg and her colleagues (Eisenberg et al 1994, Fabes & Eisenberg 1992) have demonstrated that children differ in the strategies they use in coping with anger, and that children's emotionality and emotion regulation skills are related to peer acceptance.

The attributions that siblings render to explain behavior occurring during sibling interactions will either escalate or de-escalate sibling conflict. Fincham's (1994) research on the role of attributional processes in marriage has particular relevance for understanding sibling relationships. According to Fincham's findings, conflicted siblings should be likely to locate the causes of negative events in their brothers or sisters, to consider the causes to be unchanging, to see the events as affecting many areas of their sibling relationships, to believe that the events reflect their siblings' negative intentions and selfish motives, and to blame their siblings for the events. Other empirical investigations give further support to this conjecture, indicating that similar attributional processes predict behavior in parent-child (Dix 1993), marital (Bradbury & Fincham 1992), and peer (Crick & Dodge 1994) interactions. Recent research on children's attributions for parental (Brody et al 1996a) and peer (Dodge 1993) behavior links the attributions to relational processes within the family. Communicative and responsive parent-child relationships are associated with the rendering of benign attributions for negative relational events with parents and ambiguous events with peers. Conversely, hostile parenting is linked with nonbenign attributions for such events.

The transmission of a set of norms governing sibling behavior is an important goal of the parenting process. When that process functions effectively, parents' norms for sibling behavior contribute to children's development of internalized controls that lead them not only to comply with their parents' rules and standards in the parents' presence but also to use those standards to guide their conduct in the absence of parental surveillance or constraints. Most parents want their children to settle disputes without resorting to physical and verbal aggression, to respect each other's property rights, to share resources, and to provide comfort when needed (Ross et al 1994), whether the parents are present or not. Although previous research has not addressed the internalization of sibling relationship norms specifically, relevant hypotheses can be derived from the broader internalization literature. Those processes that enhance children's sense of willing, rather than externally pressured, observance of particular norms will be more likely to foster internalization. Children with this sense of chosen compliance consider the norms to be their own and follow them even in the absence of authority figures (Brody & Shaffer 1982, Kochanska 1993). Parental use of unnecessarily power-oriented control is detrimental to norm internalization. Children who experience such control perceive parental norms to be forced upon them and attribute their behavior to external sources, resulting in rejection of the norms.

## SIBLINGS' CONTRIBUTIONS TO COGNITIVE AND PSYCHOSOCIAL OUTCOMES

At the outset of this discussion of the contributions that siblings make to various cognitive and psychosocial outcomes, a cautionary note is in order about attributing causation to sibling influences, which are only one of a myriad of ongoing contextual influences that children encounter. The linkages between sibling interactions and the behaviors attributed to those interactions are difficult to evaluate when the most critical variables—the actual attitudes, values, social behavior, and cognitive schemas that the siblings exemplify or encourage—are not directly and intensively assessed. The identification of specific contributions that sibling relationships make to child behavior is made even more difficult when similar behavior is displayed and sanctioned by various socializing agents in a child's life. Under these circumstances there is no reliable means of determining which agent originally nurtured a given competence.

In addition, very little of the research concerning sibling influences on developmental outcomes gives any attention to sibling relationship quality, even though it may be a significant moderator of the links between sibling relationship events and changes in one or both siblings as a result of those experiences. (For a notable exception, see Youngblade & Dunn 1995.) Siblings whose relationships are reasonably positive should be more likely than cold, aloof siblings to interact with one another, thus experiencing more opportunities to observe and learn from each other. Because influence processes are bidirectional, siblings who share values and emulate one another may increase their interpersonal contact and experience growing positivity in their interactions. If the sibling relationship, however, is characterized by high levels of rancor, or if one sibling observes the other receiving negative sanctions from parents and other social agents, modeled behavior will be less likely to be adopted.

### Sibling Contributions to Conceptual and Semantic Development

Siblings gain opportunities to expand their conceptual and semantic capabilities during naturally occurring interactions with one another. Bronfenbrenner

(1979) has argued that development is facilitated through interactions with persons who occupy a variety of roles. In learning and practicing a role, a child learns not only his or her own role, but also the complementary ones. Naturalistic observations of sibling interactions indicate that siblings enact asymmetrical, complementary roles with one another. Older siblings act as teachers, managers, and helpers when playing with their younger brothers and sisters, and the younger siblings assume the corresponding learner, managee, and helpee roles (Abramovitch et al 1986; Azmitia & Hesser 1993; Brody et al 1982, 1985; Dunn & Kendrick 1982). Although the potential cognitive benefits of role asymmetry have received little empirical attention thus far, two studies by Smith (1990, 1993) offer some support for the hypothesized dynamic. Seventh- to ninth-grade students who reported that they spent a small amount of time teaching their younger siblings earned higher reading and language achievement scores than did classmates who also had younger siblings but did not teach them at all. In a follow-up study conducted two years later, unique effects of older sibling teaching on overall achievement emerged.

Researchers have also considered sibling influences using Vygotsky's (1962) scaffolding theory. From this perspective, social agents with more highly developed cognitive skills structure and guide children's learning by providing them with a framework within which to practice more sophisticated reasoning. The literature indicates that older siblings in middle childhood can effectively assume this function in teaching their younger siblings (Cicirelli 1972); however, Perez-Granados & Callanan (1997) found that mothers were more proficient than early school-aged older siblings in imparting conceptual information to preschool-aged younger siblings. This difference has been linked to mothers' greater concern about the learning process compared to older siblings' greater concern about the learning product. Such findings suggest that, although older siblings are able to help their younger siblings go beyond the younger children's current states of conceptual knowledge, the older siblings' approach to the teaching situation differs from that used by adults in ways that make the older siblings less effective teachers than their parents.

Research on older siblings' contributions to language development in general, and semantic development in particular, has been sparse, but that which exists indicates that older siblings contribute to communicative development (Dunn & Shatz 1989, Hoff-Ginsberg & Krueger 1991, Tomasello et al 1990). As was the case for conceptual knowledge, however, older siblings were found to be less skilled than parents in adjusting the pragmatic aspects of their language to their younger siblings' abilities. During semistructured observations, preschool-aged older siblings emitted fewer utterances, asked fewer questions, made fewer references to objects, engaged in less joint attention, gave fewer on-topic responses, and responded to their infant siblings less frequently than did their mothers (Tomasello et al 1990). Future research would benefit from intensive analyses of the language learning opportunities that older siblings provide in daily interactions at home and their links with younger siblings' acquisition of word meanings.

## Contributions of Sibling Relationships to Psychosocial Competence

Chronic conflict between siblings has generally been conceptualized as a negative influence on psychosocial competence among children and adolescents, a view that is to some extent justifiable. The cooperative solution of sibling conflict and a general sense of good will between siblings certainly can enhance children's adjustment. Both family (Grotevant & Cooper 1986) and developmental (e.g. Erikson 1968) theorists, however, have suggested that conflict is not necessarily detrimental. Conflict can provide an opportunity for siblings to vent their emotions, express their feelings, and practice open communication. The family process literature is replete with evidence indicating that individual child and adolescent development is enhanced and family relationships are more supportive when conflict is managed in a way that allows mutual self-assertion, discussion, and compromise (Grotevant & Cooper 1986, Hauser et al 1984). Both conflict and supportiveness in sibling interactions have been linked to children's development of social-cognitive skills such as affective perspective-taking and consideration of other people's feelings and beliefs (Brown & Dunn 1992; Dunn et al 1991a,b; Howe 1991; Howe & Ross 1990; Youngblade & Dunn 1995). Howe & Ross (1990) found that sibling interactions that included both negative conflictual exchanges and positive discussion of feelings were also linked positively with caregiving during early childhood. These findings suggest that conflict and support are not simply the opposite ends of a continuum but can coexist to give children a variety of experiences in learning to deal with others. Perhaps, then, a balance of support and conflict in the sibling relationship may exert a positive effect in promoting psychosocial competence. This balance can provide a unique opportunity for children to develop social-cognitive and behavioral competencies that are linked to managing conflict and anger on the one hand and providing support and nurturance on the other.

This balance of conflict and support in sibling relationships has been found to be related to children's peer relationships and school adjustment. Hetherington (1988) found that brothers whose relationships included relatively high levels of both aggression and warmth were rated by their teachers as having more positive peer relationships and fewer externalizing problems than were children whose sibling relationships were characterized by high conflict and low support. In a more recent study (Stormshak et al 1996), children with behavior problems were assigned to one of three groups on the basis of the quality of their sibling relationships: conflictual (high conflict, low warmth), involved (moderate conflict, moderate warmth), and supportive (low conflict, high warmth). Teachers' assessments of the children's social adjustment at school indicated that those who experienced involved sibling relationships displayed greater self-control and social competence than did children with conflictual sibling relationships. Children in the conflictual group also received less favorable ratings than children in the other groups on peer sociometric like-least assessments. These results appear to support the balance hypothesis by suggesting that even aggressive children can receive support from their siblings, and that this may contribute to the development of prosocial cognitions and skills that promote relatively competent peer relations even among children with behavior problems.

The two studies described above are the only ones conducted to date in which sibling relationships have been conceptualized as opportunities to develop both prosocial skills and conflict management strategies that generalize to relationships with age-mates outside the home. In other studies, linear models have been used to examine links from positivity and negativity in the sibling relationship to measures of friendship quality and popularity. These studies have yielded inconsistent results. Some researchers found a positive association between sibling relationship and best friendship quality (McCoy et al 1994, Vandell & Wilson 1987), whereas others found a negative association (East & Rook 1992, Stocker & Dunn 1990) and still others obtained conflicting or nonsignificant results (Abramovitch et al 1986, Berndt & Bulleit 1985). A different pattern may have emerged had the relative balance between prosocial and conflicted attributes of sibling relationships been linked to the friendship parameters rather than the absolute amounts of each separate sibling relationship quality. The interpretation that Stocker & Dunn (1990) rendered upon finding sibling and peer relationship quality to be negatively associated supports this suggestion. They proposed that resolving negative sibling interactions facilitated children's development of conflict-management skills that enabled them to maintain close friendships. Defining sibling relationship quality as a balance of prosocial and conflict training opportunities may yield clearer links between sibling and peer relationships.

Sibling relationships appear to be associated with compromised psychosocial functioning when the balance of conflict and support is heavily weighted toward conflict. Chronically high sibling conflict serves as a training ground for the development and maintenance of aggressive behavior (Bank et al 1996) and is linked to academic difficulty and poor peer relations at school (Berndt & Bulleit 1985, Loeber & Tengs 1986, Patterson 1982). Practicing aggressive behaviors with siblings during childhood not only increases the risk of aggression in other childhood contexts but also leaves adolescent and young adult siblings with a sense of inadequacy, incompetence, and hostility (Bank et al 1996, Dunn et al 1994). Obviously, these associations do not develop in isolation from other contextual sources of stress, and caution is warranted in attributing causality to the sibling relationship.

Sibling relationships are rarely characterized by very high levels of support along with low levels of rivalry and aggression. Hetherington (1988), however, reported that the combination occurred in divorced and remarried families in which adult support was largely unavailable. The children in these families were nurturant and empathic with one another but were mainly unconcerned about peers' and adults' feelings; they also reported elevated levels of internalizing symptoms. These siblings were enmeshed and defensively reliant on their relationships with one another. These findings, however, do not mean that all unusually close and supportive sibling relationships are associated with psychosocial maladaptation. Siblings in close but nonenmeshed relationships, particularly younger siblings, have identified their sibling relationships as important sources of emotional and instrumental support during times of stress and family transitions (Bryant 1992, Dunn 1996, Jenkins 1992).

## CONCLUSION

Sibling relationships are, in and of themselves, important as children interact with one another and influence the social and emotional context in which they grow and develop. The psychosocial skills attained through sibling interactions are also used throughout life in a wide variety of other social relationships. The study of sibling relationships can also serve as a window through which we can look to understand general family processes and child psychological functioning. Family processes that ameliorate the risk that difficult temperaments pose for sibling relationships probably also reduce risk for the development of conduct disorders and internalizing problems. As our knowledge base concerning the transactions between child vulnerabilities and family processes that nurture sibling relationships is broadened, we are also likely to expand our understanding of the transactions that create positive developmental trajectories for vulnerable children and adolescents.

### ACKNOWLEDGMENTS

Support for the preparation of this review was provided by the following grants: #30588 from the National Institute of Child Health and Human Development, #09224 from the National Institute on Alcohol Abuse and Alcoholism.

Visit the *Annual Reviews home page* at
http://www.AnnualReviews.org.

## Literature Cited

Abramovitch R, Corter C, Pepler D, Stanhope L. 1986. Sibling and peer interaction: a final follow-up and a comparison. *Child Dev.* 57:217–29

Adams JS. 1965. Inequity in social exchange. In *Advances in Experimental and Social Psychology,* ed. L Berkowitz, 1:149–75. New York: Academic

Azmitia M, Hesser J. 1993. Why siblings are important agents of cognitive development: a comparison of siblings and peers. *Child Dev.* 64:430–44

Bandura A. 1977. Self-efficacy: toward a unifying theory of behavioral change. *Psychol. Rev.* 84:191–215

Bandura A. 1991. Self-regulation of motivation through anticipatory and self-regulatory mechanisms. In *Perspectives on Motivation: Nebraska Symposium on Motivation,* ed. RA Dinstbier, 38:69–164. Lincoln: Univ. Nebr. Press

Bank L, Patterson GR, Reid JB. 1996. Negative sibling interaction patterns as predictors of later adjustment problems in adolescent and young adult males. See Brody 1996, pp. 197–229

Berndt TJ, Bulleit TN. 1985. Effects of sibling relationships on preschoolers' behavior at home and at school. *Dev. Psychol.* 21:761–67

Boer F. 1990. *Sibling Relationships in Middle Childhood.* Leiden: DSWO Univ. Leiden Press

Boer F, Dunn J, eds. 1992. *Children's Sibling Relationships: Developmental and Clinical Issues.* Hillsdale, NJ: Erlbaum

Bradbury TN, Fincham FD. 1992. Attributions and behavior in marital interaction. *J. Pers. Soc. Psychol.* 63:613–28

Brody GH, ed. 1996. *Sibling Relationships: Their Causes and Consequences.* Norwood, NJ: Ablex

Brody GH, Arias I, Fincham FD. 1996a. Linking marital and child attributions to family processes and parent-child relationships. *J. Fam. Psychol.* 10:408–21

Brody GH, Shaffer DR. 1982. Contributions of parents and peers to children's moral socialization. *Dev. Rev.* 2:31–75

Brody GH, Stoneman Z, Burke M. 1987a. Child temperaments, maternal differential behavior, and sibling relationships. *Dev. Psychol.* 23:354–62

Brody GH, Stoneman Z, Burke M. 1987b. Family system and individual child correlates of sibling behavior. *Am. J. Orthopsychiatry* 57:561–69

Brody GH, Stoneman Z, Gauger K. 1996b. Parent-child relationships, family problem-solving behavior, and sibling relationship quality: the moderating role of sibling temperaments. *Child Dev.* 67:1289–1300

Brody GH, Stoneman Z, MacKinnon C. 1982. Role asymmetries in interactions between school-aged children, their younger siblings, and their friends. *Child Dev.* 53:1364–70

Brody GH, Stoneman Z, MacKinnon C. 1986. Contributions of maternal child-rearing practices and play contexts to sibling interactions. *J. Appl. Dev. Psychol.* 7:225–36

Brody GH, Stoneman Z, MacKinnon CE, MacKinnon R. 1985. Role relationships and behavior among preschool-aged and school-aged sibling pairs. *Dev. Psychol.* 21:124–29

Brody GH, Stoneman Z, McCoy JK. 1992a. Associations of maternal and paternal direct and differential behavior with sibling relationships: contemporaneous and longitudinal analyses. *Child Dev.* 63:82–92

Brody GH, Stoneman Z, McCoy JK. 1992b. Parental differential treatment of siblings and sibling differences in negative emotionality. *J. Marriage Fam.* 54:643–51

Brody GH, Stoneman Z, McCoy JK. 1994a. Contributions of family relationships and child temperaments to longitudinal variations in sibling relationship quality and sibling relationship styles. *J. Fam. Psychol.* 8:274–86

Brody GH, Stoneman Z, McCoy JK. 1994b. Forecasting sibling relationships in early adolescence from child temperaments and family processes in middle childhood. *Child Dev.* 65:771–84

Brody GH, Stoneman Z, McCoy JK, Forehand R. 1992c. Contemporaneous and longitudinal associations of sibling conflict with family relationship assessments and family discussions about sibling problems. *Child Dev.* 63:391–400

Bronfenbrenner U. 1979. *The Ecology of Human Development.* Cambridge, MA: Harvard Univ. Press

Brown JR, Dunn J. 1992. Talk with your mother or your sibling? Developmental changes in early family conversations about feelings. *Child Dev.* 63:336–49

Bryant B. 1992. Sibling caretaking: providing emotional support during middle childhood. See Boer & Dunn 1992, pp. 55–70

Bryant BK, Crockenberg SB. 1980. Correlates and dimensions of prosocial behavior: a study of female siblings with their mothers. *Child Dev.* 51:529–44

Buhrmester D. 1992. The developmental courses of sibling and peer relationships. See Boer & Dunn 1992, pp. 19–40

Buss A, Plomin R. 1986. The EAS approach to temperament. In *The Study of Temperament: Changes, Continuities, and Challenges,* ed. R Plomin, J Dunn, pp. 67–79. Hillsdale, NJ: Erlbaum

Christensen A, Margolin G. 1988. Conflict and alliance in distressed and nondistressed families. See Hinde & Stevenson-Hinde 1988, pp. 263–82

Cicirelli VG. 1972. The effect of sibling relationships on concept learning of young children taught by child teachers. *Child Dev.* 43:282–87

Clifford E. 1959. Discipline in the home: a controlled observational study of parental practices. *J. Genet. Psychol.* 95:45–82

Crick NR, Dodge KA. 1994. A review and reformulation of social information-processing mechanisms in children's social adjustment. *Psychol. Bull.* 115: 74–101

Cummings EM. 1987. Coping with background anger in early childhood. *Child Dev.* 58:976–84

Cummings EM, Smith D. 1989. The impact of anger between adults on siblings' emotions and social behavior. *J. Child Psychol. Psychiatry* 34:1425–33

Cummings EM, Zahn-Waxler C, Radke-Yarrow M. 1981. Young children's responses to expressions of anger and affection by others in the family. *Child Dev.* 52:1274–82

Cummings EM, Zahn-Waxler C, Radke-Yarrow M. 1984. Developmental changes in children's reactions to anger in the home. *J. Child Psychol. Psychiatry* 25: 63–74

Dix T. 1993. Attributing disposition to children: an interactional analysis of attribution and socialization. *Pers. Soc. Psychol. Bull.* 19:633–43

Dodge KA. 1993. Social-cognitive mechanisms in the development of conduct disorder and depression. *Annu. Rev. Psychol.* 44:559–84

Dubow EF, Tisak J. 1989. The relation between stressful life events and adjustment in elementary school children: the role of social support and problem-solving skills. *Child Dev.* 60:1412–20

Dunn J. 1988. Connections between relationships: implications of research on mothers and siblings. See Hinde & Stevenson-Hinde 1988, pp. 168–80

Dunn J. 1996. Brothers and sisters in middle childhood and early adolescence: continuity and change in individual differences. See Brody 1996, pp. 31–46

Dunn J, Brown J, Beardsall L. 1991a. Family talk about feeling states and children's later understanding of others' emotions. *Dev. Psychol.* 27:448–55

Dunn J, Brown J, Slomkowski C, Tesla C, Youngblade L. 1991b. Young children's understanding of other people's feelings and beliefs: individual differences and their antecedents. *Child Dev.* 62:1352–66

Dunn J, Kendrick C. 1982. *Siblings: Love, Envy, and Understanding.* Cambridge, MA: Harvard Univ. Press

Dunn J, Kendrick C, MacNamee R. 1981. The reaction of first born children to the birth of a sibling: mothers' reports. *J. Child Psychol. Psychiatry* 22:1–18

Dunn J, Munn P. 1986. Sibling quarrels and maternal intervention: individual differences in understanding and aggression. *J. Child Psychol. Psychiatry* 27:583–95

Dunn J, Munn P. 1987. Development of justification in disputes with mother and sibling. *Dev. Psychol.* 23:791–98

Dunn J, Shatz M. 1989. Becoming a conversationalist despite (or because of) having an older sibling. *Child Dev.* 60:399–410

Dunn J, Slomkowski C, Beardsall L, Rende R. 1994. Adjustment in middle childhood and early adolescence: links with earlier and contemporary sibling relationships. *J. Child Psychol. Psychiatry* 35: 491–504

East PL, Rook KS. 1992. Compensatory patterns of support among children's peer relationships: a test using school friends, nonschool friends, and siblings. *Dev. Psychol.* 28:163–72

Eisenberg N, Fabes RA, Nyman M, Bernzweig J, Pinuelas A. 1994. The relations of emotionality and regulation to children's anger-related reactions. *Child Dev.* 65: 109–28

Emery RE. 1982. Interparental conflict and the

children of discord and divorce. *Psychol. Bull.* 92:310–30

Erikson EH. 1968. *Identity: Youth and Crisis.* New York: Norton

Fabes RA, Eisenberg N. 1992. Young children's coping with interpersonal anger. *Child Dev.* 63:116–28

Fincham FD. 1994. Cognition in marriage: current status and future challenges. *Appl. Prevent. Psychol.* 3:185–98

Freud S. 1949. *An Outline of Psychoanalysis.* New York: Norton

Grotevant HD, Cooper CR. 1986. Individuation in family relationships: a perspective on individual differences in the development of identity and role-taking skill in adolescence. *Hum. Dev.* 29:82–100

Hauser ST, Powers S, Noam G, Jacobson A, Weiss B, Follansbee D. 1984. Familial contexts of adolescent ego development. *Child Dev.* 55:195–213

Hetherington EM. 1988. Parents, children, and siblings six years after divorce. See Hinde & Stevenson-Hinde 1988, pp. 311–31

Hetherington EM. 1989. Coping with family transitions: winners, losers, and survivors. *Child Dev.* 60:1–14

Hinde RA, Stevenson-Hinde J, eds. 1988. *Relationships Within Families: Mutual Influences.* Oxford: Clarendon

Hoff-Ginsberg E, Krueger W. 1991. Older siblings as conversational partners. *Merrill-Palmer Q.* 37:465–81

Howe N. 1986. *Socialization, social cognitive factors, and the development of the sibling relationship.* PhD thesis. Univ. Waterloo, Ontario

Howe N. 1991. Sibling-directed internal state language, perspective taking, and affective behavior. *Child Dev.* 62:1503–12

Howe N, Ross HS. 1990. Socialization, perspective-taking, and the sibling relationship. *Dev. Psychol.* 26:160–65

Ihinger M. 1975. The referee role and norms of equity: a contribution toward a theory of sibling conflict. *J. Marriage Fam.* 37: 515–24

Jenkins J. 1992. Sibling relationships in disharmonious homes: potential difficulties and protective effects. See Boer & Dunn 1992, pp. 125–38

Jenkins MJ, Smith MA, Graham PJ. 1989. Coping with parental quarrels. *J. Am. Acad. Child Adolesc. Psychiatry* 28: 182–89

Kelly FD, Main FO. 1979. Sibling conflict in a single-parent family: an empirical case study. *Am. J. Fam. Ther.* 7:39–47

Koch HL. 1960. *The relation of certain formal attributes of siblings to their attitudes held towards each other and towards their parents. Monogr. Soc. Res. Child Dev.* 25(4)

Kochanska G. 1993. Toward a synthesis of parental socialization and child temperament in early development of conscience. *Child Dev.* 64:325–47

Kowal A, Kramer L. 1997. Children's understanding of parental differential treatment. *Child Dev.* 68:113–26

Legg C, Sherrick I, Wadland W. 1974. Reactions of preschool children to the birth of a sibling. *Child Psychiatry Hum. Dev.* 5: 3–39

Lerner RM, Lerner JV, Windle M, Hooker K, Lenerz K, East PL. 1986. Children and adolescents in their contexts: test of a goodness of fit model. In *The Study of Temperament: Changes, Continuities, and Challenges,* ed. R Plomin, J Dunn, pp. 99–114. Hillsdale, NJ: Erlbaum

Lerner RM, Spanier GB. 1978. *Child Influences on Marital and Family Interactions: A Life-Span Perspective.* New York: Academic

Loeber R, Tengs T. 1986. The analysis of coercive chains between children, mothers, and siblings. *J. Fam. Violence* 1:51–70

MacKinnon CE. 1989. An observational investigation of sibling interactions in married and divorced families. *Dev. Psychol.* 25:36–44

Mash EJ, Johnson C. 1983. Sibling interactions of hyperactive and normal children and their relationship to reports of maternal stress and self-esteem. *J. Clin. Child Psychol.* 12:91–99

Matheny AP, Wilson RS, Thoben AS. 1987. Home and mother: relations with infant temperament. *Dev. Psychol.* 23:323–31

McCoy JK, Brody GH, Stoneman Z. 1994. Longitudinal analysis of sibling relationships as mediators of the link between family processes and youths' best friendships. *Fam. Relat.* 43:400–8

McHale SM, Crouter AC. 1996. The family contexts of children's sibling relationships. See Brody 1996, pp. 173–96

McHale SM, Crouter AC, McGuire SA, Updegraff KA. 1995. Congruence between mothers' and fathers' differential treatment of siblings: links with family relations and children's well-being. *Child Dev.* 66:116–28

Minnett AM, Vandell DL, Santrock JW. 1983. The effects of sibling status on sibling interaction: influence of birth order, age spacing, sex of child, and sex of sibling. *Child Dev.* 54:1064–72

Minuchin P. 1988. Relationships within the family: a systems perspective on development. See Hinde & Stevenson-Hinde 1988, pp. 7–26

Munn P, Dunn J. 1989. Temperament and the developing relationship between siblings. *Int. J. Behav. Dev.* 12:433–51

Parke RD, MacDonald KD, Beitel A, Bhavnagri N. 1988. The role of the family in the development of peer relationships. In *Social Learning and Systems Approaches to Marriage and the Family,* ed. RD Peters, RJ McMahon, pp. 17–44. New York: Bruner-Mazel

Patterson GR. 1982. *Coercive Family Process.* Eugene, OR: Castalia

Patterson GR. 1984. A microsocial process: a view from the boundary. In *Boundary Areas in Psychology: Social and Developmental Psychology,* ed. JC Masters, KL Yarkin, pp. 43–66. New York: Academic

Perez-Granados DR, Callanan MA. 1997. Conversations with mothers and siblings: young children's semantic and conceptual development. *Dev. Psychol.* 33:120–34

Plomin R. 1986. *Development, Genetics, and Psychology.* Hillsdale, NJ: Erlbaum

Reiss D. 1993. Genes and the environment: siblings and synthesis. In *Nature, Nurture, and Psychology,* ed. R Plomin, GE McClearn, pp. 417–32. Washington, DC: Am. Psychol. Assoc.

Ross HG, Milgram J. 1982. Important variables in adult sibling relationships: a qualitative study. In *Sibling Relationships: Their Nature and Significance Over the Lifespan,* ed. ME Lamb, B Sutton-Smith, pp. 225–47. Hillsdale, NJ: Erlbaum

Ross HS, Filyer RE, Lollis SP, Perlman M, Martin JL. 1994. Administering justice in the family. *J. Fam. Psychol.* 8:254–73

Rothbart M, Ahadi SA. 1994. Temperament and the development of personality. *J. Abnorm. Psychol.* 103:55–66

Rothbart MK, Derryberry D, Posner MI. 1994. A psychobiological approach to the development of temperament. In *Temperament: Individual Differences at the Interface of Biology and Behavior,* ed. JE Bates, TD Wachs, pp. 83–116. Washington, DC: Am. Psychol. Assoc.

Rowe DC, Plomin R. 1981. The importance of nonshared environmental influences in behavior development. *Dev. Psychol.* 17: 517–31

Rutter M. 1990. Commentary: some focus and process considerations regarding effects of depression on children. *Dev. Psychol.* 26: 60–67

Sameroff AJ, Chandler MJ. 1975. Reproductive risk and the continuum of caretaking casualty. In *Review of Child Development Research,* ed. FD Horowitz, 4:98–150. Chicago: Univ. Chicago Press

Smith TE. 1990. Academic achievement and teaching younger siblings. *Soc. Psychol. Q.* 53:352–63

Smith TE. 1993. Growth in academic achievement and teaching younger siblings. *Soc. Psychol. Q.* 56:77–85

Snyder JJ, Patterson GR. 1995. Individual differences in social aggression: a test of a reinforcement model of socialization in the natural environment. *Behav. Ther.* 26: 371–91

Sroufe LA, Fleeson J. 1986. Attachment and the construction of relationships. In *Relationships and Development,* ed. Z Rubin, pp. 51–71. New York: Cambridge Univ. Press

Stewart RB, Mobley LA, Van Tuyl SS, Salvador MA. 1987. The firstborn's adjustment to the birth of a sibling: a longitudinal assessment. *Child Dev.* 58:341–55

Stillwell R, Dunn J. 1985. Continuities in sibling relationships: patterns of aggression and friendliness. *J. Child Psychol. Psychiatry* 26:627–37

Stocker C, Dunn J. 1990. Sibling relationships in childhood: links with friendships and peer relationships. *J. Appl. Dev. Psychol.* 8:227–44

Stocker C, Dunn J, Plomin R. 1989. Sibling relationships: links with child temperament, maternal behavior, and family structure. *Child Dev.* 60:715–27

Stoneman Z, Brody GH. 1993. Sibling temperaments, conflict, warmth, and role asymmetry. *Child Dev.* 64:1786–800

Stormshak EA, Bellanti C, Bierman KL. 1996. The quality of sibling relationships and the development of social competence and behavioral control in aggressive children. *Dev. Psychol.* 32:79–89

Tesser A. 1980. Self-esteem maintenance in family dynamics. *J. Pers. Soc. Psychol.* 39:77–91

Teti DM, Gibbs ED, Bond LA. 1989. Sibling interaction, birth spacing, and intellectual development. In *Sibling Relationships Across Cultures,* ed. P Zuckow, pp. 117–39. New York: Springer-Verlag

Thomas A, Birch HG, Chess S, Robbins A. 1961. Individuality in responses of children to similar environmental situations. *Am. J. Psychiatry* 117:798–803

Thomas A, Chess S. 1977. *Temperament and Development.* New York: Brunner-Mazel

Tomasello M, Conti-Ramsden G, Ewert B. 1990. Young children's conversations with their mothers and fathers: differences in breakdown and repair. *J. Child Lang.* 17:115–30

Vandell DL, Wilson KS. 1987. Infants' interactions with mother, sibling, and peer: contrasts and relations between interaction systems. *Child Dev.* 58:176–86

Volling BL, Belsky J. 1992. The contribution of mother-child and father-child relationships to the quality of sibling interaction: a longitudinal study. *Child Dev.* 63:1209–22

Vygotsky LS. 1962. *Thought and Language.* Cambridge, MA: MIT Press

Walster E, Bercheid E, Walster GW. 1973. New directions in equity research. *J. Pers. Soc. Psychol.* 25:151–76

Werner EE, Smith RS. 1992. *Overcoming the Odds: High Risk Children from Birth to Adulthood.* Ithaca, NY: Cornell Univ. Press

Youngblade LM, Dunn J. 1995. Individual differences in young children's pretend play with mother and sibling: links to relationships and understanding of other people's feelings and beliefs. *Child Dev.* 66: 1472–92

*Annu. Rev. Psychol. 1998. 49:25–42*

# MEMORY-BASED LANGUAGE PROCESSING: Psycholinguistic Research in the 1990s

*Gail McKoon and Roger Ratcliff*

Department of Psychology, Northwestern University, Evanston, Illinois 60208;
e-mail: g-mckoon@nwu.edu

KEY WORDS:   reading, language comprehension, lexical semantics, long-term memory, syntax,
              meaning

---

### ABSTRACT

There are two main domains of research in psycholinguistics: sentence processing, concerned with how the syntactic structures of sentences are computed, and text processing, concerned with how the meanings of larger units of text are understood. In recent sentence processing research, a new and controversial theme is that syntactic computations may rely heavily on statistical information about the relative frequencies with which different syntactic structures occur in the language. In text processing, recent research has focused on what information the words and ideas of a text evoke from long-term memory quickly, passively, and at low processing cost. Research in both domains has begun to use the information that can be obtained from large corpora of naturally occurring texts.

---

## CONTENTS

0066-4308/98/0201-0025$08.00

## Introduction

> I was still staring at the portrait when a door opened far back under the stairs. It wasn't the butler coming back. It was a girl.
>
> She was twenty or so, small and delicately put together, but she looked durable. She wore pale blue slacks and they looked well on her. She walked as if she were floating. Her hair was a fine tawny wave cut much shorter than the current fashion of pageboy tresses curled in at the bottom. Her eyes were slate-gray, and had almost no expression when they looked at me. She came over near me and smiled with her mouth and she had little sharp predatory teeth, as white as fresh orange pith and as shiny as porcelain. They glistened between her thin too taut lips. Her face lacked color and didn't look too healthy.
>
> "Tall, aren't you?" she said.

These sentences are from the beginning of *The Big Sleep* by Raymond Chandler (1939). They convey a "narrative world" (Gerrig 1993)—they convey atmosphere and emotion, place and time, and they portray the girl in rich complexity. Moreover, all this is accomplished with no apparent effort on the part of the reader. Whatever we do to experience this narrative world, beyond reading the 144 individual words of the 12 sentences, little of it is available to conscious awareness. It is the job of psycholinguistic research to describe and explain how our experience of passages like this one from *The Big Sleep* comes about.

Psycholinguistics as we know it today began about 35 years ago (e.g. Miller & Isard 1963). Since then, subfields have coalesced, each formulating its own favorite questions about language processing, and many things have been learned in the course of attempts to answer these questions. But it is a fair summary to say that most of what has been learned does not address the central issue of how readers come to experience narrative worlds. More optimistically, however, current theoretical ideas and empirical methods show promise of setting the stage to begin exploration of this issue.

The largest division among the different subfields of psycholinguistics is the one between "text processing" research and "sentence processing" research. In the 1960s, psycholinguistics was an effort to document the psychological reality of the syntactic theory proposed by Chomsky (see Fodor et al 1974). Around 1970, rejecting the overemphasis on syntax, a number of researchers began to study meaning (e.g. Anderson & Bower 1973, Bransford & Franks 1971, Kintsch & Keenan 1973, Norman et al 1975). As the study of meaning grew, so the objects of interest grew from the meanings conveyed by a single sentence to the interconnecting and interacting meanings conveyed by larger texts, paragraphs, and stories, and the research came to be known as "text processing" research (or, sometimes, "discourse processing" research). Meanwhile, research continued on how the syntactic structure of a sentence is computed, and because syntactic processes are assumed to operate at the sentence level, it came to be known as "sentence processing" research.

The text processing and sentence processing domains are almost entirely separate from each other. They have separate journals (e.g. *Discourse Processes* and *The Journal of Psycholinguistic Research*) and separate conferences (e.g. the Society for Text and Discourse conference and the CUNY Sentence Processing conference). The research questions are different, and the methods used to answer the questions show little significant overlap.

In the past five years, both domains have witnessed major additions to the collection of theoretical ideas guiding research. In text processing, new consideration has been given to fast, passive, parallel retrieval processes that can make multiple complexities of meaning available to comprehension processes quickly and at low cost. In sentence processing, the new idea is that the frequency with which a particular syntactic structure occurs in natural language may be a powerful determinant of how easy it is to process. Neither of these new ways of thinking about language processing offers any immediate solution to the problem of how Raymond Chandler's words convey so much about the girl introduced at the beginning of *The Big Sleep,* but both may represent some progress in an appropriate direction. In the sections below, these ideas are described and, as a by-product of the description, current work in text processing is contrasted with current work in sentence processing. The last section reviews the possibilities offered to the study of language by a new tool—large corpora of naturally occurring text.

## Text Processing and Resonance

In the 1970s and 1980s, most text processing experiments were concerned with whether some particular kind of inference was encoded during reading. If a fish swam under a rock and a turtle was sitting on the rock, does the reader encode that the fish swam under the turtle (Bransford et al 1972)? If a janitor sweeps the floor, does the reader understand that he uses a broom (Corbett & Dosher 1978)? If an actress falls from a 14-story building, does the reader understand that she will very likely die (McKoon & Ratcliff 1986)?

Sorting out the results of many such experiments led to an enhanced appreciation of what turned out to be a crucial methodological issue. The procedures used in most early experiments did not allow inferences that were generated at the time of reading to be distinguished from inferences that were generated at the time of the inference test. Suppose, for example, that after studying a list of sentences, subjects were given a list of words and asked to recall the sentence that went with each word. Given the word "broom," for instance, the sentence to recall might have been "the janitor swept the classroom." Recall of the sentence could occur either because the subject had generated the connection between "broom" and the sweeping sentence when the sentence was read or because the subject generated the connection at the time the word "broom" was given in the recall test (see Corbett & Dosher 1978).

In response to this problem, experimenters moved to procedures by which inferences could be unequivocally attributed to processes that occurred during reading (e.g. Corbett & Chang 1983). To make the move, two theoretical ideas were borrowed from research on memory. The first was Tulving's (1974) notion of cue-dependent retrieval: A cue evokes information from memory directly and selectively; that is, it directly evokes traces of those past events of which it was a part. The second was Posner's (1978) separation of fast automatic cognitive processes from slower strategic ones. These two ideas in combination led to the use of speeded, single-word recognition as a procedure to examine inference processes. In a typical experiment, subjects read a sentence (or longer passage) and then, after some delay, one or more single test words are presented. For each test word, subjects are asked to make a recognition decision, that is, they are asked to decide whether the test word had appeared in the sentence, and they are asked to indicate their decision as quickly as possible. It is assumed that the recognition decision is based on cue-dependent retrieval: If the test word and/or its meaning was encoded as part of the studied sentence, then the test word will quickly evoke the information encoded from the sentence, allowing a fast positive response to the test word. For example, given the sentence "the janitor swept the classroom," the test word "janitor" should quickly evoke the information from the sentence, and there should be a fast positive response. If an inference was encoded about the janitor sweeping with a broom, then "broom" as a test word should also quickly evoke the information from the sentence, leading to a fast positive response, a response that would be an error because "broom" did not actually appear in the sentence (for discussion of slow responses and the use of deadline methods to ensure fast responses, see McKoon & Ratcliff 1989b). The important point for interpretation of the results of recognition experiments is that, following Posner, fast responses are assumed to come from automatic processes, processes that are not under the subject's strategic control. Because the processes are not under strategic control, it is further assumed that responses reflect information that was encoded during reading, not information that was constructed by slower strategic processes occurring at the time of the test.

Applying this reasoning, experiments looked more analytically than had been done in the past at what kinds of information were encoded during reading in circumstances in which subjects were given no special goals to encode any particular types of information. One outcome was the conclusion that in the absence of special goals, relatively few of the inferences that had been earlier studied so extensively were actually generated during reading. This conclusion was summarized by the "minimalist hypothesis" (McKoon & Ratcliff 1992a), the hypothesis that the only inferences encoded during reading, in the absence of special strategies, are those that depend on information that is easily and quickly available from memory and those that are needed to make the text that is being read locally coherent. This conclusion was not shared by all text processing researchers, and considerable debate ensued (e.g. Graesser et al 1994, Graesser & Zwaan 1995, McKoon & Ratcliff 1995, Singer et al 1994). Efforts to map out what kinds of nonminimalist inferences are generated during reading, especially those that create causal links between pieces of text information, continue (e.g. van den Broek et al 1996).

Although the new focus on fast, parallel, and passive evocation of information from memory was first reflected in new experimental procedures, a more important consequence has been its reflection in theoretical thinking. This change is part of a broader movement in cognitive psychology. In memory research, the global memory models (Gillund & Shiffrin 1984, Hintzman 1986, Murdock 1982) account for many and various empirical findings with direct access retrieval processes that are global, passive, fast, and automatic, explicit implementations of cue-dependent retrieval. In text processing, part of the minimalist hypothesis (McKoon & Ratcliff 1992a) is that not only a test word but also every word, concept, and proposition in a text evokes information from memory directly, globally, and quickly. Kintsch's (1974) model for the representation of meaning in propositional structures has acquired processes (Kintsch 1988) by which information from long-term memory is made available by fast, passive retrieval processes. A crucial aspect of this new focus is that attention is directed at what is evoked from memory by a text rather than only at what inferences need to be generated to understand the text.

There has also been a change from interest only in the content of inferences to increased interest in the processes by which they are generated—an interest in processing issues as well as representational issues. In the 1970s and 1980s, text experiments could be summarized by a list of the conceptual contents of inferences: for example, instrumental ("broom" for sentences about sweeping), causal connections ("because" to connect events and their consequences; Keenan et al 1984, Trabasso & van den Broek 1985), and predictable events ("death" from falling from a high building). The 1990s have begun to see more thought given to separating those inferences that are generated quickly and passively from long-term memory from those inferences that require strategic processing by the reader. (For reviews and examples of this research, see Britton & Graesser 1996, Gernsbacher 1994, van den Broek et al 1995, Noordman et al 1992, Noordman & Vonk 1992.)

The new focus has been signaled with key terms. We (McKoon et al 1996) use the words "memory based" text processing to describe the idea that a text's words, concepts, and propositions are understood in terms of the information they evoke from memory, individually and in combination. Myers, O'Brien, and colleagues (Albrecht & O'Brien 1993, 1995; Albrecht & Myers 1995; Albrecht et al 1995; Huitema et al 1993; Klin & Myers 1993; Myers et al 1994; O'Brien & Albrecht 1992) have brought back the term "resonance," which describes Tulving's original notion of cue-dependent retrieval (Lockhart et al 1976, Ratcliff 1978, Tulving 1974).

The long-term memory information that a piece of text evokes can be either general knowledge (of all kinds—lexical knowledge, world knowledge, semantic memory knowledge) or information from earlier parts of the text itself (McKoon & Ratcliff 1992a). Myers, O'Brien, and their colleagues have presented a number of experiments designed to demonstrate directly that pieces of information in a text evoke one another across large distances in the surface structure of the text. For example, in a story from an experiment by Myers et al (1994), a character refused to eat anything fried or cooked in grease but later ordered a cheeseburger and fries. These two pieces of information were separated from each other in the story, yet it appeared that associations among the concepts "fried," "cooked," "grease," "cheeseburger," and "fries" served to connect the two pieces of information together so that readers noticed the inconsistency. In a similar vein, we (Greene et al 1994, McKoon et al 1996; see also Grosz & Sidner 1986, O'Brien et al 1995) have shown that a pronoun can be understood to refer to a character that has not been mentioned recently in the text if the pronoun is used in a context in which the character has already been evoked by means of association to earlier encoded textual information.

Perhaps the most important feature of resonance is that the focus of attention turns to the question of what it is that a word, concept, or proposition evokes from general knowledge. With this focus, questions about whether one or another inference is required to understand a text become of secondary importance. Optimistically, the incorporation of information provided by general knowledge into the larger picture of meaning conveyed by a text, into the meaning that is constructed through a consortium of processes, might be one small step toward discovery of how it is that Chandler makes us see the girl in *The Big Sleep* so clearly.

Two different lines of research can be used to illustrate the shift toward general knowledge being investigated as a central component of comprehension: One is concerned with what information individual words evoke from general knowledge, and several examples of experiments of this type are reviewed first. The other is concerned with what information is evoked by combinations of words.

Individual words have, of course, always been assumed to evoke their meanings. What is especially new is the possibility that individual words, within themselves, also evoke structural information about their relations with the concepts that surround them. Consider the verb "cram," a member of the class of locative verbs. Not only does it have the meaning of pushing lots of stuff into some space, it also carries implications about how affected the space is by the cramming, implications that depend on the syntactic structure in which it is used (Rappaport et al 1987). To "cram the closet with boxes" suggests that the closet is quite full; to "cram boxes into the closet" suggests that it is not so full, that more stuff might still be crammed in. Empirical evidence indicates that readers understand the implications of use of verbs of this class (McKoon & Ratcliff 1989a).

Another example is verbs of implicit causality. Although these have been studied by psycholinguists for some time (e.g. Garvey & Caramazza 1974), recently their contributions to immediate comprehension have been investigated. Verbs of implicit causality can be divided according to whether they attribute causality to their subject argument or to their object argument. "Annoy," for example, attributes causality to its subject argument; if John annoys Mary, one normally assumes that the cause of the annoyance is some property or action of John's. "Admire," on the other hand, attributes causality to the argument in the object position; if Bill admires Nancy, it is usually some quality of Nancy's that causes the admiration. Recent work indicates that causal verbs evoke lexical information about which of their arguments is likely to be causal, that they do so quickly and passively, and that the causal argument becomes more salient than the other argument (Garnham et al 1996, Greene & McKoon 1995).

The examples just described illustrate what could become a profitable trend in psycholinguistics in the 1990s—the convergence of meaning and syntactic structure in empirical research (see also Marslen-Wilson et al 1994). The lexical structures that are part of the evoked information about locative verbs like "cram" and verbs of implicit causality like "admire" are structures that are as important to syntactic processing as they are to comprehension of meaning. This strand of converging research appears again below in discussion of current work in sentence processing.

The shift in attention toward what information is evoked from general knowledge by the words, concepts, and propositions of the text is also apparent in research about combinations of words. Research on combinations of words is essential because it is combinations of words that make up context, and "context" is what surrounds the reader in a narrative world. The idea that one word "primes" or "activates" words related to it dates back to Meyer & Schvaneveldt's early demonstration in 1971. In both cognitive psychology in general and psycholinguistics in particular, the idea has been updated to combinations of words. In the global memory models, combinations of words (e.g. "mint money") are familiar to the extent that the strengths of the connections between them in memory are high (McKoon & Ratcliff 1992b; McNamara 1992a,b, 1994a,b; Ratcliff & McKoon 1988, 1994, 1995). In research on semantic memory, it has been shown that which members of a category are evoked by a category label (e.g. "animal") depends on the sentence context in which the label is given (e.g. "riding an animal" versus "milking an animal"; Roth & Shoben 1983). In text processing, one example of this trend is Kintsch's (1988) context integration model. The words of a text are assumed to activate, in what can be described as a promiscuous fashion (Keenan & Jennings 1995), all the concepts in memory to which they are associated. Then activation recycles among all the concepts, those from the text and those from memory, in such a way that concepts with multiple strong connections become the most highly activated, and concepts with few and weak connections drop out. The result is that the meaning represented for the text includes concepts from long-term memory that are associated with combinations of concepts in the text; in other words, the meaning represented for the text reflects context. Another example is HAL, Burgess's (Burgess & Lund 1995) model for semantic relations. In this model, words are semantically related to the extent that they have co-occurred in large corpora of text (e.g. 100 million words of online computer conversations). This measure of semantic relatedness predicts the ease of processing of word combinations in sentences, specifically noun-verb combinations (Burgess & Lund 1995).

All of the examples just discussed illustrate the move toward investigation of memory-based comprehension processes. The trend is encouraging because combining information from general knowledge and information from the text in a fast passive way must be at least a part of the experience of narrative worlds like Chandler's. But there is a long way to go. One thing that needs to be worked out is how the structures implicit in single words like "cram" come to be integrated with the rest of the information in a text. Another problem is how to translate the idea of combinations of words evoking general knowledge into a satisfying description of the context evoked by a text and how it affects comprehension processes. Still another problem is that little attention has been paid to what emotional information is evoked during reading (but see Hirsch & Matthews 1997).

Not only is the resonance idea incomplete, there are also serious conceptual problems. Here, four are listed. First, text comprehension is much more than the product of resonance between combinations of the words of a text (elephant) and information in long-term memory. The word "elephant" in the last sentence evokes nothing relevant to the sentence but the meaning of "elephant" itself. It does not combine or interact with the other elements of the sentence to contribute to the understanding of the sentence, yet it will probably be remembered better than the other elements. Likewise, for the girl in *The Big Sleep,* "predatory teeth" does not combine in resonance with her being "small," "delicate," and "floating," yet "predatory teeth" probably has more to do with our picture of her than the other concepts that are more typically associated with beautiful girls. How to integrate the resonance idea with the prominence of never before or rarely encountered conceptual combinations is a problem that has not yet been adequately formulated.

Second, passive resonance must somehow be related to processes that yield active and conscious engagement of the reader (Gerrig 1993, Graesser et al 1994, Singer et al 1994). If there is some process by which combinations of Chandler's words passively associate "beautiful" with the girl, and some other process gives prominence to her having predatory teeth, then still another process must lead to the reader's strong feeling that she will be trouble for the Bogart-type hero of the story. In general, what is evoked passively from long-term memory must somehow lay a foundation that makes possible conscious involvement on the part of the reader.

Third, comprehension processes are able to circumvent passive resonance. Somehow, readers know and can keep separate which pieces of information are relevant to which circumstances and characters in a story. If we were to read on in *The Big Sleep,* comprehension processes would be able to keep separate what the reader is told about the girl from what the detective hero can know in the circumstances of the story (Gerrig et al 1997). By passive resonance, any mention of the girl ought to evoke all that we know about her in all circumstances (McKoon & Ratcliff 1992a), yet the reader knows which things the reader can know that the hero cannot.

In another way, however, the flow of information from long-term memory cannot be turned off. No matter how many times we read *The Big Sleep,* no matter how well we know what is going to happen, we still experience suspense and emotion; we still experience *The Big Sleep*'s narrative world. An experiment by Gerrig (1989) can be used to make the dilemma clear. In the experiment, subjects read texts that outlined circumstances that might have prevented well-known historical events from occurring. For example, one text outlined Washington's reasons for initially refusing to accept nomination as a candidate to become the first president of the United States. On the one hand, this information should evoke from long-term memory the well-known fact that Washington was the first president. On the other hand, according to Gerrig's empirical results, the pieces of information in the text about refusal to accept a nomination and the reasons for not doing so raise, in their combinations of meanings, some amount of interference. In the context of the story, the interference from these pieces of the text cannot be overridden by the sure knowledge that Washington did become president. That is, the comprehension system has both the information that, with absolute certainty, Washington was president as well as some amount of interference in verifying the proposition that Washington was president.

Overall, it is a reasonable expectation that the resonance, or memory-based retrieval, idea will lead to significant advances in research. Certainly, some part of the power of language must come from the facility with which words and the combinations of words that make up context evoke information and emotion from memory. However, we currently know almost nothing about the boundaries between resonance and other comprehension processes. Delineating the tasks served by memory from other, more constructive processes is an important task for future research.

## Sentence Processing

The central question that drives sentence processing research is how the human language processing system computes the syntactic representations of sentences. By definition, this area of research is not concerned with the narrative world readers experience when reading Chandler. Nevertheless, recent ideas and empirical findings in sentence processing show promise of being useful to explorations of readers' experiences.

From the 1970s (Bever 1970, Frazier 1978, Frazier & Fodor 1978) until the early 1990s, most research in sentence processing was guided by the hypothesis that the syntactic processing of a sentence precedes semantic processing and occurs in isolation from it (Fodor 1983). Empirical work concentrated on demonstrating the psychological validity of this claim for sentences with various types of syntactic structures. Recently, however, a competing viewpoint has been strongly advanced: The processes that compute the syntactic structures of sentences make use of "constraints" from all types of information, including semantic information and information about the frequencies with which syntactically relevant structures occur in the language (MacDonald et al 1994, Trueswell et al 1994).

The types of linguistic information used by constraint-based processes are assumed to be stored in a lexicon, the entry for each word in the lexicon having stored with it the word's possible arguments, its possible syntactic structures, and the frequencies with which the arguments and syntactic structures occur for that word. Arguments are the participant roles that can be associated with a word; for example, "eat" has associated with it an agent role, the entity who does the eating, and a theme role, the entity that gets eaten. "Eat" can participate in two possible syntactic structures, either with a subject and an object (the transitive use) or with only a subject (the intransitive use). With each argument and each syntactic structure is associated the frequency with which it occurs with "eat." So, for example, for the sentence "John ate," the lexical entry for John includes (among other things) the information that "John" is very frequently an agent noun phrase, and the lexical entry for "ate" includes that "ate" can take a noun phrase as its agent and that "ate" is more frequently used in the transitive than in the intransitive construction. The absence of a direct object in the sentence would force the intransitive construction, and the fact that it is less frequent would lead to a slight cost in processing time.

Many aspects of how a constraint-based model would actually work are unclear. Frazier (1995; see also McKoon et al 1993) has pointed out the nontrivial nature of the problem of building syntactic structures for whole sentences when all the processor has to work with are the chunks of syntax stored in the lexicon for individual words. Until a simulation model can be developed to actually produce whole-sentence syntactic structures for a large variety and number of words and constructions, satisfactory evaluation of the constraint-based approach is not possible. However, the aim here is not to present a critique of constraint-based models but rather to compare advances in the sentence processing domain to advances in the text processing domain.

In virtually all sentence processing research, it is implicitly assumed that each word in a sentence evokes all the linguistic information stored about that word in the lexicon. No discussion or investigation is devoted to the processes by which the information is evoked nor to the issue of how all the evoked information is stored and/or kept available in the course of computation. Nevertheless, the theme that a word, within itself, evokes not just its meaning but also complex structures of interrelated entities and meanings (see Stevenson 1993) is the same theme discussed above as being prominent in text processing research.

However, how this theme is carried through is considerably different in sentence processing research than in text processing research. One critical difference is that text processing researchers treat combinations of words as well as individual words as capable of evoking information from memory. "Animals" in the context of "giving milk" evokes different information than either "animals" in the context of "riding" or "animals" alone. In contrast, in sentence processing research, for the sentences "a cow milked" and "a farmer milked," exactly the same information is evoked for "milked" (but see Britt et al 1992, Taraban & McClelland 1988). The point is that for text processing, the context in which a concept appears controls the information evoked from memory; for sentence processing, the context in which a concept appears does not affect what is evoked from the lexicon (for related discussion of this issue with respect to constraint-based models, see Frazier 1995). This contrast is a fundamental theoretical difference in how the two fields of research regard the processes by which information is retrieved from memory.

There is also a critical gap in the domains of study between where sentence processing research leaves off and text processing research begins. In sentence processing research, there is typically little consideration given to the consequences of syntactic structures for understanding meaning. Consider, for example, the verbs of implicit causality. Text processing studies of these verbs make heavy use of the notions that verbs have associated argument structures, and that the verbs' agents are likely the syntactic subjects of their sentences and that the experiencers of the verbs' actions are likely in object position. This sounds like syntactic, that is, sentence processing, research. But in sentence processing research, there is nothing in the information that is assumed to be evoked from the lexicon by verbs that would indicate which argument is likely to be the cause of the action denoted by the verb.

How the gap between typical sentence processing research and meaning might be addressed is illustrated by a set of studies by Birch & Garnsey (1995; see also McKoon et al 1993). Their studies used sentences like "there was this painting that was on display in the museum," in which "painting" is put into focus by "there-insertion," and they found that in-focus concepts were better remembered than out-of-focus concepts. This is a finding about the consequences for comprehension of meaning of one aspect of syntax. Much more research of this type needs to be undertaken. Specifically, how does the syntactically relevant information encoded in the lexicon for individual words (as opposed to specialized structures like there-insertion) affect comprehension of meaning and get incorporated into meaning?

In sum, the goal of sentence processing research has usually been to develop models that can produce the syntactic structures of sentences. The goal has not been formulated to be the development of models that produce all of the syntactic information that is useful for understanding the meanings of sentences. Either semantically relevant syntactic information needs to be added to the information used by the processors of current syntactic models or new models need to be developed to link the products of current parsers to semantically relevant syntactic information. The aim would be to explore how syntax puts together and organizes concepts in context to make a contribution to the overall meaning of a text. It is likely that part of the power with which Chandler makes us "see" the girl at the beginning of *The Big Sleep* comes from the way he uses syntactic structures to organize the information he presents.

There is an additional difference between text processing research and sentence processing research that should be mentioned. Typically, the goal of sentence processing research is to develop models that can produce the *correct* syntactic structures of sentences. This is sometimes stated explicitly (MacDonald et al 1994, p. 686), and it is almost always implicit in designs of experiments and discussions of theoretical interpretations of data. The underlying assumption is that human comprehension processes produce a correct and complete syntactic interpretation of a sentence (but see Frazier & Clifton 1996). In contrast, the history of text processing research has been, in the main, an effort to find out what is understood as well as how it is understood. Therefore, for any piece of implicit information, it is always assumed that there is some possibility that a reader does not correctly or completely comprehend it. The consequences of this difference in assumptions show up empirically. In text processing research, even when processing time is the measure of main interest, there is usually some check to determine whether or not subjects actually understand correctly whatever aspect of the text is under investigation. For example, it might be hypothesized that "Jack threw a snowball at Phil, but he ducked" was more difficult to comprehend than "Jack threw a snowball at Phil, but he missed." More difficult comprehension would be predicted to lead to longer reading times, but in addition, relative success of comprehension of the pronoun would be measured by recognition response times for the single probe word "Jack" or "Phil" presented immediately following the sentence (see, for example, Corbett & Chang 1983). In contrast, in sentence processing research, processing time is the most common measure, and there is usually no check for comprehension accuracy for the aspect of the text under investigation.

Text processing research, at least implicitly, allows subjects the possibility of engaging in speed/accuracy trade-offs. Subjects might read faster but understand less, or they might read slower and understand more. Or they might understand so little that they skip rapidly through the sentence. For instance, most readers of this chapter will read "colorless green ideas sleep furiously" very quickly but claim that they understood little. Only with some measure to check comprehension can the experimenter know the difference between fast reading with excellent comprehension and fast "reading" with little comprehension.

Although the differences just outlined between text processing research and sentence processing research are important ones, there are at least hints of shared interests between the two domains, mainly in the interplay between syntactic structures and the contributions they might make to comprehension of meaning. Payoffs from research in this area might lead to progress on a wide range of different issues in text processing, issues for which a syntactic contribution may not have been contemplated previously.

## *Large Corpora*

For neither text processing nor sentence processing research can a review of recent developments neglect the increasing availability and use of large corpora of naturally occurring samples of language. For example, the Penn Treebank project (Marcus et al 1993) provides one widely available (but expensive) corpus of over three million words of text from the *Wall Street Journal.*

There are a number of different ways corpora can be used, and they are briefly listed here.

One use to which corpora are put is the calculation of statistics about frequencies of occurrence of linguistic constructions. For syntactic constructions, frequencies of occurrence assume central theoretical importance for constraint-based models of syntactic processing, as mentioned above. The constructions easiest to process are assumed to be those that occur most frequently in the language. For example, a verb will be easier to process in a transitive construction than in an intransitive construction if the verb occurs more frequently as transitive.

The assumption of such a large explanatory role for statistical information is controversial (see Frazier 1995). Consider how the processing of verbs of implicit causality might be explained. Empirical data (Caramazza et al 1977) show that, when presented with an incomplete sentence like "John admired Mary because...," subjects tend to respond with a completion that attributes causality to the object (as in "because she is so smart"). Most theorizing about this class of verbs has postulated that the linguistically relevant structure encoded in lexical memory as part of a causal verb's meaning includes information about causality, such as which argument is the direct initiator of the action described by the verb. It is also assumed that the initiator argument is given greater prominence in the representation of the sentence constructed by comprehension processes, and it is assumed that it is this prominence that leads to the initiator being chosen as the subject of a "because" clause following the verb as well as to a number of other linguistic and psycholinguistic effects (Edwards & Potter 1993, Greene & McKoon 1995, McKoon et al 1993). Replacing this chain of theoretical constructs with the simple explanation that the argument of the verb that will be used as the subject of the "because" clause is the one that has been used most frequently as the subject of the "because" clause in the past is unsatisfactory for many researchers.

In text processing, the role of statistical information has been different. The frequencies of co-occurrence of conceptual combinations are computed as the number of times two (or more) words, such as "mint" and "money," occur in the same "window" of text together, where the window might be defined as some number of consecutive words or a whole sentence. Frequencies of co-occurrence fit naturally with the text processing notion that concepts and combinations of concepts in a text evoke all the information with which they are associated in long-term memory. Frequencies of co-occurrence provide a natural empirical measure of what information is likely to be evoked during reading (Burgess & Lund 1995, Landauer & Dumais 1997). How the associations reflected in co-occurrence frequencies are handled theoretically is a separable issue from their empirical use: A theory could assume that frequencies of co-occurrence are represented directly in memory, or it could be assumed that the frequencies are derived from some other theoretical construct (such as relatedness in terms of some type of semantic features).

Setting theoretical uses aside, large corpora are extremely valuable for other purposes. Perhaps most important, they provide examples of linguistic constructions. If it is hypothesized that some linguistic construction is disallowed in English, then finding examples of the construction in corpora provides disconfirmation of the hypothesis. If the theorist seeks to find the range of uses of some word, corpora can provide the relevant examples. For example, it is often said that the verb "put" requires as arguments both an object to be put and a place to put it. However, a search of any large corpus will quickly turn up such uses as "put the question," "put it" (as in "put it succinctly"), "put into question," "put it together," "put on" (as in "put on a show"), "put an end" to something, and so on. A theorist seeking a theoretical description of the use of "put" would need to consider these examples in addition to the more typical uses.

Finally, it should not be overlooked that corpora can be a source of materials for use in experiments. In both text processing and sentence processing research, the criticism is often made that the materials used in some experiment are not natural, and therefore any conclusions drawn from the results of the experiment are suspect. Basing experimental materials on corpus examples obviates this criticism.

## Conclusion

Obviously, we are a long way from solving the problem of how readers enter narrative worlds. As with any research domain, psycholinguistic research has oscillated over time between central questions and more peripheral ones. During some periods, the major topics have been methodological ones. It could be said, however, that considerable expenditure of energy on methodology made possible current attempts at progress on more substantive issues. On another front, convergence between the currently separate domains of syntactic processing research and research more concerned with meaning might pay off in the future. We may come to see more research more directly related to the central questions of what readers understand, what they experience, and how understanding and experience come about.

Four salient avenues that might lead to significant progress present themselves: investigating interactions between syntax and meaning, investigating interactions between passively retrieved information from long-term memory and newly constructed information, investigating how emotions are evoked by texts, and testing theoretical ideas of all sorts against empirical data offered by large corpora of naturally occurring text. What progress will actually be made is an open question: Language and how it is understood present problems as difficult as any in psychology.

ACKNOWLEDGMENTS

Preparation of this article was supported by NIDCD grant R01-DC01240, NSF grant SBR-9221940, and NIMH grants HD MH44640 and MH00871. We thank Richard Gerrig and Colleen Seifert for provocative comments on an earlier version of this article.

> Visit the *Annual Reviews home page* at http://www.AnnualReviews.org.

## *Literature Cited*

Albrecht JE, Myers JE. 1995. The role of context in accessing distant information during reading. *J. Exp. Psychol.: Learn. Mem. Cogn.* 19:1459–68

Albrecht JE, O'Brien EJ. 1993. Updating a mental model: maintaining both local and global coherence. *J. Exp. Psychol.: Learn. Mem. Cogn.* 19:1061–70

Albrecht JE, O'Brien E. 1995. Goal processing and the maintenance of global coherence. In *Sources of Coherence in Reading,* ed. RF Lorch Jr, EJ O'Brien. Hillsdale, NJ: Erlbaum

Albrecht JE, O'Brien E, Mason R, Myers J. 1995. The role of perspective in the accessibility of goals during reading. *J. Exp. Psychol. Learn. Mem. Cogn.* 21: 364–72

Anderson JR, Bower GH. 1973. *Human Associative Memory.* Washington, DC: Winston

Bever TG. 1970. The cognitive basis for linguistic structure. In *Cognitive Development of Language,* ed. JR Hayes. New York: Wiley

Birch G, Garnsey S. 1995. The effect of focus on memory for words in sentences. *J. Mem. Lang.* 34:232–67

Bransford JD, Barclay JR, Franks JJ. 1972. Sentence memory: a constructive versus interpretive approach. *Cogn. Psychol.* 3: 193–209

Bransford JD, Franks JJ. 1971. The abstraction of linguistic ideas. *Cogn. Psychol.* 2: 331–50

Britt MA, Perfetti CA, Garrod S, Rayner K. 1992. Parsing in discourse: context effects and their limits. *J. Mem. Lang.* 31:293–314

Britton B, Graesser A, eds. 1996. *Models of Understanding Text.* Hillsdale, NJ: Erlbaum

Burgess C, Lund K. 1995. Automatic extraction of high-dimensional semantics from large corpora: a model of human syntactic processing constraints. In *Proc. Annu. CUNY Conf. Hum. Sent. Process., 8th*

Caramazza A, Grober E, Garvey C, Yates J. 1977. Comprehension of anaphoric pronouns. *J. Verbal Learn. Verbal Behav.* 16: 601–9

Chandler R. 1939. *The Big Sleep.* New York: Avenel

Corbett AT, Chang FR. 1983. Pronoun disambiguation: accessing potential antecedents. *Mem. Cogn.* 11:283–94

Corbett AT, Dosher BA. 1978. Instrument inferences in sentence encoding. *J. Verbal Learn. Verbal Behav.* 17:479–91

Edwards D, Potter J. 1993. Language and causation: a discursive action model of description and attribution. *Psychol. Rev.* 100:23–41

Fodor JA. 1983. *The Modularity of Mind.* Boston: MIT Press

Fodor JA, Bever TG, Garrett MF. 1974. *The Psychology of Language:An Introduction to Psycholinguistics and Ggenerative Grammar.* St. Louis: McGraw-Hill

Frazier L. 1978. *On Comprehending Sentences: Syntactic Parsing Strategies.* Bloomington: Ind. Univ. Linguist. Club

Frazier L. 1995. Issues of representation in psycholinguistics. In *Speech, Language, and Communication,* ed. JL Miller, PD Eimas. San Diego, CA: Academic

Frazier L, Clifton C. 1996. *Construal.* Cambridge, MA: MIT Press

Frazier L, Fodor JD. 1978. The sausage machine: a new two stage parsing model. *Cognition* 6:291–325

Garnham A, Traxler M, Oakhill J, Gernsbacher MA. 1996. The locus of implicit causality effects in comprehension. *J. Mem. Lang.* 35:517–43

Garvey C, Caramazza A. 1974. Implicit causality in verbs. *Linguist. Inq.* 5:459–64

Gernsbacher M. 1994. *Handbook of Psycholinguistics.* New York: Wiley

Gerrig RJ. 1989. The time course of sense creation. *Mem. Cogn.* 17:194–207

Gerrig RJ. 1993. *Experiencing Narrative Worlds.* New Haven: Yale Univ. Press

Gerrig RJ, Ohaeri JO, Brennan SE. 1997. Illusory transparency. Revisited. manuscript

Gillund G, Shiffrin RM. 1984. A retrieval model for both recognition and recall. *Psychol. Rev.* 91:1–67

Graesser A, Zwaan R. 1995. Inference generation and the construction of situation models. In *Discourse Comprehension: Essays in Honor of Walter Kintsch,* ed. CA Weaver, S Mannes, CR Fletcher. Hillsdale, NJ: Erlbaum

Graesser AC, Singer M, Trabasso T. 1994. Constructing inferences during narrative text comprehension. *Psychol. Rev.* 101: 371–95

Greene SB, Gerrig RJ, McKoon G, Ratcliff R. 1994. Unheralded pronouns and the management of common ground. *J. Mem. Lang.* 33:511–26

Greene SB, McKoon G. 1995. Telling something we can't know: experimental approaches to verbs exhibiting implicit causality. *Psychol. Sci.* 6:262–70

Grosz B, Sidner C. 1986. Attention, intentions and the structure of discourse. *Comput. Linguist.* 12:175–204

Hintzman D. 1986. "Schema abstraction" in a multiple-trace memory model. *Psychol. Rev.* 93:411–28

Hirsch C, Matthews A. 1997. Inferences when reading about uncertain emotional events. manuscript

Huitema JS, Dopkins S, Klin CM, Myers JL. 1993. Connecting goals and actions during reading. *J. Exp. Psychol.: Learn. Mem. Cogn.* 19:1053–60

Keenan JM, Baillet SD, Brown P. 1984. The effects of causal cohesion on comprehension and memory. *J. Verbal Learn. Verbal Behav.* 23:115–26

Keenan JM, Jennings TM. 1995. Priming of inference concepts in the construction-integration model. In *Discourse Compre-*

*hension: Essays in Honor of Walter Kintsch,* ed. CA Weaver, S Mannes, CR Fletcher, pp. 233–44. Hillsdale, NJ: Erlbaum

Kintsch W. 1974. *The Representation of Meaning in Memory.* Hillsdale, NJ: Erlbaum

Kintsch W. 1988. The role of knowledge in discourse comprehension: a construction-integration model. *Psychol. Rev.* 95: 163–82

Kintsch W, Keenan JM. 1973. Reading rate and retention as a function of the number of propositions in the base structure of sentences. *Cogn. Psychol.* 5:257–74

Klin C, Myers J. 1993. Reinstatement of causal information during reading. *J. Exp. Psychol. Learn. Mem. Cogn.* 19:554–60

Landauer TK, Dumais ST. 1997. A solution to Plato's problem: the latent semantic analysis theory of acquisition, induction and representation of knowledge. *Psychol. Rev.* 104:211–40

Lockhart RS, Craik FIM, Jacoby L. 1976. In *Recall and Recognition,* ed. J Brown. London: Wiley

MacDonald MC, Pearlmutter NJ, Seidenberg MS. 1994. Lexical nature of syntactic ambiguity resolution. *Psychol. Rev.* 101: 676–703

Marcus MP, Santorini B, Marcinkiewicz MA. 1993. Building a large annotated corpus of English: the Penn Treebank. *Comput. Linguist.* 19:313–30

Marslen-Wilson W, Komisarjevsky TL, Waksler R, Older L. 1994. Morphology and meaning in the Englist mental lexicon. *Psychol. Rev.* 101:3–33

McKoon G, Gerrig RJ, Greene SB. 1996. Pronoun resolution without pronouns: some consequences of memory based text processing. *J. Exp. Psychol.: Learn. Mem. Cogn.* 22:919–32

McKoon G, Greene SB, Ratcliff R. 1993. Discourse models, pronoun resolution, and the implicit causality of verbs. *J. Exp. Psychol.: Learn. Mem. Cogn.* 19:1–13

McKoon G, Ratcliff R. 1986. Inferences about predictable events. *J. Exp. Psychol.: Learn. Mem. Cogn.* 12:82–91

McKoon G, Ratcliff R. 1989a. *Inferences based on lexical information about verbs.* Presented at Annu. Meet. Psychonomic Soc., 30th, Atlanta

McKoon G, Ratcliff R. 1989b. Semantic association and elaborative inference. *J. Exp. Psychol.: Learn. Mem. Cogn.* 15:326–38

McKoon G, Ratcliff R. 1992a. Inference during reading. *Psychol. Rev.* 99:440–66

McKoon G, Ratcliff R. 1992b. Spreading activation versus compound cue accounts of priming: mediated priming revisited. *J. Exp. Psychol.: Learn. Mem. Cogn.* 18: 1155–72

McKoon G, Ratcliff R. 1995. The minimalist hypothesis: directions for research. In *Discourse Comprehension: Essays in Honor of Walter Kintsch,* ed. CA Weaver, S Mannes, CR Fletcher. Hillsdale, NJ: Erlbaum

McKoon G, Ratcliff R, Ward G, Sproat R. 1993b. Syntactic prominence effects on discourse processes. *J. Mem. Lang.* 32: 593–607

McNamara TP. 1992a. Priming and constraints it places on theories of memory and retrieval. *Psychol. Rev.* 99:650–62

McNamara TP. 1992b. Theories of priming: I. Associative distance and lag. *J. Exp. Psychol.: Learn. Mem. Cogn.* 18:1173–90

McNamara TP. 1994a. Priming and theories of memory: a reply to Ratcliff and McKoon. *Psychol. Rev.* 101:185–87

McNamara TP. 1994b. Theories of priming: II. Types of primes. *J. Exp. Psychol.: Learn. Mem. Cogn.* 20:507–20

Meyer DE, Schvaneveldt RW. 1971. Facilitation in recognizing pairs of words: evidence of a dependence between retrieval operations. *J. Exp. Psychol.* 90:227–34

Miller GA, Isard S. 1963. Some perceptual consequences of linguistic rules. *J. Verbal Learn. Verbal Behav.* 2:217–28

Murdock BB. 1982. A theory for the storage and retrieval of item and associative information. *Psychol. Rev.* 89:609–26

Myers JL, O'Brien EJ, Albrecht JE, Mason RA. 1994. Maintaining global coherence during reading. *J. Exp. Psychol.: Learn. Mem. Cogn.* 20:876–86

Noordman L, Vonk W. 1992. Reader's knowledge and the control of inference in reading. *Lang. Cogn. Process.* 7:373–91

Noordman L, Vonk W, Kempff H. 1992. Causal inferences during the reading of expository texts. *J. Mem. Lang.* 31:573–90

Norman DA, Rumelhart DE, LNR Research Group. 1975. *Explorations in Cognition.* San Francisco: Freeman

O'Brien E, Albrecht J, Hakala C, Rizzell M. 1995. Activation and suppression of antecedents during reinstatment. *J. Exp. Psychol.: Learn. Mem. Cogn.* 21:626–34

O'Brien EJ, Albrecht JE. 1992. Comprehension strategies in the development of a mental model. *J. Exp. Psychol.: Learn. Mem. Cogn.* 18:777–84

Posner MI. 1978. *Chronometric Explorations of Mind.* Hillsdale, NJ: Erlbaum

Rappaport M, Laughren M, Levin B. 1987. *Levels of Lexical Representation.* Lexicon Proj. Work. Pap., MIT

Ratcliff R. 1978. A theory of memory retrieval. *Psychol. Rev.* 85:59–108

Ratcliff R, McKoon G. 1988. A retrieval theory of priming in memory. *Psychol. Rev.* 95:385–408

Ratcliff R, McKoon G. 1994. Retrieving information from memory: spreading activation theories versus compound cue theories. *Psychol. Rev.* 101:177–84

Ratcliff R, McKoon G. 1995. Sequential effects in lexical decision: tests of compound cue retrieval theory. *J. Exp. Psychol.: Learn. Mem. Cogn.* 21:1380–88

Roth EM, Shoben EJ. 1983. The effect of context on the structure of categories. *Cogn. Psychol.* 15:346–78

Singer M, Graesser AC, Trabasso T. 1994. Minimal or global inference in comprehension. *J. Mem. Lang.* 33:421–41

Stevenson S. 1993. A competition-based explanation of syntactic attachment preferences and garden path phenomena. In *Proc. Annu. Meet. Assoc. Comput. Linguist, 31st.* Palo Alto, CA: Assoc. Comput. Linguist.

Taraban R, McClelland J. 1988. Constituent attachment and thematic role assignment in sentence processing: influences of content-based expectations. *J. Mem. Lang.* 27:592–632

Trabasso T, van den Broek P. 1985. Causal thinking and the representation of narrative events. *J. Mem. Lang.* 24:612–30

Trueswell JC, Tanenhaus MK, Garnsey SM. 1994. Semantic influences on parsing: use of thematic role information in syntactic disambiguation. *J. Mem. Lang.* 33: 285–318

Tulving E. 1974. Cue-dependent forgetting. *Am. Sci.* 62:74–82

van den Broek P, Risden K, Fletcher CR, Thurlow R. 1996. A 'landscape' view of reading: fluctuating patterns of activation and the construction of a stable memory representation. In *Models of Understanding Text,* ed. BK Britton, AC Graesser. Hillsdale, NJ: Erlbaum

van den Broek P, Risden K, Husebye-Hartmann E. 1995. The role of readers' standards for coherence in the generation of inferences during reading. In *Sources of Coherence in Reading,* ed. RF Lorch Jr, EJ O'Brien. Hillsdale, NJ: Erlbaum

*Annu. Rev. Psychol. 1998. 49:43–64*

# BRAIN PLASTICITY AND BEHAVIOR

## Bryan Kolb and Ian Q. Whishaw

Department of Psychology, University of Lethbridge, Lethbridge, Alberta, T1K 3M4
Canada; e-mail: kolb@HG.ULETH.CA

KEY WORDS: dendrite arborization, environmental enrichment, cortex, neuropsychology,
experience

---

### ABSTRACT

Brain plasticity refers to the brain's ability to change structure and function.
Experience is a major stimulant of brain plasticity in animal species as diverse as insects and humans. It is now clear that experience produces multiple, dissociable changes in the brain including increases in dendritic length,
increases (or decreases) in spine density, synapse formation, increased glial
activity, and altered metabolic activity. These anatomical changes are correlated with behavioral differences between subjects with and without the
changes. Experience-dependent changes in neurons are affected by various
factors including aging, gonadal hormones, trophic factors, stress, and brain
pathology. We discuss the important role that changes in dendritic arborization play in brain plasticity and behavior, and we consider these changes in
the context of changing intrinsic circuitry of the cortex in processes such as
learning.

---

## CONTENTS

43

0066-4308/98/0201-0043$08.00

# INTRODUCTION

One of the key principles of behavioral neuroscience is that experience can modify brain structure long after brain development is complete. Indeed, it is generally assumed that structural changes in the brain accompany memory storage (Bailey & Kandel 1993). Although the idea that experience can modify brain structure can probably be traced back to the 1890s (Ramon y Cajal 1928, Tanzi 1893), it was Hebb who made this a central feature of his neuropsychological theory (Hebb 1949). Hebb did the first experiments on the consequences of enriched rearing on the behavior of the rat (Hebb 1947). Later, the group at Berkeley began to demonstrate changes in brain weight, cortical thickness, acetylcholine levels, and dendritic structure that accompanied the behavioral changes related to experience (e.g. Diamond et al 1967, 1981; Globus et al 1973; Rosenzweig & Bennett 1978; Rosenzweig et al 1962). In the 1970s, and continuing still, William Greenough and his colleagues initiated a multidisciplinary investigation of the cellular effects of rearing animals in visually or motorically enriched environments (e.g. Greenough & Chang 1989). Perhaps the fundamental point that this group has made over the past decades is that synapses can form and dendrites can grow well beyond the period of brain development. Although this point is certainly not unique to Greenough, he and his colleagues have shown most forcefully that the adult mammalian brain (and presumably other vertebrate brains as well) can add not only dendrites and synapses in response to behavioral demands but also supportive tissue elements such as astrocytes and blood vessels.

There is now an extensive literature correlating neural and glial changes with behavioral change in species ranging from insects to humans. Because many other chapters review synaptic changes during development, our focus is on studies in which some sort of experimental manipulation has been shown to change behavior and neural structure, especially in mammals.

## Assumptions

The study of brain and behavioral correlations necessarily involves assumptions about methodology, and this review chapter is no exception. In particular, we assume that changes in the structural properties of the brain will reflect changes in brain function. Furthermore, we assume that the most likely place to identify neural changes associated with behavior is at the synapse. In order to relate synaptic change to behavioral change, it also is assumed in the current review that synaptic changes can be measured by analysis of the postsynaptic structure of cells, either by light microscope or electron microscope techniques. We do not consider neurochemical or neurophysiological changes in the current review.

## METHODS OF STUDY

### Analysis of Behavior

Three important sets of behavioral distinctions are relevant to plastic changes in the brain. The first relates to the difference between exercise and skill acquisition. Running in a treadmill is wonderful exercise as it no doubt improves cardiovascular function, reduces body fat, and improves health in old age, all of which may contribute to brain plasticity. But running may not require much in the way of plastic changes to support it. Learning a new skill, such as playing a musical instrument, learning to type, or reading Braille requires extensive practice, and this practice is likely instrumental in changing the neuropil in relevant brain regions. This distinction is methodologically important because a group receiving exercise can be used as a control for nonspecific effects in a group receiving skill training. In most of the experiments reviewed below some form of exercise regime is administered to a control group that will subsequently be compared with a group receiving skill training.

A more subtle, and often unrecognized, distinction is that between voluntary movements and supporting reactions. Most voluntary movements, such as advancing a limb to grasp food, require concomitant supporting reactions. For example, when a quadruped, such as a rat, lifts and advances a limb to reach for food in an experimental test, it must support its weight with its remaining limbs. To do so, it usually supports and shifts its weight with the diagonal couplet of the contralateral forelimb and the ipsilateral hind limb, and it sometimes assists in balancing itself and moving by using its tail (Whishaw & Miklyaeva 1996). Whereas it is widely accepted that acquiring the act of reaching is a skill that is accompanied by morphological changes in the forelimb area of motor cortex (Greenough et al 1985), it is unclear whether balancing, weight shifting, and tail use are also skills in the same sense. This could be tested empirically, but the more important point relates to how much of the brain undergoes plastic change during the acquisition of the skill of reaching. Perhaps only the neurons controlling the reaching arm undergo change, but it is more likely that the entire motor system will change to varying degrees as the animal acquires the reaching skill. Thus, experiments must be quite complex and include measures from the brain area of interest, adjacent brain regions, and the contralateral hemisphere as well as from appropriate control groups.

The third distinction is between recovery and compensation following brain injury. There is a great deal of interest in how surviving brain tissue changes to contribute to recovery following brain injury (e.g. Forgie et al 1996, Jones & Schallert 1994, Prusky & Whishaw 1996). Careful analysis of the behavior of rats recovering from injury suggests that much of what appears on cursory examination to be recovery is actually a compensatory substitution of new movements for lost movements (Whishaw & Miklyaeva 1996). Thus, the recovery of behavior following injury may not be due to spared neurons assuming the functions of lost neurons but may be due to spared neurons changing their morphology to support compensatory skills. Because both recovery and compensation are potentially important avenues for therapeutics following brain injury, this distinction, though subtle, is not unimportant.

## Analysis of the Brain

The analysis of neuronal change and behavior rests upon the assumption that changes will be found at the synapse when behavior changes. There are, however, two problems to solve. First, the visualization of morphology must provide similar results from animal to animal and study to study. Injections of neuronal tracers to identify axons will not satisfy this concern because visualization of axon terminals depends critically upon how many cells are actually affected by the injection. Furthermore, it is not always possible, a priori, to know where in the brain to look for experience-dependent change, so injections into focal areas are often impractical. Second, because there are so many neurons in the brain, it is essential that only a subset of cells is stained, at best randomly, throughout the brain. Golgi-type stains solve these concerns. Somewhere between 1%–4% of neurons are stained, and there is good evidence that the staining is random (e.g. Pasternak & Woolsey 1987). Furthermore, modern Golgi techniques (e.g. Golgi-Cox; see Gibb & Kolb 1997) provide reliable and extensive staining. Once the cells are stained with a Golgi procedure, the dendritic length can be measured with the aid of a light microscope. Cells are traced using either some sort of semiautomated imaging system or a camera lucida procedure in which cells are drawn with pen and ink. The length of dendritic arborization and the density of synaptic spines then can be estimated using various methods (e.g. Capowski 1989, Kolb et al 1997a). The rationale for selecting dendrites is based upon their special attributes. In particular, dendrites represent up to 95% of the receptor surface with which neurons form connections (Schade & Baxter 1960). The dendrites grow and retract in response to various events including neuronal activity, various chemicals, and injury to adjacent neurons. This makes dendrites one of the more sensitive indicators of change within the CNS. Finally, because dendrites form a large fraction of the neuropil, they are an important indicator of the functional capacity of neural networks. Furthermore, because the majority of excitatory synapses are found on synaptic spines, measurements of spine characteristics including their density, shape, and ultrastructural characteristics also can be made to supplement the dendritic results. (Of course, dendrites do not allow quantification of the actual number of synapses; this can only be done using electron microscopic procedures.)

# EXPERIENCE AND THE CHANGING BRAIN

We can now identify a large range of neural changes associated with experience. These include increases in brain size, cortical thickness, neuron size, dendritic branching, spine density, synapses per neuron, and glial numbers. The magnitude of these changes should not be underestimated. For example, in our own studies of the effects of housing rats in enriched environments, we consistently see changes in young animals in overall brain weight on the order of 7%–10% after 60 days (e.g. Kolb 1995). This increase in brain weight represents increases in glia, blood vessels, neuron soma size, dendritic elements, and synapses. It would be difficult to estimate the total number of increased synapses, but it is probably on the order of 20% in the cortex, which is an extraordinary change!

## Environmental Enrichment

The logic of enrichment studies is that one group of animals is placed in laboratory cages while a second group is housed in a more stimulating environment, the extreme case being Hebb's home (Hebb 1947). Hebb's enrichment procedure was extreme because Hebb's rats roamed fully around his home, whereas most studies of this sort have placed the experimental animals in large enclosures that contain visually stimulating objects and an opportunity to interact haptically with the environment, including the objects. In many studies, the objects are changed routinely and in some studies the social housing conditions may also be manipulated. As mentioned above, it was the group of Bennett, Krech, Rosenzweig, Diamond, and their colleagues at the University of California, Berkeley that first showed large changes in various measures of cortical morphology. As important and seminal as the Berkeley experiments were, they had the weakness that they did not demonstrate changes in brain organization so much as in brain size. It was not until the early 1970s that several groups, including the Berkeley group, began to look at dendritic fields (e.g. Globus et al 1973, Uylings et al 1978). The most thorough studies of this sort were done, however, by Greenough. Typical experiments showed that the dendritic fields of these neurons increased by about 20% relative to cage-reared animals (e.g. Greenough & Volkmar 1973; Volkmar & Greenough 1972). These effects were not restricted to the visual cortex, although other regions tended to show lesser effects and some cell types were relatively unaffected (e.g. Greenough et al 1973). A parallel set of studies has examined changes in the cerebellum of animals trained in complex motor tasks and, as might be anticipated, there are parallel changes in the Purkinje cells, which are the major output cell of the cerebellum. Furthermore, as in the studies of neocortical regions, there is evidence that neuronal changes are not inevitable consequences of experience because cerebellar granule cells do not show the same changes (e.g. Floeter & Greenough 1979).

Although most studies of environment-dependent changes in the cortex have been done with rodents, several studies have used monkeys or cats. In general, these studies have found similar results (e.g. Beaulieu & Colonnier 1987, Floeter & Greenough 1979, Stell & Riesen 1987). One curious difference between the rodent and primate studies appears to be the effects upon the visual system. Because monkeys are highly visual compared to rats, one might predict greater effects upon the visual cortex of monkeys; yet the opposite appears to be true. In fact, it appears that the effects upon the primary visual cortex of monkeys reared in enriched environments are negligible (e.g. Riesen et al 1977, Struble & Riesen 1978). One explanation is that much of the exploration of the visual world of monkeys is done without movement, and because monkeys in relatively impoverished housing can still visually explore their environment, this stimulation may be sufficient to ensure the development of visual cortical synapses. In contrast, the visual system of the rat has relatively poor acuity and is not designed for pattern vision so much as for spatial navigation. The gathering of spatial information likely requires movement in space. An alternate explanation is that because the visual areas of the primate have expanded dramatically, and because the primary visual cortex is multifunctional, then it is "higher" visual areas that show greater experience-dependent changes. In this case, one might predict that visual experiences that emphasized object exploration and recognition would lead to growth in the ventral visual pathway, whereas visual experiences that emphasized visuomotor guidance, such as in climbing or object manipulation, would lead to growth in the dorsal visual pathway (for a discussion of the two pathways, see Milner & Goodale 1995).

Most studies of dendritic change have used a Golgi-type technique to measure dendritic space, and from this there is an assumption that dendritic space is correlated tightly with synaptic numbers. Turner & Greenough (1983, 1985) examined this hypothesis directly by calculating the number of synapses per neuron in the cortex of animals housed in enriched environments. They found an increase of about 20% in the number of synapses per neuron in the brains of enriched versus cage-reared animals. Thus, although the density of synapses in a section of cortical tissue is relatively constant in enriched and cage-reared animals, there is more dendritic space in the enriched animals and, consequently, there are more synapses per neuron. Similarly, Beaulieu & Colonnier (1988) analyzed the number and type of synapses in cats reared in laboratory cages or in enriched housing. Like Turner & Greenough, they found that synaptic changes correlated with experience. One additional finding, however, was that experience increased the number of excitatory synapses per neuron and decreased the number of inhibitory ones in the visual cortex. Thus, enrichment had modified the excitatory-inhibitory equilibrium of the visual cortex. One prediction from this observation is that neurons in the cortex of enriched animals would be more reactive to visual stimulation than those in impoverished animals.

It is reasonable to expect that if there are increases in the size of the dendritic fields of neurons, and correspondingly in the number of synapses per neuron, then these neurons will require more support both from glial cells, especially astrocytes, and from blood vessels. In one heroic series of studies, Sirevaag & Greenough (e.g. 1987, 1988, 1991) used light and electron microscope techniques to analyze 36 different aspects of cortical synaptic, cellular, and vascular morphology in rats raised in complex or in caged-housing environments. The simple conclusion was that there is a coordinated change not only in neuronal morphology but also in glial, vascular, and metabolic processes in response to differential experiences. Thus, not only are there more synapses per neuron in animals with enriched experience, there is also more astrocytic material, more blood capillaries, and a higher mitochondria volume. (Mitochondrial volume is used as a measure of metabolic activity.) It is therefore clear that when the brain changes in response to experience there are the expected neural changes but there are also adjustments in metabolic requirements of the larger neurons. One interesting implication of this conclusion is that things that influence the maintenance and adjustment of the metabolic components of the aging brain can be expected to influence the brain's capacity for neural change as well (e.g. Black et al 1987, 1989). This speaks to the importance of examining the effects of exercise and nutrition on the brain's capacity for change, especially in senescence. It is important to note in this context, however, that merely having exercise is not sufficient to induce neuronal changes. Black et al (1990) trained animals to negotiate a complex obstacle course ("acrobat rats") or placed rats in running wheels where they obtained forced exercise. The animals in the wheels showed increased capillary formation but no change in cerebellar Purkinje cell synapses, whereas the acrobat rats showed a 30% increase in Purkinje synapses. Thus, merely increasing neuronal support does not change the neurons. The critical feature for neuronal change is presumably increased neuronal processing, which would be facilitated by a complementary increase in metabolic support.

## Training in Specific Tasks

Although it is tempting to conclude that the synaptic changes observed in animals housed in complex environments reflect changes in learning about the environment, there is little direct evidence of this. One way to approach this issue is to train animals in specific tasks and then to demonstrate specific changes in dendritic fields of neurons in regions suspected of being involved in the performance of such tasks. Perhaps the most convincing studies of this sort were done by Chang & Greenough (1982). These studies took advantage of the fact that the visual pathways of the laboratory rat are about 90% crossed. That is, about 90% of the cortical projections from the left eye project via the right lateral geniculate nucleus to the right hemisphere. Chang & Greenough placed occluders on one eye of rats and then trained the animals in a visual maze. Comparison of the neurons in the two hemispheres revealed that those in the trained hemisphere had larger dendritic fields. This experiment is compelling because the rest of the two hemispheres (e.g. auditory, somatosensory, or olfactory regions) would still have interacted with the maze, and both hemispheres would be required for the motor demands. It was only the visual cortex contralateral to the open eye that could process and/or store the task-specific visual information, however; and this was reflected by the specific dendritic changes in that hemisphere.

Another experiment is relevant here. Although they did not train animals in a visual learning task, Tieman & Hirsch (1982) raised cats with lenses that restricted visual exposure to lines oriented vertically or horizontally. Many previous studies had shown that cells in the visual cortex of cats with such restricted experience show a marked change in their tuning characteristics. Hence, neurons in cats with selective exposure to lines of vertical orientation are most excitable when presented with lines of the same orientation. The new wrinkle in the Tieman & Hirsch study was that they examined the morphology of visual cortical neurons from cats with selective horizontal or vertical visual experience. Cats raised in a normal environment showed a random distribution of orientation of dendritic fields, but cats raised with selective experiences showed a change in the orientation of the dendritic fields. These changes were specific, too, because they occurred in pyramidal cells in visual cortex and not in the adjacent stellate cells.

A second set of experiments has taken advantage of the fact that rats are very talented at using their forepaws to retrieve food from tubes, through bars, and so on. Because the cortical control of the forelimbs is largely crossed, it is possible to train one limb to reach for food and to compare the layer V neurons in the forelimb region of motor cortex, many of which form the cortical spinal tract, in the trained and untrained hemispheres. Several studies have shown dendritic changes in the expected neurons (Greenough et al 1985, Kolb et al 1997a, Withers & Greenough 1989).

The changes in dendritic fields seen in the studies of visual and motor learning are strikingly reminiscent of the changes seen in studies of enriched rearing, which have been taken as evidence that the observed changes in synaptic connectivity in animals in enriched environments are somehow involved in memory and learning (Greenough & Chang 1989). While this is a reasonable conclusion, there may be important differences in details of dendritic change in the enrichment and learning studies. It is generally found that enrichment not only increases dendritic length but also increases the density of synaptic spines on the dendrites. In contrast, animals trained in specific tasks show changes in dendritic length but not in spine density (Kolb et al 1996). Thus, it appears that although there are marked similarities between the effects of enriched rearing and specific training on dendritic fields, there may be differences in other measures of dendritic morphology, especially spine density.

## Olfactory Experience in Rodents

Rodents have a keen sense of smell so it is reasonable to suppose that experience would have significant effects upon the structure of the olfactory system. In fact, the general finding is that olfactory deprivation leads to restricted morphological development of the olfactory system, whereas olfactory training or olfactory "enrichment" leads to enhanced development (e.g. Doving & Pinching 1973, Pinching & Doving 1974, Rehn & Breipohl 1986, Rehn et al 1986) (see also the extensive studies by Leon and colleagues, e.g. Leon 1992a,b). One surprising finding is that olfactory experience not only changes the morphology of existing neurons, but it also alters the number of neurons. For example, odor deprivation results in reductions in neuronal number (e.g. Brunjes & Frazier 1986, Meisami & Safari 1981, Skeen et al 1986), whereas enriched odor exposure leads to increased neuron numbers (Rosselli-Austin & Williams 1990). This neuronal increase is not trivial, being in the order of 35-40%! Evidence of increased neuron numbers in the olfactory system is especially intriguing because it has not been seen in analyses of neocortical or cerebellar cortex. One important difference between the olfactory system and neocortical and cerebellar regions is that olfactory neurons are generated throughout the lifetime of rodents (e.g. Lois & Alvarez-Buylla 1994). Thus, it is likely that enhanced olfactory experience influences neuronal growth in the olfactory bulb throughout life. One possible reason for this could be that the addition and deletion of olfactory neurons throughout life allow a mechanism for the nervous system to form new olfactory memories and to modify existing ones. It is noteworthy that the other forebrain structure that generates neurons throughout adulthood is the dentate gyrus of the hippocampus, and this area has been implicated in certain types of learning and memory.

## Plasticity in the Avian Brain

Three general types of studies look at brain plasticity and behavior in birds. These include studies of bird song, imprinting, and one-trial learning. Studies of bird song have been reviewed extensively elsewhere (e.g. Bottjer & Arnold 1997) and largely have focused on the development of neurons and their connectivity. Our emphasis here therefore is on imprinting and one-trial learning.

Imprinting is a process whereby an organism learns, during a sensitive period in development, to restrict its social preferences to a specific class of objects (e.g. Bateson 1966). Imprinting is especially common in precocial birds such as chickens or geese. Within hours of hatching, a young bird will approach and follow a moving object, which may or may not resemble an adult female of the same species. Horn and his colleagues (for reviews, see Dudai 1989, Horn 1985) have identified a specific neural region (region IMHV) in the chick brain that changes morphologically during imprinting. For example, there is increased metabolic activity and genetic (RNA) activity in IMHV during imprinting. Morphological studies have emphasized ultrastructure where it has been shown that imprinting is correlated with an increase in the length of the postsynaptic density (PSD) of spine synapses in the IMHV, but only in the left hemisphere (Horn et al 1985). The PSD is the active receptor-dense region of the postsynaptic cell. Thus, as the PSD lengthens, the number of receptors for neurotransmitters increases (Matus et al 1981). Horn (1985) noted that small changes in the length of the postsynaptic density provide an effective way for presynaptic cells to control the firing of postsynaptic cells, or to control local synaptic interactions. Significantly, there does not seem to be an increase in synapse number in the IMHV during imprinting.

Several studies have taken advantage of the observation that one-day-old chicks peck spontaneously at a small bright chrome bead. For instance, Patel & Stewart (1988) coated the bead with either a substance with an aversive taste or nonaversive water. Chicks presented with the aversive taste learn in one trial to avoid the bead, whereas those presented with the nonaversive bead continue to peck (for a review, see Rose 1985). Various regions of the chick brain, such as the hyperstriatum, show enhanced activity following training as revealed both by electrophysiological investigations and studies of glucose accumulation.

Patel & Stewart used a Golgi technique to impregnate chick brains 25 h after training and found a twofold increase in spine density in the neurons in a region of the hyperstriatum (intermediate medial hyperstriatum ventrale) in the "trained" chicks. They concluded that this represented an increase in synapses that reflected the learning. This interpretation was supported by a second study in which Patel et al (1988) trained chicks on the passive avoidance task described above but, in their experiment, half of the trained chicks were given a subconvulsive transcranial electroshock 5 min after training. This procedure rendered about half of the trained animals amnesic for the experience. The spine density was found to be higher in the chicks that remembered the aversive nature of the training stimulus than in the chicks rendered amnesic. This finding argues strongly in favor of a specific role for dendritic spines in experience-dependent memory formation in the chick.

There is one additional study that suggests that their conclusion may not be quite correct, however. Wallhausser & Scheich (1987) presented newly hatched chicks with either a hen or an acoustic stimulus, with the goal of imprinting the chicks to the visual or auditory stimulus. The neurons in different regions of the hyperstriatum of the imprinted chicks were compared with those of isolated chicks. There was a decrease in spine density. Thus, in the first study, there was an increase 25 h after training, whereas in the latter study there was a decrease 7 days after training. The simplest conclusion from the chick studies is that the novel stimulation may cause an initial rapid increase in spine density, followed by a pruning. The critical experiment here would be to examine the neurons in the brains of animals killed at different times in the training.

## The Invertebrate Nervous System

There is a burgeoning literature on the effects of experience on the morphology of neurons of invertebrates, both during metamorphosis (e.g. Jacobs & Weeks 1990, Kent & Levine 1993) and in response to experience (e.g. Hoy et al 1985). Two studies on Drosophila are especially intriguing. In one, Technau (1984) showed that the complexity of neurons in *Drosophila melanogaster* depends upon the flies' living conditions. Flies were housed for 3 weeks either singly in small plastic vials or in groups of 200 in larger enclosures with colored visual patterns on the walls, various odor sources, and plants. Analysis of the Kenyon cell fibers in the mushroom bodies (cells in the "brain" of the fly) showed about 15% more fibers in the enriched versus impoverished flies. A subsequent study by Heisenberg et al (1995) showed that most regions of the Drosophila brain were continuously reorganized throughout life in response to specific living conditions. In particular, social and sexual activity was associated with increased brain size, as was the volume of space available. These experience-dependent changes in Drosophila are remarkable and leave little doubt that experience is a major force in shaping the nervous system of all animals. Furthermore, changes in insect brains are not only seen in artificial lab experiments but can also be seen in ecologically valid settings. For example, Withers et al (1993) examined the changes in the brain of the honey bee in relation to the division of labor in adult worker bees. Adult worker bees spend about the first 3 weeks of their 4–7-week life performing a variety of tasks within the hive, including caring for the queen and brood ("nursing"). They then make a dramatic transition in behavior and begin to forage outside for food. Food foraging is a complex behavior that requires that the animal learn the location of both the hive and the food and the nature of different foods, as well as learn to recognize and use species-typical signals about food sources from other bees. Withers et al (1993) found not only that the behavioral change is associated with striking changes in brain structure, but that these changes are dependent not on the age of the animal but on its foraging experience. This honey bee model offers a new entry into the cellular mechanisms of neural and behavioral plasticity.

## Dendrites and Behavior in Humans

On the basis of studies in laboratory animals it is reasonable to expect correlations between neuronal structure and behavior in humans. One way to approach this would be to look for a relationship between cell structure and education. Jacobs et al (1993) did, in fact, consider this question and found a relationship between extent of dendritic arborization in a cortical language area (Wernicke's area) and amount of education. Hence, the cortical neurons from the brains of deceased people with university education had more dendritic arbor than those from people with high school education who, in turn, had more dendritic material than those with less than high school education. Of course, it may have been that people with larger dendritic fields were more likely to go to university, but that is not easy to test.

Another way to look at the relationship between human brain structure and behavior is to consider the functional abilities of people and to correlate them with neuronal structure. For example, one might expect to find differences in language-related areas between people with high and low verbal abilities. This experiment is difficult to do, however, because it presupposes behavioral measures before death, and this is not normally done. However, Jacobs et al (1993) considered this possibility by taking advantage of the now well-documented observation that females have verbal abilities that are superior to those of males (for a review, see Kolb & Whishaw 1996). Thus, when they examined the structure of neurons in Wernicke's area, they found that females have more extensive dendritic arbors than males. Furthermore, in a subsequent study, Jacobs et al (1993) found that this sex difference was present as early as age 9, suggesting that such sex differences emerge within the first decade. These sex differences in cortical architecture in humans are parallel to those reported in other studies showing sex differences in cerebral blood flow and glucose metabolism, with females having a level about 15% higher than that of males (e.g. Baxter et al 1987).

Scheibel et al (1990) approached the matter in a slightly different way. They began with two hypotheses. First, they suggested that there is a relationship between the complexity of dendritic arbor and the nature of the computational tasks performed by a brain area. To test this hypothesis, they examined the dendritic structure of neurons in different cortical regions that they proposed to have functions that varied in computational complexity. For example, when they compared the structure of neurons corresponding to the somatosensory representation of the trunk versus those for the fingers, they found the latter to have more complex cells. They reasoned that the somesthetic inputs from receptive fields on the chest wall would constitute less of an integrative and interpretive challenge to cortical neurons than those from the fingers and thus that neurons representing the chest were less complex. Similarly, when they compared the cells in the finger area to those in the supramarginal gyrus (SMG), a region that is associated with higher cognitive processes, they found the SMG neurons to be more complex. The second hypothesis was that dendritic trees in all regions are subject to experience-dependent change. As a result, they hypothesized that predominant life experiences (e.g. occupation) should be reflected in the structure of dendritic trees. Although they did not test this hypothesis directly, they did have an interesting observation. In their study comparing cells in the trunk area, finger area, and the SMG, they found curious individual differences. For example, especially large differences in trunk and finger neurons were found in the brains of people who were typists, machine operators, and appliance repairmen. In each of these, a high level of finger dexterity maintained over long periods of time may be assumed. In contrast, one case with no trunk-finger difference was a salesman in whom one would not expect a good deal of specialized finger use. These results are suggestive although we would agree with Scheibel et al's caution that "a larger sample size and far more detailed life, occupation, leisure, and retirement histories are necessary" (p. 101). The preliminary findings in this study do suggest that such an investigation would be fruitful.

Finally, one can look at pathological development and see if there is a neural correlate of abnormal behavior. In one such study, Purpura (1974) examined the dendritic structure of neurons from the brains of retarded versus average intelligence children. He did not quantify the dendritic length, but he did find marked differences in dendritic structure. The retarded children had spindly dendrites that had a very much reduced spine density. This abnormal spine density is intriguing because it is reminiscent of the low spine density that we have consistently observed in rats with cortical injury in what would be equivalent to the third trimester of human development. Like retarded children, these rats have severe behavioral deficits that render them unable to learn cognitive tasks that are solved easily by animals with similar brain injuries later in life (e.g. Kolb & Gibb 1991a). More recently, there have been several studies of children with trisomic chromosomal states, such as Down's syndrome and trisomy 13 (e.g. Becker et al 1986, Jay et al 1990, Marin-Padilla 1974), the general observation being that there is anomalous spine morphology, decreased spine density, and small dendritic fields in many types of retardation.

# MODULATION OF EXPERIENCE-DEPENDENT CHANGE

The demonstration that dendritic and/or synaptic change is related to experience is intriguing, but it is not proof of a relationship. The critical experiments are those in which an experimental manipulation alters the behavior and the morphology changes in a meaningful manner. Various manipulations fit this requirement, including especially age, sex hormones, neurotrophins, stress, and injury.

## Aging

Despite nearly a century of effort by scores of investigators, many of the basic questions concerning changes in the aging brain are swirling in controversy (Coleman & Flood 1987). Buell & Coleman (1979) first noted that the aged brain showed an increase in dendritic growth that was hypothesized to compensate for the loss of neurons with age. That is, their general idea is that the number of synapses in the cortex is maintained by adding synapses to the dendrites of the adjacent neurons in the cortex. This growth would seem to be in accord with the general observation that most middle-aged people can be presumed to have suffered neuronal loss but do not appear demented. Furthermore, Buell & Coleman (1985) have shown that there is a failure of dendritic growth in the demented brain. As intriguing as the relationship between aging, dementia, and dendritic growth appears, we must caution that there nonetheless remains some controversy because not all brain regions appear to suffer cell death with age (e.g. Coleman & Flood 1987).

## Sex Hormones

There is accumulating evidence that the male brain and the female brain differ in their structure and respond differently to experience. Specifically, Juraska and her colleagues (e.g. Juraska 1984, 1986, 1990; Juraska et al 1985, 1989) were the first to report that the visual cortex is more sensitive to experience in males than it is in females. This is not a general increased sensitivity of males, however, because they have also reported that the hippocampus is more sensitive to experience in females than in males. These differences are related to the circulating gonadal hormone and therefore can be manipulated with hormone injections. Evidence of sex differences in cortical structure has now been shown to occur in the prefrontal cortical regions of lab-reared rats (e.g. Kolb & Stewart 1991, 1995), and recently it has been shown that injury to these morphologically dimorphic areas produces sexually dimorphic differences in functional recovery (Kolb & Cioe 1996).

The importance of sex hormones is not restricted to development. Stewart & Kolb (1994) have shown that ovariectomized or gonadectomized adult rats show significant change in cortical structure, especially in the females. Thus, the brains of ovariectomized rats not only grew heavier, but the cortical neurons showed a 25% increase in dendritic arbor and a 10% increase in spine density. This result implies that cortical morphology is hormone-dependent throughout the life of the animal. Because experience has sexually dimorphic effects, it seems reasonable to suppose that changes in hormonal state, especially in postmenopausal women, will alter the brain's response to experience.

## Neurotrophins

Neurotrophins, which are chemicals known to have growth-enhancing properties in the nervous system, influence dendritic structure and also interact with experience. It is known, for instance, that administration of nerve growth factor during adulthood increases both dendritic branching and spine density throughout the cortex (e.g. Kolb et al 1997b). Furthermore, experience differentially modulates the levels of different neurotrophins such as nerve growth factor which, in turn, stimulates growth (e.g. Schoups et al 1995). Thus, it is possible that one route of action of experience on the brain is to stimulate (or inhibit?) the production of neurotrophins, and these, in turn, alter neuronal structure. This promises to be an area of intense study in the near future.

## Stress

Stress has effects on the neuroendocrine system and this, in turn, has been shown to affect cell morphology (e.g. Sapolsky 1987, Sirevaag et al 1991, Stewart & Kolb 1988). Most studies to date have focused on the hippocampal formation, but there is reason to suspect that cortical neurons are also vulnerable to the effects of stress (Stewart & Kolb 1988). There is no specific evidence about whether stress interacts with experience-dependent changes in the brain, but it seems likely.

## Injury

When the cortex is damaged there are changes in the remaining cortex that are correlated with functional outcome. For example, when Kolb & Gibb (1991b) removed the frontal cortex in adult rats there was an initial drop in dendritic arborization near the injury. This atrophy slowly resolved and four months later there was a significant increase in dendritic morphology, which was correlated with partial restitution of function. In contrast, large sensorimotor cortex lesions lead only to neuronal atrophy and no evidence of functional recovery (Kolb et al 1997b).

These results are reminiscent of those seen in the aging and demented brain: When there is evidence of dendritic growth it leads to functional recovery, whereas when there is no dendritic growth there is no recovery. This principle can be seen even more clearly in the developing brain. One of our consistent findings over the past decade has been that when the cortex of the developing rat is damaged in the first few days of life, which corresponds to a time just after neural proliferation is complete but neural migration and differentiation is still ongoing, there is a marked generalized atrophy of dendritic arborization and a decrease in spine density in neurons throughout the cortical mantle (for a review, see Kolb 1995). This result is correlated with a miserable functional outcome and is reminiscent of the marked abnormalities in the brains of retarded children (Purpura 1974). In contrast, when the cortical mantle of rats is damaged in the second week of life, which corresponds to the period of rapid dendritic growth and synaptic formation, there is a generalized enhancement of dendritic arborization and/or spine density throughout the remaining cortex (Kolb & Gibb 1991a). This enhanced dendritic response is correlated with dramatic functional recovery. Thus, we see that if the injury in the cortex leads to increased dendritic space, there is a good functional outcome, whereas if the injury leads to a retarded development of dendritic material, there is a poor functional outcome. Furthermore, we have shown that with treatments that reverse the dendritic atrophy, such as administration of neurotrophins or housing in enriched environments, there is functional improvement.

## CONCLUSIONS

One of the most intriguing questions in behavioral neuroscience concerns the manner in which the brain, and especially the neocortex, can modify its function throughout one's lifetime. Taken all together, the evidence discussed above makes a strong case for a relationship between brain plasticity and behavioral change. Indeed, it is now clear that experience alters the synaptic organization of the brain in species as diverse as fruit flies and humans. Evidence that these changes are functionally meaningful is more difficult to collect, but there is little doubt that changes in synaptic organization are correlated with changes in behavior. Thus, animals with extensive dendritic growth, relative to untreated animals, show facilitated performance on many types of behavioral measures. In contrast, animals with atrophy in dendritic arborization show a decline in behavioral capacity. Similarly, factors that enhance dendritic growth (e.g. nerve growth factor) facilitate behavioral outcome, whereas factors that block dendritic growth (e.g. brain injury at birth in rats) retard functional outcomes. We should emphasize that although we have stressed changes in dendritic morphology, there are multiple, and likely dissociable, changes in the neuron morphology that correlate with behavioral change. These include increases in dendritic length, dendritic branching pattern, spine density, synapse number, synapse size, glial size and number, and metabolic activity.

The critical question that remains is how dendritic and synaptic change is related to behavioral change. The current evidence clearly shows that dendrites in the cortex may show a net proliferation, regression, or stability depending upon various factors that affect behavior. It seems likely that a net proliferation of dendrites is a response to an increased availability of afferent supply. In contrast, the net reduction in dendrites, which is seen in response to injury, for example, is likely to reflect a decline in the afferent supply to a cell. In this view, dendrites are hypothesized to be in a state in which they are constantly ready to expand or retract their territory, limited largely by the availability of afferent nourishment and by the metabolic capacities of the cell. Because changes in the dendritic length are presumed to reflect changes in synaptic connectivity, it follows that increased dendritic arbor reflects increased synapse formation, whereas decreased dendritic arbor reflects decreased synapse formation.

The putative increase (or decrease) in afferent supply to a neuron leads to the question of where these afferents arise. There is scant evidence that the adult or even the infant brain is capable of growing new projections over long distances. Thus, it seems most likely that changes in afferent supply reflect changes in axonal arborizations of relatively nearby neighbors. A recent analysis by Nicoll & Blakemore (1993) is instructive. They examined the patterns of connections of pyramidal cells, which are the almost exclusive outputs of the the neocortex. The axons of pyramidal cells make long-range connections to other cortical regions or subcortical structures, but they also have axon collaterals that form extensive arborizations with nearby cells. In fact, the most common target of pyramidal cells is other cortical pyramidal cells. Nicoll & Blakemore estimated that roughly 70% of the excitatory synapses on any layer II/III pyramidal cell are derived from pyramidal cells in the near vicinity. One way for the functioning of an intrinsic circuit to change is for the field of influence of a neuron to change. For example, the diameter of a cell's dendritic field could expand, allowing the cell to interact with a larger number of neurons. Alternatively, the axon terminal could redistribute to enlarge the field of influence, too. The fact that neurons can expand their field of influence means that if neurons die, remaining ones could enlarge their field to make up for some of the lost processing power.

It is assumed in our model that increasing the connectivity of pyramidal cells will increase their functional capacity. But why should this be? Hebb (1949) proposed the idea of cell assemblies in which networks of cortical neurons were seen as being responsible for mental activity. A key component of this model is that individual neurons have little role in behavioral control, but rather behavior is dependent upon networks of neurons. Furthermore, Hebb noted that a given neuron could participate in multiple networks, each with a different function. Calvin (1996) likened this to the person who is on multiple committees, each with a different function. Thus, if neurons have more connections, they are hypothesized to have more influence on the observed behavior.

A critical feature of this view is that afferent supply influences neuronal function. We are now left with the question of what controls afferent supply. Various factors, such as neurotrophins, can influence this supply, but they must do it through some clear mechanism. One likely candidate is gene expression. There is ample evidence that the expression of genes in the mature brain is influenced by environmental and behavioral events (e.g. Dudai 1989). Gene expression thus provides a mechanism whereby cells can synthesize new proteins needed to form more synapses. Studies in various species, especially *Aplysia,* have shown that blockade of protein synthesis blocks long-lasting changes in both synapses and behavior (Bailey & Kandel 1993). The most likely mechanism for increased gene activity is neuronal activity, which is stimulated by behavior and experience. Activity initiated by experience or behavior could therefore increase the activity of genetic mechanisms responsible for dendritic and synaptic growth and, ultimately, behavioral change.

> **Visit the *Annual Reviews home page* at**
> **http://www.AnnualReviews.org.**

## Literature Cited

Bailey CH, Kandel ER. 1993. Structural changes accompanying memory storage. *Annu. Rev. Physiol.* 55:397–426

Bateson PPG. 1966. The characteristics and context of imprinting. *Biol. Rev.* 41: 177–220

Baxter LR Jr, Mazziotta JC, Phelps ME, Selin CE, Guze GH, Fairbanks L. 1987. Cerebral glucose metabolic rates in normal human females versus normal males. *Psychol. Res.* 21:237–45

Beaulieu C, Colonnier M. 1987. Effect of the

richness of the environment on the cat visual cortex. *J. Comp. Neurol.* 266:478–94

Beaulieu C, Colonnier M. 1988. Richness of environment affects the number of contacts formed by boutons containing flat vesicles but does not alter the number of these boutons per neuron. *J. Comp. Neurol.* 274:347–56

Becker LE, Armstrong DL, Chan F. 1986. Dendritic atrophy in children with Down's syndrome. *Ann. Neurol.* 20:520–26

Black JE, Greenough WT, Anderson BJ, Isaacs KR. 1987. Environment and the aging brain. *Can. J. Psychol.* 41:111–30

Black JE, Isaacs KR, Anderson BJ, Alcantara AA, Greenough WT. 1990. Learning causes synaptogenesis, whereas motor activity causes angiogenesis, in cerebellar cortex of adult rats. *Proc. Natl. Acad. Sci. USA* 87:5568–72

Black JE, Polinsky M, Greenough WT. 1989. Progressive failure of cerebral angiogenesis supporting neural plasticity in aging rats. *Neurobiol. Aging* 10:353–58

Bottjer SW, Arnold AP. 1997. Developmental plasticity in neural circuits for a learned behavior. *Annu. Rev. Neurosci.* 20:459–81

Brunjes PC, Frazier LL. 1986. Maturation and plasticity in the olfactory system of vertebrates. *Brain Res. Rev.* 11:1–45

Buell SJ, Coleman PD. 1979. Dendritic growth in the aged human brain and failure of growth in senile dementia. *Science* 206:854–56

Buell SJ, Coleman PD. 1985. Regulation of dendritic extent in developing and aging brain. In *Synaptic Plasticity*, ed. CW Cotman, pp. 311–33. New York: Raven

Calvin WH. 1996. *The Cerebral Code.* Cambridge, MA: MIT Press

Capowski J. 1989. *Computer Techniques in Neuroanatomy.* New York: Plenum

Chang F-LF, Greenough WT. 1982. Lateralized effects of monocular training on dendritic branching in adult split-brain rats. *Brain Res.* 232:283–92

Coleman PD, Flood DG. 1987. Neuron numbers and dendritic extent in normal aging and Alzheimer's disease. *Neurobiol. Aging* 8:521–45

Diamond MC, Dowling GA, Johnson RE. 1981. Morphologic cerebral cortical asymmetry in male and female rats. *Exp. Neurol.* 71:261–68

Diamond MC, Lindner B, Raymond A. 1967. Extensive cortical depth measurements and neuron size increases in the cortex of environmentally enriched rats. *J. Comp. Neurol.* 131:357–64

Doving KB, Pinching AJ. 1973. Selective degeneration of neurones in the olfactory bulb following prolonged odour exposure. *Brain Res.* 52:115–29

Dudai Y. 1989. *The Neurobiology of Memory: Concepts, Findings, Trends.* Oxford: Oxford Univ. Press

Floeter MK, Greenough WT. 1979. Cerebellar plasticity: modification of Purkinje cell structure by differential rearing in monkeys. *Science* 206:227–29

Forgie ML, Gibb R, Kolb B. 1996. Unilateral lesions of the forelimb area of rat motor cortex: lack of evidence for use-dependent neural growth in the undamaged hemisphere. *Brain Res.* 710:249–59

Gibb R, Kolb B. 1997. A method of vibratome sectioning of Golgi-Cox stained whole rat brain. *J. Neurosci. Methods.* In press

Globus A, Rosenzweig MR, Bennett EL, Diamond MC. 1973. Effects of differential experience on dendritic spine counts in rat cerebral cortex. *J. Comp. Physiol. Psychol.* 82:175–81

Greenough WT, Chang FF. 1989. Plasticity of synapse structure and pattern in the cerebral cortex. In *Cerebral Cortex*, ed. A Peters, EG Jones, 7:391–440. New York: Plenum

Greenough WT, Larson JR, Withers GS. 1985. Effects of unilateral and bilateral training in a reaching task on dendritic branching of neurons in the rat motorsensory forelimb cortex. *Behav. Neur. Biol.* 44:301–14

Greenough WT, Volkmar FR. 1973. Pattern of dendritic branching in occipital cortex of rats reared in complex environments. *Exp. Neurol.* 40:491–504

Greenough WT, Volkmar FR, Juraska JM. 1973. Effects of rearing complexity on dendritic branching in frontolateral and temporal cortex of the rat. *Exp. Neurol.* 41:371–78

Hebb DO. 1947. The effects of early experience on problem solving at maturity. *Am. Psychol.* 2:737–45

Hebb DO. 1949. *The Organization of Behavior.* New York: Wiley

Heisenberg M, Heusipp M, Wanke C. 1995. Structural plasticity in the Drosophila brain. *J. Neurosci.* 15:1951–60

Horn G. 1985. *Memory, Imprinting, and the Brain: An Inquiry Into Mechanisms.* Oxford: Clarendon

Horn G, Bradley P, McCabe BJ. 1985. Changes in the structure of synapses associated with learning. *J. Neurosci.* 5:3161–68

Hoy RR, Nolen TG, Casaday GC. 1985. Dendritic sprouting and compensatory synaptogenesis in an identified interneuron follow auditory deprivation in a cricket. *Proc. Natl. Acad. Sci. USA* 82:7772–76

Jacobs B, Schall M, Scheibel AB. 1993. A quantitative dendritic analysis of Wernicke's area. II. Gender, Hemispheric, and environmental factors. *J. Comp. Neurol.* 237:97–111

Jacobs GA, Weeks JC. 1990. Postsynaptic changes at a sensory to motoneuron synapse contribute to the developmental loss of a reflex behavior during insect metamorphosis. *J. Neurosci.* 10:1341–56

Jay V, Chan F-W, Becker LE. 1990. Dendritic arborization in the human fetus and infant with trisomy 18 syndrome. *Dev. Brain Res.* 54:291–94

Jones TA, Schallert T. 1994. Use-dependent growth of pyramidal neurons after neocortical damage. *J. Neurosci.* 14:2140–52

Juraska JM. 1984. Sex differences in dendritic responses to differential experience in the rat visual cortex. *Brain Res.* 295:27–34

Juraska JM. 1986. Sex differences in developmental plasticity of behavior and the brain. In *Developmental Neuropsychobiology,* ed. WT Greenough, JM Juraska, pp. 409–22. New York: Academic

Juraska JM. 1990. The structure of the cerebral cortex: Effects of gender and the environment. In *The Cerebral Cortex of the Rat,* ed. B Kolb, R Tees, pp. 483–506. Cambridge, MA: MIT Press

Juraska JM, Fitch J, Henderson C, Rivers N. 1985. Sex differences in the dendritic branching of dentate granule cells following differential experience. *Brain Res.* 333:73–80

Juraska JM, Fitch JM, Washburne DL. 1989. The dendritic morphology of pyramidal neurons in the rat hippocampal CA3 area. II. Effects of gender and experience. *Brain Res.* 479:115–21

Kent KS, Levine RG. 1993. Dendritic reorganization of an identified neuron during metamorphosis of the moth Manduca sexta: the influence of interactions with the periphery. *J. Neurobiol.* 24:1–22

Kolb B. 1995. *Brain Plasticity and Behavior.* Mahwah, NJ: Erlbaum

Kolb B, Cioe J. 1996. Sex-related differences in cortical function after medial frontal lesions in rats. *Behav. Neurosci.* 110:1271–81

Kolb B, Cote S, Ribeiro-da-Silva A, Cuello AC. 1996. NGF stimulates recovery of function and dendritic growth after unilateral motor cortex lesions in rats. *Neuroscience* 76: 1139–51

Kolb B, Forgie M, Gibb R, Gorny G, Rowntree S. 1997a. Age, experience and the changing brain. *Neurosci. Biobehav. Rev.* In press

Kolb B, Gibb R. 1991a. Sparing of function after neonatal frontal lesions correlates with increased cortical dendritic branching: a possible mechanism for the Kennard effect. *Behav. Brain Res.* 43:51–56

Kolb B, Gibb R. 1991b. Environmental enrichment and cortical injury: behavioral and anatomical consequences of frontal cortex lesions in rats. *Cereb. Cortex* 1: 189–98

Kolb B, Gibb R, Gorny G, Ouellette A. 1996. Experience dependent changes in cortical morphology are age dependent. *Soc. Neurosci. Abstr.* 22:1133

Kolb B, Gorny G, Cote S, Ribeiro-da-Silva A, Cuello AC. 1997b. Nerve growth factor stimulates growth of cortical pyramidal neurons in young adult rats. *Brain Res.* 751:289–94

Kolb B, Stewart J. 1991. Sex-related differences in dendritic branching of cells in the prefrontal cortex of rats. *J. Neuroendocrinol.* 3:95–99

Kolb B, Stewart J. 1995. Changes in neonatal gonadal hormonal environment prevent behavioral sparing and alter cortical morphogenesis after early frontal cortex lesions in male and female rats. *Behav. Neurosci.* 109:285–94

Kolb B, Whishaw IQ. 1996. *Fundamentals of Human Neuropsychology.* New York: Freeman. 4th ed.

Leon M. 1992a. Neuroethology of olfactory preference development. *J. Neurobiol.* 23: 1557–73

Leon M. 1992b. The neurobiology of filial learning. *Annu. Rev. Psychol.* 43:377–98

Lois C, Alvarez-Buylla A. 1994. Long-distance neuronal migration in the adult mammalian brain. *Science* 264:1145–48

Marin-Padilla M. 1974. Structural organization of the cerebral cortex (motor area) in human chromosomal aberrations: a Golgi study. I. D½1 (13–15) trisomy, Patau syndrome. *Brain Res.* 66:375–91

Matus A, Pehling G, Wilkinson D. 1981. Gamma-aminobutyric acid receptors in brain postsynaptic densities. *J. Neurobiol.* 12:67–73

Meisami E, Safari L. 1981. A quantitative study of the effects of early unilateral olfactory deprivation on the number and distribution of mitral and tufted cells and of glomeruli in the rat olfactory bulb. *Brain Res.* 222:81–107

Milner D, Goodale MA. 1995. *The Visual*

*Brain in Action.* Oxford: Oxford Univ. Press

Nicoll A, Blakemore C. 1993. Patterns of local connectivity in the neocortex. *Neural Comput.* 5:665–80

Pasternak JF, Woolsey TA. 1987. On the "selectivityá" of the Golgi-Cox method. *J. Comp. Neurol.* 160:307–12

Patel SN, Rose SPR, Stewart MG. 1988. Training induced dendritic spine density changes are specifically related to memory formation processes in the chick, Gallus domesticus. *Brain Res.* 463:168–73

Patel SN, Stewart MG. 1988. Changes in the number and structure of dendritic spines 25 hours after passive avoidance training in the domestic chick, Gallus domesticus. *Brain Res.* 449:34–46

Pinching AJ, Doving KB. 1974. Selective degeneration in the rat olfactory bulb following exposure to different odours. *Brain Res.* 82:195–204

Prusky G, Whishaw IQ. 1996. Morphology of identified corticospinal cells in the rat following motor cortex injury: absence of use-dependent change. *Brain Res.* 714:1–8

Purpura DP. 1974. Dendritic spine "dysgenesis" and mental retardation. *Science* 186:1126–28

Ramon y Cajal S. 1928. *Degeneration and Regeneration of the Nervous System.* London: Oxford Univ. Press

Rehn B, Breipohl W. 1986. Transient postnatal impacts on the mouse olfactory epithelium proprium affect the granule cell development in the mouse olfactory bulb. In *Ontogeny of Olfaction in Vertebrates,* ed. W Breipohl, pp. 143–56. Berlin: Springer-Verlag

Rehn B, Breipohl W, Mendoza AS, Apfelbach A. 1986. Changes in granule cells of the ferret olfactory bulb associated with imprinting on prey odours. *Brain Res.* 373:114–25

Riesen AH, Dickerson GP, Struble RG. 1977. Somatosensory restriction and behavioral development in stumptail monkeys. *Ann. NY Acad. Sci.* 290:285–94

Rose SPR. 1985. The cell biological consequences of passive avoidance training in the chick. *Adv. Behav. Biol.* 28:39–49

Rosenzweig MR, Bennett EL. 1978. Experiential influences on brain anatomy and brain chemistry in rodents. In *Studies on the Development of Behavior and the Nervous System,* ed. G Gottlieb, pp. 289–387. New York: Academic

Rosenzweig MR, Krech D, Bennett EL, Diamond M. 1962. Effects of environmental complexity and training on brain chemistry and anatomy: a replication and extension. *J. Comp. Physiol. Psychol.* 55:429–37

Rosselli-Austin L, Williams J. 1990. Enriched neonatal odor exposure leads to increased numbers of olfactory bulb mitral and granule cells. *Dev. Brain Res.* 51:135–37

Sapolsky RM. 1987. Glucocorticoids and hippocampal damage. *Trends Neurosci.* 10:346–49

Schade JB, Baxter CF. 1960. Changes during growth in volume and surface area of cortical neurons in the rabbit. *Exp. Neurol.* 2:158–78

Scheibel AB, Conrad T, Perdue S, Tomiyasu U, Wechsler A. 1990. A quantitative study of dendrite complexity in selected areas of the human cerebral cortex. *Brain Cogn.* 12:85–101

Schoups AA, Elliott RC, Friedman WJ, Black IB. 1995. NGF and BDNF are differentially modulated by visual experience in the developing geniculocortical pathway. *Dev. Brain Res.* 86:326–34

Sirevaag AM, Black JE, Greenough WT. 1991. Astrocyte hypertrophy in the dentate gyrus of young male rats reflects variation of individual stress rather than group environmental complexity manipulations. *Exp. Neurol.* 111:74–79

Sirevaag AM, Greenough WT. 1987. Differential rearing effects on rat visual cortex synapses. III. Neuronal and glial nuclei, boutons, dendrites, and capillaries. *Brain Res.* 424:320–32

Sirevaag AM, Greenough WT. 1988. A multivariate statistical summary of synaptic plasticity measures in rats exposed to complex, social and individual environments. *Brain Res.* 441:386–92

Sirevaag AM, Greenough WT. 1991. Plasticity of GFA-immunoreactive astrocyte size and number in visual cortex of rats reared in complex environments. *Brain Res.* 540:273–78

Skeen LC, Due BR, Douglas FE. 1986. Neonatal sensory deprivation reduces tufted cell number in mouse olfactory bulbs. *Neurosci. Lett.* 63:5–10

Stell M, Riesen A. 1987. Effects of early environments on monkey cortex neuroanatomical changes following somatomotor experience: effects on layer III pyramidal cells in monkey cortex. *Behav. Neurosci.* 101:341–46

Stewart J, Kolb B. 1988. The effects of neonatal gonadectomy and prenatal stress on cortical thickness and asymmetry in rats. *Behav. Neural Biol.* 49:344–60

Stewart J, Kolb B. 1994. Dendritic branching in cortical pyramidal cells in response to ovariectomy in adult female rats: suppression by neonatal exposure to testosterone. *Brain Res.* 654:149–54

Struble RG, Riesen AH. 1978. Changes in cortical dendritic branching subsequent to partial social isolation in stumptail monkeys. *Dev. Psychobiol.* 11:479–86

Tanzi E. 1893. I fatti e le induzioni nell' odierna istologia del sistema nervoso. *Riv. Sper. Freniatr. Med. Leg. Alienazioni Ment.* 19:419–72

Technau G. 1984. Fiber number in the mushroom bodies of adult Drosophila melanogaster depends on age, sex and experience. *J. Neurogenet.* 1:13–26

Tieman SB, Hirsch HVB. 1982. Exposure to lines of only one orientation modifies dendritic morphology of cells in the visual cortex of the cat. *J. Comp. Neurol.* 211:353–62

Turner AM, Greenough WT. 1983. Synapses per neuron and synaptic dimensions in occipital cortex of rats reared in complex, social, or isolation housing. *Acta Sterol.* 2(Suppl. 1):239–44

Turner AM, Greenough WT. 1985. Differential rearing effects on rat visual cortex synapses. I. Synaptic and neuronal density and synapses per neuron. *Brain Res.* 329:195–203

Uylings HBM, Kuypers K, Diamond M, Veltman WAM. 1978. Environmental influences on neocortex in later life. *Prog. Brain Res.* 48:261–74

Volkmar FR, Greenough WT. 1972. Rearing complexity affects branching of dendrites in visual cortex of the rat. *Science* 176:1445–47

Wallhausser E, Scheich H. 1987. Auditory imprinting leads to differential 2-deoxyglucose uptake and dendritic spine loss in the chick rostral forebrain. *Dev. Brain Res.* 31:29–44

Whishaw IQ, Miklyaeva EI. 1996. A rat's reach should exceed its grasp: analysis of independent limb and digit use in the laboratory rat. In *Measuring Movement and Locomotion: From Invertebrates to Humans,* ed. P-K Ossenkopp, M Kavaliers, PR Sanburg, pp. 135–69. Austin, TX: Landes

Withers GS, Fahrbach SE, Robinson GE. 1993. Selective neuroanatomical plasticity and division of labour in the honey bee. *Nature* 364:238–40

Withers GS, Greenough WT. 1989. Reaching training selectively alters dendritic branching in subpopulations of layer II-III pyramids in rat motor-somatosensory forelimb cortex. *Neuropsychology* 27:61–69

*Annu. Rev. Psychol. 1998. 49:65–85*

# INTERGROUP CONTACT THEORY

## Thomas F. Pettigrew

Department of Psychology, University of California, Santa Cruz, California 95064;
e-mail: pettigr@cats.ucsc.edu

KEY WORDS:  affective ties, ingroup reappraisal, group categorization

### ABSTRACT

Allport specified four conditions for optimal intergroup contact: equal group status within the situation, common goals, intergroup cooperation and authority support. Varied research supports the hypothesis, but four problems remain. 1. A selection bias limits cross-sectional studies, since prejudiced people avoid intergroup contact. Yet research finds that the positive effects of cross-group friendship are larger than those of the bias. 2. Writers overburden the hypothesis with facilitating, but not essential, conditions. 3. The hypothesis fails to address process. The chapter proposes four processes: learning about the outgroup, changed behavior, affective ties, and ingroup reappraisal. 4. The hypothesis does not specify how the effects generalize to other situations, the outgroup or uninvolved outgroups. Acting sequentially, three strategies enhance generalization—decategorization, salient categorization, and recategorization. Finally, both individual differences and societal norms shape intergroup contact effects. The chapter outlines a longitudinal intergroup contact theory. It distinguishes between essential and facilitating factors, and emphasizes different outcomes for different stages of contact.

## CONTENTS

0066-4308/98/0201-0065$08.00

# INTRODUCTION

Social scientists began to theorize about intergroup contact after World War II (Watson 1947, Williams 1947). Allport's (1954) hypothesis proved the most influential by specifying the critical situational conditions for intergroup contact to reduce prejudice. His hypothesis has received extensive attention both for its rare theoretical status and policy importance (Pettigrew 1971). Oddly, for a discipline that focuses on face-to-face interaction, social psychology rarely decomposes situations into their basic components. Allport's attempt is a prominent exception. And it has proven useful in applied settings, such as in the distinction between racial desegregation and integration in schools (Pettigrew 1975).

## Allport's Intergroup Contact Hypothesis

Allport (1954) held that positive effects of intergroup contact occur only in situations marked by four key conditions: equal group status within the situation; common goals; intergroup cooperation; and the support of authorities, law, or custom.

EQUAL STATUS  Allport stressed equal group status *within* the situation. Most research supports this contention, although "equal status" is difficult to define and has been used in different ways (Cagle 1973, Riordan 1978). It is important that both groups expect and perceive equal status in the situation (Cohen & Lotan 1995, Cohen 1982, Riordan & Ruggiero 1980, Robinson & Preston 1976). Some writers emphasize equal group status *coming into* the situation (Brewer & Kramer 1985). Thus, Jackman & Crane (1986) show negative effects from contact with outgroup members of lower status. Yet Patchen (1982), in research on racially mixed high schools, found this to be less important than equal status within the situation. The meta-analytic results of Mullen et al (1992) clarify these disparities. They noted that ingroup bias increased with relative status in laboratory groups but decreased in field research with real groups.

COMMON GOALS  Prejudice reduction through contact requires an active, goal-oriented effort. Athletic teams furnish a prime example (Chu & Griffey 1985, Miracle 1981, Patchen 1982). In striving to win, interracial teams need each other to achieve their goal. Goal attainment, such as a winning season, furthers this process.

INTERGROUP COOPERATION    Attainment of common goals must be an inter-dependent effort without intergroup competition (Bettencourt et al 1992). Sherif (1966) demonstrated this principle vividly in his Robbers' Cave field study. Intergroup cooperation in schools provides the strongest evidence (Brewer & Miller 1984, Desforges et al 1991, Johnson et al 1984, Schofield 1989, Slavin 1983, Slavin & Madden 1979). Drawing on this thinking, Aronson's jigsaw classroom technique structures classrooms so that students strive cooperatively for common goals (Aronson & Patnoe 1997). This technique has led to positive results for a variety of children: Australians (Walker & Crogan 1997), Germans (Eppler & Huber 1990), Japanese (Araragi 1983), and Mexican Americans (Aronson & Gonzalez 1988).

SUPPORT OF AUTHORITIES, LAW, OR CUSTOM    The final condition concerns the contact's auspices. With explicit social sanction, intergroup contact is more readily accepted and has more positive effects. Authority support establishes norms of acceptance. Field research underscores its importance in military (Landis et al 1984), business (Morrison & Herlihy 1992), and religious (Parker 1968) institutions.

## INITIAL EMPIRICAL EVIDENCE

Allport (1954) derived his hypothesis from early field research. An Alabama study revealed negative effects when all four conditions were violated (Sims & Patrick 1936). White college students from the North increased on average in antiblack prejudice with each year spent in the South.

Other studies investigated optimal conditions. After desegregation of the Merchant Marine in 1948, interdependency developed on ships and in the maritime union. The more voyages the white seamen took with blacks under these conditions, the more positive their racial attitudes became (Brophy 1946). Similarly, white police in Philadelphia who had worked with black colleagues had fewer objections to black police joining their districts, teaming with a black partner, and taking orders from qualified black officers (Kephart 1957).

Studies of public housing provided robust evidence. Deutsch & Collins (1951) compared racially desegregated housing projects in New York City with similar but segregated projects in Newark. Sharp differences emerged. Desegregated white housewives held their black neighbors in higher esteem and favored interracial housing more (75% to 25%). When asked to name black faults, they listed such personal issues as feelings of inferiority. Segregated white women voiced stereotypes such as "rowdy" and "dangerous."

Later public housing research extended these findings (Wilner et al 1955). Favorable racial attitudes developed among only one third of the white tenants who just had casual greetings with their black neighbors. But half who entered into conversations and three fourths who had multiple interactions developed positive racial views. Social norms are crucial. In the desegregated projects, whites expected approval from their neighbors for their friendly interracial behavior. In the segregated projects, they feared social ostracism from other whites for such behavior. "Contact and perceived social climate tend to reinforce each other when their influence operates in the same direction, and to cancel each other out when their influence works in the opposite direction" (Wilner et al 1955, p. 106).

## RECENT EMPIRICAL EVIDENCE

Allport's formulation continues to receive support across a variety of situations, groups, and societies. Some research, conducted in situations that do not provide key conditions, uncovers negative effects. Poorly arranged entry of black workers into London's public transportation, for example, led to hostility by white workers (Brooks 1975). Interracial housing research sometimes reveals few effects on racial attitudes (Bradburn et al 1971, Meer & Freedman 1966, Zuel & Humphrey 1971). These findings support Allport, although some writers mistakenly view their results as falsifying his hypothesis. The erroneous notion that the hypothesis holds that intergroup contact "will of itself produce better relations between…groups" still persists (McGarty & de la Haye 1997, p. 155).

Most studies report positive contact effects, even in situations lacking key conditions. Although it concentrates on school and housing situations (Ford 1986), the contact literature ranges from Chinese students in the United States (Chang 1973) and interracial workers in South Africa (Bornman & Mynhardt 1991) to German and Turkish school children (Wagner et al 1989) and Australians (McKay & Pitman 1993) and Americans (Riordan 1987) getting to know Southeast Asian immigrants. It involves attitudes toward a wide range of targets beyond ethnic groups—the elderly (Caspi 1984, Drew 1988), homosexuals (Eskilson 1995, Herek & Capitanio 1996), the mentally ill (Desforges et al 1991), disabled persons (Anderson 1995), victims of AIDS (Werth & Lord 1992), and even computer programmers (McGinnis 1990). In addition, diverse research methods yield supporting results—field (Meer & Freedman 1966, Ohm 1988), archival (Fine 1979), survey (Jackman & Crane 1986; Pettigrew 1997a,b; Robinson 1980; Sigelman & Welch 1993), and laboratory (Cook 1978, 1984; Desforges et al 1991).

Research with African Americans is also supportive. Works (1961) found that both black wives and husbands in a desegregated housing project felt more positively about their white neighbors than those in a segregated project. With longitudinal data, Smith (1994) found contact meeting Allport's conditions decreased prejudice among both black and white neighbors, though there were group differences in contact effects. In a national probability sample, interracial friendships proved to be a strong predictor of blacks' racial attitudes (Ellison & Powers 1994, Powers & Ellison 1995).

These varied investigations broaden the application of the hypothesis. They also raise the question: Why does intergroup contact usually have positive effects even when the situation does not attain all of Allport's conditions? In addition, they typically do not address the basic problems with the original contact hypothesis—problems to which I now turn.

## PROBLEMS

### The Causal Sequence Problem

Selection bias limits the interpretation of many cross-sectional studies of contact. Instead of optimal contact reducing prejudice, the opposite causal sequence could be operating. Prejudiced people may avoid contact with outgroups. Three methods overcome this limitation. 1. Find an intergroup situation that severely limits choice to participate. In the Merchant Marine, police, and public-housing research, little choice was available to participants. 2. Statistical methods borrowed from econometrics allow researchers to compare the reciprocal paths (optimal contact lowers prejudice and prejudice decreases contact) with cross-sectional data. Powers & Ellison (1995) use endogenous switching regression models. Later I review the use of a nonrecursive structural equation model. 3. Although not without problems (Clogg 1986), longitudinal designs are best (Pettigrew 1996). Yet such research is rare in intergroup research; Sherif's (1966) study is a famous exception. Indeed, the major findings of the Robbers' Cave study would not have emerged without its longitudinal design (Pettigrew 1991a). The initial intergroup contact situations had little effect. Only after repeated treatments did the positive results cumulate.

### Independent Variable Specification Problem

Allport's hypothesis risks being an open-ended laundry list of conditions— ever expandable and thus eluding falsification (Pettigrew 1986, Stephan 1987). Researchers keep advancing new situational factors for optimal contact. From Germany, Wagner & Machleit (1986) concluded that positive effects require a common language, voluntary contact, and a prosperous economy. From Israel, Ben-Ari & Amir (1986) held that the group's initial views of one another cannot be too negative. From the United States, Cook (1978) insisted that stereotype disconfirmation is crucial.

This growing list of limiting conditions threatens to remove all interest from the hypothesis. Too many factors would exclude most intergroup situations. The hypothesis would rarely predict positive results from contact, although research typically finds positive results. The problem is that writers often confuse *facilitating* with *essential* conditions. Many factors suggested for optimal contact may not be essential but relate to the underlying mediating processes. This point leads to the third problem.

## Unspecified Processes of Change Problem

The original hypothesis says nothing about the *processes* by which contact changes attitudes and behavior. It predicts only *when* contact will lead to positive change, not *how* and *why* the change occurs. A broader theory of intergroup contact requires an explicit specification of the processes involved, which I provide below.

## The Generalization of Effects Problem

Nor does the hypothesis specify how the effects generalize beyond the immediate situation. Such generalization is pivotal if intergroup contact is to have broad and lasting consequences. There are three distinct types of generalization: *Situational*—do the changes generalize across situations? *Individual to group*—do the changes generalize from the specific outgroup members with whom there is contact to the outgroup? *To uninvolved outgroups*—do the changes toward the outgroup generalize to other outgroups not involved in the contact? (For analyses of the generalization of different effects, see Brewer & Miller 1988 and Hewstone 1996.) Thus, a broader theory of intergroup contact also requires explicit predictions of how the contact effects will generalize, another task I undertake below.

## FOUR PROCESSES OF CHANGE THROUGH INTERGROUP CONTACT

Recent work suggests that four interrelated processes operate through contact and mediate attitude change: learning about the outgroup, changing behavior, generating affective ties, and ingroup reappraisal.

LEARNING ABOUT THE OUTGROUP    Initial theory held this process to be the major way that intergroup contact has effects. When new learning corrects negative views of the outgroup, contact should reduce prejudice. Support for such a benign process is available, though plausible rival explanations remain. Consider Jeffries & Ransford's (1969) findings on middle-class white reactions to the Watts race riot in Los Angeles. Those who had prior interracial contact were significantly less fearful of blacks, less punitive, and less likely to view the riot as caused by outside agitators.

Yet cognitive research has uncovered a host of mechanisms that limit learning material that counters our attitudes and stereotypes. Writing from this perspective, Rothbart & John (1985) conclude that disconfirming evidence alters stereotypes only if (*a*) the outgroup's behavior is starkly inconsistent with their stereotype and strongly associated with their label, (*b*) occurs often and in many situations, and (*c*) the outgroup members are seen as typical. These restrictions eliminate most intergroup contact situations.

Nonetheless, new information about an outgroup can improve attitudes. Stephan & Stephan (1984) found that contact allowed Anglo students to learn more about Chicano culture that in turn led to more positive attitudes toward Chicano classmates. "Ignorance," they assert, "promotes prejudice..." (Stephan & Stephan 1984, p. 238). Other studies with the cultural assimilator technique of Triandis (1994) provide further evidence that learning about an outgroup can improve intergroup attitudes and stereotypes (Gardiner 1972, Weldon et al 1975).

Still, the dominant consensus of cognitive analyses denies the likelihood of positive effects from most contact situations. Yet the research literature suggests that positive effects are more common than either the contact hypothesis or cognitive analyses predict. Why the contradiction? The basic reason is that learning about the outgroup is only one of several processes involved. Cognitive analyses are not so much wrong as they are incomplete. Other processes are also involved.

CHANGING BEHAVIOR    Optimal intergroup contact acts as a benign form of behavior modification. Behavior change is often the precursor of attitude change. New situations require conforming to new expectations. If these expectations include acceptance of outgroup members, this behavior has the potential to produce attitude change. We can resolve our dissonance between old prejudices and new behavior by revising our attitudes (Aronson & Patnoe 1997). This behavioral process also benefits from repeated contact, preferably in varied settings (Jackman & Crane 1986). Repetition makes intergroup encounters comfortable and "right." Repetition itself leads to liking (Zajonc 1968). Appropriate rewards for the new behavior enhances the positive effects further.

GENERATING AFFECTIVE TIES    Emotion is critical in intergroup contact. Anxiety is common in initial encounters between groups, and it can spark negative reactions (Islam & Hewstone 1993; Stephan 1992; Stephan & Stephan 1985, 1989, 1992; Wilder 1993a,b). Such anxious, negative encounters can occur even without intergroup prejudice (Devine et al 1996). Continued contact generally reduces anxiety, though bad experiences can increase it.

Positive emotions aroused by optimal contact also can mediate intergroup contact effects. Empathy plays a role here. Reich & Purbhoo (1975) found that school contact improved cross-group role-taking ability among both majority and minority Canadian students. And empathy for a stigmatized outgroup member—a young woman with AIDS, a homeless man or a convicted murderer—can improve attitudes toward the whole outgroup (Batson et al 1997).

Positive emotions aroused by intergroup friendship also can be pivotal. The Oliners (1988) found that non-Jews who risked their lives to save Jews during World War II reported more close friendships as children with other groups. Similarly, Rippl (1995) found friendship to be decisive in shaping contact effects between West and East Germans. These findings support earlier claims by Amir (1976) concerning the importance of intimacy in intergroup contact.

The most extensive data on intergroup friendship derive from 1988 surveys in Western Europe (Pettigrew 1997a,b; Pettigrew & Meertens 1995). (For survey details, see Reif & Melish 1991; for a different, though consistent, analysis of these data, see Hamberger & Hewstone 1997). Over 3800 majority group respondents in seven probability samples of France, Great Britain, the Netherlands, and West Germany were asked their attitudes toward major minority groups in their country and whether they had friends of another nationality, race, culture, religion, or social class. In all samples, Europeans with outgroup friends scored significantly lower on five prejudice measures even after controlling for seven variables. The largest effect occurred for a two-item measure of affective prejudice. Those with intergroup friends significantly more often reported having felt sympathy and admiration for the outgroup. Few studies in the contact literature have used affective dependent variables. When they have, similar results emerge (Wright et al 1997).

Figure 1 compares the paths between intergroup friends and affective prejudice. Note that living in an intergroup neighborhood makes it more likely that a European will have an outgroup friend (+.356). There is no direct relationship, however, between mixed neighborhoods and affective prejudice. This allows a test of the paths between friendship and affective prejudice (Bollen 1989, Heist 1975). As in other research (Herek & Capitanio 1996), the prejudiced avoid intergroup contact (−.137). But the path from friendship to reduced affective prejudice is significantly stronger (−.210), a finding consistent with that of Powers & Ellison (1995). In short, like prejudice, contact involves both cognition and affect.

INGROUP REAPPRAISAL   Optimal intergroup contact provides insight about ingroups as well as outgroups. Ingroup norms and customs turn out not to be the only ways to manage the social world. This new perspective can reshape your view of your ingroup and lead to a less provincial view of outgroups in general ("deprovincialization"). In the European surveys, outgroup friendship related to significantly less "pride" in nationality even after education, age, and political conservatism are controlled (Pettigrew 1997c). (A comparable

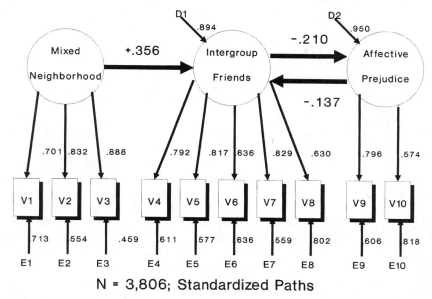

**N = 3,806; Standardized Paths**

*Figure 1* Friends—prejudice model

analysis to Figure 1 reveals similar results with a significant path from out-group friends to less national pride.)

Part of this process involves having less contact with the ingroup as a result of more contact with the outgroup. Wilder & Thompson (1980) covaried contact with the ingroup and outgroup in a laboratory study. While it had no impact on ingroup ratings, less ingroup contact led to less bias toward the outgroup. This finding is consistent with meta-analytic results that show ingroup bias is positively related with ingroup salience (Mullen et al 1992).

## THREE TYPES OF GENERALIZATION

GENERALIZATION ACROSS SITUATIONS   World War II research showed major improvements in white attitudes toward black soldiers after combat together (Stouffer et al 1949). Yet whites continued to favor racially separate post exchanges (military stores). Other early studies also demonstrated limited generalization across situations (Biesanz & Smith 1951, Deutsch & Collins 1951, Harding & Hogrefe 1952, Minard 1952, Reitzes 1953, Saenger & Gilbert 1950).

Recall that the first cooperative encounters of the Robbers' Cave study did not generalize either. Only the cumulative effect of repeated optimal situations altered the attitudes of the rival groups. Similarly, only after the US Army offered many types of optimal interracial situations could it conclude that its program of racial desegregation "works" (US Department of Defense 1955, Moscos & Butler 1996).

GENERALIZATION FROM THE OUTGROUP INDIVIDUAL TO THE OUTGROUP
Brown & Turner (1981) questioned the generalization of effects between *interpersonal* and *intergroup* phenomena. They doubted whether positive effects from getting to know an outgroup member (interpersonal) could affect attitudes about the outgroup (intergroup).

Following this reasoning, Hewstone & Brown (1986) theorized that contact effects generalize to the outgroup only when group membership is salient. When group saliency is low, the situation is interpersonal and no intergroup effects should result. Only when the interactants view one another as group representatives does the contact become an intergroup event. Research that supports this *salient categorization strategy* shows stereotype change generalizes best to the intergroup level when the individuals involved are typical group members (Johnston & Hewstone 1992, Vivian et al 1995, Weber & Crocker 1983, Wilder 1984). As typical members, their group memberships were more salient.

This poses a problem. Typical members of real groups are different in many ways, but people with similar interests and status seek each other out—the similarity principle (Byrne 1971). People from different groups who have contact, then, are more likely to share similar interests and values. And outgroup members with similar interests to the ingroup often will not typify their group or make group membership salient. Hence, Brewer & Miller (1984) advocate a *decategorization strategy*. The opposite of salient categorization, it holds that intergroup contact is most effective when group saliency is low.

So, given real differences between groups, those most likely to have intergroup contact are atypical of their groups. Yet contact effects generalize best when the participants are typical group members. Thus, people most likely to engage in intergroup contact are the least likely to evoke changes that generalize to their groups.

How, then, can effective contact take place? First, the similarity principle is not the whole story. Durkheim (1960) pointed out that similarity (mechanical solidarity) is only one form of social bond. Society could not exist without bonds across reciprocal roles—parents and children, clerks and customers. So differences (organic solidarity) also are important for social bonds. These differences, widespread in modern society, guarantee that contact takes place between dissimilar people. Further, under some conditions, optimal contact leads to positive changes that generalize even when atypical members are involved (Hamburger 1994, Werth & Lord 1992).

Second, the time sequence is crucial. Conflicting as they seem, both strategies are possible if they occur sequentially. Diminished saliency of group categories can be important when intergroup contact is initiated. Once established, salient group categorization is required for the effects to generalize to the intergroup level (Van Oudenhoven et al 1996).

In time, the Common Ingroup Identity Model emphasizes that *recategorization* becomes possible (Anastasio et al 1997; Gaertner et al 1993, 1994). After extended contact, people can begin to think of themselves in a larger group perspective. Recategorization adopts an inclusive category that highlights similarities among the interactants and obscures the "we" and "they" boundary (Perdue et al 1990). Note, however, that recategorization is the final state many interacting groups never reach. The progression through these three stages of categorization is not automatic, and recategorization into a single group often will not be attained.

Wright and his colleagues propose a further form of generalization involving friendship. Using both questionnaire and experimental methods, they show that even knowledge of an ingroup member's friendship with an outgroup member relates to more positive attitudes toward the outgroup (Wright et al 1997). Such an "extended contact effect" does not require intergroup friendship for the perceiver.

GENERALIZATION FROM THE IMMEDIATE OUTGROUP TO OTHER OUTGROUPS
This higher-order form of generalization presupposes the other forms and is seldom studied because many regard it as highly unlikely (but see Reich & Purbhoo 1975, Weigert 1976). Nonetheless, the European surveys show that such generalization is possible. Having an ingroup friend related to greater acceptance of minorities of many types (Pettigrew 1997a,b). The 3800 respondents rated how favorable they were toward eight outgroups, many of whom were not in their country. In all samples, significant relationships emerged even after seven variables were controlled. For each outgroup, those with intergroup friends were significantly more positive in their views. And a test like that of Figure 1 showed that the path from friendship to reduced prejudice is significantly stronger than the prejudice to less friendship path. These findings challenge Rose's (1981) assertion that intimate relationships cannot generalize to different persons and groups.

# A REFORMULATION OF INTERGROUP CONTACT THEORY

These considerations provide direction for a reformulation of Allport's hypothesis. At least four processes, not one, are involved, and these processes may well overlap and interact in complex ways. Intergroup friendship is potent because it potentially invokes all four mediating processes. This suggests that constructive contact relates more closely to long-term close relationships than to initial acquaintanceship—a dramatic shift for the intergroup contact research literature.

Optimal intergroup contact requires time for cross-group friendships to develop. Past work has focused chiefly on short-term intergroup contact—the very condition that Sherif's (1966) Robbers' Cave field experiment found minimally effective. Once we adopt a long-term perspective that allows cross-group friendship to develop and the full decategorization, salient categorization, and recategorization sequence to unfold, we can expect striking results. Such a revised perspective explains why extended intergroup contact often has more positive results than either the contact hypothesis or cognitive analyses predict.

The power of cross-group friendship to reduce prejudice and generalize to other outgroups demands a fifth condition for the contact hypothesis: *The contact situation must provide the participants with the opportunity to become friends.* Such opportunity implies close interaction that would make self-disclosure and other friendship-developing mechanisms possible. It also implies the potential for extensive and repeated contact in a variety of social contexts. Allport (1954) alluded to this point when he favored intimate to trivial contact; Cook (1962) called it "acquaintance potential." These European results suggest that "friendship potential" is an essential, not merely facilitating, condition for positive intergroup contact effects that generalize. Further, they suggest that Allport's conditions are important in part because they provide the setting that encourages intergroup friendship.

Instead of a list of conditions, then, I propose a longitudinal model as schematically outlined in Figure 2. Note first that this version of intergroup contact theory involves the meso-level of analysis. Yet it is placed within the micro- and macrolevel contexts of (B) the participants' experiences and characteristics as well as the larger societal setting of the situation. The basic features of this reformulated version consist of (A) the essential and facilitating situational factors and (C, D, E) the time dimension. Each of these features involves details not shown in Figure 2.

(A) From the previous discussion, the theory posits Allport's four conditions and friendship potential as essential situational factors for positive intergroup outcomes—less negative stereotyping, prejudice, and discrimination. An array of additional factors, such as equivalent group status outside the situation, act as facilitating factors for such effects. Complicating the picture further, such factors might prove important at different stages of the intergroup contact.

(C, D, E) in Figure 2 designate only three stages. As diagrammed, this time dimension is obviously oversimplified. The stages will overlap, and at any point the groups can break off contact. This heuristic, however, following the

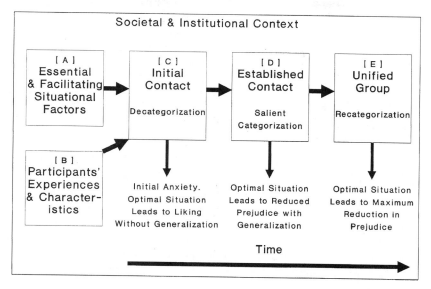

*Figure 2* Reformulated contact theory.

three research traditions on group categorization, allows the theory to predict different outcomes at different stages.

We need research on several points. While the recategorization of the unified group, if attained, appears to yield the maximum in prejudice reduction, we have little data on how this effect generalizes. Further, we must understand how the four contact processes of change are activated and become important at each stage. The thrust of the time dimension is to underline the need for longitudinal research on intergroup contact. Though rare in this literature, this reformulated theory holds that such research designs are necessary for further progress.

Conceptualizing intergroup contact as a meso-level, situational phenomenon links it to both the microindividual and macrosocietal levels of analysis (Pettigrew 1991b, 1996). Research has shown how important these cross-level links can be.

## Individual Differences Shape Contact Effects

Prior attitudes and experiences influence whether people seek or avoid intergroup contact, and what the effects of the contact will be. Figure 1 showed that prejudiced Europeans are less likely to have outgroup friends. Other characteristics also deter contact. Value differences shaped differential readiness for intergroup contact among both Israeli Arabs and Jews (Sagiv & Schwartz 1995). Cook (1984) found large individual differences in the effects of even optimal contact; 40% of his experimental subjects, compared with 12% of controls, evinced sweeping attitude changes. Yet other experimental subjects averaged little change.

High intergroup anxiety and threat also can impede both contact and its positive effects (Islam & Hewstone 1993; Stephan 1992; Stephan & Stephan 1985, 1989, 1992, 1996; Wilder 1993a,b; Wilder & Shapiro 1989). Such emotions often derive from no prior experience with the outgroup. Black and white high school students who had the most favorable earlier interracial experience were more positive toward the other race (Patchen 1982). Thus, intergroup contact and its effects are cumulative—we live what we learn. Braddock (1989) found that black graduates of segregated high schools were significantly less likely later to work with whites. Since jobs with white co-workers have better pay and promotions, this result helps to explain why black graduates of interracial schools do better in later life than those from segregated schools (Braddock 1989, Braddock et al 1984, Braddock & McPartland 1987).

## Societies Shape Contact Effects

Situations are embedded in social institutions and societies. Thus, institutional and societal norms structure the form and effects of contact situations (Kinloch 1981, 1991). Consider intergroup strife in Northern Ireland and Quebec. These societal contexts severely limit all forms of intergroup contact. Moreover, they render the contact that does occur less than optimal. Implicit in Allport's equal-status condition is equivalent group power in the situation. This is difficult to achieve when a struggle over power fuels the larger intergroup conflict.

The meager equal-status contact between groups that takes place in such societies is typically subversive in character. In Northern Ireland, neighboring Catholic and Protestant farmers cooperate in their agricultural pursuits but remain apart in other activities (Harris 1972, Kirk 1993). Even conversations are circumscribed. In both Quebec and Northern Ireland, intergroup interaction focuses on local issues and avoids divisive group concerns (Taylor et al 1986, Trew 1986). It is at best constrained discussion, not the easy banter of friends.

Russell (1961) showed how societal norms of discrimination poison intergroup contact. She tested a racially mixed neighborhood at the height of South Africa's *Apartheid* policy of intense racial segregation. This rare area had 50% whites, 20% Coloureds, and 30% Indians. Even here, modest improvements emerged in white attitudes toward their neighbors of color. Yet the larger social context constrained these effects. The improved attitudes did not generalize to Coloureds and Indians as groups, and whites were defensive about their interracial contact. Some avoided it, and the exchange that took place was not reciprocal. Whites received neighborly aid and entered nonwhite homes far more than the reverse. Many whites rationalized their interracial behavior with the exploitative nature of the relationship. All were aware that the then stern South African norms punished equal-status interracial contact. Such norms erode true neighborliness.

Alternatively, when a society embraces intergroup harmony, equal-status contact between groups is no longer subversive. Normative support makes attainment of other optimal conditions far easier.

## GENERAL EVALUATIONS OF CONTACT EFFECTS

Consider this reformulation in light of two efforts to test the chief contentions of contact theory, one with surveys and the other experimental.

In meta-analytic fashion, the European surveys tested the link between intergroup friendship and five different measures of prejudice across seven samples (Pettigrew 1997a). Weighting for sample size, the average correlations ranged between −.14 and −.32 without controls. With controls for seven variables and weighting for sample size, the average correlations ranged between −.10 and −.25. These results are consistent with the preliminary findings of a meta-analysis of the full contact literature now under way (Pettigrew et al 1998).

Cook (1984) provided the most extensive laboratory test of the intergroup contact hypothesis. He set up an ideal interracial situation featuring equal status, a stereotype-disconfirming minority member, an interdependent task, task success, high friendship potential, and equalitarian social norms. Highly prejudiced white subjects worked with two partners who were confederates, one black and one white. They operated an imaginary railroad system over 40 sessions, sharing successes and failures but eventually winning bonus money. To enhance generalization, the black confederate told of a personal experience with racial discrimination after rapport had developed. Later, the white confederate disapproved of the discriminatory practice.

Cook recorded major changes. Subjects reported highly favorable opinions of their black partner, and these views generalized. In another context, the subjects evinced on average more positive racial views toward African Americans than controls. Observe the time sequence. First, the prejudiced subjects found the stereotype-disconfirming black as similar and grew to like her in the optimal situation. Next the black confederate made race salient by telling of past discrimination. Then the white confederate emphasized the link between their friend's bad treatment and racial discrimination.

# SUMMARY

Allport's hypothesis specified four conditions for optimal contact. The situation must allow equal group status within the situation, common goals, intergroup cooperation, and authority support. Recent research adds another: The contact situation must have "friendship potential."

Varied research supports the hypothesis—from field and archival studies to national surveys and laboratory experiments. However, cross-sectional studies suffer from a selection bias. Prejudiced people avoid intergroup contact, so the causal link between contact and prejudice is two-way. Yet those studies that have tested both paths find that the positive effects of cross-group friendship are larger than those of the bias.

Three additional problems limit the contact hypothesis. 1. Writers have overburdened the hypothesis with too many facilitating, but not essential, conditions. 2. The hypothesis does not address process. It predicts only when positive contact effects will occur, not how and why. The chapter details four interrelated processes underlying contact effects: learning about the outgroup, changing behavior, generating affective ties, and ingroup reappraisal. Intergroup friendship has strong positive effects, because it potentially entails all four processes.

3. The hypothesis does not specify how the effects generalize to other situations, the entire outgroup or uninvolved outgroups. Many effects do not generalize beyond the immediate contact situation and participants. There are three strategies to enhance generalization: decategorization, salient group categorization, and recategorization. Thinking of these strategies acting sequentially removes the apparent contradiction between them. Since similarity attracts, initial stages of intergroup contact benefit from not making group membership salient. Later, as anxiety and threat subside, group membership must become salient to maximize the generalization of positive effects beyond the immediate situation. Then recategorization becomes possible if the participants adopt an all-encompassing group identification.

Both individual differences and societal norms shape intergroup contact effects. The deeply prejudiced both avoid intergroup contact and resist positive effects from it. Societies suffering intergroup conflict both restrict and undercut intergroup contact. From these considerations, the chapter advances a longitudinal reformulation of the intergroup contact hypothesis. Within the contexts of the participants' characteristics and the situation's societal setting, the chapter outlines a meso-level theory with two key features. It distinguishes between essential and facilitating situational factors. And it emphasizes the time dimension with different outcomes predicted for different stages of intergroup contact.

## ACKNOWLEDGMENTS

I wish to thank my research colleagues over the past decade, James Jackson of the University of Michigan and Roel W. Meertens of the University of Amsterdam, for their invaluable collaboration with the European survey research. I also greatly appreciate the helpful comments on earlier drafts of this chapter by John Darley, Susan Fiske, Miles Hewstone, Marylee Taylor, and Linda Tropp.

> Visit the *Annual Reviews home page* at
> http://www.AnnualReviews.org.

## *Literature Cited*

Allport GW. 1954. *The Nature of Prejudice.* Reading, MA: Addison-Wesley. 537 pp.

Amir Y. 1976. The role of intergroup contact in change of prejudice and race relations. In *Towards the Elimination of Racism,* ed. PA Katz, pp. 245–80. New York: Pergamon. 444 pp.

Anastasio P, Bachman B, Gaertner S, Dovidio J. 1997. Categorization, recategorization and common ingroup identity. See Spears et al 1997, pp. 236–56

Anderson LS. 1995. *Outdoor adventure recreation and social integration: a social-psychological perspective.* PhD thesis. Univ. Minn., Minneapolis, MN. 271 pp.

Araragi C. 1983. The effect of the jigsaw learning method on children's academic performance and learning attitude. *Jpn. J. Educ. Psychol.* 31:102–12

Aronson E, Gonzalez A. 1988. Desegregation, jigsaw, and the Mexican-American experience. See Katz & Taylor 1988, pp. 301–14

Aronson E, Patnoe S. 1997. *The Jigsaw Classroom.* New York: Longman. 150 pp. 2nd ed.

Batson CD, Polycarpou MP, Harmon-Jones E, Imhoff HJ, Mitchener EC, et al. 1997. Empathy and attitudes: can feeling for a member of a stigmatized group improve feelings toward the group? *J. Pers. Soc. Psychol.* 72:105–18

Ben-Ari R, Amir Y. 1986. Contact between Arab and Jewish youth in Israel: reality and potential. See Hewstone & Brown 1986, pp. 45–58

Bettencourt BA, Brewer MB, Rogers-Croak MR, Miller N. 1992. Cooperation and the reduction of intergroup bias: the role of re-ward structure and social orientation. *J. Exp. Soc. Psychol.* 28:301–19

Biesanz J, Smith LM. 1951. Race relations of Panama and the Canal Zone. *Am. J. Sociol.* 57:7–14

Bollen KA. 1989. *Structural Equations with Latent Variables.* New York: Wiley. 514 pp.

Bornman E, Mynhardt JC. 1991. Social identification and intergroup contact in South Africa with specific reference to the work situation. *Genet. Soc. Gen. Psychol. Monogr.* 117:437–62

Bradburn N, Sudman S, Gockel GL. 1971. *Side by Side: Integrated Neighborhoods in America.* Chicago: Quadrangle Books. 209 pp.

Braddock JH Jr. 1989. Social psychological processes that perpetuate racial segregation: the relationship between school and employment desegregation. *J. Black Stud.* 19:267–89

Braddock JH Jr, Crain RL, McPartland JM. 1984. A long-term view of racial desegregation: some recent studies of graduates as adults. *Phi Delta Kappan* 66:259–64

Braddock JH Jr, McPartland JM. 1987. How minorities continue to be excluded from equal employment opportunities: research on labor market and institutional barriers. *J. Soc. Issues* 43:5–39

Brewer MB, Kramer RM. 1985. The psychology of intergroup attitudes and behavior. *Annu. Rev. Psychol.* 36:219–43

Brewer MB, Miller N. 1984. Beyond the contact hypothesis: theoretical perspectives on desegregation. See Miller & Brewer 1984, pp. 281–302

Brewer MB, Miller N. 1988. Contact and cooperation: when do they work? See Katz & Taylor 1988, pp. 315–26

Brooks D. 1975. *Race and Labour in London Transport.* London: Oxford Univ. Press. 389 pp.

Brophy IN. 1946. The luxury of anti-Negro prejudice. *Public Opin. Q.* 9:456–66

Brown RJ, Turner JC. 1981. Interpersonal and intergroup behavior. In *Intergroup Behavior,* ed. J Turner, H Giles, pp. 33–65. Chicago, IL: Univ. Chicago Press. 277 pp.

Byrne D. 1971. *The Attraction Paradigm.* New York: Academic. 474 pp.

Cagle LT. 1973. Interracial housing: a reassessment of the equal-status contact hypothesis. *Sociol. Soc. Res.* 57:342–55

Caspi A. 1984. Contact hypothesis and inter-age attitudes: a field study of cross-age contact *Soc. Psychol. Q.* 47:74–80

Chang H. 1973. Attitudes of Chinese students in the United States. *Sociol. Soc. Res.* 58: 66–77

Chu D, Griffey D. 1985. The contact theory of racial integration: the case of sport. *Sociol. Sport J.* 2:323–33

Clogg CC. 1986. Invoked by RATE. *Am. J. Sociol.* 92:696–706

Cohen EG. 1982. Expectation states and interracial interaction in school settings. *Annu. Rev. Sociol.* 8:209–35

Cohen EG, Lotan RA. 1995. Producing equal-status interaction in the heterogeneous classroom. *Am. Educ. Res. J.* 32:99–120

Cook SW. 1962. The systematic analysis of socially significant events: a strategy for social research. *J. Soc. Issues* 18:66–84

Cook SW. 1978. Interpersonal and attitudinal outcomes in cooperating interracial groups. *J. Res. Dev. Educ.* 12:97–113

Cook SW. 1984. Cooperative interaction in multiethnic contexts. See Miller & Brewer 1984, pp. 155–85

Desforges DM, Lord CG, Ramsey SL, Mason JA, Van Leeuwen MD, et al. 1991. Effects of structured cooperative contact on changing negative attitudes toward stigmatized social groups. *J. Pers. Soc. Psychol.* 60:531–44

Deutsch M, Collins M. 1951. *Interracial Housing: A Psychological Evaluation of a Social Experiment.* Minneapolis: Univ. Minn. Press. 173 pp.

Devine PG, Evett SR, Vasquez-Suson KA. 1996. Exploring the interpersonal dynamics of intergroup contact. In *Handbook of Motivation and Cognition: The Interpersonal Context,* ed. RM Sorrentino, ET Higgins, 3:423–64. New York: Guilford. 646 pp.

Drew B. 1988. *Intergenerational contact in the workplace: an anthropological study of relationships in the secondary labor market.* PhD thesis. Rutgers Univ., New Brunswick, NJ. 285 pp.

Durkheim E. 1960. (1893). *The Division of Labor.* Glencoe, IL: Free Press. 439 pp.

Ellison CG, Powers DA. 1994. The contact hypothesis and racial attitudes among Black Americans. *Soc. Sci. Q.* 75:385–400

Epler R, Huber GL. 1990. Wissenserwerb im Team: Empirische Untersuchung von Effekten des Gruppen-Puzzles. *Psychol. Erzieh. Unterr.* 37:172–78

Eskilson A. 1995. *Trends in homophobia and gender attitudes: 1987–1993.* Presented at Annu. Meet. Am. Sociol. Assoc., 90th, Washington, DC

Fine GA. 1979. The Pinkston settlement: an historical and social psychological investigation of the contact hypothesis. *Phylon* 40:229–42

Ford WS. 1986. Favorable intergroup contact may not reduce prejudice: inconclusive journal evidence 1960–1984. *Sociol. Soc. Res.* 70:256–58

Gaertner SL, Dovidio JF, Anastasio PA, Bachman BA, Rust MC. 1993. The common ingroup identity model: recategorization and the reduction of intergroup bias. *Eur. Rev. Soc. Psychol.* 4:1–26

Gaertner SL, Rust MC, Dovidio JF, Bachman BA, Anastasio PA. 1994. The contact hypothesis: the role of a common ingroup identity on reducing intergroup bias. *Small Group Res.* 25:224–49

Gardiner GS. 1972. Complexity training and prejudice reduction. *J. Appl. Soc. Psychol.* 2:326–42

Hamberger J, Hewstone M. 1997. Inter-ethnic contact as a predictor of prejudice: tests of a model in four West European nations. *Br. J. Soc. Psychol.* In press

Hamburger Y. 1994. The contact hypothesis reconsidered: effects of the atypical outgroup member on the outgroup stereotype. *Basic Appl. Soc. Psychol.* 15:339–58

Harding J, Hogrefe R. 1952. Attitudes of white department store employees toward Negro co-workers. *J. Soc. Issues* 8:18–28

Harris R. 1972. *Prejudice and Tolerance in Ulster.* Manchester, UK: Manchester Univ. Press. 234 pp.

Heist DR. 1975. *Causal Analysis.* New York: Wiley. 301 pp.

Herek GM, Capitanio JP. 1996. "Some of my best friends": intergroup contact, concealable stigma, and heterosexuals' attitudes toward gay men and lesbians. *Pers. Soc. Psychol. Bull.* 22:412–24

Hewstone M. 1996. Contact and categorization: social-psychological interventions to change intergroup relations. In *Foundations of Stereotypes and Stereotyping,* ed. CN Macrae, C Stagnor, M Hewstone, pp. 323–68. New York: Guilford. 462 pp.

Hewstone M, Brown R, eds. 1986. *Contact and Conflict in Intergroup Encounters.* Oxford: Blackwell. 231 pp.

Islam MR, Hewstone M. 1993. Dimensions of contact as predictors of intergroup anxiety, perceived out-group variability, and out-group attitude: an integrative model. *Pers. Soc. Psychol. Bull.* 19:700–10

Jackman MR, Crane M. 1986. "Some of my best friends are black…": interracial friendship and whites' racial attitudes. *Public Opin. Q.* 50:459–86

Jeffries V, Ransford HE. 1969. Interracial social contact and middle-class white reaction to the Watts riot. *Soc. Probl.* 16: 312–24

Johnson DW, Johnson RT, Maruyama G. 1984. Goal interdependence and interpersonal-personal attraction in heterogeneous classrooms: a meta-analysis. See Miller & Brewer 1984, pp. 187–212

Johnston L, Hewstone M. 1992. Cognitive models of stereotype change: III. Subtyping and the perceived typicality of disconfirming group members. *J. Exp. Soc. Psychol.* 28:360–86

Katz PA, Taylor DA, eds. 1988. *Eliminating Racism: Profiles in Controversy.* New York: Plenum. 380 pp.

Kephart WM. 1957. *Racial Factors and Urban Law Enforcement.* Philadelphia: Univ. Pa. Press. 209 pp.

Kinloch GC. 1981. Comparative race and ethnic relations. *Int. J. Comp. Sociol.* 22: 257–71

Kinloch GC. 1991. Inequality, repression, discrimination and violence: a comparative study. *Int. J. Cont. Sociol.* 28:85–98

Kirk T. 1993. *The polarisation of Protestants and Roman Catholics in rural Northern Ireland: a case study of Glenravel Ward, County Antrim 1956 to 1988.* PhD thesis. Queen's Univ., Belfast, North. Ireland. 541 pp.

Landis D, Hope RO, Day HR. 1984. Training for desegregation in the military. See Miller & Brewer 1984, pp. 257–78

McGarty C, de la Haye AM. 1997. Stereotype formation: beyond illusory correlation. See Spears et al 1997, pp. 144–70

McGinnis SP. 1990. *Descriptive and evaluative components of stereotypes of computer programmers and their determinants.* PhD thesis. New York: City Univ. NY. 248 pp.

McKay S, Pitman J. 1993. Determinants of Anglo-Australian stereotypes of the Vietnamese in Australia. *Aust. J. Psychol.* 45: 17–23

Meer B, Freedman E. 1966. The impact of Negro neighbors on white house owners. *Soc. Forces* 45:11–19

Miller N, Brewer MB, eds. 1984. *Groups in Contact: The Psychology of Desegregation.* Orlando, FL: Academic. 316 pp.

Minard RD. 1952. Race relations in the Pocahontas coal field. *J. Soc. Issues* 8:29–44

Miracle AW. 1981. Factors affecting interracial cooperation: a case study of a high school football team. *Hum. Organ.* 40: 150–54

Morrison EW, Herlihy JM. 1992. Becoming the best place to work: Managing diversity at American Express Travel related services. In *Diversity in the Workplace,* ed. SE Jackson, pp. 203–26. New York: Guilford. 356 pp.

Moscos CC, Butler JS. 1996. *All That We Can Be.* New York: Basic Books. 198 pp.

Mullen B, Brown R, Smith C. 1992. Ingroup bias as a function of salience, relevance, and status: an integration. *Eur. J. Soc. Psychol.* 22:103–22

Ohm RM. 1988. *Constructing and reconstructing social distance attitudes.* PhD thesis. Ariz. State Univ., Tempe. 316 pp.

Oliner SP, Oliner PM. 1988. *The Altruistic Personality: Rescuers of Jews in Nazi Europe.* New York: Free Press. 419 pp.

Parker JH. 1968. The interaction of Negroes and whites in an integrated church setting. *Soc. Forces* 46:359–66

Patchen M. 1982. *Black-White Contact in Schools: Its Social and Academic Effects.* West Lafayette, IN: Purdue Univ. Press. 387 pp.

Perdue CW, Dovidio JF, Gurtman MB, Tyler RB. 1990. Us and them: social categorization and the process of intergroup bias. *J. Pers. Soc. Psychol.* 59:475–86

Pettigrew TF. 1971. *Racially Separate or Together?* New York: McGraw-Hill. 371 pp.

Pettigrew TF. 1975. The racial integration of the schools. In *Racial Discrimination in the United States,* ed. TF Pettigrew, pp. 224–39. New York: Harper & Row. 429 pp.

Pettigrew TF. 1986. The contact hypothesis revisited. See Hewstone & Brown 1986, pp. 169–95

Pettigrew TF. 1991a. The importance of cumulative effects: a neglected emphasis of Sherif's work. In *Social Judgment and Intergroup Relations: Essays in Honor of Muzafer Sherif,* ed. D Granberg, G Sarup, pp. 89–103. New York: Springer-Verlag. 280 pp.

Pettigrew TF. 1991b. Toward unity and bold theory: Popperian suggestions for two persistent problems of social psychology. In *The Future of Social Psychology,* ed. CW Stephan, W Stephan, TF Pettigrew, pp. 13–27. New York: Springer-Verlag. 121 pp.

Pettigrew TF. 1996. *How to Think Like a Social Scientist.* New York: Harper-Collins. 198 pp.

Pettigrew TF. 1997a. Generalized intergroup contact effects on prejudice. *Pers. Soc. Psychol. Bull.* 23:173–85

Pettigrew TF. 1997b. The affective component of prejudice: empirical support for the new view. In *Racial Attitudes in the 1990s: Continuity and Change,* ed. SA Tuch, JK Martin, pp. 76–90. Westport, CT: Praeger. In press

Pettigrew TF. 1997c. Ingroup reappraisal: another intergroup contact process that reduces prejudice. Univ. Calif., Santa Cruz. Unpublished manuscr.

Pettigrew TF, Meertens RW. 1995. Subtle and blatant prejudice in western Europe. *Eur. J. Soc. Psychol.* 25:57–75

Pettigrew TF, Wright S, Tropp L. 1998. Intergroup contact and prejudice: a meta-analytic test of Allport's hypothesis. Dep. Psychol., Univ. Calif., Santa Cruz. Unpublished manuscr.

Powers DA, Ellison CG. 1995. Interracial contact and black racial attitudes: the contact hypothesis and selectivity bias. *Soc. Forces* 74:205–26

Reich C, Purbhoo M. 1975. The effect of cross-cultural contact. *Can. J. Behav. Sci.* 7:313–27

Reif K, Melich A. 1991. *Euro-Barometer 30: Immigrants and Out-Groups in Western Europe, 1988.* Ann Arbor, MI: Inter-Univ. Consort. Polit. Soc. Res. 780 pp.

Reitzes DC. 1953. The role of organizational structures: union versus neighborhood in a tension situation. *J. Soc. Issues* 9(1):37–44

Riordan C. 1978. Equal-status interracial contact: a review and revision of the concept. *Int. J. Intercult. Relat.* 2:161–85

Riordan C. 1987. Intergroup contact in small cities. *Int. J. Intercult. Relat.* 11:143–54

Riordan C, Ruggiero J. 1980. Producing equal-status interracial interaction: a replication. *Soc. Psychol. Q.* 43:131–36

Rippl S. 1995. Vorurteile und personliche Beziehungen zwischen Ost- und Westdeuschen. *Z. Soziol.* 24:273–83

Robinson JL Jr. 1980. Physical distance and racial attitudes: a further examination of the contact hypothesis. *Phylon* 41:325–32

Robinson JW Jr, Preston JD. 1976. Equal-status contact and modification of racial prejudice. *Soc. Forces* 54:911–24

Rose TL. 1981. Cognitive and dyadic processes in intergroup contact. In *Cognitive Processes in Stereotyping and Intergroup Behavior,* ed. DL Hamilton, pp. 145–81. Hillsdale, NJ: Erlbaum. 366 pp.

Rothbart M, John OP. 1985. Social categorization and behavioral episodes: a cognitive analysis of the effects of intergroup contact. *J. Soc. Issues* 41:81–104

Russell MJ. 1961. *Study of a South African Inter-Racial Neighbourhood.* Durban, S. Afr: Univ. Natal, Durban. 167 pp.

Saenger G, Gilbert E. 1950. Customer reactions to the integration of Negro sales personnel. *Int. J. Opin. Attent. Res.* 4: 57–76

Sagiv L, Schwartz SH. 1995. Value priorities and readiness for out-group social contact. *J. Pers. Soc. Psychol.* 69:437–48

Schofield JW. 1989. *Black and White in School: Trust, Tension, or Tolerance?* New York: Teachers College Press. 255 pp.

Sherif M. 1966. *In Common Predicament.* Boston: Houghton Mifflin. 192 pp.

Sigelman L, Welch S. 1993. The contact hypothesis revisited: black-white interaction and positive racial attitudes. *Soc. Forces* 71:781–95

Sims VM, Patrick JR. 1936. Attitude toward the Negro of northern and southern college students. *J. Soc. Psychol.* 7:192–204

Slavin RE. 1983. *Cooperative Learning.* New York: Longman. 147 pp.

Slavin RE, Madden NA. 1979. Social practices that improve race relations. *Am. Educ. Res. J.* 16:169–80

Smith CB. 1994. Back and to the future: the intergroup contact hypothesis revisited. *Sociol. Inq.* 64:438–55

Spears R, Oakes PJ, Ellemers N, Haslam SA, eds. 1997. *The Social Psychology of Stereotyping and Group Life.* Oxford, UK: Blackwell. 422 pp.

Stephan CW. 1992. Intergroup anxiety and intergroup interaction. *Cult. Divers. Sch.* 2: 145–58

Stephan CW, Stephan WG. 1992. Reducing intercultural anxiety through intercultural contact. *Int. J. Intercult. Relat.* 16:89–106

Stephan WG. 1987. The contact hypothesis in intergroup relations. *Rev. Pers. Soc. Psychol.* 9:13–40

Stephan WG, Stephan CW. 1984. The role of

ignorance in intergroup relations. See Miller & Brewer 1984, pp. 229–56

Stephan WG, Stephan CW. 1985. Intergroup anxiety. *J. Soc. Issues* 41:157–75

Stephan WG, Stephan CW. 1989. Antecedents of intergroup anxiety in Asian-Americans and Hispanic-Americans. *Int. J. Intercult. Relat.* 13:203–19

Stephan WG, Stephan CW. 1996. *An integrated threat theory of prejudice.* Presented at Int. Psychol. Congr., 26th, Montreal

Stouffer SA, Suchman EA, DeVinney LC, Star SA, Williams RM Jr. 1949. *The American Soldier: Adjustment During Army Life.* Princeton, NJ: Princeton Univ. Press. 756 pp.

Taylor DM, Dube L, Bellerose J. 1986. Intergroup contact in Quebec. See Hewstone & Brown 1986, pp. 107–18

Trew K. 1986. Catholic-Protestant contact in Northern Ireland. See Hewstone & Brown 1986, pp. 93–106

Triandis HC. 1994. *Culture and Social Behavior.* New York: McGraw-Hill. 330 pp.

US Department of Defense. 1955. *A Progress Report on Integration in the Armed Services, 1954.* Washington, DC: US Gov. Print. Off. 165 pp.

Van Oudenhoven JP, Groenewoud JT, Hewstone M. 1996. Cooperation, ethnic salience and generalisation of interethnic attitudes. *Eur. J. Soc. Psychol.* 26:649–61

Vivian J, Brown R, Hewstone M. 1995. Changing attitudes through intergroup contact: the effects of group membership salience. Univ. Kent & Cardiff, Wales. Unpublished manuscr.

Wagner U, Hewstone M, Machleit U. 1989. Contact and prejudice between Germans and Turks. *Hum. Relat.* 42:561–74

Wagner U, Machleit U. 1986. "Gestarbeiter" in the Federal Republic of Germany: contact between Germans and migrant populations. See Hewstone & Brown 1986, pp. 59–78

Walker I, Crogan M. 1997. *Academic performance, prejudice, and the jigsaw classroom: new pieces to the puzzle.* Presented at Annu. Meet. Soc. Aust. Soc. Psychol., 3rd, Wollongong

Watson G. 1947. *Action for Unity.* New York: Harper. 165 pp.

Weber R, Crocker J. 1983. Cognitive processes in the revision of stereotypic beliefs. *J. Pers. Soc. Psychol.* 45:961–77

Weigert KM. 1976. Intergroup contact and attitudes about third-group: a survey of Black soldiers' perceptions. *Int. J. Group Tens.* 6:110–24

Weldon DE, Carlston DE, Rissman AK, Slobodin L, Triandis HC. 1975. A laboratory test of effects of culture assimilator training. *J. Pers. Soc. Psychol.* 32:300–10

Werth JL, Lord CG. 1992. Previous conceptions of the typical group member and the contact hypothesis. *Basic Appl. Soc. Psychol.* 13:351–69

Wilder DA. 1984. Intergroup contact: the typical member and the exception to the rule. *J. Exp. Soc. Psychol.* 20:177–94

Wilder DA. 1993a. The role of anxiety in facilitating stereotypic judgments of outgroup behavior. In *Affect, Cognition, and Stereotyping: Interactive Processes in Group Perception,* ed. DM Mackie, DL Hamilton, pp. 87–109. San Diego: Academic. 389 pp.

Wilder DA. 1993b. Freezing intergroup evaluations: anxiety fosters resistance to counterstereotypic information. In *Group Motivation: Social Psychological Perspectives,* ed. MA Hogg, D Abrams, pp. 68–86. London: Harvester Wheatsheaf. 240 pp.

Wilder DA, Shapiro PN. 1989. Role of competition-induced anxiety in limiting beneficial impact of positive behavior by an outgroup member. *J. Pers. Soc. Psychol.* 56:60–69

Wilder DA, Thompson JE. 1980. Intergroup contact with independent manipulations of in-group and out-group interaction. *J. Pers. Soc. Psychol.* 38:589–603

Williams RM Jr. 1947. *The Reduction of Intergroup Tensions.* New York: Soc. Sci. Res. Counc. 153 pp.

Wilner DM, Walkley R, Cook SW. 1955. *Human Relations in Interracial Housing: A Study of the Contact Hypothesis.* Minneapolis: Univ. Minn. Press. 167 pp.

Works E. 1961. The prejudice-interaction hypothesis from the point of view of the Negro minority group. *Am. J. Sociol.* 67:47–52

Wright SC, Aron A, McLaughlin-Volpe T, Ropp SA. 1997. The extended contact effect: knowledge of cross-group friendships and prejudice. Univ. Calif., Santa Cruz. Unpublished manuscr.

Zajonc RB. 1968. Attitudinal effects of mere exposure. *J. Pers. Soc. Psychol.* 9(Suppl. 2):1–27

Zuel CR, Humphrey CR. 1971. The integration of black residents in suburban neighborhoods. *Soc. Probl.* 18:462–74

*Annu. Rev. Psychol. 1998. 49:87–115*

# COGNITIVE NEUROSCIENCE OF HUMAN MEMORY

*J. D. E. Gabrieli*

Department of Psychology, Stanford University, Stanford, California 94305;
e-mail: gabrieli@psych.stanford.edu

KEY WORDS: declarative memory, skill learning, repetition priming, conditioning, functional brain imaging

## ABSTRACT

Current knowledge is summarized about long-term memory systems of the human brain, with memory systems defined as specific neural networks that support specific mnemonic processes. The summary integrates convergent evidence from neuropsychological studies of patients with brain lesions and from functional neuroimaging studies using positron emission tomography (PET) or functional magnetic resonance imaging (fMRI). Evidence is reviewed about the specific roles of hippocampal and parahippocampal regions, the amygdala, the basal ganglia, and various neocortical areas in declarative memory. Evidence is also reviewed about which brain regions mediate specific kinds of procedural memory, including sensorimotor, perceptual, and cognitive skill learning; perceptual and conceptual repetition priming; and several forms of conditioning. Findings are discussed in terms of the functional neural architecture of normal memory, age-related changes in memory performance, and neurological conditions that affect memory such as amnesia, Alzheimer's disease, Parkinson's disease, and Huntington's disease.

## CONTENTS

87

0066-4308/98/0201-0087$08.00

# INTRODUCTION

The cognitive neuroscience of human memory aims to understand how we rec-ord, retain, and retrieve experience in terms of memory systems—specific neural networks that support specific mnemonic processes. Advances in the study of the cognitive neuroscience of human memory reveal the functional neural architecture of normal human memory and illuminate why focal or de-generative injuries to specific memory systems lead to characteristic patterns of mnemonic failure.

Studies of patients with brain lesions have provided the foundations of our knowledge about the biological organization of human memory. Lesions have produced dramatic and often unexpected mnemonic deficits that provide clues about which brain regions are necessary for which memory processes. The be-havior of memory-impaired patients with brain lesions, however, does not de-lineate what process is subserved by the injured tissue. Rather, the behavior re-flects what uninjured brain regions can accomplish after the lesion. Further, naturally occurring lesions often impair multiple brain systems, either by di-rect insult or by disconnection of interactive brain regions. It is therefore diffi-cult to determine which deficit is the consequence of which part of a lesion.

Although lesion studies continue to provide new evidence, functional neu-roimaging studies using positron emission tomography (PET) or functional magnetic resonance imaging (fMRI) now permit the visualization of memory processes in the healthy brain. Functional neuroimaging studies allow for the design of psychological experiments targeted at specific memory processes. They are limited, however, by several factors. PET and fMRI derive their sig-nals not from neural activity but rather from local changes in blood flow or me-tabolism correlated with neural activity. The local vascular changes affect the distribution of an injected radionuclide (usually $O^{15}$) in PET or magnetic prop-erties that are blood-oxygen level dependent (BOLD) in fMRI. The indirect measure of neural activity limits the temporal and spatial fidelity of activations.

There is also a great deal of psychological interpretation involved in understanding the meaning of an activation, i.e. in specifying what mental process is signified by an activation. Most imaging studies report activations arising from the difference between two tasks. Such differences are not only open to a variety of interpretations but also are often confounded with factors such as task difficulty or trial duration. Further, neuroimaging constraints influence task designs, such as the need to block stimuli in homogenous conditions for between-condition comparisons where each condition often lasts for 30 seconds (fMRI) or 2 minutes (PET). Ongoing developments, however, are expanding the range of experimentation that can be performed within the constraints of fMRI measurement, including parametric task designs (Cohen et al 1997), multiple regression analyses (Courtney et al 1997), and single-trial analysis (Buckner et al 1996). Even with these improvements, remarkable progress in brain imaging techniques does not compete with the psychological analysis of behavior but instead places a new premium upon the thoughtfulness and accuracy of such analysis.

The combination of lesion and neuroimaging studies may overcome the limitations of each source of evidence and provide powerful, mutual constraints on ideas about memory systems. For example, activations for some memory tasks occur in brain regions that can be severely injured without affecting performance on that task. Those activations may represent correlated memory processes that are not participating in the form of memory being measured in the neuroimaging study. Without the lesion evidence, it would be difficult, if not impossible, to discriminate between activations signifying processes that are essential or nonessential for the specific form of memory being measured. Thus, convergent evidence from lesion and functional neuroimaging studies should help both in advancing the understanding and in avoiding the misunderstanding of human memory systems.

The present review emphasizes how lesion and functional neuroimaging evidence converge to identify the neural networks and characterize the mnemonic processes of long-term memory systems. Progress in delineating short-term and working memory systems is reviewed by Smith & Jonides (1994, 1997).

## DECLARATIVE MEMORY

Declarative memory encompasses the acquisition, retention, and retrieval of knowledge that can be consciously and intentionally recollected (Cohen & Squire 1980). Such knowledge includes memory for events (episodic memory) or facts (semantic memory) (Tulving 1983). Episodic memories are measured by direct or explicit tests of memory, such as free recall, cued recall, or recognition, that refer to a prior episode (Graf & Schacter 1985). In contrast, nondeclarative or procedural kinds of memory encompass the acquisition, retention, and retrieval of knowledge expressed through experience-induced changes in performance. These kinds of memory are measured by indirect or implicit tests where no reference is made to that experience. Skill learning, repetition priming, and conditioning are classes of implicit tests that often reveal procedural memory processes dissociable from declarative memory.

A source of common confusion and theoretical challenge lies in the distinction between test instructions and memory processes. It is easy to classify a test as explicit when subjects are asked to intentionally retrieve memories from a specified episode, or as implicit when subjects are asked to perform a task and no reference is made to any prior episode. It is not easy to determine, however, what kind of memory processes are involved when performing the test. There are many examples where memory on an implicit test is correlated with memory on a related explicit test. A parsimonious interpretation is that these implicit tests invoke some of the same declarative memory processes typically invoked by explicit memory tests. There are theories (e.g. Cohen & Eichenbaum 1993) and methods (Bowers & Schacter 1990) that address the distinction between implicit tests that measure processes associated with or dissociated from declarative memory. Presently, however, these theories and methods cannot predict in principle whether a specific implicit test will or will not invoke declarative memory processes.

## Medial-Temporal and Diencephalic Systems

Lesions to medial-temporal and diencephalic brain regions yield amnesia, a selective deficit in declarative memory with sparing of short-term memory, remote memories, and motor, perceptual, and cognitive capacities (Scoville & Milner 1957, Cohen & Squire 1980). All amnesic patients have an anterograde amnesia—an inability to learn new information after the onset of the amnesia. Amnesic patients vary in their severity and extent of their retrograde amnesia—a loss of information gained before the onset of the amnesia. Retrograde losses of memory in amnesia are usually temporally graded in that they are most severe for time periods closest to amnesia onset. Unilateral left or right lesions produce material-specific declarative memory deficits for verbal or nonverbal information, respectively (Milner 1971). Bilateral lesions produce a global amnesia that extends to verbal and nonverbal information. Global amnesia impairs the ability to acquire both episodic and semantic memories, such as the meaning of words and concepts (Gabrieli et al 1988).

Diencephalic lesions that produce amnesia, as seen in patients with alcoholic Korsakoff's syndrome, involve damage to the medial thalamus and often the mammillary nuclei. Damage to these regions is sufficient to produce severe memory impairments even when medial-temporal regions remain anatomically intact (Press et al 1989). The medial thalamic lesions appear to have a greater effect than the mammillary body lesions upon declarative memory. It is unclear at present, however, what specific aspect of the medial thalamic lesions accounts for amnesia.

Medial temporal lesions may result from resection (as in the case of the noted amnesic patient HM), anoxia, herpes simplex encephalitis, infarction, or sclerosis. The first lesions in most cases of Alzheimer's disease (AD) may occur in the medial temporal lobe (Hyman et al 1984), and this may account for amnesia being the most common initial problem in AD. Unlike patients with pure amnesia, however, AD patients have a dementia defined by the compromise of at least one additional, nonmnemonic function. Further, AD patients also have early damage to cholinergic neurons in the basal forebrain (Arendt et al 1983), and lesions in that area cause declarative memory impairments. Therefore, it is difficult to ascribe the amnesia in AD exclusively to medial-temporal injuries.

The medial temporal-lobe memory system consists of multiple structures, most of which may be classified as belonging to one of two major regions. High-level unimodal and polymodal cortical regions provide convergent inputs to the parahippocampal region, which is comprised of parahippocampal and perirhinal cortices (Suzuki & Amaral 1994). The parahippocampal region provides major inputs to the hippocampal region, which is composed of the subiculum, the CA fields, and the dentate gyrus. Entorhinal cortex is variably classified as belonging to either the hippocampal or parahippocampal region. The amygdala is located in the medial temporal lobe, but it has a limited role in declarative memory that is discussed later.

Postmortem analysis of medial-temporal damage in patients with well-characterized amnesias shows that damage restricted to a small part of the hippocampal region, the CA1 field, is sufficient to produce a clinically significant anterograde amnesia. More extensive damage to additional medial-temporal structures aggravates both the severity of the anterograde amnesia and the temporal extent of the retrograde amnesia. When lesions extend beyond the hippocampal region to entorhinal and perirhinal cortices, retrograde amnesias extend back one or two decades (Corkin et al 1997, Rempel-Clower et al 1996).

Neuroimaging studies provide convergent evidence about the participation of medial-temporal regions in declarative memory. Medial-temporal activations are observed during intentional memory retrieval (Squire et al 1992; Schacter et al 1995b, 1996a,c). These activations are associated with successful memory retrieval: Activations are greater when people make memory judgments for studied than for novel materials and for well-remembered than for poorly remembered words. Medial-temporal activations occur also during the encoding of memories. The encoding activations appear to index stimulus novelty: They are greater for stimuli seen initially rather than repeatedly (Tulving et al 1994, Stern et al 1996).

One study showed that encoding and retrieval activations occurred in different medial-temporal regions (Gabrieli et al 1997a). Retrieving well-learned memories resulted in an anterior activation in the subiculum, a component of the hippocampal region. Encoding novel memories resulted in a posterior activation in parahippocampal cortex, a component of the parahippocampal region. The two locations are in agreement with findings of a posterior locus for encoding (Stern et al 1996) and a positive correlation between the magnitude of anterior hippocampal activation and retrieval accuracy in a recognition memory test (Nyberg et al 1996).

Lesion studies showed that a medial-temporal system is critical for declarative memory, but it has been difficult to glean the specific declarative processes mediated by components of that system because lesions typically traverse multiple medial-temporal structures. Imaging studies are beginning to provide information about the specific contributions of different components of the medial-temporal memory system to declarative memory. The finding that different medial-temporal structures make different contributions to declarative memory may help explain why more extensive lesions, which may compromise multiple declarative memory processes, yield more severe anterograde and retrograde amnesias.

## Amygdala

Lesion and functional neuroimaging findings have illuminated the importance of the amygdala in emotional aspects of human memory (reviewed in Phelps & Anderson 1997). Because the amygdala is near the hippocampal formation, amnesic patients, such as HM, often have damage to both structures. It was, therefore, difficult to distinguish between the specific mnemonic roles of these adjacent limbic structures. However, a rare congenital dermatological disorder, Urbach-Weithe syndrome, leads to mineralization of the amygdala that spares the hippocampal formation. The amygdala is also resected for treatment of pharmacologically intractable epilepsy, although the resection usually involves additional medial-temporal structures. Studies with these patients have allowed for a more direct examination of the consequence of amygdala lesions in humans.

There is convergent evidence for a limited role for the amygdala in declarative memory. Normal subjects show superior memory for emotionally disturbing relative to emotionally neutral stimuli. An Urbach-Weithe patient showed normal memory for neutral slides but failed to show the normal additional memory for the emotionally salient slides (Cahill et al 1995). In one PET study, amygdala activation correlated with individual differences in later recall for emotional, but not for neutral, film clips (Cahill et al 1996). In another PET study, amygdala activation was noted during retrieval of autobiographical memories that were likely to have personal emotional salience (Fink et al 1996).

At present, lesion and neuroimaging evidence indicates that the amygdala has a circumscribed role in declarative memory for emotionally disturbing or aversive experiences. The amygdala participates not only in explicit memory for aversive stimuli but also implicit memory for aversive stimuli tested via fear conditioning (reviewed below). Patients with amygdala lesions show selective deficits in the identification of fearful or angry facial expressions (Adolphs et al 1994) or prosody (Scott et al 1997). Amygdala activations occur in PET and fMRI studies during the perception of fearful facial expressions or scenes (Morris et al 1996). Thus, the amygdala appears to have a widespread role in processing negatively salient stimuli.

## Neocortical Systems

Declarative memory is generally thought to reflect an interaction between medial-temporal/diencephalic and neocortical brain regions. The fact that medial-temporal or diencephalic lesions spare remote memories has encouraged the view that the neocortex is the ultimate repository of consolidated long-term memory. Neocortical areas are also viewed as critical for encoding (processing and analyzing) current experience. This may occur in a domain-specific fashion, with different cortical regions processing different perceptual (e.g. visual, auditory, tactual) and cognitive (e.g. verbal, spatial) features of an experience. Thus, the neocortex contributes to the encoding, storage, and retrieval of declarative memories.

CORTICAL REPRESENTATION OF KNOWLEDGE    Lesions have revealed remarkable specificity in the cortical representation of long-term memories. Some patients with cortical lesions have shown category-specific inabilities to produce the names of objects (anomias). Thus, patients have shown selective deficits for retrieving the names of (a) people and other proper nouns (Semenza & Zettin 1989); (b) fruits and vegetables (Hart et al 1985); (c) living things such as animals (Damasio et al 1996); and (d) manufactured things such as tools (Damasio et al 1996). These patients can demonstrate retention of knowledge about objects that they cannot name by, for example, selecting the names of such objects from multiple choices. Other patients appear to have category-specific losses of knowledge for objects, with disproportionate losses of knowledge for either living (Warrington & Shallice 1984) or manufactured objects (Warrington & McCarthy 1983). Even within the category of living things, a patient has exhibited a dissociation between impaired verbal versus intact pictorial knowledge (McCarthy & Warrington 1988). Yet other patients have shown focal losses of autobiographical knowledge following injury to the right anterior temporal lobe (Kapur et al 1992). These patients differ from amnesic patients in that declarative memory is relatively spared and that the retrograde amnesia is not temporally graded.

Neuroimaging studies motivated by these surprising patient findings have provided corroborating evidence. Thus, separate loci of activations are found in the left-temporal lobe during the naming of people (proper nouns), tools, and animals that correspond to the lesion sites producing selective anomias (Damasio et al 1996). The naming of tools or animals yields both shared and separate activations (Martin et al 1996) as does answering conceptual questions about corresponding pictures and words (Vandenberghe et al 1996). Listening to one's own autobiographical passage, relative to another person's autobiographical passage, results in activation of right frontal- and temporal-lobe regions (Fink et al 1996). These neuroimaging studies indicate that the unexpected dissociations of knowledge in patients are not idiosyncratic phenomena, but rather the consequence of the differential cortical geography of knowledge in the healthy brain.

Two emerging principles may be discerned from these neuroimaging studies. First, knowledge in any domain (e.g. for pictures or words, living or manufactured objects) is distributed over a specific, but extensive, neural network that often extends over several lobes. Injury to any component of that network could affect performance in that domain, with the specific effect reflecting what aspect of that knowledge is represented in that component of the network. Second, some localization appears to be a consequence of how various classes of knowledge interact with different perceptual and motor systems. Thus, we have motor experiences with tools that vary systematically in relation to each tool's function. In contrast, most people have far fewer motor experiences with animals. Perhaps for this reason, naming tools relative to naming animals, or naming an action (writing) relative to naming a color (yellow) associated with an object (pencil), yields activation in left prefrontal regions near motor cortex (Martin et al 1995, 1996).

ENCODING OF MEMORIES   Left frontal activations, especially in the anterior portion of the inferior prefrontal gyrus, have been found when subjects perform tasks that enhance memory for the encoded information. There is greater left prefrontal activation when subjects make semantic (deep) versus nonsemantic (shallow) decisions about words (Demb et al 1995, Gabrieli et al 1996a, Kapur et al 1994), study words with a mild versus a severe division of attention (Shallice et al 1994), or generate versus read words (Petersen et al 1989). In one of the first lesion studies inspired by imaging findings, it was found that patients with left frontal lesions were impaired at making the same semantic judgments that had yielded left frontal activations in healthy subjects (Swick & Knight 1996). Although the left frontal activation is evident also for nonverbal stimuli such as faces (Haxby et al 1996), it seems likely that this activation is most closely linked to semantic processes associated with language. This kind of activation, which may also be considered one of semantic memory retrieval, occurs in the right prefrontal cortex of patients who are right-hemisphere dominant for language (Desmond et al 1995).

STRATEGIC MEMORY   Declarative memory tasks differ in their strategic memory demands, i.e. in how much retrieved memories must be evaluated, manipulated, and transformed. Recognition tests given shortly after study may have minimal strategic demands as subjects quickly decide whether or not a particular stimulus had been included in a study list. Tests of free recall, delayed recognition, temporal order, and source may have much greater strategic demands because subjects have to figure out how they will recall stimuli or what time or place a familiar stimulus was encountered.

Frontal-lobe lesions can compromise performance on strategic memory tasks even when patients perform normally or near normally on recognition tests (this pattern differs from amnesia where performance on both strategic and nonstrategic memory tasks is severely impaired). Patients with frontal-lobe lesions have disproportionate impairments on tests of free recall (Janowsky et al 1989), recency or temporal order judgments (Milner 1971), frequency judgments (Smith & Milner 1988), self-ordered pointing (Petrides & Milner 1982), and recollection of the source of information (Janowsky et al 1989). An imaging study with normal subjects found frontal-lobe activation during the performance of self-ordered pointing (Petrides et al 1993a).

Strategic memory tasks may require subjects to reason about their memories, and there is evidence that the frontal lobes are important in reasoning. Frontal patients perform poorly on problem-solving or reasoning tasks that require the generation, flexible maintenance, and shifting of plans, such as the Wisconsin Card Sorting Test (Milner 1963) and the Tower-of-London Test (Shallice 1982). Neuroimaging studies have found prominent frontal-lobe activations when people reason as they perform problem-solving tasks (Baker et al 1996, Prabhakaran et al 1997). Thus, the frontal-lobe contribution to strategic memory may be one of problem-solving and reasoning in the service of difficult declarative memory demands.

Selective deficits of strategic declarative memory have been found also in degenerative or developmental diseases of the basal ganglia, such as Parkinson's disease (PD), Huntington's disease (HD), and Gilles de la Tourette's syndrome (GTS) (Gabrieli 1996). Striatal diseases also impair reasoning (Lees & Smith 1983). In addition, PD, HD, and GTS patients have significantly reduced working memory capacities, and the reductions are highly correlated with the strategic memory and reasoning deficits. Indeed, difficult tasks that tax working memory capacity routinely yield frontal activations (e.g. Cohen et al 1997, Petrides et al 1993a,b). Thus, it may be hypothesized that fronto-striatal lesions reduce working memory capacity, which limits reasoning ability and, in turn, impairs strategic memory performance. Further, the neurotransmitter dopamine may be critical for working memory. PD patients have severely reduced dopamine functioning, and dopamine treatment can enhance working memory performance in PD patients (Cooper et al 1992).

There are several reasons to hypothesize that age-related decline in fronto-striatal function may account for a great deal of normal age-related decline in memory performance (Gabrieli 1995). Working memory, reasoning, and strategic memory performance decline linearly across the life span. Similarly, dopaminergic function appears to decline linearly across the life span, with a 5–10% decline per decade. The notion that it is specifically fronto-striatal dysfunction that accounts for age-related declines in memory performance is supported by a neuroimaging study that found age-related differences in frontal but not medial-temporal regions during explicit retrieval (Schacter et al 1996c).

Associations between working memory, reasoning, and strategic memory occur in patient studies, normal aging, and functional neuroimaging. All three capacities appear to depend upon dopaminergic fronto-striatal systems. The extent to which these associations reflect shared versus neighboring processes and whether reductions in one capacity are causal or merely correlated with changes in the other capacities remains to be determined.

INTENTIONAL RETRIEVAL   A consistent but poorly understood activation occurs in right frontal cortex during intentional declarative or episodic retrieval of memory for words (Schacter et al 1996a, Shallice et al 1994, Squire et al 1992, Tulving et al 1994), faces (Haxby et al 1996), scenes (Tulving et al 1996), or meaningless objects (Schacter et al 1995b). These robust activations were unexpected because they applied to verbal and nonverbal memories, and because right frontal lesions have modest effects on declarative memory. Further, it has been difficult to specify the nature of the retrieval conditions that yield right frontal activations. In some studies, the activations occur during memory judgments for old (studied) stimuli relative to new (unstudied) stimuli, and such activations are considered to reflect retrieval success (greater for old than new stimuli) (e.g. Rugg et al 1996, Tulving et al 1994). In other studies, they occur equally for well-remembered old stimuli, poorly remembered old stimuli, and new stimuli; this pattern of results is interpreted as reflecting retrieval attempt or mode that occurs irrespective of the memorial status of the stimulus (e.g. Kapur et al 1995, Nyberg et al 1995). In yet other studies, the activations appear slightly greater for poorly remembered than well-remembered information and are interpreted as indexing retrieval effort (Schacter et al 1996a).

One speculative interpretation is that right-frontal retrieval activations reflect working memory processes that guide or evaluate the products of episodic retrieval. If right-frontal activation were required for intentional retrieval, patients with right-frontal lesions would be globally amnesic because they would be unable to retrieve memories. To the contrary, deficits after right-frontal lesions are limited to more subtle impairments in strategic memory. For example, a right-frontal lesion can result in a propensity for false recognition under some, but not all, circumstances (Schacter et al 1996b). Thus, the degree of right-frontal activation during intentional retrieval may reflect the degree of strategic monitoring of memory retrieval. If the right-frontal activations reflect working with or reasoning about memory judgments, then such activations could vary considerably depending on what strategies are encouraged by particular retrieval conditions. Such an interpretation would posit a special role for right-frontal cortex in the working memory aspects of intentional retrieval.

## SKILL LEARNING

In skill-learning tasks, subjects perform a challenging task on repeated trials in one or more sessions. The indirect or implicit measure of learning is the improvement in speed or accuracy achieved by a subject across trials and sessions. Preservation of sensorimotor, perceptual, and cognitive skill learning in amnesia indicates that such learning for some skills is not dependent upon declarative memory. Some of the neural systems underlying such skill learning have been identified in neuropyschological and neuroimaging studies.

### Sensorimotor Skills

Intact sensorimotor skill learning in amnesia is well documented for three tasks: mirror tracing, rotary pursuit, and serial reaction time (SRT). In mirror tracing, subjects trace a figure with a stylus only seeing their hand, the stylus, and the figure reflected in a mirror. With practice, subjects trace the figure more quickly and make fewer errors (departures from the figure). Such skill learning is intact in patients with declarative memory problems due to amnesia (Milner 1962) or AD (Gabrieli et al 1993). In rotary pursuit, subjects attempt to maintain contact between a hand-held stylus and a target metal disk, the size of a nickel, on a revolving turntable. With practice, subjects increase the time per trial that they are able to maintain contact with the disk. Rotary-pursuit skill learning is intact in amnesia (Corkin 1968) and in AD (Eslinger & Damasio 1986, Heindel et al 1989). In the SRT task, subjects see targets appear in one of four horizontal locations on a computer monitor and press one of four keys placed directly below those locations as soon as a target appears in the corresponding location. In the critical trials, unbeknown to subjects, targets appear in a repeating 10- or 12-trial sequence of locations. With practice, subjects perform more quickly, and pattern-specific skill learning is measured by a slowing in performance when the targets are presented in random locations. SRT learning is intact in amnesia (Nissen & Bullemer 1987) and intact in some but not all AD patients (Ferraro et al 1993, Knopman & Nissen 1987). Variability in AD performance may reflect dementia severity and perhaps specific impairment in spatial working memory.

Sensorimotor skill learning is often impaired in patients with basal ganglia diseases. Rotary-pursuit skill learning is impaired in HD patients (Gabrieli et al 1997c, Heindel et al 1989), GTS patients (Stebbins et al 1995), and, more variably, PD patients (Heindel et al 1989). SRT learning is impaired in HD patients (Willingham & Koroshetz 1993) and PD patients (Ferraro et al 1993). Basal ganglia diseases do not, however, have uniform effects on sensorimotor skill learning. In one study, HD patients showed a dissociation between impaired rotary-pursuit and intact mirror-tracing skill learning (Gabrieli et al 1997c). Cerebellar lesions, however, do impair mirror-tracing skill learning (Sanes et al 1990). In another study, HD patients showed a dissociation between impaired SRT skill learning and intact learning when subjects had to press a key one position to the right of the target (there was no repeating sequence) (Willingham & Koroshetz 1993). Further, HD patients showed a normal pattern of skill learning when tracking with a joystick a cursor that moved randomly, but impaired learning when the cursor moved in a repeating pattern (Willingham et al 1996).

Thus, the basal ganglia and cerebellum appear to make different contributions to sensorimotor skill learning. Two related hypotheses have been proposed about what differentiates those contributions. One hypothesis proposes that the learning of repetitive motor sequences depends upon the basal ganglia, whereas the learning of new mappings between visual cues and motor responses depends upon the cerebellum (Willingham et al 1996). Another hypothesis is that closed-loop skill learning, which involves continuous external, visual feedback about errors in movement, depends upon the cerebellum. In contrast, open-loop skill learning, which involves the planning of movements and delayed feedback about errors, depends upon the basal ganglia (Gabrieli et al 1997c).

Functional neuroimaging studies have not only supported the importance of the basal ganglia and cerebellum in sensorimotor skill learning but have also shed light upon the importance of motor neocortex in such learning. Rotary-pursuit skill learning is associated with increases in activation of the primary and secondary motor cortices (Grafton et al 1992). SRT skill learning, and similar tasks involving the learning of specific manual sequences, are associated with increased activations in primary and secondary motor cortices and in the basal ganglia (e.g. Doyon et al 1996, Hazeltine et al 1997, Karni et al 1995). In some studies, there is a decrease in cerebellar activation associated with the learning of finger-movement sequences (Friston et al 1992). The possibility that cerebellar activity reflects error-correction, which would decrease as skill increases, is supported by a study finding a correlation between cerebellar activity and errors in a perceptual-motor task (Flament et al 1996). Imaging studies typically report complex patterns of increases and decreases in activation that reflect not only learning but also the changes in performance that occur with learning. These studies reveal that skill learning involves a complex, dynamic set of interactive neural networks.

## Perceptual Skills

Learning to read mirror-reversed text is a perceptual skill that has been well studied in patients. Amnesic patients gain skill in reading such text at a normal rate, despite poor declarative memory for the particular words read or the episodes in which they gained their skill. In contrast, HD patients have mildly impaired mirror-reading skill learning despite relatively good declarative memory for words read and the reading experiences (Martone et al 1984).

An imaging study examined activation in posterior cortical areas as normal subjects gained skill in mirror reading (Poldrack et al 1996). As skill improved, activation increased in left inferior occipito-temporal cortex and decreased in right parietal cortex. These shifts in activity may represent a change in reliance upon visuospatial decoding of mirror-reversed words in unskilled performance to more direct reading in skilled performance. Such shifts from effortful to automatic neural networks occur also in conceptual task performance (Raichle et al 1994).

## Cognitive Skills

Cognitive skills may be acquired normally by amnesic patients, but under relatively narrow circumstances. Amnesic patients have shown normal skill learning on Tower tasks that require planning and problem-solving under some circumstances (Cohen et al 1985, Saint-Cyr et al 1988), but not other circumstances (Butters et al 1985). Amnesic patients have also shown normal learning in the early but not later stages of probabilistic classification problems (Knowlton et al 1994). Cognitive skill learning, however, is impaired in HD and PD patients for Tower tasks (Saint-Cyr et al 1988) and probabilistic classification problems (Knowlton et al 1996a,b). Thus, at least some aspects of cognitive skill learning depend upon the integrity of the basal ganglia, but not upon the medial-temporal and diencephalic structures that support declarative memory.

The basal ganglia appear to be critical for a variety of motor, perceptual, and cognitive skills. These various skill learning deficits may reflect separable damage to distinct striatal-thalamic-cortical loops (Alexander et al 1986). There is evidence, for example, of a dissociation between motor and perceptual skill learning in PD patients (Harrington et al 1991). Each loop may mediate striatal-thalamic-cortical functions in separate motor or cognitive domains, but the loops may share a common abstract or computational property. For example, each loop may provide working memory modulation of domain-relevant cortices.

## REPETITION PRIMING

Repetition priming refers to a change in the processing of a stimulus, usually words or pictures, due to prior exposure to the same or a related stimulus. In a typical experiment, participants process a set of stimuli in a study phase. In a subsequent test phase, participants perform a task with "old" stimuli identical or related to the study-phase stimuli and with "new" stimuli unrelated to the study-phase that provide a baseline measure of performance. The difference in performance with old and new stimuli constitutes the measure of repetition priming (hereafter referred to as priming).

One important distinction is that between perceptual priming, which reflects prior processing of stimulus form, and conceptual priming, which reflects prior processing of stimulus meaning (reviewed in Roediger & McDermott 1993). Perceptual priming occurs in visual, auditory, and tactual modalities. It is maximal when study-phase and test-stimuli are perceptually identical, and reduced when there is a study-test change in modality (e.g. from auditory to visual) or symbolic notation (e.g. from words to pictures). Priming has been characterized as perceptual for tasks such as identification of words presented at threshold, word-stem completion (e.g. complete STA into a word), word-fragment completion (e.g. what letters would make _ T _ M _ into a word), and picture naming. Conceptual priming is maximal when study-phase processing enhances semantic analysis of stimulus meaning, and reduced when study-phase processing diminishes semantic analysis. Priming has been characterized as conceptual for word-association generation (what word goes with KING?) and category-exemplar generation (name FRUITS). Perceptual priming is often unaffected by the level of semantic analysis at study, whereas conceptual priming is often unaffected by study-test relations in perceptual form. Although many priming tasks are well characterized as predominately perceptual or conceptual in nature, there is a growing literature of priming tasks that are difficult to characterize in terms of the perceptual/conceptual dichotomy (e.g. Vaidya et al 1997a).

Repetition priming has been dissociated from declarative memory because of two convergent sources of evidence. First, amnesic patients exhibit normal magnitudes of priming on many tasks, including word identification (Cermak et al 1985), word-stem completion (Graf et al 1984, Warrington & Weiskrantz 1970), word-fragment-completion (Vaidya et al 1995), picture naming (Cave & Squire 1992, Verfaellie et al 1996), word-association generation (Shimamura & Squire 1984), and category-exemplar generation (Graf et al 1985). Second, parallel dissociations between these forms of priming and declarative memory have been obtained in normal subjects (Roediger & McDermott 1993). Two issues of interest are what constitutes the limits of priming in the absence of declarative memory and what neural networks mediate such priming.

## Limits of Priming in Amnesia

PROCESSING/SYSTEM DEBATE    Some investigators have hypothesized that amnesia is better characterized by a distinction between impaired conceptual and intact perceptual memory processes (e.g. Blaxton 1992) than one between impaired explicit and intact implicit retrieval modes. This hypothesis constitutes the core of the "processing-systems" debate. According to the "processing" view, amnesic patients are impaired on explicit memory tests not because these tests require intentional memory retrieval but because performance on these tests is conceptually driven. Amnesic patients show intact priming on word-identification, word-stem completion, and word-fragment completion because such priming reflects perceptual processes. Indeed, the normal status of perceptual priming in amnesia has been well documented as amnesic patients have shown normal reductions in cross-modal word-stem completion (Graf et al 1985), in cross-font word-stem completion (Vaidya et al 1997b), and in cross-exemplar picture naming (Cave & Squire 1992).

The processing and systems views make contradictory predictions about the status of conceptual priming and perceptually cued recall in amnesia. The processing view holds that conceptual memory processes are impaired and perceptual memory processes are intact in amnesia regardless of the explicit or implicit nature of test-phase retrieval. The systems view posits that explicit retrieval is impaired and implicit retrieval is intact in amnesia regardless of the perceptual or conceptual nature of the test-phase retrieval. One study pitted these hypotheses against each other by using identical perceptual (word fragments) and conceptual (word associates) test-phase cues and varying explicit and implicit test-phase retrieval (Vaidya et al 1995). The results were clear: Amnesic patients showed intact perceptual and conceptual priming (implicit retrieval) and impaired perceptual and conceptual cued recall (explicit retrieval). Cermak et al 1995 report similar conclusions. Further, amnesic patients have shown normal insensitivity to modality manipulation (Vaidya et al 1995) and sensitivity to conceptual manipulation (Keane et al 1997) in their intact conceptual priming.

The hypothesis that explicit and implicit conceptual memory performance reflects a unitary process has now been controverted not only by findings in amnesia but also by similar dissociations in normal subjects (Vaidya et al 1997a), normal aging (Monti et al 1996), and schizophrenia (Schwartz et al 1993). The explicit/implicit distinction is superior to the perceptual/conceptual distinction for predicting amnesic performance, but it still cannot explain amnesic impairments on a variety of perceptual and conceptual priming tasks (e.g. Gabrieli et al 1994, Vaidya et al 1996, Schacter 1995a, Verfaellie et al 1996).

PRIMING FOR NOVEL STIMULI   A second theoretical concern was spurred by early studies indicating that amnesic patients could show priming for familiar words known before the onset of amnesia but not for novel pseudowords (Cermak et al 1985, Diamond & Rozin 1984). These results were interpreted as indicating that priming in the absence of declarative memory was limited to the activation of premorbidly acquired memory representations. There is now, however, abundant evidence that amnesic patients can show normal priming for novel information, including nonverbal patterns (Gabrieli et al 1990, Knowlton & Squire 1993) and novel pronounceable (Haist et al 1991) or unpronounceable letter strings (Keane et al 1995). In retrospect, the earlier studies appear to have encouraged normal subjects to use explicit retrieval to support their test-phase performance, a source of support unavailable to amnesic patients. Thus, priming for novel verbal and nonverbal stimuli can occur in the absence of declarative memory processes.

PRIMING FOR NOVEL ASSOCIATIONS   A related theoretical concern was whether amnesic patients could show priming for novel associations between unrelated stimuli. Priming for new associations may be measured by exposing participants to unrelated word pairs in a study phase (e.g. MARCH—SHAVE,

ABOVE—FLEET, AMAZE—VOTER). In a test phase, participants perform a task with three kinds of word pairs—1. Old pairs seen in the study phase (MARCH—SHAVE); 2. Recombined study-phase pairs (ABOVE—VOTER); and 3. New baseline pairs. Superior performance for Recombined relative to New pairs reflects single-word priming. Superior performance for Old relative to Recombined pairs must reflect new associations made between words by their arbitrary study-phase pairing because all words in Old and Recombined pairs were seen in the study phase.

Despite intact word-stem completion priming for single words, amnesic patients have failed to show normal associative priming for word-stem completion (e.g. being more likely to provide SHAVE when seeing MARCH—SHA____ than ABOVE—SHA____) (Cermak et al 1988, Schacter & Graf 1986). These findings raised the possibility that declarative memory was required for explicit and implicit associative memory processes. Amnesic patients, however, have shown normal associative priming on tasks of word identification (Gabrieli et al 1997b), reading time (Moscovitch et al 1986), and color-word naming (Musen & Squire 1993). It is unclear at present why some but not other forms of associative priming depend on the same brain structures and mental processes that mediate declarative memory. The preservation of some forms of associative priming in amnesia, however, provides a possible mechanism for intact priming for novel stimuli. Priming for novel pseudowords, for example, could reflect novel associations among the letters presented together in the pseudoword.

FLUENCY AND FAMILIARITY    The foregoing discussion has emphasized dissociations between memory for stimuli as measured by explicit tests of recall or recognition or by implicit tests of repetition priming. Some processes, however, may be shared by explicit and implicit memory performance. It has been hypothesized that explicit retrieval and perceptual priming may share a common process of fluency and familiarity (Jacoby & Dallas 1981, Mandler 1980). By this view, prior perceptual processing of a stimulus makes more fluent the later reprocessing of that stimulus. Such fluency could mediate priming in implicit tests of word identification or word-stem completion. The same fluency could give rise to a sense of familiarity with a stimulus that contributes to explicit recognition memory performance.

These speculations became testable with the development of two methods aimed at dissociating the roles of conscious recollection and automatic familiarity in explicit recognition performance. The processes dissociation procedure uses inclusion and exclusion tasks that have recollection and familiarity working in concert or in opposition so that separate values for recollection and familiarity can be calculated (Jacoby 1991). This procedure, however, indicates that both recollection and familiarity in explicit recognition are more influenced by conceptual than perceptual factors (Wagner et al 1997). Further, explicit recognition familiarity is intact in a patient with impaired visual priming on word-identification and stem-completion tasks (Wagner et al 1995). Thus, convergent behavioral and neurological evidence dissociates explicit recognition familiarity from perceptual priming.

A second method used to dissociate recollection from familiarity in explicit recognition memory is the remember/know procedure (Gardiner 1988). Subjects are asked to designate which items in a recognition test they "remember" from the study list (have a conscious recollection of the study event) and which items they "know" were on the study list but for which cannot explicitly recollect a study event. Amnesic patients were impaired on both "remember" and "know" responses on a recognition memory test (Knowlton & Squire 1995). Because amnesic patients have intact priming, it does not seem the same processes could underlie priming and "know" recognition responses. The aim of delineating processes that are shared by explicit and implicit retrieval remains an important one, but it does not appear that current methods used to isolate familiarity in explicit recognition are identifying the same processes that mediate perceptual priming.

## Brain Systems Mediating Perceptual and Conceptual Priming

The above findings indicate that perceptual and conceptual priming do not depend upon the medial-temporal and diencephalic structures that mediate declarative memory. HD patients show intact priming (Heindel et al 1989), so priming is also not dependent upon basal ganglia structures critical for skill learning. What neural systems mediate priming?

Several lines of evidence indicate that priming is mediated by neocortical areas, with perceptual priming being mediated by modality-specific cortical regions and conceptual priming by amodal language areas. One source of evidence is the performance of AD patients who exhibit severely reduced conceptual priming (Monti et al 1996) but intact perceptual priming on visual tasks (Fleischman et al 1995; Keane et al 1991, 1995). This pattern of impaired conceptual and intact perceptual priming may be interpreted in terms of the characteristic neocortical neuropathology in AD. In vivo metabolic imaging studies (e.g. Frackowiak et al 1981) and postmortem studies of late-stage AD patients (Brun & Englund 1981) find substantial damage to association neocortices in the frontal, parietal, and temporal lobes but relatively little compromise of primary visual, somatosensory, auditory, and motor cortices, the basal ganglia, or the cerebellum. The sparing of the basal ganglia and cerebellum may account for intact rotary-pursuit and mirror-tracing in AD. The sparing of modality-specific cortices and the compromise of association cortices may account, respectively, for intact perceptual and impaired conceptual priming.

There is more direct evidence that modality-specific neocortex mediates modality-specific perceptual priming. Patients with right occipital lesions have shown an absence of priming on visual word-identification tasks, and of modality and font visual specificity on word-stem completion priming (Fleischman et al 1995, Gabrieli et al 1995b, Keane et al 1995, Vaidya et al 1997b). These patients demonstrate intact performance on explicit tests of recall and recognition and on implicit tests of conceptual priming. Thus, these patients provide two double dissociations: in comparison with amnesia between visual implicit and explicit memory for words, and in comparison with AD between perceptual and conceptual priming.

Neuroimaging studies also indicate that separate cortical areas mediate perceptual and conceptual priming. Priming on visual word-stem completion tasks is associated with reduced activity, relative to baseline word-stem completion, in bilateral occipito-temporal regions (Schacter et al 1996a, Squire et al 1992). Priming on conceptual tasks is associated with reduced activity in left frontal neocortex on tasks involving abstract/concrete decisions about words (Demb et al 1995, Gabrieli et al 1996b), living/nonliving decisions about words and pictures (Wagner et al 1997), generation of verbs to nouns (Raichle et al 1994), and generation of semantically related words (Blaxton et al 1996). Amnesic patients, who show normal priming when making abstract/concrete decisions about words, also show a priming-related reduction in left frontal cortex (Gabrieli et al 1996b).

Thus, lesion and imaging studies provide convergent evidence that different forms of priming reflect process-specific plasticity in separate neocortical regions. It is hypothesized that auditory and tactual priming will be mediated by changes in auditory and somatosensory neocortices. Lexical and semantic priming may reflect changes in association areas of the frontal and temporal lobes. Thus, repetition priming in a given domain appears to reflect experience-induced changes in the same neural networks that subserved initial processing in that domain (Gabrieli et al 1996a, Raichle et al 1994). These changes facilitate or bias the subsequent reprocessing of the stimuli. The enhanced efficiency of reprocessing may diminish computational demands and thus lead to reduced activations relative to baseline conditions.

Earlier, the cortical geography of semantic memory was reviewed. It may be hypothesized that perceptual, lexical, and semantic knowledge systems must be constantly molded by experience to enhance efficiency for identifying objects and words and for using concepts. Repetition priming, psychological domain by psychological domain, and cortical area by cortical area may be revealing how experience constantly tunes the representation of perceptual and conceptual knowledge.

## CONDITIONING

The neural circuitry underlying classical and other forms of conditioning has been studied extensively in rabbits and rats. Parallel studies have now been conducted systematically in humans, and a question of interest is whether the same memory systems mediate conditioning across these mammalian species.

### Delay Conditioning

The memory system underlying classical delay eyeblink conditioning has been delineated with great precision in the rabbit (Thompson 1990). In the typical delay paradigm, a 250–500 ms tone (conditioned stimulus or CS) is repeatedly followed by an air-puff (unconditioned stimulus or US) delivered to the eye that elicits reflexively a blink, the unconditioned response (UR). The tone and air-puff coterminate. With repeated CS-US pairings, subjects learn to associate the tone with the air-puff and initiate an eyeblink (conditioned response or CR) in response to the CS before the onset of the US. In the rabbit, electrophysiological activity in the cerebellum (McCormick & Thompson 1987) and in the hippocampus (Disterhoft et al 1986) parallels the development of behavioral CRs. The convergence of CS and US projections in eyeblink conditioning occurs in the cerebellum ipsilateral to the eye receiving the air-puff. Lesions of the cerebellar dentate-interpositus nuclei prevent acquisition or abolish retention of the conditioned association. Hippocampal lesions, however, do not impair delay conditioning in the rabbit (Schmaltz & Theios 1972). Presumably, CR-correlated electrophysiological activity in the hippocampus reflects a parallel learning circuit that does not mediate delay conditioning.

Results with human beings provide three striking parallels with animal findings. First, cerebellar lesions in human beings abolish delay eyeblink conditioning (Daum et al 1993). Second, delay eyeblink conditioning is intact in amnesic patients with bilateral medial-temporal (Gabrieli et al 1995a) or bilateral thalamic lesions (Daum & Ackermann 1994). Such conditioning is somewhat impaired in HM (Woodruff-Pak 1993) and greatly impaired in alcoholic Korsakoff's patients (McGlinchey-Berroth et al 1995), but these deficits appear to reflect cerebellar damage due to chronic exposure to anticonvulsant medications or alcohol, respectively. Third, PET studies have reported both cerebellar and medial-temporal activations associated with delay conditioning that parallel the development of behavioral CRs (Blaxton et al 1996, Logan & Grafton 1995).

Delay eyeblink conditioning is not diminished by the basal ganglia lesions in HD (Woodruff-Pak & Papka 1996). It does diminish across the normal adult life span (Woodruff-Pak & Thompson 1988) and is virtually abolished in AD (Woodruff-Pak et al 1990). The brain basis for diminished delay eyeblink conditioning in aging or in AD is unknown. Such conditioning does not depend upon either the medial-temporal structures critical for declarative memory or the striatal structures critical for many forms of skill learning.

## Trace and Discrimination Reversal Conditioning

The hippocampal activation evident in human and animal recordings during delay eyeblink conditioning does not appear to be essential for such learning but it may reflect correlated learning that is essential for other forms of conditioning. In animals, medial-temporal lesions impair trace eyeblink conditioning, which differs from delay conditioning in that there is a short time period—a second or less—between the offset of the CS and the onset of the US (Solomon et al 1986). Amnesic patients with medial-temporal lesions who are unimpaired on delay conditioning show impaired trace conditioning with CS-US trace intervals as short as 500 ms (McGlinchey-Berroth et al 1997). In animals, medial-temporal lesions also impair discrimination reversal, in which the two CSs are switched in their association with the US (Berger & Orr 1983). Amnesic patients with medial-temporal lesions also have impaired conditioning for discrimination reversal (Daum et al 1989). These findings suggest that the same medial-temporal lobe structures that are essential for declarative memory also mediate processes required for more complex forms of conditioning in human beings as they do in rabbits.

## Fear Conditioning

The critical role of the amygdala in fear conditioning to aversive stimuli such as electric shocks has been well established in rats (Davis et al 1987). Two studies have shown now that amygdala damage impairs fear conditioning in humans. In both studies, participants were exposed to pairings of initially neutral conditioned visual stimuli (CS) preceding aversive unconditioned auditory stimuli (US), white-noise or boat-horn bursts, which elicited an unconditioned response measured as a change in skin conductance response (SCR). Over multiple trials, normal participants showed fear conditioning by making conditioned SCRs to the CS. An Urbach-Weithe patient (Bechara et al 1995) and patients with amygdala resections (LaBar et al 1995) showed little or no fear conditioning. The fear-conditioning deficit was dissociated from declarative memory because the patients had excellent declarative memory for the experimental experience (e.g. for the stimuli). In contrast, amnesic patients without amygdala damage demonstrated intact fear conditioning but impaired declarative memory for their experimental experience (Bechara et al 1995). Thus, the critical role of the amygdala in fear conditioning appears to be conserved in the human brain.

# PERSPECTIVE

The emergence of functional neuroimaging techniques offers unprecedented opportunities to discover how the brain learns and remembers. Understanding of the brain organization of memory had heretofore relied on the coincidence of brain injuries, and scientists prepared to understand the significance of the memory failures that followed. This path to knowledge took us a long way. We learned about the critical role of medial-temporal and diencephalic structures in declarative memory, the amygdala in emotional modulation of memory, the basal ganglia in skill learning, the cerebellum in conditioning, and the neocortex in repetition priming. In some cases, studies of human lesions guided parallel lesion research in animals (e.g. medial-temporal and diencephalic lesions), and in other cases animal lesions guided research in patients (e.g. amygdala, cerebellum).

It may be thought that the greater freedom of neuroimaging studies, where systematic experiments can be performed on many normal subjects, will render lesion studies obsolete. This thought ignores how much psychological interpretation is required to comprehend the significance of neuroimaging activations (in addition to a host of neurobiological, image analysis, and statistical issues). With imaging studies alone, it might have been concluded that (*a*) global amnesia would follow left or right frontal lesions because they would prevent the encoding or retrieval of new memories; (*b*) the hippocampus is not important for declarative memory because it often was not active during explicit retrieval (e.g. Shallice et al 1994, Tulving et al 1994); and (*c*) the hippocampus is critical for delay conditioning. Each of these conclusions would have been wrong. Thus, animal lesion, human lesion, and imaging studies will provide powerful sources of mutual constraints for a long time to come.

There is, however, a turning of the wheel in the cognitive neuroscience of human memory. For nearly a quarter of a century, our understanding of the normal brain organization of memory depended upon studies of diseased memory. Now, functional neuroimaging studies of healthy brains can begin to illuminate how and why injuries to specific memory systems result in various diseases of memory.

ACKNOWLEDGMENT

I thank Maria Carrillo, Debra Fleischman, Maggie Keane, Laura Monti, Russ Poldrack, Matthew Prull, Glenn Stebbins, Anthony Wagner, and Dan Willingham for helpful comments on this chapter and Marion Zabinski for assistance with the manuscript.

Visit the *Annual Reviews home page* at **http://www.AnnualReviews.org.**

# Literature Cited

Adolphs R, Tranel D, Damasio H, Damasio A. 1994. Impaired recognition of emotion in facial expressions following bilateral damage to the human amygdala. *Nature* 372: 669–72

Alexander G, DeLong M, Strick P. 1986. Parallel organization of functionally segregated circuits linking basal ganglia and cortex. *Annu. Rev. Neurosci.* 9:357–81

Arendt T, Bigl V, Teanstedt A. 1983. Loss of neurons in the nucleus basal of Meynert in Alzheimer's disease, paralysis agitans, and Korsakoff's disease. *Acta Neuropathol.* 61:101–8

Baker SC, Rogers RD, Owen AM, Frith CD, Dolan RJ, et al. 1996. Neural systems engaged by planning: a pet study of the tower London task. *Neuropsychologia* 34: 515–26

Bechara A, Tranel D, Damasio H, Adolphs R, Rockland C, Damasio AR. 1995. Double dissociation of conditioning and declarative knowledge relative to the amygdala and hippocampus in humans. *Science* 269: 1115–18

Berger TW, Orr WB. 1983. Hippocampectomy selectively disrupts discrimination reversal conditioning of the rabbit nictitating membrane response. *Behav. Brain Res.* 8:49–68

Blaxton TA. 1992. Dissociations among memory measures in memory-impaired subjects: Evidence for a processing account of memory. *Mem. Cogn.* 20:549–62

Blaxton TA, Bookheimer SY, Zeffiro TA, Figlozzi CM, William DD, Theodore WH. 1996. Functional mapping of human memory using PET: Comparisons of conceptual and perceptual tasks. *Can. J. Exp. Psychol.* 50:42–56

Bowers JS, Schacter DL. 1990. Implicit memory and test awareness. *J. Exp. Psychol. Learn. Mem. Cogn.* 16:404–16

Brun A, Englund E. 1981. Regional pattern of degeneration in Alzheimer's disease: neuronal loss and histopathological grading. *Histopathology* 5:549–64

Buckner RL, Bandettini PA, O'Craven KM, Savoy RL, Petersen SE, et al. 1996. Detection of cortical activation during averaged single trials of a cognitive task using functional magnetic resonance imaging. *Proc. Natl. Acad. Sci. USA* 93: 14878–83

Butters N, Wolfe J, Martone M, Granholm E, Cermak LS. 1985. Memory disorders associated with Huntington's disease: verbal recall, verbal recognition, and procedural memory. *Neuropsychologia* 6:729–44

Cahill L, Babinsky R, Markowitsch HJ, McGaugh JL. 1995. The amygdala and emotional memory. *Nature* 377:295–96

Cahill L, Haier RJ, Fallon J, Alkire MT, Tang C, et al. 1996. Amygdala activity at encoding correlated with long-term, free recall of emotional information. *Proc. Natl. Acad. Sci. USA* 93:8016–21

Cave CB, Squire LR. 1992. Intact and long-lasting repetition priming in amnesia. *J. Exp. Psychol. Learn. Mem. Cogn.* 18: 509–20

Cermak LS, Bleich RP, Blackford SP. 1988. Deficits in the implicit retention of new associations by alcoholic Korsakoff patients. *Brain Lang.* 7:312–23

Cermak LS, Talbot N, Chandler K, Wolbarst LR. 1985. The perceptual priming phenomenon in amnesia. *Neuropsychologia* 23:615–22

Cermak LS, Verfaellie M, Chase KA. 1995. Implicit and explicit memory in amnesia: an analysis of data-driven and conceptually driven processes. *Neuropsychology* 22:85–97

Cohen JD, Perlstein WM, Braver TS, Nystrom LE, Noll DC, et al. 1997. Temporal dynamics of brain activation during a working memory task. *Nature* 386:604–8

Cohen NJ, Eichenbaum H, Deacedo BS, Corkin S. 1985. Different memory systems underlying acquisition of procedural and declarative knowledge. *Ann. NY Acad. Sci.* 444:54–71

Cohen NJ, Eichenbaum HE. 1993. *Memory, Amnesia, and the Hippocampal System.* Cambridge, MA: MIT Press

Cohen NJ, Squire LR. 1980. Preserved learning and retention of pattern-analyzing skill in amnesia: dissociation of knowing how and knowing that. *Science* 210: 207–10

Cooper JA, Sagar HJ, Doherty SM, Jordan N, Tidswell P, Sullivan EV. 1992. Different effects of dopaminergic and anticholinergic therapies on cognitive and motor function in Parkinson's disease. *Brain* 115: 1701–25

Corkin S. 1968. Acquisition of motor skill after bilateral medial temporal-lobe excision. *Neuropsychologia* 6:255–65

Corkin S, Amaral DG, Gonzalez RG, Johnson KA, Hyman BT. 1997. H. M.'s medial temporal-lobe lesion: findings from MRI. *J. Neurosci.* 17:3964–79

Courtney SM, Ungerleider LG, Keil K, Haxby JV. 1997. Transient and sustained activity in a distributed neural system for human working memory. *Nature* 386:608–11

Damasio H, Grabowski TJ, Tranel D, Hichwa RD, Damasio AR. 1996. A neural basis for lexical retrieval. *Nature* 380:499–505

Daum I, Ackermann H. 1994. Dissociation of declarative and nondeclarative memory after bilateral thalamic lesions: a case report. *Int. J. Neurosci.* 75:153–65

Daum I, Channon S, Canavan AGM. 1989. Classical conditioning in patients with severe memory problems. *J. Neurol. Neurosurg. Psychiatry* 52:47–51

Daum I, Schugens MM, Ackermann H, Lutzenberger W, Dichgans J, Birbaumer N. 1993. Classical conditioning after cerebellar lesions in humans. *Behav. Neurosci.* 107:748–56

Davis M, Hitchcock JM, Rosen JB. 1987. Anxiety and the amygdala: pharmacological and anatomical analysis of the fear-potentiated startle response. In *The Psychology of Learning and Motivation,* ed. G Bower, 21:263–65. Orlando, FL: Academic

Demb JB, Desmond JE, Wagner AD, Vaidya CJ, Glover GH, Gabrieli, JDE. 1995. Semantic encoding and retrieval in the left inferior prefrontal cortex: a functional MRI study of task difficulty and process specificity. *J. Neurosci.* 15:5870–78

Desmond JE, Sum JM, Wagner AD, Demb JB, Shear PK, et al. 1995. Functional mri measurement of language lateralization in wada-tested patients *Brain* 118:1411–19

Diamond R, Rozin P. 1984. Activation of existing memories in anterograde amnesia. *J. Abnorm. Psychol.* 93:98–105

Disterhoft JF, Coulter DA, Alkon DL. 1986. Conditioning-specific membrane changes of rabbit hippocampal neurons measured in vitro. *Proc. Natl. Acad. Sci. USA* 83: 2733–37

Doyon J, Owen AM, Petrides M, Sziklas V, Evans AC. 1996. Functional anatomy of visuomotor skill learning in human subjects examined with positron emission tomography. *Eur. J. Neurosci.* 8:637–48

Eslinger PJ, Damasio AR. 1986. Preserved motor learning in Alzheimer's disease: implications for anatomy and behavior. *J. Neurosci.* 6:3006–9

Ferraro FR, Balota DA, Connor T. 1993. Implicit memory and the formation of new associations in nondemented Parkinson's disease individuals and individuals with senile dementia of the Alzheimer type: a serial reaction time (SRT) investigation. *Brain Cogn.* 21:163–80

Fink GR, Markowitsch HJ, Reinkemeier M, Bruckbauer T, Kessler J, Heiss WD. 1996. Cerebral representation of one's own past: neural networks involved in autobiographical memory. *J. Neurosci.* 16: 4275–82

Flament D, Ellermann JM, Kim SG, Ugurbil K, Ebner TJ. 1996. Functional magnetic resonance imaging of cerebellar activation during the learning of a visuomotor dissociation task. *Hum. Brain Map* 4: 210–26

Fleischman DA, Gabrieli JDE, Reminger S, Rinaldi J, Morrell F, Wilson R. 1995. Conceptual priming in perceptual identification for patients with Alzheimer's disease and a patient with a right occipital lobectomy. *Neuropsychology* 9:187–97

Frackowiak RSJ, Pozzilli C, Legg NJ, Du Boulay GH, Marshall J, et al. 1981. Regional cerebral oxygen supply and utilization in dementia: a clinical and physiological study with oxygen-15 and positron tomography. *Brain* 104:753–78

Friston KJ, Frith CD, Passingham RE, Liddle PF, Frackowiak RSJ. 1992. Motor practice and neurophysiological adaptation in the cerebellum: a positron tomography study. *Proc. R. Soc. London Ser. B Biol. Sci.* 248: 223–28

Gabrieli JDE. 1995. Contributions of the basal ganglia to skill learning and working memory in humans. In *Models of Information Processing in the Basal Ganglia,* ed. J Houk, J Davis, D Beiser, pp. 277–94. Boston: MIT Press

Gabrieli JDE. 1996. Memory systems analyses of mnemonic disorders in aging and age-related diseases. *Proc. Natl. Acad. Sci. USA* 93:13534–40

Gabrieli JDE, Brewer JB, Desmond JE, Glover GH. 1997a. Separate neural bases of two fundamental memory processes in the human medial temporal lobe. *Science* 276:264–66

Gabrieli JDE, Carrillo MC, Cermak LS, McGlinchey-Berroth R, Gluck MA, Disterhoft JF. 1995a. Intact delay-eyeblink classical conditioning in amnesia. *Behav. Neurosci.* 109:819–27

Gabrieli JDE, Cohen NJ, Corkin S. 1988. The impaired learning of semantic knowledge following bilateral medial temporal-lobe resection. *Brain Cogn.* 7:525–39

Gabrieli JDE, Corkin S, Mickel SF, Growdon JH. 1993. Intact acquisition and long-term retention of mirror-tracing skill in Alzheimer's disease and in global amnesia. *Behav. Neurosci.* 107:899–910

Gabrieli JDE, Desmond JE, Demb JB, Wagner AD. 1996a. Functional magnetic resonance imaging of semantic memory processes in the frontal lobes. *Psychol. Sci.* 7:278–83

Gabrieli JDE, Fleischman DA, Keane MM, Reminger SL, Morrell F. 1995b. Double dissociation between memory systems underlying explicit and implicit memory in the human brain. *Psychol. Sci.* 6:76–82

Gabrieli JDE, Keane MM, Stanger BZ, Kjelgaard MM, Corkin S, Growdon JH. 1994. Dissociations among structural-perceptual, lexical-semantic, and even-fact memory systems in amnesic, Alzheimer's, and normal subjects. *Cortex* 30:75–103

Gabrieli JDE, Keane MM, Zarella MM, Poldrack RA. 1997b. Preservation of implicit memory for new associations in global amnesia. *Psychol. Sci.* 7:326–29

Gabrieli JDE, Milberg WP, Keane MM, Corkin S. 1990. Intact priming of patterns despite impaired memory. *Neuropsychologia* 28:417–27

Gabrieli JDE, Stebbins GT, Singh J, Willingham DB, Goetz CG. 1997c. Intact mirror-tracing and impaired rotary-pursuit skill learning in patients with Huntington's disease: evidence for dissociable memory systems in skill learning. *Neuropsychology* 11:272–81

Gabrieli JDE, Sullivan EV, Desmond JE, Stebbins GT, Vaidya CJ, et al. 1996b. Behavioral and functional neuroimaging evidence for preserved conceptual implicit memory in global amnesia. *Soc. Neurosci.* 22:1449 (Abstr.)

Gardiner JM. 1988. Functional aspects or recollective experience. *Mem. Cogn.* 16:309–13

Graf P, Schacter DL. 1985. Implicit and explicit memory for new associations in normal and amnesic subjects. *J. Exp. Psychol. Learn. Mem. Cogn.* 11:501–18

Graf P, Shimamura AP, Squire LR. 1985. Priming across modalities and priming across category levels: extending the domain of preserved function in amnesia. *J. Exp. Psychol. Learn. Mem. Cogn.* 11:386–96

Graf P, Squire LR, Mandler G. 1984. The information that amnesic patients do not forget. *J. Exp. Psychol. Learn. Mem. Cogn.* 10:164–78

Grafton ST, Mazziotta JC, Presty S, Friston KJ, Frackowiak RSJ, Phelps ME. 1992. Functional anatomy of human procedural learning determined with regional cerebral blood flow and PET. *J. Neurosci.* 12:2542–48

Haist F, Musen G, Squire LR. 1991. Intact priming of words and nonwords in amnesia. *Psychobiology* 19:275–85

Harrington DL, Haaland KY, Yeo RA, Marder E. 1991. Procedural memory in Parkinson's disease: impaired motor but not visuoperceptual learning. *J. Clin. Exp. Neuropsychol.* 12:323–39

Hart J, Berndt RS, Caramazza A. 1985. Category-specific naming deficit following cerebral infarction. *Nature* 316:439–40

Haxby JV, Ungerleider LG, Horwitz B, Maisog JM, Rapoport SI, Grady CL. 1996. Face encoding and recognition in the human brain. *Proc. Natl Acad. Sci. USA* 93:922–27

Hazeltine E, Grafton ST, Ivry R. 1997. Attention and stimulus characteristic determine the locus of motor-sequence encoding. A pet study. *Brain* 120:123–40

Heindel WC, Salmon DP, Shults CW, Walicke PA, Butters N. 1989. Neuropsychological evidence for multiple implicit memory systems: a comparison of Alzheimer's, Huntington's, and Parkinson's disease patients. *J. Neurosci.* 9:582–87

Hyman BT, Van Hoesen GW, Damasio AR, Barnes CL. 1984. Alzheimer's disease: cell-specific pathology isolates the hippocampal formation. *Science* 225:1168–70

Jacoby LL. 1991. A process dissociation framework: Separating automatic from intentional uses of memory. *J. Mem. Lang.* 30:513–41

Jacoby LL, Dallas M. 1981. On the relationship between autobiographical memory and perceptual learning. *J. Exp. Psychol. Gen.* 110:306–40

Janowsky JS, Shimamura AP, Kritchevsky M, Squire LR. 1989. Cognitive impairment following frontal lobe damage and its relevance to human amnesia. *Behav. Neurosci.* 103:548–60

Kapur N, Ellison D, Smith MP, Mclellan DL, Burrows EH. 1992. Focal retrograde amnesia following bilateral temporal lobe pathology: a neuropsychological and magnetic resonance study. *Brain* 115:73–85

Kapur S, Craik FIM, Jones C, Brown GM, Houle S, Tulving E. 1995. Functional role of the prefrontal cortex in retrieval of memories: a pet study. *NeuroReport* 6:1880–84

Kapur S, Craik FIM, Tulving E, Wilson AA, Houle S, Brown GM. 1994. Neuroanatomical correlates of encoding in episodic memory: levels of processing effect. *Proc. Natl. Acad. Sci. USA* 91:2008–11

Karni A, Meyer G, Jezzard P, Adams MM, Turner R, Ungerleider LG. 1995. Functional MRI evidence for adult motor cortex plasticity during motor skill learning. *Nature* 377:155–58

Keane MM, Gabrieli JDE, Fennema AC, Growdon JH, Corkin S. 1991. Evidence for a dissociation between perceptual and conceptual priming in Alzheimer's disease. *Behav. Neurosci.* 105:326–42

Keane MM, Gabrieli JDE, Mapstone HC, Johnson KA, Corkin S. 1995. Double dissociation of memory capacities after bilateral occipital-lobe or medial temporal-lobe lesions. *Brain* 118:1129–48

Keane MM, Gabrieli JDE, Noland JS, McNealy SI. 1995. Normal perceptual priming of orthographically illegal words in amnesia. *J. Int. Neuropsychol. Soc.* 1:425–33

Keane MM, Gabrieli JDE, Monti LA, Fleischman DA, Cantor JM, Noland JS. 1997. Intact and impaired conceptual memory processing in amnesia. *Neuropsychology* 11:59–69

Knopman DS, Nissen MJ. 1987. Implicit learning in patients with probable Alzheimer's disease. *Neurology* 37:784–88

Knowlton BJ, Mangels JA, Squire LR. 1996a. A neostriatal habit learning system in humans. *Science* 273:1399–402

Knowlton BJ, Squire LR. 1993. The learning of categories: parallel brain systems for item memory and category knowledge. *Science* 262:1747–49

Knowlton BJ, Squire LR. 1995. Remembering and knowing: two different expressions of declarative memory. *J. Exp. Psychol. Learn. Mem. Cogn.* 21:699–710

Knowlton BJ, Squire LR, Gluck MA. 1994. Probabilistic classification in amnesia. *Learn. Mem.* 1:106–20

Knowlton BJ, Squire LR, Paulsen JS, Swerdlow NR, Swenson M, Butters N. 1996b. Dissociations within nondeclarative memory in Huntington's disease. *Neuropsychology* 10:538–48

LaBar KS, Ledoux JE, Spencer DD, Phelps EA. 1995. Impaired fear conditioning following unilateral temporal lobectomy in humans. *J. Neurosci.* 15:6846–55

Lees AJ, Smith E. 1983. Cognitive deficits in the early stages of Parkinson's disease. *Brain* 106:257–70

Logan CG, Grafton ST. 1995. Functional anatomy of human eyeblink conditioning determined with regional cerebral glucose metabolism and positron-emission tomography. *Proc. Natl. Acad. Sci. USA* 92:7500–4

Mandler G. 1980. Recognizing: the judgment of previous occurrence. *Psychol. Rev.* 87:252–71

Martin A, Haxby JV, Lalonde FM, Wiggs CL, Ungerleider LG. 1995. Discrete cortical regions associated with knowledge of color and knowledge of action. *Science* 270:102–5

Martin A, Wiggs CL, Ungerleider LG, Haxby JV. 1996. Neural correlates of category-specific knowledge. *Nature* 379:649–52

Martone M, Butters N, Payne M, Becker JT, Sax DS. 1984. Dissociations between skill learning and verbal recognition in amnesia and dementia. *Arch. Neurol.* 41:965–70

McCarthy RA, Warrington EK. 1988. Evidence for modality-specific meaning systems in the brain. *Nature* 334:428–30

McCormick DA, Thompson RF. 1987. Neuronal responses of the rabbit cerebellum during acquisition and performance of a classically conditioned NM-eyelid response. *J. Neurosci.* 4:2811–22

McGlinchey-Berroth R, Carrillo M, Gabrieli JDE, Brawn CM, Disterhoft JF. 1997. Impaired trace eyeblink conditioning in bilateral medial temporal lobe amnesia. *Behav. Neurosci.* In press

McGlinchey-Berroth R, Cermak LS, Carrillo MC, Armfield S, Gabrieli JDE, Disterhoft JF. 1995. Impaired delay eyeblink conditioning in amnesic Korsakoff's patients and recovered alcoholics. *Alcohol. Clin. Exp. Res.* 1127–32

Milner B. 1962. Les troubles de la memoire accompagnant des lesions hippocampiques bilaterales. In *Physiologie de l'hippocampe,* ed. P Passsouant, pp. 257–72. Paris: Cent. Rech. Sci.

Milner B. 1963. Effects of different brain lesions on card sorting. *Arch. Neurol.* 9:90–100

Milner B. 1971. Interhemispheric differences in the localization of psychological processes in man. *Br. Med. J.* 27:272–77

Monti LA, Gabrieli JDE, Reminger SL, Rinaldi JA, Wilson RS, Fleischman DA. 1996. Differential effects of aging and Alzheimer's disease upon conceptual implicit and explicit memory. *Neuropsychology* 10:101–12

Morris JS, Frith CD, Perrett DI, Rowland D, Young AW, et al. 1996. A differential neural response in the human amygdala to fearful and happy facial expressions. *Nature* 383:812–15

Moscovitch M, Winocur G, McLachlan D.

1986. Memory as assessed by recognition and reading time in normal and memory-impaired people with Alzheimer's disease and other neurological disorders. *J. Exp. Psychol. Gen.* 115:331–47

Musen G, Squire LR. 1993. Implicit learning of color-word associations using a Stroop paradigm. *J. Exp. Psychol.: Learn. Mem. Cogn.* 19:789–98

Nissen MJ, Bullemer P. 1987. Attentional requirements of learning: evidence from performance measures. *Cogn. Psychol.* 19: 1–32

Nyberg L, Mcintosh AR, Houle S, Nilsson LG, Tulving E. 1996. Activation of medial temporal structures during episodic memory retrieval. *Nature* 380:715–17

Nyberg L, Tulving E, Habib R, Nilsson LG, Kapur S, et al. 1995. Functional brain maps of retrieval mode and recovery of episodic information *NeuroReport* 7: 249–52

Petersen SE, Fox PT, Posner MI, Mintun M, Raichle ME. 1989. Positron emission tomographic studies of the processing of single words. *J. Cogn. Neurosci.* 1: 153–70

Petrides M, Alivisatos B, Evans AC, Meyer E. 1993a. Dissociation of human mid-dorsolateral from posterior dorsolateral frontal cortex in memory processing. *Proc. Natl. Acad. Sci. USA* 90:873–77

Petrides M, Alivisatos B, Meyer E, Evans AC. 1993b. Functional activation of the human frontal cortex during the performance of verbal working memory tasks. *Proc. Natl. Acad. Sci. USA* 90:878–82

Petrides M, Milner B. 1982. Deficits on subject-ordered tasks after frontal and temporal lobe lesions in man. *Neuropsychologia* 20:601–14

Phelps EA, Anderson AK. 1997. Emotional memory: What does the amygdala do? *Curr. Biol.* 7:311–13

Poldrack RA, Desmond JE, Glover GH, Gabrieli JDE. 1996. The neural bases of visual skill: an fMRI study of mirror reading. *Soc. Neurosci.* 22:719 (Abstr.)

Prabhakaran V, Smith JAL, Desmond JE, Glover GH, Gabrieli JDE. 1997. Neural substrates of fluid reasoning: an fMRI study of neocortical activation during performance of the Raven's Progressive Matrices Test. *Cogn. Psychol.* 33:46–63

Press GA, Amaral DG, Squire LR. 1989. Hippocampal abnormalities in amnesic patients revealed by high-resolution magnetic resonance imaging. *Nature* 341: 54–57

Raichle ME, Fiez JA, Videen TO, MacLeod AK, Pardo JV, et al. 1994. Practice-related changes in human brain functional anatomy during nonmotor learning. *Cereb. Cortex* 4:8–26

Rempel-Clower NL, Zola SM, Squire LR, Amaral DG. 1996. Three cases of enduring memory impairment after bilateral damage limited to the hippocampal formation. *J. Neurosci.* 16:5233–55

Roediger HL, McDermott K. 1993. Implicit memory in normal human subjects. In *Handbook of Neuropsychology,* ed. F Boller, J Grafman, 8:63–131. New York: Elsevier

Rugg MD, Fletcher PC, Frith CD, Frackowiak RSJ, Dolan RJ. 1996. Differential activation of the prefrontal cortex in successful and unsuccessful memory retrieval. *Brain* 119:2073–83

Saint-Cyr JA, Taylor AE, Lang AE. 1988. Procedural learning and neostriatal dysfunction in man. *Brain* 111:941–59

Sanes JN, Dimitrov B, Hallett M. 1990. Motor learning in patients with cerebellar dysfunction. *Brain* 113:103–20

Schacter DL, Alpert NM, Savage CR, Rauch SL, Albert MS. 1996a. Conscious recollection and the human hippocampal formation: evidence from positron emission tomography. *Proc. Natl. Acad. Sci. USA* 93: 321–25

Schacter DL, Church BA, Bolton E. 1995a. Implicit memory in amnesic patients: impairment of voice-specific priming. *Psychol. Sci.* 6:20–25

Schacter DL, Curran T, Galluccio L, Milberg WP, Bates JF. 1996b. False recognition and the right frontal lobe: a case study. *Neuropsychologia* 34:793–808

Schacter DL, Graf P. 1986. Preserved learning in amnesic patients: Perspectives from research on direct priming. *J. Clin. Exp. Neuropsychol.* 8:727–43

Schacter DL, Reiman E, Uecker A, Polster MR, Yun LS, Cooper LA. 1995b. Brain regions associated with retrieval of structurally coherent visual information. *Nature* 376:587–90

Schacter DL, Savage CR, Alpert NM, Rauch SL, Albert MS. 1996c. The role of hippocampus and frontal cortex in age-related memory changes: a PET study. *NeuroReport* 7:1165–69

Schmaltz LW, Theios J. 1972. Acquisition and extinction of a classically conditioned response in hippocampectomized rabbits (*Oryctolgus cuniculus*). *J. Comp. Physiol. Psychol.* 79:328–33

Schwartz BL, Rosse RB, Deutsch SI. 1993. Limits of the processing view in accounting for dissociations among memory measures in a clinical population. *Mem. Cogn.* 21:63–72

Scott SK, Young AW, Calder AJ, Hellawell DJ, Aggleton JP, Johnson M. 1997. Impaired auditory recognition of fear and anger following bilateral amygdala lesions. *Nature* 385:254–57

Scoville WB, Milner B. 1957. Loss of recent memory after bilateral hippocampal lesions. *J. Neurol. Neurosurg. Psychiatry* 20:11–21

Semenza C, Zettin M. 1989. Evidence from aphasia for the role of proper names as pure referring expressions. *Nature* 342: 678–79

Shallice T. 1982. Specific impairments of planning. *Philos. Trans. R. Soc. London Ser. B* 298:199–209

Shallice T, Fletcher P, Frith CD, Grasby P, Frackowiak RSJ, Dolan RJ. 1994. Brain regions associated with acquisition and retrieval of verbal episodic memory. *Nature* 368:633–35

Shimamura AP, Squire LR. 1984. Paired-associate learning and priming effects in amnesia: a neuropsychological study. *J. Exp. Psychol. Gen.* 113:556–70

Smith EE, Jonides J. 1994. Working memory in humans: Neuropsychological evidence. In *The Cognitive Neurosciences,* ed. M Gazzaniga, Cambridge, MA: MIT Press

Smith EE, Jonides J. 1997. Working memory: a view from neuroimaging *Cogn. Psychol.* 33:5–42

Smith ML, Milner B. 1988. Estimation of frequency of occurrence of abstract designs after frontal or temporal lobectomy. *Neuropsychologia* 26:297–306

Solomon PR, Vander Schaaf ER, Thompson RF, Weisz DJ. 1986. Hippocampus and trace conditioning of the rabbits classically conditioned nictitating membrane response. *Behav. Neurosci.* 100:729–44

Squire LR, Ojemann JG, Miezin FM, Petersen SE, Videen TO, Raichle ME. 1992. Activation of the hippocampus in normal humans: a functional anatomical study of memory. *Proc. Natl. Acad. Sci. USA* 89: 1837–41

Stebbins GT, Singh J, Weiner J, Goetz CG, Gabrieli JDE. 1995. Selective impairments of memory functioning in unmedicated adults with Gilles de la Tourette's syndrome. *Neuropsychology* 9:329–37

Stern CE, Corkin S, Gonzalez RG, Guimaraes AR, Baker JR, et al. 1996. The hippocampus participates in novel picture encoding: evidence from functional magnetic resonance imaging. *Proc. Natl. Acad. Sci. USA* 93:8660–65

Suzuki WA, Amaral DG. 1994. Perirhinal and parahippocampal cortices of the macaque monkey: cortical afferents. *J. Comp. Neurol.* 350:497–533

Swick D, Knight RT. 1996. Is prefrontal cortex involved in cued recall? A neuropsychological test of PET findings. *Neuropsychologia* 34:1019–28

Thompson RF. 1990. Neural mechanisms of classical conditioning in mammals. *Philos. Trans. R. Soc. London Ser. B* 329:161–70

Tulving E. 1983. *Elements of Episodic Memory.* London: Oxford Univ. Press

Tulving E, Kapur S, Markowitsch HJ, Craik FIM, Habib R, Houle S. 1994. Neuroanatomical correlates of retrieval in episodic memory: auditory sentence recognition. *Proc. Natl. Acad. Sci. USA* 91:2012–15

Tulving E, Markowitsch HJ, Craik FIM, Habib R, Houle S. 1996. Novelty and familiarity activations in pet studies of memory encoding and retrieval. *Cereb. Cortex* 6:71–79

Vaidya CJ, Gabrieli JDE, Demb JB, Keane MM, Wetzel LC. 1996. Impaired priming on the general knowlege task in amnesia. *Neuropsychology* 10:529–37

Vaidya CJ, Gabrieli JDE, Keane MM, Monti LA. 1995. Perceptual and conceptual memory processes in global amnesia. *Neuropsychology* 9:580–91

Vaidya CJ, Gabrieli JDE, Keane MM, Monti LA, Gutierrez-Rivas H, Zarella MM. 1997a. Evidence for multiple mechanisms of conceptual priming on implicit memory tests. *J. Exp. Psychol. Learn. Mem. Cogn.* In press

Vaidya CJ, Gabrieli JDE, Verfaellie M, Fleischman D, Askari N. 1997b. Font-specific priming following global amnesia and occipital lobe damage. *Neuropsychology.* In press

Vandenberghe R, Price C, Wise R, Josephs O, Frackowiak RSJ. 1996. Functional anatomy of a common semantic system for words and pictures. *Nature* 383:254–56

Verfaellie M, Gabrieli JDE, Vaidya CJ, Croce P. 1996. Implicit memory for pictures in amnesia: role of etiology and priming task. *Neuropsychology* 10:517–37

Wagner AD, Desmond JE, Demb JB, Glover GH, Gabrieli JDE. 1997. Semantic memory processes and left inferior prefrontal cortex: a functional MRI study of form specificity. *J. Cog. Neurosci.* In press

Wagner AD, Gabrieli JDE, Verfaellie M. 1997. Dissociations between familiarity processes in explicit-recognition and implicit-perceptual memory. *J. Exp. Psychol. Learn. Mem. Cogn.* 23:305–23

Wagner AD, Stebbins GT, Burton KW, Fleischman DA, Gabrieli JDE. 1995. Anatomic and functional dissociations between recognition fluency and perceptual fluency. *Proc. Cogn. Neurosci. Soc.* 2:41 (Abstr.)

Warrington EK, McCarthy RA. 1983. Category-specific access dysphasia. *Brain* 106:859–78

Warrington EK, Shallice T. 1984. Category specific semantic impairments. *Brain* 107: 829–53

Warrington EK, Weiskrantz L. 1970. The amnesic syndrome: consolidation or retrieval? *Nature* 228:628–30

Willingham DB, Koroshetz WJ. 1993. Evidence for dissociable motor skills in Huntington's disease patients. *Psychobiology* 21:173–82

Willingham DB, Koroshetz WJ, Peterson EW.

1996. Motor skills have diverse neural bases: Spared and impaired skill acquisition in Huntington's disease. *Neuropsychology* 10:315–21

Woodruff-Pak DS. 1993. Eyeblink classical conditioning in H. M.: delay and trace paradigms. *Behav. Neurosci.* 107:911–25

Woodruff-Pak DS, Finkbiner RG, Sasse DK. 1990. Eyeblink conditioning discriminates Alzheimer's patients from nondemented aged. *Clin. Neurosci. Neuropathol.* 1: 45–49

Woodruff-Pak DS, Papka M. 1996. Huntington's disease and eyeblink classical conditioning: normal learning but abnormal timing. *J. Int. Neuropsychol. Soc.* 2:323–34

Woodruff-Pak DS, Thompson RF. 1988. Classical conditioning of the eyeblink response delay paradigm in adults aged 18–83 years. *Psychol. Aging* 3:219–29

*Annu. Rev. Psychol. 1998. 49:117–39*

# GIFTEDNESS: An Exceptionality Examined

## Ann Robinson

University of Arkansas at Little Rock, 2801 South University, Little Rock, Arkansas 72204; e-mail: aerobinson@ualr.edu

## Pamela R. Clinkenbeard

University of Wisconsin-Whitewater, 800 West Main Street, Whitewater, Wisconsin 53190-1790; e-mail: clinkenp@uwwvax.uww.edu

KEY WORDS: gifted children, talent development, gifted education, recommended practices

### ABSTRACT

The study of giftedness has practical origins. High-level performance intrigues people. Theoretically, the study of giftedness is related to the psychology of individual differences and has focused on the constructs of intelligence, creativity, and motivation. At a practical level, the research is largely related to school and family contexts, which develop gifts and talents in children and youth. Although broadened definitions of giftedness have emerged, the most extensive body of research available for review concentrates on intellectual giftedness. The varying definitions of giftedness and the impact of social context and diversity on the development of talent pose significant challenges for the field. Finally, the study of exceptionally advanced performance provides insight into basic psychological processes and the school contexts that develop talents in children and youth.

## CONTENTS

0066-4308/98/0201-0117$08.00

## INTRODUCTION

The study of giftedness has practical origins. People are intrigued by high-level performance and wish to inspect both the performance and the performers more closely. A novel well written, a basketball maneuver well executed, a blues riff well played, an endgame well concluded, or a high school science project well designed attract attention. Fine writers, exhilarating basketball players, memorable musicians, canny chess prodigies, or youthful scientists are examples of giftedness made observable.

Theoretically, the study of giftedness is related to the psychology of individual differences. Historically, the constructs of intelligence and creativity and, to a lesser extent, motivation provided the psychological foundations for investigations of giftedness. The study of giftedness encompasses both adults and children and the development of talents across many different domains—for example, the academic content areas, the performing arts, or entrepreneurial pursuits. It involves the investigation of both cognitive and affective variables. Both retrospective and prospective studies form its research lexicon.

At a practical level, the study of giftedness is primarily concerned with issues related to the education and upbringing of children with gifts and talents. The field of gifted education generally attracts researchers and school practitioners whose interests and whose research programs are applied. Thus, the corpus of research in the field has been largely related to schooling and to family contexts that develop gifts and talents in children and youth.

The focus of this chapter is on intellectual giftedness, its description, and the nurture of such gifts and talents in the elementary and secondary school setting. Although the development of giftedness in the visual arts and in music are also productive areas of interest for the field (Clark & Zimmerman 1983, Winner & Martino 1993), the greatest body of extant research available for review remains largely in studies in which intellectual giftedness is a key variable. Definitions of intellectual giftedness, however, have evolved substantially away from equating it with IQ scores. Current research includes a richer array of variables in defining and describing giftedness.

# GIFTEDNESS AND GIFTED CHILDREN

## *Definitions of Giftedness and Talent*

Theorists, researchers, and practitioners have grappled with the definition of giftedness and talent. In the modern literature, early definitions ranged from conservative ones such as Terman's (1925) use of the top 1% of general intellectual ability to Witty's (1958) liberal conceptualization that giftedness is displayed by a child "whose performance, in a potentially valuable line of human activity, is consistently remarkable." A decade ago, Sternberg & Davidson (1986) edited a collection in which 17 conceptualizations of giftedness were discussed by the researchers who proposed them. Again, the range of conceptualizations was diverse, with some concentrating primarily on the psychological aspects of intellectual giftedness (Sternberg 1986) and others including social context in which the development of giftedness is culturally fostered in some domains, but not recognized in others (Csikszentmihalyi & Robinson 1986, Tannenbaum 1986).

Of those conceptualizations focusing on the psychological aspects, theories and definitions tended to include the constructs of intelligence, creativity, and motivation either singly or in combination. For example, Feldhusen (1986) specifically includes general intellectual ability and achievement motivation in his conceptualization of giftedness. Jackson & Butterfield (1986) concentrate primarily on variables that contribute to superior cognitive performance in children. Renzulli (1978, 1986) proposes a three-ring definition in which above average intellectual ability, creativity, and task commitment interact to produce giftedness.

An important challenge articulated by Gallagher & Courtright (1986) is that the field applies the term "gifted" to definitions that emerge out of the study of individual differences in psychology and also to definitions that are developed by policy makers and by practitioners in order to develop and deliver services to gifted children. The two kinds of definitions overlap, but according to Gallagher & Courtright (1986) they serve different functions and can cause confusion. An example of a definition developed by policy makers is found in *Education of the Gifted and Talented,* a report to Congress by Marland (1971). The definition from the Marland Report states: "Gifted and talented children are those identified by professionally qualified persons who by virtue of outstanding abilities are capable of high performance. These are children who require differentiated educational programs and services beyond those normally provided by the regular school program in order to realize their contribution to self and society (pp. I-3 to I-4)."

The report went on to enumerate six areas of giftedness: general intellectual ability, specific academic aptitude, creative or productive thinking, leadership ability, visual and performing arts, and psychomotor ability.

Later, the domain of psychomotor ability was dropped as a separate category. The Marland definition served to increase awareness beyond strict psychometric definitions like Terman's. It was criticized, however, for presenting unparallel categories and for possible misinterpretations, for example, leading practitioners to believe that a particular child would exhibit high performance in all areas (Renzulli 1978). As stated earlier, Renzulli (1978) proposed his own definition, which suggested that giftedness was an interaction among three clusters of traits: above-average general or specific abilities, task commitment, and creativity. Both the definition from the Marland Report and the definition proposed by Renzulli affected the development of educational programs for able students with the concentration being on developing services that provide general academic or creative enrichment.

More recently, Feldhusen & Jarwan (1993) reviewed the definitions of giftedness and talent and noted that they fell into six categories: psychometric definitions, trait definitions, definitions focused on social needs, educationally oriented definitions, special talent definitions, and multidimensional definitions. Their categories were not exclusive; some definitions of giftedness could be classified in more than one way. Psychometric definitions focus on attaining certain scores usually on intelligence tests. The operational definition of an IQ score of 140 used by Terman (1925) is an example of the psychometric definition. Trait definitions are those that focus on the psychological characteristics of able children and youth, although whether these definitions assume that characteristics such as motivation are stable traits rather than states is not clear. In contrast to state-trait definitions, definitions that focus on social needs include statements that giftedness is defined by what society values. Tannenbaum's (1986) conceptualization of talents emerging in response to popular demand is an example of this kind of definition. Educationally oriented definitions include statements about the need for special provisions, and in some cases use a local norm-referenced approach. For example, state or district definitions may explicitly note a percentage of the school population to be served, usually ranging from the top 20% to top 5%. Special talent definitions are those that focus on specific domains such as mathematics, the arts, and the sciences. The language used in the 1993 federal report, *National Excellence: A Case for Developing America's Talent* (Ross 1993), is an example of a definition that crosses several categories: "These children and youth exhibit high performance capability in intellectual, creative, and/or artistic areas, possess an unusual leadership capacity, or excel in specific academic fields. They require services or activities not ordinarily provided in the schools."

Giftedness and talent are often used interchangeably; however, Gagné (1985, 1991) has differentiated between the two concepts by defining giftedness as above-average competence in human ability, and talent as above-average performance in a particular field. That is, giftedness refers to human aptitudes such as intellectual or creative abilities. Talent is demonstrated in an area of human activity such as mathematics, literature, or music.

SUMMARY OF DEFINITIONS    There is no one agreed-upon definition of giftedness or talent that dominates the field. Robinson & Olszewski-Kubilius (1996) note this diversity reflects the substantial variability among exceptional children who deviate positively from the norm. Most definitions, whether they are psychologically based or educationally driven, have moved away from equating giftedness with intelligence as defined by general IQ tests. Several current definitions are broadened in terms of the constructs they consider constituents of giftedness—creativity and motivation, for example. Others are broadened by enumerating specifically the fields or domains in which high performance may be observed. And finally, some definitions are broadened by explicitly considering the societal or cultural context in which gifts and talents develop.

## Social Context and Diversity

The social context of giftedness includes the cultural values and therefore the opportunities that make it possible for gifts and talents to develop. An extreme example of the importance of social and cultural context is found in child prodigies. Feldman (1991) has proposed co-incidence theory to explain the appearance of remarkable, adult-level performance in children before the age of ten. According to Feldman, prodigies occur when the extraordinary abilities of the child, the development of the domain in which the prodigy excels, and the context of the family and learning opportunities "co-incide" to provide optimal conditions. Prodigies are generally born into families that recognize and value the talent when it emerges; they are schooled by master teachers, and their talent area is culturally valued and also accessible to children. For example, chess prodigies appear in cultures where chess is appreciated and available to the child. Thus, for Feldman (1993) the existence of a well-developed domain, its cultural acceptance, and the child's opportunity to engage with the domain are crucial determinants of the development of prodigious performance.

DIVERSITY    Social and cultural context operate in other ways as well. The definitions reviewed in the preceding section noted that acknowledging cultural context has broadened conceptualizations of giftedness. For example, children from diverse ethnic backgrounds may display their gifts and talents in areas particularly valued by members of the culture but not easily recognized by members of other cultural groups. Frasier & Passow (1994) reviewed the literature on the characteristics or attributes of gifted children from various ethnic minority groups and concluded that across all groups there were some shared attributes such as motivation, intense interests, and problem solving ability but that other distinct behavioral indicators were specific to each ethnicity.

One of the most pervasive concerns in the field is that children and youth from diverse cultural backgrounds (Harris & Ford 1991, Maker 1996) and from low-income homes (Borland & Wright 1994) or children who have learning (Whitmore & Maker 1985) or physical disabilities are less likely to be recognized as gifted (Willard-Holt 1994).

In each case, adaptations to the usual means of identifying students for specialized services have been suggested or investigated. For example, Scott and her colleagues (1996) used a series of open-ended cognitive tasks with kindergarten children and were able to identify both Black/non-Hispanic and White/Hispanic youngsters missed by more traditional identification measures and procedures. Borland & Wright (1994) used a case study approach to locate young gifted children from extremely impoverished homes. They engaged in extended observation periods in classrooms with multicultural enrichment activities and used portfolio assessment and teacher nomination to formulate a pool of children for further consideration. A second phase included nontraditional and standardized assessment and resulted in two cohorts of children being identified over the course of two years. Mills & Tissot (1995) report that the Ravens Progressive Matrices shows promise as a screening measure for culturally diverse gifted learners.

SUMMARY OF SOCIAL CONTEXT AND DIVERSITY   The development of gifts and talents in diverse populations has been addressed in at least two substantive ways. First, the conceptions of giftedness have been broadened to include explicit acknowledgment of social and cultural influences on behavioral indicators of giftedness. Second, school-based procedures for the identification of gifted and talented learners have been adapted to take diversity into account by including formal and informal measures other than standard IQ tests.

## PSYCHOLOGICAL CHARACTERISTICS OF GIFTED CHILDREN

In his classic longitudinal studies of the gifted, Terman (1925) investigated various characteristics of a high IQ (over 140) sample, followed from childhood through adulthood. He found that members of his sample, who also tended to be above average on socioeconomic and physical characteristics, generally scored average or somewhat above average on a wide variety of psychological characteristics. The fact that SES was not controlled for in Terman's studies is one of the biggest hurdles in applying his research to today's gifted students. Current broadened conceptions of giftedness are more valid for the provision of educational services, but they make it more of a challenge to create a coherent picture of the psychological characteristics of the gifted.

Definitions of giftedness vary considerably in recent research on psychological characteristics. Researchers in cognitive and metacognitive areas still tend to use a high IQ definition, probably as a way of holding constant at least some general aspects of cognitive functioning within their samples. Researchers in nonintellective areas are more likely to use whatever definition has been used to identify gifted students by the participating school systems. There is some validity to this approach: Not only does it mean that a more diverse group of students is being studied, but also it may be that the social and emotional experience of being gifted is due as much to the label as to internal psychological factors.

One more complicating factor in studying the psychological characteristics of the gifted is that underachieving gifted students may be quite different from high achievers. Some authors (Ford 1993, Luthar et al 1992) address these differences in their research, but for other studies it is not always clear whether underachieving gifted students are included in the sample.

## Cognitive Characteristics

Most research on the cognition of the gifted has investigated in what way gifted individuals (usually children) are different from others in the ways they think. While there is some overlap in the literature between what are considered cognitive skills and what are considered metacognitive skills, the research can be separated into the investigation of simpler individual cognitive skills, and processes that are more complex, strategic, and executive.

COGNITIVE DIFFERENCES    In a review of the cognitive differences between intellectually gifted (high IQ) children and others, Rogers (1986) concludes that the gifted are generally different in degree, not kind, of cognition. That is, gifted students tend to acquire and process information and solve problems better, faster, or at earlier ages than other students. However, they are probably not employing qualitatively different, unique thinking abilities, at least in the high IQ groups reviewed by Rogers.

Wilkinson (1993) analyzed the Wechsler Intelligence Scale for Children–Revised (WISC-R) profiles of 456 third grade students, all of whom had full-scale IQs of 120 or above. Compared to the norm, these students showed greater variability in their profiles. There was a greater frequency of extreme subtest scores, larger verbal-performance discrepancies (in both directions), and more scatter among subtest scores. These students scored highest on subscales reflecting more complex reasoning (for example, similarities and block design) and lowest on scales measuring lower-level thinking skills (coding, digit-span).

Butterfield & Feretti (1987) list several kinds of cognitive differences that various authors have shown distinguish between people of like ages but different IQs. Higher IQ persons have been found to: have larger, more efficient memories; have larger and more elaborately organized knowledge bases; and use more, more complex, and more active processing strategies.

Davidson (1986) measured the performance of gifted students on mathematical and verbal insight problems. Insight was defined as the selective or novel encoding, combining, or comparing of information. Gifted upper elementary school children not only scored better than others on the insight problems, they were more likely to employ selective encoding, combination, and comparison spontaneously in solving the problems. Other children were more likely to need cues in order to use these processes.

Some authors have investigated the cognition of extremely high IQ children. Lovecky (1994) focused on the cognitive differences between "moderately gifted" (IQ 140–159) and "highly gifted" (170 and above) children. From clinical testing and observation, she concluded that highly gifted children tend to make simple tasks more complex, have a need for extreme precision, understand complex patterns quickly, reason abstractly at an earlier age, and have exceptional memory. Gross (1994) adds to these characteristics of the highly gifted an early ability to transfer knowledge across domains, a verbally sophisticated sense of humor, and intuitive leaps.

A review by Sternberg & Davidson (1985) lists several cognitive abilities at which the gifted are exceptional: They tend to have both high general intelligence and specific ability in their area of expertise, they capitalize on their patterns of abilities, they shape their environment, they demonstrate problem-finding ability, and they can conceive higher-order relations. This begins to take us into the realm of metacognition.

METACOGNITIVE DIFFERENCES   Metacognition, or thinking about one's own thinking, may be an important component of giftedness. A recent review of research in this area (Alexander et al 1995, Carr et al 1996) looked at three aspects of metacognition: factual knowledge about thinking strategies, use of strategies, and cognitive monitoring. The authors conclude that gifted students show better performance than other students on only some aspects of metacognition. For instance, gifted children seem to have more factual knowledge about metacognition than other children, and this advantage seems to be present consistently across age levels. They also seem to be better at far transfer, using strategies in contexts far different from that in which strategies were learned. These authors concluded that there was limited support for the idea that gifted students are more spontaneous in their strategy use than other students, although there was some evidence for this in upper elementary age and young adolescent students. Finally, they concluded that there is no evidence that gifted children are better than other children at consistently using better strategy, monitoring their strategy use (evaluating and changing strategies as needed), or in maintenance and near transfer (using strategies in situations similar to those in which the strategy was taught).

Cheng (1993), in addition to reviewing some of the empirical research on metacognition and the gifted, notes the importance of case studies and naturalistic research in order to see more clearly the developmental path of metacognitive skills in gifted individuals. She speculates that metacognition within a particular talent domain becomes important after the early learning years, after children have learned the basics of their field and become immersed in strategy and self-analysis. Shore et al (1994) illustrate the complexity of research in this area. In a reanalysis of an earlier study comparing gifted and other students, the authors examined the problem-solving results of a group of gifted students who originally had not met the criterion for inclusion in the study (solving the first few of nine problems correctly). In contrast to their conclusions in the earlier study (that gifted students performed better metacognitively than others), it was found that these "noncriterion" gifted actually made more metacognitive (strategy) errors than the other students who did not meet the criterion, and that they seemed to be drawing on imaginary data to help solve the problem. Shore et al (1994) warn against jumping to conclusions about the overall abilities of individuals who do not perform well on specific tasks, and speculate about the role of motivation and creativity in metacognition as did Cheng (1993).

SUMMARY OF COGNITIVE CHARACTERISTICS   Gifted elementary or secondary age children, who in this research are usually defined as those with high IQ scores, show some advantages over other students particularly in quantity, speed, and complexity of cognition. They know more about metacognition and can use strategies better in new contexts, but they may not use a wider variety of metacognitive strategies than other students, and they do not apparently monitor their strategies more than other students. Several authors caution that both creativity and motivation probably influence the results of research on cognitive and metacognitive characteristics.

## Social-Emotional Characteristics

There has always been a fascination with the social and emotional characteristics of the gifted. This may be due, in part, to an anti-intellectual desire to find something "wrong" with this group. Some of the research on nonintellective characteristics compares gifted and other students; other approaches describe these characteristics in various subgroups of the gifted, or look for differences among groups of gifted seventh through ninth graders. In general, the research indicates that the stereotyped view of a maladjusted child with poor social skills is far from the truth. In a review of the literature on psychosocial development, Janos & Robinson (1985) conclude that "Being intellectually gifted, at least at moderate levels of ability, is clearly an asset in terms of psychosocial adjustment in most situations." (p. 181).

How do gifted students see their own noncognitive characteristics? Kunkel et al (1995) used a concept-mapping technique: This involved asking gifted students about their experience of being gifted, developing questionnaire items from the responses, and presenting graphically the main themes that emerged. The strongest noncognitive themes included receiving respect from others, feeling a sense of social stress, and generally feeling satisfied with themselves. These themes are found in other studies as well.

SOCIAL SKILLS AND RELATIONSHIPS   How do gifted students get along with their peers? Mayseless (1993) reports on several studies indicating that pre-adolescent and adolescent gifted students tend to be at least as popular as other students their age, but that gifted adolescents may self-report lower popularity than others. Kline & Short (1991a,b) found that both gifted girls and gifted boys scored very high on a self-report measure of "relationship with peers." However, while girls found relationships to be more important as they developed through the school-age years, boys seemed to value relationships less as they grew older. Mayseless (1993) compared the friendship styles of gifted and other students. Ninth grade gifted students reported lower levels of intimacy with their best same-sex friend than did other ninth graders (girls reported higher levels than boys). The author speculates that this may be due to higher standards of ideal friendships on the part of the gifted students, or to gifted students being more activity- and task-oriented (instrumental) than person-oriented (expressive) in their relationships.

What factors serve to assist gifted students in their social relationships? In an investigation of the social support of gifted adolescents (VanTassel-Baska et al 1994), students of higher socioeconomic status reported higher levels of support than students of lower socioeconomic status. There were significant differences between these groups on support from friends, classmates, parents, and teachers. Males overall reported more support from friends than females overall. In a factor analytic study of social coping strategies, Swiatek (1995) found three statistically reliable strategies used by highly gifted adolescents, strategies that help them deal with the social consequences of being gifted. The strategies were denial of giftedness, popularity/conformity, and peer acceptance. Swiatek found no gender differences in the strategies; she did find that the most highly gifted students were those most likely to deny being gifted, and that students who were predominantly gifted in verbal domains reported lower levels of peer acceptance than did students who were predominantly talented in mathematics. It may be that students with extremely high intellectual gifts are most concerned with living up to others' expectations, and so deny their giftedness more often. Verbal talents may be more visible to peers than mathematical talents, and so verbally gifted students may feel more "different" from peers than the mathematically gifted.

EMOTIONAL CHARACTERISTICS   Studies of the emotional and personality characteristics of the gifted generally show, like the Terman studies, that gifted students are somewhat better adjusted than students on average. However, recent research on the affect of gifted students has investigated finer distinctions within types of variables such as self-concept, and has highlighted some of the gender differences in gifted students with respect to emotion and personality.

In a review of the literature on personality and gifted children, Olszewski-Kubilius et al (1988) found that gifted students were generally at least as well adjusted as norm groups and comparison groups, and possessed more personality characteristics ordinarily considered to be favorable than comparison groups. They also found that gifted children may display personality functioning, in some domains, similar to that of older students. High IQ elementary school students tended to display lower levels of anxiety than other children, especially anxiety about school. Gifted adolescents scored within normal ranges or higher on almost every scale of major personality inventories. The authors note that the generalization of research comparing gifted and other students is hampered by lack of information on socioeconomic status and other demographic information.

Research on the self-concept of gifted children has presented conflicting results. Some studies using global measures of self-esteem indicate that gifted students score higher on these measures than other students, whereas other studies show no difference between groups or, occasionally, that gifted students score lower (Olszewski-Kubilius et al 1988). More informative are studies that look at various types of self-concept, and that investigate gender differences. Hoge & McSheffrey (1991) gave the Self-Perception Profile for Children (Harter 1985) to 280 students in grades five through eight. They found that gifted students scored slightly lower than the norm group on Social and Athletic Competence, but higher on Scholastic Competence and Global Self-Worth. They also found that academic performance seemed to be a more important factor in global self-worth for girls than for boys. Similarly, Pyryt &

Mendaglio (1994) administered a multidimensional self-concept measure and found that gifted students scored higher, on average, than their age peers, with academic self-concept contributing most to the difference. However, the gifted students scored slightly higher on social, athletic, and evaluative subscales as well.

In a study of the psychological adjustment of gifted early adolescents (Luthar et al 1992), these students were found to be more similar to college students (matched to the gifted students on cognitive maturity) than to students their own chronological age. Measures of cognitive ability, depression, anxiety, locus of control, and real and ideal self-image were administered. Gifted students were generally high on psychological adjustment and had less depression and better self-image than same-age students. The authors speculate that previous inconsistencies in the research on the adjustment of the gifted may be due to differences in achievement: that is, that underachieving gifted students may be less well-adjusted than both achieving gifted students and an unselected group of same-age students.

In contrast to most of the research presented above, Roberts & Lovett (1994) found that after experimentally induced scholastic failure, gifted adolescents demonstrated more negative emotional reactions than did two groups of their age peers: high academic achievers who had not been labeled gifted, and a randomly selected group of students. After failing to solve extremely difficult anagrams, gifted students showed greater irrational beliefs and self-oriented perfectionism, greater negative affect, and more physiological stress than students in the other two groups.

In a pair of developmental studies of social and emotional characteristics of gifted students (Kline & Short 1991a,b), it was found that gifted girls in high school had significantly less self-confidence, more perfectionism, and more discouragement than younger gifted girls. There were no age differences in hopelessness, but means were above the norms. In contrast, for gifted boys the authors found that gifted high school boys felt less discouragement and hopelessness than younger boys; there were no age differences in self-confidence or perfectionism. Scores were similar for high school girls and boys on self-confidence and perfectionism, but girls scored higher on discouragement and hopelessness.

## Motivational Characteristics

Research on the motivational characteristics of the gifted can be classified into three main categories: studies that compare gifted students to the norm on motivation, studies that describe motivation patterns of gifted students, and studies that investigate motivational differences between gifted students who perform up to potential ("achieving") and those who do not ("underachieving").

Olszewski-Kubilius et al (1988) reviewed several studies showing that gifted elementary students generally score significantly higher on internal locus of control than comparison students. High IQ students tended to score higher on measures of intrinsic motivation and autonomy than average IQ students, and are more likely to demonstrate positive attributions for success and failure, for example, attributing success to their own ability and effort, and attributing failure to bad luck or inappropriate strategy choice. Csikszentmihalyi et al (1993), in a longitudinal study of ninth and tenth grade students through their high school years, found that when compared with average students, intellectually talented adolescents showed more intrinsic motivation for reading, thinking, and solitude. They also found that the students who were the most committed to their own talent domain at the end of this longitudinal study were those who had displayed the strongest intrinsic motivation for that domain.

Benbow et al (1991) investigated correlates of educational achievement in a sample of mathematically precocious youth. They found that motivation (as measured by quantity of academic activities and participation in optional contests and exams in high school) was the third most useful predictor of educational achievement and aspiration at age 23, behind quality of instruction and home environment. Ford (1993) found that several motivational factors distinguished between achieving and underachieving gifted Black students. Achievers were less concerned with peer pressure and reported high effort and no test anxiety. Underachievers had a more external locus of control, were more ambivalent about trying hard, and reported that they felt test anxiety. Emerick (1992) identified motivational factors that led to the reversal of underachievement in several gifted adolescents. Factors included a strong intellectual or creative interest pursued outside of school, school classes that allowed for advanced and independent study, and an ability to relate school success to personal goals.

SUMMARY OF SOCIAL-EMOTIONAL AND MOTIVATIONAL CHARACTERISTICS
Gifted students (usually defined by a wide variety of school definitions in this research, including intellectual, creative, and leadership characteristics) tend to have better psychosocial adjustment than other students. They are at least as popular, though they may have different friendship styles. Their self-concepts, while heavily weighted with their academic abilities, are generally high, and they tend to score at normal or above levels on personality measures. They tend to be more internally motivated and have more positive attributions for success and failure; however, they may have more trouble coping when they do encounter failure.

These positive findings may not be true for various subgroups of the gifted. Sex differences have been found such that through adolescence, females tend to decrease and males tend to increase on several positive emotional character-istics. In addition, these psychological advantages may start to disappear as the level of giftedness increases. Students who are extremely far from the norm in-tellectually seem to have more trouble fitting in socially and emotionally as well. Gifted students who are underachievers may demonstrate considerably different psychological profiles. Finally, students from cultural or ethnic groups where the identification of giftedness has not been traditional have not been thoroughly investigated.

# RECOMMENDED PRACTICES IN EDUCATING CHILDREN WITH GIFTS AND TALENTS

## *Recommended Practices as a Framework*

The relationship between theoretically driven research and educational prac-tice in developing students' gifts and talents is frequently less direct and useful than either researchers or practitioners would like it to be. Assessments of a knowledge base in psychology or education generally take the form of an ex-pert review of the empirical literature on a specific topic. Depending upon the topic and the personal interests of the reviewer, the connections among theory, research, and practice are suggested openly or they may go begging. When the connections are not clearly made, the researcher looking for current trends or future directions is disappointed; the practitioner looking for validation of daily educational practice finds little of immediate value. To aid the connec-tion between research and practice in giftedness, Shore et al (1991) proposed that the knowledge base be examined from the practitioner's point of view. Shore and his colleagues recommended using the considered expert advice generally accessible to a concerned parent or teacher as the bridge between re-searcher and practitioner. According to the authors, there are five important elements to the notion of a recommended practice as a way of organizing the knowledge base. First, it refers to specific advice given in the form of "do," "don't," or "should" statements; for example, "Career counseling is needed, especially for girls." Second, recommended practices signal a level of agree-ment among experts in the field, but more narrowly so than standards that are generally endorsed by some organization for the purpose of certification or ac-creditation. Third, recommended practices are sufficiently broad to be generic. For example, a practice proposing the use of rigorous curriculum with able learners does not specify particular curricular materials. Fourth, recommended practices should be viewed as hypotheses—tested or untested—in the field. Fifth, the term recommended practice does not imply that the practice is thor-oughly researched and validated. Although they may have the initial appear-ance of received wisdom, recommended practices are to be held up to scrutiny.

Shore and associates made the pragmatic decision that the compilation of recommended practice should not only be based on the best information on a topic but also on the information that is most widespread and most likely to be available by parents and practitioners. In fact, very durable but scantily researched practices have found their way into the knowledge base on giftedness. The use of the recommended practice as a framework for review provides a means for determining the areas most in need of research and suggests the direction the inquiry might take.

The process used to develop the recommended practices has been fully described elsewhere (Robinson 1992, Shore et al 1991, Shore & Delcourt 1996). Briefly, from an examination of 100 textbooks, handbooks, yearbooks, and collections of readings, Shore and associates identified 101 recommended practices organized into four main groups with several subgroups. The headings provide a signpost and overview for the research subsequently reviewed in relation to each of the practices:

Noncurricular Issues
    1. Advocacy and Administration
    2. Identification and Assessment
Curricular and Teaching Strategies
    3. Curricular and Program Policies
    4. Advice to Educators
Family, Counseling and Personal Adjustment
    5. Advice to Parents
    6. Advice to Professionals
    7. Social and Emotional Adjustment
Special Groups
    8. Special Groups

Books rather than journal articles or other types of research reports were selected as the source for recommended practices because texts become the repository for widely held assumptions and shared information.

In the next phase of the investigation, the research reported in general education and gifted education journals relevant to each of the 101 practices was reviewed. Each review included an expanded statement of the practice, a summary of the current research on the practice, a set of implications for action derived from the current knowledge, and a section suggesting needed research on the practice.

## School Practices with Support

When the reviews of the individual practices were completed, an overall picture of the state of the knowledge base on giftedness emerged. In the initial assessment of 1991, approximately 40% of the recommended practices were supported by research. The practices with the most complete research support were in the area of identifying students for specialized services and in the special needs of particular groups, notably gifted girls and gifted learners with physical disabilities. The developed research base in both of these areas reflects the psychometric roots of the field and the sustained interest in special groups of gifted learners.

In 1991, those recommended practices with the least well-developed knowledge base and therefore most in need of attention from researchers tended to cluster in curricular and program policies. Thus, as the authors (Shore et al 1991) noted, some very important and widespread practices were without solid empirical support. A subsequent review by Shore & Delcourt (1996) updated the status of several of the practices related to curricular and program policies. Combining the initial review, the recent update and several large-scale studies undertaken with federal support, two major practices with research support are reviewed here.

ACCELERATION   In both the 1991 and the 1996 review, research support was found for the practice of acceleration for able learners. Although popular notions of acceleration envision only grade skipping in which a student is moved ahead of his or her agemates in grade placement, there are various forms. Southern et al (1993) compiled a list of 17 different types of educational acceleration, only 4 of which depend upon changing the classroom grade placement of students. In addition to grade skipping, these include: early entrance to kindergarten or first grade, early entrance to junior or senior high school, and early graduation from high school, typically in 3.5 years rather than 4 years. Continuous progress, concurrent enrollment programs, or Advanced Placement courses are also examples of acceleration used with gifted learners, but they do not require grade skipping.

The available literature on acceleration has been reviewed regularly over the decades (Benbow 1992, Daurio 1979, Kulik & Kulik 1984, Pollins 1983, Southern & Jones 1991). In a meta-analysis of acceleration studies, Kulik & Kulik (1984) analyzed 26 different studies in 21 reports. One set of studies compared accelerants with same-age controls; the second set compared accelerants with older-age controls on measures of achievement. In order to be included in the meta-analysis, the study had to control for aptitude between the accelerated and nonaccelerated groups. The comparison of same-age accelerants and nonaccelerants resulted in a mean effect size of +.88. In the studies comparing accelerants with older age students, the mean effect size was +.05. The authors concluded that on measures of achievement, accelerated students do not differ from older aged control students of similar aptitude (Kulik & Kulik 1984).

Shore & Delcourt (1996) characterized certain kinds of acceleration as clumsy. For example, grade skipping was not always accompanied with adaptations to the curriculum to meet the educational needs of the accelerated students.

Although research that clearly identifies and controls for the different features of the various types of acceleration is in the beginning stages (Rogers 1991), the kinds of accelerative opportunities with the greatest positive impact on student achievement are likely to be those that modify the curriculum with subject matter acceleration or with fast-paced instruction. Simply changing grade placement recognizes the prior achievement of students (Southern et al 1993), but it does not necessarily guarantee that appropriate curriculum experiences will occur in the new placement.

Acceleration is generally a response to a particular child in the classroom or school setting. That is, it is practice applied on a case-by-case basis to an individual child or adolescent rather than a practice applied regularly to large groups of children in the school. Southern et al (1993) note that because of its individual nature and the concerns many practitioners have about the grade skipping forms of acceleration, it is used conservatively by schools.

In contrast, accelerative, fast-paced content classes are more likely to be offered to students on a volunteer basis in the college or university setting. These programs, called Talent Searches, offer accelerated instruction in content areas in after-school, Saturday, or summer venues. Students with high academic performance and high aptitude scores related to the academic area in which they are studying are selected to participate in accelerated courses. The Talent Search programs have been documented extensively and provide a good deal of the research support for acceleration as a practice uniquely suited to gifted and talented learners (VanTassel-Baska 1997).

LEVEL OF CURRICULAR MATERIALS   The use of rich and varied curriculum materials has been an admonition voiced by educational reformers for a broad range of students. The practice has particular salience for students with advanced reading capabilities for two reasons. First, evidence exists that the reading levels of regular classroom texts have dropped over the past few decades (Chall 1994). Thus, capable readers are being exposed to what has been identified as "dumbing down" of textbooks. Second, students with advanced reading capability respond positively to interventions that raise the level of the material they encounter in the classroom.

McCormick & Swassing (1982) surveyed reading programs nationally and reported that educators regarded high-level reading materials an important feature of appropriate services for talented students. They noted that the Junior Great Books program was the most frequently used program of curricular materials when particular specialized materials were reported. Martin & Cramond (1983) also reported agreement that reading instruction should be taught creatively at a high level with challenging materials; however, they also report that such experiences are infrequent for students.

Recently, two large-scale federally funded studies indicate that adapting curriculum and instruction to minimize exposure to low-level materials and to increase exposure to high-level ones have benefits for academically talented students. Reis et al (1993) investigated classrooms in which teachers had condensed the grade level curriculum materials for talented learners and compared them with classrooms in which no such adaptations were made. Compacting, as this adaption is called, includes documenting, generally through pretesting or work samples, a student's knowledge and skills in the grade level curriculum. If students demonstrate mastery of the material about to be taught, they are provided with extended curriculum activities or alternatives during the time that set of skills or curriculum topic is being covered in the classroom. Reis and her colleagues demonstrated that with training, regular classroom teachers can adapt the curriculum for students with positive impacts on both student attitudes and learning.

The second investigation was an evaluation study of language arts curriculum for advanced learners in grades four through six (VanTassel-Baska et al 1996). Outcome measures included a reading assessment that focused on literary analysis, a persuasive writing assessment, and an objective assessment of grammatical understanding. In all three areas, able learners who received the specialized advanced curriculum outperformed comparison groups. The effect sizes for literary analysis, writing, and grammatical understanding were .11, .99, and 1.57, respectively. The authors note that two key curricular elements emerged as important from qualitative data provided by teachers. First, the reading levels of the selections were advanced for the grade levels in which they were introduced. Second, the curriculum emphasized abstract concepts in literary analysis: theme, motivation, tone, and mood. Again the treatment of these concepts was advanced beyond the traditional expectations for elementary students in grades four through six.

In conclusion, the practice of using high-level reading materials with academically gifted students is supported. While social justice demands that all children be given rich curricular fare that interests them, the practice, when applied to academically talented learners, implies that the materials be substantially above grade level norms.

## School Practices to be Used with Caution

Although gifted students tend to do well academically, not all school practices are beneficial for them. One example of a popular school practice that has modest positives and significant negatives for gifted students is cooperative learning. Among the general population of students, cooperative learning advocates have documented many positive outcomes for the model (Slavin 1991). A number of these positive outcomes are social ones. There are reported increases in cross-ethnic friendships (Warring et al 1985) and in acceptance for students with disabilities (Madden & Slavin 1983). However, for achievement outcomes, the picture requires a finer lens. A recent study by Kenny et al (1994) concludes that cooperative learning is a relatively weak pedagogical strategy in terms of achievement for gifted students. They noted that the absence of a gifted student in a heterogeneous cooperative learning group did not negatively affect the learning of other students in the group. A study by Lando and Schneider (1997) provides further support for the caution with which standard cooperative learning models should be used. They found differences in the types of verbal interactions among homogeneously and heterogeneously constituted cooperative learning groups. Higher-level discourse and more positive interactions occurred when gifted students were in cooperative learning groups with other high-ability students. These studies and a recent meta-analysis on small group learning within classrooms indicate that group composition on the basis of ability or prior achievement does not have consistent effects for high, average, and low attaining students (Lou et al 1996). In addition, a study by Mulryan (1992) that documents that passivity, and therefore possible disengagement from learning, occurs in heterogeneous cooperative learning groups by both high- and low-attaining members lends support to the caution with which this educational practice should be used with academically talented learners (Robinson 1997).

SUMMARY    Educational practices with research support include the use of various forms of acceleration and the use of high-level and rigorous curriculum materials. The relatively stronger research base in these areas is in part due to the use of focused identification measures that are closely related to the services provided to the students on the basis of them. For example, mathematically talented students are located on the basis of prior mathematics achievement and aptitude and provided with accelerated and enriched instruction in that content area. In contrast, other popular educational practices like cooperative learning do not provide consistently positive outcomes for gifted learners.

## FUTURE DIRECTIONS FOR RESEARCH

### Research on the Psychology of Giftedness and Talent

Although intriguing in itself, the study of an exceptionality like giftedness which deviates from the norm in a positive way can inform our understanding of human potential generally. The examination of cases of advanced development and instances of precocious performance provide a window on the conditions and processes that help children and youth maximize their potential.

In terms of research on the psychology of giftedness and talent, the most promising directions are those that take a finer-grained look at the variability among talented children and adolescents, in other words, within-group differences. The comparisons made between talented youth and the general cohort are useful, but they are not the sole standard by which exceptionality can be examined. At present, the study of these within-group differences would be most fruitfully pursued descriptively rather than comparatively. For example, studies of talented performance outside the general intellectual domain would provide empirical information about the richer array of variables that broadened definitions of giftedness include. Studies of talent development in different domains, among culturally diverse populations, and in youth with disabilities are among the most promising.

In addition to informing our understanding of human potential, the study of psychological variables in groups of gifted students allows the researcher to hold constant the effects of ability or achievement. For example, for variables that are correlated with intellectual ability such as motivation and self-esteem, it is possible to examine how they operate in depth, over time, and across age and gender without the confounding effects of differential ability. Although ability can be controlled as an independent variable, it could be fruitful to examine other variables in depth within a group of high intellectual functioning.

Finally, the study of students with high ability but low achievement (often termed "gifted underachievers") is a unique opportunity for the intensive, perhaps longitudinal, investigation of motivational variables. With intellectual ability not a factor, how do expectancy and value, competence, and control operate to depress achievement? Investigations of this sort shed light on the psychological characteristics of talented youth, but they also inform our understanding of basic psychological processes.

## Research on School Practices

One of the key interests to the field of gifted education is to determine which of its practices are uniquely suited to talented children and adolescents; which are practices defined as good in general for all learners. Additional work is needed to illuminate the distinction. Practices that are good general education can be advocated for talented learners from that context. In other words, it is no less important to advocate for such services for talented learners, but the link between general and specialized education should be acknowledged. Practices that are uniquely suited to academically talented students will benefit from further and finer grained analyses to determine under which conditions they are best implemented to develop students' gifts and talents.

---

**Visit the *Annual Reviews home page* at http://www.AnnualReviews.org.**

---

## Literature Cited

Alexander J, Carr M, Schwanenflugel P. 1995. Development of metacognition in gifted children: directions for future research. *Dev. Rev.* 15:1–37

Benbow C. 1992. Academic achievement in mathematics and science of students between ages 13 and 23: Are there differences among students in the top one percent of mathematical ability? *J. Educ. Psychol.* 84:51–61

Benbow CP, Arjmand O, Walberg HJ. 1991. Educational productivity predictors among mathematically talented students. *J. Educ. Res.* 84:215–23

Borland JH, Wright L. 1994. Identifying young, potentially gifted economically disadvantaged students. *Gifted Child Q.* 38:164–71

Butterfield EC, Feretti RP. 1987. Toward a theoretical integration of cognitive hypotheses about intellectual differences among children. In *Cognition in Special Children: Comparative Approaches to Retardation, Learning Disabilities, and Giftedness,* ed. JG Borkowski, JD Day, pp. 195–233. Norwood, NJ: Ablex. 244 pp.

Carr M, Alexander J, Schwanenflugel P. 1996. Where gifted children do and do not excel on metacognitive tasks. *Roeper Rev.* 18: 212–17

Chall J. 1994. What students were reading 100 years ago. *Am. Educ.* 18(2):26–33

Cheng P. 1993. Metacognition and giftedness: the state of the relationship. *Gifted Child Q.* 37:105–12

Clark GA, Zimmerman E. 1983. At the age of six I gave up a magnificent career as a painter: seventy years of research about identifying students with superior abilities in the visual arts. *Gifted Child Q.* 27: 180–84

Colangelo N, Davis GA, eds. 1997. *Handbook of Gifted Education.* Boston: Allyn & Bacon. 582 pp. 2nd ed.

Csikszentmihalyi M, Rathunde K, Whalen S.

1993. *Talented Teenagers: The Roots of Success and Failure.* Cambridge, UK: Cambridge Univ. Press. 307 pp.

Csikszentmihalyi M, Robinson RE. 1986. Culture, time and the development of talent. See Sternberg & Davidson 1986, pp. 264–84

Daurio SP. 1979. Educational enrichment versus acceleration: a review of the literature. In *Educating the Gifted: Acceleration and Enrichment,* ed. WC George, JC Stanley, pp. 13–63. Baltimore, MD: Johns Hopkins Univ. Press

Davidson JE. 1986. The role of insight in giftedness. See Sternberg & Davidson 1986, pp. 201–22

Emerick LJ. 1992. Academic underachievement among the gifted: students' perceptions of factors that reverse the pattern. *Gifted Child Q.* 36:140–46

Feldhusen JF. 1986. A conception of giftedness. See Sternberg & Davidson 1986, pp. 112–27

Feldhusen JF, Jarwan F. 1993. Identification of gifted and talented youth for educational programs. See Heller et al 1993, pp. 233–51

Feldman DH. 1993. Child prodigies: a distinctive form of giftedness. *Gifted Child Q.* 37:188–93

Feldman DH, Goldsmith LT. 1991. *Nature's Gambit: Child Prodigies and the Development of Human Potential.* New York: Teachers College Press

Ford DY. 1993. An investigation of the paradox of underachievement among gifted Black students. *Roeper Rev.* 16:78–84

Frasier M, Passow AH. 1994. *Toward a New Paradigm for Identifying Talent Potential.* Storrs, CT: Natl. Res. Cent. Gifted Talented

Gagné F. 1985. Giftedness and talent: reexamining a reexamination of the definitions. *Gifted Child Q.* 29:103 -12

Gagné F. 1991. Toward a differentiated model

of giftedness and talent. In *Handbook of Gifted Education.* ed. N Colangelo, GA Davis, pp. 65–80. Boston: Allyn & Bacon

Gallagher JG, Courtright RD. 1986. The educational definition of giftedness and its policy implications. See Sternberg & Davidson 1986, pp. 93–111

Gross M. 1994. The highly gifted: their nature and needs. In *Talent Development: Theories and Practice,* ed. JB Hansen, SB Hoover, pp. 257–80. Dubuque, IA: Kendall/Hunt. 338 pp.

Harris JJ, Ford DY. 1991. Identifying and nurturing the promise of gifted Black American children. *J. Negro Educ.* 60(1):3–18

Harter S. 1985. *Manual for the Self-Perception Scale for Children.* Unpublished manuscript.

Heller KA, Monks FJ, Passow AH, eds. 1993. *International Handbook of Research and Development of Giftedness and Talent.* Oxford: Pergamon. 964 pp.

Henry NB, ed. 1958. *Education of the Gifted.* (The 57th Yearbook of the National Society for the Study of Education, Part II.) Chicago: Univ. Chicago Press

Hoge RD, McSheffrey R. 1991. An investigation of self-concept in gifted children. *Except. Child.* 57:238–45

Jackson NE, Butterfield EC. 1986. A conception of giftedness designed to promote research. See Sternberg & Davidson 1986, pp. 151–81

Janos PM, Robinson NM. 1985. Psychosocial development in intellectually gifted children. In *The Gifted and Talented: Developmental Perspectives,* ed. FD Horowitz, M O'Brien, pp. 149–95. Washington, DC: Am. Psychol. Assoc. 477 pp.

Kenny DA, Archambault FX Jr, Hallmark BW. 1994. *The Effects of Group Composition on Gifted and Nongifted Elementary Students in Cooperative Learning Groups. Rep. 94108.* Storrs, CT: Univ. Conn. Natl. Res. Cent. Gifted Talented

Kline BE, Short EB. 1991a. Changes in emotional resilience: gifted adolescent boys. *Roeper Rev.* 13:184–87

Kline BE, Short EB. 1991b. Changes in emotional resilience: gifted adolescent females. *Roeper Rev.* 13:118–21

Kulik JA, Kulik CC. 1984. Effects of accelerated instruction on students. *Rev. Educ. Res.* 54:409–25

Kunkel MA, Chapa B, Patterson G, Walling DD. 1995. The experience of giftedness: a concept map. *Gifted Child Q.* 39:126–34

Lando BZ, Schneider BH. 1997. Intellectual contributions and mutual support among developmentally advanced children in homogeneous and heterogeneous work/discussion groups. *Gifted Child Q.* 42:44–57

Lou Y, Abrami PC, Spence J, Paulsen C, Chambers B, d'Apollonia S. 1996. Within-class grouping: a meta-analysis. *Rev. Educ. Res.* 66:423–58

Lovecky DV. 1994. Exceptionally different children: different minds. *Roeper Rev.* 17: 116–20

Luthar SS, Zigler E, Goldstein D. 1992. Psychosocial adjustment among intellectually gifted adolescents: the role of cognitive-developmental and experiential factors. *J. Child Psychol. Psychiatry* 33: 361–73

Madden N, Slavin R. 1983. Effects of cooperative learning on the social acceptance of mainstreamed academically handicapped students. *J. Spec. Educ.* 17:171–83

Maker CJ. 1996. Identification of gifted minority students: a national problem, needed changes and a promising solution. *Gifted Child Q.* 40:41–50

Marland SP. 1971. *Education of the Gifted and Talented. US Congr. Rep. 72–5020.* Washington, DC: US Off. Educ.

Martin CE, Cramond B. 1983. Creative reading: Is it being taught to the gifted in elementary schools? *J. Educ. Gifted* 5:34–43

Mayseless O. 1993. Gifted adolescents and intimacy in close same-sex relationships. *J. Youth Adolesc.* 22:135–46

McCormick S, Swassing RH. 1982. Reading instruction for the gifted: a survey of programs. *J. Educ. Gifted* 5:34–43

Mills CJ, Tissot SL. 1995. Identifying academic potential in students from underrepresented populations: Is using the Ravens Progressive Matrices a good idea? *Gifted Child Q.* 39:209–17

Mulryan CM. 1992. Student passivity during cooperative small groups in mathematics. *J. Educ. Res.* 85:261–73

Olszewski-Kubilius PM, Kulieke MJ, Krasney N. 1988. Personality dimensions of gifted adolescents: a review of the empirical literature. *Gifted Child Q.* 32:347–52

Pollins LD. 1983. The effects of acceleration on the social and emotional development of gifted students. In *Academic Precocity,* ed. CP Benbow, JC Stanley, pp. 160–78. Baltimore, MD: Johns Hopkins Univ. Press

Pyryt MC, Mendaglio S. 1994. The multidimensional self-concept; a comparison of gifted and average-ability adolescents. *J. Educ. Gifted* 17:299–305

Reis SM, Westberg KL, Kulikovich J, Rogers JB, Smist JM. 1993. *Why Not Let High Ability Students Start School in January?*

Storrs, CT: Natl. Res. Cent. Gifted Talented

Renzulli JS. 1978. What makes giftedness? Reexamining a definition. *Phi Delta Kappan* 60:180–84, 261

Renzulli JS. 1986. The three-ring conception of giftedness: a developmental model for creative productivity. See Sternberg & Davidson 1986, pp. 53–92

Roberts SM, Lovett SB. 1994. Examining the "F" in gifted; academically gifted adolescents' physiological and affective responses to scholastic failure. *J. Educ. Gifted* 17:241–59

Robinson A. 1992. Promising practices for talented children: What does the research say? *Understanding Our Gifted* 55(3):1–3

Robinson A. 1997. Cooperative learning for talented students: emergent issues and implications. See Colangelo & Davis 1997, pp. 243–52

Robinson NM, Olszewski-Kubilius P. 1996. Gifted and talented children: issues for pediatricians. *Pediatr. Rev.* 17(12):427–34

Rogers KB. 1986. Do the gifted think and learn differently? A review of recent research and its implications for instruction. *J. Educ. Gifted* 10:17–39

Ross P. 1993. *National Excellence: A Case for Developing America's Talent.* Washington, DC: Off. Educ. Res. Improve., US Off. Educ.

Scott MS, Deuel LLS, Jean-Francois B, Urbano RC. 1996. Identifying cognitively gifted ethnic minority children. *Gifted Child Q.* 40:147–53

Shore BM, Cornell DG, Robinson A, Ward VS. 1991. *Recommended Practices in Gifted Education: A Critical Analysis.* New York: Teachers Coll. Press

Shore BM, Delcourt MAB. 1996. Effective curricular and program practices in gifted education and the interface with general education. *J. Educ. Gifted* 20:138–54

Shore BM, Koller M, Dover A. 1994. More from the water jars: a reanalysis of problem-solving performance among gifted and nongifted children. *Gifted Child Q.* 38:179–83

Slavin RE. 1991. Synthesis of research on cooperative learning. *Educ. Leadership* 48(5):71–82

Southern WT, Jones ED. 1991. Academic acceleration: background and issues. In *The Academic Acceleration of Gifted Children,* ed. WT Southern, ED Jones, pp. 1–29. New York: Teachers College Press

Southern WT, Jones ED, Stanley JC. 1993. Acceleration and enrichment: the context and development of program options. See Heller et al 1993, pp. 387–409

Sternberg RJ. 1986. A triarchic theory of intellectual giftedness. See Sternberg & Davidson 1986, pp. 223–43

Sternberg RJ, Davidson JE, eds. 1986. *Conceptions of Giftedness.* New York: Cambridge Univ. Press. 460 pp.

Sternberg RJ, Davidson JE. 1985. Cognitive development in the gifted and talented. In *The Gifted and Talented: Developmental Perspectives,* ed. FD Horowitz, M O'Brien, pp. 37–74. Washington, DC: Am. Psychol. Assoc. 477 pp.

Swiatek MA. 1995. An empirical investigation of the social coping strategies used by gifted adolescents. *Gifted Child Q.* 39: 154–60

Tannenbaum AJ. 1986. Giftedness: a psychsocial approach. See Sternberg & Davidson 1986, pp. 21–52

Terman LM. 1925. Genetic studies of genius. *Mental and Physical Characteristics of a Thousand Gifted Children,* Vol. 1. Stanford, CA: Stanford Univ. Press

VanTassel-Baska J. 1997. Contributions to gifted education of the Talent Search concept. In *Psychometric and Social Issues Concerning Intellect and Talent,* ed. CP Benbow, D Lubinski. Baltimore, MD: Johns Hopkins Univ. Press. In press

VanTassel-Baska J, Johnson DT, Hughes CE, Boyce LN. 1996. A study of language arts curriculum effectiveness with gifted learners. *J. Educ. Gifted* 19:461–80

VanTassel-Baska J, Olszewski-Kubilius P, Kulieke M. 1994. A study of self-concept and social support in advantaged and disadvantaged seventh and eighth grade gifted students. *Roeper Rev.* 16:186–91

Warring D, Johnson D, Maruyama G, Johnson R. 1985. Impact of different types of cooperative learning on cross-ethnic and cross-sex relationships. *J. Educ. Psychol.* 77: 53–59

Whitmore JR, Maker CJ. 1985. *Intellectual Giftedness in Disabled Persons.* Rockville, MD: Aspen

Wilkinson SC. 1993. WISC-R profiles of children with superior intellectual ability. *Gifted Child Q.* 37:84–91

Willard-Holt C. 1994. *Recognizing Talent: Cross-Case Study of Two High Potential Students with Cerebral Palsy.* Storrs, CT: Natl. Res. Cent. Gifted Talented

Winner E, Martino G. 1993. See Heller et al 1993, pp. 253–82

Witty P. 1958. See Henry 1958, pp. 41–63

*Annu. Rev. Psychol. 1998. 49:141–68*

# PERFORMANCE EVALUATION IN WORK SETTINGS

## R. D. Arvey and K. R. Murphy

Industrial Relations Center, University of Minnesota, Minneapolis, Minnesota 55455;
e-mail: rarvey@csom.umn.edu

KEY WORDS: performance, appraisal, evaluation, utility, review

### ABSTRACT

Recent research from 1993 on performance evaluations in work settings is reviewed and integrated with the prior reset and historical bases. Contemporary research reflects several themes: General models of job performance are being developed, the job performance domain is being expanded, research continues to explore the psychometric characteristics of performance ratings, research is developing on potential bias in ratings, rater training is examined, and research continues in terms of efforts to attach utility values to rated performance. We conclude that research is progressing in traditional content areas as well in the exploration of new ground. Researchers are recognizing that job performance is more than just the execution of specific tasks and that it involves a wider array of important organizational activities. There is also an increased optimism regarding the use of supervisory ratings and recognition that such "subjective" appraisal instruments do not automatically translate into rater error or bias.

## CONTENTS

## INTRODUCTION

Psychologists have long been attentive to the issue of defining, understanding, and evaluating performance within work contexts. This chapter constitutes the first independent and separate treatment of recent research on this topic in an *Annual Review* format. *Annual Review* chapters on personnel selection by Landy et al (1994) and Borman et al (1997) give some treatment to perform-ance evaluation issues. These reviews primarily focus on the role of job per-formance measures as criterion variables against which personnel selection methods and systems are validated, and as such, the treatment of personnel evaluation has been embedded within the larger framework of prediction and selection systems.

Our intent in this chapter is to develop and expand on previous treatments as well as to review and integrate more recent research on performance evalua-tion. We review and discuss recent research associated with job performance and appraisal methods and instrumentation, and we attend to psychological ef-forts to understand the value of individuals to organizations vis-à-vis their work performance.

We acknowledge at the outset that the value of an individual to a firm may be more than "just" his or her work performance. An individual may be valued by an organization because he or she possesses particular personal characteristics (e.g. valuing diversity; see Chemers et al 1995, Jackson & Ruderman 1995) or skills (see Gerhart & Milkovich 1992, Lawler 1990, Lawler & Jenkins 1992). In addition, the value of an individual is likely to vary substantially depending on the job he or she holds [this is an assumption that is the basis of many job evaluation systems (Lawler 1990)]. Here we take a traditional perspective that the major contributor of an employee's worth to the organization is through work behavior and ultimately performance. In addition, we explicitly deal with individual job performance and do not consider group or team performance or individual performance within teams (for a treatment of team performance, see Guzzo & Dickson 1996). Similarly, we do not deal with economic theories of employee worth that tend to focus on economic or financial definitions and ex-planations of performance (for an economic treatment of subjectivity in per-formance appraisals, see, for example, Prendergast & Topel 1996).

The scope of the chapter includes a comprehensive review of major psycho-logical journals from 1993 to present. The decision to focus on recent research is based on a rationale used in previous Annual Review chapters (Borman et al 1997, Landy et al 1994). We reviewed relevant articles cited in *PsychInfo* and sent out a call for additional papers to over 75 professional psychologists. We also examined a variety of seminal articles, books, and reviews that provided context for this review. Many of the issues discussed in recent research can only be understood in the context of papers published before 1993, and our review includes numerous references to research published before this date. Our coverage, however, of research published before 1993 is not designed to be comprehensive.

## HISTORICAL TREATMENT AND CONTEXT

It is useful to provide brief coverage of some of the historical treatments and models of performance appraisal. Between 1950 and 1980, most research was concerned with improving the instruments used in making performance ratings. Thus, there were hundreds of studies on the advantages and disadvantages of different types of rating scales, of rating vs ranking, and of ways of eliciting ratings that would provide the most objective measures of performance.

In the early 1980s, researchers shifted their focus away from instrumentation issues and toward developing a better understanding of the way raters form impressions and judgments of their subordinates' performance. In particular, Landy & Farr (1980, 1983) directed the attention of researchers toward the links between research on information processing and cognition and the practical questions often faced by performance appraisal researchers. Feldman's (1981) review helped to introduce a number of concepts from social cognition into research on performance appraisal. The next fifteen years saw an explosion in research on information processing in performance appraisal; DeNisi (1997) provides an in-depth review of this research. Many individuals, however, expressed skepticism about the contribution this research made to our understanding of performance appraisal in organizations (DeNisi 1997, Guion & Gibson 1988, Ilgen et al 1993).

There are several noteworthy reviews that are somewhat more restricted in scope than those discussed above. Austin & Villanova (1992) described the history of research on performance criteria, from 1917 to 1992. Folger et al (1992) reviewed research on justice perceptions of fairness in appraisal and suggest a due-process metaphor for understanding many of the questions raised in that literature. Bobko & Colella (1994) reviewed research on the meaning, implications, and determination of performance standards. In a broader context, several papers addressed the impact of ongoing changes in the structure and function of organizations on performance appraisal. Organizations are becoming flatter, more decentralized, and are moving away from individual-based and toward team-based methods of production. Cascio (1995) and Fletcher (1994, 1995) examined the probable impact of these changes on the way performance appraisals will be conducted and used in organizations.

This understanding of the broader context is consistent with several papers that examined in more detail the role of the rating context and the goals pursued by various stakeholders in shaping the behavior of raters, ratees, and other users of performance appraisal. For example, Murphy & Cleveland (1991, 1995) suggest that researchers should consider the rating context before attempting to analyze or evaluate the effectiveness, accuracy, etc, of performance ratings. Cleveland & Murphy (1992) analyzed performance appraisal as goal-oriented behavior and suggested that if the goals pursued by raters were examined more closely, behaviors that are typically treated as rating errors (e.g. giving high ratings to most subordinates) would be seen as adaptive responses to forces in the rating environment.

In a similar vein, Cardy & Dobbins (1994) discussed the relationships between concepts from research on efficient production systems and Total Quality Management (TQM) and performance appraisal. They noted that performance is determined by both the behavior of the individual and the system in which he or she functions. Likewise, Waldman (1994a,b) suggested an integration of TQM principles with performance appraisal/management and noted that an adequate theory of performance should contain both person and system components.

A review of the historical literature concerning personnel evaluation also shows a substantial gap between research and practice in performance appraisal. This was perhaps most obvious during the 1980s, when many of the studies in this area were conducted in the laboratory and focused on the cognitive processes in appraisal and evaluation (Banks & Murphy 1985). However, concerns about the links between appraisal research and practice still remain. Bretz et al (1992) noted that researchers have not typically asked what practitioners and managers regard as the most important questions and that the results of performance appraisal research have had little impact on the practice of appraisal in organizations. There are clearly opportunities for good research-practice linkages (Banks & Murphy 1985). For example, Latham et al (1993) illustrated the interface between practical issues and salient research findings. However, these links are seldom as strong as they could or should be.

One place where a concerted effort has been made to link research and practice is in the Armed Services Joint Performance Measurement project (Wigdor & Green 1991). Substantial efforts on the parts of several branches of the Armed Services were directed at developing the best practical measures of job performance. This project resulted in the development of several "hands-on" performance measures, which typically involved demonstrating proficiency in specific job tasks.

Another area where historically there is an active research-practice interchange is within the legal arena. In court cases involving Title VII charges of bias and discrimination, performance appraisal evaluations often come under attack. Expert witnesses often rely on the published literature to help them reach informed opinions about the adequacy of the appraisal system and instrumentation used by organizations. Reviews by Feild & Holley (1982), Kleiman & Durham (1981), Bernardin & Beatty (1984), and Cascio & Bernardin (1984) analyzed case law to develop principles and themes associated with appraisal systems and formats that appear to influence how courts and juries review the relative fairness of such evaluation systems.

The groundwork for utility analysis was laid decades ago (Brogden 1949, Cronbach & Gleser 1965), and the conceptual models guiding this work have changed little over time. In the area of personnel and human resource management, utility analysis has been used to (a) forecast the effect of some intervention (e.g. a test, a training program) on the performance of employees, and (b) attach a value, often framed in a dollar metric, to that performance. Research on utility estimation over the past several decades has mostly focused on elaborating and applying the basic models developed by Brogden and others.

## DEFINITION OF JOB PERFORMANCE

The first broad area of recent performance evaluation research focuses on defining job performance. First, there are several efforts outlining general models of job performance and the determinants of job performance. Drawing from the long-term Selection and Classification project (Project A) sponsored by the military, Campbell et al (1993) proposed the view of job performance as multidimensional in nature and comprised of an eight-factor latent structure. In addition, Campbell et al proposed several broad individual determinants of performance (i.e. Declarative Knowledge, Procedural Knowledge and Skill, and Motivation). Empirical support for this model is presented by McCloy et al (1994), who show significant relationships between the measured and latent variables of performance and specified performance determinants indicating a good fit to their model.

Waldman & Spangler (1989) also developed an integrated model of job performance focusing on characteristics of the individual (e.g. experience, ability), outcomes (e.g. feedback, job security), and the immediate work environment. Campbell et al (1996) reviewed and discussed other models of job performance (e.g. the "classical" general factor model, the critical deficiency model) but again affirmed their belief that performance is best understood as multifactor in nature.

Further specification of the taxonomic structure of job performance is developed in Borman & Brush (1993). Using the results of published and unpublished studies of managerial performance, expert judges sorted performance dimensions into similar content domains. Further psychometric methods were used to develop an 18-factor solution. These 18 factors (e.g. planning and organizing, training, coaching, developing subordinates, technical proficiency) compared well with previous research efforts to derive a taxonomic structure of performance in managerial jobs.

Viswesvaran (1996) suggested that there is a general factor underlying most common performance measures but that there are also important subfactors, including task-specific as well as conscientiousness-oriented factors. One question that surfaces here is whether there might be a "general factor" in performance that corresponds to a "g" factor in cognitive intelligence. Along these lines, Arvey (1986) earlier called attention to a possible general factor (a "p" factor?) resulting from factor analyzing job-analytic information for a number of petrochemical jobs. The implication of this type of research is that performance measures might be differentiated in terms of both performance dimensions and level of abstraction/specificity.

Campbell et al (1996) also drew specific attention to the need to examine more fully the nature of job performance variability across employees. They discussed different methods of estimating variation in job performance (i.e. the coefficient of variation) and the meaning of variance in terms of economic value. Sackett et al (1988) and DuBois et al (1993) also called attention to distributional aspects of performance in their discussion of maximum and typical measures of performance, essentially referring to range difference within ratees.

A second theme is that the job performance domain is expanding. This theme is sounded somewhat broadly by Cascio (1995) and Ilgen & Hollenbeck (1991), who argue that the nature of work is changing and therefore so are the different definitions of what jobs and job performance are all about. There appears to be a general move toward more flexible definitions of work roles and jobs, where jobs are viewed as dynamic and more interchangeable and are defined with less precision. The focus is on the personal competencies required to perform various work roles and jobs rather than a narrow review of specific tasks and duties inherent in fixed jobs and work roles. Hedge & Borman (1995) suggested that different rater types (i.e. peers, self, subordinates) will capture different and valued perspectives in measuring performance, that electronic monitoring devices might be used for measurement purposes, and that attitudes toward appraisal systems will be examined more thoroughly.

Consistent with this theme is that broad distinctions might be made between measures of task proficiency in job performance and what is being called "contextual" performance. Borman & Motowidlo (1993) suggested that task performance relates to the proficiency with which incumbents perform core technical activities that are important for their jobs, whereas contextual performance is defined as extratask proficiency that contributes more to the organizational, social, and psychological environment to help accomplish organizational goals. These contextual factors include such aspects as persisting with enthusiasm and extra effort, volunteering to carry out duties not formally part of one's job, and endorsing and supporting organizational objectives (Borman & Motowidlo 1993). This notion is consistent with the work by Organ (1988), who discusses organizational citizenship behavior; prosocial behavior as discussed by Brief & Motowidlo (1986); and organizational spontaneity (George & Brief 1992). All these labels refer to constructs contributing to organizational goals and reflect the polar opposites of constructs of employee deviance and counterproductivity that detract from organizational goals. Such contextual behaviors serve to facilitate communications, lubricate social communications, and reduce tension and/or disruptive emotional responses, and are viewed as important and contributing to organizational goals.

Recent awareness that it is important for individuals to develop and possess skills that facilitate teamwork that are distinct and are different from specific on-task performance is also consistent with this theme (McIntyre & Salas 1995). Likewise, there is a growing recognition that counterproductive behaviors that detract from organizational goals should also be specified and treated as aspects of performance—perhaps as conditions of employment.

Schmidt (1993) sounded a note of caution regarding the idea of creating a new performance construct called contextual performance, because it appears to be defined as something absent from a job description. He further made the argument that as soon as it becomes part of such a description, it ceases being part of contextual performance. Part of the problem might lie in whether the distinction is only conceptual or whether it has an empirical basis. As such, there are several empirical research efforts to support this distinction. Using supervisory ratings from over 18,000 employees in 42 different entry-level jobs in retail settings, Hunt (1996) developed a taxonomy of "generic" work behavior, or behavior that contributes to performance of jobs independent of technical job roles. These included the following dimensions: Adherence to Confrontational Rules, Industriousness, Thoroughness, Schedule Flexibility, Attendance, Off-Task Behavior, Unruliness, Theft, and Drug Misuse. Motowidlo & Van Scotter (1994) tested the distinction between task and contextual performance using supervisory ratings of over 400 Air Force mechanics. Results showed that both task and contextual performance factors contributed independently to overall performance and showed that personality variables were more highly correlated with contextual performance in accordance with their expectations.

Conway (1996) used a multitrait-multirater database and confirmatory factor analysis to support the validity of task and contextual performance as separate domains. Further, the distinction was more pronounced for nonmanagerial than for managerial jobs. Nonetheless, the two domains show substantial intercorrelations (in the .5–.6 range), indicating that they are certainly not entirely independent from each other. Van Scotter & Motowidlo (1996) added more empirical support to refine the construct of contextual performance by dividing it into two narrower constructs, interpersonal facilitation and job dedication. Results from supervisory ratings of 975 Air Force mechanics indicate that task performance is distinguishable from interpersonal facilitation but not from job dedication. Werner (1994) showed that extrarole behaviors such as citizenship behaviors strongly influenced rater search strategies as well as the eventual ratings given by supervisors evaluating secretarial performance.

One might ask why this kind of distinction has not been developed previously. Part of the answer to this question may be due to the historical attachment of the field of I/O psychology to a pronounced behavioristic/objective orientation which emphasized on-task performance as the only important performance domain. Schmidt et al (1981) called attention to the "behavioral fractionation" of criterion measures and task-oriented job performance measures that were virtually set in concrete in the federal government's Uniform Guidelines on Employee Selection Procedures.

Research suggesting that performance consists of both task-oriented and contextually oriented facets has led to the question of whether the attributes that lead some applicants to excel in specific aspects of performance (e.g. performing individual job tasks) might be different from those that lead some applicants to excel in other aspects of job performance (e.g. working well with others). Several studies suggest that there are differences in the variables that predict task vs contextual performance (Borman et al 1997, Day & Silverman 1989, McCloy et al 1994, McHenry et al 1990, Motowidlo & Van Scotter 1994, Rothstein et al 1994). On the whole, this research suggests that cognitive abilities might be more relevant for predicting task performance, whereas personality variables might be more critical for predicting contextual performance. Arvey et al (1997) hypothesized that constructs associated with individual differences in emotionality might also predict contextual aspects of performance.

Another issue explored in terms of definition of performance is the work by Hofmann et al (1993), who discussed the dynamic nature of performance measures across time. While researchers have previously addressed the issue of whether work performance measures are dynamic, Hofmann et al suggested that emphasis should be placed on decomposing change into the study of intra- and interindividual differences in observed change.

## MEASUREMENT OF JOB PERFORMANCE

The second broad area of performance evaluation research focuses on performance appraisal techniques that are used to measure job performance. We have organized this section of the review by thematically grouping relevant research that reflects similar content domains. This grouping was driven by the research and therefore should be considered inductive in nature.

## Construct Validity/Psychometric Considerations

Recent research continues to explore the construct validity and other psychometric properties of performance measures. Vance et al (1988) reported a study involving the assessment of construct validity using multitrait-multimethod data obtained for a sample of 256 jet engine mechanics. They used confirmatory factor analysis to support the construct validity of performance ratings provided by self, supervisors, and peers and to relate each to performance data gathered using an objective test of task proficiency. Convergence among the three different rating sources was found as well as significant discriminant validity. Similarly, Conway (1996) reported analyses of multitrait-multimethod designs and estimated the proportion of trait and method variance in ratings.

Viswesvaran et al (1996) reported the results of a meta-analysis of the interrater and intrarater reliabilities of job performance ratings. Their findings indicated that supervisory ratings appear to have higher interrater reliability than peer ratings (m = .52 for supervisors, m = .42 for peers) and that intrarater estimates of reliability (e.g. coefficient alphas) tend to be higher than interrater estimates. They conclude that the use of intrarater reliability estimates to correct for measurement error will lead to potentially biased research results and recommend the use of interrater reliability estimates. There also appears to be some evidence for differential reliabilities depending on which specific job performance dimension is being used. For example, supervisors rate performance on communication competence and interpersonal competence less reliably, on average, than productivity or quality. This finding suggests that the contextual performance factors mentioned above might be less reliably rated dimensions of performance compared with more task-specific factors.

Finally, Ganzach (1995) challenged the notion that there is a linear relationship between ratings of various dimensional ratings or attributes and an overall performance evaluation and showed that more weight is given to negative attributes than to positive attributes, and that the combination of attributes may be configural in nature. McIntyre & James (1995) showed that rater policies on weighting and combining information about target ratees are target-specific and particularly sensitive to negative information about target ratees.

## Alternative Measures of Performance

A number of recent studies have examined the relative value and interchangeability of different types of performance measures. Bommer et al (1995) assessed the relationships between relatively objective and subjective measures of employee performance. Using meta-analytic techniques to summarize the relationships for over 50 independent samples, the overall corrected mean correlation between the two types of measures was .39 (.32 observed), suggesting that the two measures were significantly and moderately related but not totally substitutable. Subsequent moderator analyses revealed that when objective and subjective measures tapped the same construct, their convergent validity improved substantially and that the measures were reasonably substitutable, a finding that is not surprising. Their discussion is valuable in that they summarize arguments that differences between these two types of measurement may not be as distinctive as once believed (e.g. there is subjectivity in the choice of objective measures and metrics). Likewise, Harris et al (1995) examined the psychometric properties of performance ratings collected for research versus administrative purposes. They found that administrative-based ratings were more lenient, that ratings obtained only for research purposes demonstrated significant correlations with a predictor, and that the two types of ratings were substantially correlated with each other (.58). Gottfredson (1991) outlined factors to be used to evaluate the equivalence of alternative measures of performance: validity, reliability, susceptibility to compromise (i.e. changes in validity or reliability with extensive use), financial cost, and acceptability to interested parties. This article represents an excellent summary of various psychometric and theoretical issues in assessing the equivalence or nonequivalence of criterion measures.

A discussion of the relative costs of alternative performance measures was provided by Stone et al (1996). As an alternative to a more expensive "hands-on" performance measure, a low-cost, readily available measure of performance was developed for Air Force specialty jobs using an existing data base that rank-ordered individuals. More research is needed to explore the relative advantages of low-fidelity and low-cost performance measures. Conceivably the relative value of such instruments might be better than more highly specific, high-fidelity instruments if relatively molar decisions are being made about individuals (e.g. promote versus not-promote, high versus low performance). A paper by Yang et al (1996) addressed this concern. They described substituting a low-cost proxy criterion measure for a higher-cost criterion measure to illuminate that such a strategy can pay off when evaluating training programs.

Absenteeism as a criterion measure continues to be the subject of research. Johns (1994) examined the psychometric properties and theoretical perspectives for self-reported absence measures as well as the possibilities of bias in such measures due to common measurement error or distortions due to memory, for example. He provided a number of recommendations for measuring and using self-reports of absence. Likewise, Harrison & Shaffer (1994) examined biases in self-reports of absences and suggested the presence of an under-reporting bias when describing oneself and an over-reporting bias when describing perceived norms or others.

Kulick & Ambrose (1993) reported a study comparing performance ratings given for secretarial performance observed under videotaped conditions as well as when typing performance data were delivered in a computerized summary format. Results showed that when evaluating performance, subjects used visual sources of information, but the computerized data were used only when evaluating typing performance. The authors suggested that different processing strategies are used when viewing performance presented via these different modalities. Future research might focus more on potential differential processing and evaluations that could occur as a result of using computer-delivered performance information.

## Rating Accuracy and Rating Error

A number of recent studies have examined a number of different variables and processes relating to the accuracy of performance ratings. Several studies have examined the role of affect in performance appraisal. Many studies in this area have focused on the potential biases that may occur when a supervisor likes or dislikes a subordinate (see Cardy & Dobbins 1994 for a review). However, more recent studies of affect and rating have suggested that affective influences on ratings may not represent rating biases. In a well-designed laboratory study, Robbins & DeNisi (1994) showed how affect toward ratees can influence the acquisition and processing of performance information. However, they argued that affect is likely to be a function of how well or poorly a person performs his or her job and is therefore more likely to represent a valid piece of information than an irrelevant source of bias. In a subsequent field study, Varma et al (1996) presented evidence consistent with this argument. Likewise, Ferris et al (1994) proposed a model wherein supervisors' affect toward subordinates was a major influence of rated performance. They tested their model using a sample of 95 staff nurses and 28 nurse supervisors and found a good fit; supervisors' affect toward subordinates correlated .74 with performance ratings.

Sanchez & De La Torre (1996) explored the influence of accuracy of memories on the accuracy of ratings of ratee's strengths and weaknesses. Not surprisingly, results show that the accuracy of dimensional ratings are a function of the accuracy of memories. In contrast, their results also show that overall holistic ratings are not related to the accuracy of memories. They suggest that raters overcome memory loss over time by relying on their on-line impressions when forming holistic or overall ratings. Kinicki et al (1995) explored the impact of activating performance prototypes (by giving raters prototypical trait adjectives of effective and ineffective performers) and found that such priming minimally affected ratings of videotaped performance, regardless of whether ratings were made immediately or under a delayed condition. A priming effect was observed when using pencil-and-paper vignettes as opposed to more richly embedded stimuli using videotape methods.

Ryan et al (1995) also investigated the impact of using videotaped performance (in an assessment center context) on rating accuracy and concluded that viewing performance through a videotape modality rather than directly does not affect the accuracy of ratings. Using in-basket and videotape methods to present stimulus information about ratees, Mero & Motowidlo (1995) showed that raters are more accurate in their ratings when they are made to feel accountable by having to justify their evaluations.

In perhaps the only field study investigating the impact of cognitive processes on performance evaluations, DeNisi & Peters (1996) showed that structuring diary-keeping and recall methods helped in terms of recalling information, differentiating among ratees, and generating more positive reactions to the appraisal process. The use of a field study to investigate these issues is very encouraging. However, no direct measurement of the proposed cognitive processes was undertaken in this study.

Some other studies have investigated more traditional rater error topics even though the topic is now thought to be not as important as it was in the past. Murphy et al (1993) reviewed the definitions of rater halo error and noted that the major conceptions about this construct are either wrong or problematic. Their review of the evidence is that halo error is not pervasive, that inflated correlations among rating dimensions are not the norm, and that there are a number of contextual factors that influence when halo might be observed. However, Lance et al (1994) tested the notion that the type of halo that occurs varies as a function of rating context and found that halo is best considered as a unitary phenomenon and should be defined as the influence of a rater's general impression on ratings of specific ratee qualities. Kane (1994) developed a model of the determinants of rater error, hypothesizing that such error has conscious antecedents where raters make decisions to introduce distortion into ratings. The model he developed draws upon subjective expected utility concepts where raters evaluate the relative utility of rating accurately and rating inaccurately, and the probability of being detected for giving inaccurate ratings. No empirical data are presented to substantiate this model, however.

Sumer & Knight (1996) examined the impact of rating previous performance on ratings of subsequent performance from the framework of contrast effects (inappropriate high or low ratings because of prior evaluations). Their findings showed that individuals who reviewed but did not rate the previous performance demonstrated an assimilation effect by rating a second rating in the direction of the previous performance. In addition, individuals who reviewed and actually rated the previous performance engaged in a contrast effect by rating the second performance away from the direction of the previous performance. However, the effect sizes for the main and interaction effects were low. Maurer et al (1993) also investigated contrast effects and showed that the use of checklists and diaries did not reduce potential contrast effects and may even strengthen such effects.

Woehr & Roch (1996) examined the impact of prior evaluations that varied in terms of performance level and ratee gender on subsequent evaluations and on recall of either a male or female of average performance. Results showed that both the performance level and the gender of the target ratee's prior evaluation influenced the subsequent rating. Relatively low performance for the prior target influenced subsequent evaluations differentially for male and female target ratees such that males were given relatively higher evaluations than females. Thus, recent research confirms complex interactions in the rating environment that influence performance ratings.

Schrader & Steiner (1996) reported the results of a study where they investigated the impact of different comparison standards on the ratings of supervisors and on self-ratings. They hypothesized that ratings in which employees are evaluated against clear and specific objective standards will differ from those in which such objective criteria are not specified and the standards are ambiguous. Results supported this proposition. However, ratings made when using internal, relative, or multiple standards of comparison were not terribly different from those made under the more objective conditions both in terms of mean differences and supervisor-self agreement. Thus, a conclusion that employee standards that involve objective and specific standards against which to evaluate individuals are the one "best" method seems premature given the results of this study. A potential problem with this study is that it involves dimensions of performance that lend themselves to precise and objective measurement, a condition that does not generalize to many dimensions of job performance.

## Performance Ratings as a Function of Rater Source

Several recent investigations have focused on relative differences in performance ratings generated by groups compared with ratings generated by individuals. This topic is important given the contemporary trend toward the use of teams and groups in organizational settings. Using experimental laboratory methods and students as subjects, Jourden & Heath (1996) showed that after completing a task, most individuals ranked their own performance below the median (a negative performance illusion), whereas most group members ranked their group performance above the median (a positive performance illusion), contradicting previous research showing a positive illusion for both individuals and group members. The authors labeled the differences between group and individual perceptions of performance as the "evaluation gap."

Martell & Borg (1993) examined the relative accuracy of having individuals or groups of individuals provide ratings on a behavioral checklist after reviewing a pencil-and-paper vignette depicting the work behavior of a police officer. Ratings were made either immediately or after a five-day delay. Results showed that groups remembered more accurately than individuals under a delayed condition, but no differences were observed when ratings were made immediately. They argued that using groups to provide ratings may be a help but not a panacea for dealing with rating accuracy. Research is just starting to examine the issue of group versus individual rating sources. Before we progress too much further, it might be wise to develop more theoretical specifications of when and why groups may provide more accurate evaluations of performance.

The use of peers as sources of ratings continues to be investigated. Saavedra & Kwun (1993) showed, in a laboratory context, that peer evaluations in self-managed work groups are conditional on self-other comparisons. Individuals who were outstanding contributors tended to be the most discerning evaluators when evaluating their peers. Borman et al (1995) showed that peers and supervisors differed slightly with regard to the different sources of information they use in providing performance ratings of US soldiers.

Self-ratings were examined by Yu & Murphy (1993) across several samples in China. As typically found in Western research, Chinese workers showed leniency effects in their self-ratings, contradicting earlier results demonstrating that Chinese workers would produce modesty bias or self-rate themselves lower than their peers or supervisors.

There is a substantial increase of interest lately in so-called "360-degree" performance measures. Such measures incorporate evaluations from a number of different rater perspectives—supervisor, peer, subordinate, self, and even customers—and are used for feedback and/or personnel decisions. London & Smither (1995) developed a model and propositions regarding the impact of such a multisource system on perceptions of goal accomplishment, reevaluation of self-image, and changes in performance-related outcomes (i.e. goals, development, behavior, and subsequent performance). These authors also articulated a number of potential moderators of the major components of the model.

An excellent starting point in terms of becoming aware of 360-degree instruments and systems is a special issue of *Human Resource Management* (Tornow 1993). Included in this issue is a cluster of articles focusing on understanding the relationship between the self and other ratings (Nilsen & Campbell 1993, Van Velsor et al 1993, Yammarino & Atwater 1993), a cluster focusing on improving the value of others' feedback, and a final cluster dealing with the impact of 360-degree feedback as a management intervention.

Antonioni (1994) presented the results of a field study using 38 managers and their subordinates and showed that subordinates preferred providing appraisal feedback to their managers anonymously. However, managers viewed upward appraisals more positively when such feedback was provided under conditions of accountability or when they were aware of the identity of the subordinates. Under conditions of accountability, subordinates tended to inflate their rating of managers, suggesting that ratee identification may influence such feedback information.

## Rating Fairness and Bias Issues

The topic of subgroup differences on performance ratings is an important one. However, the topic has received only modest attention recently, especially given the persistent finding that subgroups receive systematically different scores on a variety of performance measures. Past literature has established that racial differences in performance persistently are found. For example, Ford et al (1986) conducted a meta-analysis across 53 studies, showing that blacks receive slightly lower performance scores than whites on both subjective and objective measures (the corrected point biserial correlations were respectively .209 and .204). Studying a sample of supermarket cashiers, DuBois et al (1993) showed that black-white ratee differences also were significant. The evaluations favored whites on four different performance criteria that reflected two separate performance domains (accuracy and speed) as well as measures of "typical" performance (using computer-monitored operational measures) and "maximum" performance (using work sample tests). These differences were less extreme on the measures of maximum performance.

Kraiger & Ford (1985) conducted a meta-analysis of 74 studies across field and laboratory settings and concluded that an interaction effect existed: White raters rate white ratees higher than black ratees, whereas black raters evaluated black ratees higher than white ratees. Moderator effects were found also for group composition and research setting: Effect sizes increased as the proportion of blacks in the group decreased, and field studies generated larger effect sizes than laboratory studies. Pulakos et al (1989) examined performance ratings for racial differences using a military sample of 8642 enlisted personnel as rating targets. Both between-subjects and within-subjects (where each ratee was evaluated by both a black and white rater and therefore performance is held constant) designs were used. While statistical differences were observed, the amount of variance accounted for by race effects (main and interactions) was quite small across both within- and between-subjects analyses. These authors interpreted their data as being at odds with Kraiger & Ford (1985) but suggested that the military sample was not representative of the larger population.

Sackett & DuBois (1991) represents perhaps the most contemporary investigation of this topic. They challenge the conclusion that raters generally give more favorable ratings to members of their own race. Using a civilian sample of over 36,000 individuals in 174 jobs, and using again a between- and within-subjects design, they showed black employees to be rated lower by both black and white raters, but the difference between black and white ratees was not as great for black ratees as for white raters. Comparisons were made between the Pulakos et al (1989) military study and the Kraiger & Ford (1985) meta-analysis. Sackett & DuBois found great similarities between their results and those found in the military studies, but both their results and the data from the Pulakos et al (1989) were at odds with the meta-analytic study conducted by Kaiger & Ford (1985). The conclusion that black raters rate black ratees higher than they rate white ratees was not confirmed by either the civilian or the military studies. They suggest that the differences between these two conclusions rest in that the Kraiger & Ford (1985) study involved a limited sample size and that the observed effect was limited to laboratory studies using peer and student samples.

Oppler et al (1992) noted that differences observed between black and white ratees in performance do not necessarily imply bias; such differences could reflect actual and true differences between such samples. One method to tease out whether such differentials reflect bias is to attempt to control for as many job-relevant variables as possible. After controlling for a number of non-rated variables (i.e. Awards and Letters, Disciplinary Actions, Training Achievement), the differences between black and white ratees as rated by supervisors diminished but did not disappear.

Age-performance relationships, a popular topic of past research, has not received much attention within the past few years. Waldman & Avolio (1986) reviewed 40 samples using meta-analytic methods and found that age was significantly positively correlated (mean r = .27) with measures of productivity (i.e. unit output over time, number of patents) but negatively correlated with supervisory ratings (mean r = −.14). There was some evidence that job type moderated the relationships observed; performance ratings showed more positive relationships with age for professionals compared with nonprofessionals.

A more recent meta-analysis of the age-performance relationship including 96 independent studies was reported by McEvoy & Cascio (1989). Their meta-analysis showed that age and performance generally were unrelated. No evidence was found for moderators of the relationship, either by job type or type of performance measure.

The relationship between gender and performance has received little recent investigation. One exception is the study by Pulakos et al (1989), cited above, which found that males were rated significantly higher than females by peers. However, this difference was not observed for supervisors. All main and interactive effects associated with rater and ratee gender on performance ratings were small, accounting for a minimal amount of rating variance. The study noted earlier by Woehr & Roch (1996) showed that females tend to receive relatively lower ratings compared with males when being rated after the evaluation of a low-performing ratee (either male or female). One hypothesis sometimes put forth to explain why groups might differ is that the antecedents of job performance may not be the same for men and women, or for members of different racial or ethnic groups. Pulakos et al (1996) tested this hypothesis using structural modeling, and their data suggest that the antecedents of performance are similar across gender and racial groups.

The issue of whether rating type or format has anything to do with differential ratings given to racial minorities, women, or older employees is explored in an excellent review by Bernardin et al (1995). They observed that "expert witnesses" working for plaintiffs in discrimination cases often testify that age, race, or gender bias in performance ratings is due to the use of performance-appraisal systems that are too subjective or insufficiently specific. Their review makes it clear that there is no scientific support for the opinion that the format or specificity of appraisal systems has a significant effect on race or gender bias in performance ratings. They note that an "expert" who wishes to link bias or discrimination to specific characteristics of performance appraisal systems will be hard pressed to provide firm scientific support for such testimony.

Traditional treatments of the relative fairness of performance ratings and appraisal systems focus on whether subgroups differ significantly and meaningfully on performance ratings themselves. However, consistent with contemporary treatments of fairness in selection contexts (Arvey & Sackett 1993), researchers are beginning to examine the relative fairness of the appraisal process itself via concepts of dueprocess and procedural justice. Folger et al (1992) developed three characteristics of a due-process appraisal system. The first is that "adequate notice" be given such that employing organizations publish, distribute, and explain performance evaluation standards and processes. The second is that a "fair hearing" should be provided with a formal review meeting in which an employee is informed of his/her evaluation. A third characteristic is that raters apply performance standards consistently across employees, without distortion by external pressure, corruption, or personal biases ("judgment based on evidence").

Taylor et al (1995) described the results of a study where a performance-appraisal system was designed to ensure that due-process components were embedded in the evaluation processes. Their methodology involved randomly assigning employee-manager pairs to train for and implement the due-process system or to continue using the appraisal system as it was. Results showed that those employees evaluated by managers trained in the due-process system displayed significantly more favorable reactions along a variety of measures (e.g. perceived system fairness, appraisal accuracy, attitudes toward the system). An interesting finding was that the due-process employees received significantly lower evaluations than control employees, suggesting that such an intervention might be helpful in controlling rating inflation.

Other research has focused on the attitudes resulting from the appraisal process. Dickinson (1993) provided a nice review of this research showing that a number of appraisal variables can influence the opinions and attitudes about the fairness, accuracy, and acceptability of appraisal ratings.

## Performance Evaluation Training

Recent research has examined the impact of "frame of reference" (FOR) training on rating outcomes and processes. The primary goal of FOR training is to train raters to share and use common conceptualizations of performance when making evaluations (Woehr 1994). Woehr & Huffcutt (1994) found an average effect size of .83 for studies comparing FOR training with control or no training on the dependent variables of rating accuracy. They concluded that FOR-trained raters typically provide substantially more accurate ratings than do untrained raters. Along these lines, Stamoulis & Hauenstein (1993), investigating FOR training for raters evaluating the performance of job interviewers, found such training to be more effective in terms of some types of rater accuracy than others.

Several recent studies have explored the mechanics of why FOR training improves rater accuracy. Woehr & Feldman (1993) articulated an information-processing model where they suggested that rating are based on both memory and contextual factors. Their study showed that performance accuracy and recall depend on the instructional set given to ratees (i.e. learning versus evaluating) as well as the order in which the evaluation and recall tasks were elicited. In a follow-up study, Woehr (1994) again hypothesized that FOR training will be used by raters as the basis of information processing in the evaluation process and will be demonstrated through improved ratings using different indices of accuracy (i.e. differential elevation, differential accuracy) as dependent variables.

Day & Sulsky (1995) examined the accuracy of ratings after FOR training under various time delays, hypothesizing that different types of accuracy (differential accuracy, distance accuracy) and recall would be better or worse under various time delays based on the notion that raters who receive FOR training will be more capable of correctly categorizing ratees on various performance dimensions even when specific information is forgotten. Some support for the hypotheses was found, but the experiment did not involve direct assessment of any categorization process among raters. They also examined whether the manner in which performance information was presented to subjects (i.e. blocked by person versus some unpredictable mixture of information) might moderate the beneficial impact of FOR training. Support for the moderating hypothesis was not found; instead, both FOR training and the manner in which the performance information was presented exhibited main effects on performance-rating accuracy.

Somewhat noticeable across these FOR studies is that little attempt is made to measure directly the information processing that hypothetically goes on as a result of such training. We also worry that research exploring the impact of training tends to use similar stimulus materials (e.g. standard videotapes of performance) and generally to use students as subjects. Thus, research in this area seems to have limited generalizability across jobs and subjects.

## ATTACHING VALUE TO EMPLOYEES: UTILITY ASSESSMENT

The third broad area of performance-evaluation research focuses on utility analysis. In its most basic form, Brogden's model for estimating utility used linear regression both to forecast future performance and to attach specific values to that performance, using an equation similar to:

Predicted value $= (rxy \times Zx \times SD_y) - C$,

where $rxy$ refers to the validity of the intervention, or the relationship between the intervention and the criterion; $Zx$ refers to the "score" (in $z$-score form) that an individual receives on the intervention (e.g. test score, whether an individual receives training); $SD_y$ refers to the variability of the criterion (typically in dollar terms); and $C$ refers to the cost, per person, of implementing the intervention. Thus, the results of a utility analysis provide an estimate of the relative benefits over costs of a planned intervention.

A great deal of recent research reflects elaborations on this model. Boudreau (1991) reviewed the increasing complexity and sophistication of utility models that have built on the equation shown above. Adjustments have been proposed to (a) take into account a variety of financial parameters (Cascio 1991, 1993); (b) include a wider range of costs (e.g. recruiting costs; see Law & Myors 1993, Martin & Raju 1992) and a more realistic assessment of benefits [e.g. relatively lower performance and higher turnover during probationary periods (De Corte 1994)]; (c) appropriately take into account range restriction (Raju et al 1995); (d) reflect uncertainties in the forecasting process (e.g. re-

jected job offers, Murphy 1986); and (*e*) integrate the effects of both recruitment and selection strategies on the quality of the set of individuals who eventually occupy jobs (De Corte 1996). Most discussions of utility analysis have
focused on selection testing, but Klaas & McClendon (1996) demonstrated the
application of these techniques in evaluating pay policies.

A long-standing barrier to implementing utility analysis has been the difficulty in estimating the dollar value of the variability in job performance (i.e.
$SD_y$). Schmidt et al (1979) proposed a method of obtaining direct estimates by
supervisors of the value of employees performing at different levels and showed
how this might be used to estimate $SD_y$. The validity and meaning of such direct estimates of employee value have been examined in detail in numerous studies (for reviews of utility analysis, see Bobko et al 1987, Vance & Colella 1990),
and debate still rages concerning the accuracy of $SD_y$ estimates. For example,
Judiesch et al (1992) suggested that supervisory estimates of $SD_y$ are down-
wardly biased, but they also claimed that estimates of the coefficient of variation (i.e. ratio of $SD_y$ to the mean of the performance value distribution) are not
seriously biased and may be preferable to direct $SD_y$ estimates. Becker & Huselid (1992) also suggested that traditional procedures underestimate $SD_y$ and
illustrated the use of organizational productivity indices in estimating utility.

Recent research on the accuracy of $SD_y$ estimates does not yield clear conclusions about which procedure is best or about which type of estimate is most
trustworthy, but it has shed some light on the processes involved in judging the
value of employees. Most notably, estimates of the value of employee performance appear to be strongly related to salary levels. Judiesch et al (1992) noted
that when supervisors are asked to judge the value of an average employee, these
estimates are very close to the average wage for that job. $SD_y$ estimates obtained
from supervisory judgments are typically 40–70% as large as mean salaries. One
possibility is that judgments of the value of employees are themselves based
on salary (Bobko et al 1987). That is, an employee who receives substantial rewards is likely to be judged to be worth more than another who receives lower
rewards. However, Roth et al (1994) found factors other than salary (e.g. output levels, initiative) to be the most critical determinants of perceived worth.

Cesare et al (1994) examined a number of factors that may affect these estimates of the value of an employee to an organization and showed what appears
to be a very global bias. Estimates of the value of employees to the organization appear to be very closely tied to the supervisor's estimate of his or her own
value to the organization (in estimating value of average performer, correlation between self-worth and employee worth is above .90). Thus, while job-
oriented factors such as skills, personal qualities of subordinates, and job characteristics are rated as being important in evaluating worth, evaluations of
one's own worth to the organization may be a critical anchor.

Boudreau et al (1994) suggested that the meaning of utility estimates is often unclear because of a failure to adequately identify and measure the criterion variable $Y$. In particular, these authors noted that the criteria of interest in utility analyses are usually complex and multivariate but that the analyses themselves are usually simple and univariate. Earlier, we noted that discussions of the construct of job performance have broadened considerably, with a general recognition that both core task proficiency and contextual performance represent critical aspects of job performance. To date, few studies of utility have incorporated this perspective. Most studies instead focus almost exclusively on the correlation between tests, intervention, and the like, and measures of core task performance.

Boudreau et al (1994) suggested that very different conclusions about the utility of various tests and interventions might be reached if a broader conception of the performance domain is adopted. Murphy & Shiarella (1996) presented evidence from a simulation study that supports this suggestion. Their study examined the validity and utility of a selection test battery for predicting a multidimensional criterion, using the two-facet model discussed earlier to characterize the criterion space (i.e. job performance is assumed to represent a composite of task and contextual performance). They showed that both validity and utility could vary considerably, depending on the relative emphasis given to individual- versus group-oriented facets of the criterion domain.

Raju et al (1990) and Becker & Huselid (1992) presented alternative approaches for addressing the criterion problem in utility analysis. Raju et al (1990) suggested that the relationship between performance evaluations and an employee's value to the organization is linear, and they presented a method for directly estimating value without any separate estimate of troublesome parameters such as SD$_y$, in effect bypassing the criterion problem. This suggestion has received some criticism (Judiesch et al 1993; for a reply, see Raju et al 1993). Becker & Huselid (1992) took another approach, suggesting that utility analyses should be based on organizational-level indices (e.g. overall firm performance) rather than on unreliable estimates of individual-level performance.

Macan & Highhouse (1994) documented the use of utility analysis by human resource specialists, and noted that the dollar metric favored by researchers in this area is not the only useful one; Vance & Colella (1990) made a similar suggestion. However, Latham & Whyte (1994) cautioned that utility analysis may not be useful or credible to managers. In a carefully designed study, they showed that presenting dollar-value utility estimates could *lower* managers' willingness to adopt an intervention.

The sheer volume of research and debate on the estimation of SD$_y$ might suggest that this is a critically important parameter. There are reasons to believe that it is not. First, as noted above, practitioners do not always use a dollar metric for communicating their utility estimates, and when they do, those figures do not seem convincing or credible to managers. Second, as Murphy & Cleveland (1991, 1995) have noted, the scaling of utility estimates rarely has any impact on actual decisions. For example, if an organization is choosing between two different testing programs, it does not matter if utility estimates are phrased in terms of dollars, units of productivity, or completely arbitrary units. The dollar metric is useful if and only if all costs and benefits of each of the options being considered can be accurately scaled in terms of dollars. Rather than focusing so much attention on the estimation of $SD_y$, we suggest that utility researchers should focus on understanding exactly what $Y$ represents. We expect that future research on utility will feature multivariate rather than univariate models and will take advantage of our growing understanding of the domain of job performance to create more realistic estimates of the impact of tests, interventions, etc, on an organization's effectiveness.

## OBSERVATIONS AND SUMMARY

This review suggests that research on performance evaluation is alive and well in the psychological and management literatures. Our review of recent (and some past) literatures suggests that research is progressing in traditional content areas as well as exploring new ground. Perhaps the most exciting areas of research are the development and elaboration around the notion of contextual aspects of job performance. The notion that job performance is more than just the execution of specific tasks and that it involves a wide variety of organizational activities has important implications for the understanding and measurement of job performance. Such a focus will result in a greater likelihood that performance will be more predictable within job contexts through the use of a larger number of predictor vehicles tapping different constructs. Perhaps a larger trend is the tendency to view performance evaluation in a broader context, in general. One thought here is that ultimately the effects of contextual variables will be observed through their interactions with the rater who ultimately provides an evaluation of performance.

Much progress has been made in terms of delineating broad taxonomies of job performance that cut across most, if not all, jobs. Such a trend will almost surely enhance our understanding of job performance. We note, however, that for practical purposes, organizations will perhaps continue to need more narrow and job-focused measures of performance, often for legal defense purposes as well as to help to provide feedback to employees. It is also true that organizations have very practical needs to limit the costs of measurement and to provide instrumentation that provides for the assessment of performance in terms of broader domains and fluid aspects of performance due to rapidly changing work roles, assignments, etc. The movement toward broader measurement is perhaps consistent with this reality; perhaps there will be more convergence between the research and practitioner domains in the future.

We also find a trend in terms of an increased optimism regarding the use of supervisory ratings and other "subjective" appraisal instruments and formats. There is increased recognition that subjectivity does not automatically translate into rater error or bias and that ratings are most likely valid reflections of true performance and represent a low-cost mechanism for evaluating employees. The notion that performance evaluations and particularly supervisory ratings of performance are biased against racial and gender groups is simply not supported by the empirical data. Such differentials, when exhibited, are typically small and are as likely to be a reflection of true differences as they are to be indications of bias in performance appraisals. This optimism is shared by others as well (e.g. Cardy, as cited in Church 1995).

A similar observation might be made in terms of how contemporary researchers view rater "error"; the trend is not to view such variances and discrepancies as error but true variance that can be traced to a variety of different sources. Thus, such concepts as contrast error, central tendency, halo, etc, which occupied so much research space, are thought to be relatively unimportant, trivial, and due to understandable factors.

We are pleased to see additional progress with regard to utility components of performance estimation, and it is likely that we will see more of this. Efforts to model complex and multidimensional performance patterns that are nonlinear in nature are emerging and will likely receive greater attention in the next few years.

ACKNOWLEDGMENTS

We thank the following individuals for their input and help during the various phases in writing this paper: Paul Sackett, Fred Oswald, Melissa Gruys, Sarah Hustis, Maria Rotundo, Jill Ellingson, Tim Landon, Walter Borman, Frank Landy, George Thornton, Mike Campion, and Jan Cleveland.

> **Visit the _Annual Reviews home page_ at**
> **http://www.AnnualReviews.org.**

## Literature Cited

Anderson N, Herriot P, eds. 1994. _Assessment and Selection in Organizations: Methods and Practice for Recruitment and Appraisal._ New York: Wiley

Antonioni D. 1994. The effects of feedback accountability on upward appraisal ratings. _Pers. Psychol._ 47:349–56

Arvey RD. 1986. General ability in employment: a discussion. _J. Vocat. Behav._ 29:415–20

Arvey RD, Renz G, Watson T. 1997. Individual differences in emotionality as predictors of job performance. In *Research in Personnel and Human Resources Management*, ed. GR Ferris, KM Rowland, Vol. 15. Greenwich, CT: JAI. In press

Arvey RD, Sackett PR. 1993. Fairness in selection: current developments and perspectives. See Schmitt et al 1993, pp. 171–202

Austin JT, Villanova P. 1992. The criterion problem: 1917–1992. *J. Appl. Psychol.* 77(6):836–74

Banks CG, Murphy KR. 1985. Toward narrowing the research-practice gap in performance appraisal. *Pers. Psychol.* 38(2): 335–45

Becker BE, Huselid MA. 1992. Direct estimates of $SD_y$ and the implications for utility analysis. *J. Appl. Psychol.* 77(3): 227–33

Bernardin HJ, Beatty RW. 1984. *Performance Appraisal: Assessing Human Behavior at Work.* Boston: Kent

Bernardin HJ, Hennessey HW Jr, Peyrefitte J. 1995. Age, racial, and gender bias as a function of criterion specificity: a test of expert testimony. *Hum. Resour. Manage. Rev.* 5(1):63–77

Bobko P, Colella A. 1994. Employee reactions to performance standards: a review and research propositions. *Pers. Psychol.* 47(1): 1–29

Bobko P, Karren R, Kerkar SP. 1987. Systematic research needs for understanding supervisory-based estimates of SDy in utility analysis. *Organ. Behav. Hum. Decis. Process.* 40(1):69–95

Bommer WH, Johnson JL, Rich GA, Podsakoff PM, MacKenzie SB. 1995. On the interchangeability of objective and subjective measures of employee performance: a meta-analysis. *Pers. Psychol.* 48(3): 587–605

Borman WC, Brush DH. 1993. More progress toward a taxonomy of managerial performance requirements. *Hum. Perform.* 6(1):1–21

Borman WC, Hanson M, Hedge J. 1997. Personnel selection. *Annu. Rev. Psychol.* 48: 299–337

Borman WC, Motowidlo SJ. 1993. Expanding the criterion domain to include elements of contextual performance. See Schmitt et al 1993, pp. 71–98

Borman WC, White LA, Dorsey DW. 1995. Effects of ratee task performance and interpersonal factors on supervisor and peer performance ratings. *J. Appl. Psychol.* 80(1):168–77

Boudreau JW. 1991. Utility analysis for decisions in human resource management. See Dunnette & Hough 1991, pp. 621–745

Boudreau JW, Sturman MC, Judge TA. 1994. Utility analysis: What are the black boxes, and do they affect decisions? See Anderson & Herriot 1994, pp. 77–96

Bretz RD, Milkovich GT, Read W. 1992. The current state of performance appraisal research and practice: concerns, directions, and implications. *J. Manage.* 18(2):321–52

Brief AP, Motowidlo SJ. 1986. Prosocial organizational behaviors. *Acad. Manage. Rev.* 10:710–25

Brogden HE. 1949. When testing pays off. *Pers. Psychol.* 2:171–83

Campbell JP, Gasser MB, Oswald FL. 1996. The substantive nature of job performance variability. In *Individual Differences and Behavior in Organizations,* ed. KR Murphy, pp. 258–99. San Francisco: Jossey-Bass

Campbell JP, McCloy RA, Oppler SH, Sager CE. 1993. A theory of performance. See Schmitt et al 1993, pp. 35–70

Cardy RL, Dobbins GH. 1994. *Performance Appraisal: Alternative Perspectives.* Cincinnati, OH: Southwest

Cascio WF. 1991. *Costing Human Resources: The Financial Impact of Behavior in Organizations.* Boston: Kent. 3rd ed.

Cascio WF. 1993. Assessing the utility of selection decisions: theoretical and practical considerations. See Schmitt et al 1993, pp. 310–40

Cascio WF. 1995. Whither industrial and organizational psychology in a changing world of work? *Am. Psychol.* 50(11): 928–39

Cascio WF, Bernardin HJ. 1984. Implications of performance appraisal litigation for personnel decisions. *Pers. Psychol.* 34(2): 211–26

Cesare SJ, Blankenship MH, Giuannetto PW. 1994. A dual focus of Sdy estimations: a test of the linearity assumption and multivariate application. *Hum. Perform.* 7(4): 235–55

Chemers MM, Oskamp S, Costanzo MA, eds. 1995. *Diversity in Organizations: New Perspectives for a Changing Workplace.* Thousand Oaks, CA: Sage

Church AH. 1995. Performance appraisal: practical tools or effective measures. *Ind. Organ. Psychol.* 33(2):57–64

Cleveland JN, Murphy KR. 1992. Analyzing performance appraisal as goal-directed behavior. In *Research in Personnel and Human Resources Management,* ed. GR Ferris, KM Rowland, 10:121–85. Greenwich, CT: JAI

Conway JM. 1996. Analysis and design of multitrait-multirater performance appraisal studies. *J. Manage.* 22(1):139–62

Cronbach LJ, Gleser GC. 1965. *Psychological Tests and Personnel Decisions.* Urbana: Univ. Ill. Press. 2nd ed.

Day DV, Silverman SB. 1989. Personality and job performance: evidence of incremental validity. *Pers. Psychol.* 42(1):25–36

Day DV, Sulsky LM. 1995. Effects of frame-of-reference training and information configuration on memory organization and rating accuracy. *J. Appl. Psychol.* 80(1):158–67

De Corte W. 1994. Utility analysis for the one-cohort selection-retention decision with a probationary period. *J. Appl. Psychol.* 79(3):402–11

De Corte W. 1996. Recruitment and retention decisions that maximize the utility of a probationary selection to obtain a fixed quota of successful selectees. *Pers. Psychol.* 49(2):399–428

DeNisi AS. 1997. *A Cognitive Approach to Performance Appraisal: A Program of Research.* London: Routledge. In press

DeNisi AS, Peters LH. 1996. Organization of information in memory and the performance appraisal process: Evidence from the field. *J. Appl. Psychol.* 81(6):717–37

Dickinson TL. 1993. Attitudes about performance appraisal. In *Personnel Selection and Assessment: Individual and Organizational Perspectives,* ed. H Schuler, JL Farr, M Smith, pp. 141–62. Hillsdale, NJ: Erlbaum

DuBois CL, Sackett PR, Zedeck S, Fogli L. 1993. Further exploration of typical and maximum performance criteria: definitional issues, prediction, and white-black differences. *J. Appl. Psychol.* 78(2):205–11

Dunnette MD, Hough LM, eds. 1991. *Handbook of Industrial and Organizational Psychology,* Vol. 2. Palo Alto, CA: Consult. Psychol. Press. 2nd ed.

Dunnette MD, Hough LM, eds. 1992. *Handbook of Industrial and Organizational Psychology,* Vol. 3. Palo Alto, CA: Consult. Psychol. Press. 2nd ed.

Feild HS, Holley WH. 1982. The relationship of performance appraisal system characteristics to verdicts in selected employment discrimination cases. *Acad. Manage. J.* 25(2):392–406

Feldman JM. 1981. Beyond attribution theory: cognitive processes in performance appraisal. *J. Appl. Psychol.* 66(2):127–48

Ferris GR, Judge TA, Rowland KM, Fitzgibbons DE. 1994. Subordinate influence and the performance evaluation process: test of a model. *Organ. Behav. Hum. Decis. Process.* 58:101–35

Fletcher C. 1994. Performance appraisal in context: organizational changes and their impact on practice. See Anderson & Herriot 1994, pp. 41–55

Fletcher C. 1995. New directions for performance appraisal: some findings and observations. *Int. J. Select. Assess.* 3(3):191–201

Folger R, Konovsky MA, Cropanzano R. 1992. A due process metaphor for performance appraisal. In *Research in Organizational Behavior,* ed. BM Staw, LL Cummings, 14:129–77. Greenwich, CT: JAI

Ford JK, Kraiger K, Schechtman SL. 1986. Study of race effects in objective indices and subjective evaluations of performance: a meta-analysis of performance criteria. *Psychol. Bull.* 99(3):330–37

Ganzach Y. 1995. Negativity (and positivity) in performance evaluation: three field studies. *J. Appl. Psychol.* 80(4):491–99

George RA, Brief AP. 1992. Feeling good-doing good: a conceptual analysis of the mood at work-organizational spontaneity relationship. *Psychol. Bull.* 112(2):310–29

Gerhart B, Milkovich GT. 1992. Employee compensation: research and practice. See Dunnette & Hough 1992, pp. 481–569

Gottfredson LS. 1991. The evaluation of alternative measures of job performance. In *Performance Assessment for the Workplace, Tech. Issues,* ed. AK Wigdor, BF Green Jr, 2:75–126. Washington, DC: Natl. Acad. Sci.

Guion RM, Gibson WM. 1988. Personnel selection and placement. *Annu. Rev. Psychol.* 37:349–74

Guzzo RA, Dickson MW. 1996. Teams in organizations: recent research on performance and effectiveness. *Annu. Rev. Psychol.* 47:307–38

Harris MM, Smith DE, Champagne D. 1995. A field study of performance appraisal purpose: research- versus administrative-based ratings. *Pers. Psychol.* 48(1):151–60

Harrison DA, Shaffer MA. 1994. Comparative examinations of self-reports and perceived absenteeism norms: wading through Lake Wobegon. *J. Appl. Psychol.* 79(2):240–51

Hedge JW, Borman WC. 1995. Changing conceptions and practices in performance appraisal. In *The Changing Nature of Work,* ed. A Howard, pp. 451–81. San Francisco: Jossey-Bass

Hofmann DA, Jacobs R, Baratta JE. 1993. Dynamic criteria and the measurement of change. *J. Appl. Psychol.* 78(2):194–204

Hunt S. 1996. Generic work behavior: an investigation into the dimensions of entry-level, hourly job performance. *Pers. Psychol.* 49(1):51–83

Ilgen DR, Barnes-Farrell JL, McKellin DB. 1993. Performance appraisal process research in the 1980s: What has it contributed to appraisals in use? *Organ. Behav. Hum. Decis. Process.* 54(3):321–68

Ilgen DR, Hollenbeck JR. 1991. The structure of work: job design and roles. See Dunnette & Hough 1991, pp. 165–207

Jackson SE, Ruderman MN. 1995. *Diversity in Work Teams: Research Paradigms for a Changing Workplace.* Washington, DC: Am. Psychol. Assoc.

Johns G. 1994. How often were you absent? A review of the use of self-reported absence data. *J. Appl. Psychol.* 79(4):574–91

Jourden FJ, Heath C. 1996. The evaluation gap in performance perceptions: illusory perceptions of groups and individuals. *J. Appl. Psychol.* 81(4):369–79

Judiesch MK, Schmidt FL, Hunter JE. 1993. Has the problem of judgment in utility analysis been solved? *J. Appl. Psychol.* 78(6):903–11

Judiesch MK, Schmidt FL, Mount MK. 1992. Estimates of the dollar value of employee output in utility analyses: an empirical test of two theories. *J. Appl. Psychol.* 77(3): 234–50

Kane JS. 1994. A model of volitional rating behavior. *Hum. Resour. Manage. Rev.* 4(3):83–310

Kinicki AJ, Hom PW, Trost MR, Wade KJ. 1995. Effects of category prototypes on performance-rating accuracy. *J. Appl. Psychol.* 80(3):354–70

Klaas BS, McClendon JA. 1996. To lead, lag, or match: estimating the financial impact of pay level policies. *Pers. Psychol.* 49(1): 121–41

Kleiman LS, Durham RS. 1981. Performance appraisal, promotion, and the courts: a critical review. *Pers. Psychol.* 34(1): 103–21

Kraiger K, Ford JK. 1985. A meta-analysis of ratee race effects in performance ratings. *J. Appl. Psychol.* 70(1):56–65

Kulick CT, Ambrose ML. 1993. Category-based and feature-based processes in performance appraisal: integrating visual and computerized sources of performance data. *J. Appl. Psychol.* 78(5):821–30

Lance CE, LaPointe JA, Stewart AM. 1994. A test of the context dependency of three causal models of halo rater error. *J. Appl. Psychol.* 79(3):332–40

Landy FJ, Farr JL. 1980. Performance rating. *Psychol. Bull.* 87(1):72–107

Landy FJ, Farr JL. 1983. *The Measurement of Work Performance: Methods, Theory, and Applications.* New York: Academic

Landy FJ, Shankster LJ, Kohler SS. 1994. Personnel selection and placement. *Annu. Rev. Psychol.* 45:261–96

Latham GP, Skarlicki D, Irvine D, Siegel JP. 1993. The increasing importance of performance appraisals to employee effectiveness in organizational settings in North America. *Int. Rev. Ind. Organ. Psychol.* 8:87–132

Latham GP, Whyte G. 1994. The futility of utility analysis. *Pers. Psychol.* 47(10): 31–46

Law KS, Myors B. 1993. Cutoff scores that maximize the total utility of a selection program: Comment on Martin and Raju's (1992) procedure. *J. Appl. Psychol.* 78(5): 736–40

Lawler EE III. 1990. *Strategic Pay.* San Francisco: Jossey-Bass

Lawler EE III, Jenkins GD Jr. 1992. Strategic reward systems. See Dunnette & Hough 1992, pp. 1009–55

London M, Smither JW. 1995. Can multi-source feedback change perceptions of goal accomplishment, self-evaluations, and performance-related outcomes? Theory-based applications and directions for research. *Pers. Psychol.* 48(4):803–39

Macan TH, Highhouse S. 1994. Communicating the utility of human resource activities: a survey of I/O and HR professionals. *J. Bus. Psychol.* 8(4):425–36

Martell RF, Borg MR. 1993. A comparison of the behavioral rating accuracy of groups and individuals. *J. Appl. Psychol.* 78(1): 43–50

Martin SL, Raju NS. 1992. Determining cutoff scores that optimize utility: a recognition of recruiting costs. *J. Appl. Psychol.* 77(1): 15–23

Maurer TJ, Palmer JK, Ashe DK. 1993. Diaries, checklists, evaluations and contrast effects in measurement of behavior. *J. Appl. Psychol.* 78(2):226–31

McCloy RA, Campbell JP, Cudeck R. 1994. A confirmatory test of a model of performance determinants. *J. Appl. Psychol.* 79(4): 493–505

McEvoy GM, Cascio WF. 1989. Cumulative evidence of the relationship between employee age and job performance. *J. Appl. Psychol.* 74(1):11–17

McHenry JJ, Hough LM, Toquam JL, Hanson MA, Ashworth S. 1990. Project A validity results: the relationship between predictor and criterion domains. *Pers. Psychol.* 43(2):335–55

McIntyre MD, James LR. 1995. The inconsistency with which raters weight and combine information across targets. *Hum. Perform.* 8(2):95–111

McIntyre RM, Salas E. 1995. Measuring and managing for team performance: emerging principles from complex environments. In *Team Effectiveness and Decision Making in Organizations,* ed. R Guzzo, E Salas, pp. 9–45. San Francisco: Jossey-Bass

Mero NP, Motowidlo SJ. 1995. Effects of rater accountability on the accuracy and the favorability of performance ratings. *J. Appl. Psychol.* 80(4):517–24

Motowidlo SJ, Van Scotter JR. 1994. Evidence that task performance should be distinguished from contextual performance. *J. Appl. Psychol.* 79(4):475–80

Murphy KR. 1986. When your top choice turns you down: Effect of rejected offers on the utility of selection tests. *Psychol. Bull.* 99(1):133–38

Murphy KR, Cleveland JN. 1991. *Performance Appraisal: An Organizational Perspective.* Needham Heights, MA: Allyn & Bacon

Murphy KR, Cleveland JN. 1995. *Understanding Performance Appraisal: Social, Organizational and Goal-Based Perspectives.* Thousand Oaks, CA: Sage

Murphy KR, Jako RA, Anhalt RL. 1993. Nature and consequences of halo error: a critical analysis. *J. Appl. Psychol.* 78(2):218–25

Murphy K, Shiarella A. 1996. *Estimating the validity and utility of selection test batteries in relation to multi-attribute criteria.* Presented at Annu. Meet. Soc. Ind. Organ. Psychol., 11th, San Diego

Nilsen D, Campbell DP. 1993. Self-observer rating discrepancies: Once an overrater, always an overrater? *Hum. Resour. Manage.* 32(2/3):265–81

Oppler SH, Campbell JP, Pulakos ED, Borman WC. 1992. Three approaches to the investigation of subgroup bias in performance measurement: review, results, and conclusions. *J. Appl. Psychol.* 77(2):201–17

Organ DW. 1988. *Organizational Citizenship Behavior: The Good Soldier Syndrome.* Lexington, MA: Lexington

Prendergast C, Topel RH. 1996. Favoritism in organizations. *J. Polit. Econ.* 104(5):958–78

Pulakos ED, Schmitt N, Chan D. 1996. Models of job performance ratings: an exami-

nation of ratee race, ratee gender, and rater level effects. *Hum. Perform.* 9:103–19

Pulakos ED, White LA, Oppler SH, Borman WC. 1989. Examination of race and sex effects on performance ratings. *J. Appl. Psychol.* 74(5):770–80

Raju NS, Burke MJ, Maurer TJ. 1995. A note on direct range restriction corrections in utility analysis. *Pers. Psychol.* 48(1):143–49

Raju NS, Burke MJ, Normand J. 1990. A new approach for utility analysis. *J. Appl. Psychol.* 75(1):3–12

Raju NS, Burke MJ, Normand J, Lezotte DV. 1993. What would be if what is wasn't? Rejoinder to Judiesch, Schmidt, and Hunter (1993). *J. Appl. Psychol.* 78(6):912–16

Robbins TL, DeNisi AS. 1994. A closer look at interpersonal affect as a distinct influence on cognitive processing in performance appraisal *J. Appl. Psychol.* 79(3):341–53

Roth PL, Pritchard RD, Stout JD, Brown SH. 1994. Estimating the impact of variable costs on $SD_y$ in complex situations. *J. Bus. Psychol.* 8(4):437–54

Rothstein MG, Paunonen SV, Rush JC, King GA. 1994. Personality and cognitive ability predictors of performance in graduate business school. *J. Educ. Psychol.* 86(4):516–30

Ryan AM, Daum D, Bauman T, Grisez M, Mattimore K, et al. 1995. Direct, indirect, and controlled observation and rating accuracy. *J. Appl. Psychol.* 80(6):664–70

Saavedra R, Kwun SK. 1993. Peer evaluation in self-managing work groups. *J. Appl. Psychol.* 78(3):450–62

Sackett PR, DuBois CL. 1991. Rater-ratee race effects on performance evaluation: challenging meta-analytic conclusions. *J. Appl. Psychol.* 76(6):873–77

Sackett PR, Zedeck S, Fogli L. 1988. Relations between measures of typical and maximum job performance. *J. Appl. Psychol.* 73(3):482–86

Sanchez JI, De La Torre P. 1996. A second look at the relationship between rating and behavioral accuracy in performance appraisal. *J. Appl. Psychol.* 81(1):3–10

Schmidt FL. 1993. Personnel psychology at the cutting edge. See Schmitt et al 1993, pp. 497–515

Schmidt FL, Hunter JE, McKenzie RC, Muldrow TW. 1979. Impact of valid selection procedures on work-force productivity. *J. Appl. Psychol.* 64(6):609–26

Schmidt FL, Hunter JE, Pearlman K. 1981. Task differences as moderators of aptitude test validity in selection: a red herring. *J. Appl. Psychol.* 66(5):166–85

Schmitt N, Borman WC, Associates, eds. 1993. *Personnel Selection in Organizations.* San Francisco: Jossey-Bass

Schrader BW, Steiner DD. 1996. Common comparison standards: an approach to improving agreement between self and supervisory performance ratings. *J. Appl. Psychol.* 81(6):813–20

Stamoulis DT, Hauenstein NMA. 1993. Rater training and rating accuracy: training for dimensional accuracy versus training for ratee differentiation. *J. Appl. Psychol.* 78(6):994–1003

Stone BM, Turner KL, Wiggins VL, Looper LT. 1996. Measuring airman job performance using occupational survey data. *Mil. Psychol.* 8(3):143–60

Sumer HC, Knight PA. 1996. Assimilation and contrast effects in performance ratings: effects of rating the previous performance on rating subsequent performance. *J. Appl. Psychol.* 81(4):436–42

Taylor MS, Tracy KB, Renard MK, Harrison JK, Carroll SJ. 1995. Due process in performance appraisal: a quasi-experiment in procedural justice. *Adm. Sci. Q.* 40:495–523

Tornow WW. 1993. Perceptions or reality? Is multi-perspective measurement a means or an end? *Hum. Resour. Manage.* 32:2211–29

Vance RJ, Colella A. 1990. The utility of utility analysis. *Hum. Perform.* 3(2):123–39

Vance RJ, MacCallum RC, Coovert MD, Hedge JW. 1988. Construct validity of multiple job performance measures using confirmatory factor analysis. *J. Appl. Psychol.* 73(1):74–80

Van Scotter JR, Motowidlo SJ. 1996. Interpersonal facilitation and job dedication as separate facets of contextual performance. *J. Appl. Psychol.* 81(5):525–31

Van Velsor E, Taylor S, Leslie JB. 1993. An examination of the relationships among self-perception accuracy, self-awareness, gender, and leader effectiveness. *Hum. Resour. Manage.* 32(2&3):249–63

Varma A, DeNisi AS, Peters LH. 1996. Interpersonal affect and performance appraisal: a field study. *Pers. Psychol.* 49(2):341–60

Viswesvaran C. 1996. *Modeling job performance: Is there a general factor?* Presented at Annu. Meet. Soc. Ind. Organ. Psychol., 11th, San Diego

Viswesvaran C, Ones DS, Schmidt FL. 1996.

Comparative analysis of the reliability of job performance ratings. *J. Appl. Psychol.* 81(5):557–74

Waldman DA. 1994a. Contributions of total quality management to the theory of work performance. *Acad. Manage. Rev.* 19:510–36

Waldman DA. 1994b. Designing performance management systems for total quality implementation. *J. Organ. Change* 7(2):31–44

Waldman DA, Avolio BJ. 1986. A meta-analysis of age differences in job performance. *J. Appl. Psychol.* 71(1):33–38

Waldman DA, Spangler WD. 1989. Putting together the pieces: a closer look at the determinants of job performance. *Hum. Perform.* 2(1):29–59

Werner JM. 1994. Dimensions that make a difference: examining the impact of in-role and extrarole behaviors on supervisory ratings. *J. Appl. Psychol.* 79(1):98–107

Wigdor AK, Green BF Jr, eds. 1991. *Performance Assessment for the Workplace,* Vols. 1, 2. Washington, DC: Natl. Acad. Sci.

Woehr DJ. 1994. Understanding frame-of-reference training: the impact of training on the recall of performance information. *J. Appl. Psychol.* 79(4):525–34

Woehr DJ, Feldman J. 1993. Processing objective and question order effects on the causal relation between memory and judgment in performance appraisal: the tip of the iceberg. *J. Appl. Psychol.* 78(2):232–41

Woehr DJ, Huffcutt AI. 1994. Rater training for performance appraisal: a quantitative review. *J. Occup. Organ. Psychol.* 67:189–205

Woehr DJ, Roch SG. 1996. Context effects in performance evaluation: the impact of ratee sex and performance level on performance ratings and behavioral recall. *Organ. Behav. Hum. Decis. Process.* 66(1):31–41

Yammarino FJ, Atwater LE. 1993. Understanding self-perception accuracy: implications for human resource management. *Hum. Resour. Manage.* 32(2&3):231–48

Yang H, Sackett PR, Arvey RD. 1996. Statistical power and cost in training evaluation: some new considerations. *Pers. Psychol.* 49(3):651–68

Yu J, Murphy KR. 1993. Modesty bias in self-ratings of performance: a test of the cultural relativity hypothesis. *Pers. Psychol.* 46(2):357–63

*Annu. Rev. Psychol. 1998. 49:169–97*

# PSYCHOLOGY AND THE STUDY OF MARITAL PROCESSES

## John Mordechai Gottman

Department of Psychology, University of Washington, Seattle, Washington 98195;
e-mail: johng@u.washington.edu

KEY WORDS: marriage, relationships, divorce, children, sex

---

### ABSTRACT

The divorce rate in the United States is extremely high. It is estimated that between 50% and 67% of first marriages end in divorce. For second marriages, failure rates are even higher. There are strong negative consequences to separation and divorce on the mental and physical health of both spouses, including increased risk for psychopathology, increased rates of automobile accidents, and increased incidence of physical illness, suicide, violence, homicide, significant immunosuppression, and mortality from diseases. In children, marital distress, conflict, and disruption are associated with depression, withdrawal, poor social competence, health problems, poor academic performance, and a variety of conduct-related difficulties. Though intervention techniques might be expected to reduce these grim statistics, our best scholars have concluded that marital therapy is at a practical and theoretical impasse. This article discusses the progress of research on the study of marriage.

---

## CONTENTS

169

0066-4308/98/0201-0169$08.00

# WHY STUDY MARRIAGE?

The divorce rate remains extremely high in the United States. Current estimates of the chances of first marriages ending in divorce range between 50% and 67% (Martin & Bumpass 1989). Failure rates for second marriages are about 10% higher than for first marriages.

We now know that separation and divorce have strong negative consequences for the mental and physical health of both spouses. These negative effects include increased risk for psychopathology; increased rates of automobile accidents including fatalities; and increased incidence of physical illness, suicide, violence, homicide, significant immunosuppression, and mortality from diseases (for a review, see Bloom et al 1978, Burman & Margolin 1992). Marital distress, conflict, and disruption are also associated with a wide range of deleterious effects on children, including depression, withdrawal, poor social competence, health problems, poor academic performance, and a variety of conduct-related difficulties (Cowan & Cowan 1987, 1990; Cowan et al 1991; Cummings & Davies 1994; Easterbrooks 1987; Easterbrooks & Emde 1988; Emery 1982, 1988; Emery & O'Leary 1982; Forehand et al 1986; Gottman & Katz 1989; Hetherington 1988; Hetherington & Clingempeel 1992; Hetherington et al 1978, 1982; Howes & Markman 1989; Katz & Gottman 1991a,b; Peterson & Zill 1986; Porter & O'Leary 1980; Rutter 1971; Shaw & Emery 1987; Whitehead 1979). There is evidence from two US national probability samples that adults who experienced a divorce as a child are under considerably more stress than those who did not (Glenn & Kramer 1985, Kulka & Weingarten 1979). These adults report less satisfaction with family and friends, greater anxiety, that bad things more frequently happen to them, and that they find it more difficult to cope with life's stresses in general. In a recent report based on the Terman longitudinal study of gifted children (Friedman et al 1995), survival curves show that the combination of one's parents having divorced and one's own divorce reduced longevity by an average of approximately eight years.

Intervention techniques such as marital therapy might be expected to reduce these grim statistics. Our best scholars have concluded that, unfortunately, marital therapy is at a practical and a theoretical impasse (Jacobson & Addis 1993). Outcome results suggest the following. 1. Most couples (75%) report improvement in marital satisfaction immediately following marital therapy. 2. All therapies are about equally effective in this regard, regardless of the "school" of therapy, once replication studies have been done. 3. There is a strange effect that separate "components" of an intervention are often equally effective, and about as effective as the combined treatment; thus, it has proven difficult to build a theory of change based on dismantling a complex intervention. 4. There is a large relapse effect. In general, after long-term follow-up, only between 30% and 50% of couples stay improved. In fact, the relapse data are probably much more grim than these conclusions suggest. As far as we know, long-term follow-up is likely to yield evidence of even greater relapse.

## PSYCHOLOGY'S EARLY YEARS IN STUDYING MARRIAGE

Psychology was a latecomer to the study of marriage. Sociologists had been studying marriages for 35 years before psychologists became interested in the topic, although the first published study on marriage was by a psychologist—Louis Terman—in 1938 (Terman et al 1938). What psychologists initially brought to the study of marriage was the use of observational methods, the design and evaluation of intervention programs, and an unbridled optimism that changing marriages was going to be easy and quick work. These contributions have had an enormous impact on the study of marriage. Psychologists were initially skeptical about studying marriage, in part because personality theory was facing a severe challenge in the 1970s from the work of Walter Mischel. In *Personality and Assessment* (Mischel 1968), Mischel reviewed research on personality and suggested that personality theory had come far short of being able to predict and understand behavior. He concluded that correlations were quite low on the whole, that the field was plagued with common method variance (mostly self-reports predicting self-reports), and that the best predictors of future behavior were past behavior in similar situations. This book was a great stimulus to many researchers. It encouraged a new look at personality measurement, validity, and reliability (Wiggins 1973) and stimulated new kinds of research in personality. It contributed, however, to a pessimistic view that research in interpersonal psychology would have very little payoff. In hindsight, however, this view was wrong. We are in fact learning that much of the order in individual personality exists at the interpersonal level. For example, Patterson (1982), in his conclusion that there is a great deal of consistency across time and situations in aggression, suggested that the aggressive trait should be rethought in interpersonal terms as the aggressive boy's recasting people in his social world to play out dramatic coercive scenes shaped in his family. The same is true of gender differences: They appear to emerge primarily in the context of relationships (Maccoby 1990).

The use of self-report measures, including personality measures, had initially dominated the field of marriage research. Unfortunately, even with the problem of common method variance, the self-report paper-and-pencil personality measures yielded relatively weak correlations of marital satisfaction (Burgess et al 1971). As an example, psychoanalysis initially embraced Winch's complementarity of need theory (Winch 1958), which proposed that happy marriage would be associated with spouses who have complementary needs (such as she needs to dominate and he needs to be dominated). No other theory in this field has ever been as soundly rejected as Winch's. Not until studies asked spouses to fill out questionnaires about their spouse's personality were substantial correlations discovered with marital satisfaction. Unhappily married couples were found to endorse nearly every negative trait as characteristic of their spouses (the negative halo effect), whereas happily married spouses were found to endorse nearly every positive trait as characteristic of their spouses (the positive halo effect) (Nye 1988).

## THE GLOP PROBLEM AND REFUSING TO LIVE WITH GLOP

Bank et al (1990) wrote an important paper subtitled "Living with Glop." Glop refers to high correlations among variables obtained using a common method of measurement, usually with just one reporter. In the marital field, this usually refers to self-report data obtained from a single reporter. The point to be made about glop is an old one. Bank et al noted that reviews by Rutter (1979) and Emery (1982) showed consistent correlations between marital discord and child adjustment problems, but that Emery & O'Leary (1984) pointed out that, in most of these studies, both variables come from one person (usually the mother), who uses self-report measures. It was the experience of Emery & O'Leary and other investigators that the correlations between parents' and teachers' reports of child behaviors were essentially zero. Structural Equations Modeling (SEM) was developed in part to deal with the problem of increasing reliability and validity in measurement of constructs. The SEM methods hark back to a classic paper in measurement by Campbell & Fiske (1959), in which they argued for the use of a multitrait-multimethod matrix. It is quite common to be able to create beautiful SEM models when all the data are collected by the same agent and self-report data are employed. However, once the issue of validity is introduced to the model (just adding the requirement that the data correlate with measurement of the same construct using a different reporter or different method), the models typically fall apart.

In studying marriage, the glop problem is also of great theoretical concern. For example, it is commonly observed that measures of neuroticism are correlated with marital satisfaction (Kurdek 1993). It is, however, difficult to demonstrate that one is really measuring neuroticism rather than distress associated with being unhappily married. It is well known that unhappily married people are more depressed, more anxious, more distressed, less optimistic, and so on. Is the personality measure assessing an enduring trait or a state of wellness, distress, or the current quality of life, which is essentially the same thing that the marital satisfaction measure taps?

The glop problem also occurs when one uses different reporters, as Kelly & Conley (1987) did when they had friends and acquaintances of the couple fill out the personality measures. Clearly, friends are likely to be familiar with the general dysphoria of their unhappily married friends, and they are likely to use the items of the personality tests they are given to report this fact. The conclusion we must reach from these studies is clear: *We should refuse to accept constructs as explanatory if they have not dealt adequately with the glop problem.* It is absolutely critical that any theory of marriage be very careful about how a construct was measured in drawing conclusions. This is an admonition that all studies of marriage employ multiple methods to operationalize constructs.

## THE RELUCTANCE TO OBSERVE COUPLES

Researchers have been reluctant to use systematic observation to study couples, primarily because it is very costly and frustrating. In addition, it takes lots of time and experience to develop a good coding system for marital interaction, and then more time to obtain actual numbers from tapes of the interaction. The researcher must persistently deal with issues of reliability of measurement and problems with defining categories and interobserver reliability drift and decay (Reid 1970). It is so much easier to hand out a packet of questionnaires. In addition, observational measures are often somewhat atheoretical. They usually are designed to exhaustively describe all the behavior within a particular framework that can be observed in a particular situation. In contrast, a questionnaire measures a specific set of constructs, such as egalitarianism in the marriage, paranoid ideation in each partner, and so on. After an observation, it is often unclear what has been measured. Consequently, a purely descriptive, hypothesis-generating phase of research is required to validate the observational measures—an added time-consuming phase that is often skipped. While observational data are often a richer source of hypotheses and are more satisfying to the truly voyeuristic researcher, they also require much more psychometric work to know what one has actually measured.

Moreover, underlying the selection of categories for any observational system are a set of assumptions and some rudimentary theory about what behaviors are important to observe. For example, the Marital Interaction Coding System (MICS) emerged from behavioral marital therapy in which it was considered important to "pinpoint" the marital issue; as such, for example, vague statements of the problem were considered "negative," whereas specific statements were considered "positive." Only recently have Heyman et al (1995) been able to conduct an important study of the structure of the MICS and provide an empirically based guide about what it may measure. They used an archival data set of 995 couples' interactions coded with the Marital Interaction Coding System–IV (MICS). Their factor analysis yielded four factors: hostility, constructive problem discussion, humor, and responsibility discussion.

Furthermore, observational approaches to the study of families in the 1960s by General Systems theorists failed miserably. (The General Systems theorists were a group of researchers and clinicians who began to view the family as an interactive system and to emphasize communication patterns as a potential etiology of psychopathology.) The story of this failure is very dramatic. First, a few maverick psychologists, psychiatrists, and anthropologists in the 1950s observed a strange pattern of interaction between adult schizophrenics and their mothers when they visited them in the hospital. The mothers would greet their children with warmth and then stiff coldness, all packaged in one embrace. The researchers called this the "double bind" theory of schizophrenia (Bateson et al 1956), which maintained that the mother sent a mixed message to her child and that this message put the child in a "double bind," meaning that he was damned if he responded to one part of the message and damned if he responded to the other (contradictory) part of the message. The General Systems theorists thought that the resulting double bind created the emotional withdrawal we have come to associate with schizophrenia. The way out of the double bind was to "meta-communicate," that is, to raise the communication to a new level through commenting on the communication itself.

In 1964, a new journal, *Family Process,* was formed and was dedicated to research on possible family origins of mental disorders. A lot of this research was observational, because the theories focused on communication. Unfortunately, this early quantitative observational research was very weak. Not a single hypothesis of these General Systems theorists received clear support from research, except for the finding that the communication of families with a schizophrenic member was more confusing than that of normal families (see Jacob 1987). This hardly encouraged others to do observational research on families.

In the early 1970s, however, several psychology laboratories did begin to use direct observation to study marital interaction.[1] These investigators were motivated by the idea that marriages could be helped with a behavioral approach that essentially taught couples new social skills for resolving conflict. Because these researchers all came from a behavioral perspective, observational methods were part of the assumed assessment battery. The historical reason for this is worth noting. Early in the intervention research on families with children who had problems, researchers (Robert Weiss, Hyman Hops, JR Patterson) at the Oregon Social Learning Center had noted that even if the children did not improve, the parents' claimed that their children were greatly improved in self-reports of their satisfaction with treatment. These outcomes bred a distrust among researchers of parental reports of child status and a reliance on direct observation. They also decided to design an intervention for marriages in distress and naturally employed observational methods to help distressed couples resolve their conflicts. Thus, from a classic book chapter published by Weiss et al (1973), observational research on marriage was born. The chapter was titled "A Framework for Conceptualizing Marital Conflict: A Technology for Altering It, Some Data for Evaluating It." It was an optimistic attempt to define an entire field in one paper. It did just that.

The first question that marital researchers tackled was the same question raised by Terman: "What makes some marriages happy and others miserable?" Although it continues to be criticized today, marital satisfaction had shown itself to be a venerable criterion variable, and so the search began for the observational correlates of marital satisfaction. There was a faith that an adequate theoretical background would be provided by social learning theory—broadly conceptualized and coupled with principles of communication that had been described by General Systems theorists and by behavior exchange theorists (Thibaut & Kelley 1959). The hope was that by bringing precision to the study of marriage, a superior theory would emerge and lead the way to effective marital therapies. Two paths were simultaneously pursued: the attempt to answer Terman's question with psychological constructs, and the design and evaluation of new therapies.

---

[1] Only a handful of laboratories have consistently included observational methods in their study of couples. These researchers include J Alexander, D Baucom, S Beach, G Birchler, T Bradbury, A Christensen, F Fincham, FJ Floyd, M Fitzpatrick, WC Follette, M Forgatch, H Hops, G Howe, N Jacobson, G Margolin, H Markman, C Notarius, KD O'Leary, J Vincent, R Weiss, C Schaap (in Holland), the Max Planck group (in Germany, including L Schindler, K Hahlweg, and D Revenstorf), HB Vogel, K Halford (in Australia), and P Noller.

## LABORATORY OBSERVATION OF COUPLES START GETTING CONSISTENT RESULTS

### New Methods, New Concepts

In the 1970s, developmental psychology converged methodologically with the psychological study of marriage, and a common approach to the study of social interaction began to emerge. Important works included Lewis & Rosenblum's (1974) *The Effect of the Infant on Its Caregiver,* and RQ Bell's (1968) paper on the bidirectionality of effects between parent and child. These works led researchers to view interaction as sequences of behavior unfolding over time. In 1974, the landmark *Communication, Conflict, and Marriage* appeared; the authors, Raush et al, had followed a cohort of newlyweds completing the transition to parenthood. Raush et al introduced the use of Markov models of sequential interaction and an idea they called "adaptive probabilism." They claimed that marriages and families should be studied as systems, and suggested how this could be done mathematically using "information theory" (Shannon & Weaver 1949) for the study of sequential patterns of interaction, showing that the mathematics were a new approach to interaction. Instead of this systems concept remaining a vague metaphor, or a mathematical procedure for analyzing data, Raush et al realized that it was a whole new way of thinking. It was their intention to introduce the idea of stochastic models, which are uniquely designed for thinking in terms of systems rather than individual behavior. Stochastic models refer to the conceptualization of behavior sequences in terms of probabilities and the reduction of uncertainty in predicting patterns of interaction. (For a systematic development of these concepts and their mathematics, see Bakeman & Gottman 1986, Bakeman & Quera 1995, and Gottman & Roy 1990.)

### New Findings

Because of space limitations, only a sampler, some general conclusions, and a flavor of the findings are presented. Focusing on studies that included some sequential analyses of the data, this review is restricted to the research of Weiss (Oregon), Raush (Massachusetts), Gottman (Washington), Schapp (Holland), Ting-Toomey (New Jersey), the Max Planck group (Revenstorf, Hahlweg, Schindler, and Vogel in Munich), and Fitzpatrick (Wisconsin). What were the results of various laboratories that investigated the Terman question, and in particular, what were the results of sequential analyses?

Of the many studies that have observed marital interaction, few have employed sequential analyses. There are only two such studies that use the MICS. Margolin & Wampold (1981) reported the results of interaction with 39 couples, combined from two studies conducted in Eugene, Oregon, and Santa Barbara, California. Codes were collapsed into three global categories: positive (problem-solving, verbal and nonverbal positive), negative (verbal and nonverbal negative), and neutral. Distressed couples showed negative reciprocity through Lag 2, whereas nondistressed couples did not demonstrate this effect to any significant extent. For positive reciprocity, Margolin and Wampold found that, "whereas both groups evidenced positive reciprocity through Lag 2, this pattern appears to continue even into Lag 3 for distressed couples" (p. 559). Thus, reciprocating positive acts were more likely between distressed than for nondistressed couples. Gottman (1979) had reported similar results, suggesting that distressed couples showed greater rigidity and interactional structure than nondistressed couples.

Margolin & Wampold also defined a sequence called "negative reactivity," which involves a positive response to a negative antecedent by one's spouse. They proposed that there is a suppression of positivity following a negative antecedent in distressed couples. They found this for all four lags for distressed couples, but they found no evidence for this suppression of positivity by negativity for any lag for nondistressed couples.

Revenstorf et al (1980), studying 20 German couples, collapsed the MICS categories into six summary codes. These codes were positive reaction, negative reaction, problem solution, problem description, neutral reaction, and filler; interrupts, disagrees, negative solution, and commands were considered negative. They employed both lag sequential analyses that allowed them to examine sequences out for four lags and the multivariate information theory that Raush et al (1974) had employed. From the multivariate information analysis, Revenstorf et al (p. 103) concluded that

> In problem discussions distressed couples respond differently from nondistressed couples....In particular [distressed couples] are more negative and less positive following positive (+) and negative (−) reactions. At the same time they are more negative and more positive, that is more emotional, following problem descriptions (P) of the spouse. Above all distressed couples are more negative and less positive in general than nondistressed couples.

They also found 17 sequences that differentiated the two groups. There is some inconsistency in the group differences for sequences with similar names (e.g. "reconciliation"), so I summarize only their clearest results. For what might be called constructive interaction sequences, they found that nondistressed couples engaged in more validation sequences (problem description followed by positivity) and positive reciprocity sequences (positive followed by positivity). On the destructive side, they found that distressed couples engaged in more devaluation sequences (negative follows positive), negative continuance sequences (which they called "fighting on" or "fighting back" in three-chain sequences), and negative startup sequences (which they called "yes-butting," meaning that somewhere in the four-chain sequence, negative follows positive) than nondistressed couples. After an analysis of the sequences following a problem description, Revenstorf et al (p. 107) concluded that

> It appears as if the distressed couples would interact like nondistressed—had they only higher positive response rates following a problem description of the spouse. And vice versa. The nondistressed would react equally detrimentally as the distressed—were they to respond more negatively to problem description of their spouse. The way they handle problems [problem description statements] seems to be the critical issue—not the sheer number of problems stated.

Revenstorf et al also continued their sequential analyses for five lags and found that these reciprocity differences held across lags. They wrote (p. 109):

> In summary, different patterns of response tendencies emerge for distressed and nondistressed couples. After a positive statement the partner continues to reciprocate it positively in nondistressed, whereas no immediate response is likely in distressed couples. After a negative statement no immediate response is most likely in nondistressed, whereas in distressed couples both partners continue to reciprocate negatively. A problem description finally is repeatedly followed by a positive response in nondistressed. In distressed couples, negative statements follow repeatedly.

Revenstorf et al then described four types of sequences. The first type of sequence is continued negativity (they called it "distancing"). This sequence measures the extent to which negativity becomes an absorbing state. The second sequence type was positive reciprocity (which they called "attraction"). This sequence measures the extent to which positivity becomes an absorbing state. The third sequence consisted of alternating problem descriptions and negativity (they called it "problem escalation"). The fourth type of sequence consists of validation sequences—sequences of alternating problem descriptions and positive responses to them (they called it "problem acceptance"). In most instances (e.g. for positive reciprocity), the differences between the groups were not very great. The evidence, however, was very clear that negativity represented an absorbing state for distressed couples but not for nondistressed couples. By Lag 2, nondistressed couples begin to escape from the negativity, but distressed couples could not escape. Graphs of the data provide dramatic information of group differences reflected in sequential patterning of MICS codes. The consistent findings in these two studies and other studies that have employed sequential analysis (Fitzpatrick 1988, Gottman 1979, Raush et al 1974, Schaap 1982, Ting-Toomey 1982; for a review, see Gottman 1994) are that (*a*) unhappily married couples appear to engage in long chains of re-ciprocated negativity, and (*b*) there is a climate of agreement created in the in-teraction of happily married couples.

Most of these studies collapsed their codes into a global positive or nega-tive. However, using a new method developed by Sackett (see Bakeman & Gottman 1986) called "lag sequential analysis," Gottman, Notarius, and Mark-man (see Gottman 1979) examined sequences using specific codes of their Couples Interaction Scoring System (CISS). These analyses revealed the anat-omy of distressed and nondistressed marital interaction, both in the laboratory and at home. In a series of studies that combined observation with behavior ex-change principles (using a "talk table" device in which spouses rated each ex-change), and individual assessments of social competence, Gottman and his students developed an empirically based intervention, which they evaluated. In three separate studies significant results were obtained on marital satisfac-tion and interaction (Gottman 1979).

## NEGATIVE AFFECT RECIPROCITY AS THE FAILURE OF REPAIR ATTEMPTS

The basic sequential result that held across laboratories was that greater recip-rocated negative affective interaction is an absorbing state for dissatisfied cou-ples. This result has profound implications for interaction process. The result means that negativity becomes an absorbing state for dissatisfied couples, that is, it is a state that is difficult to exit once entered.

We need to know two additional facts about marital interaction to under-stand the implications of this finding. Vincent et al (1979) studied the interac-tion of distressed and nondistressed couples in the Inventory of Marital Con-flicts, a problem-solving task. The two groups could be discriminated from each other on five out of six MICS summary codes, positive problem solving, and verbal and nonverbal positive and negative codes. Vincent et al then asked the couples to try either to fake good or to fake bad during the next 10 minutes. Both groups of couples were unable to fake their nonverbal behaviors. Hence, nonverbal behavior may be a better discriminator of distressed and nondis-tressed groups than verbal behavior alone. Second, Gottman (1979) found that most couples express the most negative affect during the middle arguing phase of the conflict resolution, and their major attempts at repair of the interaction are usually delivered in this phase as well. Attempts at interaction repair are of-ten delivered with negative affect. For example, statements like "Stop inter-rupting me!" or "We're getting off the subject" may be accompanied by irrita-tion, tension, sadness, or some other form of distress. Thus, repair attempts usually have two components, a negative affective nonverbal component and a metacommunicative content component attempting to repair the interaction.

The implication of greater negativity being an absorbing state for dissatisfied couples is that they may attend primarily to the negative affect component of repair attempts, whereas satisfied couples attend primarily to the repair component. Thus, it can be concluded that repair processes do work very well in dissatisfied marriages. Instead, what predominates in dissatisfied couples' attempts to use these social processes is the negative affect. Hence, in various sequential analyses of the stream of behavior, if one spouse attempts a repair mechanism with negative affect, the other spouse is more likely to respond to the negative affect component with reciprocated negative affect in a dissatisfied marriage than in a satisfied one. The usual social processes present during conflict that repair the interaction (such as metacommunication) do not work in unhappy marriages. These processes are the mechanisms used by satisfied couples for exiting a negative state (Gottman 1979). They include metacommunication, feeling probes that explore feelings, information exchange, social comparison, humor, distraction, gossip, finding areas of common ground, and appeals to basic philosophy and expectations in the marriage. What goes hand in glove with this phenomena is a constriction of social processes in distressed couples. The constriction of available social processes is the fascinating structural dynamic that maintains the absorbing state.

How does this constriction work? For example, assume that a message has two parts, one positive and one negative, such as "Stop interrupting me," which is an attempt to repair the interaction, but may have also been said with some irritation. In a happy marriage, there is a greater probability that the listener will focus on the repair component of the message and respond by saying, "Sorry, what were you saying?" In an unhappy marriage, there is a greater probability that the listener will respond only to the irritation in the message and say something like, "I wouldn't have to interrupt if I could get a word in edgewise." In this case the attempted repair mechanism does not work. The response to the negativity now continues for long chains of reciprocated negative affect in dissatisfied marriages. Negativity as an absorbing state implies that all these social processes have less of a chance of working because what people attend to, and respond to, is the negativity. An interesting side effect of this analysis is that the interactions of dissatisfied couples show a higher degree of interaction structure, more predictability of one spouse's behaviors from those of the other, and less statistical independence than is found in the interactions of satisfied couples. The interaction of happy married couples is more random than that of unhappily married couples. This is precisely what Raush et al (1974) predicted. One finding that may be related to this phenomenon is that greater structure may come to pervade positive as well as negative interaction. This latter result is not as consistently found across laboratories, but this may not be so much a failure to replicate as the inconsistency across laboratories in conceptualizing, generating, and measuring "positivity" and in the lack of studies that do sequential analyses of data.

# WHAT IS DYSFUNCTIONAL IN AILING MARRIAGES?

Research on the correlates of marital satisfaction represents only one way to address the Terman question. The second approach is to ask the longitudinal question about which marital interaction patterns and other variables predict marital stability and eventual happiness. There have been many suggestions about what is dysfunctional about ailing marriages. For example, Lederer & Jackson's (1968) book *Mirages of Marriage* spelled out what is dysfunctional about ailing marriages and how therapists should go about fixing them. They said that the sine qua non of marriage was the quid pro quo, that in good marriages there was a reciprocal exchange of positive behaviors, and that in bad marriages there was for various reasons (like romanticism) the breakdown of these agreements, these contracts. This point of view was consistent with an economically based behavior exchange theory recommended 10 years earlier by Thibaut & Kelly. (Romanticism, they argued, sets up false expectations that lead to the quid pro quo being violated.) The Lederer & Jackson book had an enormous impact. In marital behavior therapy, for example, it led to the method of contingency contracting.

The claim about quid pro quo turned out to be totally wrong (Murstein et al 1977). Not only were happy marriages not characterized by the quid pro quo, but it actually characterized unhappy marriages! This erroneous and untested assumption not only spawned a new marital therapy, even when it was confirmed it continued on as a major ingredient of marital therapy.

Marital therapy must be guided by a theory of both what is dysfunctional in ailing marriages and what is functional in marriages that are working. This knowledge helps spell out the objectives of the treatment and the assessment of the marriage, although not necessarily the methods for producing change. Two important hypotheses about what is dysfunctional in ailing marriages were suggested by Rausch et al (1974). In their book, they raised two critical questions. The first was why in some marriages do minor conflicts "escalate far beyond their apparent triviality" (p. 2). Rausch et al's question was also more broadly about what makes conflict constructive or destructive in marriages. Rausch et al gave the example of a couple given the task of deciding about which television show to watch. They were impressed by the fact that many couples got quite involved with the role-play improvisations. One wife became extremely upset and said, "Damn it, you always watch what you want to see. You're always drinking beer and watching football. Nothing else seems important to you, especially my wishes." The seemingly small discussion of which TV show to watch had led her to escalate and to express her complete exasperation with her partner and with the marriage. Raush et al's second question was whether the avoidance of conflict in marriage was functional or dysfunctional. They concluded that conflict avoidance is dysfunctional and that conflict or bickering about trivial issues is also dysfunctional (indicative of what they called "symbolic conflict").

Many other hypotheses have been proposed, most of them stated as if they were, without much empirical backing. In addition to the two proposed by Raush, a baker's dozen have been suggested: 1. a dominance structure is dysfunctional (Gottman 1979); 2. the lack of a dominance structure is dysfunctional (Kolb & Straus 1974); 3. a "demand-withdraw" pattern or a "pursuer-distancer" pattern is dysfunctional (e.g. Heavey et al 1995); 4. not being able to change each other's behavior is dysfunctional (Jacobson & Margolin 1979); 5. a good marriage is characterized by acceptance, in which spouses accept each other as they are and do not try to get behavior change (Jacobson & Christensen 1997); 6. poor problem solving is dysfunctional (Jacobson 1989); 7. "mindreading," or attributing motives or behaviors to one's spouse is dysfunctional (Watzlawick et al 1967); 8. not metacommunicating is dysfunctional (Bateson et al 1956); 9. need complementarity is functional (Winch 1958); 10. healthy marriage is not possible unless neuroses in one's primary family are resolved (Scharff & Scharff 1991); 11. most marital conflict is projection (Meissner 1978); first the marriage needs to become "conscious" (Hendrix 1988); 12. marriages start off happy, but over time reinforcement erosion occurs and that is the source of marital dysfunction (Jacobson & Margolin 1979); 13. only equalitarian marriage is functional (Schwartz 1994).

The questions we must ask are, first, are any of these contentions supportable, and second, are these results fundamental or epiphenomenal? It will be important to consider this latter question when discussing the construction of theory. As to the first question, the two primary approaches taken to date involve finding the correlates of marital satisfaction and the predictors of long-term stability and satisfaction.

## The Criterion of Correlates with Marital Satisfaction

Gottman (1979) defined a dominance structure as asymmetry in predictability of one partner's behavior compared with the other's and used time-series analysis to assess its existence. Distressed couples had significantly greater asymmetry in predictability, with husbands being dominant. A study of 122 societies by Gray (1984) showed that female power is related to more positive sexual relations; however, a review by Gray & Burks (1983) concluded that wife-dominant marriages are the least happy. However, because of the difficulty of operationalizing dominance and the lack of agreement among various measures of power and dominance (Rushe 1996), it cannot be concluded that the lack of a dominance structure is dysfunctional. The "demand-withdraw" pattern or a "pursuer-distancer" pattern as characteristic of unhappy marriage has been replicated a number of times (Gottman & Levenson 1988, Heavey et al 1995). In this pattern, it is the wife who raises and pursues the issues and the husband who attempts to avoid the discussion and tends to withdraw. A few results must qualify this conclusion. First, the pattern is also, to some degree, characteristic of happy marriages. Second, the pattern depends to some degree on whether the issue is the husband's or the wife's (Christensen & Heavey 1990). To date, there has been no research on the hypothesis that not being able to change each other's behavior is dysfunctional or that a good marriage is characterized by acceptance in which spouses accept one another as they are and do not try to get behavior change. The hypothesis that poor problem solving is dysfunctional has yet to be tested independent of other processes of communication, such as negative affect. In therapeutic interventions, the two aspects of interaction are also confounded. Mindreading is a frequent way that couples begin discussing an event or probing feelings (Gottman 1979). There is no evidence that mindreading by itself is dysfunctional. However, a potentially related process of negative trait attributions to one's spouse is characteristic of unhappily married couples. The simple leap from mindreading to negative trait attributions is manifested in phrases such as "You always" or "You never." The genesis of the transformation from simple, specific complaints to these global complaints is unknown and unexplored, but Fincham & Bradbury (1992) offered a clue when they reported that attributions of responsibility were correlated with the amount of anger displayed by wives during a problem-solving interaction and the amount of whining by both husbands and wives. There is no evidence that not metacommunicating is dysfunctional; Gottman (1979) found that the amount of metacommunication was the same for happily and unhappily married couples. However, sequential analyses showed that happily married couples used short chains of metacommunication often with agreement in the chain, whereas unhappily married couples used reciprocated metacommunication with metacommunication. This latter sequence shows that metacommunication in distressed couples was an ineffective repair technique. There has been little support for the other hypotheses of what is dysfunctional in ailing marriages.

## The Longitudinal Criterion: Divorce Prediction Research

Gottman (1994) reported that there were three types of stable couples. One type of stable couple, called "volatile," was very much like Raush's bickering couple, another type of stable couple was very much like Raush's conflict avoiding couples, while a third type of stable couple, called "validators," was like Raush's harmonious couples. That is, all three types of couples Raush et al had identified turned out to be stable. The three types of couples differed most dramatically in the amount and timing of persuasion attempts: Volatile couples had the most persuasion attempts and began them almost immediately; validators waited to begin their persuasion attempts until the middle of the conversation; and conflict avoiders avoided all persuasion attempts. The three types of couples also differed in how emotionally expressive they were, with volatile couples highest, validators intermediate, and avoiders lowest in emotionality. The three stable types of couples differed from couples on a trajectory toward divorce in many ways. First, using a balance theory of marriage, Gottman (1994) reported that the ratio of positive to negative codes during the conflict discussion was about 5.0 for the three types of stable marriages, while it was 0.8 for the unstable marriage. Second, couples headed for divorce were high on four behaviors that Gottman (1994) called the "Four Horsemen of the Apocalypse"; they are criticism, defensiveness, contempt, and stonewalling (or listener withdrawal). Consistent with the demand-withdraw pattern, women were significantly more likely than men to criticize, whereas men were more likely than women to stonewall.

## WHAT WE HAVE LEARNED: THE PSYCHOLOGY OF MARRIAGE

### The View from Observing

Only a few patterns seem to be consistently characteristic of ailing marriages. The first is negative affect reciprocity, which this review has suggested is a result of the failure of repair processes. Second is the demand-withdraw pattern. Third is a greater amount of negative than positive behaviors. Fourth is the presence of particular forms of negativity, namely criticism, contempt, defensiveness, and stonewalling.

### The View from Cognitive Psychology

A thorough review of this productive area in the study of marriage is not possible here (see Fincham et al 1990). There is a universal phenomenon in marriage that has to do with how spouses in happy and unhappy marriages think about positive and negative actions of their partner. In a happy marriage, if one partner does something negative, the other partner tends to think that the negativity is fleeting and situational. For example, the thought might be something like, "Oh, well, he's in a bad mood. He's been under a lot of stress lately and needs more sleep." So the negativity is viewed as unstable, and the cause is viewed as situational. In an unhappy marriage, however, the same behavior is likely to be interpreted as stable and internal to the partner. The accompanying thought might be something like, "He is inconsiderate and selfish. That's the way he is. That's why he did that." On the other hand, in a happy marriage, if someone does something positive, the behavior is likely to be interpreted as stable and internal to the partner. The accompanying thought might be something like, "He is a considerate and loving person. That's the way he is. That's why he did that." But in an unhappy marriage, the same positive behavior is likely to be seen as fleeting and situational hence as unstable. The accompanying thought might be, "Oh, well, he's nice because he's been successful this week at work. It won't last and it doesn't mean much." Holtzworth-Munroe & Jacobson (1985) used indirect probes to investigate when a couple might spontaneously search for causes of events and what they conclude when they do search for causes. They found evidence that distressed couples engaged in more attributional activity than nondistressed couples, and that attributional thoughts primarily surrounded events with negative impact. Nondistressed couples engaged in relationship-enhancing attributions while distressed couples engaged in distress-maintaining attributions. Distress-maintaining attributions maximize the impact of negativity and minimize the impact of positivity of the partner's behavior.

Moreover, there was an important gender difference. Distressed husbands generated more attributions than nondistressed husbands, but the two groups of wives did not differ. They suggested that, normally, males may not engage in much attributional activity but that they outstrip women once relationship conflict develops. Relationship-enhancing attributions were responses to positive partner behavior in both groups of couples. Relationship-enhancing attributions minimize the impact of negative and maximize the impact of positive behaviors of the partner. In an experimental study by Jacobson et al (1985b), distressed and nondistressed couples were randomly instructed to "act positive" or to "act negative." They found that distressed couples were likely to attribute their partner's negative behavior to internal factors, whereas nondistressed couples were likely to attribute their partner's positive behavior to internal factors. Thus, these attributions, once established, make change less likely to occur. Behaviors that should disconfirm the attributional sets tend to get ignored, whereas behaviors that confirm the attributional set receive attention. Attributional processes may tap the way couples think in general about the marital interaction as it unfolds in time. For example, Berley & Jacobson (1984) noted that Watzlawick et al (1967) were referring to attributional processes when they discussed the punctuation fallacy. The punctuation fallacy is that each spouse views himself or herself as the victim of the partner's behavior, which is seen as the causal stimulus. Attributions and general thought patterns about negative behaviors may thus be theoretically useful in providing a link between the immediate patterns of activity seen in behavioral interaction and physiological response and more long-lasting and more global patterns that span longer time periods. It might be the case that these more stable aspects of the marriage are better for predicting long-term outcomes such as divorce than can be obtained from behavioral observation.

The content dimensions of negative attributions that have been studied include locus (partner, self, relationship, or outside events), stability (e.g. due to partner's trait, or a state that is situationally determined), globality (how many areas of the marriage are affected), intentionality (negative intent—selfish versus unselfish motivation), controllability, volition, and responsibility (e.g. blameworthiness). For attributions about negative events, all of the studies reviewed supported differences between happily and unhappily married couples on the two dimensions of globality and selfish versus unselfish motivation. It is likely that these attributional phenomena are what make the self-report measurement of any aspects of the quality of the marriage so strongly related. It is also what becomes problematic in attaching any specificity to the measurement of marital satisfaction or marital quality (see Fincham & Bradbury 1987).

Another important cognitive dimension, called "sentiment override," was introduced by Weiss (1980). Weiss suggested that reactions during marital interaction may be determined by a global dimension of affection or disaffection rather than by the immediately preceding valence of the stimulus. Notarius et al (1989) evaluated the validity of this hypothesis in a remarkably creative study in which they employed a sequential stream of behavior and cognitions to operationalize a number of hypotheses linking behavior and cognition. They found that distressed wives were more negative, were more likely to evaluate their partner's neutral and negative messages as negative (suggesting the operation of a negative sentiment override), and, given a negative evaluation of their partner's antecedent message, were more likely to offer a negative reply than were all other spouses. Vanzetti et al (1992) reported that distressed couples have more negative and less positive expectations. They measured "relational efficacy," which is a shared belief that a couple can solve its problems, and found that couples high in relational efficacy choose relationship-enhancing attributions more often than do low-efficacy couples. Low-efficacy marriages showed strong preferences for distress-maintaining attributions.

To assess a larger cognitive unit than attributions, Buehlman et al (1992) coded interviews with couples to assess the shared beliefs and narratives of couples about the history of their marriage and their philosophy of marriage. A few simple variables (such as the husband's fondness for his wife) were able to predict divorce or marital stability over a three-year period with a great degree of accuracy (100% for the divorcing couples, and 94% overall).

## The View from Psychophysiology

A recent and productive approach to studying marriages has been a social psychophysiological procedure. Beginning with Kaplan et al (1964), simultaneous psychophysiological recording was taken of two conversing individuals. The initial finding was that the galvanic skin responses of the two interacting people were correlated only when they disliked each other. Levenson & Gottman (1983) later extended this finding to the construct of physiological linkage, i.e. predictability of one person's physiology (across channels) from the other's (controlling for autocorrelation), and reported greater physiological linkage for unhappily married compared with happily married couples. The linkage variable accounted for over 60% of the variance in marital satisfaction. Levenson & Gottman (1985) later reported that measures of physiological arousal in cardiovascular channels and in skin conductance were able to predict drops in marital satisfaction over three years, controlling for the initial level of marital satisfaction. The pattern was later used by Gottman (1990) to suggest that diffuse physiological arousal, that is, arousal in more than one physiological channel (but not necessarily more than one physiological system, e.g. increased heart rate as well as contractility, or blood velocity) would be associated with decreased information processing capability and a reliance on overlearned patterns of behavior and cognition, particularly those associated with fight or flight. Brown & Smith (1992) studied 45 married couples and found that husbands attempting to persuade their wives showed the greatest increase in systolic blood pressure before and during the discussion. In males, physiological effects were accompanied by increased anger and a hostile and coldly assertive interpersonal style. Although wives showed behavior patterns that were similar to husbands to some degree, they displayed neither elevated systolic blood pressure nor anger. In addition, Fan2) found that both the size of the systolic blood pressure responses of husbands during marital conflict and their recovery times exceeded those of their wives. Malarkey et al (1994) simultaneously studied the secretion of stress-related hormones in five samples of blood taken during the conflict interactions of 90 newlywed couples. Hostile behavior (coded with the MICS) correlated with decreased levels of prolactin and increases in epinephrine, norepinephrine, ACTH, and growth hormone, but not cortisol.

Physiological approaches have added something important theoretically. The general contribution they provide is in directing the organization and search for patterns of behavior and cognition within *balance theories,* in which positivity and negativity are in a state of dynamic balance around a steady state, or set point (for a mathematical model, see Cook et al (1995). In the body, many systems are in a state of dynamic homeostatic balance around a steady state through the action of opponent processes (e.g. the regulation of the heart's rate through the parasympathetic and sympathetic branches of the autonomic nervous system).

Three additional concepts are discussed here. First, negative affect reciprocity may exist as a function of spouses' inability to soothe themselves and each other. Second, this variable of soothing may be the basis for the large relapse effect in marital therapy. In therapy the therapist plays the role of soother instead of the spouses, and when therapy ends the spouses are unable to soothe each other, and old patterns of behavior and cognition reassert themselves. Third, Gottman & Levenson found that the husband's stonewalling (withdrawal as a listener) was related to his physiological arousal (reported in Gottman 1994). In addition, Levenson et al (1995), in a study of older long-term marriages, reported that the husband's but not the wife's physiological arousal was related to his self-report of feeling negative (in a video recall paradigm); they speculated that the husband's withdrawal in the demand-withdraw pattern may be related to his physiological arousal, since it is known that males are more aware of their own physiology than women. Thus, physiological measures suggest a biological basis for the gender effect in the demand-withdraw pattern. This observation is not intended to mean that such a biological basis is unrelated to socialization.

## The View from Intervention

A major contribution by psychologists to the study of marriage was the idea of systematically evaluating marital therapy. Unfortunately, as is typical of psychotherapy in general, new therapies emerged in this field largely from speculative writings by therapists instead of from careful empirical work. There have been a number of reviews of the marital therapy literature to date (e.g. Baucom & Hoffman 1986, Bray & Jouriles 1997, Dunn & Schwebel 1995, Hahlweg & Markman 1983, Jacobson & Addis 1993, Pinsof & Wynne 1995, Prince & Jacobson 1997). Their major conclusions are summarized here. Meta-analytic studies of marital therapy outcome appear at first blush to present a more optimistic picture than the one presented here, but meta-analytic studies tend to ask a very global question about "effectiveness" relative to a control group, which obscures issues of which therapies are successful on which outcome measures (e.g. only self-report?), issues of clinical versus statistical significance, and issues of longitudinal follow-up and relapse. In addition, meta-analyses tend to lump good and bad studies together and examine effect sizes; as is well known, studies with the best control groups necessarily have the smallest effect sizes because they attempt to control everything except what they suppose to be the active ingredients of the intervention.

The most frequently evaluated marital intervention is behavioral. Baucom & Hoffman (1986) noted that the skills usually taught by behavioral marital therapy (BMT) are communication and problem solving, and contingency contracting (based on the quid pro quo assumption). They distinguished these communication skills as problem solving in nature, as opposed to communication skill programs oriented toward the expression of emotions and listening skills. Baucom & Hoffman concluded that (a) couples receiving BMT (compared with a wait-list control group) improve significantly in negative communication and self-reports of problems (Jacobson's program was the only one to report improvements in positive communication); (b) BMT is superior to nonspecific and attention control groups; and (c) there are no major differences in the effectiveness of two components of BMT, nor in their order of administration. However, Jacobson et al (1985b, 1987) reported some evidence that the communication/problem-solving (CO) training was superior to the behavior exchange (contingency contracting) (BE) condition. Upon two-year follow-up, couples in the CO condition were most likely to be happily married and least likely to be separated or divorced. They also noted, however, that while statistically significant changes were obtained by BMT compared with a waiting list (and other) control group, "60–65% of the couples either remained somewhat distressed or failed to change during treatment" (p. 605). In a more recent review, Jacobson & Addis (1993) reached similar conclusions to those of Baucom & Hoffman (1986). They estimated that about 50% of couples cannot be considered successes. They are considerably more pessimistic than Baucom & Hoffman about the long-term effectiveness of BMT. Recently, Snyder et al (1991) reported that the insight-oriented and BMT groups were equivalent at termination. At four-year follow-up, however, they found that the divorce rate was 38% for the BMT group and only 3% for the insight-oriented group. Jacobson (1993), however, challenged the meaning of the Snyder et al results; in a comparison of treatment manuals for the two groups, he concluded that their BMT manual was 10 years out of date and that the insight-oriented manual was far closer to current BMT treatments. Regardless of how one labels the intervention, the Snyder et al four-year follow-up results are quite encouraging.

## Summary

First, if one requires replicated effects, treatment gains are not generally maintained over time. Second, it does not seem to matter very much what one does in treatment. In general, the effect sizes are roughly the same, regardless of the exact nature of the intervention. This latter fact is remarkable when "dismantling" studies done in BMT are considered. Rather than having identified an active ingredient of BMT, they suggest the conclusion that any of the parts equals the whole. Furthermore, it appears possible that all parts may be as effective as contingency contracting, an approach based on an erroneous assumption about what makes marriages work. If this remarkable conclusion were true, almost all marital treatment effects to date would be due to nonspecifics such as trust in the therapist, hope, the existence of a structured program, all of which could be considered to be placebo effects.

## SUMMARY: AN INTEGRATIVE MODEL OF HOW MARRIAGES MAY DYSFUNCTION AND FUNCTION

### The Stable Phenomena of Marital Process and Outcomes

To date, research on marriage by psychologists has been remarkably productive. We can identify seven consistent patterns across laboratories. These patterns are (a) greater negative affect reciprocity in unhappy couples, which may be related to the failure of repair; (b) lower ratios of positivity to negativity in unhappy couples and couples headed for divorce (this includes a greater climate of agreement in happily married couples); (c) less positive sentiment override in unhappy couples; (d) the presence of criticism, defensiveness, contempt, and stonewalling in couples headed for divorce; (e) greater evidence of the wife demand–husband withdraw pattern in unhappy couples (though it is probably also there to some extent in happily married couples); (f) negative and lasting attributions about the partner and more negative narratives about the marriage and partner in unhappy couples; and (g) greater physiological arousal in unhappy couples. What is needed at this juncture is a theoretical model of how these various patterns may fit together. The search for a theory needs to be guided by two questions, the question of what is dysfunctional in marriages (i.e. how the seven negative patterns are related and the ontogeny of the seven negative patterns in ailing marriages), and the question of what is functional, that is, what couples whose marriages are doing well are doing (thinking, feeling, etc) differently. Both questions are necessary—identifying negative dysfunctional patterns does not imply that one has also simultaneously identified positive functional patterns.

### What Is Dysfunctional in Unhappy, Unstable Marriages?

Gottman (1994) proposed a theory of dysfunction based on longitudinal research and the correlates of marital satisfaction. Unstable marriages are likely to be unable to work out over time one of three stable adaptations Gottman discovered: volatile, validating, conflict avoiding. In their attempts to accomplish a stable adaptation, some couples fall into a pattern that does not maintain the balance of positivity to negativity at a high level. Spouses tend to formulate their complaints as criticisms and contempt; they tend to respond defensively and eventually withdraw from each other. At the core of this formulation is a balance theory, an ecology of marital behaviors in which a ratio of positivity to negativity that is highly tilted toward positivity needs to be maintained. This ratio is suggested as the quantity that needs to be regulated at a high level, approximately 5.0. Related to marital interaction is the subtext of how the interaction is perceived by each partner. If the ratio of 5.0 is significantly violated, the perception of well-being is replaced by one of distress, which is some combination of hurt and anger (fight, or the "righteous indignation" perception) and/or hurt and perceived attack (flight, or the "innocent victim" perception). The length of time in a state of distress, in turn, determines feeling flooded by one's partner's negative affect, with accompanying diffuse physiological arousal (DPA), negative subjective affective states, and negative attributions of the partner. Flooding begins the Distance and Isolation Cascade, which entails perceiving one's marital problems as severe, as better worked out alone rather than with the spouse, arranging one's lives so that they are more in parallel than they used to be, and loneliness within the marriage. Eventually, even one's perception of the entire relationship is affected, and the couple's narratives change. In the oral history interview, people (particularly husbands) express disappointment with the marriage, declare little fondness for the partner, and present themselves as separate entities who do not see the past the same way or share a common philosophy of marriage. They also tend to see their lives as chaotic and out of control, and they see all the marital conflict as pointless and empty. This grim formulation is balanced by the reverse results that couples whose marriages are stable use positive affect and persuasion in very different ways—ways that buffer them from the physiological stresses of DPA and from the perception of their partner's negative emotions as horrible, disgusting, terrifying, overwhelming, disorganizing, and impossible to predict.

## An Intergrative Account: the Bank Account Model

What is the etiology of these dysfunctional patterns, which are predictive of unhappiness and divorce? This review introduces a new theory, called the Bank Account Model (BAM). The first premise of the BAM is that the answer to the question of the ontogeny of the seven negative patterns in ailing marriages lies in asserting that psychologists have been looking in the wrong place. They have studied almost exclusively the resolution of conflict, and BAM suggests that the seven dysfunctional patterns reviewed here reflect the endpoint of the failure of three related processes. The first process is the couple's ratio of fairly low-level positivity to negativity in nonconflict interaction. Nonconflict interaction consists primarily of the mundane, everyday interactions of married life, each of which holds the possibility of what might be called either "turning toward" or "turning away" from one's partner. An example follows: One spouse is in the bathroom in the morning, in a hurry getting ready for the day, when the partner comes into the bathroom and says, "I just had a disturbing dream." An example of turning away would be, "I don't have time for this right now," while an example of turning toward would be, "I'm in a real hurry, but tell me about your dream." A greater balance of turning away compared with turning toward implies that there will be many moments of what could be called "unrequited interest and excitement," in which one person's interest and excitement is not responded to by the partner, and many moments of "unrequited irritability," in which one person's low-intensity anger is not responded to by the partner. This lack of responsiveness leads to the presence of the first of the Four Horsemen, criticism. Criticism leads to the other horsemen.

The theory proposes that a greater proportion of turning toward compared with turning away leads to positive sentiment override (Weiss 1980), whereas a greater proportion of turning away compared with turning toward leads to negative sentiment override. Physiological soothing of one's partner using a variety of positive affects (e.g. interest, affection, validation, empathy, humor) during everyday stress reduction interactions (typically events-of-the-day discussions and errand talk) is central to contributing to positive sentiment override, and this is accomplished through the simple mechanism of escape conditioning. The second process is the amount of cognitive room that couples allocate for the relationship and for their spouse's world. We call this the "love map." The husband's love map is particularly predictive of the longitudinal course of marriages. This process has to do with knowing one's partner's world and continually updating that knowledge. The third process, which is another contributor to positive sentiment override is the existence of what we call the Fondness and Admiration System (tapped by the oral history interview). Admiration is the antidote for contempt. Couples who are on a stable and happy trajectory express spontaneous admiration and affection for their partner much more than couples on the trajectory toward divorce. The Fondness and Admiration System affects and is affected by both cognition and behavior.

The existence of either positive or negative sentiment override determines the success or failure of repair processes (Gianino & Tronick 1988 discussed these in mother-infant interaction) in conflict interaction. The success of repair minimizes negative affect reciprocity. Positive sentiment override, however, also leads to the presence of three other processes (in addition to successful repair) during conflict interaction. The first has been called "editing." Part of breaking the chain of negative-affect reciprocity, editing is assessed as a lowered conditional probability of becoming a negative-affect speaker after one has been a negative-affect listener. There is a fair amount of evidence that happily married couples are more likely to edit than unhappily married couples (Gottman 1979, Notarius et al 1989). Editing is responsible for decreasing the probability of what the Patterson group has called "negative startup," which means moving from one's partner's neutral affect to one's own negative affect. It is related to the beginning of the demand-withdraw pattern, and it is more characteristic of wives than husbands (Gottman 1994, 1996). The second process is one we call "respectful influence." Respectful influence involves using positive affect in the service of the de-escalation of conflict while attempting to influence one's partner without using the Four Horsemen, and it also involves accepting influence from one's partner. Rushe (1996), in a detailed analysis of persuasion and influence tactics during marital conflict resolution, found that assertive means of persuasion during conflict resolution was the one discriminator between happily married and distressed nonviolent couples. Coan et al (1997) described rejecting influence as characteristic of violent couples. The third process is positive affect, which this theory hypothesizes is used carefully to avoid one's partner's defensiveness and to reduce physiological arousal. Our laboratory has evidence that among newlyweds the Time-1 positive affects of interest, affection, humor, and validation predict and discriminate whether couples will eventually divorce, be stable and happily married, or stable and unhappily married (in a five-year follow-up). These processes affect the couple's narratives, the stories they tell themselves and each other about the marriage and the partner. The current evidence is that these narratives are quite powerful predictors of marital trajectory (Buehlman et al 1992). Narratives may guide cognition and attributions even when the couple is not together.

---

**Visit the *Annual Reviews* home page at
http://www.AnnualReviews.org.**

---

## Literature Cited

Bakeman R, Gottman J. 1986. *Observing Interaction: An Introduction to Sequential Analysis.* New York: Cambridge Univ. Press

Bakeman R, Quera V. 1995. *Analyzing Interaction: Sequential Analysis with SDIS and GSEQ.* New York: Cambridge Univ. Press

Bank L, Dishion T, Skinner M, Patterson GR. 1990. Method variance in structural equation modeling: living with "glop." In *Depression and Aggression in Family Inter-*

*action,* ed. GR Patterson, pp. 247–79. Hillsdale, NJ: Erlbaum

Bateson G, Jackson DD, Haley J, Weakland J. 1956. Toward a theory of schizophrenia. *Behav. Sci.* 1:251–64

Baucom DH, Hoffman JA. 1986. The effectiveness of marital therapy: current status and application to the clinical setting. In *Clinical Handbook of Marital Therapy,* ed. N Jacobson, A Gurman, pp. 597–620. New York: Guilford

Bell RQ. 1968. A reinterpretation of the direction of effects in studies of socialization. *Psychol. Rev.* 75:81–95

Berley RA, Jacobson NS. 1984. Causal attributions in intimate relationships: toward a model of cognitive behavioral marital therapy. In *Advances in Cognitive-Behavioral Research and Therapy,* ed. P Kendall, 3:2–90. New York: Academic

Bloom B, Asher S, White S. 1978. Marital disruption as a stressor: a review and analysis. *Psychol. Bull.* 85:867–94

Bray JH, Jouriles EN. 1997. Treatment of marital conflict and prevention of divorce. *J. Marital Fam. Ther.* In press

Brown PC, Smith TW. 1992. Social influence, marriage, and the heart: cardiovascular consequences of interpersonal control in husbands and wives. *Health Psychol.* 11:88–96

Buehlman K, Gottman JM, Katz L. 1992. How a couple views their past predicts their future: predicting divorce from an oral history interview. *J. Fam. Psychol.* 5: 295–318

Burgess EW, Locke HJ, Thomes MM. 1971. *The Family: From Traditional to Companionship.* New York: Van Nostrand Reinhold

Burman B, Margolin G. 1992. Analysis of the association between marital relationships and health problems: an interactional perspective. *Psychol. Bull.* 112:39–63

Campbell DT, Fiske DW. 1959. Convergent and discriminant validation by the multitrait-multimethod matrix. *Psychol. Bull.* 56:81–105

Christensen A, Heavey CL. 1990. Gender and social structure in the demand/withdraw pattern. *J. Pers. Soc. Psychol.* 59(1):73–81

Coan J, Gottman JM, Babcock J, Jacobson NS. 1997. Battering and the male rejection of influence from women. *Aggress. Behav.* In press

Cook J, Tyson R, White J, Rushe R, Gottman J, Murray J. 1995. The mathematics of marital conflict: qualitative dynamic mathematical modeling of marital interaction. *J. Fam. Psychol.* 9:110–30

Cowan CP, Cowan PA, Heming G, Miller NB. 1991. Becoming a family: marriage, parenting and child development. In *Family Transitions,* ed. PA Cowan, EM Hetherington. Hillsdale, NJ: Erlbaum

Cowan PA, Cowan CP. 1987. *Couple's relationships, parenting styles and the child's development at three.* Presented at Meet. Soc. Res. Child Dev., Baltimore, MD

Cowan PA, Cowan CP. 1990. Becoming a family: research and intervention. In *Family Research,* ed. I Sigel, A Brody. Hillsdale, NJ: Erlbaum

Cummings EM, Davies P. 1994. *Children and Marital Conflict: The Impact of Family Dispute Resolution.* New York: Guilford

Dunn R, Schwebel AI. 1995. Meta-analytic review of marital therapy outcome research. *J. Fam. Psychol.* 9(1):58–68

Easterbrooks MA. 1987. *Early family development: longitudinal impact of marital quality.* Presented at Meet. Soc. Res. Child Dev., Baltimore, MD

Easterbrooks MA, Emde RA. 1988. Marital and parent-child relationships: the role of affect in the family system. In *Relationships Within Families: Mutual Influence,* ed. RA Hinde, J Stevenson-Hinde, pp. 27–45. Oxford: Clarendon

Emery RE. 1982. Interparental conflict and the children of discord and divorce. *Psychol. Bull.* 92:310–30

Emery RE. 1988. *Marriage, Divorce, and Children's Adjustment.* Newbury Park, CA: Sage

Emery RE, O'Leary KD. 1982. Children's perceptions of marital discord and behavior problems of boys and girls. *J. Abnorm. Child Psychol.* 10:11–24

Emery RE, O'Leary KD. 1984. Marital discord and child behavior problems in a nonclinical sample. *J. Abnorm. Child Psychol.* 12:411–20

Fankish CJ. 1992. Warning! Your marriage may be hazardous to your health: spousepair risk factors and cardiovascular reactivity. *Diss. Abstr. Int.* 52:5532

Fincham FD, Bradbury TN. 1987. The assessment of marital quality: a reevaluation. *J. Marriage Fam.* 49:797–809

Fincham FD, Bradbury TN. 1992. Assessing attributions in marriage: the relationship attribution measure. *J. Pers. Soc. Psychol.* 62:457–68

Fincham FD, Bradbury TN, Scott CK. 1990. Cognition in marriage. In *The Psychology of Marriage,* ed. FD Fincham, TD Bradbury, pp. 118–49. New York: Guilford

Fitzpatrick MA. 1988. *Between Husbands and Wives: Communication in Marriage.* Beverly Hills, CA: Sage

Forehand R, Brody G, Long N, Slotkin J, Fauber R. 1986. Divorce/divorce potential and interparental conflict: the relationship to early adolescent social and cognitive functioning. *J. Adolesc. Res.* 1:389–97

Friedman HS, Tucker JS, Schwartz JE, Tomilson KC. 1995. Psychosocial and behavioral predictors of longevity: the aging and death of the "Termites." *Am. Psychol.* 50: 69–78

Gianino A, Tronick EZ. 1988. The mutual regulation model: the infant's self and interactive regulation coping and defense. In *Stress and Coping,* ed. T Field, P McCabe, N Schnieiderman, pp. 47–68. Hillsdale, NJ: Erlbaum

Glenn ND, Kramer KB. 1985. The psychological well-being of adult children of divorce. *J. Marriage Fam.* 40:269–82

Gottman JM. 1979. *Marital Interaction: Empirical Investigations.* New York: Academic

Gottman JM. 1990. How marriages change. In *Depression and Aggression in Family Interaction,* ed. GR Patterson, pp. 110–35. Hillsdale, NJ: Erlbaum

Gottman JM. 1994. *What Predicts Divorce?* Hillsdale, NJ: Erlbaum

Gottman JM, ed. 1996. *What Predicts Divorce: The Measures.* Hillsdale, NJ: Erlbaum

Gottman JM, Katz L. 1989. Effects of marital discord on young children's peer interaction and health. *Dev. Psychol.* 25: 373–81

Gottman JM, Levenson RW. 1988. The social psychophysiology of marriage. In *Perspectives on Marital Interaction,* ed. P Noller, MA Fitzpatrick, pp. 182–200. Clevedon, Engl: Multilingual Matters

Gottman JM, Roy AK. 1990. *Sequential Analysis: A Guide for Behavioral Researchers.* New York: Cambridge Univ. Press

Gray JP. 1984. The influence of female power in marriage on sexual behaviors and attitudes: a holocultural study. *Arch. Sex. Behav.* 13:223–31

Gray LB, Burks N. 1983. Power and satisfaction in marriage: a review and critique. *Psychol. Bull.* 93:513–38

Hahlweg K, Markman HJ. 1983. Effectiveness of behavioral marital therapy: empirical status of behavioral techniques in preventing and alleviating marital distress. *J. Consult. Clin. Psychol.* 56: 440–47

Heavey CL, Christensen A, Malamuth NM. 1995. The longitudinal impact of demand and withdrawal during marital conflict. *J. Consult. Clin. Psychol.* 63:797–801

Hendrix H. 1988. *Getting the Love You Want.* New York: Holt

Hetherington EM. 1988. Coping with family transitions: winners, losers and survivors. *Child Dev.* 60:1–14

Hetherington EM, Clingempeel WG. 1992. Coping with marital transitions. *Monogr. Soc. Res. Child Dev.* 57(227):1–242

Hetherington EM, Cox M, Cox R. 1978. The aftermath of divorce. In *Mother-Child, Father-Child Relations,* ed. JH Stevens, M Matthews, pp.117–45. Washington, DC: Natl. Assoc. Educ. Young Children

Hetherington EM, Cox M, Cox R. 1982. Effects of divorce on parents and children. In *Nontraditional Families,* ed. M Lamb, pp. 233–88. Hillsdale, NJ: Erlbaum

Heyman RE, Eddy JM, Weiss RL, Vivian D. 1995. Factor analysis of the Marital Interaction Coding System (MICS). *J. Fam. Psychol.* 9:209–15

Holtzworth-Munroe A, Jacobson NS. 1985. Causal attributions of married couples: When do they search for causes? What do they conclude when they do? *J. Pers. Soc. Psychol.* 48:1398–412

Howes P, Markman HJ. 1989. Marital quality and child functioning: a longitudinal investigation. *Child Dev.* 60:1044–51

Jacob T. 1987. Family interaction and psychopathology: historical overview. In *Family Interaction and Psychopathology,* ed. T Jacob, pp. 3–24. New York: Plenum

Jacobson NS. 1989. The maintenance of treatment gains following social learning-based marital therapy. *Behav. Ther.* 20: 325–36

Jacobson NS, Addis ME. 1993. Research on couple therapy: What do we know? Where are we going? *J. Consult. Clin. Psychol.* 61(1):85–93

Jacobson NS, Christensen A. 1997. *Integrated Cognitive Behavioral Marital Therapy.* New York: Guilford. In press

Jacobson NS, Follette VM, Follette WC, Holtzworth-Munroe A, Katt JL, Schmaling KB. 1985a. A component analysis of behavioral marital therapy: 1-year followup. *Behav. Res. Ther.* 23:549–55

Jacobson NS, Margolin G. 1979. *Marital Therapy.* New York: Brunner/Mazel

Jacobson NS, McDonald DW, Follette WC, Berley RA. 1985b. Attributional processes in distressed and nondistressed married couples. *Cogn. Ther. Res.* 9:35–50

Jacobson NS, Schmaling K, Holtzworth-Munroe A. 1987. Component analysis of behavioral marital therapy: 2-year followup and prediction of relapse. *J. Marital Fam. Ther.* 13:187–95

Kaplan HB, Burch NR, Bloom SW. 1964. Physiological covariation in small peer groups. In *Psychological Approaches to Social Behavior,* ed. PH Liederman, D Shapiro, pp.21–43. Stanford, CA: Stanford Univ. Press

Katz LF, Gottman JM. 1991a. Marital discord and child outcomes: a social psychophysiological approach. In *The Development of Emotion Regulation and Disregulation,* ed. K Dodge, J Garber, pp.129–58. New York: Cambridge Univ. Press

Katz LF, Gottman JM. 1991b. *Marital interaction processes and preschool children's peer interactions and emotional development.* Presented at Meet. Soc. Res. Child Dev.

Kelly LE, Conley JJ. 1987. Personality and compatibility: a prospective analysis of marital stability and marital satisfaction. *J. Pers. Soc. Psychol.* 52:27–40

Kolb JM, Straus MA. 1974. Marital power and marital happiness in relation to problemsolving. *J. Marriage Fam.* 36:756–66

Kulka RA, Weingarten H. 1979. The longterm effects of parental divorce on adult adjustment. *J. Soc. Issues* 35:50–78

Kurdek LA. 1993. Predicting marital dissolution: a 5-year prospective longitudinal study of newlywed couples. *J. Pers. Soc. Psychol.* 64:221–42

Lederer WJ, Jackson DD. 1968. *The Mirages of Marriage.* New York: Norton

Levenson RW, Carstensen LL, Gottman JM. 1994. The influence of age and gender on affect, physiology and their interactions: A study of long-term marriages. *J. Pers. Soc. Psychol.* 67:56–68

Levenson RW, Gottman JM. 1983. Marital interaction: physiological linkage and affective exchange. *J. Pers. Soc. Psychol.* 45: 587–97

Levenson RW, Gottman JM. 1985. Physiological and affective predictors of change in relationship satisfaction. *J. Pers. Soc. Psychol.* 49:85–94

Lewis M, Rosenblum LA, eds. 1974. *The Effect of the Infant on Its Caregiver.* New York: Wiley

Maccoby EE. 1990. Gender and relationships: a developmental account. *Am. Psychol.* 45(4):513–20

Malarkey WB, Kiecolt-Glaser JK, Pearl D, Glaser R. 1994. Hostile behavior during marital conflict alters pituitary and adrenal hormones. *Psychosom. Med.* 56:41–51

Margolin G, Wampold BE. 1981. Sequential analysis of conflict and accord in distressed and nondistressed marital partners. *J. Consult. Clin. Psychol.* 49:554–67

Martin TC, Bumpass L. 1989. Recent trends in marital disruption. *Demography* 26: 37–51

Meissner WW. 1978. The conceptualization of marriage and family dynamics from a psychoanalytic perspective. In *Marriage and Marital Therapy,* ed. TJ Paolino, BS McCrady, pp. 25–88. New York: Brunner/Mazel

Mischel W. 1968. *Personality and Assessment.* New York: Wiley

Murstein BI, Cerreto M, MacDonald MG. 1977. A theory and investigation of the effect of exchange-orientation on marriage and friendship. *J. Marriage Fam.* 39: 543–48

Notarius CI, Benson PR, Sloane D, Vanzetti NA. 1989. Exploring the interface between perception and behavior: an analysis of marital interaction in distressed and nondistressed couples. *Behav. Assess.* 11: 39–64

Nye FI. 1988. Fifty years of family research 1937–1987. *J. Marriage Fam.* 50:305–16

Patterson GR. 1982. *Coercive Family Process.* Eugene, OR: Castalia

Peterson JL, Zill N. 1986. Marital disruption, parent-child relationships, and behavior problems in children. *J. Marriage Fam.* 48:295–307

Pinsof WM, Wynne LC. 1995. The effectiveness of marital and family therapy: an empirical overview, conclusions and recommendations. *J. Marital Fam. Ther.* 21(4):339–623

Porter B, O'Leary KD. 1980. Marital discord and childhood behavior problems. *J. Abnorm. Child Psychol.* 8:287–95

Prince SE, Jacobson NS. 1997. A review and evaluation of marital and family therapies for affective disorders. *J. Marital Fam. Ther.* 21:377–402

Raush HL, Barry WA, Hertel RK, Swain MA. 1974. *Communication, Conflict, and Marriage.* San Francisco: Jossey-Bass

Reid JB. 1970. Reliability assessment of observational data: a possible methodolgical problem. *Child Dev.* 41:1143–50

Revenstorf D, Vogel B, Wegener C, Halweg K, Schindler L. 1980. Escalation phenomena in interaction sequences: an empirical comparison of distressed and nondistressed couples. *Behav. Anal. Modif.* 2: 97–116

Rushe R. 1996. *Tactics of power and influence in violent marriages.* PhD thesis. Univ. Wash., Seattle

Rutter M. 1971. Parent-child separation: psychological effects on the children. *J. Child Psychol. Psychiatry* 12:233–60

Rutter M. 1979. Protective factors in children's responses to stresss and disadvantage. In *Primary Prevention in Psychopathology:* Vol. 3. *Social Competence in Children,* ed. MW Kent, JE Rold, pp. 3–27. Hanover, NH: Univ. Press New England

Schaap C. 1982. *Communication and Adjustment in Marriage.* Netherlands: Swets Zeitlinger

Scharff DE, Scharff SS. 1991. *Object Relations Couple Therapy.* Northvale, NJ: Aronson

Schwartz P. 1994. *Peer Marriage.* New York: The Free Press

Shannon CE, Weaver W. 1949. *The Mathematical Theory of Communciation.* Urbana: Univ. Ill. Press

Shaw DS, Emery RE. 1987. Parental conflict and other correlates of the adjustment of school-age children whose parents have separated. *J. Abnorm. Child Psychol.* 15:269–81

Snyder DK, Wills RM, Grady FA. 1991. Long-term effectiveness of behavioral versus insight-oriented marital therapy: a 4-year followup study. *J. Consult. Clin. Psychol.* 59(1):138–41

Terman LM, Buttenweiser P, Ferguson LW, Johnson WB, Wilson DP. 1938. *Psychological Factors in Marital Happiness.* New York: McGraw-Hill

Thibaut JW, Kelley HH. 1959. *The Social Psychology of Groups.* New York: Wiley

Ting-Toomey S. 1982. An analysis of verbal communication patterns in high and low marital adjustment groups. *Hum. Commun. Res.* 9:306–19

Vanzetti NA, Notarius CI, NeeSmith D. 1992. Specific and generalized expectancies in marital interaction. *J. Fam. Psychol.* 6:171–83

Vincent JP, Friedman LC, Nugent J, Messerly L. 1979. Deman characteristics in observations of marital interaction. *J. Consult. Clin. Psychol.* 47:557–66

Watzlawick P, Beavin JH, Jackson DD. 1967. *Pragmatics of Human Communication.* New York: Norton

Weiss RL. 1980. Strategic behavioral and marital therapy: toward a model for assessment and intervention. In *Advances in Family Intervention, Assessment and Theory,* ed. JP Vincent, 1:229–71. Greenwich, CT: JAI Press

Weiss RL, Hops H, Patterson GR. 1973. A framework for conceptualizing marital conflict, a technique for altering it, some data for evaluating it. In *Behavior Change,* ed. LA Hamerlynck, LC Handy, EJ Mash. Champaign, IL: Research Press

Whitehead LB. 1979. Sex differences in children's responses to family stress. *J. Child Psychol. Psychiatry* 20:247–54

Wiggins JS. 1973. *Personality and Prediction.* Reading, MA: Addison-Wesley

Winch RF. 1958. *Mate Selection: The Study of Complimentary Needs.* New York: Harper Brothers

*Annu. Rev. Psychol. 1998. 49:199–227*

# MODELS OF THE EMERGENCE OF LANGUAGE

*Brian MacWhinney*

Department of Psychology, Carnegie Mellon University, Pittsburgh, Pennsylvania 15213; e-mail: macw@cmu.edu

KEY WORDS: development, syntax, connectionism, nativism, lexicon, children, meaning, phonology, neural networks

## ABSTRACT

Recent work in language acquisition has shown how linguistic form emerges from the operation of self-organizing systems. The emergentist framework emphasizes ways in which the formal structures of language emerge from the interaction of social patterns, patterns implicit in the input, and pressures arising from general aspects of the cognitive system. Emergentist models have been developed to study the acquisition of auditory and articulatory patterns during infancy and the ways in which the learning of the first words emerges from the linkage of auditory, articulatory, and conceptual systems. Neural network models have also been used to study the learning of inflectional markings and basic syntactic patterns. Using both neural network modeling and concepts from the study of dynamic systems, it is possible to analyze language learning as the integration of emergent dynamic systems.

## CONTENTS

199

# INTRODUCTION

Language is a uniquely human achievement. All of the major social achievements of human culture—architecture, literature, law, science, art, and even warfare—rely on the use of language. Although there have been attempts to teach language to primates (Allen & Gardner 1969, Savage-Rumbaugh et al 1988), the successful learning of human language seems to be a tightly copyrighted component of our basic human nature.

This view of language as a Special Gift has led some researchers (Bickerton 1990) to hypothesize that some small set of evolutionary events may have triggered the emergence of language in the human species. Others (Chomsky 1980, Fodor 1983) have argued that the capacity to learn language is a unique property of the human mind that is represented neurologically in a separate cognitive module. These scholars believe that this modular architecture allows the shape and form of human language to be largely independent of other aspects of cognitive processing or social functioning. Studies of language learning stimulated by this nativist perspective have tended to focus attention onto a small set of syntactic structures that are thought to constitute the core of Chomsky's Universal Grammar (Chomsky 1965). According to the "principles and parameters" model of language structure (Hyams & Wexler 1993), the learning of particular languages occurs through parameter-setting. During parameter setting, children identify the exact shape of their mother tongue by choosing the proper settings on a small set of binary oppositions. For example, a positive setting on the pronoun omission parameter will select for languages like Italian or Chinese, whereas a negative setting will select for English.

Recent studies of the neural basis of communication systems in organisms such as crickets (Wyttenback & Hoy 1996), quail, and song birds (Marler 1991) have emphasized the extent to which species-specific communication patterns are stored in highly localized hard-wired neurological structures. However, even these lower organisms display some developmental plasticity in the ways in which communication is supported by the brain. When we look at human language learning, we see that children learn language gradually and inductively, rather than abruptly and deductively. There is little evidence for a tight biological timetable of developments of the type that we see in other species. In fact, children can learn language even when they have been isolated until an age of even 6 years (Davis 1947). Throughout the protracted period of human language learning, it is impossible to find evidence for some discrete moment at which a child sets some crucial parameter (Hyams 1995, MacWhinney & Bates 1989) that can determine the shape of the native language. Moreover, it is very difficult to use standard experimental methods to prove that children have acquired some of the more abstract categories and structures required by Universal Grammar, such as argument chains, empty categories, landing sites, or dominance relations (Gopnik 1990, van der Lely 1994). Despite these empirical problems, the nativist approach remains dominant for studies that investigate the acquisition of formal linguistic structures. For a comprehensive survey of nativist approaches to the acquisition of grammar, consult Atkinson (1992). Similarly, Markman (1989) summarizes evidence supporting a nativist approach to the acquisition of the lexicon.

## NATIVISM AND EMERGENTISM

The inability of nativist accounts to provide accurate or testable accounts of the details of language acquisition has led many language development researchers to explore alternatives to genetically wired modules. These alternative frameworks emphasize the ways in which the formal structures of language emerge from the interaction of social patterns, patterns implicit in the input, and pressures arising from the biology of the cognitive system. The emergentist approach to language acquisition views language as a structure arising from interacting constraints, much as the shape of the coastline arises from pressures exerted by ocean currents, underlying geology, weather patterns, and human construction. The formalisms that are used to express these nonlinear patterns of interaction include neural network modeling (Fausett 1994), dynamic systems theory (Port & van Gelder 1995), and structured approaches such as Optimality Theory (Tesar & Smolensky 1997). In this chapter, I examine the extent to which neural network models can account for what we currently know about the early states of language development.

## THE EMERGENCE OF AUDITORY PATTERNS

During the first year of life, the child goes through a complex set of experi-ences that lay down an extensive perceptual and motoric framework for the learning of the first words. On the perceptual side, the child actively encodes the raw sound patterns of her native language, organizing these patterns into types and sequences. At one time, researchers thought that the learning of per-ceptual contrasts, such as the ones that allow us to distinguish between "pin" vs "bin," occurred during the second year of life when words are being learned (Jakobson 1968, Shvachkin 1948). This picture changed radically when Eimas et al (1971) showed that the ability to detect the contrast between /b/ and /p/ is present soon after birth. Initially, it was thought that these abilities were innate components of a species-specific language gift. However, researchers soon showed that these abilities were shared with other mammals, such as chinchil-las (Kuhl & Miller 1975, 1978) and monkeys (Kuhl & Padden 1982, 1983). It now appears that the ability to discriminate the sounds of language is grounded on raw perceptual abilities of the mammalian auditory system. The sharpness and accuracy of this ability declines during the first year, as children learn to lump together sounds that their language treats as equivalent (Polka & Werker 1994). In effect, children spend much of the first year of life losing the ability to make contrasts that are not used in the speech they hear about them. Kuhl (1991) has interpreted these findings as evidence for a "preceptual magnet" ef-fect. This effect can be understood by imagining that there is a magnet at the center of each phonemic category that tends to draw in the edges of the cate-gory, thereby shortening the distance and leading to an inability to make fine distinctions within this compressed region.

Given the fact that children do not yet understand the words they are hear-ing, their attentiveness to sound is all the more remarkable. Recent research shows that they are attending not just to the individual phonemes they hear, but even to longer range patterns, such as syllabic sequences. For example, Saffran et al (1996) have shown that when 8-month-old children listen to long sound sequences such as "dabigogatanagotidabigo," they appear to pull out repeated sequences such as "dabigo." They demonstrate this by tending to listen to these familiar sequences more than to similar new sequences.

Infants also demonstrate an early attentiveness to the prosodic characteris-tics of the language they are hearing. Soon after birth, infants tend to prefer sounds produced by their own mothers to those produced by other women (De-Casper & Fifer 1980). They also prefer their native languages to other lan-guages (Moon et al 1993). These preferences are probably dependent both on the infant's ability to detect speaker-specific vocal characteristics and on the detection of language-specific prosodic patterns. Infants seem to be sensitive early on to the presence of intonational organization in the language they listen to. Using the sucking habituation technique, Mandel et al (1994) showed that 2-month-olds tend to remember word strings better when they are presented with normal sentence intonation, than when they are presented as unintegrated lists of words with flat prosody. It appears that stressed intonation may have a particularly important role in picking up auditory strings. Jusczyk & Aslin (1995) have shown that children tend to pick up and learn stressed syllables above unstressed syllables. However, it also appears that syllables that directly follow after a stressed syllable are also well encoded (Aslin et al 1997). As a result, many of the first sound sequences recorded by the child consist of a stressed peak followed by one or two further weak syllables. This pattern of sound learning has been discussed as a "trochaic bias." However, it can also be viewed as emerging from the combination of a bias to track stressed syllables together with a linear sequence recorder that fires when a stressed syllable is detected.

## THE EMERGENCE OF ARTICULATORY PATTERNS

During the first year of life, the infant's articulatory abilities also progress through radical transformations. The basic shape of these changes has been documented since the beginning of the century. We know that children's first vocalizations include the birth cry, the pain cry, the hunger cry, and the pleasure cry. These cries are tightly linked to clear emotional states (Lewis 1936). By the age of 3 months, children begin a type of social vocalization known as cooing. Around the age of 6 months, children begin a form of sound play that we call babbling. At first, babbling involves the sporadic production of a few simple sounds. These sounds include some strange sounds like clicks that are not found in the input. However, it is not true that each child babbles all the sounds of all the world's languages. Nor is there much evidence for any tight linkage before nine months between the form of the child's babbling and the shape of the input language (Atkinson et al 1970, Boysson-Bardies & Vihman 1991). However, around 11 months, there is increasing evidence for a drift toward the segments and prosody of the target language (Levitt et al 1993), as the child begins to move into the period of the first words.

Initially, it appears that auditory and articulatory development proceed as if largely decoupled. The fact that deaf children babble normally at the age of six months is particularly strong evidence for this conclusion. Given the fact that the brain areas subserving audition (inferior parietal, superior temporal) and articulation (motor cortex) are distant neurologically, this initial decoupling is not too surprising. By the age of nine months, evidence starts to emerge of a connection between babbling and audition. By this age, deaf children, who are not receiving adequate auditory feedback, cease babbling. Normal children start to show the first movement in the prosodic shape of their babbling toward the forms of the input language.

# THE EMERGENCE OF THE FIRST WORDS

One of the most active areas of current research in the child language is the study of early word learning. Philosophers like Quine (1960) have emphasized the extent to which word learning needs to be guided by ideas about what might constitute a possible word. For example, if the child were to allow for the possibility that word meanings might include disjunctive Boolean predicates (Hunt 1962), then it might be the case that the word "grue" would have the meaning "green before the year 2000 and blue thereafter." Similarly, it might be the case that the name for any object would refer not to the object itself, but to its various undetached parts. When one thinks about the word learning task in this abstract way, it appears to be impossibly hard.

## *Lexical Principles*

Markman (1989) and Golinkoff et al (1994) have proposed that Quine's problem can be solved by imagining that the child's search for word meanings is guided by lexical principles. For example, children assume that words refer to whole objects rather than to parts of objects. Thus, a child would assume that the word "rabbit" refers to the whole rabbit and not just some part of the rabbit. However, there is reason to believe that such principles are themselves emergent properties of the cognitive system. For example, Merriman & Stevenson (1997) have argued that the tendency to avoid learning two names for the same object emerges naturally from the competition (MacWhinney 1989) between closely related lexical items.

Another proposed lexical principle is the tendency to focus on object names and nominal categories over other parts of speech. Gentner (1982) compared the relative use of nominal terms, predicative terms, and expressive terms in English, German, Japanese, Kaluli, and Turkish. She found that, in all five languages, words for objects constituted the largest group of words learned by the child. Like Gentner, Tomasello (1992) has argued that nouns are easier to "package" cognitively than verbs. Nouns refer to objects that can be repeatedly touched and located in space, whereas verbs refer to transitory actions that are often hard to repeat and whose contour varies markedly for different agents. However, Gopnik & Choi (1990) and Choi & Bowerman (1991) have reported that the first words of Korean-speaking children include far more verbs than do those of English-speaking children. Findings of this type indicate that the nominal bias emerges only in languages that tend to emphasize nouns.

Even in English, we know that children will often treat a new word as a verb or an adjective (Hall et al 1993), because words like "run," "want," "hot," and "good" are included in some of the child's first words. Children are also quick to pick up socially oriented words such as "hi" and "please." As Bloom et al (1993) and Vihman & McCune (1994) have argued, the nominal bias is far from a predominant force, even in English.

## Social Support

The idea that early word learning depends heavily on the spatio-temporal contiguity of a novel object and a new name can be traced back to Aristotle, Plato, and Augustine. Recently, Baldwin (1991) has shown that children try to acquire names for the objects that adults are specifically attending to. Similarly, Akhtar et al (1996) and Tomasello & Akhtar (1995) have emphasized the crucial role of mutual gaze between mother and child in the support of early word learning. Moreover, Tomasello has argued that human mothers differ significantly from primate mothers in the ways that they encourage mutual attention during language. While not rejecting the role of social support in language learning, Samuelson & Smith (1997) have noted that one can also interpret the findings of Akhtar, Carpenter, and Tomasello in terms of low-level perceptual and attentional matches that help focus the child's attention to novel objects to match up with new words.

## Child-Based Meanings

Several researchers have emphasized the extent to which the shape of the meanings of the first words is governed by a "child-based agenda" (Mervis 1984, Slobin 1985). Children seem to be particularly interested in finding ways of talking about their favorite toys, friends, and foods (Dromi 1997). They also like to learn words to discuss social activities and functions. In fact, Ninio & Snow (1988) have argued that the basic orientation of the child's first words and early grammar is not toward some objective, nominal, cognitive reality, but toward the interpersonal world involving people and social roles.

## Overgeneralization and Undergeneralization

We can refer to the formation of a link between a particular referent and a new name as "initial mapping." This initial mapping is typically fast, sketchy, and tentative. Most lexical learning occurs after the formation of this initial mapping. As the child is exposed repeatedly to new instances of an old word, the semantic range of the referent slowly widens. Barrett (1995), Huttenlocher (1974), and others have viewed this aspect of meaning growth as "decontextualization." Harris et al (1988) have shown that the initial representations of words contain components that are linked to the first few contacts with the word in specific episodes or specific contexts. Gradually, the process of generalization leads to a freeing of the word from irrelevant aspects of the context.

Over time, words develop a separation between a "confirmed core" (MacWhinney 1984, 1989) and a peripheral area of potential generalization. As long as the child sticks closely to attested instances of the category inside the confirmed core, she will tend to undergeneralize the word "car." Anglin (1977) and Dromi (1987) have argued that the frequency of such undergeneralizations is typically underestimated, because undergeneralizations never lead to errors. If one does a careful analysis of the range of uses of new words, it appears that undergeneralization is closer to the rule than the exception. As the confirmed core of the meaning of a word widens and as irrelevant contextual features are pruned out, the word begins to take on a radial or prototype form (Lakoff 1987, Rosch & Mervis 1975). In the center of the category, we find the best instances that display the maximum category match. At the periphery of the category, we find instances whose category membership is unclear and which compete with neighboring categories (MacWhinney 1989).

According to the core-periphery model of lexical structure, overgeneralizations arise from the pressures that force the child to communicate about objects that are not inside any confirmed core. Frequently enough, children's overgeneralizations are corrected when the parent provides the correct name for the object (Brown & Hanlon 1970). The fact that feedback is so consistently available for word learning increases our willingness to believe that major determinants of word learning are social feedback, rather than innate constraints or even word learning biases.

## The Shape of Vocabulary Growth

Researchers have often noted that the growth of the overall size of the lexicon does not follow a smooth linear trend. After the child has acquired an initial vocabulary of about 100 words, the learning of new words seems to progress more and more rapidly. This rapid rise in the size of the vocabulary, which has been called the "vocabulary spurt" (Bates & Carnevale 1993, Bloom 1993), is more evident in some children than in others. However, Mervis & Bertrand (1994) and Dromi (1997) have shown that accurate detection of the timing of the vocabulary spurt may require following children well past the first 100 words. Mervis & Bertrand (1995) argue that the timing of the vocabulary spurt is dependent on the rate of cognitive development, with slower developers having a later spurt. They further claim that, before the beginning of the vocabulary spurt, children cannot pick up words through a few exposures. However, recent experimental work by Woodward et al (1994) and Schafer & Plunkett (1997) has indicated that infants who have not yet gone through the vocabulary shift are still capable of quick learning of new words in an experimental context.

Three accounts have been offered for the timing of the vocabulary burst and the causes of the burst. One account attributes the burst to the development of control over articulatory representations. Schwartz (1988) and Schwartz & Leonard (1981) have shown that young children tend to avoid producing difficult phonological forms. Once these output limitations are surmounted, the child is free to produce words that had been difficult to produce during earlier periods.

A second account (MacWhinney 1982) focuses on the role of syntactic patterns in the learning of new words. Often parents make extensive use of stable syntactic frames such as "Here's the nice (toy name)" or "Show me your (body part name)." Having learned these frames, children can quickly pick up a large quantity of new words in the context of each frame. In this way, the vocabulary spurt could be dependent upon syntactic development. In fact, Bates et al (1988) reported a correlation of between .70 and .84 between lexical size at 20 months and syntactic abilities at 28 months. This level of correlation is exactly what is predicted by a model that views lexical learning as facilitated by the appearance of words in the context of well-understood syntactic frames.

In accord with the Piagetian emphasis on cognitive determination of developmental stages, a third group of authors has attributed the vocabulary spurt to the underlying growth in those cognitive capacities (Bloom 1970, Gopnik & Meltzoff 1987) that allow children to understand the meanings of new words. For example, one could argue that 14-month-olds are not yet ready conceptually to acquire the meanings of comparative adjectives, conjunctions, abstract nouns, speech act verbs, and superordinates. To be sure, very young children have not yet acquired complex relational concepts, such as the ones required to support the learning of form like "nonetheless," "preamble," or "next Thursday" (Kenyeres 1926). However, attempts to relate overall aspects of linguistic development to fundamental changes or shifts in cognitive development have seldom demonstrated strong linkages (Corrigan 1978, 1979). Instead, it appears that the links between cognitive and lexical development are fragmentary and specific to particular lexical fields (Gopnik & Meltzoff 1986).

Each of these three accounts is compatible with attempts (Bates & Carnevale 1993, van Geert 1991) to model vocabulary growth as a dynamic system using logistic growth functions. The nonlinear effects that emerge during the vocabulary spurt can be viewed as arising from the dynamic coupling of the lexical system with a quickly developing system of syntactic patterns, phonological advances, or cognitive advances. As these various patterns develop, they feed into vocabulary growth in a nonlinear and interactive fashion, as growth in vocabulary leads to further growth in syntactic structures, at least during the several months of the vocabulary spurt.

## Components of a Model of Word Learning

We are now ready to explore ways in which these facts about lexical develop-ment can be captured in an emergentist model based on neural network theory. The preceding sections indicate that a good model of lexical learning will need seven components. First, it must provide a system for representing auditory contrasts. Second, it must be able to use this system to store frequently heard auditory sequences. Third, the model must be able to account for the develop-ment from unconstrained babbling to the controlled articulation of real words. Fourth, the model must be able to account for both social and child-based in-fluences on the meanings underlying the first words. Fifth, the model has to ac-count for the ways in which parents can provide social scaffolding that focuses children's attention on referents. Sixth, the model must be able to account for both fast initial learning and slow subsequent tuning of the meaning of new words. Seventh, the model must be able to capture facts about the induction of word meanings from syntactic frames.

Neural network models are systems based on the use of a common language of units, connections, weights, and learning rules. Within this common lan-guage of connectionism, architectures differ markedly both in their detailed patterns of connectivity and in the specific rules used for activation and learn-ing. There are now many excellent readable introductions to the theory and practice of neural network modeling. The reader who is interested in learning more about the mechanics of this framework may wish to consult Bechtel & Abrahamsen (1991) or Fausett (1994).

## Lexical Learning as Self-Organization

One emergentist framework that allows us to model many of these aspects of lexical learning is the self-organizing feature map (SOFM) architecture of Ko-honen (1982), Miikkulainen (1990), and Miikkulainen & Dyer (1991). These self-organizing networks treat word learning as occurring in maps of con-nected neurons in small areas of the cortex. Three local maps are involved in word learning: an auditory map, a concept map, and articulatory maps. Emer-gent self-organization on each of these three maps uses the same learning algo-rithm. Word learning involves the association of elements between these three maps. What makes this mapping process self-organizing is the fact that there is no preestablished pattern for these mappings and no preordained relation be-tween particular nodes and particular feature patterns.

Evidence regarding the importance of syllables in early child language (Bijeljac et al 1993, Jusczyk et al 1995) suggests that the nodes on the auditory map may best be viewed as corresponding to full syllabic units, rather than separate consonant and vowel phonemes. The recent demonstration by Saffran et al (1996) of memory for auditory patterns in 4-month-old infants indicates that children are not only encoding individual syllables but are also remembering sequences of syllables. In effect, prelinguistic children are capable of establishing complete representations of the auditory forms of words. Within the SOFM framework, these capabilities can be represented in two alternative ways. One method uses a slot-and-frame featural notation from MacWhinney et al (1989). An alternative approach views the encoding as a temporal pattern that repeatedly accesses a basic syllable map. A lexical learning model developed by Gupta & MacWhinney (1997) uses serial processes to control word learning. This model couples a serial order mechanism known as an "avalanche" (Grossberg 1978) with a lexical feature map model. The avalanche controls the order of syllables within the word. Each new word is learned as a new avalanche.

The initial mapping process involves the association of auditory units to conceptual units. Initially, this learning links concepts to auditory images (Naigles & Gelman 1995, Reznick 1990). For example, the 14-month-old who has not yet produced the first word may demonstrate an understanding of the word "dog" by turning to a picture of a dog, rather than a picture of a cat, when hearing the word "dog." It is difficult to measure the exact size of this comprehension vocabulary in the weeks preceding the first productive word, but it is probably at least 20 words in size.

In the self-organizing framework, the learning of a word is viewed as the emergence of an association between a pattern on the auditory map and a pattern on the concept map through Hebbian learning (Hebb 1949, Kandel & Hawkins 1992). When the child hears a given auditory form and sees an object at the same time, the coactivation of the neurons that respond to the sound and the neurons that respond to the visual form produces an association across a third pattern of connections which maps auditory forms to conceptual forms. Initially, the pattern of these interconnections is unknown, because the relation between sounds and meanings is arbitrary (de Saussure 1966). This means that the vast majority of the many potential connections between the auditory and conceptual maps will never be used, making it a very sparse matrix (Kanerva 1993). In fact, it is unlikely that all units in the two maps are fully interconnected (Shrager & Johnson 1995). In order to support the initial mapping, some researchers (Schmajuk & DiCarlo 1992) have suggested that the hippocampus may provide a means of maintaining the association until additional cortical connections have been established. As a result, a single exposure to a new word is enough to lead to one trial learning. However, if this initial association is not supported by later repeated exposure to the word in relevant social contexts, the child will no longer remember the word.

## Word Learning and Working Memory

The account of word learning we have been examining so far has focused on the learning of the auditory form of the word. In the infant, learning of the articulatory form is typically more delayed. For adults, the task of articulating a newly perceived word is a simple one. However, for the child in the second year of life, matching up articulations to auditions is a major challenge. The simple control of the articulatory system is still a major challenge for the 2-year-old. Apart from this, the child must acquire a mapping from individual auditory features to articulatory gestures, and must also encode the sequence and prosodic contour of each of the syllables in the word. Just like the learning of auditory sequences requires the mediation of memory systems, the learning of articulatory sequences may involve support from rehearsal loops or hippocampal systems.

Models of word learning in adults (Burgess & Hitch 1992; Grossberg 1978, 1987; Houghton 1990) have tended to emphasize the role of working memory. Gupta & MacWhinney (1997) have shown that a model based on the encoding of syllable strings for output phonology in avalanches does a good job of accounting for a wide variety of well-researched phenomena in the literature on word learning, immediate serial recall, interference effects, and rehearsal in both adults and children (Gathercole & Baddeley 1993).

## The Organization of Semantic Fields

Parallel with the growth of the auditory map, the child is working on the development of an extensive system for conceptual coding. As we have noted, studies of concept development in the preverbal infant (Piaget 1954, Stiles-Davis et al 1985, Sugarman 1982) indicate that the child comes to the language-learning task already possessing a fairly well-structured coding of the basic objects in the immediate environment. Children treat objects such as dogs, plates, chairs, cars, baby food, water, balls, and shoes as fully structured separate categories (Mervis 1984). They also show good awareness of the nature of particular activities such as falling, bathing, eating, kissing, and sleeping.

Like auditory categories, these basic conceptual categories can be represented in self-organizing feature maps. Schyns (1991) applied a self-organizing feature map to the task of learning three competing categories with prototype structures. The individual exemplars of each category were derived from geometric patterns that were blurred by noise to create a prototype structure, although the actual prototypes were never displayed. The simulations showed that the network could acquire human-like use of the categories. When presented with a fourth new word that overlapped with one of the first three words, the system broke off some of the territory of the old referent to match up with the new name. This competitive behavior seems to reflect the process of competition between old words and new words discussed for children's word learning by Markman (1989), Clark (1987), and MacWhinney (1989).

Another simulation of meaning development by Li & MacWhinney (1996) used a standard backpropagation architecture to model the learning of reversive verbs that used the prefix "un-" as in "untie" or "dis-" as in "disavow." The model succeeded in capturing the basic developmental stages for reversives reported by Bowerman (1982) and Clark et al (1995). In particular, the model was able to produce overgeneralization errors such as "*unbreak" or "*disbend." The network's performance was based on its internalization of what Whorf (1938, 1941) called the "cryptotype" for the reversive, which involved a "covering, enclosing, and surface-attaching meaning" that is present in a word like "untangle" but absent in a form such as "*unbreak." Whorf viewed this category as a prime example of the ways in which language reflects and possibly shapes thought.

A similar neural network model of the learning of fine differences in the meaning of the word "over" was developed by Harris (1990, 1994). The Harris model is capable of taking new input test sentences of the type "the pin rolled over the table" and deciding on the basis of past learning that the meaning involved is "across," rather than "covering" or "above." It does this only on the basis of the co-occurrence patterns of the words involved, rather than on information from their individual semantics. Thus, it learns that combinations like "ball," "roll," and "table" tend to activate "across" without regard to facts such as knowing that balls are round and can roll or knowing that tables are flat and that rolling involves movement.

## THE EMERGENCE OF INFLECTIONAL MARKING

One of the most active areas in recent work on language acquisition has been the study of the child's learning of inflectional marking. In English, inflections are short suffixes that occur at the ends of words. For example, the word "dogs" has a final /s/ suffix that marks the fact that it is plural. There are now well over 30 empirical studies and simulations investigating the learning of inflectional marking. The majority of work on this topic has examined the learning of English verb morphology with a particular focus on the English past tense. These models are designed to learn irregular forms such as "went" or "fell," as well as regular past tense forms such as "wanted" and "jumped." Other areas of current interest include German noun declension, Dutch stress placement, and German participle formation. Although the learning of inflectional markings is a relatively minor aspect of language learning, our ability to quantify this process has made it an important testing ground not only for the study of child language, but for developmental psychology and cognitive science more generally.

## A Sample Model for Inflectional Learning

To illustrate how connectionist networks can be used to study the learning of inflectional morphology, let us take as an example the model of German gender learning developed by MacWhinney et al (1989). This model was designed to explain how German children learn to select one of the six different forms of the German definite article. In English, we have a single word "the" that serves as the definite article. In German, the article can take the form "der," "die," "das," "des," "dem," or "den." Which of the six forms of the article should be used to modify a given noun in German depends on three additional features of the noun: its gender (masculine, feminine, or neuter), its number (singular or plural), and its role within the sentence (subject, possessor, direct object, prepositional object, or indirect object). To make matters worse, assignment of nouns to gender categories is often quite nonintuitive. For example, the word for "fork" is feminine, the word for "spoon" is masculine, and the word for "knife" is neuter. Acquiring this system of arbitrary gender assignments is particularly difficult for adult second language learners. Mark Twain expressed his consternation at this aspect of German in a treatise entitled "The aweful German language" (Twain 1935), in which he accuses the language of unfairness in assigning young girls to the neuter gender, while allowing the sun to be feminine and the moon masculine. Along a similar vein, Maratsos & Chalkley (1980) argued that, because neither semantic nor phonological cues can predict which article accompanies a given noun in German, children could not learn the language by relying on simple surface cues.

Although these relations are indeed complex, MacWhinney et al (1989) show that it is possible to construct a connectionist network that learns the German system from the available cues. The MacWhinney et al model, like most current connectionist models, involves a level of input units, a level of hidden units, and a level of output units (Figure 1). Each of these levels or layers contains a number of discrete units or nodes. For example, in the MacWhinney et al model, the 35 units within the input level represent features of the noun that is to be modified by the article. Each of the two hidden unit levels includes multiple units that represent combinations of these input-level features. The six output units represent the six forms of the German article.

As noted above, a central feature of such connectionist models is the many connections among processing units. As shown in Figure 1, each input-level unit is connected to first-level hidden units; each first-level hidden unit is connected to second-level hidden units; and each second-level hidden unit is connected to each of the six output units. None of these hundreds of individual node-to-node connections is illustrated in Figure 1, since graphing each individual connection would lead to a blurred pattern of connecting lines. Instead,

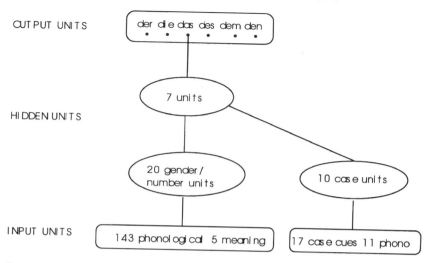

*Figure 1*   A network model of the acquisition of German declensional marking.

a single line is used to stand in place of a fully interconnected pattern between levels. Learning is achieved by repetitive cycling through three steps. First, the system is presented with an input pattern that turns on some but not all of the input units. In this case, the pattern is a set of sound features for the noun being used. Second, the activations of these units send activations through the hidden units and on to the output units. Third, the state of the output units is compared to the correct target and, if it does not match the target, the weights in the network are adjusted so that connections that suggested the correct answer are strengthened and connections that suggested the wrong answer are weakened.

MacWhinney et al tested this system's ability to master the German article system by repeatedly presenting 102 common German nouns to the system. Frequency of presentation of each noun was proportional to the frequency with which the nouns are used in German. The job of the network was to choose which article to use with each noun in each particular context. After it did this, the correct answer was presented, and the simulation adjusted connection strengths so as to optimize its accuracy in the future. After training was finished, the network was able to choose the correct article for 98% of the nouns in the original set.

To test its generalization abilities, we presented the network with old nouns in new case roles. In these tests, the network chose the correct article on 92% of trials. This type of cross-paradigm generalization is clear evidence that the network went far beyond rote memorization during the training phase. In fact, the network quickly succeeded in learning the whole of the basic formal paradigm for the marking of German case, number, and gender on the noun. In addition, the simulation was able to generalize its internalized knowledge to solve the problem that had so perplexed Mark Twain—guessing at the gender of entirely novel nouns. The 48 most frequent nouns in German that had not been included in the original input set were presented in a variety of sentence contexts. On this completely novel set, the simulation chose the correct article from the six possibilities on 61% of trials, versus 17% expected by chance. Thus, the system's learning mechanism, together with its representation of the noun's phonological and semantic properties and the context, produced a good guess about what article would accompany a given noun, even when the noun was entirely unfamiliar.

The network's learning paralleled children's learning in a number of ways. Like real German-speaking children, the network tended to overuse the articles that accompany feminine nouns. The reason for this is that the feminine forms of the article have a high frequency, because they are used both for feminines and for plurals of all genders. The simulation also showed the same type of overgeneralization patterns that are often interpreted as reflecting rule use when they occur in children's language. For example, although the noun *Kleid* (which means clothing) is neuter, the simulation used the initial "kl" sound of the noun to conclude that it was masculine. Because of this, it invariably chose the article that would accompany the noun if it were masculine. Interestingly, the same article-noun combinations that are the most difficult for children proved to be the most difficult for the simulation to learn and to generalize to on the basis of previously learned examples.

How was the simulation able to produce such generalization and rule-like behavior without any specific rules? The basic mechanism involved adjusting connection strengths between input, hidden, and output units to reflect the frequency with which combinations of features of nouns were associated with each article. Although no single feature can predict which article would be used, various complex combinations of phonological, semantic, and contextual cues allow quite accurate prediction of which articles should be chosen. This ability to extract complex, interacting patterns of cues is a characteristic of the particular connectionist algorithm, known as back-propagation, that was used in the MacWhinney et al simulations. What makes the connectionist account for problems of this type particularly appealing is the fact that an equally powerful set of production system rules for German article selection would be quite complex (Mugdan 1977), and learning of this complex set of rules would be a challenge in itself.

## Cues vs Rules

The central issue being addressed in the study of the learning of inflectional markings is whether one can model this process without using formal rules. Rumelhart & McClelland (1986) were the first to provide a demonstration of how rules could emerge from the behavior of neural networks without being explicitly learned. Conceding that irregular forms are indeed produced by connectionist networks, Pinker (1991) nonetheless argues that regular forms are produced by a regular rule. This dual-route model echoes an earlier account by MacWhinney (1978) and related dual-route models in the study of reading by Coltheart et al (1993).

These attempts to preserve a role for rules in human cognition have run into problems with the fact that even the most regular patterns or "rules" display phonological conditioning and patterns of gradience (Bybee 1997) of the type that are well captured in a connectionist network. Moreover, the existence of differences between regular and irregular processing does not, in itself, provide strong evidence for the existence of rules. Kawamoto (1994) has shown that regular and irregular forms display quite different activation patterns, even within a homogeneous neural network. Therefore, differences in the processing of regular and irregular verbs that have recently been demonstrated through neural imaging work (Jaeger et al 1996, Weyerts et al 1996) do not provide strong evidence for the separate existence of rule system.

## U-Shaped Learning

A major shortcoming of nearly all connectionist models of inflectional learning has been their inability to capture the patterns of overgeneralization and recovery from overgeneralization that have been called "u-shaped" learning. In u-shaped learning, the child begins by correctly producing an irregularly inflected form such as "went." Next, under the pressure of the general pattern, the child produces the overgeneralized form "goed." Finally, the child recovers from overgeneralization and returns to saying "went." Some writers have mistakenly assumed that this type of u-shaped learning applies across all verbs to create three major periods in language learning. However, empirical work by Marcus et al (1992) has shown that strong u-shaped learning patterns occur only for some verbs and only for some children.

The modeling of these weaker u-shaped patterns has proven difficult for neural networks. In order to correctly model the child's learning of inflectional morphology, models must go through a period of virtually error-free learning of irregulars, followed by a period of learning of regulars accompanied by the first overregularizations (Marcus et al 1992). No current model consistently displays all of these features in exactly the right combination. MacWhinney

(1997) has argued that models that rely exclusively on back-propagation will never be able to display the correct combination of developmental patterns and that a two-process connectionist approach may be needed (Kawamoto 1994, Stone 1994). The basic process is one that learns new inflectional formations, both regular and irregular, as items in self-organizing feature maps. The secondary process is a network that generalizes the information inherent in feature maps to extract secondary productive generalizations. Unlike Pinker's dual-route account, this proposed account works on a uniform underlying connectionist architecture without relying on formal, symbolic linguistic rules.

## The Role of Semantic Factors

The first attempts to model morphological learning focused exclusively on the use of phonological features as both input and output. However, it is clear that the formation of past-tense forms must also involve semantic factors. In English, the use of semantic information is associated with the irregular patterns of inflection. The idea is that, because we cannot access "went" by combining "go" and "-ed," it might be that we can access it directly by a semantic route. Of course, this idea is much like that underlying the dual-route theory. In German gender, the role of semantic information is much clearer. Köpcke & Zubin (Köpcke 1994; Köpcke & Zubin 1983, 1984; Zubin & Köpcke 1981, 1986) have shown that a wide variety of both phonological and semantic factors are used in predicting the gender of German nouns and their plural. Some of the features involved include alcoholic beverages, superordinates, inherent biological gender, gem stones, body parts, rivers inside Germany, and light vs heavy breezes. Simulations by Cottrell & Plunkett (1991) and Gupta & MacWhinney (1992) have integrated semantic and phonological information in various ways. However, a better understanding of the ways in which semantic factors interact during word formation will require a more extensive modeling of lexical items and semantic features.

## Extensions of Irregular Patterns to New Words

Extending earlier work by Bybee & Slobin (1982) with older children, Prasada & Pinker (1993) examined the abilities of adult native English speakers to form the past tense for nonsense words like "plink," "plup," or "ploth." They found that, the further the word diverged from the standard phonotactic rules for English verbs, the more likely the subjects were to form the past tense by just attaching the regular "-ed" suffix. Ling & Marinov (1993) noted that the original verb-learning model developed by Rumelhart & McClelland (1987) failed to match these new empirical data, largely because of its tendency to overapply irregular patterns. To correct this problem, Ling & Marinov created a nonconnectionist symbolic pattern associator that did a better job modeling the Prasada & Pinker data. However, MacWhinney (1993a) found that the network model of MacWhinney & Leinbach (1991) worked as well as Ling & Marinov's symbolic model in terms of matching up to the Prasada & Pinker generalization data.

## Inflections and the Logical Problem of Language Acquisition

In the network we have been discussing, a single lexical feature map can produce both a rote form like "went" and a productive form like "*goed." The fact that both can be produced in the same lexical feature map allows us to develop a general solution to the "logical problem of language acquisition" (Baker & McCarthy 1981; Gleitman 1990; Gleitman et al 1984; Morgan & Travis 1989; Pinker 1984, 1989; Wexler & Culicover 1980). The logical problem of language acquisition arises from the (incorrect) assumption that recovery from overgeneralization must depend on corrective feedback. Because corrective feedback is seldom available for grammatical patterns (as opposed to semantic and lexical patterns), it can be shown that language learning from input data is impossible. Therefore, it is argued, the acquisition of grammar constitutes a logical problem and requires the postulation of innate constraints on the form of language. The solution to this problem proposed by MacWhinney (1993b) focuses on the competition between regular and irregular forms. In the case of the competition between "went" and "*goed," we expect "went" to become solidified over time because of its repeated occurrence in the input. The form "*goed," however, is supported only by the presence of the -ed form. Figure 2 illustrates this competition.

This particular competition is an example of what Baker (1979) calls a "benign exception to the logical problem." The exception is considered benign because the child can learn to block overgeneralization by assuming that there is basically only one way of saying "went." This Uniqueness Constraint is thought to distinguish benign and nonbenign exceptions to the logical problem. However, from the viewpoint of the Competition Model account we are constructing here, all exceptions are benign.

The basic idea here is that, when a child overgeneralizes and produces "*goed," the system itself contains a mechanism that eventually forces recovery. Thus, the solution to the logical problem of language acquisition emerges from the competition between alternative competing expressions. One of these forms receives episodic support from the actual linguistic input. This episodic support grows slowly over time. The other form arises productively from the operation of analogistic pressures. When episodic support does not agree with these analogistic pressures, the episodic support eventually comes to dominate, and the child recovers from the overgeneralization. This is done without

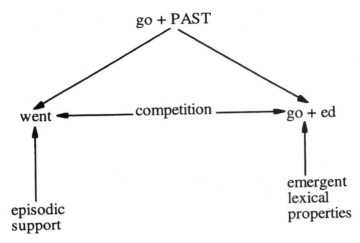

*Figure 2*    Competition between episodic and combinatorial knowledge.

negative evidence, solely on the basic of positive support for the form receiving episodic confirmation.

## THE EMERGENCE OF SYNTACTIC PATTERNS

### Induction from Syntactic Frames

Many aspects of word meaning can be acquired from individual words without relying on the role that the word plays in sentences. However, other aspects of meaning require close attention to the ways in which words are combined. In an early demonstration of these effects, Katz et al (1974) gave children a human and a nonhuman figure and asked them either to "Show me the zav" or to "Show me Zav." When "zav" was treated syntatically as a proper noun by omitting the definite article, 2-year-olds tended to hand the experimenter the figure of a doll. When "zav" was treated syntatically as a common noun by use of the definite article, children tended to hand the experimenter the nonhuman figure. In this way, even children as young as 20 months of age showed how syntactic context can serve as a powerful guide to word learning.

Similar effects have now been demonstrated for a wide variety of syntactic constructions. Brown (1957) found that children could use a sentence frame like "in this picture you see sibbing" to infer that "sib" is a verb. Carey (1978) and Landau et al (1992) found that when asked to choose "not the red one, but the xerillium one," children would assume that "xerillium" was a color name.

Golinkoff et al (1987) showed children movies in which Big Bird and Cookie Monster were either turning separately or turning each other. When 27-month-old children heard "Big Bird is gorping with Cookie Monster," they tended to look at the video with both characters turning separately. However, when they heard "Big Bird is gorping Cookie Monster," they tended to look at the video with Big Bird turning Cookie Monster. These results indicate that children can use the transitive syntactic frame to induce some aspects of the meaning of the new word "gorp." Similarly, if we ask children to "please repulsate Big Bird the banana," they will assume that "repulsate" is a verb of transfer that permits a double-object construction. However, if we tell children to "please repulsate the tub with water," they will assume that "repulsate" is a verb like "fill" that takes a goal as direct object and a transferred object in an instrumental phrase.

Gleitman (1990) has argued that the meanings of words can be induced largely on the basis of this syntactic information. In addition, she has argued that certain aspects of argument structure can only be reliably induced from syntactic frames. However, P Bloom (1994) argued that the fact that representations acquired in this way would be incomplete. Since children have access to both semantic and syntactic information, it seems likely that both types of information are used whenever they are reliable. In a detailed computational model of verb argument frame induction, Siskind (1996) has shown that if the child has access to a basic situational representation along with surface co-occurrence information, the argument frames of verbs, which are in fact the backbone of the language (Goldberg 1995, MacWhinney 1988, Pinker 1989), can be learned easily even from fairly noisy input data.

## The Emergence of Parts of Speech

Psycholinguists working in the standard symbolic tradition (Chomsky 1965, Fodor & Pylyshyn 1988, Lachter & Bever 1988) have pointed to the learning of syntax as a quintessential problem for connectionist approaches. One of the key abilities involved in the learning of syntax is the abstraction of syntactic classes or "parts of speech," such as nouns, verbs, or prepositions. In the theory of universal grammar, these categories are innately given. However, their actual realization differs so much from language to language that it makes sense to explore accounts that induce these categories from the input data.

Bates & MacWhinney (1982) and MacWhinney (1988) emphasize the extent to which the assignment of words to syntactic classes is heavily dependent upon semantic category structure. Although not all nouns are objects, the best or most prototypical nouns all share this feature. As the category of "noun" radiates out (Lakoff 1987), noncentral members start to share fewer of the core features of the prototype. Maratsos & Chalkley (1980) point out that words like "justice" and "lightning" are so clearly nonobjects that their membership in the class of nouns cannot be predicted from their semantic status and can only be inferred from the fact that the language treats them as nouns. Although Bates & MacWhinney (1982) and Maratsos & Chalkley (1980) staked out strongly contrasting positions on this issue, each of the approaches granted the possibility that both co-occurrence and semantic factors play a major role in the emergence of the parts of speech.

At this point, language researchers are primarily interested in exploring detailed models that show exactly how the parts of speech and argument frames can be induced. Elman (1993) has presented a connectionist model that does just this. The model relies on a recurrent architecture of the type presented in Figure 3. This model takes the standard three-layer architecture of pools A, B, and C and adds a fourth input pool D of context units that has recurrent connections to pool B. Because of the recurrent or bidirectional connections between B and D, this architecture is known as "recurrent backpropagation."

A recurrent backpropagation network encodes changes over time by storing information regarding previous states in the pool of units labeled as D. Consider how the network deals with the processing of a sentence such as "Mommy loves Daddy." When the first word comes in, pool C is activated and this activation is passed on to pool B and then pools A and D. The complete state of pool B at Time 1 is stored in pool D. The activation levels in pool D are preserved, while pools A, B, and C are set back to zero. At time 2, the network hears the word "love" and a new pattern of activations is established on pool C. These activations are passed on to pools B, C, and D. However, because pool D has stored activations from the previous word, the new state is blended with the old state and pool C comes to represent aspects of both "Mommy" and "love."

Processing in a network of this type involves more than just storage of a superficial sequence of words or sounds. For example, in the simulations of sentence processing developed by Elman (1993), the output units are trained to predict the identity of the next word. In order to perform in this task, the network needs to implicitly extract part-of-speech information from syntactic co-occurrence patterns. Alternatively, the output units can be used to represent comprehension decisions, as in the model of MacWhinney (1997). In that model, part-of-speech information is assumed and the goal of the model is to select the agent and the patient using a variety of grammatical and pragmatic cues.

The training set for Elman's model consists of dozens of simple English sentences such as "The big dog chased the girl." By examining the weight patterns on the hidden units in the fully trained model, Elman showed that the model was conducting implicit learning of the parts of speech. For example, after the word "big" in our example sentence, the model would be expecting to

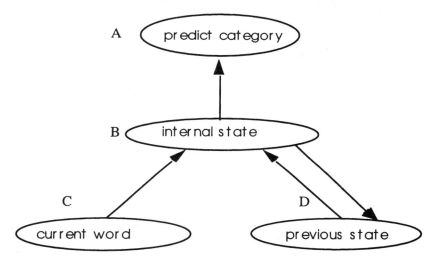

*Figure 3*    A recurrent network.

activate a noun. The model was also able to distinguish between subject and object relative structures, as in "the dog the cat chased ran" and "the dog that chased the cat ran."

## The Emergence of Argument Structures

The machinery governing word combinations depends not only on part of speech information, but also on information regarding detailed aspects of argument structure. Consider the use of verbs like "pour" and "fill." Bowerman (1988) discusses cases in which the child says "I poured the tub with water" instead of "I poured water into the tub," and "I filled water into the tub" instead of "I filled the tub with water." We can describe these errors by saying that the child has overgeneralized the "pour" pattern to the word "fill" or overgeneralized the "fill" pattern to the word "pour." In order to avoid these overgeneralizations and to recover from them once they are made, children have to organize verbs into semantic fields. Extending the self-organizing topological network approach we examined earlier, we can model this process by building a network in which the use of the pattern "V N with N" is correlated with the semantic features of words like "fill," "stuff," and "load," and in which the use of the pattern "V N into N" is correlated with the semantic features of words like "fill," "paint," "cover," and "load." Because a network of this type uses semantic features to achieve a separation on the argument frame map, it is able to implement both the semantic proposals of Bates & MacWhinney (1982) and the co-occurrence proposals of Maratsos & Chalkley (1980).

## CONCLUSION

In this chapter, we have seen how neural network models can help us organize our growing understanding of auditory, articulatory, lexical, inflectional, and syntactic development. There are many aspects of language development to which these models have not yet been applied. We do not yet have models that can learn to control sociolinguistic relations, conversational patterns, narrative structures, intonational contours, and gestural markings. Even in the areas to which they have been applied, emergentist models are limited in many ways. The treatment of the more complex aspects of syntax remains unclear, the modeling of lexical extensions is still quite primitive, and the development of the auditory and articulatory systems is not yet sufficiently grounded in physiological and neurological facts. Despite these limitations, we can see that, by treating language learning as an emergent process, these models have succeeded in providing an exciting new perspective on questions about language learning that have intrigued scholars for centuries.

---

Visit the *Annual Reviews home page* at
http://www.AnnualReviews.org.

---

*Literature Cited*

Akhtar N, Carpenter M, Tomasello M. 1996. The role of discourse novelty in early word learning. *Child Dev.* 62:635–45

Allen R, Gardner B. 1969. Teaching sign language to a chimpanzee. *Science* 165: 664–72

Anglin JM, ed. 1977. *Word, Object, and Conceptual Development.* New York: Norton

Aslin R, Jusczyk P, Pisoni D. 1997. Speech and auditory processing during infancy: constraints on and precursors to language. In *Handbook of Child Psychology,* Vol. 2, ed. D Kuhn, R Siegler. New York: Wiley. In press

Atkinson K, MacWhinney B, Stoel C. 1970. An experiment on the recognition of babbling. *Pap. Rep. Child Lang. Dev.* 5:1–8

Atkinson M. 1992. *Children's Syntax.* Oxford: Blackwell

Baker CL. 1979. Syntactic theory and the projection problem. *Linguist. Inq.* 10: 533–81

Baker CL, McCarthy JJ, eds. 1981. *The Logical Problem of Language Acquisition.* Cambridge: MIT Press

Baldwin DA. 1991. Infants' contribution to the achievement of joint reference. *Child Dev.* 62:875–90

Barrett M. 1995. Early lexical development. In *Handbook of Child Language,* ed. P Fletcher, B MacWhinney. Oxford: Blackwell

Bates E, Bretherton I, Snyder L. 1988. *From First Words to Grammar: Individual Differences and Dissociable Mechanisms.* Cambridge, MA: Cambridge Univ. Press

Bates E, Carnevale G. 1993. New directions in research on language development. *Dev. Rev.* 13:436–70

Bates E, MacWhinney B. 1982. Functionalist

approaches to grammar. See Wanner & Gleitman 1982, pp. 173–218

Bechtel W, Abrahamsen A. 1991. *Connectionism and the Mind: An Introduction to Parallel Processing in Networks.* Cambridge, MA: Blackwell

Bickerton D. 1990. *Language and Species.* Chicago: Chicago Univ. Press

Bijeljac BR, Bertoncini J, Mehler J. 1993. How do four-day-old infants categorize multisyllabic utterances? *Dev. Psychol.* 29:711–21

Bloom L. 1970. *Language Development: Form and Function in Emerging Grammars.* Cambridge, MA: MIT Press

Bloom L. 1993. *The Transition from Infancy to Language: Acquiring the Power of Expression.* Cambridge, MA: Cambridge Univ. Press

Bloom L, Tinker E, Margulis C. 1993. The words children learn: evidence against a noun bias in early vocabularies. *Cogn. Psychol.* 8:431–50

Bloom P. 1994. Overview: controversies in language acquisition. In *Language Acquisition: Core Readings,* ed. P Bloom, pp. 5–48. Cambridge, MA: MIT Press

Bowerman M. 1982. Reorganizational processes in lexical and syntactic development. See Wanner & Gleitman 1982, pp. 73–104

Bowerman M. 1988. The "no negative evidence" problem. In *Explaining Language Universals,* ed. J Hawkins. London: Blackwell

Boysson-Bardies B, Vihman MM. 1991. Adaption to language: evidence from babbling and first words in four languages. *Language* 67:297–320

Brown R. 1957. Linguistic determinism and the part of speech. *J. Abnorm. Soc. Psychol.* 55:1–5

Brown R, Hanlon C. 1970. Derivational complexity and order of acquisition in child speech. In *Cognition and the Development of Language,* ed. JR Hayes, pp. 11–54. New York: Wiley

Burgess N, Hitch G. 1992. Toward a network model of the articulatory loop. *J. Mem. Lang.* 31:429–60

Bybee J. 1997. Regular morphology and the lexicon. *Cognition.* In press

Bybee JL, Slobin DI. 1982. Rules and schemas in the development and use of the English past. *Language* 58:265–89

Carey S. 1978. The child as word learner. In *Linguistic Theory and Psychological Reality,* ed. M Halle, J Bresnan, G Miller, pp. 264–93. Cambridge, MA: MIT Press

Choi S, Bowerman M. 1991. Learning to express motion events in English and Korean: the influence of language-specific lexicalization patterns. *Cognition* 41: 83–121

Chomsky N. 1965. *Aspects of the Theory of Syntax.* Cambridge, MA: MIT Press

Chomsky N. 1980. *Rules and Representations.* New York: Columbia Univ. Press

Clark E. 1987. The principle of contrast: a constraint on language acquisition. See MacWhinney 1987, pp. 1–34

Clark E, Carpenter K, Deutsch W. 1995. Reference states and reversals: undoing actions with verbs. *J. Child Lang.* 22:633–52

Coltheart M, Curtis B, Atkins P, Haller M. 1993. Models of reading aloud: dual-route and parallel distributed processing approaches. *Psychol. Rev.* 100:589–608

Corrigan R. 1978. Language development as related to stage 6 object permanence development. *J. Child Lang.* 5:173–89

Corrigan R. 1979. Cognitive correlates of language: differential criteria yield differential results. *Child Dev.* 50:617–31

Cottrell G, Plunkett K. 1991. Learning the past tense in a recurrent network: acquiring the mapping from meaning to sounds. *Proc. Annu. Conf. Cogn. Sci. Soc., 13th,* ed. K Hammond, D Gentner. Hillsdale, NJ: Erlbaum

Davis K. 1947. Final note on a case of extreme social isolation. *Am. J. Sociol.* 52:432–37

DeCasper AJ, Fifer WP. 1980. Of human bonding: newborns prefer their mothers' voices. *Science* 208:1174–76

de Saussure F. 1966. *Course in General Linguistics.* New York: McGraw-Hill

Dromi E. 1987. *Early Lexical Development.* New York: Cambridge Univ. Press

Dromi E. 1997. Early lexical development. In *The Development of Language,* ed. M Barrett. London: UCL. In press

Eimas PD, Siqueland ER, Jusczyk P, Vigorito J. 1971. Speech perception in infants. *Science* 171:303–6

Elman J. 1993. Incremental learning, or the importance of starting small. *Cognition* 48:71–99

Fausett L. 1994. *Fundamentals of Neural Networks.* Englewood Cliffs, NJ: Prentice Hall

Fodor J. 1983. *The Modularity of Mind: An Essay on Faculty Psychology.* Cambridge, MA: MIT Press

Fodor J, Pylyshyn Z. 1988. Connectionism and cognitive architecture: a critical analysis. *Cognition* 28:3–71

Gathercole V, Baddeley A. 1993. *Working Memory and Language.* Hillsdale, NJ: Erlbaum

Gentner D. 1982. Why nouns are learned before verbs: linguistic relativity versus natural partitioning. In *Language Development: Language, Culture, and Cognition,* ed. S Kuczaj, pp. 301–34. Hillsdale, NJ: Erlbaum

Gleitman L. 1990. The structural sources of verb meanings. *Lang. Acquis.* 1:3–55

Gleitman LR, Newport EL, Gleitman H. 1984. The current status of the motherese hypothesis. *J. Child Lang.* 11:43–79

Goldberg A. 1995. *Constructions.* Chicago: Univ. Chicago Press

Golinkoff R, Hirsh-Pasek K, Cauley K, Gordon L. 1987. The eyes have it: lexical and syntactic comprehension in a new paradigm. *J. Child Lang.* 14:23–46

Golinkoff RM, Mervis CB, Hirsh-Pasek K. 1994. Early object labels: the case for a developmental lexical principles framework. *J. Child Lang.* 21:125–55

Gopnik A, Choi S. 1990. Do linguistic differences lead to cognitive differences? A crosslinguistic study of semantic and cognitive development. *First Lang.* 10:199–215

Gopnik A, Meltzoff A. 1987. The development of categorization in the second year and its relation to the other cognitive and linguistic developments. *Child Dev.* 58:1523–31

Gopnik A, Meltzoff AN. 1986. Relations between semantic and cognitive development in the one-word stage: the specificity hypothesis. *Child Dev.* 57:1040–53

Gopnik M. 1990. Feature blindness: a case study. *Lang. Acquis.* 1:139–64

Grossberg S. 1978. A theory of human memory: self-organization and performance of sensory-motor codes, maps, and plans. *Prog. Theoret. Biol.* 5:233–374

Grossberg S. 1987. Competitive learning: from interactive activation to adaptive resonance. *Cogn. Sci.* 11:23–63

Gupta P, MacWhinney B. 1992. Integrating category acquisition with inflectional marking: a model of the German nominal system. *Proc. 14th Annu. Conf. Cogn. Sci. Soc.* Hillsdale, NJ: Erlbaum

Gupta P, MacWhinney B. 1997. Vocabulary acquisition and verbal short-term memory: computational and neural bases. *Brain Lang.* In press

Hall D, Waxman S, Hurwitz W. 1993. How two- and four-year-old children interpret adjectives and count nouns. *Child Dev.* 64:1651–64

Harris C. 1990. Connectionism and cognitive linguistics. *Connect. Sci.* 2:7–33

Harris CL. 1994. Back-propagation representations for the rule-analogy continuum. In *Analogical Connections,* ed. J Barnden, K Holyoak, pp. 282–326. Norwood, NJ: Ablex

Harris M, Barrett MD, Jones D, Brookers S. 1988. Linguistic input and early word meaning. *J. Child Lang.* 15:77–94

Hebb D. 1949. *The Organization of Behavior.* New York: Wiley

Houghton G. 1990. The problem of serial order: a neural network model of sequence learning and recall. In *Current Research in Natural Language Generation,* ed. R Dale, C Mellish, M Zock, pp. 287–319. London: Academic

Hunt E. 1962. *Concept Learning: An Information Processing Approach.* New York: Wiley

Huttenlocher J. 1974. The origins of language comprehension. In *Theories in Cognitive Psychology: The Loyola Symposium,* ed. R Solso, pp. 331–88. Potomac, MD: Erlbaum

Hyams N. 1995. Nondiscreteness and variation in child language: implications for principle and parameter models of language development. In *Other Children, Other Languages,* ed. Y Levy, pp. 11–40. Hillsdale, NJ: Erlbaum

Hyams N, Wexler K. 1993. On the grammatical basis of null subjects in child language. *Linguist. Inq.* 24(3):421–59

Jaeger JJ, Lockwood AH, Kemmerer DL, Van Valin RD, Murphy BW. 1996. A positron emission tomographic study of regular and irregular verb morphology in English. *Language* 72:451–97

Jakobson R. 1968. *Child Language, Aphasia and Phonological Universals.* The Hague: Mouton

Jusczyk P, Aslin R. 1995. Infants' detection of the sound patterns of words in fluent speech. *Cogn. Psychol.* 29:1–23

Jusczyk PW, Jusczyk AM, Kennedy LJ, Schomberg T, Koenig N. 1995. Young infants' retention of information about bisyllabic utterances. *J. Exp. Psychol.: Hum. Percept. Perform.* 21:822–36

Kandel ER, Hawkins RD. 1992. The biological basis of learning and individuality. *Sci. Am.* 266:40–53

Kanerva P. 1993. Sparse distributed memory and related models. In *Associative Neural Memories: Theory and Implementation,* ed. M Hassoun. New York: Oxford Univ. Press

Katz N, Baker E, Macnamara J. 1974. What's in a name? A study of how children learn common and proper names. *Child Dev.* 45:469–73

Kawamoto A. 1994. One system or two to handle regulars and exceptions: how time-course of processing can inform this debate. In *The Reality of Linguistic Rules,* ed. SD Lima, RL Corrigan, GK Iverson. Amsterdam: Benjamins

Kenyeres E. 1926. *A gyermek elsö szavai es a szófajók föllépése.* Budapest: Kisdednevelés

Kohonen T. 1982. Self-organized formation of topologically correct feature maps. *Biol. Cybern.* 43:59–69

Köpcke K-M. 1994. Funktionale Untersuchungen zur deutschen Nominal- und Verbalmorphologie. *Linguist. Arb.* 319: 81–95

Köpcke K-M, Zubin DA. 1983. Die kognitive Organisation der Genuszuweisung zu den einsilbigen Nomen der deutschen Gegenwartssprache. *Z. Ger. Linguist.* 11:166–82

Köpcke K-M, Zubin DA. 1984. Sechs Prinzipien fur die Genuszuweisung im Deutschen: ein Beitrag zur natürlichen Klassifikation. *Linguist. Ber.* 93:26–50

Kuhl PK. 1991. Human adults and human infants show a "perceptual magnet effect" for the prototypes of speech categories, monkeys do not. *Percept. Psychophys.* 50: 93–107

Kuhl PK, Miller JD. 1975. Speech perception by the chinchilla: voiced-voiceless distinction in alveolar plosive consonants. *Science* 190:69–72

Kuhl PK, Miller JD. 1978. Speech perception by the chinchilla: identification functions for synthetic VOT stimuli. *J. Acoust. Soc. Am.* 63:905–17

Kuhl PK, Padden DM. 1982. Enhanced discriminability at the phonetic boundaries for the voicing feature in macaques. *Percept. Psychophys.* 32:542–50

Kuhl PK, Padden DM. 1983. Enhanced discriminability at the phonetic boundaries for the voicing feature in macaques. *J. Acoust. Soc. Am.* 73:1003–10

Lachter J, Bever T. 1988. The relation between linguistic structure and associative theories of language learning: a constructive critique of some connectionist learning models. *Cognition* 28:195–247

Lakoff G. 1987. *Women, Fire, and Dangerous Things.* Chicago: Chicago Univ. Press

Landau B, Smith L, Jones S. 1992. Syntactic context and the shape bias in children's and adults' lexical learning. *J. Mem. Lang.* 31:807–25

Levitt AG, Utman J, Aydelott J. 1993. From babbling towards the sound systems of English and French: a longitudinal two-case study. *J. Child Lang.* 19:19–49

Lewis MM. 1936. *Infant Speech: A Study of the Beginnings of Language.* New York: Harcourt, Brace

Li P, MacWhinney B. 1996. Cryptotype, overgeneralization, and competition: a connectionist model of the learning of English reversive prefixes. *Connect. Sci.* 8:3–30

Ling C, Marinov M. 1993. Answering the connectionist challenge. *Cognition* 49:267–90

MacWhinney B. 1978. The acquisition of morphophonology. *Monogr. Soc. Res. Child Dev.* 43(1):1–123

MacWhinney B. 1982. Basic syntactic processes. In *Language Acquisition,* Vol. 1: *Syntax and Semantics,* ed, ed. S Kuczaj, pp. 73–136. Hillsdale, NJ: Erlbaum

MacWhinney B. 1984. Where do categories come from? In *Child Categorization,* ed. C Sophian, pp. 407–18. Hillsdale, NJ: Erlbaum

MacWhinney B, ed. 1987. *Mechanisms of Language Acquisition.* Hillsdale, NJ: Erlbaum

MacWhinney B. 1988. Competition and teachability. In *The Teachability of Language,* ed. R Schiefelbusch, M Rice. New York: Cambridge Univ. Press

MacWhinney B. 1989. Competition and lexical categorization. In *Linguistic Categorization,* ed. R Corrigan, F Eckman, M Noonan, pp. 195–242. New York: Benjamins

MacWhinney B. 1993a. Connections and symbols: closing the gap. *Cognition* 49: 291–96

MacWhinney B. 1993b. The (il) logical problem of language acquistion. *Proc. 15th Annu. Conf. Cogn. Sci. Soc.* Hillsdale, NJ: Erlbaum

MacWhinney B. 1997. Lexical connectionism. In *Models of Language Acquisition: Inductive and Deductive Approaches,* ed. P Broeder, J Murre. Cambridge, MA: MIT Press. In press

MacWhinney B, Bates E, eds. 1989. *The Crosslinguistic Study of Sentence Processing.* New York: Cambridge Univ. Press

MacWhinney B, Leinbach J. 1991. Implementations are not conceptualizations: revising the verb learning model. *Cognition* 29: 121–57

MacWhinney BJ, Leinbach J, Taraban R, McDonald JL. 1989. Language learning: Cues or rules? *J. Mem. Lang.* 28:255–77

Mandel DR, Jusczyk PW, Kemler Nelson DG. 1994. Does sentence prosody help infants to organize and remember speech information? *Cognition* 53:155–80

Maratsos M, Chalkley M. 1980. The internal language of children's syntax: the ontogenesis and representation of syntactic categories. In *Children's Language,* ed. K Nelson, 2:127–214. New York: Gardner

Marcus G, Ullman M, Pinker S, Hollander M, Rosen T, Xu F. 1992. Overregularization in language acquisition. *Monogr. Soc. Res. Child Dev.* 57(4)

Markman E. 1989. *Categorization and Naming in Children: Problems of Induction.* Cambridge, MA: MIT Press

Marler P. 1991. Song-learning behavior: the interface with neuroethology. *Trends Neurosci.* 14:199–206

Merriman WE, Stevenson CM. 1997. Restricting a familiar name in response to learning a new one: evidence for the mutual exclusivity bias in young 2-year-olds. *Child Dev.* In press

Mervis C. 1984. Early lexical development: the contributions of mother and child. In *Origins of Cognitive Skills,* ed. C Sophian, pp. 339–70. Hillsdale, NJ: Erlbaum

Mervis C, Bertrand J. 1994. Acquisition of the novel name-nameless category (NC3) principle. *Child Dev.* 65:1646–62

Mervis C, Bertrand J. 1995. Early lexical acquisition and the vocabulary spurt: a response to Goldfield and Reznick. *J. Child Lang.* 22:461–68

Miikkulainen R. 1990. A distributed feature map model of the lexicon. *Proc. 12th Annu. Conf. Cogn. Sci. Soc.* Hillsdale, NJ: Erlbaum

Miikkulainen R, Dyer M. 1991. Natural language processing with modular neural networks and distributed lexicon. *Cogn. Sci.* 15:343–99

Moon C, Cooper RP, Fifer WP. 1993. Two-day infants prefer their native language. *Infant Behav. Dev.* 16:495–500

Morgan J, Travis L. 1989. Limits on negative information in language input. *J. Child Lang.* 16:531–52

Mugdan J. 1977. *Flexionsmorphologie und Psycholinguistik.* Tübingen: Gunter Narr

Naigles LG, Gelman SA. 1995. Overextensions in comprehension and production revisited: preferential looking in a study of dog, cat, and cow. *J. Child Lang.* 22:19–46

Ninio A, Snow C. 1988. Language acquisition through language use: the functional sources of children's early utterances. In *Categories and Processes in Language Acquisition,* ed. Y Levy, I Schlesinger, M Braine, pp. 11–30. Hillsdale, NJ: Erlbaum

Piaget J. 1954. *The Construction of Reality in the Child.* New York: Basic Books

Pinker S. 1984. *Language Learnability and Language Development.* Cambridge, MA: Harvard Univ. Press

Pinker S. 1989. *Learnability and Cognition: The Acquisition of Argument Structure.* Cambridge: MIT Press

Pinker S. 1991. Rules of language. *Science* 253:530–35

Polka L, Werker JF. 1994. Developmental changes in perception of nonnative vowel contrasts. *J. Exp. Psychol.: Hum. Percept. Perform.* 20:421–35

Port RF, van Gelder T, eds. 1995. *Mind as Motion.* Cambridge, MA: MIT Press

Prasada S, Pinker S. 1993. Generalisation of regular and irregular morphological patterns. *Lang. Cogn. Proc.* 8:1–56

Quine WVO. 1960. *Word and Object.* Cambridge, MA: MIT Press

Reznick S. 1990. Visual preference as a test of infant word comprehension. *Appl. Psycholinguist.* 11:145–66

Rosch E, Mervis CB. 1975. Family resemblances: studies in the internal structure of categories. *Cogn. Psychol.* 7:573–605

Rumelhart DE, McClelland JL. 1986. On learning the past tense of English verbs. In *Parallel Distributed Processing: Explorations in the Microstructure of Cognition,* ed. JL McClelland, DE Rumelhart, pp. 216–71. Cambridge: MIT Press

Rumelhart DE, McClelland JL. 1987. Learning the past tenses of English verbs: implicit rules or parallel distributed processes? See MacWhinney 1987, pp. 195–248

Saffran J, Aslin R, Newport E. 1996. Statistical learning by 8-month-old infants. *Science* 274:1926–28

Samuelson LK, Smith LB. 1997. Memory and attention make smart word learning: an alternative account of Akhtar, Carpenter, and Tomasello. *Child Dev.* In press

Savage-Rumbaugh S, Sevcik RA, Hopkins WD. 1988. Symbolic cross-modal transfer in two species of chimpanzees. *Child Dev.* 59:617–25

Schafer G, Plunkett K. 1997. Rapid word learning by 15-month-olds under tightly controlled conditions. *Child Dev.* In press

Schmajuk N, DiCarlo J. 1992. Stimulus configuration, classical conditioning, and hippocampal function. *Psychol. Rev.* 99:268–305

Schwartz RG. 1988. Phonological factors in early lexical acquisition. In *The Emergent Lexicon: The Child's Development of a Linguistic Vocabulary,* ed. MD Smith, JL Locke, pp. 118–40. New York: Academic

Schwartz RG, Leonard LB. 1981. Do children pick and choose? An examination of phonological selection and avoidance in early lexical acquisition. *J. Child Lang.* 9:319–36

Schyns P. 1991. A modular neural network

model of concept acquisition. *Cogn. Sci.* 15:461–508

Shrager JF, Johnson MH. 1995. Waves of growth in the development of cortical function: a computational model. In *Maturational Windows and Adult Cortical Plasticity,* ed. B Julesz, I Kovacs, pp. 31–44. New York: Addison-Wesley

Shvachkin N. 1948. Razvitiye fonematicheskogo vospriyatiya rechi v rannem vozraste. *Izv. Akad. Pedagog. Nauk RSFSR* 13:101–32

Siskind JM. 1996. A computational study of cross-situational techniques for learning word-to-meaning mappings. *Cognition* 61: 39–91

Slobin D. 1985. Crosslinguistic evidence for the language-making capacity. In *The Crosslinguistic Study of Language Acquisition,* Vol. 2: *Theoretical Issues,* ed. D Slobin, pp. 1157–256. Hillsdale, NJ: Erlbaum

Stiles-Davis J, Sugarman S, Nass R. 1985. The development of spatial and class relations in four young children with right-cerebral-hemisphere damage: evidence for an early spatial constructive deficit. *Brain Cogn.* 4(4):388–412

Stone G. 1994. Combining connectionist and symbolic properties in a single process. In *The Reality of Linguistic Rules,* ed. SD Lima, RL Corrigan, GK Iverson, pp. 417–44. Amsterdam: Benjamins

Sugarman S. 1982. Developmental change in early representational intelligence: evidence from spatial classification strategies and related verbal expressions. *Cogn. Psychol.* 14:410–49

Tesar B, Smolensky P. 1997. Learnability in Optimality Theory. *Linguist. Inq.* In press

Tomasello M. 1992. *First Verbs: A Case Study of Early Grammatical Development.* Cambridge: Cambridge Univ. Press

Tomasello M, Akhtar N. 1995. Two-year-olds use pragmatic cues to differentiate reference to objects and actions. *Cogn. Dev.* 10:201–24

Twain M. 1935. The aweful German language.

*In The Family Mark Twain.* New York: Harper Brothers

van der Lely H. 1994. Canonical linking rules: forward vs. reverse linking in normally developing and Specifically Language Impaired children. *Cognition* 51:29–72

van Geert P. 1991. A dynamic systems model of cognitive and language growth. *Psychol. Rev.* 98:3–53

Vihman MM, McCune L. 1994. When is a word a word? *J. Child Lang.* 21:517–42

Wanner E, Gleitman L, eds. 1982. *Language Acquisition: The State of the Art.* New York: Cambridge Univ. Press

Wexler K, Culicover P. 1980. *Formal Principles of Language Acquisition.* Cambridge, MA: MIT Press

Weyerts H, Penke M, Dohrn U, Clahsen H, Münte T. 1996. Brain potentials indicate differences between regular and irregular German noun plurals. *Essex Res. Rep. Linguist.* 13:54–67

Whorf B. 1938. Some verbal categories of Hopi. *Language* 14:275–86

Whorf B. 1941. The relation of habitual thought and behaviour to language. In *Language, Culture, and Personality: Essays in Memory of Edward Sapir,* ed. L Spier, pp. 75–93. Ogden, UT: Univ. Utah Press

Woodward AL, Markman EM, Fitzsimmons CM. 1994. Rapid word learning in 13- and 18-month-olds. *Dev. Psychol.* 30:553–66

Wyttenback M, Hoy D. 1996. Categorical perception of sound frequency by crickets. *Science* 273:1542–44

Zubin DA, Köpcke KM. 1981. Gender: a less than arbitrary grammatical category. In *Pap. 17th Region. Meet.,* ed. R Hendrick, C Masek, M Miller, pp. 439–49. Chicago: Chicago Linguist. Soc.

Zubin DA, Köpcke KM. 1986. Gender and folk taxonomy: the indexical relation between grammatical and lexical categorization. In *Noun Classes and Categorization,* ed. C Craig, pp. 139–80. Amsterdam: Benjamins

*Annu. Rev. Psychol. 1998. 49:229–58*

# RECONCILING PROCESSING DYNAMICS AND PERSONALITY DISPOSITIONS

*Walter Mischel*

Department of Psychology, Columbia University, New York, New York 10027;
e-mail: wm@psych.columbia.edu

*Yuichi Shoda*

Department of Psychology, University of Washington, Seattle, Washington 98195;
e-mail: yshoda@u.washington.edu

KEY WORDS: traits, person-situation interactions, cognitive-affective system, personality stability, dispositions, dynamics, social cognition

## ABSTRACT

Developments in personality-social psychology, in social cognition, and in cognitive neuroscience have led to an emerging conception of personality dynamics and dispositions that builds on diverse contributions from the past three decades. Recent findings demonstrating a previously neglected but basic type of personality stability allow a reconceptualization of classic issues in personality and social psychology. It reconstrues the nature and role of situations and links contextually sensitive processing dynamics to stable dispositions. It thus facilitates the reconciliation within a unitary framework of dispositional (trait) and processing (social cognitive–affective–dynamic) approaches that have long been separated. Given their history, however, the realization of this promise remains to be seen.

## CONTENTS

229

# INTRODUCTION

Throughout the history of the field, two different approaches to personality have competed (often bitterly) in the search for an adequate theory of the person as an individual and of the important differences between persons. In this chapter we ask if they can be reconciled in light of developments within personality-social-cognitive psychology in the past three decades and make the case that the answer is affirmative—at least theoretically, although the depths of the splits that have occurred have made such reconciliation difficult to realize.

# TWO APPROACHES TO PERSONALITY: PROCESSING DYNAMICS AND BEHAVIORAL DISPOSITIONS

In one approach, personality is construed as a system of mediating units (e.g. encodings, expectancies, goals) and psychological processes or cognitive-affective dynamics, conscious and unconscious, that interact with the situation. In this view, in the past twenty years, the basic question has been to understand how the person functions psychologically in terms of the mediating processes that underlie stable individual differences in social behavior and that can make sense of intra-individual variability across situations (e.g. Bandura 1986; Cantor 1994; Cantor & Kihlstrom 1987; Higgins 1990, 1996; Mischel 1973, 1984, 1990; Pervin 1990a,b).

The second approach, dispositional or trait theory, in recent years personified in the Big Five approach (e.g. Costa & McCrae 1997; Wiggins & Trapnell 1997), posits broad stable traits, factors, or behavioral dispositions as its basic units. Its fundamental goal is to characterize individuals in terms of a comprehensive but finite, preferably small set of stable dispositions that remain invariant across situations and that are distinctive for the individual, determining a wide range of important behaviors (e.g. Allport 1937, Funder 1991, Goldberg 1993, Wiggins & Pincus 1992). Thus, traditionally, as textbooks regularly teach, the processing approach tends to focus on the interaction of the specific situation with the social-cognitive-emotional processing system of the individual. The dispositional approach, in contrast, focuses on the broad stable characteristics that differentiate individuals consistently, seeking evidence for the breadth and durability of these differences across diverse situations.

## Divergent Goals

The uneasy, often even antagonistic relationship between these two approaches over many decades in part reflects that their advocates tend to be committed passionately to different goals that seem to be in intrinsic conflict and even mutually preemptive. Consequently, the field has long been divided into two subdisciplines, pursuing two distinct sets of goals—either personality processes or personality dispositions—with different agendas and strategies that often seem in conflict (Cervone 1991; Cronbach 1957, 1975; Mischel & Shoda 1994). Currently these debates on the relative virtues and limitations of these alternatives occupy center stage in personality theory, with special issues and handbooks devoted both to explicating the distinctive contributions of each of the two approaches and to pointing out the limitations of the other side, as each either critiques or ignores the other (e.g. Cervone 1991, Funder 1991, Goldberg 1993, Pervin 1994, Wiggins & Pincus 1992). A good example of this dualistic approach to personality is seen in pursuit of the question of whether human personality is malleable or stable over the life course, with trait conceptions of personality generally demonstrating stability and process conceptions of personality typically finding change (Heatherton & Weinberger 1994, Heatherton & Ambady 1993).

## Two Fields—Or One?

The most common, and often justified, critique of processing approaches is that they neglect the stable dispositional differences between individuals and thus bypass a core aspect of the personality construct. Studies conducted within these approaches tend to focus on the effects of situational character-istics on people in general, and as a consequence they are often viewed as un-deremphasizing the role of individual differences, or even as relegating them to the role of unwanted, "error" variance. They thus are easily criticized as los-ing the person and the phenomena of personality in their focus on processes. Objecting to such a neglect, Funder (1991), for example, advocates a return to an intuitively appealing neo-Allportian global dispositional approach, remind-ing advocates of processing approaches that people are characterizable in broad dispositional terms, as in the person who is always (or mostly) miserable-and-complaining, and arguing that such information has potential explanatory as well as predictive value (Funder 1994). A failure to take ac-count of such differences in temperament or other dispositions on which peo-ple differ would at the least highly constrain any personality theory and risks creating an oxymoron.

Even assuming, however, the existence of broad temperamental and other pervasive human characteristics, the question still remains: What is the nature of the basic invariances that form the core of each person's personality? What are the intra-individual dynamics and psychological processes that mediate be-tween these invariances and their experiential and behavioral expression? As Epstein (1994) put it, articulating his concerns about trait theory generally and the Big Five in particular, "a description of surface attributes, although useful for some purposes, provides a poor basis for understanding process. If one wishes to understand what makes people tick, and what to do about their off-beat ticking, a more dynamic interactive approach capable of elucidating cause-and-effect relations is necessary" (p. 121).

## PERSONALITY AT THE CROSSROADS

Given this history, the field is now at a major choice point: to try to carve an overarching framework that integrates the two disciplines to pursue both goals within one field, or to show that such an integration is impossible or un-constructive. Absent such a reconciliation, personality psychology is likely to continue to split itself in half, as the partitions that separate basic processes and individual differences in its mainstream journal already institutionalize, at best indifferent to each other, at worst undermining each other, and in ei-ther case risking making it more difficult to become a cumulative coherent sci-ence.

A vivid illustration of the unfortunate consequences of this division can be found in research on coping with stress, which traditionally has been pursued either in a dispositional framework—*coping styles*—or in a *coping processes* approach (e.g. Lazarus 1993). The styles approach assumes that each person is characterized by a type of coping strategy consistently across a wide range of situations. It measures the individuals' typical coping strategy, either by reports of typical strategy use or by averaging behavior in multiple situations into a single coping style index. The process approach, on the other hand, focuses on what people do in a specific stressful encounter, focusing on the change over time and across situations, and asks: What type of coping strategies do people use in what situations?

While each approach makes a contribution, they leave an important gap. One casualty, for example, is the phenomenon of flexibility in adaptation of coping styles (Chiu et al 1995, Shoda 1996). As the process approach stresses, such flexibility may be valuable because no single type of coping behavior is effective in all situations. For example, sometimes it is better to blunt anxiety-provoking events and sometimes it is better to monitor for them, and it is important to discriminate which one to use and when (Chiu et al 1995, Miller 1987). Therefore, a person with a situationally invariant global coping style is bound to be less effective in at least some situations. To capture such differences among individuals in flexible use of coping styles in response to different situational characteristics, however, requires a perspective that focuses on stable individual differences in coping that is situationally contextualized and process connected, "specifying meaningful patterning and regularities in person-environment transactions" (Coyne & Gottlieb 1996, p. 971). That is, it will require the integration of both approaches.

This point is also relevant to, and is being taken increasingly seriously in, behavioral medicine and health psychology (Baumeister & Heatherton 1996; Miller et al 1996a,b; Taylor & Aspinwall 1996). Likewise, the interactional, indeed transactional, perspective has allowed an analysis of emotions as "responses to the appraised person-environment *relationship*" (emphasis in original) that has reinvigorated the research in that area (e.g. Smith & Pope 1992, p. 32). And in the same vein, current analyses of the self construe it as experienced and defined in part in relation to significant others, again requiring a transactional dynamic perspective (e.g. Andersen et al 1997). Any personality theory that wishes to be relevant to these areas also needs to take that perspective into account. The message here is easy to misconstrue. Dispositions, no matter how conceptualized, are key aspects of the personality construct. The point is that personality theory needs to analyze dispositions in a way that allows us to understand how individuals interact with situations and, most importantly, to identify and assess the dynamic intra-individual processes that underlie these interactions.

## *Steps Toward Reconciliation*

To reconcile the two approaches to personality requires first an understanding of their differences. Some of these differences sound greater than they are and seem more to be matters of differential emphases and preferred levels of analysis than fundamental incompatibilities. Indeed there are grounds for reconciliation. It has long been recognized that the existence of overall enduring important differences between individuals in such qualities as temperament, chronic mood and affective states, and skills does not necessarily create any theoretical conflict with processing approaches (e.g. Cantor 1994; Mischel 1968, 1973, 1990, 1993; Pervin 1990a,b). Nor are process-oriented approaches incompatible with evidence for substantial genetic contributions to personality. On the contrary, they assume such contributions and incorporate them into the framework (Mischel 1993, Mischel & Shoda 1995).

Rather than denying the importance of individual differences in personality and behavior, processing approaches have helped to identify diagnostic situations in which such differences, for example with regard to aggressive tendencies or self-control abilities, are likely to become particularly visible (e.g. Baumeister et al 1993, Shoda et al 1990, Wright & Mischel 1987).

Other process-oriented researchers have examined the stable correlates and consequences of individual differences in such social cognitive person variables as the goals and personal projects pursued over time (e.g. Cantor 1994, Cantor & Fleeson 1994), the person's beliefs and goal structures (Weary & Edwards 1994), and the type of focus primed in goal pursuit such as gain-oriented versus loss-avoidant (Higgins 1996b,c). They even have probed the implications of the person's own implicit theories about personality in terms of stable traits versus modifiable processes have and shown the importance of these theories for how individuals experience their worlds and act within them (e.g. Dweck & Leggett 1988, Dweck et al 1995; Y Hong, C Chiu & CS Dweck, submitted for publication).

Studies of basic cognitive-attentional processes during self-control efforts in young children in the past decade also have identified dramatic threads of long-term continuity and stability in the course of development (e.g. Mischel et al 1989). The results show significant and substantial links between seconds of delay of gratification in certain diagnostic laboratory situations in preschool and behavioral outcomes years later in adolescence and early adulthood (e.g. Mischel et al 1989, Shoda et al 1990). For example, seconds of preschool delay time significantly predicted verbal and quantitative scores on the Scholastic Aptitude Test (SAT) administered in adolescence (Shoda et al 1990). It also correlated significantly with parental ratings of competencies, including ability to use and respond to reason, planfulness, ability to handle stress, ability to delay gratification, self-control in frustrating situations, and ability to concentrate without becoming distracted. The preschoolers' self-control strategies in the delay of gratification situations, in turn, seem to be foreshadowed by the types of strategies they use in certain mother-toddler interactions three years earlier (Sethi & Shoda 1997). Such levels of stability and meaningful networks of associated developmental outcomes seem clearly indicative of long-term personality coherence. They also provide support for the construct of social-emotional intelligence (Cantor & Kihlstrom 1987, Goleman 1995, Mischel et al 1996, Salovey & Mayer 1990). Provocative, albeit still tentative, connections to findings on temperament and attention processes early in life are also emerging (e.g. Rothbart et al 1995).

Moves toward integration also are visible from at least some dispositional theorists who increasingly seem to allow room for the contextualized, situation-bound expressions of traits, and who seek to incorporate motivational and processing-dynamic concepts into their models (e.g. Revelle 1995). In one direction is the trait-state distinction, with emphasis on the state that is evoked with the particular context as influencing the behavior within that situation, whereas the broader trait disposition is seen as underlying the types of states likely to be readily activated within the person. Research in this vein increasingly is aimed at specifying the boundary conditions within which traits will be selectively activated (e.g. Stemmler 1997). Most notably, a quiet but potentially profound transformation may be occurring in the very definition of personality dispositions. For many researchers, the construct seems to be moving away from the global and uncontextualized trait construct, criticized thirty years earlier for the empirically unviable assumption of cross-situational consistency (Mischel 1968), to: "likelihood and rates of change in behavior in response to particular situational cues" (Revelle 1995, p. 315)—a definition independent of cross-situational consistency that any process theorist could happily accept.

A viable theoretical reconciliation requires crossing many conceptual and methodological barriers that underlie the historical divisions. That calls, first of all, for a framework for an adequately rich and comprehensive processing model. Such a framework must be capable of dealing with the complexity of human personality and the cognitive-affective dynamics, conscious and unconscious—both "cool" and "hot," cognitive and emotional—that underlie the individual's distinctive, characteristic internal states and external behavioral expressions (see Metcalfe & Jacobs 1998). It also requires a reconceptualization of the situation in psychological terms that captures the interaction of context with the dynamic processing system in the generation of those distinctive behavioral expressions. And it requires a conceptual and methodological bridge from the dynamic processing system that characterizes individuals idiographically (when $N = 1$) to the characterization and classification of disposi-tional types and subtypes nomothetically (when $N =$ many). We consider be-low some of the most relevant developments.

## Evolving Models of Processing Dynamics

Attempts to build a theory of processing dynamics that respects the complexity of the human mind and its often contrary, conflictful, perplexing behavioral expressions, in the tradition pioneered by Freud and advanced over the century by such theorists as Henry Murray, Gardner Murphy, Kurt Lewin, and George Kelly, continue and seem to be having a resurgence in contemporary personality-social psychology (see Cervone 1991, Gollwitzer & Bargh 1996, Higgins & Kruglanski 1996, Mischel et al 1996, Pervin 1990a,b). Although there are many differences among particular processing models in specific variables, they share a focus on the social-cognitive-emotional mediating pro-cesses that underlie, motivate, and guide behavior. Many use language and theoretical constructs that draw extensively on social, cognitive, and social learning theories and concepts as well as on self theories and research (e.g. Bandura 1982, 1986; Baumeister & Heatherton 1996; Cantor 1990, 1994; Dodge 1986, 1993; Downey & Walker 1989; Dweck & Leggett 1988; Fiske & Taylor 1991; Higgins 1987, 1996b,c; Kihlstrom & Cantor 1984; Markus & Ki-tayama 1991; Mischel 1973, 1990; Scheier & Carver 1988a,b; Shoda & Mischel 1993; Vallacher & Wegner 1987). They tend to be predominantly "so-cial cognitive" in their theoretical language, but they also are sensitive to the role of automatic and unconscious processing (e.g. Kihlstrom 1987, 1990; Uleman & Bargh 1989) and to the goals and motivations that underlie behavior (e.g. Gollwitzer & Bargh 1996, Pervin 1989, Read & Miller 1989a,b, Westen 1990) in interaction with the situation or psychological context.

Most of these approaches draw heavily on information processing models and it is here that some particularly exciting developments for personality the-ory have unfolded. In recent years models of information processing have be-come available that promise to have some of the richness and complexity needed to make them relevant for a dynamic conception of personality. Going beyond the "cool cognitions" of the early models based on serial, central, and logical computing analogues, they take account of the fact that personally im-portant information processing is affect-laden, encompassing not just cool cognitions but hot representations and emotional states (e.g. Kahneman & Snell 1990, Smith & Lazarus 1990) that impact profoundly on decisions and behaviors (e.g. Mischel & Shoda 1995, Wright & Mischel 1982).

A key development that makes such processing models germane for the analysis of cognitive-affective personality dynamics is a shift in their focus. The focus now is not just on how much of a particular unit (e.g. self-efficacy expectations or anxiety states or achievement goals) a person has, but also on how the units relate to each other within that person, forming a unique network of interconnections that functions as an organized whole. Such a dynamic interacting processing system can operate rapidly in parallel at multiple levels of accessibility, awareness, and automaticity, able to exceed the limitation of conscious awareness (Kihlstrom 1990). It goes beyond the conceptualization of the individual as a bundle of mediating variables or as a flow chart of discrete procedures and decision rules to a more parallel and distributed (rather than serial, centralized) processing system. It is also congruent with the insights coming from cognitive neuroscience in the past decade, such as the neural network theories and connectionist models (e.g. Anderson 1996, Kandel & Hawkins 1992, Rumelhart & McClelland 1986). The unifying theme is that the key to complex human information processing is in the organization of the relationships among the units through which they are interassociated. These developments make it possible to begin to conceptualize social information processing as a dynamic organized network of interconnected and interacting cognitions and affects (e.g. Kunda & Thagard 1996, Read & Miller 1998, Shoda & Mischel 1998, Shultz & Lepper 1996), operating at various levels of awareness (e.g. Westen 1990).

## AN EMERGING CONCEPTION OF THE INDIVIDUAL: THE COGNITIVE-AFFECTIVE PERSONALITY SYSTEM

Growing out of these contributions, a unifying framework has emerged (articulated in Mischel & Shoda 1995) called the cognitive-affective processing system approach, reviewed next.

### Individual Differences in Chronic Accessibility of Units

In the cognitive-affective personality system (CAPS) approach, individual differences are seen as reflecting in part difference in the chronic accessibility or activation levels of the particular mental-emotional representations—the cognitions and affects—the person has available. For twenty-five years these types of cognitive-emotional mediating units have been conceptualized in terms of five relatively stable person variables on which individuals differ in processing self-relevant information (Mischel 1973). In the intervening years, these units have been enriched, modified, and supplemented by extensive research (reviewed in Mischel & Shoda 1995, Mischel et al 1996) and are summarized in Table 1. These units refer to various types of mental events— thoughts and affects—that become activated characteristically and stably within a given individual in relation to certain features of situations or of the self.

Note that affects and goals, as well as encodings, expectancies, and beliefs, and competencies and self-regulatory plans and strategies constitute the types

**Table 1**   Types of cognitive-affective units in the personality mediating system[a]

1. Encodings: Categories (constructs) for the self, people, events, and situations (external and internal).
2. Expectancies and Beliefs: About the social world, about outcomes for behavior in particular situations, about self-efficacy.
3. Affects: Feelings, emotions, and affective responses (including physiological reactions).
4. Goals and Values: Desirable outcomes and affective states; aversive outcomes and affective states; goals, values, and life projects.
5. Competencies and Self-Regulatory Plans: Potential behaviors and scripts that one can do, and plans and strategies for organizing action and for affecting outcomes and one's own behavior and internal states.

[a]From Mischel & Shoda (1995). Reprinted with permission.

of units within the CAPS system. Individual differences in chronic accessibility are reflected in the finding that, for example, some individuals tend to encode ambiguous negative events as instances of personal rejection (e.g. Downey & Feldman 1996), whereas others may be prone to feel angry even when they hear a mumbled greeting (e.g. Dodge 1993), and others characteristically experience irritability and distress (e.g. Eysenck & Eysenck 1985).

## Individual Differences in Stable Organization of Relations

In this type of CAPS model, stable individual differences also, and importantly, reflect the distinctive organization of relationships among the cognitions and affects, which characterizes how they change in their salience, or activation, over time and in relation to different situations. It is this organization that guides and constrains the activation of the particular cognitions, affect, and actions that are available within the system in relation to one another and to situational features. And it is this organization that constitutes the basic stable structure of personality and that underlies and reflects the person's characteristic distinctiveness. This stable organization or network of interrelations is conceptualized as the product of the individual's cognitive social learning history in interaction with the biological history, such as temperamental, and genetic-biochemical determinants (e.g. Plomin et al 1994, Posner 1997, Rothbart et al 1994, Wachs & King 1994).

The stable structure of personality emerges in the course of development, and it reflects both experience and genetics, generating the distinctive stable patterns of behavior characteristic of the individual (Mischel & Shoda 1995). The system is intrinsically interactive with the social world in which it is contextualized, and it is continuously activated, partly by external features, partly by its own internal cognitive and affective activities—such as its fantasy, daydreaming, planning, and self-regulatory attempts (Mischel et al 1996, Shoda & Mischel 1998). In turn, the behaviors that the personality system generates impact on the social world, partly shaping and selecting the interpersonal situations the person subsequently faces in a dynamic transaction (Buss 1987).

To recapitulate, the CAPS analysis begins with the assumption that individuals differ stably in the chronic accessibility or activation levels of the particular mental representations available to them (e.g. Higgins 1996a, Higgins & Bargh 1987, Mischel 1973) but adds a second assumption—namely, stable individual differences in the distinctive organization of relationships among the cognitions and affects available in the system. The latter is consistent with the emerging connectionist models of social information processing (Read & Miller 1994) as well as with contemporary models of the biological bases of human information processing (e.g. Anderson 1996, Rumelhart & McClelland 1986) and of the brain (e.g. Crick & Koch 1990, Churchland & Sejnowski 1992, Edelman 1987, Kandel & Hawkins 1992).

## Dynamic, Transactional System: The Active/Proactive Person

A schematic, highly simplified illustration of such a personality system is in Figure 1, which shows that a personality system is characterized by the available cognitive and affective units (Table 1), organized in a distinctive network of interrelations. When certain configurations of situation features are experienced by an individual, a characteristic subset of cognitions and affects (shown schematically as *circles*) becomes activated through this distinctive network of connections in the encoding process. Within any individual a rich system of interconnections among the cognitive and affective units guides and constrains further activation of other units throughout the network, ultimately activating plans, strategies, and potential behaviors in the behavior generation process. Within each person, the organization of this system is assumed to be stable and unique. In this type of system, mediating units become activated in relation to some situation features, are deactivated or inhibited in relation to others, and are not affected by the rest. That is, the connections among units within the stable network that characterizes the person may be positive, increasing the activation, or negative (shown as *broken lines* in Figure 1), which decreases the activation. It should be evident that in this view the personality system is active and indeed proactive, not just reactive—a system that anticipates, influences, rearranges, and changes situations as well as reacts to them. Thus the personality system and the behavior it generates selects, modifies, and shapes the environment in reciprocal transactions (see Mischel & Shoda 1995, Figure 5, p. 264).

## Incorporating Context

One important implication of this view of personality is that individuals may differ characteristically in the particular situational features (e.g. being teased, being approached socially) that are the salient active ingredients for them (Mischel & Shoda 1995). When they are present, they activate the individual's distinctive dynamics, i.e. their predictable characteristic pattern of cognitive, affective, and behavioral reactions to those situations. However, these dynamics are not just activated by external features of situations (as when milk that is spilled on an adolescent in line at the cafeteria is encoded as a violation) (cf Dodge 1993) but also by feedback from one's own cognitions and affects activated by such internal events as one's affective state and thoughts, such as "when sad," "when lonely" (Wright & Mischel 1988), and from situations that are simply imagined or anticipated (e.g. Cantor et al 1982). Thus, to reiterate, there also are internal feedback loops within the system through which self-generated stimuli (as in thinking, fantasy, daydreaming) activate their distinctive pathways of connections (e.g. Shoda & Mischel 1998). The behaviors the person constructs may in turn affect the interpersonal environment and social ecology, which changes the situational features that are encountered subsequently, in continuous transactions, that connects the behavioral patterns constructed by the personality system back to the situations encountered (e.g. Dodge 1986, 1993, 1997a,b).

## The System in Action: Identifying Dynamics and Linking Them to Dispositional Types

To illustrate such a system in action, consider a person for whom potentially conflictful social interactions reliably activate rejection expectancies. When beginning to discuss a troublesome relationship issue with a romantic partner, for example, the individual's anxious expectations thus trigger scripts such as scanning for evidence of imminent rejection and focusing on those features of the situation most likely to provide such evidence (Downey & Feldman 1996). These expectations, affects, and behaviors interact and combine to lower the individual's threshold for perceiving rejection. Ambiguous partner behavior thus may be perceived as rejection, leading, within this distinctive processing system, to the activation of behavioral scripts for hostility (Ayduk et al 1997). The individual's enacted hostility can elicit partner rejection and, ultimately, relationship erosion, thus fulfilling and maintaining rejection expectations in a positive feedback loop reflecting dynamic interaction between the individual's cognitive-affective processing system and features of the environment (Downey et al 1997). Note that behavior generation ultimately depends both on the situational features and on the cognitive-affective organization of the system. When the relevant situational features are present, characteristic processes become activated in a predictable pattern.

A particular noteworthy characteristic of this pattern is that hostile behavior becomes activated specifically in relation to perceived rejection from a roman-

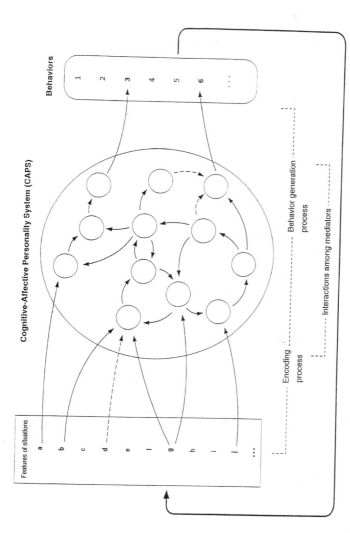

*Figure 1*  Simplified illustration of types of cognitive-affective mediating processes that generate an individual's distinctive behavior patterns. Situational features activate a given mediating unit (the encoding process), which activates specific subsets of other mediating units through a stable network of relations that characterize an individual, generating distinctive cognition, affect, and behavior in response to different situations. The relation may be positive (*solid line*), which increases the activation, or negative (*dashed line*), which decreases the activation. (Adapted from Mischel & Shoda 1995, Figure 4, p. 254.)

tic partner. The same individual can behave exceptionally caringly in other situations (e.g. early in the relationship). Linking this type of processing dynamic to the dispositional construct—in this case rejection sensitivity (Downey & Feldman 1996)—requires identifying the people who share these cognitive-affective unit organization by assessing the similarity in the *if...then* patterns that characterize them in their intimate relationships (Downey & Feldman 1996, Wright & Mischel 1987). Such a strategy allows construction of dispositional taxonomies based on the shared dynamic processes that underlie the distinctive *if...then* behavioral signatures that can distinguish a particular dynamic prototype.

This example illustrates that although intra-individual dynamics exist within a given individual, they need not just be studied idiographically with $N = 1$. By categorizing dynamics into types, one can work at a level when $N =$ many, applying an idiographic person-centered framework to do nomothetic research (Shoda et al 1994). This approach allows one to focus not just on the average overall differences between persons on particular dimensions but also on the characteristic ways they behave distinctively in relation to particular types of contexts. Note also that observers' dispositional judgments in fact depend on the *if...then* patterns in which the behavior unfolds in context (Shoda et al 1994), not just on the mean level of a type of behavior observed (e.g. average level of friendly behaviors). If the pattern changes, so does the dispositional judgment (Shoda et al 1989).

## COMPLEX BEHAVIORAL EXPRESSIONS OF THE PERSONALITY SYSTEM'S STABILITY

By definition, an information processing system like CAPS is sensitive to changing external and internal conditions. Just as one can say that "if it changes, it must be processes" (Folkman & Lazarus 1985), the reverse in this case may be true: If it is a processing system, then it must respond to changing conditions. But an important and often unrecognized point here is that changes in the behavioral expression of a processing system do not imply that the structure of the system itself is unstable or inconsistent. An extremely stable pattern and organization may characterize and constrain the surface changes in the individual's behavior. As in a musical piece, the notes played at any moment may change, but they follow a pattern that reflects the underlying structure of the composition. Thus the consistency and stability in the underlying structure of the processing system may be reflected in patterns of change in the observable behavior (Larsen 1989). During the past decade, several empirical approaches to operationalizing consistency at a higher level have been proposed and explored, as indicated below.

## Variations Across Situations: Stable Individual Differences in Situation-Behavior If...Then Relations

It follows from the assumptions of the CAPS model that the behavioral variation in relation to changing situations in part constitutes a potentially meaningful reflection of the personality system itself. Whereas different cognitions, affects, and behaviors become activated as the situation and its features change, the interconnections among them remain unchanged across situations. That is, the personality system determines the relationships between the types of situations encountered and the cognitive, affective, and behavioral responses. As the *if's* change, so do the *then's,* but the relationship between them is stable as long as the personality system remains unchanged.

This assumption leads this approach to expect characteristic, predictable patterns of variation in the individual's behavior across situations. If personality is a stable system that processes the information about the situations, external or internal, then it follows that as individuals encounter different situations, their behaviors should vary across the situations, reflecting important differences among them in their psychological by active features (Mischel & Shoda 1995). Over time this will generate distinctive *if...then* situation-behavior profiles of characteristic elevation and shape like those illustrated in Figure 2. To illustrate with a simple example, suppose that in situation A people rarely initiate personal interactions, whereas in situation B such interactions are relatively frequent. Suppose also that Person 1 tends to become irritated when she thinks she is being ignored, whereas person 2 is happier when he is left alone, and even becomes irritated when people tell him personal stories. Then Person 1 will become irritated in situation A, but not in situation B; Person 2 will show the opposite *if...then* pattern, irritated in situation B but not in A. These affects further activate other cognitions and feelings in each situation, following the pathways of activation distinctive for each person. These individual differences reflect the particular acquired meanings of the situational features in terms of the cognitions and affects associated with them, so that even if both people are similar in their overall levels of "irritability," they will display distinctive, predictable patterns of behavioral variability in their *if...then* signatures.

Consistent with the clinical wisdom of such classic processing theories as Freud's conception of psychodynamics, clues about peoples' underlying processing dynamics and qualities—the construals and goals, the motives and passions, that drive the individual—may be seen not only in its overall average frequency but also in when and where the person manifests a type of behavior. In short, this type of model expects that the stable patterns of situation-behavior relationships that unfold provide a key to the personality—an expression of personality coherence, not a source of error to be eliminated systemati-

Child # 9  profile stability: r = 0.89

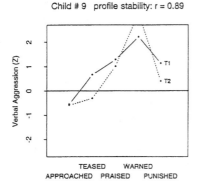

Child # 28  profile stability: r = 0.49

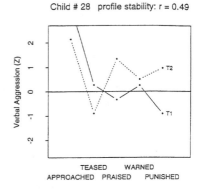

*Figure 2*  Illustrative intra-individual, situation-behavior profiles for verbal aggression in relation to five situations in two time samples (*solid* and *dotted lines*). Data are shown in standardized
scores (*Z*) relative to the normative levels of verbal aggression in each situation. (From Shoda et
al 1994, Figure 1, p. 678.)

cally by aggregating out the situation. It thus broadens the concept of the invariances in the expression of personality to include the profile of situation-
behavior relations that might characterize the person, not just the overall average level of particular types of behavior aggregated across diverse situations.

## Empirical Evidence for Stable If...Then Profiles

These theoretical expectations have received direct empirical support in a series of studies of the social behavior (e.g. "verbal aggression," "compliance")
of children who were systematically observed in relation to the interpersonal
situations in which the behavior occurred in vivo in a residential summer camp
setting (e.g. Shoda et al 1993a, 1994). To illustrate, some children were found
to be consistently more verbally aggressive than others when warned by an
adult but were much less aggressive than most peers when peers approached
them positively. In contrast, another group of children with a similar overall
average level of aggression were distinguished by a striking and opposite pattern: They were more aggressive than any other children when peers approached them positively, but were exceptionally unaggressive when warned
by an adult. To test the overall hypothesis, the profile stabilities for each individual were ipsatively computed, and the statistical significance of the group
mean stability was tested. The results were highly significant for such behaviors as verbal aggression and compliance (Shoda et al 1994).

It is noteworthy that in classic trait approaches to behavioral dispositions,
such intra-individual variations in a type of behavior across situations (after

the main effects of situations are removed by standardization) is assumed to reflect only intrinsic unpredictability or measurement error. From that perspective, the stability of the intra-individual pattern of variation should on average
be zero. The obtained findings obviously contradict this expectation and reveal
that meaningfully patterned behavioral expressions of personality, contextualized within particular situations, characterize individuals. They yield distinctive profiles of variability for particular types of behavior, forming a behavioral signature of personality (Shoda et al 1994). Note that such profiles, illustrated in Figure 2, have a meaningful shape as well as elevation. They reflect
when a given individual becomes particularly angry or depressed, anxious or
relieved, in a stable pattern, such as the following: He A when X but B when Y,
and does A most when Z. Ironically, by focusing on the effects of the situation
on the organization of behavior in depth and detail it became possible to find
this second type of personality stability, enriching rather than undermining the
personality construct.

## Behavioral Roots of Self-Perceived Consistency

Recent evidence shows that these more-complex manifestations of personality
stability and coherence also are linked to self-perceptions of consistency. It is
noteworthy that the individual's self-perception of consistency with regard to
a dimension of behavior or trait in recent research has been related to the intra-
individual *if...then* profile stability, not to the level of cross-situational consistency. This was found in a reanalysis by Mischel & Shoda (1995) of the Carle-
ton College field study (Mischel & Peake 1982). In that study, college students
were repeatedly observed on campus in various situations relevant to their conscientiousness in the college setting (such as in the classroom, in the dormi-
tory, in the library), assessed over repeated occasions in the semester. Students
who perceived themselves as consistent did not show greater consistency
cross-situationally than did those who perceived themselves as variable in conscientiousness.

Mischel & Shoda (1995) reexamined those data to test the hypothesis that
the students' self-perceptions of consistency would be related to the stability
of their situation-behavior profiles. As the first set of two columns of Figure 3
show (and as reported in Mischel & Peake 1982), those who perceived themselves as consistent (the first light column) did not show greater overall cross-
situational consistency than those who did not. Note, however, that for individuals who perceived themselves as consistent (the second set of columns),
the average situation-behavior profile stability correlation was near 0.5, but it
was trivial for those who viewed themselves as inconsistent. It is the stability
in the situation-behavior profiles, not the cross-situational consistency of behavior, that seems to underlie the perception of consistency.

In sum, such stable situation-behavior profiles reflect characteristic intra-individual patterns in how the person relates to different psychological conditions, forming a sort of behavioral signature of personality (Shoda et al 1994). Most striking is not so much that this type of behavioral signature of personality exists but rather that it has so long been treated as error and purposefully removed by simply averaging behavior over diverse situations. Whereas such aggregation was intended to capture personality, it actually can remove data that can alert us to the individual's most distinctive qualities and unique intra-individual patterning.

## The Personality Paradox Demystified

The types of *if...then* situation-behavior relations that a dynamic personality system like CAPS necessarily generates has important implications for the field, particularly the classic "personality paradox" (Bem & Allen 1974). As Bem & Allen noted two decades ago, on the one hand, the person's behavior across situations yields only modest cross-situational consistency coefficients (Hartshorne & May 1928, Newcomb 1929), but on the other hand, personality theory's fundamental assumption, and our intuition, insist that personality surely is stable (e.g. Bem & Allen 1974; Heatherton & Weinberger 1994; Krahe 1990; Mischel 1968; Moskowitz 1982, 1994).

This paradox dissolves, however, by recognizing that the variability of behaviors within individuals across situations is neither all "error" nor is it "due to the situation rather than to the person." Instead, it is at least partly an essential expression of the enduring but dynamic personality system itself and its stable underlying organization. Thus the person's behaviors in a domain will necessarily change from one type of situation to another because when the *if* changes, so will the *then,* even when the personality structure remains entirely unchanged. Just how the individual's behavior and experience change across situations is part of the essential expression of personality (Mischel & Shoda 1995) and becomes a key focus for personality assessment. From this perspective, the person's ability to make subtle discriminations among situations and to take these cues into account in the self-regulation of behavior in order to adapt it to changing situational requirements is a basic aspect of social competence, not a reflection of inconsistency (Chiu et al 1995, Shoda et al 1993a). This type of discriminative facility seems to be a component of social intelligence, a sensitivity to the subtle cues in the situation that influences behavior. Such discriminative facility, for example, by encoding spontaneously social information in conditional versus global dispositional terms, was found to predict the quality of the person's social interaction (Chiu et al 1995). Indeed such *discriminative facility* is an index of adaptive behavior and constructive func-

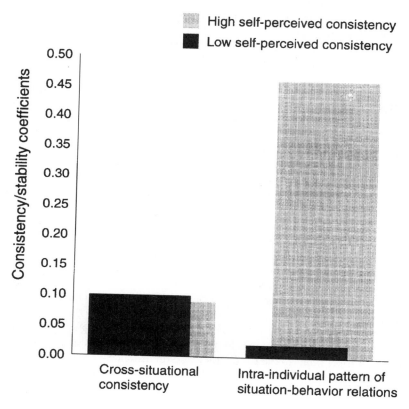

*Figure 3*   Self-perceived consistency and the organization of behavior. Cross-situational consistency and the stability of person-situation profiles for people high versus low in perceived consistency in conscientiousness (based on data in Mischel & Peake 1982). (From Mischel & Shoda 1995, Figure 3, p. 251.)

tioning, whereas consistency regardless of subtle contextual cues can be a sign of rigidity (Chiu et al 1995).

## Redefining Situations in Terms of Active Psychological Ingredients: The Ifs and Thens of Personality

Situations have been difficult to incorporate into personality theory in part because they have been defined in nominal rather than psychological terms (e.g. "playground," "arts and crafts"). Specific nominal situations, like school playground, however, may provide information about individual differences only in relation to such specific places and be of limited interest if they are not generalizable beyond them.

In the CAPS approach, one seeks to analyze situations in terms of their *active ingredients* or *psychological features,* i.e. those in relation to which the person's characteristic dynamics become activated (Mischel & Shoda 1995, Shoda et al 1994). In the case of rejection-sensitive individuals (Downey & Feldman 1996), for example, such features include criticism or lack of attention in the context of an intimate relationship. In the presence of those diagnostic psychological ingredients, regardless of the nominal setting (at school, at home), the characteristic dynamics and their typical behavioral expressions should become activated and predictable. For example, individuals characterized by dynamics in which angry feelings and aggressive impulses become activated in relation to aversive and frustrating experiences tend to show their prototypic behavior depending on competency demands of the situation (Wright & Mischel 1987). By identifying and classifying diverse nominal situations in terms of their functional equivalence with regard to psychological features (e.g. the types of competencies they demand), it becomes possible to specify the types of diagnostic conditions in which characteristic dynamics and their behavioral expressions will be seen.

To identify such potentially diagnostic *if*s, one can analyze the open-ended descriptions provided by people who know each other well (Wright & Mischel 1988). Such analyses suggest that even children tend to spontaneously qualify their characterizations of people they know well with conditional modifiers. These modifiers point to the psychological circumstances, both interpersonal (e.g. when teased by peers) and intrapsychic (e.g. when mad) in which the individual's characteristic behaviors (e.g. verbal aggression) are expressed and contextualized.

In addition to identifying the relevant *if*s, an analysis of intra-individual dynamics also requires specifying the *then*s. Research from many directions is providing relevant strategies for the assessment of experiences and behaviors (Cervone & Williams 1982, Mischel 1993, Mischel et al 1996). The strategies encompass systematic time sampling of tasks, behavior, and perceptions at the moment in the everyday course of life (e.g. Cantor et al 1991, Moskowitz et al 1994), self-reports of reactions to daily stressors (e.g. Bolger & Shilling 1991), sampling of physical symptoms and emotional reactions to them (Larsen & Kasimatis 1991) as well as records of personal strivings and well-being (Emmons 1991), and therapeutic interventions to facilitate emotional processing of traumatic events (Foa & Riggs 1993). All these methods allow systematic analyses of the types of *if*s and *then*s significant in the lives of individuals, relevant to different characteristic behavioral patterns generated by the underlying system.

## Stable Patterns of Change over Time

Evidence for stability in the patterning of change also comes from studies of the frequency and regularity of daily mood changes over time when individuals are assessed repeatedly (Larsen 1987, 1989). For example, some college students reliably exhibit a pronounced weekly pattern of change in their affects, while others do not (Larsen & Kasimatis 1990). And for some individuals, different affects covary over time so that on some days they might experience most of the negative affects, while on others the positive affects occur. Other individuals, however, are characterized by the fact that their affects do not covary to a high degree, so that on some days they may be happy but not necessarily contented, and on other days they are sad but not angry. Such differences in the degree to which distinct affects covary in turn have been related to emotional reactivity, and among men to psychosomatic complaints (Larsen & Cutler 1996). In a related direction, research by Cantor and colleagues has pioneered ways to make visible the types of psychosocial dynamics that underlie the coping process as people pursue their life projects over time (e.g. Cantor & Fleeson 1994).

# CROSSING THE GAP?

So far we have considered the links from dynamics to dispositions. It is, of course, also possible to reconcile the two approaches to personality by starting on the other end and trying to identify the dynamic processes that characterize members of dispositional types. Such a route is particularly appealing to the degree that there is consensus about the dispositional types themselves. Historically and currently such consensus is widely seen as essential for the field of personality psychology. Indeed, the subjective sense of well-being in the field has swung over the years in a series of cycles from depression to euphoria, back and forth, in direct relation to the perceived degree of agreement achieved (or claimed) for that consensus.

## From Dispositions to Dynamics

The most popular candidate for such consensus and durability in recent years has been the Big Five approach. Hailed by its enthusiasts as a quiet revolution (e.g. Goldberg 1992), its claim of an achieved consensus for representing the structure of different personalities in terms of the Big Five factors has been widely embraced. This reception is understandable in a field tired of self-criticism and eager to go beyond a potentially endless array of intercorrelated personality constructs to a small set of factors or basic dispositions. Consequently, the Big Five provides a promising taxonomy that could be linked to the types of processing dispositions conceptualized within the CAPS approach. This connection certainly merits exploration.

Concurrently, however, there also are signs of disagreements in the consensus, and growing concern about the limitations of the approach. In a special journal issue devoted to an analysis of current trait theory and the Big Five approach, for example, Pervin (1994) reviews the claims about the Big Five (e.g. Brody 1988, Goldberg 1993, Wiggins & Pincus 1992) and finds them remarkably discrepant from the data. Pervin's critique is only one strong voice in a chorus of many, all expressing diverse concerns lest the contributions of this approach be lost among the exaggerated and even preemptive claims made by overenthusiastic advocates. Especially worrisome is the slippage from the summary meaning of trait terms to the causal-explanatory meaning that seems to have developed as the Big Five, originally presented as psycholexical descriptive dimensions about behavior, metaphorphize into the basic units used to explain what underlies and generates those behaviors (see also John & Robins 1993, McAdams 1992). Localizing someone in the factor space defined by psycholexical dimensions does not necessarily help to explain and predict why and when a person behaves in characteristic ways. The goal of explanation in personality psychology includes understanding the intra-individual psychological mediating dynamic processes that underlie individual differences. As Block put it, after a penetrating critique of the Big Five on conceptual, empirical, and methodological grounds, "my final most ambitious suggestion is that, in the conceptual/empirical arguments to be made for specific dimensions, of whatever number, these constructs be situated within a coherent, *intra-individual* theoretical framework" (emphasis in original) (1995, p. 210).

Because the Big Five are cast at a highly general, global, unconditionalized level, it is understandable that their empirical links to specific behavioral outcomes, such as performance measures, are modest. Relevant to this, for example, Pervin (1994) questions Goldberg's (1993, p. 31) assertion that "reviews of the literature have concluded that personality measures when classified within the Big-Five domains, are systematically related to a variety of criteria of job performance" and that they are "valid predictors" that show incremental validities over measures of cognitive ability for predicting job proficiency. To illustrate, the best correlations averaged 0.22 for conscientiousness (for the other four trait factors the estimated true correlations ranged from 0.00 to 0.18). To those who still remember how those types of correlations felt when they were first noted in 1968 (e.g. Mischel 1968, Peterson 1968), not to mention earlier (e.g. Vernon 1964), Pervin's conclusion will seem familiar: "What is clear…is that the personality measures did not show incremental validity over measures of cognitive ability for the measures of core job proficiency…. In areas such as this, I'm still not sure that we have gone much beyond the .30

correlation barrier between trait measures and measures of behavior" (1994, p. 108).

However, such critiques may apply only to the degree that dispositional approaches focus on traits at a very high level of abstraction in which they are not contextualized in relation to the situations in which they function. While the trait construct seems to have become less global and more contextualized for some personologists (e.g. Baumeister et al 1993, Bornstein et al 1996, Larsen 1989, Revelle 1995, Stemmler 1997), such movement toward the conditionalization of dispositions is, of course, contradicted to the degree that researchers focus exclusively on the abstract, broad level of analysis of the Big Five approach without also incorporating more contextualized levels and dispositional subtypes.

The encouraging news, however, for the goal of reconciling dispositional and processing approaches is that a number of researchers are showing how dispositions like those in the Big Five can be analyzed in terms of the cognitive-affective process dynamic characteristic of them. For example, attempts to forge a link between trait and process orientations to personality are exemplified in research by Bolger to delineate several of the processes whereby neuroticism leads to heightened distress (Bolger 1990, Bolger & Schilling 1991, Bolger & Zuckerman 1995). In a series of studies using a daily diary methodology, Bolger and colleagues (1996) found that neuroticism affects distress through increasing both exposure and reactivity to stressful events, especially interpersonal conflict. Furthermore, neuroticism-related differences in reactivity seem to be due in part to differential choice of coping efforts (e.g. high neuroticism people were more likely to use confrontative coping) and differential effectiveness of those efforts (e.g. when used by high neuroticism people, self-control was ineffective in reducing depression).

The search for types of people who differ in the types of behavior they show in relation to different types of situations is also facilitated by a triple typology model and methodology developed by Vansteelandt & Mechelen (1997). Drawing on the conditional analysis of dispositions proposed by Wright & Mischel (1987) and Mischel & Shoda (1995), the triple typology model of individual differences yields typologies of person, situation, and behavior classes. Their method simultaneously identifies clusters of people, situations, and behaviors such that each cluster of people is characterized by distinctive *if...then* relations, using the clusters of situation identified as the units of *ifs* and the clusters of behaviors indentified as the units of *thens*. This method makes it possible, for example, to differentiate subtypes of hostile people in terms of the types of hostile behavior they are likely to manifest in different types of frustrating situations (Vansteelandt & Mechelen 1997).

## Genetic Determinants of Cognitive-Affective Dynamics

The individual's cognitive-affective processing system arises in the course of development from a foundation that is both biochemical and psychosocial, genetically guided, as well as shaped by experience and learning in the course of development (Mischel & Shoda 1995). To link processing dynamics and predispositions requires clarifying not only the structure and organization of the cognitive-affective-behavioral processing system but also its biochemical-genetic foundations (Saudino & Plomin 1996). These individual differences in genetic foundations presumably affect how people construe or encode—and shape—their environments, which in turn produce important person-context interactions throughout the life course (Plomin 1994, Plomin et al 1997, Rutter 1997, Saudino & Plomin 1996). Dispositions like those identified in the Big Five approach may be a useful step in that direction, a promising guide for where to look, but it is unlikely to be the conclusion.

The study of the biochemical foundations of dispositions, although still at an early phase, already points to some temperamental characteristics that seem particularly important influences on the structure and organization of CAPS. These largely heritable characteristics, such as activity level, visible early in development, seem particularly relevant to the person's emotional life (e.g. Bates & Wachs 1994, Buss & Plomin 1984, Plomin et al 1990), and they are likely to have important, albeit complex, links to emotional-attentional-self-regulatory processes (e.g. Posner 1997, Rothbart et al 1994, 1997). Theoretically, these influences should be manifested not just in the mean levels of particular types of behavior as traditional dispositional approaches expect, but also in the patterns of stable *if...then* relations in which they are expressed, as dynamic processing approaches predict, in ways that are contextualized and interactive with features of situations.

## Personality as a Unified Field

To the degree that the boundary between dispositional and process approaches to personality becomes fuzzy and even evaporates, there are theoretical implications for the study of personality that need to be made explicit. Suppose, for example, that the *if...then* relationship, rather than the unconditionalized global trait, becomes a basic unit in personality assessment and theory. Then the analyses of just how and why variation in the situation is predictably linked to variation in the characteristic response pattern distinctive for the person becomes a fundamental route for personality assessment. That requires recognition of the high cost of decontextualizing personality. It highlights the need for collaboration rather than confrontation with disciplines bifurcated from personality psychology, such as cognitive and social psychology, by a historical definition of personality that pits it against the situation rather than rooting it within it.

Traditionally, the "situation" has been deliberately eliminated in the assessment of personality in order to distill those stable aspects that characterize the individual, no matter what the context, i.e. across diverse situations. From that perspective, the analysis of situations and of what determines behavior within them becomes the province of social psychology (pioneered by Floyd Allport), whereas the study of individuals and individual differences regardless of the situation becomes the mission of personality psychology, founded by Gordon Allport (the other brilliant brother in the team that created this partition of the two fields). This division seems to have served both disciplines well for many of their early years, but it may have outlived its usefulness, with the boundaries becoming increasingly fuzzy as social psychologists focus on person-situation interactions and personality psychologists incorporate the role of situations into the analysis of dispositions (e.g. Higgins & Kruglanski 1996).

As Gordon Allport (1937, p. 61) emphasized since the start of the field, the stable intra-individual patterns that characterize each person are at the core of personality, yet curiously much of modern personality psychology has searched for dispositions while losing those internal processes and dynamics. The two goals of personality psychology, to understand both dispositions and dynamics, have long had separate histories driven by different conceptions and commitments, more in competition than in the service of building a cumulative coherent science of personality. Might both goals be enhanced if pursued as two sides of the same unitary system within one field?

ACKNOWLEDGMENT

Preparation of this chapter and the research for it by the authors were supported in part by Grants MH39349 and MH45994 to Walter Mischel from the National Institute of Mental Health.

> **Visit the *Annual Reviews home page* at**
> **http://www.AnnualReviews.org.**

## Literature Cited

Allport GW. 1937. *Personality: A Psychological Interpretation.* New York: Holt, Rinehart & Winston

Andersen SM, Reznik I, Chen S. 1997. The self in relation to others: motivational and cognitive underpinnings. In *The Self Across Psychology: Self-Recognition, Self*

*Awareness, and the Self-Concept,* ed. JG Snodgrass, RL Thompson, pp. 233–75. New York: NY Acad. Sci.

Anderson JR. 1996. (1983). *The Architecture of Cognition.* Mahwah, NJ: Erlbaum

Ayduk O, Downey G, Testa A, Shoda Y, Ying Y. 1997. Does rejection elicit hostility in rejection sensitive women? *Soc. Cogn.* In press

Bandura A. 1982. Self-efficacy mechanism in human agency. *Am. Psychol.* 37:122–47

Bandura A. 1986. *Social Foundations of Thought and Action: A Social Cognitive Theory.* Englewood Cliffs, NJ: Prentice Hall

Bates JE, Wachs TD, eds. 1994. *Temperament: Individual Differences at the Interface of Biology and Behavior.* Washington, DC: Am. Psychol. Assoc.

Baumeister RF, Heatherton TF. 1996. Self-regulation failure: an overview. *Psychol. Inq.* 7:1–15

Baumeister RF, Heatherton TF, Tice D. 1993. When ego threats lead to self-regulation failure: negative consequences of high self-esteem: *J. Pers. Soc. Psychol.* 64:141–56

Bem DJ, Allen A. 1974. On predicting some of the people some of the time: the search for cross-situational consistencies in behavior. *Psychol. Rev.* 81:506–20

Block J. 1995. A contrarian view of the five-factor approach to personality description. *Psychol. Bull.* 117:187–215

Bolger N. 1990. Coping as a personality process: a prospective study. *J. Pers. Soc. Psychol.* 59:525–37

Bolger N, Schilling EA. 1991. Personality and the problems of everyday life: the role of neuroticism in exposure and reactivity to daily stressors. *J. Pers.* 59:355–86

Bolger N, Zuckerman A. 1995. A framework for studying personality in the stress process. *J. Pers. Soc. Psychol.* 69:890–902

Bornstein RF, Riggs MJ, Hill EL, Calabrese C. 1996. Activity, passivity, self-denigration, and self-promotion: toward an interactionist model of interpersonal dependency. *J. Pers.* 64:637–73

Brody N. 1988. *Personality: In Search of Individuality.* New York: Academic

Buss AH, Plomin R. 1984. *Temperament: Early Developing Personality Traits.* Hillsdale, NJ: Erlbaum

Buss DM. 1987. Selection, evocation and manipulation. *J. Pers. Soc. Psychol.* 53:1214–21

Cantor N. 1990. From thought to behavior: "having" and "doing" in the study of personality and cognition. *Am. Psychol.* 45:735–50

Cantor N. 1994. Life task problem-solving: situational affordances and personal needs. Presidential address Soc. Pers. Soc. Psychol. (Div. 8 Am. Psychol. Assoc.), 1993, Toronto, Can. *Pers. Soc. Psychol. Bull.* 20:235–43

Cantor N, Fleeson W. 1994. Social intelligence and intelligent goal pursuit: a cognitive slice of motivation. In *Integrative Views of Motivation, Cognition, and Emotion. Nebr. Symp. Motiv.*, ed. W Spaulding, 41:125–79. Lincoln: Univ. Nebr. Press

Cantor N, Kihlstrom JF. 1987. *Personality and Social Intelligence.* Englewood Cliffs, NJ: Prentice Hall

Cantor N, Mischel W, Schwartz JC. 1982. A prototype analysis of psychological situations. *Cogn. Psychol.* 14:45–77

Cantor N, Norem J, Langston C, Zirkel S, Fleeson W, Cook-Flannagan C. 1991. Life tasks and daily life experience. *J. Pers.* 59:425–51

Cervone D. 1991. The two disciplines of personality psychology: review of Handbook of Personality: Theory and Research. *Psychol. Sci.* 2:371–77

Cervone D, Williams SL. 1982. Social cognitive theory and personality. In *Modern Personality Psychology: Critical Reviews and New Directions*, ed. GV Caprara, GL Van Heck, pp. 200–52. New York: Harvester Wheatsheaf/Simon & Schuster

Chiu C, Hong Y, Mischel W, Shoda Y. 1995. Discriminative facility in social competence: conditional versus dispositional encoding and monitoring-blunting of information. *Soc. Cogn.* 13:49–70

Churchland PS, Sejnowski TJ. 1992. *The Computational Brain.* Cambridge, MA: MIT Press

Costa PT, McCrae RR. 1997. Longitudinal stability of adult personality. In *Handbook of Personality Psychology*, ed. R Hodan, J Johnson, S Briggs, pp. 269–90. San Diego, CA: Academic

Coyne JC, Gottlieb BH. 1996. The mismeasure of coping by checklist. *J. Pers.* 64:959–91

Crick F, Koch C. 1990. Towards a neurobiological theory of consciousness. *Semin. Neurosci.* 2:263–75

Cronbach LJ. 1957. The two disciplines of scientific psychology. *Am. Psychol.* 12:671–84

Cronbach LJ. 1975. Beyond the two disciplines of scientific psychology. *Am. Psychol.* 30:116–27

Dodge KA. 1986. A social information processing model of social competence in children. *Cogn. Perspect. Child. Soc. Behav. Dev., Minn. Symp. Child Psychol.* 18:77–125

Dodge KA. 1993. Social-cognitive mechanisms in the development of conduct disorder and depression. *Annu. Rev. Psychol.* 44:559–84

Dodge KA. 1997a. *Testing developmental theory through prevention trials.* Presented at Bienn. Meet. Soc. Res. Child Dev., Apr., Washington, DC

Dodge KA. 1997b. *Early peer social rejection and acquired autonomic sensitivity to peer conflicts: conduct problems in adolescence.* Presented at Bienn. Meet. Soc. Res. Child Dev., Apr., Washington, DC

Downey G, Feldman S. 1996. Implications of rejection sensitivity for intimate relationships. *J. Pers. Soc. Psychol.* 70:1327–43

Downey G, Freitas A, Michaelis B, Khouri H. 1997. The self-fulfilling prophecy in close relationships: Do rejection sensitive women get rejected by their partners? Dep. Psychol., Columbia Univ., NY. Unpubl. manuscr.

Downey G, Walker E. 1989. Social cognition and adjustment in children at risk for psychopathology. *Dev. Psychol.* 25:835–45

Dweck CS, Chiu C, Hong Y. 1995. Implicit theories and their role in judgments and reactions: a world from two perspectives. *Psychol. Inq.* 6:267–85

Dweck CS, Leggett EL. 1988. A social-cognitive approach to motivation and personality. *Psychol. Rev.* 95:256–73

Edelman GM. 1987. *Neural Darwinism: The Theory of Neuronal Group Selection.* New York: Basic Books

Emmons RA. 1991. Personal strivings, daily life events, and psychological and physical well-being. *J. Pers.* 59:453–72

Epstein S. 1994. Trait theory as personality theory: Can a part be as great as the whole? *Psychol. Inq.* 5:120–22

Eysenck HJ, Eysenck MW. 1985. *Personality and Individual Differences: A Natural Science Approach.* New York: Plenum

Fiske ST, Taylor SE. 1991. *Social Cognition.* New York: McGraw-Hill. 2nd ed.

Foa E, Riggs D. 1993. Post-traumatic stress disorder in rape victims. In *American Psychiatric Press Review of Psychiatry,* ed. J Oldham, M Riba, A Tasman, 12:273–303. Washington, DC: Am. Psychiatr.

Folkman S, Lazarus RS. 1985. If it changes it must be a process: study of emotion and coping during three stages of a college examination. *J. Pers. Soc. Psychol.* 48:150–70

Funder DC. 1991. Global traits: a neo-Allportian approach to personality. *Psychol. Sci.* 2:31–39

Funder DC. 1994. Explaining traits. *Psychol. Inq.* 5:125–27

Goldberg LR. 1992. The development of markers for the Big-Five factor structure. *Psychol. Assess.* 4:26–42

Goldberg LR. 1993. The structure of phenotypic personality traits. *Am. Psychol.* 48:26–34

Goleman D. 1995. *Emotional Intelligence.* New York: Bantam

Gollwitzer PM, Bargh JA, eds. 1996. *The Psychology of Action: Linking Cognition and Motivation to Behavior.* New York: Guilford

Hartshorne H, May MA. 1928. *Studies in Deceit: Studies in the Nature of Character,* Vol. 1. New York: Macmillan

Heatherton TF, Ambady N. 1993. Self-esteem, self-prediction, and living up to commitments. In *Self-Esteem: The Puzzle of Low Self-Regard,* ed. RF Baumeister, pp. 131–45. New York: Plenum

Heatherton TF, Weinberger JL, eds. 1994. *Can Personlity Change?* Washington, DC: Am. Psychol. Assoc.

Higgins ET. 1987. Self-discrepancy: a theory relating self and affect. *Psychol. Rev.* 94:319–40

Higgins ET. 1990. Personality, social psychology, and person-situation relations: standards and knowledge activation as a common language. See Pervin 1990a, pp. 301–38

Higgins ET. 1996a. Knowledge activation: accessibility, applicability, and salience. See Higgins & Kruglanski 1996, pp. 133–68

Higgins ET. 1996b. Ideals, oughts, and regulatory focus: affect and motivation from distinct pains and pleasures. See Gollwitzer & Bargh 1996, pp. 91–114

Higgins ET. 1996c. Emotional experiences: the pains and pleasures of distinct regulatory systems. In *Emotion: Interdisciplinary Perspectives,* ed. RD Kavanaugh, B Zimmerberg, S Fein, pp. 203–41. Mahwah, NJ: Erlbaum

Higgins ET, Bargh JA. 1987. Social cognition and social perception. *Annu. Rev. Psychol.* 38:369–425

Higgins ET, Kruglanski AW, eds. 1996. *Social Psychology: Handbook of Basic Principles.* New York: Guilford

John OP, Robins RW. 1993. Gordon Allport: father and critic of the Five-Factor model. In *Fifty Years of Personality Psychology,* ed. KH Craik, pp. 215–36. New York: Plenum

Kahneman D, Snell J. 1990. Predicting utility. In *Insights in Decision Making: A Tribute to Hillel J. Eihorn,* ed. RM Hogarth, pp. 295–310. New York: Univ. Chicago Press

Kandel ER, Hawkins RD. 1992. The biological basis of learning and individuality. *Sci. Am.* 267:78–86

Kihlstrom JF. 1987. The cognitive unconscious. *Science* 237:1445–52

Kihlstrom JF. 1990. The psychological unconscious. See Pervin 1990a, pp. 445–64

Kihlstrom JF, Cantor N. 1984. Mental representations of the self. In *Advances in Experimental Social Psychology. Theorizing in Social Psychology: Special Topics,* ed. L Berkowitz, 17:2–40. New York: Academic

Krahe B. 1990. *Situation Cognition and Coherence in Personality: An Individual-Centered Approach.* Cambridge, England: Cambridge Univ. Press

Kunda Z, Thagard P. 1996. Forming impressions from sterotypes, traits, and behaviors: a parallel-constraint-satisfaction theory. *Psychol. Rev.* 103:284–308

Larsen RJ. 1987. The stability of mood variability: a spectral analytic approach to daily mood assessments. *J. Pers. Soc. Psychol.* 52:1195–204

Larsen RJ. 1989. A process approach to personality psychology: utilizing time as a facet of data. In *Personality Psychology: Recent Trends and Emerging Directions,* ed. D Buss, N Cantor, pp. 177–93. New York: Springer-Verlag

Larsen RJ, Cutler SE. 1996. The complexity of individual emotional lives: a within-subject analysis of affect structure. *J. Soc. Clin. Psychol.* 15:206–30

Larsen RJ, Kasimatis M. 1990. Individual differences in entrainment of mood to the weekly calendar. *J. Pers. Soc. Psychol.* 58:164–71

Larsen RJ, Kasimatis M. 1991. Day-to-day physical symptoms: individual differences in the occurrence, duration, and emotional concomitants of minor daily illnesses. *J. Pers.* 59:387–423

Lazarus RS. 1993. Coping theory and research: past, present, and future. *Psychosom. Med.* 55:234–47

Markus HR, Kitayama S. 1991. Culture and the self: implications for cognition, emotion, and motivation. *Psychol. Rev.* 98:224–53

McAdams DP. 1992. The Five-Factor model in personality. *J. Pers.* 60:329–61

Metcalfe J, Jacobs WJ. 1998. Emotional memory: the effects of stress on "cool" and "hot" memory systems. In *Psychology of Learning and Motivation: Advances in Research and Theory,* ed. DL Medin, 38: In press. San Diego, CA: Academic

Miller SM. 1987. Monitoring and blunting: validation of a questionnaire to assess styles of information seeking under threat. *J. Pers. Soc. Psychol.* 52:345–53

Miller SM, Mischel W, O'Leary A, Mills M. 1969. From human papillomavirus (HPV) to cervical cancer: psychosocial processes in infection, detection, and control. *Ann. Behav. Med.* 18:219–28

Miller SM, Shoda Y, Hurley K. 1996b. Applying cognitive-social theory to health-protective behavior: breast self-examination in cancer screening. *Psychol. Bull.* 119: 70–94

Mischel W. 1968. *Personality and Assessment.* New York: Wiley. Republished 1996. Mahwah, NJ: Erlbaum

Mischel W. 1973. Toward a cognitive social learning reconceptualization of personality. *Psychol. Rev.* 80:252–83

Mischel W. 1984. On the predictability of behavior and the structure of personality. In *Personality and the Prediction of Behavior,* ed. RA Zucker, J Aronoff, AI Rabin, pp. 269–305. New York: Academic

Mischel W. 1990. Personality dispositions revisited and revised: a view after three decades. See Pervin 1990a, pp. 111–34

Mischel W. 1993. *Introduction to Personality.* Fort Worth, TX: Harcourt Brace Jovanovich. 5th ed.

Mischel W, Cantor N, Feldman S. 1996. Principles of self-regulation: the nature of willpower and self-control. See Higgins & Kruglanski 1996, pp. 329–60

Mischel W, Peake PK. 1982. Beyond déjà vu in the search for cross-situational consistency. *Psychol. Rev.* 89:730–55

Mischel W, Shoda Y. 1994. Personality psychology has two goals: Must it be two fields? *Psychol. Inq.* 5:156–58

Mischel W, Shoda Y. 1995. A cognitive-affective system theory of personality: reconceptualizing situations, dispositions, dynamics, and invariance in personality structure. *Psychol. Rev.* 102:246–68

Mischel W, Shoda Y, Rodriguez ML. 1989. Delay of gratification in children. *Science* 244:933–38

Moskowitz DS. 1982. Coherence and cross-situational generality in personality: a new analysis of old problems. *J. Pers. Soc. Psychol.* 43:754–68

Moskowitz DS. 1994. Cross-situational generality and the interpersonal circumplex. *J. Pers. Soc. Psychol.* 66:921–33

Moskowitz DS, Suh EJ, Desaulniers J. 1994. Situational influences on gender differences in agency and communion. *J. Pers. Soc. Psychol.* 66:753–61

Newcomb TM. 1929. *Consistency of Certain Extrovert-Introvert Behavior Patterns in 51 Problem Boys.* New York: Columbia Univ., Teach. Coll., Bur. Publ.

Pervin LA, ed. 1989. *Goal Concepts in Personality and Social Psychology.* Hillsdale, NJ: Erlbaum

Pervin LA, ed. 1990a. *Handbook of Personality: Theory and Research.* New York: Guilford

Pervin LA. 1990b. Goal concepts: themes, issues, and questions. See Pervin 1990a, pp. 473–79

Pervin LA. 1994. A critical analysis of current trait theory. *Psychol. Inq.* 5:103–13

Peterson DR. 1968. *The Clinical Study of Social Behavior.* New York: Appleton

Plomin R. 1994. *Genetics and Experience: The Developmental Interplay Between Nature and Nurture.* Newbury Park, CA: Sage

Plomin R, Chipuer HM, Loehlin JC. 1990. Behavioral genetics and personality. See Pervin 1990a, pp. 225–43

Plomin R, DeFries JC, McClearn GE, Rutter M. 1997. *Behavioral Genetics.* New York: Freeman. 3rd ed.

Plomin R, Owen MJ, McGuffin P. 1994. The genetic basis of complex human behaviors. *Science* 264:1733–39

Posner MI. 1997. *Cognitive neuroscience and the development of attention.* Presented at Bienn. Meet. Soc. Res. Child Dev., Apr., Washington, DC

Read SJ, Jones DK, Miller LC. 1990. Traits as goal-based categories: the importance of goals in the coherence of dispositional categories. *J. Pers. Soc. Psychol.* 58: 1048–61

Read SJ, Miller LC. 1989a. The importance of goals in personality: toward a coherent model of persons. In *Social Intelligence and Cognitive Assessments of Personality. Advances in Social Cognition,* ed. RS Wyer, TK Srull, 2:163–74. Hillsdale, NJ: Erlbaum

Read SJ, Miller LC. 1989b. Inter-personalism: toward a goal-based theory of persons in relationships. See Pervin 1989, pp. 413–72

Read SJ, Miller LC. 1993. Rapist or "regular guy": explanatory coherence in the construction of mental models of others. *Pers. Soc. Psychol. Bull.* 19:526–40

Read SJ, Miller LC. 1994. Dissonance and balance in belief systems: the promise of parallel constraint satisfaction processes and connectionist modeling approaches. In *Beliefs, Reasoning, and Decision Making: Psycho-Logic in Honor of Bob Abelson,* ed. RC Schank, E Langer, pp. 209–35. Hillsdale, NJ: Erlbaum

Read SJ, Miller LC, eds. 1998. *Connectionist Models of Social Reasoning and Social Behavior.* Mahwah, NJ: Erlbaum. In press

Revelle W. 1995. Personality processes. *Annu. Rev. Psychol.* 46:295–328

Rothbart MK, Derryberry D, Posner MI. 1994. A psychobiological approach to the development of temperament. See Bates & Wachs 1994, pp. 83–116

Rothbart MK, Posner MI, Gerardi GM. 1997. *Effortful control and the development of temperament.* Presented at Bienn. Meet. Soc. Res. Child Dev., Apr., Washington, DC

Rothbart MK, Posner MI, Hershey KL. 1995. Temperament, attention, and developmental psychopathology. In *Manual of Developmental Psychopathology,* ed. D Cicchetti, DJ Cohen, 1:315–40. New York: Wiley

Rumelhart DE, McClelland JL. 1986. *Parallel Distributed Processing: Explorations in the Microstructure of Cognition: Foundations,* Vol. 1. Cambridge, MA: MIT Press/ Bradford Books

Salovey P, Mayer JD. 1990. Emotional intelligence. *Imagin. Cogn. Pers.* 9:185–211

Saudino KJ, Plomin R. 1996. Personality and behavioral genetics: Where have we been and where are we going? *J. Res. Pers.* 30:335–47

Scheier MF, Carver CS. 1988a. A model of behavioral self-regulation: translating intention into action. In *Advances in Experimental Social Psychology: Social Psychological Studies of the Self: Perspectives and Programs,* ed. L Berkowitz, 21: 303–46. San Diego: Academic

Scheier MF, Carver CS. 1988b. Individual differences in self-concept and self-process. In *The Self in Social Psychology,* ed. DM Wegner, RR Vallacher, pp. 229–51. New York: Oxford Univ. Press

Sethi A, Shoda Y. 1997. *The relationships between maternal responsivity, secure base behavior, and emotion regulation: a molecular analysis.* Presented at Bienn. Meet. Soc. Res. Child Dev., Apr., Washington, DC

Shoda Y. 1996. Discriminative facility as a determinant of coping. *Am. Psychol. Soc., 8th, San Francisco*

Shoda Y, Mischel W. 1993. Cognitive social approach to dispositional inferences: What if the perceiver is a cognitive-social theorist? *Pers. Soc. Psychol. Bull.* 19:574–85

Shoda Y, Mischel W. 1998. The person as a cognitive-affective activation network: characteristic patterns of behavior variation emerging from a stable personality structure. See Read & Miller 1998, pp. 175–208

Shoda Y, Mischel W, Peake PK. 1990. Predicting adolescent cognitive and self-regulatory competencies from preschool delay of gratification: identifying diagnostic conditions. *Dev. Psychol.* 26:978–86

Shoda Y, Mischel W, Wright JC. 1989. Intuitive interactionism in person perception: effects of situation-behavior relations on dispositional judgments. *J. Pers. Soc. Psychol.* 56:41–53

Shoda Y, Mischel W, Wright JC. 1993a. The role of situational demands and cognitive competencies in behavior organization and personality coherence. *J. Pers. Soc. Psychol.* 65:1023–35

Shoda Y, Mischel W, Wright JC. 1993b. Links between personality judgments and contextualized behavior patterns: situation-behavior profiles of personality prototypes. *Soc. Cogn.* 11:399–429

Shoda Y, Mischel W, Wright JC. 1994. Intraindividual stability in the organization and patterning of behavior: incorporating psychological situations into the idiographic analysis of personality. *J. Pers. Soc. Psychol.* 67:674–87

Shultz TR, Lepper MR. 1996. Cognitive dissonance reduction as constraint satisfaction. *Psychol. Rev.* 103:219–40

Smith CA, Lazarus RS. 1990. Emotion and adaptation. See Pervin 1990a, pp. 609–37

Smith CA, Pope LK. 1992. Appraisal and emotion: the interactional contributions of dispositional and situational factors. In *Emotion and Social Behavior. Review of Personality and Social Psychology,* ed. MS Clark, 14:32–62. Newbury Park, CA: Sage

Stemmler G. 1997. Selective activation of traits: boundary conditions for the activation of anger. *Pers. Individ. Differ.* 22:213–33

Taylor SE, Aspinwall LG. 1996. Mediating and moderating processes in psychosocial stress: appraisal, coping, resistance, and vulnerability. In *Psychosocial Stress: Per-spectives on Structure, Theory, Life-Course, and Methods,* ed. HB Kaplan, pp. 71–110. San Diego, CA: Academic

Uleman JS, Bargh JA, eds. 1989. *Unintended Thought.* New York: Guilford

Vallacher RR, Wegner DM. 1987. What do people think they're doing? Action identification and human behavior. *Psychol. Rev.* 94:3–15

Vansteelandt K, Mechelen IV. 1997. Individual difference in situation-behavior profiles: a triple typology model. *Res. Rep. No. 97-2,* pp. 1–33. Catholic Univ. Leuven, Dep. Psychol., Leuven, Belg.

Vernon PE. 1964. *Personality Assessment: A Critical Survey.* New York: Wiley

Wachs TD, King B. 1994. Behavioral research in the brave new world of neuroscience and temperament: a guide to the biologically perplexed. See Bates & Wachs 1994, pp. 307–36

Weary G, Edwards JA. 1994. Individual differences in causal uncertainty. *J. Pers. Soc. Psychol.* 67:308–18

Westen D. 1990. Psychoanalytic approaches to personality. See Pervin 1990a, pp. 21–65

Wiggins JS, Pincus AL. 1992. Personality: structure and assessment. *Annu. Rev. Psychol.* 43:473–504

Wiggins JS, Trapnell PD. 1997. Personality structure: the return of the Big Five. In *Handbook of Personality Psychology,* ed. R Hogan, J Johnson, S Briggs, pp. 737–65. San Diego, CA: Academic

Wright J, Mischel W. 1982. Influence of affect on cognitive social learning person variables. *J. Pers. Soc. Psychol.* 43:901–14

Wright JC, Mischel W. 1987. A conditional approach to dispositional constructs: the local predictability of social behavior. *J. Pers. Soc. Psychol.* 53:1159–77

Wright JC, Mischel W. 1988. Conditional hedges and the intuitive psychology of traits. *J. Pers. Soc. Psychol.* 55:454–69

*Annu. Rev. Psychol. 1998. 49:259–87*

# BIASES IN THE INTERPRETATION AND USE OF RESEARCH RESULTS

## *Robert J. MacCoun*

Richard and Rhoda Goldman School of Public Policy, University of California, Berkeley, California 94720-7320: e-mail: maccoun@socrates.berkeley.edu

KEY WORDS: advocacy, ideology, judgment, methodology, politics, values

### ABSTRACT

The latter half of this century has seen an erosion in the perceived legitimacy of science as an impartial means of finding truth. Many research topics are the subject of highly politicized dispute; indeed, the objectivity of the entire discipline of psychology has been called into question. This essay examines attempts to use science to study science: specifically, bias in the interpretation and use of empirical research findings. I examine theory and research on a range of cognitive and motivational mechanisms for bias. Interestingly, not all biases are normatively proscribed; biased interpretations are defensible under some conditions, so long as those conditions are made explicit. I consider a variety of potentially corrective mechanisms, evaluate prospects for collective rationality, and compare inquisitorial and adversarial models of science.

CONTENTS

259

0066-4308/98/0201-0259$08.00

# INTRODUCTION

The claim that a social scientist is "biased" is rarely a neutral observation. In our culture, it can be a scathing criticism, a devastating attack on the target's credibility, integrity, and honor. Rather than coolly observing that "Professor Doe's work is biased," we are apt to spit out a phrase like "...is *completely* biased" or "...is biased *as hell.*" Such expressions of righteous indignation are generally a sure sign that some kind of norm has been violated. The sociologist Robert Merton (1973) articulated four norms of science that are widely shared in our culture by both scientists and nonscientists alike. *Universalism* stipulates that scientific accomplishments must be judged by impersonal criteria; the personal attributes of the investigator are irrelevant. *Communism* (as in "communalism") requires scientific information to be publicly shared. *Disinterestedness* admonishes investigators to proceed objectively, putting aside personal biases and prejudices. Finally, *organized skepticism* requires the scientific community to hold new findings to strict levels of scrutiny, through peer review, replication, and the testing of rival hypotheses.[1] This chapter examines theory and research on the violation—or the perceived violation—of Merton's norms, by social scientists and by those who use our research.

## Accusations and Controversies

In recent years, psychological researchers have been criticized for interpreting our data in ways that promote liberal political views, disparage conservative views (Ray 1989, Suedfeld & Tetlock 1991, Tetlock 1994, Tetlock & Mitchell 1993), and ignore radical views (e.g. Fox 1993). The psychological research literature has been criticized for being sexist (see Eagly 1995, Gannon et al 1992, Tavris 1992), racist (see Yee et al 1993), anti-Semitic (Greenwald & Schuh 1994), homophobic (Herek et al 1991), ageist (Schaie 1988), antireligious (e.g. Richards & Davison 1992), and biased toward a Western individual-

---

[1]Koehler (1993) presents evidence that scientists endorse such norms.

ist world view (e.g. Sampson 1989). Within the American Psychological Association, there have been spirited debates about the propriety of legislative and judicial advocacy by the organization and its members (Barrett & Morris 1993; Fiske et al 1991; Jarrett & Fairbank 1987; Saks 1990, 1993).

Sadly, there is no shortage of politicized research topics, where the motives of researchers and the interpretation of their findings are fiercely disputed (Alonso & Starr 1987, Maier 1991, Porter 1995, Suedfeld & Tetlock 1991). Some topics are matters of perpetual dispute; examples include research on the effects of gun control (Nisbet 1990), the death penalty (Costanzo & White 1994), pornography (Linz & Malamuth 1993), and drug prohibition (MacCoun 1993a, MacCoun & Reuter 1997). And recent years have seen the emergence of new battlegrounds involving research on global warming (Gelbspan 1997), HIV/AIDS (Epstein 1996), the addictiveness of tobacco (Cummings et al 1991, Glantz 1996), the biological basis of sexual orientation (LeVay 1996), the effects of gay and lesbian service personnel on military cohesion (Herek et al 1996, MacCoun 1993b), and the validity of therapeutically elicited repressed memories (Pezdek & Banks 1996) and racial stereotypes (Gilbert 1995, Lee et al 1995). But surely the most explosive example involving our own discipline is the long-standing dispute about racial differences and their heritability (Gould 1981), most recently resurrected by Herrnstein & Murray's (1994) *The Bell Curve* and the huge critical literature that has emerged in response (e.g. Fraser 1995, Fischer et al 1996, Neisser et al 1996).

The very decision to study certain topics is sufficient to prompt some observers to infer that the investigator is biased. Not infrequently, government officials have denounced or attempted to ban entire topics of research. A notorious example involves federal efforts to discredit early studies documenting that some diagnosed alcoholics are able to engage in sustained "controlled drinking"—drinking at reduced and less problematic levels (see Chiauzzi & Liljegren 1993, Marlatt et al 1993). Other examples include the cancellation of an NIH-funded conference on genetic influences on violence (see Johnson 1993), congressional efforts to end epidemiological research on gun violence by the Centers for Disease Control (see Herbert 1996), various congressional attempts to block survey research on adolescent and adult sexual behavior (see Gardner & Wilcox 1993, Miller 1995), and Representative Dick Solomon's ongoing efforts to pass the Anti-Drug Legalization Act, which states that "no department or agency of the United States Government shall conduct or finance, in whole or in part, any study or research involving the legalization of drugs."[2] The private sector is also guilty of research censorship, as illustrated

[2]My own research on this topic (MacCoun 1993a, MacCoun & Reuter 1997) is funded by a private source, the Alfred P. Sloan Foundation.

by the recent disclosure that a pharmaceutical company blocked publication of a study equating the effectiveness of its drug and less expensive generic alternatives (Dong et al 1997, Rennie 1997).

## Chapter Overview

The focus of this essay is on actual and perceived violations of these norms; specifically, judgmental biases in the selection and interpretation of research evidence. I focus on psychological theory and research on biases in the interpretation and use of scientific evidence, by both scientists and nonscientists. For convenience, I use the term "judge" to refer generically to both scientists who collect and present data and consumers who interpret it; context will make clear that some discussions are more relevant for the former role, others the latter.

I refer the interested reader elsewhere for discussion of bias in the *conduct* of research, including research design (Campbell & Stanley 1963), choice of study populations (e.g. Graham 1992, Hambrecht et al 1993), statistical analysis (e.g. Abelson 1995, Rosenthal 1994), data presentation (e.g. Huff 1954, Monmonier 1996), experimenter gender (e.g. Eagly & Carli 1981), and experimenter expectancies (Campbell 1993, Harris 1991, Rosenthal 1994).

Given the need to bound this topic, I must give short shrift to important contributions that other academic disciplines have made to our understanding of biases in the interpretation and use of research findings. For example, I will only briefly touch on findings from the extensive sociology literature on the effects of institutional factors, professional incentives, social networks, and demographic stratification on the scientific research process (see Cole 1992, Merton 1973, Zuckerman 1988). Similarly, I assume most readers of the *Annual Review* have at least a passing familiarity with the major developments in twentieth century philosophy of science (see Gholson & Barker 1985, Laudan 1990, Shadish 1995, Thagard 1992), so I limit my discussion to a few points where developments in philosophy inform a psychological debate, or vice versa.

I also sidestep the burgeoning postmodernist literatures on social constructivism, deconstructionism, hermeneutics, and the like (Best & Kellner 1991; cf Gross & Levitt 1994). Much of the material discussed here resonates with those perspectives, but there are also fundamental philosophical differences. While postmodernist thought has profoundly stirred many academic disciplines, it has created only modest ripples in mainstream psychology (see Gergen 1994, Smith 1994, Wallach & Wallach 1994). Though some attribute this to our discipline's collective naïveté about these heady intellectual currents, there are other plausible explanations. The mind's role in constructing our world is already a focal concern of all but the most radically behaviorist psychologists. Yet our discipline attracts few who endorse a radically idealist ontology; if there's no *there* out there to study, the practice of scientific psychology would seem fairly pointless beyond the fun and profit, or at least the fun. Nevertheless, few mainstream psychologists resemble the hypothetico-deductive "straw positivist" depicted in postmodern critiques (see Shadish 1995). Cook (1985) has provided a stylish label—"post-positivist critical multiplism"—for the dominant view in empirical psychology at least since Campbell & Stanley (1963): The choice of research methods poses inevitable trade-offs, and we can at best hope to approximate truth through a strategy of triangulation across multiple studies, investigators, and fallible methodologies. The psychological study of biased use of evidence is an essential part of that program, and systematic empirical methods have played a crucial role in identifying those biases.

In the following section, I briefly highlight the hazards of attributing bias and summarize the dominant strategies for scientifically studying the biased use of science. In the next three sections, I briefly review theory and research on three different sources of biased evidence processing: cold cognitive mechanisms, motivated cognition, and asymmetric standards of proof. Explicating these mechanisms makes clear that some forms of bias are more forgivable than others; indeed, some seem normatively defensible. In the final section, I discuss corrective practices for mitigating bias, including debiasing techniques, falsification and other hypothesis testing strategies, and institutional practices like peer reviewing, replication, meta-analysis, and expert panels. I consider the conditions under which collective judgment attenuates or exacerbates bias, and I compare adversarial and inquisitorial models of science.

## THE SCIENTIFIC STUDY OF BIASED SCIENCE

### Bias in the Eye of the Beholder?

The notion that observers' personal prejudices and interests might influence their interpretation of scientific evidence dates back at least to Francis Bacon (Lord et al 1979). But talk is cheap—it is easier to accuse someone of bias then to actually establish that a judgment is in fact biased. Moreover, it is always possible that the bias lies in the accuser rather than (or in addition to) the accused. There are ample psychological grounds for taking such attributions with a grain of salt.

For example, research using the attitude attribution paradigm (see Nisbett & Ross 1980) suggests that we might be quick to "shoot the messenger," viewing unpalatable research findings as products of the investigator's personal dispositions rather than properties of the world under study. Research on the "hostile media phenomenon" (Vallone et al 1985, Giner-Sorolla & Chaiken

1994) shows that partisans on both sides of a dispute tend to see the exact same media coverage as favoring their opponents' position. Keltner & Robinson (1996) argue that partisans are predisposed to a process of *naïve realism*; by assuming that their own views of the world are objective, they infer that subjectivity (e.g. due to personal ideology) is the most likely explanation for their opponents' conflicting perceptions. Because this process tends to affect both sides of a dispute, Robinson, Keltner, and their colleagues have demonstrated that the gap between partisans' perceptions in a variety of settings are objectively much smaller than each side believes.

Thus, we should be wary about quickly jumping to conclusions about others' biases. For example, "everyone knows" that scientists sponsored by tobacco companies are biased, having sold out their objectivity for a lucrative salary. Thus, it may come as a surprise—it did to me—to learn from surveys that a majority of these scientists asknowledge that cigarette smoking is addictive and a cause of lung cancer (Cummings et al 1991)—though this finding does not exonerate them from responsibility for their professional conduct. In a related vein, lawyer Peter Huber (e.g. Foster et al 1993) has received considerable attention for his argument that scientists who serve as expert witnesses are guilty of "junk science," spewing out whatever pseudoscientific conclusions are needed to support their partisan sponsors. While Huber's general conclusion might be correct, the cases he makes against specific experts are vulnerable to a host of inferential biases, including many of the same methodological shortcomings he identifies in their research (MacCoun 1995).

## Operationalizing Bias

Rather than attempt a theory-free definition of bias, I'll make use of Hastie's & Rasinski's (1988, Kerr et al 1996) taxonomy of "logics" for demonstrating that judgments are biased.[3]

One such logic is the one most observers use in attributing bias to others—a direct comparison of judgments across judges. (Or across groups of judges that differ in some attribute, e.g. men vs women, liberals vs conservatives, etc.) If the judgments are discrepant, then even in the absence of external criteria one can arguably infer bias. (As we see, Bayesians may disagree.) The problem is, bias on who's part? A weakness of this logic is that the observed discrepancy tells us nothing about whether either judge (or group of judges) is actually correct; both could be wrong. I'll return to this logic at the end of this essay when I examine the efficacy of collective strategies for bias reduction.

---

[3]As distinguished from taxonomies of bias *mechanisms,* discussed below.

In a second logic, bias or error is established directly by measuring the discrepancy between the judgment and the true state being judged. This logic has been quite fruitful in psychophysics, perhaps less so in social psychology, where we often lack objective measures of the "true" state of the sociopolitical environment. The third and fourth logics have been most productive in cognitive and social psychology and form the basis for much of the research discussed here. In these logics, the presence and content of various informational cues is manipulated in a between- or within-subjects experiment. In the third logic, a bias is established by showing that a judge is "using a bad cue"—i.e. overutilizing a cue relative to normative standards (e.g. legal rules of evidence, a rational choice model, or the cue's objective predictive validity). In the fourth, a bias is established by demonstrating that the judge is "missing a good cue"—underutilizing a cue relative to normative standards. These are "sins of commission" and "sins of omission," respectively (Kerr et al 1996).

## An Experimental Paradigm

Mahoney (1977) conducted the earliest rigorous demonstration of biased evidence processing using the experimental approach. Behavioral modification experts evaluated one of five randomly assigned versions of a research manuscript on the "effects of extrinsic reward on intrinsic motivation," a hypothesis in potential conflict with the experts' own paradigm. The five versions described an identical methodology but varied with respect to the study's results and discussion section. Mahoney found that the methodology and findings were evaluated more favorably, and were more likely to be accepted for publication, when they supported the experts' views. Perhaps the most intriguing finding of Mahoney's study was unintentional; reviewers who received a version of the manuscript with undesirable results were significantly more likely to detect a truly accidental, but technically relevant, typographical mistake.

Lord et al (1979) conceptually replicated Mahoney's results and extended them in several important ways. Because their study has inspired considerable research on these phenomena, it is worth describing their paradigm in some detail. Based on pretesting results, 24 students favoring capital punishment and 24 opposing it were recruited; each group believed the existing evidence favored their views. They were then given descriptions of two fictitious studies, one supporting the deterrence hypothesis, the other failing to support it. For half the respondents, the prodeterrence paper used a cross-sectional methodology (cross-state homicide rates) and the antideterrent paper used a longitudinal methodology (within-state rates before and after capital punishment was adopted); for the remaining respondents, the methodologies were reversed. Each description contained a defense of the particular methodology and a critique of the opposing approach. Students received and provided initial reactions to each study's results before being given methodological details to evaluate.

Analyses of student ratings of the quality and persuasiveness of these studies revealed a *biased assimilation* effect—students more favorably evaluated whichever study supported their initial views on the deterrent effect, irrespective of research methodology. Students' open-ended comments reveal how either methodology—cross-sectional or longitudinal—could be seen as superior or inferior, depending on how well its results accorded with one's initial views. For example, when the cross-sectional design yielded prodeterrence results, a death-penalty proponent praised the way "the researchers studied a carefully selected group of states...," but when the same design yielded antideterrence results, another death-penalty advocate argued that "there were too many flaws in the picking of the states...." Having been exposed to two studies with imperfect designs yielding contradictory results, one might expect that Lord et al's participants would have become more moderate in their views; if not coming to an agreement, at least shifting toward the grey middle zone of the topic. But Lord et al argue that such situations actually produce *attitude polarization.* Thus, in their study, respondents in each group actually became *more* extreme in the direction of their initial views. Lord and colleagues argued that "our subjects' main inferential shortcoming...did not lie in their inclination to process evidence in a biased manner....Rather, their sin lay in their readiness to use evidence to bolster the very theory or belief that initially 'justified' the processing bias."

There have been numerous conceptual replications and extensions of the Lord et al findings (Ditto & Lopez 1992, Edwards & Smith 1996, Koehler 1993, Kuhn & Lao 1996, Lord et al 1985, Miller et al 1993, Munro & Ditto 1997, Plous 1991, Sherman & Kunda, cited in Kunda 1990). For example, Plous (1991) noted that biased assimilation and attitude polarization imply that "people will feel *less* safe after a noncatastrophic technological breakdown if they already oppose the particular technology, but will feel *more* safe after such a breakdown if they support the technology." He supported this prediction in several studies of the reactions of psychology students, ROTC cadets, and professional antinuclear activists to information about a noncatastrophic nuclear breakdown. In a variation on the Lord et al paradigm, Koehler (1993) instilled weak or strong beliefs regarding two fictitious issues, then exposed respondents to studies with either low- or high-quality evidence. Studies that were consistent with instilled beliefs were rated more favorably, and the effect was stronger for those with strong beliefs (see also Miller et al 1993). In a second study, Koehler (1993) replicated the biased assimilation effect with professional experts on opposite sides of ESP debate; intriguingly, the effect was stronger among "hard-nosed" skeptics than among the parapsychologists. McHoskey

(1995) found that identical evidence regarding the JFK assassination was judged to be supportive by both conspiracy theorists and their detractors.

The biased assimilation phenomenon fit comfortably into an already burgeoning literature on biased information processing. The attitude polarization finding—the notion that exposure to mixed evidence moves opposing groups farther apart rather than closer together—was more novel. Yet Miller et al (1993) and Kuhn & Lao (1996) each note with surprise that this finding was so widely cited and accepted without critical challenge. As Kuhn & Lao note, "the findings contradict an assumption basic to much educational thought and prevalent in our culture more broadly—the assumption that engaging people in thinking about an issue will lead them to think better about the issue" (p. 115).

Happily, subsequent studies suggest possible boundary conditions on these phenomena. The biased assimilation effect is robust among judges with extreme attitudes but difficult to replicate among those with moderate views (Edwards & Smith 1996, McHoskey 1995, Miller et al 1993). Several studies have found that attitude polarization is limited to self-reported change ratings (Kuhn & Lao 1996, Miller et al 1993, Munro & Ditto 1997), though McHoskey (1995) found polarization in direct measures of attitude change. Miller et al (1993) found that neutral raters did not perceive any significant attitude polarization in essays written by the judges. Kuhn & Lao (1996) also found that polarization was just as common among respondents who wrote essays and/or discussed the topic in lieu of examining mixed research evidence.

In a paper on biased evidence evaluation, one offers conclusions about mixed evidence with some trepidation! But I think it is safe to say that the studies just cited, and additional evidence reviewed elsewhere in this chapter, provide strong support for the existence of biased assimilation effects and weak support for attitude polarization effects. Attitude polarization in response to mixed evidence, if it does exist, is a remarkable (and remarkably perverse) fact about human nature, but the mere fact that participants *believe* it is occurring is itself noteworthy. And even in the absence of attitude polarization, biased assimilation is an established phenomenon with troubling implications for efforts to ground contemporary policy debates in empirical analysis.

## Overview of Theoretical Perspectives

We are blessed with a wealth of theoretical perspectives for explaining biased evidence processing. As we shall see, these accounts are not mutually exclusive (and are probably not mutually exhaustive). Integrating them into a grand theory seems premature. Instead, I first sketch five prototypes of biased evidence processing. The prototypes vary with respect to intentionality, motivation, and normative justifiability. By *intentionality,* I refer to the combination of consciousness and controllability; a bias is intentional when the judge is aware of a bias yet chooses to express it when she could do otherwise (see Fiske 1989). *Motivation* is shorthand for the degree to which the bias has its origins in the judge's preferences, goals, or values; intentional bias is motivated, but not all motivated biases are intentional. Finally, *normative justification* distinguishes appropriate or defensible biases from inappropriate or indefensible biases; justification is always relative to some normative system, and I'll refer to several, including Merton's norms of science, Bayesian and decision theoretic norms of inference, ethical norms, and legal norms.

The first prototype is *fraud*: intentional, conscious efforts to fabricate, conceal, or distort evidence, for whatever reason—material gain, enhancing one's professional reputation, protecting one's theories, or influencing a political debate. There is a growing literature on such cases (see Fuchs & Westervelt 1996, Woodward & Goodstein 1996), though we still lack estimates on their prevalence. At a macro level, they are often explicable from sociological, economic, or historical perspectives (Cole 1992, Zuckerman 1988). At a micro level, they are sometimes explicable in terms of individual psychopathology. These cases are extremely serious, but I give them short shrift here, focusing instead on generic psychological processes that leave us all vulnerable to bias. I should note, however, that scarce funding and other institutional pressures can blur the lines between fraud and less blatant sources of bias; see recent examinations of tobacco industry research (Cummings et al 1991, Glantz 1996), drug prevention evaluations (Moskowitz 1993), risk prevention research (Fischhoff 1990), global warming testimony (Gelbspan 1997), and the Challenger disaster (Vaughan 1996).

A second prototype is *advocacy*: the selective use and emphasis of evidence to promote a hypothesis, without outright concealment or fabrication. As I discuss below, advocacy is normatively defensible provided that it occurs within an explicitly advocacy-based organization, or an explicitly adversarial system of disputing. Trouble arises when there is no shared agreement that such adversarial normative system is in effect.

I suspect the general public tends to jump to fraud or advocacy as explanations for findings they find "fishy," but contemporary psychologists recognize that most biased evidence processing can occur quite unintentionally through some combination of "hot" (i.e. motivated or affectively charged) and "cold" cognitive mechanisms. The prototypical *cold bias* is unintentional, and unconscious, and it occurs even when the judge is earnestly striving for accuracy. The prototypical *hot bias* is unintentional and perhaps unconscious, but it is directionally motivated—the judge wants a certain outcome to prevail. Though the distinction is useful, Tetlock & Levi (1982) made a persuasive case for the difficulty of definitively establishing whether an observed bias is due to hot vs cold cognition; the recent trend has been toward integrative "warm" theories.

Research on biased processing of scientific evidence has given somewhat less attention to the final prototype, which might be called *skeptical* processing. In skeptical processing, the judge interprets the evidence in an unbiased manner, but her conclusions may differ from those of other judges because of her prior probability estimate, her asymmetric standard of proof, or both. This is arguably normative on decision theoretic grounds, but those grounds are controversial.

# COLD COGNITIVE SOURCES OF BIAS

## Strategy-Based Errors

Numerous mechanisms have been identified in basic cognitive psychological research on memory storage and retrieval, inductive inference, and deductive inference that can produce biased evidence processing even when the judge is motivated to be accurate and is indifferent to the outcome. Arkes (1991) and Wilson & Brekke (1994) offer taxonomies for organizing these different sources of judgmental bias or error and detailed reviews of the relevant research.

For Arkes (1991), *strategy-based errors* occur when the judge, due to ignorance or mental economy, uses "suboptimal" cognitive algorithms. (Wilson & Brekke 1994 offer a similar category of "failures to know or apply normative rules of inference.") Examples that might influence the interpretation of research findings include: (*a*) using fallacious deductive syllogisms (e.g. affirming the consequent, denying the antecedent), (*b*) failing to adjust for nonindependence among evidentiary items, (*c*) confusing correlation with causation, and (*d*) relying on heuristic persuasive cues (e.g. appeals to an investigator's prestige or credentials).

One pervasive mental heuristic with special relevance to scientific evidence processing is *positive test strategy* (Klayman & Ha 1987), whereby hypotheses are tested by exclusively (or primarily) searching for events that occur when the hypothesis says they should occur. For example, to test the hypothesis that environmental regulations reduce employment rates, one simply cites jurisdictions with strict regulations and high unemployment (and, perhaps, jurisdictions with lax regulations and low unemployment). The evidence suggests that this kind of strategy is pervasive even in the absence of any particular outcome motivations (Fischhoff & Beyth-Marom 1983, Nisbett & Ross 1980, Snyder 1981). Positive test strategy clearly falls short of normative standards of inference, which would require data analysis strategies that take equal account of jurisdictions with strict regulations and low unemployment, or lax regulations and high unemployment. This kind of hypothesis testing is often called *confirmatory bias* (or confirmation bias), because the hypothesis is more likely to be confirmed than disconfirmed irrespective of its truth value. But in an insightful set-theoretic analysis, Klayman & Ha (1987; also see Friedrich 1993) demonstrate that in some classes of situations, the positive strategy can be an efficient means of reaching correct conclusions. Of course, we seldom know when we are in such situations.

## Mental Contamination

Wilson & Brekke (1994) call their category of nonstrategic error *mental contamination,* which they define as "the process whereby a person has an unwanted judgment, emotion, or behavior because of mental processing that is unconscious or uncontrollable" (p. 117). One type of mental contamination involves the unwanted consequences of automatic cognitive processing. For example, schematic principles of memory suggest that once a particular theory about the world becomes well learned, it filters our attention to and interpretation of incoming data (e.g. Nisbett & Ross 1980). A second subcategory is *source confusion,* whereby dissassociation or misattribution breaks the link between information and its source. From a scientific perspective, this separation is arguably a good thing if the source information in question involves things like a study author's race, gender, or nationality; the separation is much more serious when the source information includes key caveats about the study's methodology.

Arkes (1991) also identifies two categories of nonstrategic error, both of which might be classified as sources of mental contamination. *Psychophysical-based errors* stem from nonlinear relationships between objective stimuli and their subjective representations. Examples include framing effects, anchoring effects, and context effects. *Association-based errors* are perverse side effects of otherwise adaptive principles of spreading activation in semantic memory. One example might be *hindsight bias*; e.g. the exaggerated tendency for research results to seem "obvious" ex post, relative to ex ante predictions (Slovic & Fischhoff 1977). Other examples might include priming effects, and perhaps the availability and representativeness heuristics (Kahneman et al 1982, Nisbett & Ross 1980).

## MOTIVATED COGNITION

### The Psychodynamics of Science

A recent paper by Elms (1988) helps to illustrate the limitations of the psychodynamic literature on scientific practice. Elms argues that Freud's psychobiographical analysis of the scientific career of Leonardo da Vinci was distorted by Freud's own "projected identification with Leonardo, incorporating aspects of his own sexual history and his anxieties about the future of the psychoanalytic movement." But it is difficult to see how one might falsify such hypotheses, even in principle (Popper 1959). Moreover, Elms' psychodynamic analysis of Freud's psychodynamic analysis of da Vinci opens up an infinite regress, challenging us to analyze Elm's own motivations (an opportunity I'll forgo.)

## Cognitive Dissonance Theory

A more tractable motivational account is Festinger's (1957) theory of cognitive dissonance. An early prediction was that dissonance aversion should encourage judges to seek out supportive information and shun potentially unsupportive information—the "selective exposure" hypothesis. In essence, this is a motivationally driven form of confirmatory bias. Despite a skeptical early review (Freedman & Sears 1965), subsequent research has shown that these effects do occur when judges have freely chosen to commit to a decision and the decision is irreversible—two conditions that should promote maximal dissonance and discourage belief change as its mode of resolution (Frey 1986). While this research shows that dissonance reduction is *sufficient* to produce confirmatory biases, research cited earlier shows that it isn't necessary.

Berkowitz & Devine (1989; Munro & Ditto 1997) argue that dissonance theory provides a parsimonious account of biased evidence assimilation. In brief, the notion is that discovering that research findings contradict one's hypothesis may well create dissonance, which might be resolved by discrediting the research that produced the findings. But dissonance could also be resolved by changing one's belief in the hypothesis. A weakness of the theory is its inability to clearly predict the choice of resolution mode (see Kunda 1990, Lord 1989, Schlenker 1992). Lord (1989) contends that biased assimilation is cognitive rather than motivational in nature. He notes that Lord et al (1985) were able to eliminate the effect using cognitive instructions (consider how you'd evaluate the study given opposite results) but not motivational instructions (try to be unbiased)—though his implicit argument that cognitive instructions can only eliminate cognitive biases seems questionable. At any rate, this kind of motivational vs cognitive debate rarely produces clear winners (Tetlock & Levi 1982). It may be the case that purely motivational biases play their strongest role not in the initial evaluation of evidence but rather in researchers' resistance to reconsidering positions they've publically endorsed in the past (see, for example, Staw & Ross 1989, on organizational research on sunk costs and escalating commitments).

## Motive-Driven Cognition; Cognition-Constrained Motivation

Recent theories of motivated cognition are notable for integrating motivational and cognitive processes. For example, dual process theories of persuasion (e.g. Chaiken et al 1989, Petty & Cacioppo 1986) propose that a judge will only evaluate information rigorously and systematically if she is both motivated and able to do so; if both conditions aren't met, judgments will be formed heuristically using superficial cues or cognitive shortcuts. Although the motivation posited in these models was a desire for accuracy, Chaiken and her colleagues (e.g. Chaiken et al 1989, Giner-Sorolla & Chaiken 1997, Liberman & Chaiken 1992) have extended this work by examining the effects of defensive and impression management motives. For instance, under defensive motivation, judges will use heuristic processing if it leads to congenial conclusions, only resorting to systematic processing if it does not.

Kruglanski (1989, Kruglanski & Webster 1996) has offered a taxonomy of motives organized around their epistemic objectives, rather than their psychological origins. At one extreme of a continuum, one has a *need for cognitive closure;* at the other, a *need to avoid closure.* The closure that is desired or avoided is *specific* when one seeks or shuns a particular answer, or *nonspecific* if one seeks or avoids closure irrespective of its content. The need for closure creates tendencies to reach a conclusion as quickly as possible ("seizing") and stick to it as long as possible ("freezing"). In an imaginative research program, Kruglanski and his colleagues have demonstrated a variety of ways in which these motives influence information search, hypothesis formation, causal attributions, and inductive and deductive inference. Kruglanski & Webster (1996) discuss advantages of this framework over earlier concepts such as intolerance of ambiguity, authoritarianism, and dogmatism.

Pyszczynski & Greenberg (1987) and Kunda (1990) review much of the recent work on the effects of directional motives—where the judge prefers a particular outcome—on the generation and evaluation of hypotheses about the world. Pyszcynski & Greenberg (1987) argue that while motivation influences hypothesis testing, most of us feel constrained by the desire to maintain an "illusion of objectivity." Similarly, Kunda (1990, p. 482) argues that directional biases "are not unconstrained: People do not seem to be at liberty to conclude whatever they want to conclude merely because they want to. Rather…people motivated to arrive at a particular conclusion attempt to be rational and to construct a justification of their desired conclusion that would persuade a dispassionate observer." For example, Sherman & Kunda (cited in Kunda 1990) found that caffeine drinkers' prior understanding of research methodology constrained their willingness to reject findings about the hazards of caffeine. Along similar lines, McGuire & McGuire (1991) have found only weak support for a "wishful thinking" effect, in which the desirability of a proposition enhances perceptions of its likelihood; they argue that this "autistic" effect is largely offset by other, more rational cognitive principles.

Kalven & Zeisel's (1966) "liberation hypothesis" is essentially a corollary of the principle that the expression of bias is constrained by objective evidence. They argued that jurors are most likely to allow personal sentiments to influence their verdicts when the trial evidence is ambiguous. In support, MacCoun (1990,

Kerr et al 1996) cites several lines of individual- and group-level research demonstrating enhanced extra-evidentiary bias when evidence is equivocal.

Two recent studies indicate that the kind of biased assimilation effect documented by Lord et al is largely mediated by more stringent processing of evidence supporting views contrary to one's own. Ditto & Lopez (1992) found that students were significantly more likely to scrutinize a medical test when they tested positive for a potentially dangerous (fictitious) enzyme; they were also more than twice as likely to retest themselves. These reactions might appear to be normatively reasonable, but Ditto & Lopez also found that relative to students testing negative, students testing positive perceived the disease as less serious and more common; findings that argue in favor of a defensive motivational account and against a rational interpretation. Similarly, Edwards & Smith (1996) found support for a "disconfirmation bias," in which evidence inconsistent with the judge's prior beliefs was scrutinized more extensively. Moreover, this effect was heightened among participants with strongest emotional convictions about the issue. Munro & Ditto (1997) present evidence that affective responses play a significant role in mediating biased evidence assimilation.

## BAYESIAN PRIORS AND ASYMMETRIC STANDARDS

Some of the most sophisticated thinking about evidence evaluation has come from the decision theory tradition, especially in the domains of medical and legal decision making, signal detection theory, and statistical inference. Psychologists are especially well acquainted with the latter domain. Our slavish adherence to the conventional 0.05 alpha level has been blamed for many sins, and here I'll add one more. By fixing alpha, we've basically opted out of the most interesting part of the decision theoretic process: deciding how we should best trade off errors in a particular judgment context. This may explain why psychological explanations of biased evidence processing have largely overlooked the decision theoretic distinction between inductive judgments and standards of proof.

In a highly simplified decision theoretic analysis of scientific evidence evaluation, the judge assesses $p(H|D)$, the conditional probability of the hypothesis (H) given the data (D). Of course, in a simplified Bayesian model, $p(H|D)$ equals the product of a likelihood ratio denoting the diagnosticity of the evidence, $p(D|H)/p(D)$, and the judge's *prior probability* (or "prior"), $p(H)$. (More sophisticated models appear in Howson & Urbach 1993, Schum & Martin 1982). For a Bayesian, the prior probability component is an open door to personal bias; so long as diagnosticity is estimated in a sound manner and integrated coherently with one's prior, the updated judgment is normatively defensible (see Koehler 1993). Of course, the normative status of this framework is a source of continuing controversy among philosophers and statisticians (see Cohen 1989, Mayo 1996), especially the notion of subjective priors. Moreover, challenges to the theory's descriptive status (Arkes 1991, Kahneman et al 1982, Nisbett & Ross 1980, Pennington & Hastie 1993) leave its normative applicability in doubt. And much of the evidence reviewed here implies that the diagnosticity component is itself a major locus of bias, irrespective of the judge's prior.

But decision theory also identifies a second, less-controversial locus of potentially defensible "bias." Our probabilistic assessment of the hypothesis yields a continuous judgment on a 0-1 metric, yet circumstances often demand that we reach a *categorical* verdict: Will we accept or reject the hypothesis? This conversion process requires a *standard of proof*. Statistical decision theory, signal detection theory, and formal theories of jurisprudence share a notion that this standard should reflect a tradeoff among potential decision errors. A simple decision-theoretic threshold for minimizing one's regret is $p^* = u(\text{FP})/[u(\text{FN}) + u(\text{FP})]$, where $u(\text{FP})$ equals one's aversion to false positive errors, and $u(\text{FN})$ denotes one's aversion to false negative errors (see DeKay 1996, MacCoun 1984). The standard of proof, $p^*$, cleaves the assessment continuum into rejection and acceptance regions. Thus the standard of proof reflects one's evaluation of potential errors. This evaluation is a policy decision, not just a scientific decision, arguably even in the case of the conventional 0.05 alpha level.

When one error is deemed more serious than the other, the standard of proof becomes asymmetrical and can easily produce greater scrutiny of arguments favoring one position over another. Thus, even for most non-Bayesians, there is a plausible normative basis for "bias" in assessments of scientific research (see Hammond et al 1992). Note, however, that this form of bias is limited to qualitative, categorical decisions ("it's true," "he's wrong"); it cannot justify discrepancies across judges (or across experimental manipulations of normatively irrelevant factors) in their quantitative interpretations of the diagnosticity of evidence, $p(\text{D/H})/p(\text{D})$.

Mock jury research has established that various prejudicial factors influence jurors' standards of proof (Kerr 1993). A variety of methods have been developed for estimating mock jurors' $p^*$ values. Interestingly, $p^*$ as estimated indirectly from self-reported aversion to decision errors allows more accurate prediction of verdicts that direct self-reports of $p^*$, suggesting that jurors may be unwilling or unable to articulate their standards (see Hastie 1993, MacCoun 1984). Yet even the best estimates of $p^*$ have fairly poor predictive power. Pennington & Hastie's (1993a) story model departs from this decision theoretic framework, replacing the $p(H)$ vs $p^*$ comparison with a more complex cognitive process of mapping the evidence onto alternative narrative structures and selecting the one with the best "goodness of fit." Thagard's (1992) explanatory coherence model (ECHO) offers a similar interpretation using a connectionist constraint satisfaction network. Interestingly, Thagard describes his model as being purely cognitive; he considers a "Motiv-ECHO" model incorporating motivational postulates but ultimately rejects it as being superfluous. Still, it should be noted that several similar constraint satisfaction models have incorporated strong motivational components (see Read et al 1997).

This error tradeoff might explain Wilson et al's (1993) demonstration of a "leniency bias," such that professional scientists were more willing to publish studies with important findings, and an "oversight bias," in which the scientists actually rated the identical methodology more favorably when the topic was important. The oversight bias is difficult to justify, but the leniency bias is arguably normative. In general, scientists seem to believe the decision to publish findings should be influenced by their perceived importance, but only up to a point. Studies reporting truly revolutionary findings are held to perhaps the highest standards of all, leaving a field open to claims that it is biased against novel or radical ideas. In a remarkable journal editorial, Russett (1988) described the angst involved in his decision to publish a paper asserting that group transcendental meditation reduced regional violence in the Middle East. Bem & Honorton (1994) describe a similar dilemma. Bem, who considered himself a skeptic regarding telepathy, joined forces with nonskeptic Charles Honorton to conduct a rigorous meta-analytic review of studies using the ganzfeld procedure. Honorton then passed away before the conclusion of the research, leaving Bem in the personally awkward position of deciding whether to try to publish results that seemingly document the existence of telepathy. [He did (see Bem & Honorton 1994).]

## CORRECTIVE PRACTICES

### Debiasing

Behavioral decision researchers have produced a burgeoning literature on *debiasing* techniques (Arkes 1991, Koehler 1991, Nisbett 1993, Lerner & Tetlock 1994, Lord et al 1985, Schum & Martin 1982, Wilson & Brekke 1994). Examples include increasing incentives for accuracy, holding judges accountable for their judgments, enhancing outcome feedback, providing inferential training, task decomposition, and encouraging the consideration of alternative hypotheses. It should be noted that none of these techniques provides "silver bullet" solutions to the bias problem. Researchers are still trying to understand why some techniques work for some biases but not others (Arkes 1991, Wilson & Brekke 1994). Limited forms of these debiasing techniques are already built into traditional scientific practice through methodological training and professional socialization, replication, peer review, and theory competition.

## Falsification, Strong Inference, and Condition Seeking

Scientific training and socialization emphasize self scrutiny, rooted in part in Popper's (1959) principle of falsificationism. Acknowledging Hume's argument that induction can never confirm a hypothesis, Popper contended that induction might permit one to *falsify* a hypothesis, via the *modus tollens* syllogism: "If p then q; not q; therefore, not p." For Popper, falsification permits a particular sort of scientific progress; at best we can weed out bad ideas while seeing how our leading hypotheses hold up under attack. Popper's claim that falsificationism distinguishes science from pseudoscience has comforted psychologists seeking to distinguish our efforts from those of self-help gurus, astrologers, and the like. But many have noted that in practice, it is exceedingly difficult to achieve agreement that one has falsified a hypothesis (see Greenwald et al 1986, Julnes & Mohr 1989, Laudan 1990, McGuire 1983, cf Klayman & Ha 1987). A resourceful theorist can generally invoke ancillary theoretical principles to explain away a disconfirming finding, often with justification. McGuire (1983) goes so far as to conjecture that all psychological hypotheses are correct under *some* conditions, "provided that the researcher has sufficient stubbornness, stage management skills, resources, and stamina" (p. 15) to find those conditions.

In a classic paper, Platt (1964), a practicing biologist, argued that our personal attachment to our hypotheses clouds our judgment and sets science up as a conflict among scientists, rather than among ideas. He suggested that rapidly advancing research programs share a common strategy that mitigates these confirmationist tendencies. Under this *strong inference* strategy, the researcher designs studies to test not a single hypothesis, but an array of plausible competitors. Greenwald et al (1986, Greenwald & Pratkanis 1988) applaud Platt's intent but suggest that his strategy is rooted in a naïve faith in falsificationism. Instead, they recommend a strategy they called *condition seeking,* in which a researcher deliberately attempts to "discover which, of the many conditions that were confounded together in procedures that have obtained a finding, are indeed necessary or sufficient" (McGuire 1983, p. 223). Condition seeking is data driven rather than theory driven. Critics have countered that condition seeking will lead to a proliferation of special-case findings, undermining the development of more general theories (Greenberg et al 1986, MacKay 1988, Moser et al 1988). Greenwald & Pratkanis (1988) reply that results-centered research strategies will yield findings with greater shelf life than theory-centered research findings and ultimately provide the grist for better theory formulation. Related strategies that deserve wider recognition include devil's advocacy (Schwenk 1990), the "consider the opposite" heuristic (Koehler 1991, Lord et al 1985), and Anderson's & Anderson's (1996) "destructive testing" approach.

## Peer Reviewing, Replication, Meta-Analysis, Expert Panels

When self-scrutiny fails, we rely on institutional safeguards such as peer reviewing, research replication, meta-analysis, expert panels, and so on. A detailed review of these topics is beyond the scope of this essay, but it should be noted that many of these practices have themselves been scrutinized using empirical research methods. For example, Peters & Ceci (1982) provided a dramatic demonstration of the unreliability of the peer review process. A dozen scientific articles were retyped and resubmitted (with fictitious names and institutions) to the prestigious journals that had published them 18–32 months earlier. Three were recognized by the editors; eight of the remaining nine not only went unrecognized but got rejected the second time around. (One suspects that many articles would get rejected the second time around even when recognized.) Cicchetti (1991) and Cole (1992) provide equally sobering but more rigorously derived evidence on the noisiness of the peer review process, citing dismally low interreferee reliabilities in psychology journals (in the 0.19 to 0.54 range), medical journals (0.31 to 0.37), and the NSF grant reviewing process (0.25 in economics, 0.32 in physics). To make matters worse, at least some of this small proportion of stable variance in ratings is probably attributable to systematic bias, though the limited research base precludes any strong conclusions (see Blank 1991, Gardner & Wilcox 1993, Gilbert et al 1994, Laband & Piette 1994, Rennie 1997).

Traditionally, replications have been viewed as the most essential safeguard against researcher bias. Of course, this can only work if replications are attempted, and in fact, exact replications are fairly rare (Bornstein 1990), in part because editors and reviewers are biased against publishing replications (Neuliep & Crandall 1990, 1993). Moreover, replications can't eliminate any bias that's built into a study's methodology. In keeping with the critical multiplist perspective noted earlier (Cook 1985), the fact that most replications in the social sciences are "conceptual" rather than exact is probably a healthy thing (Berkowitz 1992), providing the opportunity for triangulation across diverse methodologies.

Despite some initial resistance, social scientists have come to recognize the tremendous corrective benefits of metaanalysis, the statistical aggregation of results across studies (e.g. Cooper & Hedges 1994, Schmidt 1992). Conducting a meta-analysis frequently uncovers errors or questionable practices missed by journal referees. And meta-analyses are sufficiently explicit that dubious readers who dispute a meta-analyst's conclusions can readily conduct their own reanalysis, adding or subtracting studies or coding new moderator variables. Most importantly, early conclusions about the effects of publication bias on meta-analytic results have led to new standards for literature reviewing that seem likely to attenuate the citation biases that plague traditional reviews (e.g. Greenwald & Schuh 1994).

## Will "Truth Win" Via Collective Rationality?

Our reliance on replication, peer review, and expert panels reveals that we are unwilling to place all our faith in training and socialization as means for guaranteeing unbiased judgments by individual researchers. Institutional practices like peer review, expert panels (e.g. Neisser et al 1996), and expert surveys (e.g. Kassin et al 1989) are premised on a belief that collective judgment can overcome individual error, a principle familiar to small-group psychologists as the *Lorge-Solomon Model A* (Lorge & Solomon 1955) (Model B having long since been forgotten). In this model, if $p$ is the probability that any given individual will find the "correct" answer, then the predicted probability that a collectivity of size $r$ will find the answer is $P = 1 - (1 - p)^r$. Implicit in this equation is the assumption that if at least one member finds the answer, it will be accepted as the collectivity's solution—the so-called *Truth Wins* assumption (e.g. Laughlin 1996). This can only occur to the extent that group members share a normative framework that establishes the "correctness" of the solution. That framework might be acknowledged by most academicians (the predicate calculus, Bayes Theorem, organic chemistry), or it might not (e.g. astrology, numerology, the I Ching).

For almost half a century, social psychologists have tested the "truth wins" assumption for a variety of decision tasks (see Kerr et al 1996, Laughlin 1996). Though much of this work involves the domain of small, face-to-face group discussion, the basic social aggregation framework and many of the findings can and have been generalized to wider and more diffuse social networks (e.g. Latané 1996). First and foremost, "truth" rarely wins, at least not in the strict version where a solution is adopted if at least a single member identifies or proposes it. At best, "truth supported wins"—at least some social support is needed for a solution to gain momentum, indicating that truth seeking is a social as well as intellective process (see Laughlin 1996, Nemeth 1986). Second, when members lack a shared conceptual scheme for identifying and verifying solutions—what Laughlin calls "judgmental" as opposed to "intellective" tasks—the typical influence pattern is *majority amplification,* in which a majority faction's influence is disproportionate to their size, irrespective of the truth value of their position (see Kerr et al 1996).

Collective decision making (or statistical aggregation of individual judgments) is well suited for reducing *random error* in individual judgments. Indeed, this is a major rationale underlying the practices of replication and metaanalysis (Schmidt 1992). What about bias? A common assertion is that group decision making will correct individual biases, but whether in fact this actually occurs depends on many factors, including the strength of the individual bias, its prevalence across group members, heterogeneity due to countervailing biases, and the degree to which a normative framework for recognizing and correcting the bias is shared among group members (see Kerr et al 1996, Tindale et al 1996). Elsewhere, my colleagues and I (Kerr et al 1996) demonstrate that under a wide variety of circumstances, collective decision making will significantly amplify individual bias, rather than attenuate it.

## Adversarial Science

Collective decision making is most likely to amplify bias when it is *homogeneous* across participants. Heterogeneous biases create the potential for bias correction through constructive conflict. In the Anglo-American adversarial legal system, this notion is captured by the phrase "truth will out." Yet the Western scientific tradition is quite self-consciously inquisitorial, rather than adversarial (Burk 1993, Lind & Tyler 1988, Thibaut & Walker 1978). In the inquisitorial model, the investigator strives to be neutral and objective, actively seeking the most unbiased methods for arriving at the truth. This dispassionate approach extends to the presentation of results; ideally, the investigator simply "tells it like it is" irrespective of who's ox gets gored. She "calls it like she sees it" yet in theory anyone else should see it and call it the same way if they examine the evidence she's gathered. In contrast, in an adversarial system, the investigator is an explicit advocate, actively seeking and selectively reporting the most favorable evidence for her position. Sociologists of science (see Cole 1992, Zuckerman 1988) paint a picture of scientific practice that is a dissonant blend of these seemingly unblendable models.

Thibaut & Walker (1978) proposed a normative "theory of procedure" for choosing between inquisitorial and adversarial processes. They argued that the inquisitorial method is to be preferred for "truth conflicts," purely cognitive disagreements in which the parties are disinterested (or have shared interests) and simply want to discover the correct answer. The adversarial approach is to be preferred for "conflicts of interest" in which the parties face a zero-sum (or constant sum) distribution of outcomes. According to Thibaut & Walker, in the latter context, the goal is not to find truth but to provide justice—a fair procedure for resolving the conflict.

The problem is that social science research problems rarely fit into this tidy dichotomy. Many of the issues we study involve a messy blend of truth conflicts and conflicts of interest, making it difficult to separate factual disputes from value disputes (see Hammond 1996, Hammond et al 1992). Many researchers (e.g. Sears 1994) and research organizations (e.g. the Society for Psychological Study of Social Issues; see Levinger 1986) have explicitly embraced an adversarial or advocacy-oriented view of social research, and many of us were attracted to the social sciences by social activist motives. But merging the adversarial and inquisitorial modes is problematic (see Burk 1993, Foster et al 1993). The adversarial legal system has many key features that are lacking in scientific practice. Here, I'll note four. First, the adversarial roles of the participants are quite explicit; no one mistakes an American trial lawyer for a dispassionate inquisitor. Second, at least two opposing sides are represented in the forum—though their resources may differ profoundly. Third, there is explicit agreement about the standard of proof, burden of proof (who wins in a tie?), and ultimate decision maker (i.e. the judge or jury). And fourth, in many (though not all) legal disputes, the opposing positions "bound" the truth, either because one of the positions is in fact true, or because the truth lies somewhere between the two positions.

Scientific practice is clearly very different. As expressed by Merton's (1973) norms, citizens in our culture have very clear role expectations for scientists; if one claims the authority of that role, one is bound to abide by its norms or risk misleading the public. This surely doesn't preclude advocacy activities on the part of scientists, but it does mean that we must be quite explicit about which hat we are wearing when we speak out, and whether we are asserting our facts (e.g. the death penalty has no marginal deterrent effect) or asserting our values (e.g. the death penalty degrades human life). Graduate training in schools of public policy analysis is much more explicit about managing these conflicting roles. For example, Weimer & Vining's (1992) textbook provides a neutral discussion of three different professional models: the *objective technician* who maintains a distance from clients but lets the data "speak for itself," avoiding recommendations; the *client's advocate* who exploits ambiguity in the data to strike a balance between loyalty to the facts and loyalty to a client's interests; and the *issue advocate* who explicitly draws on research opportunistically in order to promote broader values or policy objectives.

Moreover, as noted at the outset, many have argued that social science as represented in our major journals is too homogeneous—too liberal, too Anglocentric, too male, and so on. It should be noted that the viewpoints reflected in published research are surely endogenous; if our leanings influence our findings, our findings surely influence our leanings as well. But if scientists' prejudices influence their research, there is little hope that "truth will out" in the absence of a sizable or at least vigorous representation of alternative viewpoints (see Brenner et al 1996, Nemeth 1986). But as Latane' (1996) demonstrated, minority viewpoints often survive via processes of clustering and isolation; in the social sciences, this seems to manifest itself in separate journals, separate conferences, separate networks, and even separate academic departments.

Third, disputes over scientific findings typically lack an explicit burden and standard of proof, and an explicit final decision maker. This contributes to the seeming intractability of many debates; when each observer is free to establish her own $p*$, there is no grounds for consensus on who "won." Expert panels assembled by the National Academy of Sciences and other organizations attempt to circumvent this problem, with mixed success. This is surely a blessing as well as a curse. In a democratic society, we should be wary of philosopher kings. Research findings are rarely a direct determinant of policy decisions, a fact that is only partially attributable to policymakers' self-serving selectivity (Weiss & Bucuvalas 1980). Social scientists are sometimes strikingly naïve about the gaps between our research findings and the inputs needed for sound policy formation (see MacCoun & Reuter 1997, Weimer & Vining 1992).

But more importantly, the history of science (e.g. Gholson & Barker 1985, Thagard 1992) reveals little basis for assuming that the truth is represented among those factual positions under dispute at any given moment (also see Klayman & Ha 1987). This underscores the inherent ambiguity of using discrepancies among judges to locate and measure bias (Kerr et al 1996)—all of us might be completely off target.

## CONCLUSION

I have cited a wealth of evidence that biased research interpretation is a common phenomenon, and an overdetermined one, with a variety of intentional, motivational, and purely cognitive determinants. But there is danger of excessive cynicism here. The evidence suggests that the biases are often subtle and small in magnitude; few research consumers see whatever they want in the data. The available evidence constrains our interpretations—even when intentions are fraudulent—and the stronger and more comprehensive the evidence, the less wiggle room available for bias. In addition, far from condemning the research enterprise, the evidence cited here provides grounds for celebrating it; systematic empirical research methods have played a powerful role in identifying biased research interpretation and uncovering its courses.

Nor are all biases indefensible. There are some normative grounds for accepting differing opinions about imperfect and limited research on complex, multifaceted issues. There is nothing inherently wrong with differing standards of proof and nothing shameful about taking an advocacy role—provided we are self-conscious about our standards and our stance and make them explicit. Fostering hypothesis competition and a heterogeneity of views and methods can simultaneously serve the search for the truth and the search for the good. But there is a pressing need to better articulate the boundary between adversarialism and what might be called heterogeneous inquisitorialism—a partnership of rigorous methodological standards, a willingness to tolerate uncertainty, a relentless honesty, and the encouragement of a diversity of hypotheses and perspectives.

Visit the *Annual Reviews home page* at
http://www.AnnualReviews.org.

## Literature Cited

Abelson RP. 1995. *Statistics as Principled Argument.* Hillsdale, NJ: Erlbaum

Alonso W, Starr P. 1987. *The Politics of Numbers.* New York: Russell Sage

Anderson CA, Anderson KB. 1996. Violent crime rate studies in philosophical context: a destructive testing approach to heat and southern culture of violence effects. *J. Pers. Soc. Psychol.* 70:740–56

Arkes HR. 1991. Costs and benefits of judgment errors: Implications for debiasing. *Psychol. Rev.* 110:486–98

Barrett GV, Morris SB. 1993. The American Psychological Association's amicus curiae brief in Price Waterhouse v. Hopkins: the values of science versus the values of the law. *Law Hum. Behav.* 17:201–15

Bem DJ, Honorton C. 1994. Does psi exist? Replicable evidence for an anomalous process of information transfer. *Psychol. Bull.* 115:4–18

Berkowitz L. 1992. Some thoughts about conservative evaluations of replications. *Pers. Soc. Psychol. Bull.* 18:319–24

Berkowitz L, Devine PG. 1989. Research traditions, analysis, and synthesis in social psychological theories: the case of dissonance theory. *Pers. Soc. Psychol. Bull.* 15: 493–507

Best S, Kellner D. 1991. *Postmodern Theory.* New York: Guilford

Blank RM. 1991. The effects of double-blind versus single-blind reviewing: experimental evidence from *The American Economic Review. Am. Econ. Rev.* 81:1041–67

Bornstein RF. 1990. Publication politics, experimenter bias and the replication process in social science research. *J. Soc. Behav. Pers.* 5:71–81

Brenner LA, Koehler DJ, Tversky A. 1996. On the evaluation of one-sided evidence. *J. Behav. Decis. Mak.* 9:59–70

Burk DL. 1993. When scientists act like lawyers: the problem of adversary science. *Jurimetr. J.* 33:363–76

Campbell DT. 1993. Systematic errors to be expected of the social scientist on the basis of a general psychology of cognitive bias. In *Interpersonal Expectations: Theory, Research, and Applications,* ed. PD Blanck, pp. 25–41. Cambridge, UK: Cambridge Univ. Press

Campbell DT, Stanley JC. 1963. *Experimental and Quasi-Experimental Designs for Research. New York:* Houghton Mifflin

Chaiken S, Liberman A, Eagly AH. 1989. Heuristic and systematic information processing within and beyond the persuasion context. See Uleman & Bargh 1989, pp. 212–52

Chiauzzi EJ, Liljegren S. 1993. Taboo topics in addiction treatment: an empirical review of clinical folklore. *J. Subst. Abuse Treat.* 10:303–16

Cicchetti DV. 1991. The reliability of peer review for manuscript and grant submissions: a cross-disciplinary investigation. *Behav. Brain Sci.* 14:119–86

Cohen LJ. 1989. *An Introduction to the Philosophy of Induction and Probability.* Oxford, UK: Oxford Univ. Press

Cole S. 1992. *Making Science: Between Nature and Society.* Cambridge, MA: Harvard

Cook TD. 1985. Post-positive critical multiplism. In *Social Science and Social Policy,* ed. L Shotland, MM Mark, pp. 21–62. Beverly Hills, CA: Sage

Cooper H, Hedges LV. 1994. *The Handbook of Research Synthesis.* New York: Russell Sage Found.

Costanzo M, White LT, eds. 1994. The death penalty in the United States (special issue). *J. Soc. Issues* 50:1–197

Cummings KM, Russell S, Gingrass A, Davis R. 1991. What scientists funded by the tobacco industry believe about the hazards of cigarette smoking. *Am. J. Public Health* 81:894–96

DeKay ML. 1996. The difference between Blackstone-like error ratios and probabilistic standards of proof. *Law Soc. Inq.* 21: 95–132

Ditto PH, Lopez DF. 1992. Motivated skepticism: use of differential decision criteria for preferred and nonpreferred conclusions. *J. Pers. Soc. Psychol.* 63: 568–84

Dong BJ, Hauck WW, Gambertoglio JG, Gee L, White JR. 1997. Bioequivalence of generic and brand-name levothyroxine products in the treatment of hypothyroidism. *JAMA* 277:1205–13

Eagly AH. 1995. The science and politics of comparing women and men. *Am. Psychol.* 50:145–58

Eagly AH, Carli LL. 1981. Sex of researchers and sex-typed communications as determinants of sex differences in influenceability: a meta-analysis of social influence studies. *Psychol. Bull.* 90:1–20

Edwards K, Smith EE. 1996. A disconfirmation bias in the evaluation of arguments. *J. Pers. Soc. Psychol.* 71:5–24

Elms AC. 1988. Freud as Leonardo: Why the first psychobiography went wrong. *J. Pers.* 56:19–40

Epstein S. 1996. *Impure Science: AIDS, Activism, and the Politics of Knowledge.* Berkeley: Univ. Calif. Press

Festinger L. 1957. *A Theory of Cognitive Dissonance.* Stanford, CA: Stanford Univ. Press

Fischer CS, Hout M, Jankowski MS, Lucas SR, Swidler A, Voss K. 1996. *Inequality by Design: Cracking the Bell Curve Myth.* Princeton, NJ: Princeton

Fischhoff B. 1990. Psychology and public policy: tool or toolmaker? *Am. Psychol.* 45: 647–53

Fischhoff B, Beyth-Marom R. 1983. Hypothesis evaluation from a Bayesian perspective. *Psychol. Rev.* 90:239–60

Fiske ST. 1989. Examining the role of intent: toward understanding its role in stereotyping and prejudice. See Uleman & Bargh 1989, pp. 253–83

Fiske ST, Bersoff DN, Borgida E, Deaux K, Heilman ME. 1991. Social science research on trial: use of sex stereotyping research in Price Waterhouse v. Hopkins. *Am. Psychol.* 46:1049–60

Foster KR, Bernstein DE, Huber PW. 1993. *Phantom Risk: Scientific Inference and the Law.* Cambridge, MA: MIT Press

Fox DR. 1993. Psychological jurisprudence

and radical social change. *Am. Psychol.* 48:234–41

Fraser S, ed. 1995. *The Bell Curve Wars: Race, Intelligence, and the Future of America.* New York: Basic Books

Freedman JL, Sears DO. 1965. Selective exposure. *Adv. Exp. Soc. Psychol.* 2:57–97

Frey D. 1986. Recent research on selective exposure to information. *Adv. Exp. Soc. Psychol.* 19:41–80

Friedrich J. 1993. Primary error detection and minimization (PEDMIN) strategies in social cognition: a reinterpretation of confirmation bias phenomena. *Psychol. Rev.* 100:298–319

Fuchs S, Westervelt SD. 1996. Fraud and trust in science. *Perspect. Biol. Med.* 39:248–70

Gannon L, Luchetta T, Rhodes K, Pardie L, Segrist D. 1992. Sex bias in psychological research: progress or complacency? *Am. Psychol.* 47:389–96

Gardner W, Wilcox BL. 1993. Political intervention in scientific peer review: research on adolescent sexual behavior. *Am. Psychol.* 48:972–83

Gelbspan R. 1997. *The Heat is On: The High Stakes Battle Over Earth's Threatened Climate.* New York: Addison Wesley

Gergen KJ. 1994. Exploring the postmodern: perils or potentials? *Am. Psychol.* 49:412–16

Gholson B, Barker P. 1985. Kuhn, Lakatos, and Laudan: applications in the history of physics and psychology. *Am. Psychol.* 40: 755–69

Gilbert JR, Williams ES, Lundberg GD. 1994. Is there gender bias in *JAMA*'s peer review process? *JAMA* 272:139–42

Gilbert N. 1995. *Was It Rape? An Examination of Sexual Assault Statistics.* Menlo Park, CA: Henry J Kaiser Family Found.

Giner-Sorolla R, Chaiken S. 1994. The causes of hostile media judgments. *J. Exp. Soc. Psychol.* 30:165–80

Giner-Sorolla R, Chaiken S. 1997. Selective use of heuristic and systematic processing under defense motivation. *Pers. Soc. Psychol. Bull.* 23:84–97

Glantz SA. 1996. *The Cigarette Papers.* Berkeley: Univ. Calif. Press

Gould SJ. 1981. *The Mismeasure of Man.* New York: Norton

Graham S. 1992. "Most of the subjects were white and middle class": trends in published research on African Americans in selected APA journals 1970–1989. *Am. Psychol.* 47:629–39

Greenberg J, Solomon S, Pyszczynski T, Steinberg L. 1988. A reaction to Greenwald, Pratkanis, Leippe, and Baumgardner (1986): Under what conditions does research obstruct theory progress? *Psychol. Rev.* 95:566–71

Greenwald AG, Pratkanis AR. 1988. On the use of "theory" and the usefulness of theory. *Psychol. Rev.* 95:575–79

Greenwald AG, Pratkanis AR, Leippe MR, Baumgardner MH. 1986. Under what conditions does theory obstruct research progress? *Psychol. Rev.* 93:216–29

Greenwald AG, Schuh ES. 1994. An ethnic bias in scientific citations. *Eur. J. Soc. Psychol.* 24:623–39

Gross PR, Levitt N. 1994. *Higher Superstition: The Academic Left and Its Quarrels with Science.* Baltimore: Johns Hopkins Univ. Press

Hambrecht M, Maurer K, Hafner H. 1993. Evidence for a gender bias in epidemiological studies of schizophrenia. *Schizophr. Res.* 8:223–31

Hammond KR. 1996. *Human Judgment and Social Policy: Irreducible Uncertainty, Inevitable Error, Unavoidable Injustice.* New York: Oxford Univ. Press

Hammond KR, Harvey LO, Hastie R. 1992. Making better use of scientific knowledge: separating truth from justice. *Psychol. Sci.* 3:80–87

Harris MJ. 1991. Controversy and cumulation: meta-analysis and research on interpersonal expectancy effects. *Pers. Soc. Psychol. Bull.* 17:316–22

Hastie R. 1993a. Algebraic models of juror decision processes. See Hastie 1993b, pp. 84–115

Hastie R, ed. 1993b. *Inside the Juror: the Psychology of Juror Decision Making.* New York: Cambridge Univ. Press

Hastie R, Rasinski KA. 1988. The concept of accuracy in social judgment. In *The Social Psychology of Knowledge,* ed. D Bar-Tal, AW Kruglanski, pp. 193–208. New York: Cambridge Univ. Press

Herbert B. 1996. More N. R. A. mischief. *New York Times,* July 5, p. A15

Herek GM, Jobe JB, Carney R, eds. 1996. *Out in Force: Sexual Orientation and the Military.* Chicago: Univ. Chicago Press

Herek GM, Kimmel DC, Amaro H, Melton GB. 1991. Avoiding heterosexist bias in psychological research. *Am. Psychol.* 46:957–63

Herrnstein RJ, Murray C. 1994. *The Bell Curve: Intelligence and Class Structure in American Life.* New York: Free

Howson C, Urbach P. 1993. *Scientific Reasoning: The Bayesian Approach.* Chicago: Open Court. 2nd ed.

Huff D. 1954. *How to Lie with Statistics.* New York: Norton. 142 pp.

Jarrett RB, Fairbank JA. 1987. Psychologists' views: APA's advocacy of and resource expenditure on social and professional issues. *Prof. Psychol. Res. Pract.* 18:643–46

Johnson D. 1993. The politics of violence research. *Psychol. Sci.* 4:131–33

Julnes G, Mohr LB. 1989. Analysis of no-difference findings in evaluation research. *Eval. Rev.* 13:628–55

Kahneman D, Slovic P, Tversky A, eds. 1982. *Judgment Under Uncertainty: Heuristics and Biases.* New York: Cambridge Univ. Press

Kalven H, Zeisel H. 1966. *The American Jury.* Boston: Little, Brown

Kassin SM, Ellsworth PC, Smith VL. 1989. The "general acceptance" of psychological research on eyewitness testimony: a survey of the experts. *Am. Psychol.* 44:1089–98

Keltner D, Robinson RJ. 1996. Extremism, power, and the imagined basis of social conflict. *Curr. Direct. Psychol. Sci.* 5:101–5

Kerr NL. 1993. Stochastic models of juror decision making. See Hastie 1993b, pp. 116–35

Kerr NL, MacCoun RJ, Kramer G. 1996. Bias in judgment: comparing individuals and groups. *Psychol. Rev.* 103:687–719

Klayman J, Ha YW. 1987. Confirmation, disconfirmation, and information in hypothesis testing. *Psychol. Rev.* 94:211–28

Koehler JJ. 1991. Explanation, imagination, and confidence in judgment. *Psychol. Bull.* 110:499–519

Koehler JJ. 1993. The influence of prior beliefs on scientific judgments of evidence quality. *Organ. Behav. Hum. Decis. Proc.* 56:28–55

Kruglanski AW. 1989. *Lay Epistemics and Human Knowledge: Cognitive and Motivational Bases.* New York: Plenum

Kruglanski AW, Webster DM. 1996. Motivated closing of the mind: "seizing" and "freezing". *Psychol. Rev.* 103:263–83

Kuhn D, Lao J. 1996. Effects of evidence on attitudes: Is polarization the norm? *Psychol. Sci.* 7:115–20

Kunda Z. 1990. The case for motivated reasoning. *Psychol. Bull.* 108:480–98

Laband DN, Piette MJ. 1994. A citation analysis of the impact of blinded peer review. *JAMA* 272:147–49

Latané B. 1996. Strength from weakness: the fate of opinion minorities in spatially distributed groups. See Witte & Davis 1996, pp. 193–220

Laudan L. 1990. *Science and Relativism: Controversies in the Philosophy of Science.* Chicago: Univ. Chicago Press

Laughlin PR. 1996. Group decision making and collective induction. See Witte & Davis 1996, pp. 61–80

Lee YT, Jussim LJ, McCauley CR, eds. 1995. *Stereotyped Accuracy: Toward Appreciating Group Differences.* Washington, DC: Am. Psychol. Assoc.

Lerner JS, Tetlock PE. 1994. Accountability and social cognition. *Encycl. Hum. Behav.* 1:1–10

LeVay S. 1996. *Queer Science: The Use and Abuse of Research into Homosexuality.* Cambridge, MA: MIT Press

Levinger G, ed. 1986. SPSSI at 50: historical accounts and selected appraisals (special issue). *J. Soc. Issues* 42:1–147

Liberman A, Chaiken S. 1992. Defensive processing of personally relevant health messages. *Pers. Soc. Psychol. Bull.* 18:669–79

Lind EA, Tyler TR. 1988. *The Social Psychology of Procedural Justice.* New York: Plenum

Linz D, Malamuth N. 1993. *Pornography.* Newbury Park, CA: Sage

Lord CG. 1989. The "disappearance" of dissonance in an age of relativism. *Pers. Soc. Psychol. Bull.* 15:513–18

Lord CG, Lepper MR, Preston E. 1985. Considering the opposite: a corrective strategy for social judgment. *J. Pers. Soc. Psychol.* 47:1231–43

Lord CG, Ross L, Lepper MR. 1979. Biased assimiliation and attitude polarization: the effects of prior theories on subsequently considered evidence. *J. Pers. Soc. Psychol.* 37:2098–109

Lorge I, Solomon H. 1955. Two models of group behavior in the solution of Eureka-type problems. *Psychometrika* 20:139–48

MacCoun RJ. 1984. Modeling the impact of extralegal bias and defined standards of proof on the decisions of mock jurors and juries. *Dissert. Abstr. Int.* 46:700B

MacCoun RJ. 1990. The emergence of extralegal bias during jury deliberation. *Crim. Just. Behav.* 17:303–14

MacCoun RJ. 1993a. Drugs and the law: a psychological analysis of drug prohibition. *Psychol. Bull.* 113:497–512

MacCoun RJ. 1993b. Unit cohesion and military performance. In *Sexual Orientation and U. S. Military Personnel Policy: Policy Options and Assessment,* pp. 283–331. Santa Monica, CA: RAND

MacCoun RJ. 1995. Review of K. R. Foster, D. E. Bernstein, & P. W. Huber (1993). *J. Policy Anal. Manage.* 14:168–71

MacCoun RJ, Reuter P. 1997. Interpreting Dutch cannabis policy: reasoning by analogy in the legalization debate. *Science* 278:47–52

MacKay DG. 1988. Under what conditions can theoretical psychology survive and prosper? Integrating the rational and empirical epistemologies. *Psychol. Rev.* 95:559–65

Mahoney MJ. 1977. Publication prejudices: an experimental study of confirmatory bias in the peer review system. *Cogn. Ther. Res.* 1:161–75

Maier MH. 1991. *The Data Game: Controversies in Social Science Statistics.* New York: Sharpe

Marlatt GA, Larimer ME, Baer JS, Quigley LA. 1993. Harm reduction for alcohol problems: moving beyond the controlled drinking controversy. *Behav. Ther.* 24:461–504

Mayo DG. 1996. *Error and the Growth of Experimental Knowledge.* Chicago: Univ. Chicago Press

McGuire WJ. 1983. A contextualist theory of knowledge: its implications for innovation and reform in psychological research. *Adv. Exp. Soc. Psychol.* 16:1–47

McGuire WJ, McGuire CV. 1991. The content, structure, and operation of thought systems. In *The Content, Structure, and Operation of Thought Systems,* ed. RS Wyer, TK Srull, pp. 1–78. Hillsdale, NJ: Erlbaum

McHoskey JW. 1995. Case closed? On the John F. Kennedy assassination: biased assimilation of evidence and attitude polarization. *Basic Appl. Soc. Psychol.* 17:395–409

Merton RK. 1973. *The Sociology of Science.* Chicago: Univ. Chicago Press

Miller AG, McHoskey JW, Bane CM, Dowd TG. 1993. The attitude polarization phenomenon: role of response measure, attitude extremity, and behavioral consequences of reported attitude change. *J. Pers. Soc. Psychol.* 64:561–74

Miller PV. 1995. They said it couldn't be done: the National Health and Social Life Survey. *Public Opin. Q.* 59:404–19

Monmonier M. 1996. *How to Lie with Maps.* Chicago: Univ. Chicago Press. 2nd ed.

Moser K, Gadenne V, Schroder J. 1988. Under what conditions does confirmation seeking obstruct scientific progress? *Psychol. Rev.* 95:572–74

Moskowitz JM. 1993. Why reports of outcome evaluations are often biased or uninterpretable: examples from evaluations of drug abuse prevention programs. *Eval. Plan.* 16:1–9

Munro GD, Ditto PH. 1997. Biased assimilation, attitude polarization, and affect in reactions to stereotype-relevant scientific information. *Pers. Soc. Psychol. Bull.* 23: 636–53

Neisser U, Boodoo G, Bouchard TJ, Boykin AW, Brody N, et al. 1996. Intelligence: knowns and unknowns. *Am. Psychol.* 51: 77–101

Nemeth CJ. 1986. Differential contributions of majority and minority influence. *Psychol. Rev.* 93:23–32

Neuliep JW, Crandall R. 1990. Editorial bias against replication research. *J. Soc. Behav. Pers.* 5:85–90

Neuliep JW, Crandall R. 1993. Reviewer bias against replication research. *J. Soc. Behav. Pers.* 8:21–29

Nisbet L, ed. 1990. *The Gun Control Debate.* Buffalo, NY: Prometheus Books

Nisbett RE. 1993. *Rules for Reasoning.* Hillsdale, NJ: Erlbaum

Nisbett RE, Ross L. 1980. *Human Inference: Strategies and Shortcomings of Social Judgment.* Englewood Cliffs, NJ: Prentice Hall

Pennington N, Hastie R. 1993. The story model of juror decision making. See Hastie 1993b, pp. 192–221

Peters DP, Ceci SJ. 1982. Peer-reviewed practices of psychological journals: the fate of accepted published articles, submitted again. *Behav. Brain Sci.* 5:187–95

Petty RE, Cacioppo JT. 1986. *Communication and Persuasion: Central and Peripheral Routes to Attitude Change.* New York: Springer-Verlag

Pezdek K, Banks WP, eds. 1996. *The Recovered Memory/False Memory Debate.* San Diego: Academic

Platt JR. 1964. Strong inference. *Science* 146: 347–53

Plous S. 1991. Biases in the assimiliation of technological breakdowns: Do accidents make us safer? *J. Appl. Soc. Psychol.* 21: 1058–82

Popper KR. 1959. *The Logic of Scientific Discovery.* New York: Basic Books

Porter TM. 1995. *Trust in Numbers: the Pursuit of Objectivity in Science and Public Life.* Princeton, NJ: Princeton Univ. Press

Pyszczynski T, Greenberg J. 1987. Toward an integration of cognitive and motivational perspectives on social inference: a biased hypothesis-testing model. *Adv. Exp. Soc. Psychol.* 20:297–340

Ray JJ. 1989. The scientific study of ideology is too often more ideological than scientific. *Pers. Indiv. Differ.* 10:331–36

Read SJ, Vanman EJ, Miller LC. 1997. Connectionism, parallel constraint satisfaction processes, and gestalt principles: (Re)Introducing cognitive dynamics to social psychology. *Pers. Soc. Psychol. Rev.* 1:26–53

Rennie D. 1997. Thyroid storm. *JAMA* 277: 1238–42

Richards PS, Davison ML. 1992. Religious bias in moral development research: a psychometric investigation. *J. Sci. Study Relig.* 31:467–85

Rosenthal R. 1994. Science and ethics in conducting, analyzing, and reporting psychological research. *Psychol. Sci.* 5:127–34

Russett B. 1988. Editor's comment. *J. Confl. Resolut.* 32:773–75

Saks MJ. 1990. Expert witnesses, nonexpert witnesses, and nonwitness experts. *Law Hum. Behav.* 14:291–313

Saks MJ. 1993. Improving APA science translation amicus briefs. *Law Hum. Behav.* 17: 235–47

Sampson EE. 1989. The challenge of social change for psychology: globalization and psychology's theory of the person. *Am. Psychol.* 44:914–21

Schaie KW. 1988. Ageism in psychological research. *Am. Psychol.* 43:179–83

Schlenker BR. 1992. Of shape shifters and theories. *Psychol. Inq.* 3:342–45

Schmidt FL. 1992. What do data really mean? Research findings, meta-analysis, and cumulative knowledge in psychology. *Am. Psychol.* 47:1173–81

Schum DA, Martin AW. 1982. Formal and empirical research on cascaded inference. *Law Soc. Rev.* 17:105–51

Schwenk CR. 1990. Effects of devil's advocacy and dialectical inquiry on decision making: a meta-analysis. *Organ. Behav. Hum. Decis. Process.* 47:161–76

Sears DO. 1994. Ideological bias in political psychology: the view from scientific hell. *Polit. Psychol.* 15:547–56

Shadish WR. 1995. Philosophy of science and the quantitative-qualitative debates: thirteen common errors. *Eval. Program Plan.* 18:63–75

Slovic P, Fischhoff B. 1977. On the psychology of experimental surprises. *J. Exp. Psychol.: Hum. Percept. Perform.* 3:544–51

Smith MB. 1994. Selfhood at risk: postmodern perils and the perils of postmodernism. *Am. Psychol.* 49:405–11

Snyder M. 1981. Seek and ye shall find: testing hypotheses about other people. In *Social Cognition: The Ontario Symposium on Personality and Social Psychology,* ed. ET Higgins, CP Heiman, MP Zanna, pp. 277–303. Hillsdale, NJ: Erlbaum

Staw BM, Ross J. 1989. Understanding behavior in escalation situations. *Science* 246: 216–46

Suedfeld P, Tetlock PE, eds. 1991. *Psychology and Social Policy.* New York: Hemisphere

Tavris C. 1992. *The Mismeasure of Woman.* New York: Simon & Schuster

Tetlock PE. 1994. Political psychology or politicized psychology: Is the road to scientific hell paved with good moral intentions? *Polit. Psychol.* 15:509–29

Tetlock PE, Levi A. 1982. Attribution bias: on the inconclusiveness of the cognition-motivation debate. *J. Exp. Soc. Psychol.* 18:68–88

Tetlock PE, Mitchell G. 1993. Liberal and conservative approaches to justice: conflicting psychological portraits. In *Psychological Perspectives on Justice: Theory and Applications,* ed. BA Mellers, J Baron, pp. 234–55. New York: Cambridge Univ. Press

Thagard P. 1992. *Conceptual Revolutions.* Princeton, NJ: Princeton Univ. Press

Thibaut J, Walker L. 1978. A theory of procedure. *Calif. Law Rev.* 26:1271–89

Tindale RS, Smith CM, Thomas LS, Filkins J, Sheffey S. 1996. Shared representations and asymmetric social influence processes in small groups. See Witte & Davis 1996, pp. 81–104

Uleman JS, Bargh JA, eds. 1989. *Unintended Thought.* New York: Guilford

Vallone RP, Ross L, Lepper MR. 1985. The hostile media phenomenon: biased perception and perceptions of media bias in coverage of the Beirut massacre. *J. Pers. Soc.*

*Psychol.* 49:577–85

Vaughan D. 1996. *The Challenger Launch Decision.* Chicago: Univ. Chicago Press

Wallach L, Wallach MA. 1994. Gergen versus the mainstream: Are hypotheses in social psychology subject to empirical test? *J. Pers. Soc. Psychol.* 67:233–42

Weimer DL, Vining AR. 1992. *Policy Analysis: Concepts and Practice.* Englewood Cliffs, NJ: Prentice Hall. 2nd ed.

Weiss CH, Bucuvalas MJ. 1980. Truth tests and utility tests: decision-makers' frames of reference for social science research. *Am. Sociol. Rev.* 45:302–13

Wilson TD, Brekke N. 1994. Mental contamination and mental correction: unwanted influences on judgments and evaluation. *Psychol. Bull.* 116:117–42

Wilson TD, DePaulo BM, Mook DG, Klaaren KJ. 1993. Scientists' evaluations of research: the biasing effects of the importance of the topic. *Psychol. Sci.* 4:322–25

Witte E, Davis JH, eds. 1996. *Understanding Group Behavior,* Vol. 1: *Consensual Action by Small Group.* Matwah, NJ: Erlbaum

Woodward J, Goodstein D. 1996. Conduct, misconduct and the structure of science. *Am. Sci.* 84:479–90

Yee AH, Fairchild HH, Weizmann F, Wyatt GE. 1993. Addressing psychology's problem with race. *Am. Psychol.* 48:1132–40

Zuckerman H. 1988. The sociology of science. In *Handbook of Sociology,* ed. NJ Smelser, pp. 511–74. Beverly Hills, CA: Sage

*Annu. Rev. Psychol. 1998. 49:289–318*

# THE COGNITIVE NEUROSCIENCE OF CONSTRUCTIVE MEMORY

*Daniel L. Schacter, Kenneth A. Norman, and Wilma Koutstaal*

Harvard University, Psychology Department, 33 Kirkland Street, Cambridge, Massachusetts 02138; e-mail: dls@wjh.harvard.edu

KEY WORDS:    false recognition, confabulation, memory disorders, medial temporal lobes, frontal lobes

---

### ABSTRACT

Numerous empirical and theoretical observations point to the constructive nature of human memory. This paper reviews contemporary research pertaining to two major types of memory distortions that illustrate such constructive processes: (*a*) false recognition and (*b*) intrusions and confabulations. A general integrative framework that outlines the types of problems that the human memory system must solve in order to produce mainly accurate representations of past experience is first described. This constructive memory framework (CMF) emphasizes processes that operate at encoding (initially binding distributed features of an episode together as a coherent trace; ensuring sufficient pattern separation of similar episodes) and also at retrieval (formation of a sufficiently focused retrieval description with which to query memory; postretrieval monitoring and verification). The framework is applied to findings from four different areas of research: cognitive studies of young adults, neuropsychological investigations of brain-damaged patients, neuroimaging studies, and studies of cognitive aging.

---

## CONTENTS

# INTRODUCTION

Beginning with the pioneering studies of Bartlett (1932), psychologists have recognized that memory is not a literal reproduction of the past but instead depends on constructive processes that are sometimes prone to errors, distortions, and illusions (for recent reviews, see Estes 1997; Johnson et al 1993; Roediger 1996; Schacter 1995, 1996). Contemporary cognitive psychologists have been especially concerned with constructive aspects of memory, in part as a result of real-world controversies concerning the suggestibility of children's memory (e.g. Ceci & Bruck 1995, Schacter et al 1995b) and the accuracy of memories recovered in psychotherapy (e.g. Lindsay & Read 1996, Loftus 1993, Schacter et al 1996c). In contrast, neuropsychologists and neuroscientists who have focused on brain substrates of remembering and learning have tended to pay less attention to memory errors, distortions, and related phenomena. During the past several years, however, cognitive neuroscientists have been increasingly interested in phenomena that illuminate constructive aspects of remembering, such as false recognition and confabulation (cf Moscovitch 1995, Schacter & Curran 1995, Squire 1995). This review attempts to integrate diverse empirical and theoretical observations concerning constructive memory phenomena from four different areas of research: cognitive studies of young adults, neuropsychological investigations of brain-damaged patients, studies of cognitive aging, and research using brain-imaging techniques.

We begin by sketching a general framework that places the study of constructive memory phenomena in a broader conceptual context. We then examine observations from relevant research domains concerning two major types of memory distortions: (*a*) false recognition and (*b*) intrusions and confabulations.

## Constructive Memory: A General Framework

Our conceptualization of constructive memory functions, which we will refer to as the constructive memory framework (CMF), draws on notions put forward previously by Johnson et al (1993), McClelland et al (1995), Moscovitch (1994), Norman & Schacter (1996), and Squire (1992), among others. We begin by noting that representations of new experiences can be conceptualized as patterns of features, with different features representing different facets of the experience: the outputs of perceptual modules that analyze specific physical attributes of incoming information, interpretation and evaluation of these physical attributes by conceptual or semantic modules, and actions undertaken in response to incoming information (cf Johnson & Chalfonte 1994, Metcalfe 1990, Moscovitch 1994, Schacter 1989). Constituent features of a memory representation are distributed widely across different parts of the brain, such that no single location contains a complete record of the trace or engram of a specific experience (Damasio 1989, Squire 1992). Retrieval of a past experience involves a process of pattern completion (McClelland et al 1995), in which a subset of the features comprising a particular past experience are reactivated, and activation spreads to the rest of the constituent features of that experience.

A memory system that operates in such a manner must solve a number of problems if it is to produce mainly accurate representations of past experience. Features comprising an episode must be linked together at encoding to form a bound or "coherent" representation (Moscovitch 1994, Schacter 1989). Inadequate feature binding can result in source memory failure, where people retrieve fragments of an episode but are unable to recollect how or when the fragments were acquired (Johnson et al 1993, Schacter et al 1984, Squire 1995). As we shall see, source memory failure is an important contributor to various memory illusions and distortions. Source memory failures may also occur when binding processes are unimpaired, but not enough information that is diagnostic of the item's source is included in the bound representation. A closely related encoding process, sometimes referred to as pattern separation (McClelland et al 1995), is required to keep bound episodes separate from one another in memory. If episodes overlap extensively with one another, individuals may recall the general similarities (Hintzman & Curran 1994) or gist (Reyna & Brainerd 1995) common to many episodes, but fail to remember distinctive, item-specific information that distinguishes one episode from another.

Similar kinds of problems arise when retrieving information from memory. Retrieval cues can potentially match stored experiences other than the sought-after episode (Nystrom & McClelland 1992). Thus, retrieval often involves a preliminary stage in which the rememberer forms a more refined description of the characteristics of the episode to be retrieved (Burgess & Shallice 1996, Norman & Bobrow 1979). We have referred to this as a process of "focusing" (Norman & Schacter 1996). Poor retrieval focus can result in recollection of information that does not pertain to the target episode, or may produce impaired recall of an episode's details, insofar as activated information from nontarget episodes interferes with recall of target information.

When the pattern completion process produces a match, a decision must be made about whether the information that is delivered to conscious awareness constitutes an episodic memory, as opposed to a generic image, fantasy, or thought. This phase of retrieval involves a criterion setting process in which the rememberer needs to consider the diagnostic value of perceptual vividness, semantic detail, and other kinds of information for determining the origin of the retrieved pattern (Johnson et al 1993). As Johnson et al point out, the use of lax source monitoring criteria increases the probability of accepting images, fantasies, or other internally generated information as evidence of external events that never happened. If retrieved information is accepted as an episodic memory, the rememberer must also determine whether the memory pertains to the sought-after episode or to some other stored episode.

A wide variety of brain regions are likely implicated in these and other aspects of constructive memory functions. For example, recent brain imaging studies, using such techniques as positron emission tomography (PET) and functional magnetic resonance imaging (fMRI), indicate that distributed networks of structures are involved in both episodic encoding and retrieval (for reviews, see Buckner & Tulving 1995, Ungerleider 1995). Nonetheless, two brain regions are especially relevant to phenomena of constructive memory: the medial temporal area, including the hippocampal formation, and the prefrontal cortex. It has long been known that the medial temporal region is implicated in memory functions, because damage to this area produces severe impairment of episodic memory for recent events (Squire 1992). Recent neuroimaging data indicate that the medial temporal area is involved in encoding novel events into episodic memory (Stern et al 1996, Tulving et al 1994b). Indeed, a consensus account has begun to emerge regarding how exactly the hippocampus implements feature binding and pattern separation (most recently expressed by McClelland et al 1995; see also Squire & Alvarez 1995, Treves & Rolls 1994). According to this account, distributed patterns of activity in the neocortex (corresponding to individual episodes) are linked to sparse neuronal representations in region CA3 of the hippocampus; essentially, each episode is assigned its own hippocampal "index." Pattern separation is achieved to the extent that the hippocampus is able to assign nonoverlapping CA3 representations to different episodes; some minimal amount of difference needs to exist between episodes, or else the pattern separation process will fail (O'Reilly & McClelland 1994). The hippocampal index corresponding to a particular episode may only need to last until the neocortex "consolidates" the episode (by directly linking all the constituent features of the episode to one another), at which point the index can be assigned to a new episode (Squire & Alvarez 1995; but see Nadel & Moscovitch 1997).

The medial temporal region is also thought to play a role in pattern completion at retrieval (cf Moscovitch 1994). In the account of McClelland et al (1995), during retrieval of recent episodes (for which there is still a hippocampal index corresponding to the episode), cues activate the episode's index in region CA3 of the hippocampus, and activation spreads from the index to all the features comprising that episode. Once an episode has been consolidated in the neocortex, however, activation can spread directly between the episode's features, and the hippocampus no longer plays a crucial role in pattern completion. Although the neuroimaging data on medial temporal contributions to episodic retrieval are not entirely clear cut—many studies have failed to observe medial temporal activity during retrieval (for discussion, see Buckner et al 1995, Shallice et al 1994, Ungerleider 1995)—a number of brain imaging studies have implicated the medial temporal area in the successful recollection of recently acquired information (Nyberg et al 1996; Schacter et al 1995c, 1996a,e; Squire et al 1992).

Prefrontal cortex has also been implicated in episodic memory retrieval. Neuroimaging studies have consistently revealed evidence of prefrontal activity during episodic retrieval, especially in the right hemisphere (for reviews, see Buckner 1996, Nyberg et al 1996, Tulving et al 1994a), and recent data from electrophysiological studies using event-related potentials have provided converging evidence (Johnson et al 1996, Wilding & Rugg 1996). Although the exact nature of the functions indexed by these activations remains to be determined, they appear to tap effortful aspects of retrieval (Schacter et al 1996a) related to focusing or entering the "retrieval mode" (Nyberg et al 1995), post-retrieval monitoring and criterion setting (Johnson et al 1997, Rugg et al 1996), or both (Norman & Schacter 1996).

In summary, CMF emphasizes encoding processes of feature binding and pattern separation, and retrieval processes of focusing, pattern completion, and criterion setting. We have suggested further that medial temporal and prefrontal regions play important roles in various aspects of these component processes. We next consider phenomena of constructive memory in light of this general framework.

## PHENOMENA OF CONSTRUCTIVE MEMORY

We have organized our review of recent studies by considering two major phenomena that are central to CMF: false recognition, where people claim that a novel word, object, or event is familiar, and intrusions and confabulations, where people produce nonstudied information in memory experiments (intrusions) or narrative descriptions of events that never happened (confabulations). We subdivide relevant research into four domains of investigation: cognitive experiments with intact individuals, neuropsychological studies of brain-damaged patients, research on aging memory, and brain imaging experiments.

### False Recognition: Illusory Familiarity and Recollection

COGNITIVE STUDIES OF NORMAL SUBJECTS   One of the most extensively studied examples of false recognition arises in investigations of the effects of misleading postevent suggestions, pioneered by Loftus and her colleagues (for a recent review, see Loftus et al 1995). Such studies typically involve two phases. Participants first view slides or a videotape depicting a sequence of events, and then they are asked questions about the events; some questions contain suggestions of incidents that never occurred. Loftus and colleagues have shown that people falsely recognize as "old" some of the suggested events. Although Loftus's early claim that suggested information replaces or overwrites the initial event has been challenged (McCloskey & Zaragoza 1985), more recent studies indicate that false recognition in the misleading information paradigm is largely attributable to source monitoring confusions, with people failing to recollect whether the suggested information was originally presented in the videotape or slides, or occurred only in the postevent narrative (e.g. Belli et al 1994, Johnson et al 1993, Lindsay 1990, Zaragoza & Lane 1994). Insofar as thinking about an event frequently involves mentally picturing the event, mere contemplation of a suggested event can result in a vivid and detailed representation that is difficult to distinguish from stored representations of events that were actually perceived. This could sometimes lead individuals to mistakenly ascribe their recollections of an event to the original videotape even though they are also aware that references to the event occurred during postretrieval questioning (Zaragoza & Mitchell 1996; see also Fiedler et al 1996). In addition, participants may not always recognize the need for, or consistently implement, adequate source monitoring. Dodson & Johnson (1993) have shown that false recognition can be reduced by requiring participants to adopt strict source monitoring criteria: College students were less likely to claim that they had seen a picture of an object they had only read about when they were probed about source than when they were given a forced-choice recognition test.

Although studies of misleading suggestions provide a prominent example of false recognition, recent interest in the phenomenon is partly attributable to a demonstration of exceptionally high levels of false recognition by Roediger & McDermott (1995; see also Read 1996). They revived and modified a procedure originally described by Deese (1959) for producing large numbers of intrusions on a free recall test. College students studied a list of semantic associates (presented auditorily), all of which converged on a single nonpresented "theme" word; later, at test, participants frequently false alarmed to the nonpresented word (e.g. subjects who studied *drowsy, bed, tired, pillow, rest, pajamas,* and other associated words later claimed to remember having been exposed to the nonpresented theme word *sleep*). False alarm rates exceeded 70% in some conditions and were nearly as high as the hit rates. Participants expressed as much confidence in these false recognitions as they did in accurate recognitions of previously studied words. Moreover, when asked whether they possessed a specific recollection of having encountered the word (a "remember" response; cf Gardiner & Java 1993, Tulving 1985) or whether it just seemed familiar (a "know" response), subjects provided as many "remember" responses to nonstudied theme words as they did to studied words. (For an example of false "remembering" in the domain of autobiographical memory, see Conway et al 1996). Finally, the strength of the false recognition effect is a direct function of the number of associates presented during study (Robinson & Roediger 1997).

CMF provides two potential explanations for this false recognition effect. One possibility is that false recognition in the Deese/Roediger-McDermott paradigm results from a failure of pattern separation: Studying numerous semantically related words might result in unacceptably high levels of overlap between item representations. Pattern separation failure (i.e. assigning multiple similar items to the same hippocampal index) leads to excellent memory for what the items have in common ("gist" information) but impaired recall of distinctive, item-specific information. Because they lack specific recollection, participants are forced to rely on memory for gist, which does not discriminate well between studied items and nonstudied theme words. This idea is consistent with data from Mather et al (1997) and Norman & Schacter (1997), who examined the qualitative characteristics of subjects' memories and found that both true and false recognition were driven by retrieval of semantic associations (that is, participants typically claimed to "remember" nonpresented lures because they recalled associated items), and also that participants retrieved little item-specific information overall. The idea is also consistent with experiments by Israel & Schacter (1997) in which memory for item-specific information was increased by presenting, at the time of study, distinctive line drawings representing each associated word. Compared with a group that studied only lists of associated words, participants who also studied pictures showed greatly reduced false recognition of semantic associates.

It is also possible to explain false recognition of semantically related lures by appealing to the notion of "implicit associative responses"—the idea that people overtly or covertly generate a nonpresented lure word at the time of study in response to an associate (Underwood 1965). From this perspective, false recognition is viewed as a kind of source confusion, where people fail to recollect whether they actually saw or heard a word at study or generated it themselves. Both of these ideas are consistent with the finding reported by Mather et al (1997) that false recognition effects were larger when semantic associates related to a particular theme word were all presented consecutively (in blocks) than when associates of different theme words were intermixed. Insofar as blocking increases the salience of list themes, it should result in increased generation of theme words, and it should also increase the likelihood that people will notice and encode commonalities between same-theme items, thereby decreasing pattern separation.

Both Mather et al and Norman & Schacter (1997) found that although participants recalled little specific information overall, veridical recognition of previously presented words was accompanied by recollection of more auditory detail from the study phase (i.e. what the word sounded like when it was initially presented) and related contextual information (e.g. reactions triggered by the item at study) than was false recognition. Importantly, however, people were not able to make use of these small qualitative differences to reject theme words; both studies found that requiring subjects to carefully scrutinize their memories during the recognition test, by asking them to indicate whether they could recollect various qualitative details of the items they designated as old, did not reduce the magnitude of the false recognition effect after blocked study (although increased scrutiny did result in diminished false recognition following randomly intermixed study in the Mather et al experiment).

Mather et al also found that, in a situation where different speakers read different study lists, participants were willing to assign a source to a majority of their false recognitions (see also Payne et al 1996). Furthermore, participants did better than chance at choosing the "correct" source for the lures they falsely recognized (i.e. the speaker who read words semantically related to the lure). However, Mather et al found that participants reported no greater vividness of auditory detail for "correct" than for "incorrect" source identifications.

In the Deese/Roediger-McDermott paradigm, it is extremely difficult to tease apart the "implicit associative response" and "pattern separation failure" accounts of false recognition. In other situations, however, interpretation is less ambiguous. The idea that false alarms can be driven by implicit associative responses is supported by studies by Wallace and colleagues (Wallace et al 1995a,b) on false recognition of spoken words. Participants heard a series of spoken sound stimuli in which a nonpresented target word (e.g. January) was disqualified as a candidate early in a nonword (e.g. Jatuary) or late (e.g. Januaty). On a subsequent test, false recognition rates were considerably higher for lure words that had been disqualified late during initial exposure than for those that had been disqualified early. Wallace et al argued that increased false recognition of late-disqualified words could be attributed to the increased probability that subjects internally generated the lure word as part of an activated cohort of physically similar words (Marslen-Wilson & Zwitserlood 1989).

Evidence consistent with false recognition driven by pattern separation failure is provided by Koutstaal & Schacter (1997), who showed people pictures from various categories (e.g. cars, footwear) intermixed with unrelated pictures that did not belong to any of the categories. After a three-day delay, they tested recognition of previously studied pictures, nonstudied pictures that were perceptually and conceptually similar to those previously studied, and new unrelated pictures. Despite the fact that recognition memory for pictures usually yields high hit rates and low false alarm rates, participants showed robust false recognition to similar pictures, particularly when many instances of a category had been presented during study. Koutstaal & Schacter reasoned that it is highly unlikely that participants generated the related picture during the study phase of the experiment, in the same sense that they might generate "sweet" when hearing a list of associates. Rather, false recognition in this experiment appears to be caused by high inter-item similarity, resulting in robust memory for "gist" information about perceptual or conceptual features of studied pictures, but poor memory for picture-specific details.

False recognition also occurs when people miscombine elements of words or other stimuli they have recently studied (e.g. Underwood et al 1976). Drawing on previous work concerning similar kinds of miscombinations in perception (Treisman & Schmidt 1982), Reinitz et al (1992) labeled such distortions "memory conjunction errors." Reinitz et al found significant numbers of memory conjunction errors with stimuli comprised of nonsense syllables; people claimed to have seen conjunction stimuli in which syllables from two previously studied stimuli were recombined. They also demonstrated similar conjunction errors during recognition of faces, when features from separate previously studied faces were conjoined in a single face. Furthermore, Reinitz et al (1994) found that requiring participants to divide their attention between tasks while they studied faces reduced the hit rate for actually studied faces to the same level as the false alarm rate for conjunction faces. Taken together, these results suggest that focal attention during encoding is critically important for binding facial features into a unified representation, and less important for encoding individual facial features.

NEUROPSYCHOLOGICAL STUDIES OF BRAIN-DAMAGED PATIENTS   Although neuropsychological studies of memory disorders have long been concerned with the status of recognition memory after brain damage, it is only recently that systematic investigations of false recognition in patients with brain lesions have appeared. Delbecq-Derouesné et al (1990) described a patient (RW) who, after an operation to repair a ruptured anterior communicating artery aneurysm, made an abnormally large number of confident false recognitions. RW showed relatively more preserved free recall of studied items, although he did make many recall intrusions. A CT scan revealed bilateral areas of hypodensity in the medial aspects of the frontal lobes, as well as in the right temporal pole and the fusiform and parahippocampal gyri. Delbecq-Derouesné et al suggested that RW suffered from an impairment in a postretrieval verification or criterion setting process.

Parkin et al (1996) have recently described another patient (JB) who suffered a ruptured anterior communicating artery aneurysm; CT scans showed atrophy in the left frontal lobe. Like RW, JB made a large number of false recognitions that were accompanied by high confidence—he often said that he was "sure" that he had been exposed to target materials that had never been shown to him previously. When asked to make remember/know judgments about previously studied words and nonstudied words, all of JB's false alarms to nonstudied words were accompanied by "know" responses—that is, JB felt that these items were familiar, and thus was certain that they had appeared in the study list, but he did not have a specific recollection of having encountered them. When JB studied and was tested on various kinds of visual patterns, Parkin et al found that JB did not make excessive numbers of false alarms when distractor items on a recognition test were perceptually dissimilar from studied items.

Schacter & Curran and their colleagues (Curran et al 1997, Schacter et al 1996b) have described a patient (BG) with an infarction of the posterior aspects of the right frontal lobe who in some respects resembles patients RW and JB. BG showed pathologically high rates of false recognition to a wide variety of experimental materials, including words, sounds and pictures, and pseudowords. This phenomenon is not limited to lures that are semantically related to studied items; for example, when BG studied a list of unrelated words, he false alarmed excessively to nonstudied unrelated words. However, as with patient JB, Schacter et al (1996b) found that BG's pathological false recognition could be sharply reduced by testing him with items that differed substantially from those he had studied earlier (e.g. after studying pictures of inanimate objects from various categories, BG almost never made false recognition responses to pictures of animals). Unlike JB, when asked to make remember/know judgments about test items, most of BG's false alarms were accompanied by "remember" responses.

Schacter et al (1996b) suggested that BG's false recognition deficit stems from use of inappropriate decision criteria at test. According to this account, BG claimed to "remember" an item when that item matches the general characteristics of the study episode, whereas control subjects claimed to "remember" that a word or picture had appeared on a study list only when they retrieved specific information about that item's presentation at study. This criterion-setting deficit might stem from an inability to form an appropriately focused description of the study episode. It is also possible that, in addition to (or instead of) faulty criterion-setting, BG's false recognition deficit results from failure to encode distinctive item attributes at study. From the perspective of CMF, this would result in excessive feelings of familiarity for attributes common to multiple items at study (including new occurrences of those attributes in lure items), and poor memory for item-specific details.

Using signal detection analyses, Curran et al (1997) found that BG consistently used excessively liberal response criteria compared with matched controls, but there was also evidence of impaired sensitivity. When Curran et al (1997) increased BG's ability to recollect specific details about presented words by providing a semantic encoding task, BG assigned "remember" responses to more than 80% of studied items, but all of his false alarms were "know" responses. These observations suggest that BG can discriminate well between studied and nonstudied items when he has access to "high quality" recollective information about specific studied items; otherwise he relies on a signal that reflects the general similarity between study and test items.

Finally, Curran et al (1997) analyzed exactly what BG claims to recall when he makes a "remember" false alarm and found that he tends to provide associations to other words or sometimes to events in his life—specific information from an inappropriate context. In light of other evidence that frontal lobe damage is associated with impaired memory for source information (Butters et al 1994, Janowsky et al 1989, Milner et al 1991, Schacter et al 1984), it seems likely that deficient source monitoring (inability to assess whether an association triggered by an item at test is a memory from the study phase, or comes from some other episode, or is being generated for the first time at test) contributes to the character of BG's false recollections.

Excessive levels of false recognition of related lures have also been reported in studies of patients whose cerebral hemispheres have been surgically separated. Phelps & Gazzaniga (1992) showed two split-brain patients, JW and VP, slide sequences depicting everyday scenes (making cookies, bowling) and then tested yes/no recognition of previously studied slides, "schema-consistent" lures that had not been studied but that fit with the studied scene, and "schema-inconsistent" lures that were unrelated to the studied scene. Hits and false alarm rates to studied slides and unrelated lures did not differ as a function of hemisphere, but left hemisphere responses were associated with more false alarms to schema-consistent lures than right hemisphere responses. Metcalfe et al (1995) tested split-brain patient JW, and found that JW's left hemisphere made more false alarms than the right hemisphere to related words, faces, and visual patterns. The authors of both studies explain their findings in terms of hemispheric differences in encoding: The left hemisphere is thought to be biased toward "schematic" (categorical, gist) information, whereas the right hemisphere encodes more item-specific details and hence is better positioned to discriminate between studied and nonstudied schema-consistent items (cf. Chiarello & Beeman 1997).

The foregoing studies indicate that increased susceptibility to false recognition is associated with ventromedial and posterior frontal lobe damage, and with left hemisphere functioning in split-brain patients. More research is needed to pinpoint the exact kinds of frontal lobe damage that trigger increased false recognition. In any case, none of these patients exhibited the severe and pervasive memory loss observed in amnesic syndromes associated with damage to the medial temporal lobes, which have been the focus of extensive neuropsychological study (e.g. Parkin & Leng 1993, Squire 1992). Several recent experiments have begun to explore false recognition in amnesic patients, with sharply contrasting results emerging from different types of false recognition paradigms.

Two recent studies have examined memory conjunction errors using variants of the procedures introduced by Reinitz et al (1992). Reinitz et al (1996) found that normal controls made more "old" responses to studied compound words (e.g. *handstand* and *shotgun*) than to conjunction lures in which features of studied words were recombined (e.g. *handgun*), but amnesic patients failed to discriminate between studied words and conjunction lures (primarily because they made fewer "old" responses to studied words than controls). Kroll et al (1996) reported increased memory conjunction errors to recombined words in patients with left but not right hippocampal lesions, and increased conjunction errors to combined faces for both types of patients. Conjunction errors to words were more pronounced when items from which features were combined were separated by only a single item during the study phase than when they were separated by five items (lag was not manipulated for face stimuli). Kroll et al suggested that hippocampal lesions produce disinhibited binding, such that the damaged system binds features from different stimuli across an excessively broad temporal window.

In contrast to the aforementioned findings of normal or even increased levels of false recognition to conjunction lures in patients with medial temporal lobe damage, two recent experiments have revealed reduced levels of false recognition in these patients. Schacter et al (1996f), using a procedure similar to Roediger & McDermott (1995), found that amnesic patients showed reduced levels of false recognition to semantic associates of previously studied words. These findings imply that encoding, retention, and/or retrieval of the information that drives false recognition in this paradigm depend on the medial temporal and/or diencephalic brain regions that are damaged in amnesic patients. Schacter et al (1997b) replicated the Schacter et al (1996f) results with a different set of semantically related words (Shiffrin et al 1995) and extended them to the domain of perceptual false recognition: Amnesic patients made fewer false alarms than did matched controls to nonstudied words (e.g. *fate*) that were orthographically and phonologically similar to previously studied words (e.g. *lake, fake*). Conceptual false recognition in the control group was associated primarily with "remember" responses, whereas perceptual false recognition was associated primarily with "know" responses. The fact that amnesic patients showed similarly reduced levels of false recognition for both types of responses implies that structures that are damaged in amnesic patients are relevant to both of these forms of explicit memory (cf Knowlton & Squire 1995).

In all the foregoing neuropsychological investigations, false recognition occurred in the context of an episodic memory test: Participants were asked to make their old and new judgments with respect to a specific episode (the study phase). Rapcsak and colleagues (Rapcsak et al 1994, 1996) have recently described a different kind of false recognition in which patients, asked whether they have ever seen a particular face, claim that unfamiliar faces are familiar to them. These patients are characterized by damage to posterior regions of the right hemisphere and, in some instances, damage to the right frontal lobe. Rapcsak et al argue that in most patients, false recognition is attributable to impaired face perception; patients tend to rely on isolated facial features when making recognition decisions. However, one of these patients (with a right frontal lesion) did not suffer from obvious perceptual deficits. Rapcsak et al argue that this patient's false recognition problem stems from an inability to engage strategic monitoring and criterion setting processes. Although the relationship between false recognition of this sort and false recognition on episodic memory tests (e.g. Curran et al 1997, Parkin et al 1996, Schacter et al 1996b) remains to be elucidated, the fact that both kinds of impairment can occur after right frontal lobe damage suggests that the relation between the two merits closer examination in future studies.

AGING MEMORY    Early studies of aging memory reported that elderly adults show increased false recognition of semantically related distractors in paradigms, where young adults show relatively small false recognition effects (Hess 1984, Rankin & Kausler 1979, Smith 1975). More recent studies have replicated these findings (Isingrini et al 1995) and extended them to paradigms that produce high levels of false recognition even in younger adults (see Schacter et al 1997c).

Norman & Schacter (1997) reported that older adults show increased susceptibility to false recognition of semantic associates in the Deese/Roediger-McDermott converging associates paradigm (discussed above). Like younger adults, elderly individuals expressed high confidence in their false memories, frequently claimed to "remember" nonpresented words, and, when asked to rate various qualitative features of their memories, indicated that false recognitions were based primarily on recollection of semantically associated items. However, memory for auditory details of the initial presentation discriminated less well between true and false recollections in older than in younger adults, suggesting that failure to retrieve specific sensory details is related to age-related increases in false recognition (although it is unclear whether sensory details are not encoded in the first place, or whether they are encoded but not recalled due to interference from similar studied items). Because older adults showed increased susceptibility to false recognition even when they were instructed to rate the qualitative characteristics of their memories (Experiment 2) or to provide explanations of what they remembered (Experiment 1), the age effect is probably not attributable to a failure to consider relevant memorial attributes (cf Multhaup 1995). Tun et al (1996) have reported additional evidence of age-related increases in false recognition with a similar paradigm, using both accuracy and latency measures.

Although the foregoing experiments all used verbal materials, two recent studies examined whether older adults show increased false recognition after studying scenes or pictures. Schacter et al (1997b) exposed participants to videotaped scenes of everyday events and later showed them photographs of some previously viewed actions, together with actions that had not been seen previously. On a subsequent recognition test, participants were given brief verbal descriptions of individual objects or actions and instructed to respond "old" only when they specifically remembered seeing the object or action in the videotape; participants were explicitly warned that some of the items on the recognition test occurred only in photographs. Older adults showed greater false recognition of objects and actions that had appeared only in photographs than did younger adults.

The false recognition effect observed by Schacter et al (1997a) is clearly attributable to source confusion on the part of elderly adults; participants had actually seen photographs of the falsely recognized actions earlier. This observation fits with other evidence indicating that older adults often exhibit disproportionately impaired source memory compared with younger adults (e.g. Brown et al 1995, Johnson et al 1995, Schacter et al 1994). Additional analyses conducted by Schacter, Koutstaal, and colleagues (on data from their Experiment 2) showed that, as with the results described earlier from the Deese converging associates paradigm, elderly subjects were not successful at retrieving perceptual and contextual details that could be used to differentiate sources. Therefore, in this paradigm, source confusions are not simply a matter of recollecting useful contextual information and then failing to make use of it.

Koutstaal & Schacter (1997) compared older and younger adults using their picture recognition paradigm (discussed above), in which participants study exemplars of pictures from various categories intermixed with unrelated pictures, and later make old/new recognition judgments about previously studied pictures, related lure pictures, and unrelated lure pictures. Older adults consistently exhibited higher levels of false recognition of related pictures than did younger adults; older adults also showed normal hit rates to studied pictures from large categories and impaired hit rates to unrelated pictures. Overall, this pattern of results indicates age-related preservation of access to general similarity information (driving both hits and false alarms to items from studied categories) together with age-related impairment of access to item-specific, distinctive information (thereby explaining impaired hit rates to unrelated pictures).

Although the exact mechanisms remain to be elucidated, within CMF such effects could be attributable to impaired pattern separation in older adults, caused either by generally indistinct encoding or by specific impairment of the hippocampal mechanisms involved in pattern separation and binding. This latter idea is consistent with PET evidence indicating decreased hippocampal activation during encoding of novel faces in the elderly (Grady et al 1995). Alternatively, the effects described above could be attributable to a failure to engage in effortful focusing processes that facilitate retrieval of item-specific information. This idea is consistent with PET evidence showing abnormal frontal lobe activations in the elderly in test conditions that require effortful retrieval (Schacter et al 1996e). One final possibility is that elderly adults do successfully recollect item-specific information but fail to use this information when making their recognition decisions (i.e. a criterion-setting deficit).

BRAIN IMAGING STUDIES    Despite the recent surge of brain imaging studies of memory noted earlier, only a handful of recent studies have examined false recognition. In a PET study, Schacter et al (1996d) adapted procedures from Deese (1959) and Roediger & McDermott (1995) to examine brain activity of healthy young individuals during true versus false recognition. Compared with a control condition in which participants fixated on a crosshair, a variety of brain regions showed significant blood flow increases for both true and false recognition, including several areas previously implicated in episodic retrieval: anterior prefrontal cortex, medial parietal cortex, left middle temporal gyrus, cerebellum, and left parahippocampal gyrus. Although direct comparison between true and false recognition yielded little evidence of significant blood flow differences, two suggestive trends were evident in this comparison. First, there was evidence of increased left superior temporal activity during veridical recognition; the activity may reflect memory for auditory rehearsal at study, which presumably occurred more for studied items than nonstudied associates. Second, there was a trend toward increased right anterior prefrontal activity during false recognition. This trend was replicated and extended in an fMRI study conducted by Schacter et al (1997a). In addition, using new fMRI procedures that allow analysis of the time course of blood flow increases (Buckner et al 1996), they documented a late onset of anterior prefrontal activations relative to other brain areas. This latter finding suggests that anterior prefrontal activations during false recognition reflect processes that operate on the output of the memory system, such as postretrieval monitoring or criterion setting (cf Rugg et al 1996, Schacter et al 1996d).

Johnson et al (1997) used ERPs to investigate true and false recognition of semantically related words. They found that when studied words, nonstudied semantic associates, and nonstudied unrelated words were tested for recognition in separate blocks (as required by PET), ERP differences between true and false recognition were observed at frontal and left parietal electrode sites, providing a good fit with the PET data. However, when the word types were randomly intermixed during recognition testing (as is usually done in purely cognitive experiments), differences were greatly attenuated (cf Düzel et al 1997). Johnson et al (1997) noted that, in the randomly intermixed testing condition, participants could do reasonably well by relying on semantic similarity information alone (i.e. they could reject nonstudied unrelated items). However, with blocked testing, semantic similarity information does not discriminate well between items of a particular type, and hence participants may have used stricter criteria (e.g. trying to recall perceptual details) in this condition.

## Intrusions and Confabulations

Evidence concerning false recognition leaves open the question of whether people recall on their own nonpresented items or events that never happened. This question is addressed by research concerning recall intrusions, where nonstudied information is produced together with previously studied information, and confabulation, where people provide narrative accounts of events that did not occur.

COGNITIVE STUDIES OF NORMAL SUBJECTS    It is known that people sometimes produce incorrect items on free recall tests, but such recall intrusions are usually infrequent. In contrast, using the lists of semantic associates described earlier with respect to false recognition, Deese (1959) demonstrated that participants often intrude nonpresented false targets that are strong associates of previously presented words. A large number of recent studies, beginning with Roediger & McDermott (1995), have explored the parameters of this false recall effect. In general, manipulations that affect false recognition of semantic associates in the Deese/Roediger-McDermott paradigm affect false recall in a similar fashion. For example, McDermott (1996) found that false recall occurs more frequently when semantic associates of a particular theme word are studied in a block, as opposed to being randomly intermixed with associates of other theme words.

An important observation is that false recall appears to be more enduring than recall of studied items: McDermott (1996) found that when participants were tested two days after study, false recall of critical lures exceeded correct recall of studied words (see Payne et al 1996, for a similar finding with false recognition). Moreover, Robinson & Roediger (1997) found that while veridical recall is reduced by adding unrelated filler items to the study list, false recall is unaffected by this manipulation. McDermott (1996) also found that false recall persisted even when associate lists were repeatedly presented and tested, thereby providing multiple opportunities for participants to notice that lure words were not actually presented. There was some reduction of false recall across repeated trials, implying that people could make use of increasingly available item-specific information to suppress false recalls (cf Brainerd et al 1995, Hintzman et al 1992), but even after five trials participants still produced over 30% of the critical lure words.

Although it may seem paradoxical for false recall to be more robust than accurate recall, this follows from the fact that semantic features of the nonpresented theme word occur multiple times at study (insofar as they are shared and activated by several individual list items), whereas the features that distinguish a specific list item from other items occur less frequently (unless study lists are presented repeatedly). Payne et al (1996) found that providing repeated recall tests (without any intervening study trials) resulted in consistent but small increases in false recall across trials, whereas veridical recall showed little evidence of across-test increases; this may occur because list items cue the critical lure but do not cue each other.

False recall in the Deese/Roediger-McDermott paradigm (like false recognition in this paradigm) could result from subjects having generated the lure at study (and then making a source monitoring error), or simply from the semantic features of the lure having been strongly activated at study. As such, it belongs to a large class of intrusion phenomena in which the intruding information was either activated or generated earlier in the experiment. Along these lines, Roediger et al (1996) reported that subjects in post-event misinformation experiments will intrude misleading post-event suggestions on free recall tests. Another relevant example is the memory distortion known as "boundary extension": After having viewed a partial photograph of a scene, people tend to recall having seen a larger expanse of the scene than they actually did; the boundaries of the scene are "extended" in memory (Intraub et al 1992, 1996). Intraub et al argue that boundary extension reflects the fact that during scene perception, information about the expected layout of a scene is automatically activated.

From the perspective of CMF, recall distortion can also occur when people fail to construct a retrieval cue that is fully consistent with information in the target trace. Insofar as recall is a pattern completion process that seamlessly merges the retrieval cue with retrieved information, any inaccuracies in the cue might be carried over to the output of the pattern completion process. For example, during the phase of retrieval we have called "focusing," people may use schematic knowledge (information that is easily accessed because it has been encountered on multiple occasions) and information that is present in the test environment to construct cues, which in turn are used to access specific past episodes. Normally, this process produces reasonably accurate memory, but distortions of recall can arise when schematic knowledge or physical retrieval cues fail to accurately describe a particular episode. For example, Bahrick et al (1996) found that students with high grade-point averages tended to inflate their grades in classes where they did not get As, in keeping with the general idea that they received As most of the time (for another example of schema-driven recall errors, see Vicente & Brewer 1993). Also relevant here are studies of retrospective bias: distorted recollection of past perceptions and attitudes that is driven by present knowledge and beliefs (cf Dawes 1988, Ross 1989). For example, when supporters of Ross Perot recalled after the November 1992 election how they felt when Perot temporarily dropped out of the race in July 1992, their recollections were systematically biased by their present feelings toward Perot (Levine 1997). Retrospective bias can be thought of as a special case of the general principle that recall distortion will occur when the retrieval target (e.g. what one thought of Ross Perot in June 1992) is inconsistent with presently available knowledge (e.g. what one thinks of Ross Perot now).

Ochsner et al (1997) have reported a somewhat different, but related, type of recall bias. College students studied faces while listening to a corresponding voice speaking in an angry or happy tone. Ochsner et al reported that participants later tended to recall that faces with slightly positive expressions had been accompanied by a happier tone of voice than faces with slightly negative expressions, even though there was no relation between facial expression and tone of voice. This is yet another situation in which information present in the retrieval cue overshadows information present in the target trace. Although contemporary models allow for such effects (e.g. McClelland 1995), there has been little attempt thus far to consider them from a cognitive neuroscience perspective.

The studies of intrusions and retrospective biases reviewed thus far do not address whether normal adults can be induced to recall entire events that never happened. In a well-known study by Loftus (1993), young adults were asked by their relatives to try to remember a childhood event that had never occurred—being lost in a shopping mall. After repeated questioning, four of five participants in an initial study developed detailed recollections of the false event. Studying a larger sample, Loftus & Pickrell (1995) reported that approximately 25% of participants developed detailed false recollections. One limitation of such a procedure is that the experimenter has no way of knowing whether the suggested event did, in fact, occur. Since most people presumably have been lost at least sometime in their lives, it is possible that such veridical experiences may provide the basis for the false recollection. Using a slightly different procedure, Hyman and colleagues queried college students about actual events from their childhood, as well as fabricated but exceedingly improbable events, such as causing an accident by releasing a parking brake when left alone in a car. Hyman et al (1995) reported that none of their sample provided false memories when initially queried about such events, but after being repeatedly questioned, about 25% falsely recalled at least one of the fabricated events. In follow-up studies, Hyman & Pentland (1996) found that the probability of false event recall was increased significantly by instructions to imagine the suggested event. Imagery has also been implicated in the related phenomenon of "imagination inflation," where simply imagining an event leads to increases in subjective estimates of the likelihood that the event actually occurred (cf Garry et al 1996).

Although the mechanisms of these "confabulatory" false recall effects remain poorly understood, source confusions may play a role: As people repeatedly think about or imagine an event, they may retrieve fragments of other actual events, without recognizing them as such. Furthermore, the more that a person thinks about an event, the easier it becomes to retrieve details pertaining to that event; numerous studies have shown that retrieval fluency is a key determinant of whether a particular conscious experience is interpreted as a memory (cf Jacoby et al 1989, Lindsay & Kelley 1996; see also Rankin & O'Carroll 1995). In addition, a PET study conducted by Kosslyn et al (1993) found that visual imagery activated some of the same brain regions as visual perception. These results suggest that visual imagery may enhance the subjective reality of falsely recalled events because it draws on some of the same neural circuitry as does veridical perception (see also Silbersweig et al 1995).

NEUROPSYCHOLOGICAL STUDIES OF BRAIN-DAMAGED PATIENTS    Confabulatory responses in brain-damaged patients—spontaneous narrative reports of events that never happened—have been known to neurologists and neuropsychologists for decades (for reviews, see Johnson 1991, Moscovitch 1995). In addition, more recent experimental studies have examined intrusions on free recall tests in various patient populations. Although confabulations and intrusions are sometimes treated synonymously (e.g. Kern et al 1992), we prefer to examine them separately and leave open questions about the nature of their relations. We first summarize recent studies of intrusions and then consider confabulatory phenomena.

Schacter et al (1996f) examined false recall of semantically related lures in amnesic patients using the previously described procedures developed by

Deese (1959) and Roediger & McDermott (1995). They found that, while both veridical and false recall were impaired in amnesics, false recall was relatively more preserved. The robustness of false recall can be explained in terms of the fact, discussed above, that the constituent semantic features of nonpresented theme words were activated multiple times at study (presumably resulting in increased trace strength). Overall, the results from this experiment suggest that amnesics' free recall consists entirely of degraded semantic gist information, whereas normal controls recall both gist information and specific information about individual items.

Dalla Barba & Wong (1995) found that both amnesic patients and patients with memory deficits attributable to Alzheimer's disease (AD) made an abnormally large number of intrusions when they studied items from various categories and were cued with category names. Neither patient group showed an excessive number of intrusions on a free recall test. From this, we can conclude that intrusions are likely to occur when subjects are faced with strong retrieval cues ("strong" in the sense that it is easy to think of specific fruits in response to the category cue "fruit"), but memory traces are degraded. Studying items along with category names helped alleviate cued-recall intrusions in patients with intact semantic memory but not in patients with impaired semantic memory.

A major focus in recent studies of intrusion errors concerns whether and to what extent the tendency to make intrusion errors is related to frontal lobe damage. Two of the frontally lesioned patients discussed earlier who showed robust false recognition (JB, studied by Parkin et al 1996, and RW, described by Delbecq-Derouesné et al 1990) also made an abnormally high number of intrusion errors on free recall tests. These patients both suffered damage to the ventromedial regions of the frontal lobes (and possibly adjoining brain regions), brought on by ruptured anterior communicating artery aneurysms. Interestingly, patient BG (Curran et al 1997, Schacter et al 1996b), whose lesion is limited to the posterior lateral frontal lobe (and does not include ventromedial frontal cortex), is extremely susceptible to false recognition errors but does not show abnormally high levels of intrusion errors on free recall tests (KA Norman, W Koutstaal, DL Schacter & L Galluccio, unpublished data).

Group studies of recall intrusions in frontal-damaged patients have found mixed results, which is not surprising in light of the heterogeneity of lesion sites and etiologies in these patients (as well as the heterogeneity of recall paradigms used in these studies). Stuss et al (1994) failed to find abnormally high intrusion rates in patients with unilateral and bilateral frontal lobe damage on immediate free recall of categorized and unrelated word lists. By contrast, I Daum, A Mayes, Y Schwarz & R Lutgehetman (manuscript in preparation) found that patients with unilateral frontal lobe lesions made more intrusion errors than patients with posterior cortical lesions and normal controls on delayed recall of stories, categorized word lists, and dot patterns. Kern et al (1992) found that intrusion errors on story recall, design recall, and object recall tests were slightly (nonsignificantly) greater in Alzheimer's disease (AD) patients with relatively impaired frontal functioning than in AD patients with relatively intact frontal functioning. However, it is unclear whether this association is specifically related to frontal lobe dysfunction or whether it simply reflects global severity of deficit.

Following up on Dalla Barba & Wong's (1995) findings, Dalla Barba et al (1995) also used a category-cued recall test to examine the relation between intrusion errors, performance on neuropsychological tests of frontal lobe dysfunction, and awareness of memory deficit (anosognosia; McGlynn & Schacter 1989) in AD patients. Dalla Barba et al found a strong relationship between intrusion errors and degree of anosognosia, such that patients who were unaware of their memory deficits made more intrusion errors than those who exhibited awareness of deficit. Since anosognosia is often associated with frontal lobe impairment (McGlynn & Schacter 1989, Stuss 1991), this relationship indirectly suggests a link between intrusion errors and frontal impairment. The only "frontal" measure that correlated with intrusion errors and awareness of deficit was verbal fluency; intrusion errors and awareness of deficit were uncorrelated with performance on tests thought to tap (primarily dorsolateral) frontal functioning, including card sorting, sequencing, and cognitive estimation.

Questions concerning the role of frontal lobe damage have also assumed paramount importance in discussions of confabulation. The general features of confabulation are well summarized by Johnson (1991), Moscovitch (1995), and Burgess & Shallice (1996). Confabulations are typically false narrative accounts of personal experiences, although under some conditions patients may confabulate about factual knowledge (cf Dalla Barba 1993, Moscovitch 1995, Moscovitch & Melo 1997). Confabulations usually draw upon bits and pieces of the patient's actual past experiences, with episodes confused in time and place, but confabulated autobiographical memories may sometimes incorporate knowledge acquired from other sources. Confabulations are typically not intentionally produced and do not appear to be measured attempts to attract attention or compensate for memory loss (though also see Conway & Tacchi 1997). Patients typically present confabulations without awareness that their memories are false, and are more generally unaware of their own memory deficits (e.g. McGlynn & Schacter 1989). Confabulation usually occurs together with anterograde amnesia (i.e. poor memory for recent events). Finally, confabulations may sometimes contain bizarre or "fantastic" content (Kopelman 1987, Talland 1965) that patients nonetheless accept as veridical.

A number of early case reports of confabulation described patients with damage to the ventromedial aspects of the frontal lobes (e.g. Stuss et al 1978), particularly on the right (e.g. Joseph 1986). Damage limited to dorsolateral frontal regions does not appear to produce confabulation; conversely, confabulating patients frequently perform well on tasks that are sensitive to dorsolateral frontal damage, such as cognitive estimation and card sorting (Dalla Barba 1993, Dalla Barba et al 1990). More recently, Benson et al (1996) described a case of alcohol-induced Korsakoff amnesia in which the patient exhibited spontaneous confabulation together with severe memory loss during the early phases of the disorder. Single photon emission (SPECT) scanning at this time revealed hypoperfusion (low blood flow) in the medial diencephalic brain region typically associated with memory loss in Korsakoff patients, as well as hypoperfusion in the orbitomedial frontal lobe. When the patient was assessed again four months later, amnesia persisted but confabulation had disappeared. Repeat SPECT scanning revealed continuing hypoperfusion in the medial diencephalic region but normal perfusion in the frontal regions that had previously shown abnormal blood flow (see also Conway & Tacchi 1997).

Importantly, observations of patients with ruptured aneurysms of the anterior communicating artery (ACoA) suggest that ventromedial frontal lesions are not sufficient to produce confabulation. Ruptured ACoA aneurysms can result in damage to a wide range of structures in the general region of the ventromedial frontal lobes, including (but not limited to) the basal forebrain and the head of the caudate nucleus. The basal forebrain is closely linked to the hippocampus, and ACoA patients with basal forebrain damage show a form of amnesia (for a review of the neuropsychological consequences of ACoA damage, see DeLuca & Diamond 1995; Moscovitch & Melo 1997). Confabulation is reasonably common following ruptured ACoA aneurysms (especially during the acute phase that immediately follows rupture), and a number of recent studies have examined groups of ACoA patients with the goal of relating confabulatory symptoms to underlying neuroanatomical damage. These studies have established that both ventromedial frontal lobe damage and amnesia subsequent to basal forebrain damage must be present in order for lasting confabulation to occur; neither kind of damage on its own seems to suffice (DeLuca 1993).

While some progress has been made in understanding the brain regions associated with confabulation, and the domains of confabulation are beginning to be specified (e.g. episodic vs semantic memory; cf Dalla Barba 1993, Moscovitch 1995), there has been relatively little experimental work that allows firm conclusions about the nature of the memory processes that are compromised in patients who confabulate and/or show robust free recall intrusions. In general, theoretical attention has focused on impaired criterion setting and monitoring processes (e.g. Burgess & Shallice 1996, Conway & Tacchi 1997, Johnson 1991, Moscovitch 1995). Norman & Schacter (1996) point out that theories of confabulation need to explain why incorrect information comes to mind in the first place (in addition to why subjects fail to reject this incorrect information). From the perspective of CMF, one possibility is that focusing processes are impaired in confabulating patients (i.e. they submit vague cues to memory, or cues that are inordinately biased by the individual's present internal and external environment). Another possibility is that the process of pattern completion is itself dysfunctional. Regarding this latter possibility, the basal forebrain (which is damaged in ACoA patients who confabulate) is a major source of the neurotransmitter acetylcholine, and Hasselmo (1995) has argued that acetylcholine plays a key role in regulating the dynamics of pattern completion processes in the hippocampus and other brain structures.

One final unresolved issue is the relationship between intrusions, confabulation, and false recognition. Neuroanatomically, all three deficits appear to require damage to either posterior or ventromedial prefrontal cortex. Functionally, this damage probably relates to monitoring and criterion-setting deficits that are present, to some extent, in all three syndromes (if these processes were unimpaired, patients would be able to reject nontarget information). Based on data from patient BG (whose lesion is limited to posterior prefrontal cortex), it appears that frontal damage by itself is sufficient to cause false recognition. However, at least in ACoA patients, both ventromedial frontal and basal forebrain damage must be present in order for confabulations or robust free-recall intrusions to occur. The fact that the critical lesion for intrusions and confabulations extends outside of prefrontal cortex is consistent with the claim that poor monitoring (resulting from frontal lobe damage), in and of itself, is not sufficient to explain retrieval of incorrect information; some other functional deficit has to be present. Finally, it appears that free-recall intrusions can occur in the absence of confabulation (e.g. Parkin's patient JB shows a strong tendency to make free-recall intrusions despite the fact that he no longer confabulates spontaneously), suggesting that confabulation involves additional functional deficits or that confabulation is a more extreme manifestation of the same functional deficits that are responsible for free-recall intrusions.

AGING MEMORY   There has been comparatively little systematic investigation of false recall in normal aging. Two recent studies have shown that older adults are more susceptible to false recall of semantic associates in the Deese (1959) paradigm than are younger adults. In each of two experiments, Norman & Schacter (1997) found that older adults recalled fewer previously studied items and intruded more related false targets than did younger adults. In Norman & Schacter's experiments, associate lists were presented together in blocks, as in Roediger & McDermott (1995). Tun et al (1996) randomly intermixed the associate lists during presentation and found that whereas older adults recalled fewer studied items than younger adults, they produced just as many semantically related lures. As with false recognition, these age-related increases in false recall (relative to correct recall) could be attributable to source confusions, over-reliance on gist information, or both.

## CONCLUDING COMMENTS

Cognitive neuroscience has embraced the strategy of attempting to understand how a particular process works by studying how it malfunctions. In memory research, this strategy has led to productive investigations of amnesic syndromes in which patients recall little new information, either correct or incorrect. This research has yielded a rich body of knowledge specifying which neural circuits are responsible for storing and retrieving episodic memories. However, this focus on "absent" memory has diverted researchers from studying situations where memory is present but wrong; that is, situations in which people claim to remember past episodes that did not actually occur (cf Koriat & Goldsmith 1996). In this review, we have examined evidence concerning memory inaccuracies from the perspective of CMF.

A large part of CMF is concerned with the need for pattern separation at encoding, and focusing at retrieval. That is, episodes need to be stored in a manner that allows them to be accessed separately at test, and retrieval cues need to be specific enough to activate only a single episode. If either of these conditions is not met, then multiple episodes will be accessed at test; when this occurs, details that differ from episode to episode will compete, resulting in poor memory for differentiating or "source specifying" (Johnson et al 1993) details. However, between-episode competition should not adversely affect features that are common to many episodes—the gist or general similarity information that is often implicated in memory distortions and that has been the focus of theoretical interest (Hintzman & Curran 1994, Reyna & Brainerd 1995).

Once information has been retrieved, decision-making or criterion-setting processes need to be engaged, to evaluate whether it pertains to the target episode. Decision making/criterion setting is logically distinct from the retrieval process we have called focusing, but we should note that postretrieval monitoring processes require a focused description of the target episode (otherwise, there would be no way of assessing whether or not retrieved information is accurate; for additional discussion, see Norman & Schacter 1996). An important area for future research, particularly with brain imaging techniques, will be to examine the relation between processes involved in focusing and postretrieval monitoring/verification.

We have found CMF to be useful in classifying and thinking about different kinds of memory distortions. However, the vast majority of extant data on memory distortions cannot be classified or understood unambiguously. For example, false recognition of nonstudied pictures from studied categories can, at first pass, be explained by either pattern separation failure at encoding or lax criterion-setting or poor focusing at retrieval. Clearly, these are quite different (although not mutually exclusive) claims about the nature of the underlying deficit. We hope that by articulating different ideas regarding how and why different memory distortions occur, we will spur researchers to generate experiments that disentangle and specifically test such alternative hypotheses.

In conclusion, the problems inherent in retrieving accurate, episode-specific information from a system with the biological and functional properties of human memory are complex. Our attempts to understand how the brain accomplishes this difficult task are still in their infancy, and much theoretical and empirical work remains to be done. Fortunately, the neurobiology of memory has progressed to the point where this is a reasonable and even promising enterprise; we see in the research reviewed here the seeds of a cognitive neuroscience of constructive memory that should bear much fruit in the years to come.

ACKNOWLEDGMENTS

Preparation of this paper was supported by the National Institute on Aging grant AG08441 and by a grant to the second author from the Sackler Scholar Programme on Psychobiology. We would also like to thank Lissa Galluccio for her assistance.

---

Visit the *Annual Reviews home page* at
http://www.AnnualReviews.org.

---

## Literature Cited

Bahrick HP, Hall LK, Berger SA. 1996. Accuracy and distortion in memory for high school grades. *Psychol. Sci.* 7:265–71

Bartlett FC. 1932. *Remembering.* Cambridge: Cambridge Univ. Press

Belli RF, Lindsay DS, Gales MS, McCarthy TT. 1994. Memory impairment and source misattribution in postevent misinformation experiments with short retention intervals. *Mem. Cogn.* 22:40–54

Benson DF, Djenderedjian A, Miller BL, Pachana NA. 1996. Neural basis of confabulation. *Neurology* 46:1239–43

Brainerd CJ, Reyna VF, Kneer R. 1995. False-recognition reversal: when similarity is distinctive. *J. Mem. Lang.* 34:157–85

Brown AS, Jones EM, Davis TL. 1995. Age differences in conversational source monitoring. *Psychol. Aging* 10:111–22

Buckner RL. 1996. Beyond HERA: contributions of specific prefrontal brain areas to long-term memory retrieval. *Psychonom. Bull. Rev.* 3:149–58

Buckner RL, Bandettini P, O'Craven K, Savoy R, Petersen SE, et al. 1996. Detection of cortical activation during averaged single trials of a cognitive task using functional magnetic resonance imaging. *Proc. Natl. Acad. Sci. USA* 93:14878–83

Buckner RL, Petersen SE, Ojemann JG, Miezin FM, Squire LR, et al. 1995. Functional anatomical studies of explicit and implicit memory retrieval tasks. *J. Neurosci.* 15:12–29

Buckner RL, Tulving E. 1995. Neuroimaging studies of memory: theory and recent PET results. In *Handbook of Neuropsychology*, ed. F Boller, J Grafman, 10:439–66. Amsterdam: Elsevier

Burgess PW, Shallice T. 1996. Confabulation and the control of recollection. *Memory* 4:359–411

Butters MA, Kasniak AW, Glisky EL, Eslinger PJ, Schacter DL. 1994. Recency discrimination deficits in frontal lobe patients. *Neuropsychology* 8:343–53

Ceci SJ, Bruck M. 1995. *Jeopardy in the Courtroom*. Washington, DC: APA Books

Chiarello C, Beeman M. 1997. Toward a veridical interpretation of right-hemisphere processing and storage. *Psychol. Sci.* 8:343–44

Conway MA, Collins AF, Gathercole SE, Anderson SJ. 1996. Recollections of true and false autobiographical memories. *J. Exp. Psychol. Gen.* 125:69–95

Conway MA, Tacchi PC. 1997. Motivated confabulation. *Neurocase*. 2:325–39

Curran T, Schacter DL, Norman KA, Galluccio L. 1997. False recognition after a right frontal lobe infarction: memory for general and specific information. *Neuropsychologia* 35:1035–49

Dalla Barba G. 1993. Confabulation: knowledge and recollective experience. *Cogn. Neuropsychol.* 10:1–20

Dalla Barba G, Cipolotti L, Denes G. 1990. Autobiographical memory loss and confabulation in Korsakoff's syndrome: a case report. *Cortex* 26:525–34

Dalla Barba G, Parlato V, Iavarone A, Boller F. 1995. Anosognosia, intrusions, and "frontal" functions in Alzheimer's disease and depression. *Neuropsychologia* 33:247–59

Dalla Barba G, Wong C. 1995. Encoding specificity and intrusion in Alzheimer's disease. *Brain Cogn.* 27:1–16

Damasio AR. 1989. Time-locked multiregional retroactivation: a systems-level proposal for the neural substrates of recall and recognition. *Cognition* 33:25–62

Dawes R. 1988. *Rational Choice in an Uncertain World*. San Diego: Harcourt, Brace, Jovanovich

Deese J. 1959. On the prediction of occurrence of particular verbal intrusions in immediate recall. *J. Exp. Psychol.* 58:17–22

Delbecq-Derouesné J, Beauvois MF, Shallice T. 1990. Preserved recall versus impaired recognition. *Brain* 113:1045–74

DeLuca J. 1993. Predicting neurobehavioral patterns following anterior communicating artery aneurysm. *Cortex* 29:639–47

DeLuca J, Diamond BJ. 1995. Aneurysm of the anterior communicating artery: a review of neuroanatomical and neuropsychological sequelae. *J. Clin. Exp. Neuropsychol.* 17:100–21

Dodson CS, Johnson MK. 1993. Rate of false source attributions depends on how questions are asked. *Am. J. Psychol.* 106:541–57

Düzel E, Yonelinas AP, Mangun GR, Heinze HJ, Tulving E. 1997. Event-related brain potential correlates of two states of conscious awareness in memory. *Proc. Natl. Acad. Sci. USA* 94:5973–78

Estes WK. 1997. Processes of memory loss, recovery, and distortion. *Psychol. Rev.* 104:148–69

Fiedler K, Walther E, Armbuster T, Fay D, Naumann U. 1996. Do you *really* know what you have seen? Intrusion errors and presuppositions effects on constructive memory. *J. Exp. Soc. Psychol.* 32:484–511

Gardiner JM, Java RI. 1993. Recognising and remembering. In *Theories of Memory*, ed. AF Collins, SE Gathercole, MA Conway, PE Morris, pp. 163–88. Hove, UK: Erlbaum

Garry M, Manning C, Loftus EF, Sherman SJ. 1996. Imagination inflation: imagining a childhood event inflates confidence that it occurred. *Psychonom. Bull. Rev.* 3:208–14

Grady CL, McIntosh AR, Horwitz B, Maisog JM, Ungerleider LG, et al. 1995. Age-related reductions in human recognition memory due to impaired encoding. *Science* 269:218–21

Hasselmo ME. 1995. Neuromodulation and coritcal function: modeling the physiological basis of behavior. *Behav. Brain Res.* 67:1–27

Hess TM. 1984. Effects of semantically related and unrelated contexts on recognition memory of different-aged adults. *J. Gerontol.* 39:444–51

Hintzman DL, Curran T. 1994. Retrieval dynamics of recognition and frequency judgments: evidence for separate processes of familiarity and recall. *J. Mem. Lang.* 33:1–18

Hintzman DL, Curran T, Oppy B. 1992. Effects of similarity and repetition on memory: registration without learning? *J. Exp. Psychol. Learn. Mem. Cogn.* 18:667–80

Hyman IE, Husband TH, Billings FJ. 1995. False memories of childhood experiences. *Appl. Cogn. Psychol.* 9:181–97

Hyman IE, Pentland J. 1996. The role of mental imagery in the creation of false childhood memories. *J. Mem. Lang.* 35:101–17

Intraub H, Bender RS, Mangels JA. 1992.

Looking and pictures but remembering scenes. *J. Exp. Psychol. Learn. Mem. Cogn.* 18:180–91

Intraub H, Gottesman CV, Willey EV, Zuk IJ. 1996. Boundary extension for briefly glimpsed photographs: Do common perceptual processes result in unexpected memory distortions? *J. Mem. Lang.* 35: 118–34

Isingrini M, Fontaine R, Taconnat L, Duportal A. 1995. Aging and encoding in memory: false alarms and decision criteria in a word-pair recognition task. *Int. J. Aging Hum. Dev.* 41:79–88

Israel L, Schacter DL. 1997. Pictorial encoding reduces false recognition of semantic associates. *Psychonom. Bull. Rev.* In press

Jacoby LL, Kelley CM, Dywan J. 1989. Memory attributions. *Varieties of Memory and Consciousness: Essays in Honour of Endel Tulving,* ed. HL Roediger, III, FIM Craik, pp. 391–422. Hillsdale, NJ: Erlbaum

Janowsky JS, Shimamura AP, Squire LR. 1989. Memory and metamemory: comparisons between patients with frontal lobe lesions and amnesic patients. *Psychobiology* 17:3–11

Johnson MK. 1991. Reality monitoring: evidence from confabulation in organic brain disease patients. In *Awareness of Deficit After Brain Injury: Clinical and Theoretical Issues,* ed. GP Prigatano, DL Schacter, pp. 176–97. New York: Oxford Univ. Press

Johnson MK, Chalfonte BL. 1994. Binding of complex memories: the role of reactivation and the hippocampus. See Schacter & Tulving 1994, pp. 311–50

Johnson MK, De Leonardis DM, Hashtroudi S, Ferguson SA. 1995. Aging and single versus multiple cues in source monitoring. *Psychol. Aging* 10:507–17

Johnson MK, Hashtroudi S, Lindsay DS. 1993. Source monitoring. *Psychol. Bull.* 114:3–28

Johnson MK, Kounios J, Nolde SF. 1996. Electrophysiological brain activity and memory source monitoring. *NeuroReport* 7:2929–32

Johnson MK, Nolde SF, Mather M, Kounios J, Schacter DL, et al. 1997. Test format can affect the similarity of brain activity associated with true and false recognition memory. *Psychol. Sci.* 8:250–57

Joseph R. 1986. Confabulation and delusional denial: frontal lobe and lateralized influences. *J. Clin. Psychol.* 42:507–20

Kern R, Van Gorp W, Cummings J, Brown W, Osato S. 1992. Confabulation in Alzheimer's Disease. *Brain Cogn.* 19:172–82

Knowlton BJ, Squire LR. 1995. Remembering and knowing: two different expressions of declarative memory. *J. Exp. Psychol. Learn. Mem. Cogn.* 21:699–710

Kopelman MD. 1987. Two types of confabulation. *J. Neurol. Neurosurg. Psychiatry* 50: 1482–87

Koriat A, Goldsmith M. 1996. Monitoring and control processes in the strategic regulation of memory accuracy. *Psychol. Rev.* 103:490–517

Kosslyn SM, Alpert NM, Thompson WL, Chabris CF, Rauch SL, et al. 1993. Visual mental imagery activates topographically organized visual cortex: PET investigations. *J. Cogn. Neurosci.* 5:263–87

Koutstaal WK, Schacter DL. 1997. Gist-based false recognition of pictures in older and younger adults. *J. Mem. Lang.* In press

Kroll NEA, Knight RT, Metcalfe J, Wolf ES, Tulving E. 1996. Cohesion failure as a source of memory illusions. *J. Mem. Lang.* 35:176–96

Levine LJ. 1997. Reconstructing memory for emotions. *J. Exp. Psychol. Gen.* 126: 165–77

Lindsay DS. 1990. Misleading suggestions can impair eyewitnesses' ability to remember event details. *J. Exp. Psychol. Learn. Mem. Cogn.* 16:1077–83

Lindsay DS, Kelley CM. 1996. Creating illusions of familiarity in a cued recall remember/know paradigm. *J. Mem. Lang.* 35: 197–211

Lindsay DS, Read JD. 1996. 'Memory work' and recovered memories of childhood sexual abuse: Scientific evidence and public, professional, and personal issues. *Psychol. Public Policy Law* 1:1–61

Loftus EF. 1993. The reality of repressed memories. *Am. Psychol.* 48:518–37

Loftus EF, Feldman J, Dashiell R. 1995. The reality of illusory memories. See Schacter et al 1995a, pp. 47–68

Loftus EF, Pickrell JE. 1995. The formation of false memories. *Psychiatric Ann.* 25: 720–25

Marslen-Wilson WD, Zwitserlood P. 1989. Accessing spoken words: the importance of word onsets. *J. Exp. Psychol. Hum. Percept. Perform.* 15:576–85

Mather M, Henkel LA, Johnson MK. 1997. Evaluating characteristics of false memories: Remember/know judgments and memory characteristics questionnaire compared. *Mem. Logn.* In press

McClelland JL. 1995. Constructive memory and memory distortions: a parallel-distributed processing approach. See Schacter et al 1995a, pp. 69–90

McClelland JL, McNaughton BL, O'Reilly RC. 1995. Why there are complementary learning systems in the hippocampus and neocortex: insights from the successes and failures of connectionist models of learning and memory. *Psychol. Rev.* 102: 419–57

McCloskey M, Zaragoza M. 1985. Misleading postevent information and memory for events: arguments and evidence against memory impairment hypotheses. *J. Exp. Psychol. Gen.* 114:1–16

McDermott KB. 1996. The persistence of false memories in list recall. *J. Mem. Lang.* 35: 212- 30

McGlynn SM, Schacter DL. 1989. Unawareness of deficits in neuropsychological syndromes. *J. Clin. Exp. Neuropsychol.* 11: 143–205

Metcalfe J. 1990. Composite holographic associative recall model (CHARM) and blended memories in eyewitness testimony. *J. Exp. Psychol. Gen.* 119:145–60

Metcalfe J, Funnell M, Gazzaniga MS. 1995. Right-hemisphere memory superiority: studies of a split-brain patient. *Psychol. Sci.* 6:157–64

Milner B, Corsi P, Leonard G. 1991. Frontal-lobe contribution to recency judgments. *Neuropsychologia* 29:601–18

Moscovitch M. 1994. Memory and working-with-memory: evaluation of a component process model and comparisons with other models. See Schacter & Tulving 1994, pp. 269–310

Moscovitch M. 1995. Confabulation. See Schacter et al 1995a, pp. 226–54

Moscovitch M, Melo B. 1997. Strategic retrieval and the frontal lobes: Evidence from confabulation and amnesia. *Neuropsychologia* 35:1017–34

Multhaup K. 1995. Aging, source, and decision criteria: When false fame errors do and do not occur. *Psychol. Aging* 10: 492–97

Nadel L, Moscovitch M. 1997. Memory consolidation, retrograde amnesia, and the hippocampal complex. *Curr. Opin. Neurobiol.* 7:217–27

Norman DA, Bobrow DG. 1979. Descriptions: an intermediate stage in memory retrieval. *Cogn. Psychol.* 11:107–23

Norman KA, Schacter DL. 1996. Implicit memory, explicit memory, and false recollection: a cognitive neuroscience perspective. In *Implicit Memory and Metacognition*, ed. LM Reder, pp. 229–59. Hillsdale, NJ: Erlbaum

Norman KA, Schacter DL. 1997. False recognition in young and older adults: exploring the characteristics of illusory memories. *Mem. Cogn.* In press

Nyberg L, Cabeza R, Tulving E. 1996. PET studies of encoding and retrieval: the HERA model. *Psychonom. Bull. Rev.* 3: 135–48

Nyberg L, McIntosh AR, Houle S, Nilsson L-G, Tulving E. 1996. Activation of medial temporal structures during episodic memory retrieval. *Nature* 380:715–17

Nyberg L, Tulving E, Habib R, Nilsson L-G, Kapur S, et al. 1995. Functional brain maps of retrieval mode and recovery of episodic information. *NeuroReport* 6: 249–52

Nystrom LE, McClelland JL. 1992. Trace synthesis in cued recall. *J. Mem. Lang.* 31: 591–614

Ochsner K, Schacter DL, Edwards K. 1997. Illusory recall of vocal affect. *Memory.* 5: 433–55

O'Reilly RC, McClelland JL. 1994. Hippocampal conjunctive encoding, storage, and recall: avoiding a trade-off. *Hippocampus* 4:661–82

Parkin AJ, Bindschaedler C, Harsent L, Metzler C. 1996. Verification impairment in the generation of memory deficit following ruptured aneurysm of the anterior communicating artery. *Brain Cogn.* 32: 14–27

Parkin AJ, Leng NRC. 1993. *Neuropsychology of the Amnesic Syndrome.* Hillsdale, NJ: Erlbaum

Payne DG, Elie CJ, Blackwell JM, Neuschatz JS. 1996. memory illusions: recalling, recognizing, and recollecting events that never occurred. *J. Mem. Lang.* 35:261–85

Phelps E, Gazzaniga MS. 1992. Hemispheric differences in mnemonic processing: the effects of left hemisphere interpretation. *Neuropsychologia* 30:293–97

Rankin JS, Kausler DH. 1979. Adult age differences in false recognitions. *J. Gerontol.* 34:58–65

Rankin PM, O'Carroll PJ. 1995. Reality discrimination, reality monitoring and disposition towards hallucination. *Br. J. Clin. Psychol.* 34:517–28

Rapcsak SZ, Polster MR, Comer JF, Rubens AB. 1994. False recognition and misidentification of faces following right hemisphere damage. *Cortex* 30:565–83

Rapcsak SZ, Polster MR, Glisky ML, Comer JF. 1996. False recognition of unfamiliar faces following right hemisphere damage: neuropsychological and anatomical observations. *Cortex* 32:593–611

Read JD. 1996. From a passing thought to a false memory in 2 minutes: confusing real and illusory events. *Psychonom. Bull. Rev.* 3:105–11

Reinitz MT, Lammers WJ, Cochran BP. 1992. Memory conjunction errors: miscombination of stored stimulus features can produce illusions of memory. *Mem. Cogn.* 20: 1–11

Reinitz MT, Morrissey J, Demb J. 1994. Role of attention in face encoding. *J. Exp. Psychol. Learn. Mem. Cogn.* 20:161–68

Reinitz MT, Verfaellie M, Milberg WP. 1996. Memory conjunction errors in normal and amnesic subjects. *J. Mem. Lang.* 35: 286–99

Reyna VF, Brainerd CJ. 1995. Fuzzy-trace theory: an interim synthesis. *Learn. Individ. Diff.* 7:1–75

Robinson KJ, Roediger HL III. 1997. Associative processes in false recall and false recognition. *Psychol. Sci.* 8:231–37

Roediger HL III. 1996. Memory illusions. *J. Mem. Lang.* 35:76–100

Roediger HL III, Jacoby JD, McDermott KB. 1996. Misinformation effects in recall: creating false memories through repeated retrieval. *J. Mem. Lang.* 35:300–18

Roediger HL III, McDermott KB. 1995. Creating false memories: remembering words not presented in lists. *J. Exp. Psychol. Learn. Mem. Cogn.* 21:803–14

Ross M. 1989. Relation of implicit theories to the construction of personal histories. *Psychol. Rev.* 96:341–57

Rugg MD, Fletcher PC, Frith CD, Frackowiak RSJ, Dolan RJ. 1996. Differential response of the prefrontal cortex in successful and unsuccessful memory retrieval. *Brain* 119:2073–83

Schacter DL. 1989. Memory. In *Foundations of Cognitive Science,* ed. MI Posner, pp. 683–725. Cambridge, MA: MIT Press

Schacter DL. 1995. Memory distortion: history and current status. See Schacter et al 1995a, pp. 1–43

Schacter DL. 1996. *Searching for Memory: The Brain, the Mind, and the Past.* New York: Basic Books

Schacter DL, Alpert NM, Savage CR, Rauch SL, Albert MS. 1996a. Conscious recollection and the human hippocampal formation: evidence from positron emission tomography. *Proc. Natl. Acad. Sci. USA* 93: 321–25

Schacter DL, Buckner RL, Koutstaal W, Dale AM, Rosen BR. 1997a. Late onset of anterior prefontal activity during true and false recognition: An event-related FMRI study. *NeuroImage.* In press

Schacter DL, Coyle JT, Fischbach GD, Mesulam MM, Sullivan LE, eds. 1995a. *Mem-*

*ory Distortion: How Minds, Brains and Societies Reconstruct the Past.* Cambridge, MA: Harvard Univ. Press

Schacter DL, Curran T. 1995. The cognitive neuroscience of false memories. *Psychiatric Ann.* 25:726–30

Schacter DL, Curran T, Galluccio L, Milberg WP, Bates JF. 1996b. False recognition and the right frontal lobe: a case study. *Neuropsychologia* 34:793–808

Schacter DL, Harbluk JL, McLachlan DR. 1984. Retrieval without recollection: an experimental analysis of source amnesia. *J. Verb. Learn. Verb. Behav.* 23:593–611

Schacter DL, Kagan J, Leichtman MD. 1995b. True and false memories in children and adults: a cognitive neuroscience perspective. *Psychol. Public Policy Law* 1:411–28

Schacter DL, Koutstaal W, Johnson MK, Gross MS, Angell KA. 1997b. False recollection induced via photographs: a comparison of older and younger adults. *Psychol. Aging.* 12:203–15

Schacter DL, Koutstaal W, Norman KA. 1996c. Can cognitive neuroscience illuminate the nature of traumatic childhood memories? *Curr. Opin. Neurobiol.* 6: 207–14

Schacter DL, Koutstaal W, Norman KA. 1997c. False memories and aging. *Trends Cog. Sci.* In press

Schacter DL, Osowiecki DM, Kaszniak AF, Kihlstrom JF, Valdiserri M. 1994. Source memory: extending the boundaries of age-related deficits. *Psychol. Aging* 9:81–89

Schacter DL, Reiman E, Curran T, Yun LS, Bandy D, McDermott KB, Roediger HL III. 1996d. Neuroanatomical correlates of veridical and illusory recognition memory: Evidence from positron emission tomography. *Neuron* 17:267–74

Schacter DL, Reiman E, Uecker A, Polster MR, Yun LS, et al. 1995c. Brain regions associated with retrieval of structurally coherent visual information. *Nature* 376: 587–90

Schacter DL, Savage CR, Alpert NM, Rauch SL, Albert MS. 1996e. The role of hippocampus and frontal cortex in age-related memory changes: a PET study. *NeuroReport* 7:1165–69

Schacter DL, Tulving E, eds. 1994. *Memory Systems 1994.* Cambridge, MA: MIT Press

Schacter DL, Verfaellie M, Anes MD. 1997d. Illusory memories in amnesic patients: conceptual and perceptual false recognition. *Neuropsychology.* 11:331–42

Schacter DL, Verfaellie M, Pradere D. 1996f. The neuropsychology of memory illusions: false recall and recognition in amnesic patients. *J. Mem. Lang.* 35:319–34

Shallice T, Fletcher P, Frith CD, Grasby P, Frackowiak RSJ, et al. 1994. Brain regions associated with acquisition and retrieval of verbal episodic memory. *Nature* 368:633–35

Shiffrin RM, Huber DE, Marinelli K. 1995. Effects of category length and strength on familiarity in recognition. *J. Exp. Psychol. Learn. Mem. Cogn.* 21:267–87

Silbersweig DA, Stern E, Frith C, Cahill C, Holmes A, et al. 1995. Functional neuroanatomy of hallucinations in schizophrenia. *Nature* 378:176–79

Smith AD. 1975. Partial learning and recognition memory in the aged. *Int. J. Aging Hum. Dev.* 6:359–65

Squire LR. 1992. Memory and the hippocampus: a synthesis from findings with rats, monkeys, and humans. *Psychol. Rev.* 99:195–231

Squire LR. 1995. Biological foundations of accuracy and inaccuracy in memory. See Schacter et al 1995a, pp. 197–225

Squire LR, Alvarez P. 1995. Retrograde amnesia and memory consolidation: a neurobiological perspective. *Curr. Opin. Neurobiol.* 5:169–77

Squire LR, Ojemann JG, Miezin FM, Petersen SE, Videen TO, et al. 1992. Activation of the hippocampus in normal humans: a functional anatomical study of memory. *Proc. Natl. Acad. Sci. USA* 89:1837–41

Stern CE, Corkin S, Gonzalez RG, Guimaraes AR, Baker JR, et al. 1996. The hippocampal formation participates in novel picture encoding: evidence from functional magnetic resonance imaging. *Proc. Natl. Acad. Sci. USA* 93:8660–65

Stuss DT. 1991. Disturbance of self-awareness after frontal system damage. *Awareness of Deficit After Brain Injury: Clinical and Theoretical Issues,* ed. GP Prigatano, DL Schacter, pp. 63–83. New York: Oxford Univ. Press

Stuss DT, Alexander MP, Lieberman A, Levine H. 1978. An extraordinary form of confabulation. *Neurology* 28:1166–72

Stuss DT, Alexander MP, Palumbo CL, Buckle L, Sayeer L, et al. 1994. Organizational strategies of patients with unilateral or bilateral frontal lobe injury in word list learning tasks. *Neuropsychology* 8:355–73

Talland GA. 1965. *Deranged Memory: a Psy-chonomic Study of the Amnesic Syndrome.* New York: Academic

Treisman A, Schmidt H. 1982. Illusory conjunctions in the perception of objects. *Cogn. Psychol.* 14:107–41

Treves A, Rolls ET. 1994. Computational analysis of the role of the hippocampus in memory. *Hippocampus* 4:374–91

Tulving E. 1985. Memory and consciousness. *Can. Psychol.* 26:1–12

Tulving E, Kapur S, Markowitsch HJ, Craik FIM, Habib R, et al. 1994a. Neuroanatomical correlates of retrieval in episodic memory: auditory sentence recognition. *Proc. Natl. Acad. Sci. USA* 91:2012–15

Tulving E, Markowitsch HJ, Kapur S, Habib R, Houle S. 1994b. Novelty encoding networks in the human brain: positron emission tomography data. *NeuroReport* 5:2525–28

Tun PA, Wingfield A, Blanchard L, Rosen MJ. 1996. *Cognitive Aging Conf., Atlanta, GA*

Underwood BJ. 1965. False recognition produced by implicit verbal responses. *J. Exp. Psychol.* 70:122–29

Underwood BJ, Kapelak SM, Malmi RA. 1976. Integration of discrete verbal units in recognition memory. *J. Exp. Psychol. Hum. Learn. Mem.* 2:293–300

Ungerleider LG. 1995. Functional brain imaging studies of cortical mechanisms for memory. *Science* 270:760–75

Vicente KJ, Brewer WF. 1993. Reconstructive remembering of the scientific literature. *Cognition* 46:101–28

Wallace WP, Stewart MT, Malone CP. 1995a. Recognition memory errors produced by implicit activation of word candidates during the processing of spoken words. *J. Mem. Lang.* 34:417–39

Wallace WP, Stewart MT, Sherman HL, Mellor MD. 1995b. False positives in recognition memory produced by cohort activation. *Cognition* 55:85–113

Wilding EL, Rugg MD. 1996. An event-related potential study of recognition memory with and without retrieval of source. *Brain* 119:889–905

Zaragoza MS, Lane SM. 1994. Source misattributions and the suggestibility of eyewitness memory. *J. Exp. Psychol. Learn. Mem. Cogn.* 20:934–45

Zaragoza MS, Mitchell KJ. 1996. Repeated exposure to suggestion and the creation of false memories. *Psychol. Sci.* 7:294–300

*Annu. Rev. Psychol. 1998. 49:319–44*

# CONSUMER BEHAVIOR:
# A Quadrennium

## J. Jacoby[1], G. V. Johar[2], M. Morrin[3]

[1]Marketing Department, New York University, New York, NY 10012; e-mail:
jjacoby@rnd.stern.nyu.edu; [2]Marketing Department, Columbia University, New
York, NY 10027; e-mail: gvj1@columbia.edu; [3]Marketing Department, Boston
University, Boston, Massachusetts 02215; e-mail: mmorrin@acs.bu.edu

KEY WORDS:  marketing, buyer behavior, consumer psychology, information processing,
           attitude formation

## ABSTRACT

Consumer behavior continued to attract additional researchers and publication outlets from 1993 through 1996. Both general interest and domain-
specific scholarly contributions are discussed, along with limitations and
suggested areas for future research. A concluding section observes that the
integrity of consumer research is unnecessarily compromised by the failure
of the major scholarly association in the field to develop and adopt a code of
researcher ethics.

## CONTENTS

0066-4308/98/0201-0319$08.00

# INTRODUCTION

Consumer behavior has been defined as the "acquisition, consumption and disposition of products, services, time and ideas by decision making units" (Jacoby 1975, 1976). While the number of disciplines, researchers, and publishing outlets now studying consumer behavior continues to increase, of necessity attention in this review is confined primarily to work published in the *Journal of Consumer Research, Journal of Marketing, Journal of Marketing Research, Journal of Public Policy and Marketing,* and *Journal of Consumer Psychology* from 1993 through 1996. The first three journals have traditionally published the most rigorous research in the field. The contributors and content of the latter two journals, of more recent origin, suggest that they are approaching the former in repute. Because of space constraints, the works cited in this review are representative rather than comprehensive. Not covered but worthy of attention are papers appearing in *Advances in Consumer Research,* the annual proceedings of the Association for Consumer Research.

# CONTRIBUTIONS OF BROAD RELEVANCE

## *Philosophy of Science*

GENERAL   Several papers possess relevance well beyond consumer research. Particularly noteworthy are the very readable philosophy of science papers that constitute an extended debate between Hunt (1992, 1993, 1994) in defense of scientific realism and others (e.g. Peter 1992) propounding a social reconstructionist perspective. Because these papers rely on general examples, which for the most part are not tied to marketing, they make excellent reading for PhD students and scholars across the social sciences.

POSTMODERNISM   Sherry (1991) recognized a certain "tension animating the conduct of inquiry in recent years" among consumer researchers. This tension, which continues to be evident, revolves around differences in philosophical and methodological approaches to the field. Historically, the disciplines of psychology (especially cognitive and social) and economics provided the theoretical foundation for most consumer research. Recently, this hegemony has been challenged by postmodern approaches that focus on other avenues of inquiry such as anthropology, sociology, and history. In the past few years, the field saw numerous postmodern methodological approaches advocated and/or explicated, including projective techniques (McGrath et al 1993), ethnography (Arnould & Wallendorf 1994), historical methodology (Smith & Lux 1993), reader-response theory (Scott 1994), critical theory (Hetrick & Lozada 1994), deconstruction (Stern 1996), hermeneutics (e.g. Arnold & Fisher 1994, Thompson 1996), and feminist thought (e.g. Bristor & Fischer 1993, Stern 1993). Disagreement was evident: While Gould (1995) advocated introspection, Wallendorf & Brucks (1993) contended that this approach offers little opportunity for theory-building.

Postmodern techniques were used to examine several less traditional areas of inquiry such as skydiving (Celsi et al 1993), gift giving (Belk & Coon 1993), abortion (Patterson et al 1995), baseball spectating (Holt 1995), and pet (Hirschman 1994) and motorcycle (Schouten & McAlexander 1995) ownership. At this point, while some tension continues to be evident, a schism between the positivist and postmodern camps is unlikely. Instead, it looks as if multiple approaches to consumer inquiry will be accommodated in the traditional research outlets.

## Methodological Advances

GENERAL   Other papers of general interest focused on research methodology. While many psychological phenomena such as information search, attitude formation, and choice are postulated to operate as dynamic, often sequential processes, these phenomena generally have been studied using static, pre-versus-post methodologies. As an alternative, Jacoby et al (1994) outlined a procedure for capturing and studying the dynamic, ongoing molecular changes in such processes and illustrated how the procedure could be used by studying changes in risk perception as consumers acquired and integrated information.

Other papers addressed issues such as the use of conjoint analysis (Carroll & Green 1995), effect sizes (Fern & Monroe 1996), ANOVA interactions (Ross & Creyer 1993), and nonparametric approaches to signal detection theory (Cradit et al 1994). Researchers also ventured beyond the traditional relative frequency approach to probability theory by using Bayesian techniques to assess the value of manipulation checks (Sawyer et al 1995) and replications (Raman 1994).

SURVEY AND QUESTIONNAIRE DESIGN   Much consumer research relies on surveys, and a considerable amount of work has been devoted to questionnaire and survey design. Bickart (1993) and Simmons et al (1993) examined question order effects in surveys, while Menon (1993, Menon et al 1995) examined the memory processes underlying consumers' responses to behavioral frequency questions. Rose et al (1993) suggest that comparative measures (e.g. "Is Brand A superior to Brand B?") are more sensitive in detecting persuasion than noncomparative measures. Webster (1996) found that response quality for surveys is highest when interviewer and interviewee are of the same gender or ethnicity.

VALIDITY AND RELIABILITY   Several papers addressed issues concerning validity and reliability. Peterson (1994) conducted a meta-analysis of Cronbach's coefficient alpha across 832 studies and found that the average value of 0.77 was not affected by research design characteristics. Bagozzi & Yi (1993) discussed shortcomings associated with the multitrait-multimethod approach, while Peter et al (1993) addressed reliability problems associated with the use of difference scores. Fisher (1993) and Mick (1996) examined social desirability bias. Darley & Lim (1993) contended that the incidence of demand artifact is higher than that accounted for by subjects who correctly guess a research hypothesis. They suggest that subjects underreport such behavior because they are unaware of conforming. Shimp et al (1993) responded by noting there is little actual evidence for such a contention.

CONSTRUCT DEVELOPMENT   Several studies developed or clarified constructs such as expertise (e.g. Mitchell & Dacin 1996, Park et al 1994), satisfaction (e.g. Mano & Oliver 1993), materialism (e.g. Richins 1994), vanity (Netemeyer et al 1995), and consumer innovativeness (Manning et al 1995).

## DOMAIN-SPECIFIC RESEARCH

By focusing on the 42 most published scholars in the *Journal of Consumer Research* during its first 15 years, Hoffman & Holbrook (1993) provided interesting perspective on those whose scholarly contributions exerted the greatest influence upon research published in that journal. Admonishing the field for its changed and, what he believes are, misdirected priorities, Wells (1993) proposed guidelines designed to produce more meaningful and useful research. These include being interdisciplinary in nature, stimulating industry and government participation, and expanding the focus beyond the US marketplace. Research has tended to focus on the mental processes of individual decision makers when acquiring and consuming; scant attention was devoted to disposition (an exception is Taylor & Tod 1995). Much of this work is decidedly psychological in nature, relying largely on the experimental method. While other orientations abound, the cognitive perspective remains dominant. Below we summarize the domain-specific literature in an order suggested by stages in consumer decision-making: the processing of information, formation of attitudes, choice, and factors affecting these processes.

### Information Processing

SENSATION AND PERCEPTION   Historically, sensation and perception have been accorded little attention by consumer researchers. Not surprisingly, work is confined primarily to visual or auditory processes, as most forms of marketing communications rely on one (i.e. print, radio) or both (i.e. television) of these modes. An exception is work examining the impact of odors on consumer behavior (e.g. Mitchell et al 1995, Spangenberg et al 1996). Raghubir & Krishna (1996) introduced the notion of spatial perceptions to the field. The relatively underresearched sensory processes of smell, taste, and touch suggest promising avenues for future work.

ATTENTION   Attention refers to the momentary focusing of processing capacity on a particular stimulus. Research in this area focuses predominantly on advertising applications. For example, several field studies examined the impact of "zipping" (or fast-forwarding a VCR during commercials) and "zapping" (or changing channels during commercial breaks) on attention. Finding zapped ads more effective than uninterrupted ads in affecting purchase behavior, Zufryden et al (1993) speculate that this is due to increased attention during the zapping process. Attention to packages on store shelves, as measured by eye fixations, was examined in a supermarket simulation by Russo & Leclerc (1994). Janiszewski (1993) examined the impact of pre-attentive ad processing on affective response to brand names.

CATEGORIZATION   After being detected and attended to, stimuli must be identified or given meaning, that is, categorized. Goodstein (1993) utilized categorization theory to explain why ads that are atypical of an ad schema tend to provoke more extensive processing. Categorization theory also played a major role in issues related to brand equity and extension strategies (e.g. Broniarczyk & Alba 1994a, Dacin & Smith 1994, Peracchio & Tybout 1996). Ratneshwar et al (1996) used the concept of goal-derived categories to explain when and why consideration sets may include alternatives from different product categories. Lefkoff-Hagins & Mason (1993) showed that products perceived to be similar are not always similarly liked, because cognitive judgments of similarity are based on different product attributes than are judgments of preference.

The use of metaphors, which may be thought of as special types of categories, is gaining favor among consumer researchers. Spiggle (1994) discussed metaphors as a way to interpret qualitative data. Interest in metaphors and analogies is likely to increase, as advertisers of ever more technological products seek ways to communicate product features in an easily understandable manner.

INFERENCE MAKING   Consumers may choose to think more about stimuli after they have been categorized and develop additional beliefs based on the stimulus information, that is, engage in inference making. Consumer inference making has generally been examined in terms of applications to advertising communications, and this continued to be true in the past several years. Johar (1995) showed that highly involved consumers draw inferences from incomplete comparison ad claims at the time of processing the ad; however, brand belief questions may induce less involved consumers to draw such inferences at the time of measurement. Campbell (1995) examined the negative inferences consumers make about advertiser intent when attention-getting tactics, such as identifying the brand name late in a commercial, are used. Consumer inference making was also examined in terms of pricing (Pechmann 1996), warranties (Boulding & Kirmani 1993), and alpha-numeric brand names (Pavia & Costa 1993). Carpenter et al (1994) examined the brand differentiation inferences consumers make when exposed to product attributes that only appear to create meaningful differences, and Broniarczyk & Alba (1994b) examined the formation of spontaneous inferences about missing attribute information.

INFORMATION SEARCH   Most of this work focuses on consumers' conscious efforts to obtain information about durable goods or those associated with high financial or social risk. For example, Putsis & Srinivasan (1994) modeled the search patterns of new car buyers. Leong (1993), on the other hand, examined information search for low-involvement goods among Hong Kong consumers, and Grewal & Marmorstein (1994) examined the amount of price search that takes place as a function of the absolute size of the price of an item. The effects of information type (i.e. search versus experience attributes) on search behavior were examined by Wright & Lynch (1995). Cole & Balasubramanian (1993) found that the elderly were less likely than the young to search for nutritional information. Much of this work now takes place using computer simulations (e.g. Coupey 1994), and this trend is likely to continue. Web site navigation is a natural area for future research.

MEMORY   Alba et al (1991) suggested that memory has had a subordinate role in theorizing about consumer decision processes because the majority of this research has focused on advertising effects rather than on choice behavior. This continued to be true in the last several years, but the impact of memory was felt in other areas, such as brand equity (Keller 1993, Loken & Roedder John 1993), and consideration set formation (e.g. Hutchinson et al 1994, Kardes et al 1993). Broniarczyk & Alba (1994a), for example, found that brand-specific associations moderate the well-documented effects of brand affect and product category similarity on consumer evaluations of brand extensions.

Much work on memory continued to revolve around factors that affect memory for advertising. Friestad & Thorson (1993) examined variables, such as encoding strategy, that affect ad retrieval. Although it is generally thought that advertising clutter reduces recall, Brown & Rothschild (1993) found that consumer memory remained steady or improved as number of ads increased.

Singh et al (1994) found that it is better for ads to have been spaced with a significant (short) time lag when memory is measured after a long (short) delay.

Schmitt et al (1994) examined differences in brand recall as a function of ad modality (and memory mode) for consumers with an alphabetic (e.g. English) versus idiographic (e.g. Chinese) native language. Unnava et al (1994) found that message order affected persuasion only for radio, not print, ads. It was suggested that this results from a first-in first-out retrieval strategy used only in the auditory mode. Schmitt et al (1993) reported that congruency among print ad elements facilitates consumer memory. Kellaris et al (1993) also examined the notion of ad memory and congruency but in the context of whether background music evokes message-congruent thoughts.

## Attitudes

Research on attitude structure, formation, and change remained a dominant focus, with theoretical models borrowed from social psychology applied and extended in the consumer behavior domain. The uniqueness of the consumer context is illustrated by Friestad & Wright's (1994) persuasion knowledge model. They suggest that knowledge about persuasion agents' goals and tactics can influence attitudes, and that researchers need to incorporate this factor into their models. Relatedly, Kover (1995) reports that even copywriters hold implicit theories of how their ads persuade consumers.

An important issue concerns whether attitudes are cognitive or affective in nature. Fishbein & Middlestadt (1995) argue in favor of the traditional cognitive or belief-based models and suggest that other, more recent models (e.g. mere exposure, affective transfer, peripheral routes) may be the result of methodological artifacts. In contrast, Herr (1995) argues that Fishbein's theory of reasoned action, widely adopted by consumer researchers, is not falsifiable and may apply only to high-involvement purchases.

ATTITUDE FORMATION AND PERSUASION    Advertising messages differ from other messages examined in social psychology in that they are more complex, have a persuasion goal, and often contain both verbal and visual elements. Much work on persuasion in advertising applies the Elaboration Likelihood Model (Petty & Cacioppo 1981, Chaiken 1980) or extends one of the central tenets of the model. Haugtvedt & Wegener (1994) offered extent of message-relevant elaboration as a moderator of order effects (primacy vs recency) in persuasion. Meyers-Levy & Peracchio (1995) showed that use of color in an ad improves persuasion only when consumers have the ability (processing resources) to process the message, while Pham (1996) challenged the prevailing view that diminished ability increases reliance on an ad's peripheral cues. Heath et al (1994) found that peripheral ad cues, such as spokesperson fame and copy vividness, influenced attitudes only in competitive settings. This research has also found that peripheral cues can be processed elaborately and be effective even when involvement is high. Further support for this notion comes from Li & Wyer (1994) and Maheswaran (1994) who examined country-of-origin as an extrinsic cue.

Peracchio & Meyers-Levy (1994) focused on images in advertising and found that cropping objects irrelevant to verbal ad claims enhanced product evaluations of subjects motivated to process the ad. Burnkrant & Unnava (1995) found that the use of self-referencing in ads (e.g. "You know that...") increased message elaboration and persuasion when message arguments were strong. Meyers-Levy & Peracchio (1996) found that, for subjects motivated to attend to an ad, a moderate increase in self-referencing enhances persuasion, whereas an extreme increase undermines it. Research has also focused on attitude toward the advertisement (e.g. Tripp et al 1994).

CONDITIONING   Classical conditioning theory suggests that the repeated pairing of a neutral stimulus (such as an ad or brand) with a stimulus known to elicit a desired response (such as pleasant music) will result in a transfer of affect from the latter to the former. While there had been disagreement in the field over whether prior studies had demonstrated conditioning effects or merely demand artifacts, Janiszewski & Warlop (1993) found evidence for classical conditioning effects, reporting that they also increased attention and transferred meaning. Kim et al (1996) found that brand attitudes can be conditioned not only through direct affect transfer but also through the formation of inferential beliefs.

ATTITUDES AND BEHAVIOR   Instead of measuring the relationship between attitudes and actual purchase or usage, most research examines purchase intent. Lacher & Mizerski (1994), for example, found that different types of affective responses to music were related to purchase intent. Results from Morwitz et al (1993) suggest that measuring purchase intent is reactive—asking questions about intention to buy increased purchase likelihood, but asking those with low levels of intent several times about their intention to buy decreased purchase likelihood.

Some research examined actual behavior. Rook & Fisher (1995) found that impulse buying was affected by normative beliefs about its appropriateness. Smith (1993) examined how advertising attitudes and brand beliefs influence brand attitudes after product trial.

## Affect

AFFECT AS INDEPENDENT VARIABLE   Affect as an independent variable has been most commonly investigated in terms of the impact of mood on consumer behavior. Consumers in a positive mood were found to engage in more variety-seeking behaviors except when negative product features were made salient (Kahn & Isen 1993). In a study of stereo speakers, Gorn et al (1993) found that good mood improved product evaluations, unless subjects were made aware that music heard on the evaluated product was the source of their mood. Kellaris & Kent (1994) explored specific characteristics of music, such as tempo, tonality, and texture, on consumer affective responses such as pleasure, arousal, and surprise. Swinyard (1993) found that good mood resulted in more positive shopping intentions only among high involvement subjects with a good shopping experience.

Other research has classified affect as a moderator variable. For example, Holbrook & Gardner (1993) found that the emotion of pleasure moderates the relationship between arousal and consumption duration.

AFFECT AS DEPENDENT VARIABLE    Much of this research studies affective reactions to advertising. Bagozzi & Moore (1994) found that compared to rational appeals, emotional appeals in public service announcements led to greater negative emotions, greater empathy, and a desire to help. Further, the greater the magnitude of negative emotions, the stronger the empathic response. Positive emotions may influence evaluations via simple decision heuristics, whereas negative emotions may motivate detailed analysis of the event (Murry & Dacin 1996).

Other research has examined measurement of affect and changes in affect over time. The warmth monitor is an example of a continuous measure of emotional reactions where respondents viewing an ad move a pencil line steadily down the page and to the right when warmth is experienced (Aaker et al 1986). Abeele & Maclachlan (1994) found this measure to be reliable and proposed measuring variations in warmth over different ad segments rather than using the entire ad as the stimulus.

## Choice

HEURISTICS AND BIASES    Contrary to standard economic theory, which assumes people engage in fully rational, optimizing choice behavior, behavioral decision theory suggests that consumers often use a number of simplifying decision rules or heuristics. Mazumdar & Jun (1993), for example, found that consumers evaluate multiple price decreases more favorably than single price decreases, and a single price increase more favorably than multiple price increases, in accord with Thaler's work (1985) on mental accounting. In a similar vein, Yadav (1994) examined the effects of anchoring and adjustment on evaluations of product bundles. Simonson et al (1993) showed how irrelevant preference arguments bias consumer choice. Heath et al (1995) examined the effects of stating discounts in percentage versus absolute dollar terms. Research has also investigated the impact of new brand entry on brand preferences (e.g. Heath & Chatterjee 1995, Lehmann & Pan 1994), and of number and type of product features on brand choice and judgment (e.g. Nowlis & Simonson 1996). Sethuraman et al (1994) analyzed consumers' use of brand versus attribute-based processing strategies when consumers use cutoff decision rules. Additional research is needed to develop theoretical explanations for the heuristic strategies uncovered to date.

Interestingly, a backlash to this line of work has become evident, with several articles focusing on how supposedly nonoptimal heuristic strategies can, in fact, be quite appropriate and optimizing in given situations. Wernerfelt (1995), for example, demonstrates how the compromise effect can be a fully rational decision process when understood in terms of how consumers use market data to infer utilities. West et al (1996) demonstrated that consumers exhibit more consistent preferences when provided with a consumption vocabulary, and Kahn & Baron (1995) found that although consumers do not want to use compensatory decision processes when choosing high-stakes products (such as financial investments or medical procedures), they do want their agents/advisers to do so. Baumgartner (1995) showed how consumers' prior expectations can actually improve the accuracy of covariation judgments and hence that prior expectations should not necessarily be considered biasing or dysfunctional.

VARIETY SEEKING AND DECISION TIMING    Greenleaf & Lehmann (1995) classified the reasons people delay making consumer decisions. In the related area of variety-seeking behavior, Menon & Kahn (1995) found that behavior is moderated by the amount of stimulation provided by other sources in a given choice context.

SATISFACTION    Research on consumer satisfaction has tried to pin down its determinants and to differentiate it from other constructs, such as evaluation. Spreng et al (1996) proposed a new model of satisfaction that builds on the well-established expectation disconfirmation paradigm by including attribute satisfaction, information satisfaction, and the impact of marketing communications in a single model. Arnould & Price (1993) examined satisfaction derived from white-water rafting and described the experience as one of hedonic consumption; they also suggested a weak link between expectations and satisfaction. Ostrom & Iacobucci (1995) suggest customer satisfaction is based on different attributes for different types of services. Mohr & Henson (1996) demonstrated greater customer satisfaction when employees are of the expected gender in gender-typed jobs. Johnson et al (1995) proposed that expectations and satisfaction are dynamic in nature. Gardial et al (1994) differentiated satisfaction from postpurchase evaluation experiences and found that consumers understand the two constructs differently. However, consumers' interpretations of satisfaction do not appear to differ from their evaluations of service quality (Iacobucci et al 1995).

## Factors Affecting Information Processing, Attitudes, and Choice

INTRINSIC FACTORS   *Age*   Young consumers have received considerable attention (cf Peracchio 1993). Macklin (1994, 1996) examined the effects of ad visuals on children's recall of product information and found most effective encoding for dual-mode messages (audio and visual). Macklin (1994) and Gregan-Paxton & John (1995) found developmental differences when comparing preschoolers with school age children. Antismoking (vs control) advertising was found to decrease adolescent nonsmokers' ratings of a smoker's common sense, personal appeal, maturity, and glamour (Pechmann & Ratneshwar 1994), suggesting that nonsmoking adolescents are well aware of the dangers of smoking.

Although the population is aging, little research has examined elderly consumers. An exception is work by Tepper (1994) that studied how and why age segmentation cues inhibit responsiveness to discount offerings made to the elderly. Her findings support a stage model such that consumers progress over time through phases of responsiveness to "senior citizen" labeling. Holbrook has taken a different perspective on age by examining nostalgia preferences (1993, Holbrook & Schindler 1994). This research suggests that age and nostalgia proneness (an individual difference variable) act independently to influence nostalgia preferences and that consumers tend to form enduring preferences during a sensitive period in their lives. Some researchers argue that cognitive age (i.e. how old one feels), rather than chronological age, is the important construct (Auken & Barry 1995).

*Gender and ethnicity*   Iacobucci & Ostrom (1993) found that women base their evaluations of services more on relational aspects of the encounter, whereas men base their evaluation more on core aspects of the service and goals achieved.

Research on minority groups has been scarce. Deshpande & Stayman (1994) found that members of minority groups consider an ad spokesperson from their own ethnic group to be more trustworthy and that this leads to more positive brand attitudes. Webster (1994), using Hispanic couples living in the United States, reported that at lower levels of cultural assimilation (as measured by language spoken in the home), husbands were more likely to dominate the decision processes. Some work suggests that numerical minorities in consumption settings (e.g. restaurants) adjust their distinctiveness by reducing perceived dissimilarities rather than increasing perceived similarities between themselves and nonminority members (Wooten 1995).

*Personality*   Research in the area of personality has focused on defining and measuring traits such as materialism (Hunt et al 1996), material possession attachment (Klein et al 1995), vanity (Netemeyer et al 1995), deal proneness (Lichtenstein et al 1995), and compulsiveness (Faber et al 1995). For example, Lichtenstein et al (1995) found that deal proneness is domain specific (e.g. coupon proneness vs sale proneness). Other work has investigated the effects of these variables on attributions, judgments, and choice (e.g. Hunt et al 1996).

Values can also be viewed as a personality variable. Research suggests that values differ across countries and can predict behaviors such as tipping (Lynn & Zinkhan 1993). One stream of research argues that the value of possessions resides in the public and private meaning they have for consumers and that materialistic consumers can be perceived, as well as perceive other people, in terms of their possessions (Hunt et al 1996, Richins 1994).

*Perceptions*   Consumer perceptions of price and risk have been examined. Krishna & Johar (1996) found that offering different deal prices over time affects perceptions of deal frequency, average deal price, and price consumers are willing to pay for the brand. Alba et al (1994) found that frequency of price advantage exerted a dominating influence beyond that of price expectations (i.e. prior beliefs) to influence consumer price perceptions.

Perceived risk has been examined in terms of its antecedents (Grewal et al 1994, Jacoby et al 1994) and consequences (Dowling & Staelin 1994, Morris et al 1994). Grewal et al found that the effect of price on performance risk perceptions is greater when the message is framed negatively (vs positively) and when source credibility is low (vs high). Muthukrishnan (1995) found that decision ambiguity creates advantages for incumbent (vs attack) brands because of overconfidence in the superiority of incumbent brands and consumers' risk aversion. Perceived risk is an important construct that affects risk-handling activities such as search behavior, especially when product-specific risk (an element of perceived risk) is greater than the acceptable risk (Dowling & Staelin 1994).

EXTRINSIC FACTORS   *Family, interpersonal, and group influences*   Family appears to be an important influence on purchase incidence and choice (e.g. Beatty & Talpade 1994). Some research (Schaninger & Danko 1993) has examined family life-cycle stages. Wilkes (1995) validated the household life-cycle concept by showing that as households pass from one stage of the life cycle to another, their expenditure patterns change.

A number of studies examined interpersonal and group influences from a social influence viewpoint. For example, Howard et al (1995) found that interpersonal influence measured via compliance was greater when the source remembers the target's name, which is perceived as a compliment. Other research on interpersonal and group influences relied on a negotiation paradigm. For example, Corfman & Lehmann (1993) found that negotiators may be influenced by issues other than their own gain (e.g. the opponent's outcomes) during negotiating processes.

*Social roles and identity*    Otnes et al (1993) suggested that gift-givers express different social roles in relation to different gift recipients. Kleine et al (1993) suggested that consumers are attracted to products congruent with their own social identity or role. Research also examined changing social roles and their impact on consumption (Lavin 1995, Oropesa 1993).

*Culture*    Within the United States, Hispanic consumers perceive advertisers of ads that are partly or fully in Spanish as more sensitive to Hispanic culture and prefer these to English ads (Koslow et al 1994). Research also focused on the relation of culture to consumption (Sirsi et al 1996) and suggested that intracultural variation (e.g. between experts and novices) is important.

*Source credibility and reputation*    Some research has examined the consequences of source credibility (e.g. Grewal & Marmorstein 1994). Johar (1996) found contrasting effects of corrective advertising on brand vs advertiser beliefs and attitudes depending on the advertiser's reputation.

*Type of claim*    Much research has focused on the effectiveness of different types of appeals such as fear, comparison, and humor for different product categories. Keller & Block (1996) found that the inverted-U relationship between amount of fear and persuasion is driven by elaboration. Grewal et al (1996) also invoked a processing interpretation to explain why a consumer's response to a semantic price cue (e.g. compare at $x$) depends on the discount size. Stern (1994) contrasted classical TV advertising from vignette advertising and proposed that the two have different effects on consumer attributions and on empathy vs sympathy. Wansink & Ray (1996) differentiated between product-comparison ads and situation-comparison ads and found that the latter were more effective than the former in increasing brand usage in the target situation. Wansink (1994) also showed that brand usage could be increased by encouraging consumers to substitute the brand in situations for which it is not normally used through attributes featured in an ad. Malaviya et al (1996) found that ads for cameras featuring attribute-focused pictures resulted in more favorable judgments when presented in the context of competing brands. Crowley & Hoyer (1994) offered an integrative framework of how two-sided messages including both positive and negative information work and introduced message structure variables such as the amount and order of each type of information, refutation, importance, etc.

Message framing has also been a research focus. The effects of framing and perceived efficacy on message processing were explored by Block & Keller (1995). Darley & Smith (1993) found that objective claims featuring tangible attributes and factual descriptions are more effective than subjective claims.

Researchers also examined advertising from a social viewpoint. Sen & Morwitz (1996) reported that consumer consumption behaviors were affected by a provider's position on a social issue and the manner in which the position was communicated. Several studies have been devoted to "green" advertising and have tried to suggest how support for the environment can be communicated as an impetus to green consumption behaviors (cf *Journal of Advertising,* Summer 1995).

*Ad repetition*   Advertising repetition was found to have positive effects on brand awareness and preference (D'Souza & Rao 1995) and on attitude persistence (Haugtvedt et al 1994). Haugtvedt et al (1994) demonstrated that repeating varied ads resulted in greater resistance to counterattack compared with other types of repetition and single exposure.

*Context*   Studies have examined how various contextual factors, such as time, service quality, and product form, affect consumer perceptions and behavior. Leclerc et al (1995) found that consumers are risk-averse with regard to losses of time (vs risk seeking for money losses according to prospect theory) and the marginal value of time was higher for shorter (vs longer) waiting times. Hui & Tse (1996) contrasted the effects of waiting duration information (i.e. expected length of wait) with that of queuing information (i.e. position in queue) on acceptability of the wait and affective responses to the wait and service evaluation. Taylor (1994) found that delays do affect service evaluations and this relationship is mediated by negative affective reactions to the delay. Zeithaml et al (1996) suggest that service evaluations are important because of their relationship to customer behaviors that signal whether a customer will remain with or defect from a company.

Product-related context effects include propositions about how product form (Bloch 1995) and package size (Wansink 1996) affect consumers' psychological and behavioral responses. The decision making context—in-store vs at home—was also identified as a key moderator of the relation between type of semantic cue claim and consumer response (Grewal et al 1996). Finally, exposure to political poll results was itself found to affect voter expectations about election outcome, attitudes to candidates, voting intentions, and choice (Morwitz & Pluzinski 1996).

# PUBLIC POLICY AND CONSUMER BEHAVIOR

Along with the emergence of consumer behavior as an arena meriting scholarly attention has come recognition of the role of consumer research when developing and evaluating public policy. While relevant work appears in a variety of sources, the principal outlet for such research is the *Journal of Public Policy and Marketing*. A ten-year retrospective on public policy articles appearing in this and other journals is provided by Laverie & Murphy (1993).

## Labeling Effects

One major interest in this arena is the effects of warning messages. A review by Stewart & Martin (1994) concluded that consumers selectively attend to warning messages, with the principal impact of such messages being informative rather than persuasive. Related research on the effectiveness of disclaimer labeling suggests that often such labeling is not even attended to; hence, it may never reach being informative (Jacoby & Szybillo 1994). McCarthy et al (1995) provide a thoughtful discussion of criteria for product warnings.

Much attention has focused on the alcohol warning labels federally mandated in 1988. An overview of findings is provided by Hilton (1993). Research has examined warnings on alcoholic beverage containers (Laughery et al 1993), in magazine and television advertising (Barlow & Wogalter 1993), and in posters (Fenaughty & MacKinnon 1993, Kalsher et al 1993). Also examined have been cognitive responses as mediators of label effectiveness (Andrews et al 1993), changes in public attitudes (Kaskutas 1993), and US-Canadian comparisons (Graves 1993). While one study examined the effects of alcohol warning labels during pregnancy (Hankin et al 1993), another linked risk perception to product use (Morris et al 1994). Studies have also looked at alcohol and tobacco cues in daytime soap operas (Diener 1993), and recovering addicts' responses to the cinematic portrayal of alcohol and drug addiction (Hirschman & McGriff 1995).

Food labeling issues are thoughtfully reviewed by Ippolito & Mathios (1993). Research has examined the effects of various nutrition labeling formats (Burton et al 1994) and how providing summary information affects the usage of nutrition information (Viswanathan 1994). Ippolito & Mathios (1994) find producer claims to be an important source of information for consumers. Federal Trade Commission policy toward food advertising is discussed by Beales (1995), and the complex problems associated with the labeling of new biotech foods are discussed by Miller & Huttner (1995) and Douthitt (1995).

## Health Care

Moorman & Matulich (1993) developed and tested a model of the effects of various consumer characteristics on information acquisition and health maintenance behaviors. Their survey provided mixed results regarding the importance of motivation in this process. Roth (1994) modeled how to enhance consumer involvement in health care. Sofaer (1994) discusses the need for objective, salient, user-friendly information for consumers making health care decisions. While Franzak et al (1995) discuss how to improve health care delivery to rural residents, Gooding (1994) studied when and why consumers bypass local hospitals in favor of more distant facilities. Scammon et al (1994) studied how to increase the supply of health care professionals for the medically underserved. While communicating with consumers is a thread running through many of these articles, it is a principal focus of Frankenberger & Sukhdial's (1994) paper on segmenting teens for AIDS preventive behaviors and Hoy's (1994) discussion of what needs to be done when prescription drugs are "switched" to over-the-counter status.

## Advertising

Advertising is among the most examined issues in the public policy arena (e.g. Johar 1995, 1996). Pollay & Mittal (1993) described the factors, determinants, and segments in consumer criticism of advertising. Williams et al (1995) described a field experiment on racially exclusive real estate advertising, and Bristor et al (1995) discussed racial images in TV advertising. Darley & Smith (1993) tested advertising claim objectivity; "puffery," the other side of the coin, was analyzed by Simonson & Holbrook (1993). Billboard advertising provided the focus for Taylor & Taylor (1994). An enduring focus has been Federal Trade Commission policies and actions in regard to advertising. Simonson (1995) and Preston (1995) discussed the FTC's "clear and conspicuous" standard. Andrews & Maronick (1995) discussed the treatment of consumer research in *FTC* v. *Stouffer*. Details of the deceptive advertising research proffered in *FTC* v. *Kraft* were debated by the researchers themselves, Jacoby & Szybillo (1995), and Stewart (1995), with additional commentary provided by Sudman (1995).

## CONCLUSION

In an earlier review, Jacoby (1976, p. 345) concluded: "As much as 85% of what had been published under the rubric of consumer psychology prior to 1968 was rather low level and of questionable worth. At most, probably only 50% of the 1975 crop of articles belongs in this category. The amount of truly 'good' work...is certainly increasing. Surely the next octennium will witness even greater strides." It did; yet considerable room for improvement remains. Despite a notable increase in the proper application of experimental design, it is often coupled with a tendency to eschew a priori theorizing in favor of constructing a posteriori hypotheses to fit the data. Relying on tests of a single product, too small a proportion of the research reflects a concern with generalizability. Other research generalizes from tests of hypothetical products neglecting external validity. Too small a proportion of the work employs multiple measures of the independent or dependent variables or provides data on the validity and/or reliability of the measures used. Much work seems obsessed with significance testing, unmindful of its limitations for constructing science and arriving at practical findings (cf Cohen 1990, 1994; Schmidt 1996). In the senior author's opinion, these problems pale in comparison to that noted below.

Mindful of Alberts & Shine's (1994) important message, our concluding observations pertain to what has been transpiring in the field of consumer research regarding ethics during the period encompassed by this review. Respectively, the presidents of the National Academy of Sciences and National Institutes of Medicine, Alberts & Shine (1994, p. 1660) write: "The responsibility for scientific conduct falls on all parts of the research community, including...*the leaders of scientific societies*..." (italics supplied). Consumer researchers belonging to the American Psychological Association are required to adhere to and be accountable under APA's Code of Ethics. However, consumer psychology and consumer behavior are studied by researchers from a great many disciplines, the large majority of whom are not APA members. Many belong to no organization having a detailed code of researcher ethics.[1] Yet, because the field focuses on understanding consumer behavior and because its findings may be used to influence such behavior, consumer researchers bear a special responsibility for research integrity and ethical conduct.

Now nearly 30 years old and 2,000 members strong, the Association for Consumer Research has emerged as the preeminent scholarly organization in the field. It has no Code of Ethics—and is witnessing controversy in this regard (e.g. Jacoby 1995). At its October 1995 Board of Directors meeting, its Executive Secretary acknowledged having received more than 40 complaints over the past several years regarding ethical misconduct involving ACR members. In each and every instance, given no Code of Ethics, nothing was done. ACR surveyed its members and found approximately 83% wanted ACR to prepare

---

[1]Although most consumer researchers tend to belong to several organizations, the majority are members of the American Marketing Association. A professional organization of more than 50,000, less than 2,500 of whom are scholars, that organization's one-page Code of Ethics focuses on marketing practice and contains only a few sentences pertaining to researchers.

and subscribe to some statement on ethics. Yet in March 1997, ACR's leaders sent a Mission Statement to its members that explicitly excluded ethics from the organization's purview. The reasons for this omission were given as follows:

> First, any detailed code would attempt to anticipate the specific types of ethical issues that arise given the topics and methods employed. Because consumer researchers are so diverse in their disciplinary roots, it would be extremely difficult to compile an adequately exhaustive list, and harder still to get consensus among the members in the individual provisions of such a list. Second, ACR is not equipped to be in the business of enforcement. We lack the financial and human resources for handling the legal complexities of even a single ethics case per year. We view ethics to be the responsibility of the individual ACR member....
>
> *ACR Newsletter* (1997)

For scientists, the logic is strange; it implies that researchers from different disciplines would find it difficult to agree that misrepresenting one's findings, misrepresenting the work of others, plagiarism, etc, are examples of misconduct that ACR, as the leading scholarly organization in the field, will not tolerate among its members. As for lacking the resources, unexplained is why other scholarly organizations of similar size, scope, membership, background, and resources (e.g. The American Association of Public Opinion Research) are able to develop and have their members subscribe to a code of research ethics. Most ACR members belong to several scholarly organizations. Although "bystander intervention" research may explain why ACR feels it need not take a position, it does not absolve it of its responsibilities as a scholarly society nor render its position defensible (see Alberts & Shine 1994). The matter would not be so critical were ACR not considered by most to be the preeminent organization in the field.

Thus, while the quality of consumer research seems much improved, without a Code of Ethics and enforcement procedures to hold consumer researchers accountable, questions may be raised regarding the integrity of consumer research. It remains to be seen what the next quadrennium will bring.

## Literature Cited

Aaker DA, Stayman DM, Hagerty MR. 1986. Warmth in advertising: measurement, impact, and sequence effects. *J. Consum. Res.* 12(4):365–81

Abeele PV, Maclachlan DL. 1994. Process tracing of emotional responses to TV ads: revisiting the warmth monitor. *J. Consum. Res.* 20(4):586–600

ACR Mission Statement. 1997. *ACR News, Assoc. Consum. Res.,* Mar. 6–8

Alba JW, Broniarczyk SM, Shimp TA, Urbany JE. 1994. The influence of prior beliefs, frequency cues and magnitude cues on consumers: perceptions of comparative price data. *J. Consum. Res.* 21(2):219–35

Alba JW, Hutchinson JW, Lynch JG Jr. 1991. Memory and decision making. See Robertson & Kassarjian 1991, pp. 1–49

Alberts B, Shine K. 1994. Scientists and the integrity of research. *Science* 226:1660–61

Andrews JC, Maronick TJ. 1995. Advertising research issues from FTC versus Stouffer Foods Corporation. *J. Public Policy Mark.* 14(2):301–9

Andrews JC, Netemeyer RG, Durvasula S. 1993. The role of cognitive responses as mediators of alcohol warning label effects. *J. Public Policy Mark.* 12(1):57–68

Arnould SJ, Fisher E. 1994. Hermeneutics and consumer research. *J. Consum. Res.* 21(1): 55–70

Arnould EJ, Price LL. 1993. River magic: extraordinary experience and the extended service encounter. *J. Consum. Res.* 20(1): 24–45

Arnould EJ, Wallendorf M. 1994. Market-oriented ethnography: interpretation building and marketing strategy formulation. *J. Mark. Res.* 31(4):484–504

Auken SV, Barry TE. 1995. An assessment of the trait validity of cognitive age measures. *J. Consum. Psychol.* 4(2):107–32

Bagozzi RP, Moore DJ. 1994. Public service advertisements: emotions and empathy guide prosocial behavior. *J. Mark.* 58(1): 56–70

Bagozzi RP, Yi Y. 1993. Multitrait-multimethod matrices in consumer research: critique and new developments. *J. Consum. Psychol.* 2(2):143–70

Barlow T, Wogalter MS. 1993. Alcoholic beverage warnings in magazine and television advertisements. *J. Consum. Res.* 20(1): 147–56

Baumgartner H. 1995. On the utility of consumers' theories in judgments of covariation. *J. Consum. Res.* 21(4):634–43

Beales JH. 1995. Regulatory consistency and common sense: FTC policy toward food advertising under revised labeling regulations. *J. Public Policy Mark.* 14(1): 154–63

Beatty SE, Talpade S. 1994. Adolescent influence in family decision making: a replication with extension. *J. Consum. Res.* 21(2): 332–41

Belk RW, Coon GS. 1993. Gift giving as agapic love: an alternative to the exchange paradigm based on dating experiences. *J. Consum. Res.* 20(3):393–417

Bickart BA. 1993. Carryover and backfire effects in marketing research. *J. Mark. Res.* 30(1):52–62

Bloch PH. 1995. Seeking the ideal form: product design and consumer response. *J. Mark.* 59(3):16–29

Block LG, Keller PA. 1995. When to accentuate the negative: the effects of perceived efficacy and message framing on intentions to perform a health-related behavior. *J. Mark. Res.* 32(2):192–203

Boulding W, Kirmani A. 1993. A consumer-side experimental examination of signaling theory: do consumers perceive warranties as signals of quality? *J. Consum. Res.* 20(1):111–23

Bristor JM, Fischer E. 1993. Feminist thought: implications for consumer research. *J. Consum. Res.* 19(4):518–36

Bristor JM, Lee RG, Hunt MR. 1995. Race and ideology: African-American images in television advertising. *J. Public Policy Mark.* 14(1):48–59

Broniarczyk SM, Alba JW. 1994a. The importance of the brand in brand extension. *J. Mark. Res.* 31(2):214–28

Broniarczyk SM, Alba JW. 1994b. The role of consumers' intuitions in inference making. *J. Consum. Res.* 21(3):393–407

Brown TJ, Rothschild ML. 1993. Reassessing the impact of television advertising clutter. *J. Consum. Res.* 20(1):138–46

Burnkrant RE, Unnava R. 1995. Effects of self-referencing on persuasion. *J. Consum. Res.* 22(1):17–26

Burton S, Biswas A, Netemeyer R. 1994. Effects of alternative nutrition label formats and nutrition reference information on consumer perceptions, comprehension, and product evaluations. *J. Public Policy Mark.* 13(1):36–47

Campbell MC. 1995. When attention-getting advertising tactics elicit consumer inferences of manipulation intent: the importance of balancing benefits and investments. *J. Consum. Psychol.* 4(3):225–54

Carpenter GS, Glazer R, Nakamoto K. 1994. Meaningful brands from meaningless differentiation: the dependence on irrelevant attributes. *J. Mark. Res.* 31(3):339–50

Carroll JD, Green PE. 1995. Psychometric methods in marketing research. I. Conjoint analysis. *J. Mark. Res.* 32(4):385–91

Celsi RL, Rose RL, Leigh TW. 1993. An exploration of high-risk leisure consumption through skydiving. *J. Consum. Res.* 20(1): 1–23

Chaiken S. 1980. Heuristic versus systematic information processing and the use of source versus message cues in persuasion. *J. Pers. Soc. Psychol.* 39:752–66

Cohen J. 1990. Things I have learned (so far). *Am. Psychol.* 45:1304–12

Cohen J. 1994. The earth is round (p < .05). *Am. Psychol.* 49:997–1003

Cole CA, Balasubramanian SK. 1993. Age differences in consumers' search for information: public policy implications. *J. Consum. Res.* 20(1):157–69

Corfman KP, Lehmann DR. 1993. The importance of others' welfare in evaluating bargaining outcomes. *J. Consum. Res.* 20(1): 124–37

Coupey E. 1994. Restructuring: constructive processing of information displays in consumer choice. *J. Consum. Res.* 21(1): 83–99

Cradit JD, Tashchian A, Hofacker CF. 1994. Signal detection theory and single observation designs: methods and indices for advertising recognition testing. *J. Mark. Res.* 31(1):117–27

Crowley AE, Hoyer WD. 1994. An integrative framework for understanding two-sided persuasion. *J. Consum. Res.* 20(4):561–74

Dacin PA, Smith DC. 1994. The effect of brand portfolio characteristics on consumer evaluations of brand extensions. *J. Mark. Res.* 31(2):229–42

Darley WK, Lim J. 1993. Assessing demand artifacts in consumer research: an alternative perspective. *J. Consum. Res.* 20(3): 489–95

Darley WK, Smith RE. 1993. Advertising claim objectivity: antecedents and effects. *J. Mark.* 57(4):100–13

Deshpande R, Stayman DM. 1994. A tale of two cities: distinctiveness theory and advertising effectiveness. *J. Mark. Res.* 31(Feb.):57–64

Diener BJ. 1993. The frequency and context of alcohol and tobacco cues in daytime soap opera programs: fall 1986 and fall 1991. *J. Public Policy Mark.* 12(2):252–57

Douthitt RA. 1995. Consumer risk perception and recombinant bovine growth hormone: the case for labelling dairy products made from untreated herd milk. *J. Public Policy Mark.* 14(2):328–30

Dowling GR, Staelin R. 1994. A model of perceived risk and intended risk-handling activity. *J. Consum. Res.* 21(1):119–34

D'Souza G, Rao RC. 1995. Can repeating an advertisement more frequently than the competitor affect brand preference in a mature market? *J. Mark.* 59(2):32–42

Faber RJ, Christenson GA, DeZwaan M. 1995. Two forms of compulsive buying and binge eating. *J. Consum. Res.* 22(3): 296–304

Fenaughty AM, MacKinnon DP. 1993. Immediate effects of the Arizona alcohol warning poster. *J. Public Policy Mark.* 12(1): 69–77

Fern EF, Monroe KB. 1996. Effect size estimates: issues and problems in interpretation. *J. Consum. Res.* 23(2):89–105

Fishbein M, Middlestadt S. 1995. Noncognitive effects on attitude formation and change: fact or artifact? *J. Consum. Psychol.* 4(2):181–202

Fisher RJ. 1993. Social desirability and the validity of indirect questioning. *J. Consum. Res.* 20(2):303–15

Frankenberger KD, Sukhdial AS. 1994. Segmenting teens for AIDS preventive behaviors with implications for marketing communications. *J. Public Policy Mark.* 13(1): 133–50

Franzak FJ, Smith TJ, Desch CE. 1995. Marketing cancer care to rural residents. *J. Public Policy Mark.* 14(1):76–82

Friestad M, Thorson E. 1993. Remembering ads: the effects of encoding strategies, retrieval cues, and emotional response. *J. Consum. Psychol.* 2(1):1–24

Friestad M, Wright P. 1994. The persuasion knowledge model: how people cope with persuasion attempts. *J. Consum. Res.* 21(1):1–31

Gardial SF, Clemons DS, Woodruff RB, Schumann DW, Burns MJ. 1994. Comparing consumers' recall of prepurchase and postpurchase product evaluation experiences. *J. Consum. Res.* 20(4):548–60

Gooding SK. 1994. Hospital outshopping and perceptions of quality: implications for public policy. *J. Public Policy Mark.* 13(2):271–80

Goodstein RC. 1993. Category-based applications and extensions in advertising: motivating more extensive ad processing. *J. Consum. Res.* 20(1):87–99

Gorn GJ, Goldberg ME, Basu K. 1993. Mood,

awareness and product evaluation. *J. Consum. Psychol.* 2(3):237–56

Gould SJ. 1995. Researcher introspection as a method in consumer research: applications, issues, and implications. *J. Consum. Res.* 21(4):719–22

Graves KL. 1993. An evaluation of the alcohol warning label: a comparison of the United States and Ontario, Canada in 1990 and 1991. *J. Public Policy Mark.* 12(1):19–29

Greenleaf EA, Lehmann DR. 1995. Reasons for substantial delay in consumer decision making. *J. Consum. Res.* 22(2):186–99

Gregan-Paxton J, John DR. 1995. Are young children adaptive decision makers? A study of age differences in information search behavior. *J. Consum. Res.* 21(4): 567–79

Grewal D, Gotlieb J, Marmorstein H. 1994. The moderating effects of message framing and source credibility on the price-perceived value risk relationship. *J. Consum. Res.* 21(1):145–53

Grewal D, Marmorstein H. 1994. Market price variation, perceived price variation, and consumers' price search decisions for durable goods. *J. Consum. Res.* 21(3):453–60

Grewal D, Marmorstein H, Sharma A. 1996. Communicating price information through semantic cues: the moderating effect of situation and discount size. *J. Consum. Res.* 23(Sept.):148–55

Hankin JR, Firestone IJ, Sloan JJ, Ager JW, Goodman AC, et al. 1993. The impact of the alcohol warning label on drinking during pregnancy. *J. Public Policy Mark.* 12(1):10–18

Haugtvedt CP, Schumann DW, Schneier WL, Warren WL. 1994. Advertising repetition and variation strategies. Implication for the understanding attitude strength. *J. Consum. Res.* 21(1):176–89

Haugtvedt CP, Wegener D. 1994. Message order effects in persuasion: an attitude strength perspective. *J. Consum. Res.* 21(1):205–18

Heath TB, Chatterjee S. 1995. Asymmetric decoy effects on lower-quality versus higher-quality brands: meta-analytic and experimental evidence. *J. Consum. Res.* 22(3): 268–84

Heath TB, Chatterjee S, France KR. 1995. Mental accounting and changes in price: the frame dependence of reference dependence. *J. Consum. Res.* 22(1):90–97

Heath TB, McCarthy MS, Mothersbaugh DL. 1994. Spokesperson fame and vividness effects in the context of issue-relevant thinking: the moderating role of competitive setting. *J. Consum. Res.* 20(4):520–34

Herr PA. 1995. Whither fact, artifact, and attitude: reflections on the theory of reasoned action. *J. Consum. Psychol.* 4(4):371–80

Hetrick WP, Lozada HR. 1994. Construing the critical imagination: comments and necessary diversions. *J. Consum. Res.* 21(3): 548–58

Hilton ME. 1993. An overview of recent findings on alcoholic beverage warning labels. *J. Public Policy Mark.* 12(1):1–9

Hirschman EC. 1994. Consumers and their animal companions. *J. Consum. Res.* 20(4):616–32

Hirschman EC, McGriff JA. 1995. Recovering addicts' responses to the cinematic portrayal of drug and alcohol addiction. *J. Public Policy Mark.* 14(1):95–107

Hoffman D, Holbrook MB. 1993. The intellectual structure of consumer research: a bibliometric study of author cocitations in the first 15 years of the JCR. *J. Consum. Res.* 19(4):505–17

Holbrook MB. 1993. Nostalgia and consumption preference: some emerging patterns of consumer tastes. *J. Consum. Res.* 20(2): 245–56

Holbrook MB, Gardner MP. 1993. An approach to investigating the emotional determinants of consumption duration. Why do people consume what they consume for as long as they consume it? *J. Consum. Psychol.* 2(2):123–42

Holbrook MB, Schindler RM. 1994. Age, sex, and attitude toward the past as predictors of consumers' aesthetic tastes for cultural products. *J. Mark. Res.* 31(Aug.):412–22

Holt DB. 1995. How consumers consume: a typology of consumption practices. *J. Consum. Res.* 22(1):1–16

Howard DJ, Jengler C, Jain A. 1995. What's in a name? A complimentary reason of persuasion. *J. Consum. Res.* 22(20):200–11

Hoy MG. 1994. Switch drugs vis-à-vis Rx and OTC: policy, marketing, and research considerations. *J. Public Policy Mark.* 13(1): 85–96

Hui MK, Tse DK. 1996. What to tell consumers in waits of different lengths: an integrative model of service evaluation. *J. Mark.* 60(Apr.):81–90

Hunt JM, Kernan JB, Mitchell DJ. 1996. Materialism as social cognition: people, possessions and perception. *J. Consum. Psychol.* 5(1):65–83

Hunt SD. 1992. For reasons of realism in marketing. *J. Mark.* 56(2):89–102

Hunt SD. 1993. Objectivity in marketing theory and research. *J. Mark.* 57(2):76–91

Hunt SD. 1994. A realist theory of empirical testing: resolving the theory ladenness/objectivity debate. *Philos. Soc. Sci.* 24(2): 133–58

Hutchinson JW, Raman K, Mantrala M. 1994. Finding choice alternatives in memory: Probability models of brand name recall. *J. Mark. Res.* 31(4):441–61

Iacobucci D, Ostrom A. 1993. Gender differences in the impact of core and relational aspects of services on the evaluation of services encounters. *J. Consum. Psychol.* 2(3):257–86

Iacobucci D, Ostrom A, Grayson K. 1995. Distinguishing service quality and customer satisfaction: the voice of the consumer. *J. Consum. Psychol.* 4(3):277–303

Ippolito PM, Mathios AD. 1993. New food labeling regulations and the flow of nutrition information to consumers. *J. Public Policy Mark.* 12(2):188–205

Ippolito PM, Mathios AD. 1994. Information, policy, and the sources of fat and cholesterol in the U.S. diet. *J. Public Policy Mark.* 13(2):200–17

Jacoby J. 1975. Consumer psychology as a social psychological sphere of action. *Am. Psychol.* 30(10):977–87

Jacoby J. 1976. Consumer psychology: an octennium. *Annu. Rev. Psychol.* 27:331–58

Jacoby J. 1995. Ethics, the dark side of ACR: implications for our future. *Adv. Consum. Res.* 22:21–47

Jacoby J, Jaccard JJ, Currim I, Kuss A, Ansari A, Troutman T. 1994. Tracing the impact of information acquisition on higher-order mental processes: the shape of uncertainty reduction. *J. Consum. Res.* 21(2): 291–303

Jacoby J, Szybillo GJ. 1994. Why disclaimers fail. *Trademark Rep.* 84(2):224–44

Jacoby J, Szybillo GJ. 1995. Consumer research in FTC versus Kraft (1991): a case of heads we win, tails you lose? *J. Public Policy Mark.* 14(1):1–14

Janiszewski C. 1993. Preattentive mere exposure effects. *J. Consum. Res.* 20(3):376–92

Janiszewski C, Warlop L. 1993. The influence of classical conditioning procedures on subsequent attention to the conditioned brand. *J. Consum. Res.* 20(2):171–89

Johar GV. 1995. Consumer involvement and deception from implied advertising claims. *J. Mark. Res.* 32(3):267–79

Johar GV. 1996. Intended and unintended effects of corrective advertising on beliefs and evaluations: an exploratory analysis. *J. Consum. Psychol.* 5(3):209–30

Johnson MD, Anderson EW, Fornell C. 1995. Rational and adaptive performance expectations in a customer satisfaction framework. *J. Consum. Res.* 21(4):695–707

Kahn BE, Baron J. 1995. An exploratory study of choice rules favored for high-stakes decisions. *J. Consum. Psychol.* 4(4):305–28

Kahn BE, Isen AM. 1993. The influence of positive affect on variety seeking among safe, enjoyable products. *J. Consum. Res.* 20(2):257–70

Kalsher MJ, Clarke SW, Wogalter MS. 1993. Communication of alcohol facts and hazards by a warning poster. *J. Public Policy Mark.* 12(1):78–90

Kardes FR, Kalyanaram G, Chandrashekaran M, Dornoff RJ. 1993. Brand retrieval, consideration set composition, consumer choice, and the pioneering advantage. *J. Consum. Res.* 20(1):62–75

Kaskutas LA. 1993. Changes in public attitudes toward alcohol control policies since the warning label mandate of 1988. *J. Public Policy Mark.* 12(1):30–37

Kellaris JJ, Cox AD, Cox D. 1993. The effect of background music on ad processing: a contingency explanation. *J. Mark.* 57(4): 114–25

Kellaris JJ, Kent RJ. 1994. An exploratory investigation of responses elicited by music varying in tempo, tonality, and texture. *J. Consum. Psychol.* 2(4):381–401

Keller KL. 1993. Conceptualizing, measuring, and managing customer-based brand equity. *J. Mark.* 57(1):1–22

Keller PA, Block L. 1996. Increasing the persuasiveness of fear appeals: the effect of arousal and elaboration. *J. Consum. Res.* 22(4):448–59

Kim J, Allen CT, Kardes FR. 1996. An investigation of the mediational mechanisms underlying attitudinal conditioning. *J. Mark. Res.* 33(Aug.):318–28

Klein SS, Klein RE, Allen CT. 1995. How is a possession 'me' or 'not me'? Characterizing types and an antecedent of material possession attachment. *J. Consum. Res.* 22(3):327–43

Kleine RE, Kleine SS, Kerman JB. 1993. Mundane consumption and the self: a social identity perspective. *J. Consum. Psychol.* 2(3):209–36

Koslow S, Shamdasami PN, Torchstone EE. 1994. Exploring language effects in ethnic advertising: a sociolinguistic perspective. *J. Consum. Res.* 20(4):575–85

Kover A. 1995. Copywriters' implicit theories of communication: an exploration. *J. Cons. Res.* 21(4):596–611

Krishna AK, Johar GV. 1996. Consumer perceptions of deals: biasing effects of varying deal prices. *J. Exp. Psychol. Appl.* 2(3): 187–206

Lacher KT, Mizerski R. 1994. An exploratory study of the responses and relationships involved in the evaluation of, and in the intention to purchase new rock music. *J. Consum. Res.* 21(2):336–80

Laughery KR, Young SL, Vaubel KP, Brelsford JW Jr. 1993. The noticeability of warnings on alcoholic beverage containers. *J. Public Policy Mark.* 12(1):38–56

Laverie DA, Murphy PE. 1993. The marketing and public policy literature: a look at the past ten years. *J. Public Policy Mark.* 12(2):258–67

Lavin M. 1995. Creating consumers in the 1930s: Irma Phillips and the radio soap opera. *J. Consum. Res.* 22(1):75–89

Leclerc F, Schmitt BH, Dube L. 1995. Waiting time and decision making: Is time like money? *J. Consum. Res.* 22(1):110–19

Lefkoff-Hagins H, Mason CH. 1993. Characteristic, beneficial and image attributes in consumer judgements of similarity and preference. *J. Consum. Res.* 20(1):100–10

Lehmann DR, Pan Y. 1994. Context effects, new brand entry, and consideration sets. *J. Mark. Res.* 31(Aug.):364–74

Leong SM. 1993. Consumer decision making for common, repeat-purchase products: a dual replication. *J. Consum. Psychol.* 2(2): 193–208

Li W, Wyer RS Jr. 1994. The Role of country of origin in product evaluations: informational and standard-of-comparison effects. *J. Consum. Psychol.* 3(2):187–212

Lichtenstein DR, Netemeyer RG, Burton S. 1995. Assessing the domain specificity of deal proneness: a field study. *J. Consum. Res.* 22(3):413–26

Loken B, Roedder John D. 1993. Diluting brand beliefs: When do brand extensions have a negative impact? *J. Mark.* 57(3):71–84

Lynn M, Zinkhan GM. 1993. Consumer tipping: a cross-country study. *J. Consum. Res.* 20(3):478–88

Macklin MC. 1994. The impact of audiovisual information on children's product-related recall. *J. Consum. Res.* 21(1):154–64

Macklin MC. 1996. Preschoolers' learning of brand names from visual cues. *J. Consum. Res.* 23(3):251–61

Maheswaran D. 1994. Country of origin as a stereotype: effects of consumer expertise and attribute strength on product evaluations. *J. Consum. Res.* 21(2):354–65

Malaviya P, Kiselius J, Sternthal B. 1996. The effect of type of elaboration on advertisement processing and judgement. *J. Mark. Res.* 33(Nov.):410–21

Manning KC, Bearden WO, Madden TJ. 1995.

Consumer innovativeness and the adoption process. *J. Consum. Psychol.* 4(4): 329–45

Mano H, Oliver RL. 1993. Assessing the dimensionality and structure of the consumption experience: evaluation, feeling, and satisfaction. *J. Consum. Res.* 20(3): 451–66

Mazumdar T, Jun SY. 1993. Consumer evaluations of multiple versus single price change. *J. Consum. Res.* 20(3):441–50

McCarthy RL, Ayres TJ, Wood CT, Robinson JM. 1995. Risk and effectiveness criteria for using on-product warnings. *Ergonomics* 38(11):2164–75

McGrath MA, Sherry JF, Levy SJ. 1993. Giving voice to the gift: the use of projective techniques to recover lost meanings. *J. Consum. Psychol.* 2(2):171–91

Menon G. 1993. The effects of accessibility of information in memory on judgments of behavioral frequencies. *J. Consum. Res.* 20(3):431–40

Menon G, Raghubir P, Schwartz N. 1995. Behavioral frequency judgments: an accessibility-diagnosticity framework. *J. Consum. Res.* 22(2):212–28

Menon S, Kahn B. 1995. The impact of context on variety seeking in product choices. *J. Consum. Res.* 22(3):285–95

Meyers-Levy J, Peracchio LA. 1995. Understanding the effects of color: how the correspondence between available and required resources affects attitudes. *J. Consum. Res.* 22(2):121–38

Meyers-Levy J, Peracchio LA. 1996. Moderators of the impact of self-reference or persuasion. *J. Consum. Res.* 22(4):408–23

Mick DV. 1996. Are studies of dark side variables confounded by socially desirable responding? The case of materialism. *J. Consum. Res.* 23(2):106–19

Miller HI, Huttner SL. 1995. Food produced with new biotechnology: can labelling be anti-consumer? *J. Public Policy Mark.* 14: 330–33

Mitchell AA, Dacin PA. 1996. The assessment of alternative measures of consumer expertise. *J. Consum. Res.* 23(3):219–39

Mitchell DJ, Kahn BE, Knasko SC. 1995. There's something in the air: effects of congruent or incongruent ambient odor on consumer decision making. *J. Consum. Res.* 22(2):229–38

Mohr LA, Henson SW. 1996. Impact of employee gender and job congruency on customer satisfaction. *J. Consum. Psychol.* 5(2):161–87

Moorman C, Matulich E. 1993. A Model of

consumers' preventive health behaviors: the role of health motivation and health ability. *J. Consum. Res.* 20(2):208–20

Morris LA, Swasy JL, Mazis MB. 1994. Accepted risk and alcohol use during pregnancy. *J. Consum. Res.* 21(1):135–45

Morwitz VG, Johnson E, Schmittlein D. 1993. Does measuring intent change behavior? *J. Consum. Res.* 20(1):46–61

Morwitz VG, Pluzinski C. 1996. Do polls reflect opinions or do opinions reflect polls? The impact of political polling on voters' expectations, preferences, and behavior. *J. Consum. Res.* 23(1):53–67

Murry JP Jr, Dacin PA. 1996. Cognitive moderators of negative-emotion effects: implications for understanding media context. *J. Consum. Res.* 22(4):439–47

Muthukrishnan AV. 1995. Decision ambiguity and incumbent brand advantage. *J. Consum. Res.* 22(1):98–109

Netemeyer RG, Burton S, Lichtenstein DR. 1995. Trait aspects of vanity: measurement and relevance to consumer behavior. *J. Consum. Res.* 21(4):612–26

Nowlis SM, Simonson I. 1996. The effect of new product features on brand choice. *J. Mark. Res.* 33(1):36–46

Oropesa RS. 1993. Female labor force participation and time-saving household technology: a case study of the microwave from 1978 to 1989. *J. Consum. Res.* 19(4):567–79

Ostrom A, Iacobucci D. 1995. Consumer trade-offs and the evaluation of services. *J. Mark.* 59(1):17–28

Otnes C, Lowry TM, Kim YC. 1993. Gift selection for easy and difficult recipients: a social roles interpretation. *J. Consum. Res.* 20(2):229–44

Park CW, Mothersbaugh DL, Feick L. 1994. Consumer knowledge assessment. *J. Consum. Res.* 21(1):71–82

Patterson MJ, Hill RP, Maloy K. 1995. Abortion in America: a consumer-behavior perspective. *J. Consum. Res.* 21(4):677–94

Pavia TM, Costa JA. 1993. The winning number: consumer perceptions of alphanumeric brand names. *J. Mark.* 57(3):85–98

Pechmann C. 1996. Do consumers overgeneralize one-sided comparative price claims, and are more stringent regulations needed? *J. Mark. Res.* 33(May):150–62

Pechmann C, Ratneshwar S. 1994. The effects of antismoking and cigarette advertising on young adolescents' perceptions of peers who smoke. *J. Consum. Res.* 21(2):236–50

Peracchio LA. 1993. Young children's processing of a televised narrative: is a picture really worth a thousand words? *J. Consum. Res.* 20(2):281–93

Peracchio LA, Meyers-Levy J. 1994. How ambiguous cropped objects in ad photos can affect product evaluations. *J. Consum. Res.* 21(1):190–204

Peracchio LA, Tybout A. 1996. The moderating role of prior knowledge in schema-based product evaluation. *J. Consum. Res.* 23(3):177–92

Peter JP. 1992. Realism or relativism for marketing theory and research: a comment on Hunt's "Scientific Realism." *J. Mark.* 56(2):72–79

Peter JP, Churchill GA Jr, Brown TJ. 1993. Caution in the use of difference scores in consumer research. *J. Consum. Res.* 19(4):655–62

Peterson RA. 1994. A meta-analysis of Cronbach's coefficient alpha. *J. Consum. Res.* 21(2):381–91

Petty RE, Cacioppo JT. 1981. *Attitudes and Persuasion: Classic and Contemporary Approaches.* Dubuque, IA: Brown

Pham TM. 1996. Representation and selection effects of arousal on persuasion. *J. Consum. Res.* 22(4):373–87

Pollay RW, Mittal B. 1993. Here's the beef: factors, determinants, and segmentation in consumer criticism of advertising. *J. Mark.* 57(3):99–114

Preston IL. 1995. Unfairness developments in FTC advertising cases. *J. Public Policy Mark.* 14(2):318–20

Putsis WP, Srinivasan N. 1994. Buying or just browsing? The duration of purchase deliberation. *J. Mark. Res.* 31(3):393–402

Raghubir P, Krishna A. 1996. As the crow flies: bias in consumers' map-based distance judgments. *J. Consum. Res.* 23(1):26–39

Raman K. 1994. Inductive inference and replications: a Bayesian perspective. *J. Consum. Res.* 20(4):633–43

Ratneshwar S, Pechmann C, Shocker AD. 1996. Goal-derived categories and the antecedents of across-category consideration. *J. Consum. Res.* 23(3):240–50

Richins ML. 1994. Special possessions and the expression of material values. *J. Consum. Res.* 21(3):522–33

Robertson TS, Kassarjian HH, eds. 1991. *Handbook of Consumer Behavior.* Englewood Cliffs, NJ: Prentice Hall

Rook DW, Fisher RJ. 1995. Normative influences on implusive buying behavior. *J. Consum. Res.* 22(3):305–13

Rose RL, Miniard PW, Barone MJ, Manning KC, Till BD. 1993. When persuasion goes undetected: the case of comparative advertising. *J. Mark. Res.* 30(3):315–30

Ross WT Jr, Creyer EH. 1993. Interpreting interactions: raw means or residual means? *J. Consum. Res.* 20(2):330–38

Roth MS. 1994. Enhancing consumer involvement in health care: the dynamics of control, empowerment, and trust. *J. Public Policy Mark.* 13(1):115–32

Russo JE, Leclerc F. 1994. An eye-fixation analysis of choice processes for consumer nondurables. *J. Consum. Res.* 21(2): 274–90

Sawyer AG, Lynch JG Jr, Brinberg DL. 1995. A Bayesian analysis of the information value of manipulation and confounding checks in theory tests. *J. Consum. Res.* 21(4):581–95

Scammon DL, Li LB, Williams SD. 1994. Increasing the supply of providers for the medically underserved: marketing and public policy issues. *J. Public Policy Mark.* 13(2):35–47

Schaninger CM, Danko WD. 1993. A conceptual and empirical comparison of alternative household life cycle models. *J. Consum. Res.* 19(4):580–94

Schmidt FL. 1996. Statistical significance testing and cumulative knowledge in psychology: implications for training researchers. *Psychol. Methods* 1:115–29

Schmitt BH, Pan Y, Tavassoli NT. 1994. Language and consumer memory: the impact of linguistic differences between Chinese and English. *J. Consum. Res.* 21(3): 419–31

Schmitt BH, Tavassoli NT, Millard RT. 1993. Memory for print ads: understanding relations among brand name, copy, and picture. *J. Consum. Psychol.* 2(1):55–81

Schouten JW, McAlexander JH. 1995. Subcultures of consumption: an ethnography of the new bikers. *J. Consum. Res.* 22(1): 43–61

Scott LM. 1994. The bridge from text to mind: adapting reader-response theory to consumer research. *J. Consum. Res.* 21(3): 461–80

Sen S, Morwitz VG. 1996. Consumer reactions to a provider's position on social issues: the effect of varying frames of reference. *J. Consum. Psychol.* 5(1):27–48

Sethuraman R, Cole C, Jain D. 1994. Analyzing the effect of information format and task on cutoff search strategies. *J. Consum. Psychol.* 3(2):103–36

Sherry JF Jr. 1991. Postmodern alternatives: the interpretive turn in consumer research. See Robertson & Kassarjian 1991, pp. 548–91

Shimp TA, Hyatt EM, Snyder DJ. 1993. A critique of Darley and Lim's 'Alternative perspective.' *J. Consum. Res.* 20(3):496–501

Simmons CJ, Bickart BA, Lynch JG. 1993. Capturing and creating public opinion in survey research. *J. Consum. Res.* 20(2): 316–29

Simonson A. 1995. "Unfair" advertising and the FTC: structural evolution of the law and implications for marketing and public policy. *J. Public Policy Mark.* 14(2): 321–27

Simonson A, Holbrook MB. 1993. Permissible puffery versus actionable warranty in advertising and salestalk: an empirical investigation. *J. Public Policy Mark.* 12(2): 216–33

Simonson I, Nowlis SM, Simonson Y. 1993. The effect of irrelevant preference arguments on consumer choice. *J. Consum. Psychol.* 2(3):287–306

Singh S, Mishra S, Bendapudi N, Linville D. 1994. Enhancing memory of television commercials through message spacing. *J. Mark. Res.* 31(3):384–92

Sirsi AJ, Ward JC, Reingin PH. 1996. Microcultural analysis of variation in sharing of causal reasoning about behavior. *J. Consum. Res.* 22(4):345–72

Smith RA, Lux DS. 1993. Historical methods in consumer research: developing causal explanations of change. *J. Consum. Res.* 19(4):595–610

Smith RE. 1993. Integrating information from advertising and trial: processes and effect on consumer response to product information. *J. Mark. Res.* 30(May):204–19

Sofaer S. 1994. Empowering consumers in a changing health care market: the need for information and the role of marketing. *J. Public Policy Mark.* 13(2):321–22

Spangenberg ER, Crowley AE, Henderson PW. 1996. Improving the store environment: do olfactory cues affect evaluations and behaviors? *J. Mark.* 60(Apr.):67–80

Spiggle S. 1994. Analysis and interpretation of qualitative data in consumer research. *J. Consum. Res.* 21(3):491–503

Spreng RA, MacKenzie SG, Olshavsky RW. 1996. A reexamination of the determinant of consumer satisfaction. *J. Mark.* 60 (July):15–32

Stern BB. 1993. Feminist literary criticism and the deconstruction of ads: a postmodern view of advertising and consumer responses. *J. Consum. Res.* 19(4):556–66

Stern BB. 1994. Classical and vignette television advertising dramas: structural models, formal analysis, and consumer effects. *J. Consum. Res.* 20(4):601–15

Stern BB. 1996. Deconstructive strategy and consumer research: concepts and illustrative exemplar. *J. Consum. Res.* 23(2):136–47

Stewart DW. 1995. Deception, materiality, and survey research: some lessons from Kraft. *J. Public Policy Mark.* 14(1):15–28

Stewart DW, Martin IM. 1994. Intended and unintended consequences of warning messages: a review and synthesis of empirical research. *J. Public Policy Mark.* 13(1):1–19

Sudman S. 1995. When experts disagree: comments on the articles by Jacoby and Szybillo and Stewart. *J. Public Policy Mark.* 14(1):29–34

Swinyard WR. 1993. The effects of mood, involvement, and quality of store experience on shopping intentions. *J. Consum. Res.* 20(2):271–80

Taylor CR, Taylor JC. 1994. Regulatory issues in outdoor advertising: a content analysis of billboards. *J. Public Policy Mark.* 13(1):97–107

Taylor S. 1994. Waiting for service: the relationship between delays and evaluations of service. *J. Mark.* 58(Apr.):56–69

Taylor S, Tod P. 1995. Understanding household garbage reduction behavior: a test of an integrated model. *J. Public Policy Mark.* 14(2):192–204

Tepper K. 1994. The role of labeling processes in elderly consumers' responses to age segmentation cues. *J. Consum. Res.* 20(4):503–19

Thaler R. 1985. Mental accounting and consumer choice. *Mark. Sci.* 4(Summer):199–214

Thompson CJ. 1996. Caring consumers: gendered consumption meanings and the juggling lifestyle. *J. Consum. Res.* 22(4):388–407

Tripp C, Jensen TD, Carlson L. 1994. The effects of multiple product endorsements by celebrities on consumers' attitudes and intentions. *J. Consum. Res.* 20(4):535–47

Unnava HR, Burnkrant RE, Erevelles S. 1994. Effects of presentation order and communication modality on recall and attitude. *J. Consum. Res.* 21(3):481–90

Viswanathan M. 1994. The influence of summary information on the usage of nutrition informaiton. *J. Public Policy Mark.* 13(1):48–60

Wallendorf M, Brucks M. 1993. Introspection in consumer research: implementation and implications. *J. Consum. Res.* 20(3):339–59

Wansink B. 1994. Advertising's impact on category substitution. *J. Mark. Res.* 31(Nov.):505–15

Wansink B. 1996. Can package size accelerate usage volume? *J. Mark.* 60(3):1–14

Wansink B, Ray ML. 1996. Advertising strategies to increase usage frequency. *J. Mark.* 60(1):31–46

Webster C. 1994. Effects of Hispanic ethnic identification on marital roles in the purchase decision process. *J. Consum. Res.* 21(2):319–31

Webster C. 1996. Hispanic and Anglo interviewer and respondent ethnicity and gender: the impact on survey response quality. *J. Mark. Res.* 33(1):62–72

Wells WD. 1993. Discovery-oriented consumer research. *J. Consum. Res.* 19(4):489–504

Wernerfelt B. 1995. A rational reconstruction of the compromise effect: using market data to infer utilities. *J. Consum. Res.* 21(4):627–33

West PM, Brown CL, Hoch SJ. 1996. Consumption vocabulary and preference formation. *J. Consum. Res.* 23(2):120–35

Wilkes RE. 1995. Household life-cycle stages, transitions, and product expenditures. *J. Consum. Res.* 22(1):27–42

Williams JD, Qualls WJ, Grier SA. 1995. Racially exclusive real estate advertising: public policy implications for fair housing practices. *J. Public Policy Mark.* 14(2):225–44

Wooten DB. 1995. One-of-a-kind in a fall house: some consequences of ethnic and gender distinctiveness. *J. Consum. Psychol.* 4(3):205–24

Wright AA, Lynch JG Jr. 1995. Communication effects of advertising versus direct experience when both search and experience attributes are present. *J. Consum. Res.* 21(4):708–18

Yadav MS. 1994. How buyers evaluate product bundles: a model of anchoring and adjustment. *J. Consum. Res.* 21(2):342–53

Zeithaml VA, Berry LL, Parasuraman A. 1996. The behavioral consequences of service quality. *J. Mark.* 60(Apr.):31–46

Zufryden FS, Pedrick JH, Sankaralingam A. 1993. Zapping and its impact on brand purchase behavior. *J. Advert. Res.* 33(1):58–66

*Annu. Rev. Psychol. 1998. 49:345–75*

# SOCIAL CONSTRUCTIVIST PERSPECTIVES ON TEACHING AND LEARNING

*A. Sullivan Palincsar*

Educational Studies, University of Michigan, 610 East University, Ann Arbor, Michigan 48109-1259; e-mail: annemari@umich.edu

KEY WORDS: teaching, learning, context, collaboration

## ABSTRACT

Social constructivist perspectives focus on the interdependence of social and individual processes in the co-construction of knowledge. After the impetus for understanding the influence of social and cultural factors on cognition is reviewed, mechanisms hypothesized to account for learning from this perspective are identified, drawing from Piagetian and Vygotskian accounts. The empirical research reviewed illustrates (*a*) the application of institutional analyses to investigate schooling as a cultural process, (*b*) the application of interpersonal analyses to examine how interactions promote cognition and learning, and (*c*) discursive analyses examining and manipulating the patterns and opportunities in instructional conversation. The review concludes with a discussion of the application of this perspective to selected contemporary issues, including: acquiring expertise across domains, assessment, educational equity, and educational reform.

## CONTENTS

345

# INTRODUCTION

Recent chapters in the *Annual Review of Psychology* closely related to the general subject matter of teaching and learning (Glaser & Bassok 1989, Sandoval 1995, Snow & Swanson 1992, Voss et al 1995) have generally examined issues of cognition from an individualistic perspective. Voss et al (1995) indicated that the recent decade has witnessed the "sociocultural revolution," with its focus on learning in out-of-school contexts and on the acquisition of intellectual skills through social interaction (p. 174). In this review, I examine the nature and consequences of this revolution.

The review begins by intellectually situating social constructivist perspectives. Following an explication of the tenets of this approach, I explore issues of teaching and learning that are particularly salient from social constructivist perspectives. These issues are presented using institutional, interpersonal, and discursive levels of analysis. I then proceed to the application of social constructivist views to contemporary issues of importance to education; namely, the acquisition of expertise across subject matter, assessment practices, the education of linguistic and culturally diverse children, and school reform. The review concludes with a critique of this perspective and a discussion of future directions.

# INTELLECTUALLY SITUATING THE SOCIOCULTURAL REVOLUTION IN INSTRUCTIONAL RESEARCH

Instructional research in the West was initially informed by behaviorist accounts of learning found in classic writings such as those of Thorndike (1906). Thorndike postulated that learning took place through the differential strengthening of bonds between situations and actions. Teaching, in turn, was a matter of shaping the responses of the learner through using instructional procedures such as modeling, demonstration, and reinforcement of closer approximations to the targeted response. From this perspective, academic tasks were analyzed to determine their component parts, and the curriculum was carefully sequenced to ensure that students were acquiring the necessary prerequisite skills before the introduction of more advanced material. The instructional model that best reflects the tenets of behaviorism is referred to as direct instruction teaching. The hallmark of direct instruction is the active and directive role assumed by the teacher, who maintains control of the pace, sequence, and content of the lesson (Baumann 1988, p. 714):

> The teacher, in a face-to-face-reasonably formal manner, tells, shows, models, demonstrates, *teaches* the skill to be learned. The key word here is *teacher,* for it is the teacher who is in command of the learning situation and leads the lesson, as opposed to having instruction "directed" by a worksheet, kit, learning center, or workbook.

The research regarding direct instruction suggests that while it is an effective means of teaching factual content, there is less evidence that this instruction transfers to higher order cognitive skills such as reasoning and problem solving, nor is there sufficient evidence that direct-instruction teaching results in the flexibility necessary for students to use the targeted strategies in novel contexts (Peterson & Walberg 1979). In addition to these practical concerns with the limitations of direct instruction, there are significant theoretical limitations of the behavioral perspective; namely, this perspective offers no satisfactory explanation of the mechanisms that account for learning.

With increased interest in human information processing in complex cognitive activity, the cognitive perspective assumed prominence. Bruner (1990) argues that the cognitive revolution was meant to do more than simply be an improvement on behaviorism; it was also meant to promote a psychology that focused on "meaning making." To explain meaning making, cognitive psychologists introduced cognitive structures (such as schemata and heuristics) as the representations of knowledge in memory. These cognitive structures are assumed to underlie such phenomena as problem solving and transfer ability. Virtually all cognitive science theories entail some form of constructivism to the extent that cognitive structures are typically viewed as individually constructed in the process of interpreting experiences in particular contexts. However, there are many versions of constructivism, suggesting a continuum anchored by trivial constructivism at one end, which stresses the individual as constructing knowledge but is concerned with whether or not the constructions are correct representations, to radical constructivism, which rejects the notion of objective knowledge and argues instead that knowledge develops as one engages in dialogue with others.

In this review, I consider research on teaching and learning that has been conducted from postmodern constructivist perspectives (cf Prawat 1996).

What unifies postmodern constructivist perspectives is rejection of the view that the locus of knowledge is in the individual; learning and understanding are regarded as inherently social; and cultural activities and tools (ranging from symbol systems to artifacts to language) are regarded as integral to conceptual development. What distinguishes various postmodern constructivist perspectives is a bit murkier. For example, Cobb & Yackel (1996), distinguishing a perspective they call "emergent" from a sociocultural perspective, argue that while sociocultural approaches frame instructional issues in terms of *transmission* of culture from one generation to the next, the emergent perspective conceives of instructional issues in terms of the *emergence* of individual and collective meanings in the classroom. However, John-Steiner & Mahn (1996) argue that this is not an accurate interpretation of sociocultural theory which, in fact, has as its overarching focus the interdependence of the social and individual processes in the co-construction of knowledge.

While not wishing to trivialize differences among social constructivist perspectives, we also don't wish to become mired in them. Furthermore, given the fairly emergent state of this perspective—especially when considering its implications for teaching and learning, the revolution is perhaps best characterized as under way. Hence, the focus of this review is on the social dimensions of constructivism generally speaking. Where researchers have drawn distinctions among perspectives, these are identified.

Interest in social constructivism has been motivated by a number of factors, many of which were actually informed by cognitive perspectives on teaching and learning (cf Bruer 1994). As psychological research called attention to the strategic activity of experts (e.g. Flower et al 1992), intervention researchers investigated the use of think-alouds as a means of making problem-solving skills public and accessible to those with less expertise. An example is the research of Duffy et al (1986) in which they determined the value of engaging teachers in public modeling, via think-alouds, of the use of reading strategies such as using context for the purpose of figuring out the meaning of an unknown word. They determined that the children of teachers (in third and fifth grades) who were skilled in modeling the mental processing they were using when experiencing difficulty understanding text recalled more from the lessons and indicated a greater awareness of why they were learning particular strategies.

In another line of research, Palincsar & Brown (1984, 1989; Brown & Palincsar 1989; Palincsar et al 1993b) designed an intervention, called reciprocal teaching, in which teachers and children used discussion structured with four strategies—predicting, questioning, summarizing, and clarifying—to engage readers in constructing the meaning of a text and monitoring to determine that they were making sense of the text. While the teachers were encouraged to explicitly model the strategies, they were also urged to cede control of using the strategies to the children by asking them to take turns leading the discussion. As children led the discussions, the teachers provided whatever support each child needed to use the strategies. This intervention was designed for students who, while fairly adequate decoders, were very poor comprehenders. A program of research indicated that these discussions were a successful means of enhancing comprehension skills; furthermore, the research provided evidence of a relationship between the quality of the interaction between children and teachers, as well as among children, and the nature of the learning that occurred. For example, heterogeneous groups of children with diverse comprehension skills attained competence by using the learning dialogues more quickly than groups of more homogenous ability (Palincsar & Brown 1984). Furthermore, the children of teachers adept at providing specific feedback to children were able to extend children's contributions to the discussions by building upon their ideas. Consequently, these children made greater gains than those of teachers who were less effective at scaffolding children's contributions to the discussions (Palincsar 1986).

As cognitive research clarified the demands of expert reasoning and problem solving, interest emerged in distributing the cognitive work (Bruer 1994). Researchers hypothesized that by drawing upon a larger collective memory and the multiple ways in which knowledge could be structured among individuals working together, groups could attain more success than individuals working alone. Research in writing provides examples. Daiute & Dalton (1993) investigated how children aged seven to nine used diverse capabilities as they taught one another how to write stories. The peer collaboration resembled interactions between teachers and children, resulting in the generation of new story elements and more mature forms of writing than children had demonstrated alone. Furthermore, the researchers speculated that the peer interaction was more facilitative than teacher and child interactions, given the shared perspectives and life experiences that the children were able to bring to the collaborative writing process. This notion will be examined more fully below in discussions of Piagetian and Vygotskian perspectives on learning.

Another explanation for interest in the social dimensions of cognition is derived from awareness of the role that language production plays in promoting learning. Explaining one's thinking to another leads to deeper cognitive processing (Scardamalia & Bereiter 1989).

A final impetus to understanding how social and cultural factors influence cognition is the perspective that thought, learning, and knowledge are not just influenced by social factors but are social phenomena. From this perspective, cognition is a collaborative process (see Rogoff 1997), thought is internalized discourse, and the purpose of inquiry regarding cognitive development is to examine the transformation of socially shared activities into internalized processes (see John-Steiner & Mahn 1996). In the next section, we explore two perspectives on the mechanisms accounting for learning from social constructivist perspectives.

## MECHANISMS ACCOUNTING FOR LEARNING FROM SOCIAL CONSTRUCTIVIST PERSPECTIVES

### The Sociocognitive Conflict Theory of Piaget

There are several theoretical perspectives that have been proffered, in fairly well-developed terms, as explanations of the mechanism by which social interaction leads to higher levels of reasoning and learning. The first, sociocognitive conflict, is derived principally from the work of Piaget and his disciples: "Cognitive conflict created by social interaction is the locus at which the power driving intellectual development is generated" (Perret-Clermont 1980, p. 12). From this perspective, contradiction between the learner's existing understanding and what the learner experiences gives rise to disequilibration, which, in turn, leads the learner to question his or her beliefs and to try out new ideas. In Piaget's words, "disequilibrium forces the subject to go beyond his current state and strike out in new directions" (1985, p. 10). Piaget further suggested that the social exchanges between children were more likely to lead to cognitive development than exchanges between children and adults. This observation was premised on the belief that among age peers there is mutual control over the interaction.

Among studies that have investigated sociocognitive conflict theory is the research by Bell et al (1985). Using conservation tasks, they determined that children working with peers showed more cognitive growth than children working alone. However, there were particular conditions that were in place for children who derived the most from this opportunity. For example, the child had to be actively engaged in the problem-solving activity and not merely observing the more advanced peer. In addition, if the partner's cognitive level were too much in advance of the child's, the outcome mirrored that expected of interactions with adults: the partner's answer was merely accepted and did not stimulate the process of "strik[ing] out in directions."

In search of evidence that peer interaction provides greater opportunities for learning than adult-child interactions, Radziszewska & Rogoff (cited in Rogoff 1991) compared children's interactions with adults and peers, using one group of peer partners who had been taught to use an optimal strategy for completing an errand-planning task and another who had received no special preparation. When the children were later asked to plan without assistance, those children who had collaborated with adults were more successful than those who had worked with prepared or unprepared peers. In an effort to reconcile these differential outcomes of Piagetian studies, Damon (1984) argued that it is important to attend to the nature of the shift the child must make. For example, he suggested that development that requires giving up current understanding to reach a new perspective might best be attained through interaction with peers, whereas learning that does not require a transformation of perspective but rather is characterized as the accretion of a new skill or strategy might be best attained by working with more skillful and experienced partners, such as adults.

Suggesting that verbal interaction is the key to co-construction and cognitive change, Forman & Kraker (1985) cautioned that cognitive conflict may not be enough if there is insufficient verbal interaction or if the social structure permits passive compliance. The importance of considering social status within the group was demonstrated in the research by Russell et al (1990), who observed that social dominance influenced whether a child's conserving answer was adopted by the second child. Merely having the right answer was not consistently enough to persuade the other child.

## The Sociocultural Theory of Vygotsky

The role of social processes as a mechanism for learning is usually identified with Vygotsky, who suggested: "The social dimension of consciousness is primary in time and in fact. The individual dimension of consciousness is derivative and secondary" (Vygotsky 1978, p. 30, cited in Wertsch & Bivens 1992). From this perspective, mental functioning of the individual is not simply derived from social interaction; rather, the specific structures and processes revealed by individuals can be traced to their interactions with others. Wertsch (1991) has proposed three major themes in Vygotsky's writings that elucidate the nature of this interdependence between individual and social processes in learning and development.

The first theme is that individual development, including higher mental functioning, has its origins in social sources. This theme is best represented in Vygotsky's "genetic law of development" (Valsiner 1987, p. 67):

> Every function in the cultural development of the child comes on the stage twice, in two respects: first in the social, later in the psychological, first in relations between people as an interpsychological category, afterwards within the child as an intrapsychological category....All higher psychological functions are internalized relationships of the social kind, and constitute the social structure of personality.

From this perspective, as learners participate in a broad range of joint activities and internalize the effects of working together, they acquire new strate-

gies and knowledge of the world and culture. Typically, this tenet has been illustrated by examining the interactions between individuals with disparate
knowledge levels; for example, children and their caregivers or experts and
novices. Illustrative is the cross-cultural research of Rogoff, who studied the
supportive contexts in which Mayan children acquire knowledge and strategies (Rogoff 1991, p. 351):

> The routine arrangements and interactions between children and their care-
> givers and companions provide children with thousands of opportunities to
> observe and participate in the skilled activities of their culture. Through re-
> peated and varied experience in supported routine and challenging situa-
> tions, children become skilled practitioners in the specific cognitive activi-
> ties in their communities.

Perhaps as a consequence of these research contexts, contemporary critics
of a sociocultural perspective argue that it is a "transfer of knowledge model"
(e.g. Cobb et al 1993). However, scholars of this perspective have argued that
this interpretation is simplistic and misinterprets the transformative nature of
internalization that has been described by sociocultural researchers. For example, Leontiev suggested that "the process of internalization is not the trans-
ferral of an external activity to a preexisting internal 'plane of consciousness';
it is the process in which this plane is formed" (Wertsch & Stone 1985, p. 163).

In contrast with prevailing views of his time, in which learning was regarded as an external process and development an internal process, Vygotsky
was concerned with the unity and interdependence of learning and development. For example, he was critical of Piaget's theory in which "maturation is
viewed as a precondition of learning but never the result of it" (Vygotsky 1978,
p. 80). In contrast, Vygotsky proposed that (p. 90):

> Learning awakens a variety of internal developmental processes that are able
> to operate only when the child is interacting with people in his environment
> and with his peers….[L]earning is not development; however, properly or-
> ganized learning results in mental development and sets in motion a variety
> of developmental processes that would be impossible apart from learning.
> Thus learning is a necessary and universal aspect of the process of develop-
> ing culturally organized, specifically human, psychological functions.

In support of this perspective, Vygotsky (1978) introduced the construct of
the zone of proximal development (ZPD) as a fundamentally new approach to
the problem that learning should be matched in some manner with the child's
level of development. He argued that to understand the relationship between
development and learning we must distinguish between two developmental
levels: the actual and the potential levels of development. The actual refers to
those accomplishments a child can demonstrate alone or perform independ-

ently. This is in contrast with potential levels of development as suggested by the ZPD—what children can do with assistance: "the distance between the actual developmental level as determined by independent problem solving and the level of potential development as determined through problem solving under adult guidance or in collaboration with more capable peers" (p. 85). The ZPD was regarded as a better, more dynamic and relative indicator of cognitive development than what children accomplished alone. In summary, productive interactions are those that orient instruction toward the ZPD. Otherwise, instruction lags behind the development of the child. "The only good learning is that which is in advance of development" (Vygotsky 1978, p. 89). Hence, from a Vygotskian perspective, cognitive development is studied by examining the processes that one participates in when engaged in shared endeavors and how this engagement influences engagement in other activities. Development occurs as children learn general concepts and principles that can be applied to new tasks and problems, whereas from a Piagetian perspective, learning is constrained by development.

The second Vygotskian theme that Wertsch (1991) has identified is that human action, on both the social and individual planes, is mediated by tools and signs—semiotics. The semiotic means include: "language; various systems of counting; mnemonic techniques; algebraic symbol systems; works of art; writing; schemes, diagrams, maps and mechanical drawings; all sorts of conventional signs and so on" (Vygotsky 1981, p. 137). These semiotic means are both the tools that facilitate the co-construction of knowledge and the means that are internalized to aid future independent problem-solving activity. Leontiev (1981), a colleague of Vygotsky, used the term "appropriation" to characterize this process (quoted in Newman et al 1989, p. 63): "[Children] cannot and need not reinvent artifacts that have taken millennia to evolve in order to appropriate such objects into their own system of activity. The child has only to come to an understanding that it is adequate for using the culturally elaborated object in the novel life circumstances he encounters." It is in this sense that the process of collaboration is at the same time the product of collaboration.

The third theme that Wertsch (1991) proposes from Vygotsky's writing is that the first two themes are best examined through genetic, or developmental, analysis (Vygotsky 1978, pp. 64–65):

> To study something historically means to study it in the process of change; that is the dialectical method's basic demand. To encompass in research the process of a given thing's development in all its phases and changes—from birth to death—fundamentally means to discover its nature, its essence, for it is only in movement that a body shows what it is. Thus the historical study of behavior is not an auxiliary aspect of theoretical study, but rather forms its very base.

There are four aspects essential to developmental analysis from a Vygot-skian perspective, all of which are interwoven. *Phylogenetic* development is concerned with what distinguishes humans from other animals. Of particular interest in this analysis is human use of tools—especially the psychological tools of signs and symbols, including language (Vygotsky & Luria 1993). A second level of analysis, *cultural/historical,* calls attention to the profound role that the practices of particular cultures and of the same cultural group play, over time, in development. *Ontogenetic* analysis calls our attention to ways in which individual characteristics, such as physical or mental challenge, age, temperament, and the fruits of individual history influence development. Finally, *microgenetic* analysis deals with the actual processes of interaction between the individual and his or her environment; hence microgenetic analyses take into account the interplay of individual, interpersonal, and social/cultural factors simultaneously.

In summary, from a sociocultural perspective, learning and development take place in socially and culturally shaped contexts, which are themselves constantly changing; there can be no universal scheme that adequately represents the dynamic interaction between the external and the internal aspects of development. There is no generic development that is independent of communities and their practices (Rogoff et al 1995). Hence, it is with the use of genetic analysis that the complex interplay of mediational tools, the individual, and the social world is explored to understand learning and development and the transformation of tools, practices, and institutions.

In the next section, I explicate these tenets by examining research that enhances our understanding of social constructivist perspectives on teaching and learning. Given the highly interactive ways in which social constructivists view the world, the challenge in presenting this research is determining the appropriate grain size. From social constructivist perspectives, separating the individual from social influences is not regarded as possible. The sociocultural contexts in which teaching and learning occur are considered critical to learning itself, and learning is viewed as culturally and contextually specific. Furthermore, cognition is not analyzed as separate from social, motivational, emotional, and identity processes, and the study of generalization is the study of processes rather than the study of personal or situational attributes. Given these complexities, researchers are still developing research methods consistent with the assumptions of this perspective. Commonly used methods include: microgenetic analysis (described above), conversational analysis as opposed to protocol analysis, and the use of activity rather than the individual as the unit of analysis.

Rogoff (1997) suggests that "[t]he parts making a whole activity or event can be considered separately as foreground without losing track of their inherent interdependence in the whole....Foregrounding one plane of focus still involves the participation of the backgrounded planes of focus" (pp. 2–3). In this spirit, the next portion of this review foregrounds institutional, interpersonal, and discursive levels of analysis in turn (cf Cobb et al 1993, Forman et al 1993), examining the literature to determine how research conducted from social constructivist perspectives might contribute to our understanding and improvement of teaching and learning.

# ANALYSES OF SOCIAL CONSTRUCTIVIST PERSPECTIVES

## Institutional Analyses

It is interesting to consider the extent to which contemporary interest in social constructivist perspectives is propelled by recent educational reform efforts encouraging students to assume a more active role in their learning, to explain their ideas to one another, to discuss disagreements, and to cooperate in the solution of complex problems, while teachers participate in the design of these contexts and the facilitation of this kind of activity (cf Resnick et al 1993). All these notions have enormous implications for the culture of schools: "the meaningful traditions and artifacts of a group; ideas, behaviors, verbalization, and material objects" (Fine 1987; cited in Cole 1996, p. 302).

For example, given the tenets of postmodern constructivism, one of the challenges for those interested in its application to education is the development, among learners, of an *intersubjective attitude* about the joint construction of meaning; a commitment to find a common ground on which to build shared understanding (Crook 1994, Rommetveit 1974). This is a particular challenge in Western societies in which individualistic traditions have prevailed. For example, Ellis & Gauvain (1992) conducted cross-cultural research in which they observed that pairs of nine-year-old Navajo children who were asked to teach seven-year-olds to play a game were much more likely to build on each other's comments than were European-American children who more often gave parallel, unrelated lines of instruction. Furthermore, while the Navajo children stayed engaged observing their partners when they were not controlling the game moves, the European-American children lost interest when they were no longer in control of the game, sometimes even leaving the task.

The study of schooling as a cultural process and the school as a cultural system is a fairly recent endeavor. Illustrative is the research of Matusov et al (1997), in which they studied how children who were attending an innovative public school that was structured around collaboration throughout the day, and throughout the curriculum, approached decision-making and assisted younger children in problem-solving activities. Participants were 48 9–11-year-old children recruited from two public schools. One was an innovative school, and the second was a traditional school. The innovative school included activity-based learning, parent participation in the classroom, adult and child direction of the lesson plans, and a problem-solving curriculum. In addition, learning to work in small groups was an explicit part of the curriculum. Twelve pairs of children were recruited from each of the two schools. Working in same-sex pairs, consisting of one third grader and one fourth grader, the children completed a card sorting task and three math problems. The fourth grader was asked to help the third grader to solve each problem in such a way that the third grader would be able to solve the problem alone over time. The children's interactions were rated to provide global characterizations of prevalent approaches to (a) working together (which ranged from nonshared decision-making to working together through consensus), and (b) providing guidance (such as quizzing, directing actions with no rationale, pure instruction, and instruction embedded in collaboration).

Dyads from the traditional school used more quizzing in their interactions with their tutees, and instruction embedded in collaboration was more frequently used by the children from the innovative school.

While the researchers acknowledge the problems inherent in the fact that the children were not randomly assigned to the innovative school, they nonetheless suggest that their work provides useful evidence about how schools must be considered not just in terms of different teaching methods but also in terms of different cultural systems, representing different educational, social, and communicative norms and priorities.

Research on *The Fifth Dimension* conducted by Cole, Griffin, and their collaborators (Cole 1996, Nicolopoulou & Cole 1993) examined institutional and cultural contexts for collaborative activity. The *Fifth Dimension* is a computerized play-world that is constituted by a system of rules. When children join the *Fifth Dimension,* they are provided the rules and embark on a journey through a maze of problems that involve increasing mastery of a sequence of activities. Nicolopoulou & Cole (1993) conducted "cross cultural" research investigating children's engagement in the *Fifth Dimension* across two sites: a Boys and Girls Club and a library. Striking differences observed in the cultures (e.g. norms for interacting, use of time and space) of these two contexts resulted in significant differences in the amount and kinds of learning that occurred in the *Fifth Dimension.* In the Boys and Girls Club, there was no overall growth in the level at which the game was played, whereas in the library there was marked and sustained progress as shared knowledge regarding the game grew in that context.

Another line of research has examined the culture of classrooms. For example, Roth (1996) studied a fourth/fifth grade classroom in which children were using a curriculum entitled *Engineering for Children: Structures*. This program is designed to engage children in the practical application of science concepts as they work collaboratively on open-ended engineering problems. The study occurred over 13 weeks and involved using extensive data sources, including video, field notes, students' and teachers' documentation, as well as interviews. The focus of this study was on the diffusion of knowledge in the classroom; knowledge was represented in terms of resources, tool-related practices, and intellectual practices. Roth observed that facts and resources readily spread throughout the classroom, principally driven by the students. Tool-related practices also spread, though less readily, and again were principally driven by students. However, intellectual practices (in this case the use of triangular constructions) were relatively slow to suffuse the classroom, and to the extent that they did they were largely promoted by the teacher. It is useful to draw upon constructs introduced in earlier descriptions of sociocultural theory to understand this finding. Specifically, the failure of students to appropriate the use of triangular constructions may have been a function of the fact that their experiences were not sufficient to transform their understanding of the relationship between form and function. Support for this explanation may be found in the fact that some children did indeed appropriate the use of triangles in their constructions, but only for aesthetic purposes.

The critical role of the teacher was captured in another exemplary study of the culture of classrooms, conducted by Cobb et al (1991) as they explored the analogies between scientific communities and the social life in a second grade classroom in mathematics. Their work revealed how the teacher created a classroom where the children were validators of one another's ideas, including establishing norms such as persisting in the solution of personally challenging problems, explaining personal solutions to one's partner, listening to and making sense of the partner's explanation and attempting to achieve consensus about the answer, and a solution process. By the end of five months, these norms were in place, and the teacher had to do less to guide children toward these norms.

## Interpersonal Analyses

From social constructivist perspectives, interactions such as those achieved through classroom discussion are thought to provide mechanisms for enhancing higher-order thinking. There are a number of ways in which interpersonal interactions have been studied from this perspective. For example, Forman et al (1995) examined this issue in terms of the activity structures in place in a middle school mathematics class. Their analyses indicated that 71% of the two hours analyzed was spent in student-centered activity structures (15% devoted to student presentations and 55% devoted to pair or small group work). Furthermore, of the 29% of the time that was rated as teacher-centered, the teacher's interactions were facilitative rather than directive. These findings are a striking contrast with the use of time in more traditional settings. For example, Stodolsky (1988) reported that 40% of instructional time in a fifth grade math class was spent on independent seatwork, 29% was spent on whole class, teacher-directed recitations, and 1% was devoted to small group work.

Taylor & Cox (1997) were also interested in characterizing the learning of mathematics as a social enterprise. They hypothesized that children construct and invent mathematical competence rather than learn it through modeling or imitation. In their study, conducted with fourth graders, there were two peer interaction conditions (socially assisted learning and modeling) as well as a classroom control. The researchers selected word problems that would encourage students to focus on the underlying problem representation rather than to simply "graft numbers onto words." Included in the socially assisted learning were: (a) use of a reflection board in which members could share publicly their representation of the problem; (b) peer collaboration; (c) reflective questioning; (d) scaffolding; (e) shared ownership; (f) quizzes, feedback, and rewards; and (g) daily math lessons in the regular classroom. The modeling condition was identical but did not include reflective questioning, scaffolding, or shared ownership. Results indicated that the quiz scores for both interactive groups were superior to the control group, but the scores for the socially assisted were better than the scores of students in either the modeling or control conditions. Furthermore, children in the modeling group had difficulty linking the number quantities to the quantities of objects mentioned and in applying the appropriate operations; that is, they were not as adept at constructing a representation that linked numbers to world knowledge. Finally, in a microanalytic study of the interactions of the tutors with the groups, the researchers determined that the support offered by the tutor was not a function of the number of statements that the tutor made but rather that the statements came at the right time, when they would indeed serve to scaffold understanding.

In explaining the different outcomes, Taylor & Cox (1997) speculated that success with this type of learning was a function of the extent to which there was shared ownership of the learning, which discouraged the division of labor in favor of the negotiation of shared meaning. Instrumental to promoting the negotiation of shared meaning were expectations that: (a) all members of the group work on the same aspect of the problem at the same time, (b) members externalize their thoughts, including possible wrong procedures and answers, (c) members come to agreement among themselves before proceeding, and (d) as instruction moves forward, more of the regulative activity be transferred from the adult to children.

In the work of Taylor & Cox, there are integral relationships between cognitive and social processes. These relationships can raise a host of thorny issues.

For example, social relationships can work against group sense making and the negotiation of meaning. O'Connor (1998) examined this issue in the research that she conducted as a participant observer in a sixth grade mathematics class over two years. Her close study of students' interactions revealed the ways in which ideas were often subordinated to social processes that arose from past interactions among students, suggesting ways in which learning opportunities were filtered through complex interpersonal contexts. Specific phenomena included: discounting or dismissing individual contributions and resistance to the spirit of the entire enterprise. Anderson et al (1997) reported a similar set of findings in their study of sixth graders engaged in collaborative problem solving. Research of this nature reveals the increased complexity for the teacher who must attend to socializing students into new ways of dealing with peers as intellectual partners, as well as new ways of thinking about subject matter learning (see also, Hatano & Inagaki 1991).

The research of Chan et al (1997) refines our understanding of conditions likely to enhance the effectiveness of peer interaction to promote learning. Students from grades 9 and 12/13 were randomly assigned to one of four conditions: (*a*) individual assimilation, (*b*) individual conflict, (*c*) peer assimilation, and (*d*) peer conflict. Assimilation in this research refers to the presentation of probe statements that were maximally congruent with the participants' conceptual understanding of the topic of evolution. Conflict refers to the presentation of probes that maximally contradicted the students' understanding. The presentation of probes was accompanied by the opportunity for participants to revise original ratings of agreement or disagreement with factor statements. In the peer conditions, the students had to negotiate and attain consensus on any changes in their ratings.

While there were a number of interesting findings, I focus on those most central to this review. Older students performed better in the peer condition, while younger students performed better in the individual condition. In addition, students in the conflict condition earned higher scores on quality of post-test knowledge building and experienced greater conceptual changes than students in the assimilation condition. However, conflict was instrumental only to the extent that the learner engaged in some form of knowledge building that aided the restructuring of understanding. Examples of knowledge building included: (*a*) treating new information as something problematic that needs explaining (such as constructing explanations that would reconcile knowledge conflict), and (*b*) using new information to construct coherence in understanding (for example, seeking connections among diverse pieces of information).

By examining the discourse that occurred in the peer conditions, the researchers contribute to our understanding of the differential effects of peer interaction. In discourse that the researchers identified as "[debilitating]," statements that should have caused conflict were simply ignored or treated superficially, whereas in "productive" discourse, there was careful uptake and problematizing of statements that were conflictual in nature.

Webb & Farivar (1997), extending Webb's program of research regarding peer interactions in cooperative learning contexts, used an experimental design to systematically examine the processes of preparing students to work in collaboration with one another. The components of the intervention included: (a) engaging the students in activities to ensure that they knew one another; (b) teaching communication skills, such as norms for interaction; (c) devising activities designed to develop students' abilities to help one another while working on problems, and (d) developing skills for generating explanations. The experimental program was implemented in six seventh grade general-math classes. Two teachers taught three grades each. In one condition, the classes received all the preparatory activities and worked in collaborative arrangements for a semester. In the second condition, the students did not receive preparation to develop skills of explanation. Students who received the three phases of preliminary instruction were more effective in using communication skills, helping behaviors, and explaining skills. Mirroring the findings of Chan et al (1997), Webb & Farivar (1997) found that while the level of help peers received was an important predictor of achievement, this was predicated on the help leading to constructive activity. Furthermore, while there was some improvement in explanations over time, they were not explanations of a high level, raising the question about whether it is perhaps necessary to teach ways of supporting explanations that are specific to the cognitive demands of the domain in which the students are working [see Coleman (1992) and Palincsar et al (1993a) below].

Using a case study approach, Cobb et al (1993) investigated the extent to which children engaged in inquiry mathematics when they worked together in small groups. They also examined the extent to which small group collaborative activity facilitated children's mathematical learning. Stable groups' interactions were studied over 10 weeks to determine the relationship between learning opportunities and the different types of interactions in which the children engaged. Their findings suggested that the stability in the children's small group relationships across the 10 weeks of study was matched by the stability in each pair of children's cognitive capabilities relative to those of the partner. Children's cognitive capabilities and social relationships may have constrained each other in the sense of limiting possibilities for change. Furthermore, interactions in which one child routinely attempted to explain his or her thinking were not necessarily productive for either child's learning. Finally, harmony in a group's relationship did not appear to be a good indicator of learning opportunities. In fact, contentious relationships in which the children's expectations for each other were in conflict were often productive. What led to productive relationships was the development of taken-as-shared bases for mathematical communication and the routine engagement in interactions in which neither child was the authority.

## Discursive Analyses

From a social constructivist perspective, discourse is the primary symbolic, mediational tool for cognitive development. This notion is captured by Bakhtin (1981, p. 293): "[A]s a living, socio-ideological thing, language for the individual consciousness lies on the borderline between oneself and the other." For discourse to be an effective context for learning, it must be communicative. Much research has been conducted to understand the qualities of discourse that enhance its effectiveness. In this section I consider a subset of this research, drawing from various subjects. There are at least two approaches to the study of discourse. One is the investigation of naturally occurring instructional discourse to examine its patterns and opportunities, and the other is the systematic manipulating of features of discourse to determine the effects on learning.

We begin with Roschelle's (1992) inquiry on the processes by which individuals achieve convergence in collaborative activity. There is considerable research in science education examining the tendency of students to construct naive or alternative conceptions. Roschelle has argued that any serious account of science learning must provide an analysis of how convergence is achieved despite these tendencies. Toward this end, Roschelle conducted a microgenetic study of two high school students engaged in discovery learning with *The Envisioning Machine,* which is a software program that enables direct manipulation and graphical simulation of velocity and acceleration. His analyses of two one-hour sessions revealed how these students cooperatively constructed an understanding of acceleration that represented a significant conceptual change from their previous understanding and approximated the scientific meaning of acceleration.

Roschelle asserts that the students attained convergent conceptual change to the extent that, by the end of the session, important aspects of velocity and acceleration were shared, including: change of speed, change of direction, and the implications of these changes in application. Furthermore, the conversation revealed how the students responded to one another with mutual concern for shared knowledge, exerting a deliberate effort to create convergence and avoid divergence. How did this convergence happen? Roschelle suggests that it included the construction of situations at an intermediate level of abstraction from the literal features of the physical world, which was achieved through (*a*) the interplay of metaphors in relation to each other and in reference to the constructed situation, (*b*) iterative cycles of displaying, confirming, and repairing meanings, and (*c*) the application of progressively more stringent standards of evidence. Furthermore, Roschelle suggests that *The Envisioning Machine* played an essential role, simultaneously supporting individual reasoning and facilitating the negotiation of meaning.

The program of research by Raphael and her colleagues, studying elementary-aged students engaged in Book Club discussions (Raphael et al 1992), reveals the value of naturalistic study of discourse in another complex learning environment. The leading question of this research was: How do book club discussions influence fourth and fifth grade students' abilities to discuss literature? By studying children's conversations across time and across texts, we learn about the role of the constitution of the groups, literature selection, and assigned writing activities. For example, in the selection of a text, it needed to have the potential for controversy and the power to elicit emotional responses—in addition to high quality, the proper reading level, availability, and suitability for meeting curricular goals. Furthermore, writing activities that offered more flexibility in responses were more beneficial and led to more interesting discussions than did more carefully structured responses. Finally, the research speaks to the multiple roles played by the teacher in Book Club discussions: guiding students in using text comprehension strategies, modeling ways to articulate personal responses to literature, and illustrating interaction patterns that would promote improved interactions in Book Clubs.

The crucial role that the teacher plays in promoting the co-construction of knowledge in classrooms was also demonstrated in the research of Forman et al (1995). In the micro-analytic study of the discourse of middle school children and their teacher (introduced above), these researchers captured the dynamic role of the teacher in guiding classroom discussions in the context of mathematical problem solving. In addition to evaluating the frequency of teacher and student contributions, they analyzed the functions of these contributions. The scheme that they devised revealed a broad range of conversational turns. For example, there were *initiations* in the service of requesting an answer or explanation; *responses;* and *reconceptualizations* that included restatements, rephrasing, expansion, and evaluation. The research of Forman et al suggests the importance of moving beyond the traditional static treatments of I-R-E (initiation-response-evaluation) patterns in classroom discourse. While an initial pass at the discourse in this classroom might suggest it fit the I-R-E framework, the students rather than the teacher were engaged in significant evaluative activity, and the responses of the teacher expanded on students' contributions to the discussion. Forman et al also note another crucial feature of the teacher's role, which they refer to as "discussion orchestration," which served to focus student attention and facilitate negotiation in the interest of consensus building.

Lampert (1990), reflecting on her own teaching activity in mathematics, captures the role that she has played in this negotiation process (p. 41):

> The role I took in classroom discourse, therefore, was to follow and engage in mathematical arguments with students; this meant that I needed to know more than the answer or the rule for how to find it, and I needed to do something other than explain to them why the rules work. I needed to know how to *prove* it to them, in the mathematical sense, and I needed to be able to evaluate their proofs of their own mathematical assertions. In the course of classroom discussions, I also initiated my students into the use of mathematical tools and conventions.

In this manner, Lampert clearly joins the dialogue as a knowing participant, but she is not the arbiter of truth. The burden of mathematical judgment is distributed to the classroom as a community of mathematical thinkers.

Naturally occurring differences across four classrooms enabled Smagorinsky & Fly (1993) to determine how the discourse in teacher-led discussion groups influenced the nature of subsequent small group discussions. The discussions were in the service of interpreting short coming-of-age stories and took place in four sophomore high school classes. By examining transcripts of discussion across whole class and small group contexts, the researchers were able to determine that the skill with which students engaged in productive discussions during small group discussions was related to the experiences of the students in the whole-class work. Specific teacher moves in whole-class discussion that subsequently served to scaffold small group discussions included: posing questions that encouraged students to make connections between the text and their own life experiences, and stepping outside the discussion for the purpose of making analytic/interpretive procedures explicit (for example, the need to pose a question, the need to support a generalization with evidence).

Finally, we report on two studies of small groups engaged in peer-editing activities, unassisted by a teacher. Daiute & Dalton (1993) studied the interactions between 14 seven-to-nine–year-old children in an urban setting and the impact of collaboration on their abilities to write stories. The study traces how the children internalized the fruits of their collaboration by examining individually generated written work before, during, and following collaboration. This study was conducted in an urban school over eight weeks. The researchers found that the children brought diverse areas of expertise related to story structure knowledge, style, and schema to the story-writing activity. Furthermore, they described the writing processes in terms of initiating and contesting. Analyses of independent writing samples indicated that the participants used significantly more story elements following collaboration.

In another study of peer collaboration in writing, Nystrand (1986) found that students who worked in groups demonstrated greater gains than those who did not. Furthermore, students who had experienced group work came to think of revision as reconceptualization, whereas those who worked alone continued to think of revision as principally editing. However, he also found remarkable variability in the discourse across groups. For example, some groups felt they had accomplished their task if they labeled the problem, failing to examine the trouble source in any detail, while other groups would talk at length about ideas. Successful groups focused on issues of genre and the most successful groups engaged in "extensive collaborative problem solving," in which members joined together to address rhetorical problems in concrete, cooperative ways.

Next we turn to those studies that have been designed to manipulate features of discourse to learn more about how they operate to promote learning. We begin with a study by Teasley (1995), which was designed to study *collaboration* and *talk* as separate variables. Questions driving this research asked: Does the production of talk affect performance? What kinds of talk affect performance? Does the presence of a partner affect the kinds of talk produced? Teasley used a microworld (designed by Klahr and his colleagues) to investigate scientific reasoning. The task required figuring out the effect of a mystery key and then designing experiments to test the hypotheses. The 70 fourth grade participants were assigned to work alone or with a same-sex partner for one 20-min session. Within each condition, half of the children were asked to talk as they worked and half were asked not to talk. There was a main effect for talk that was more pronounced for talk-dyads than for talk-alones. Talk-dyads produced more talk and more specific types of talk than talk-alones. However, neither simply having a partner nor talking a lot improved learning. What was crucial was that children produced interpretive types of talk; that is, talk that supported reasoning about theories and evidence. Furthermore, while dyads directed more of their talk to evaluating and explaining the program outcomes, students working alone simply remarked on the behavior of the spaceship without making any assessment of that behavior.

Teasley's findings are supported by research on reasoning indicating that children's performance on reasoning tasks is significantly affected by their ability to coordinate hypotheses and evidence (Klahr et al 1993, Kuhn et al 1988, Schauble 1990). Findings of this nature informed the design of an intervention study conducted by Coleman (1992), in which she sought to define the merits of collaborative learning more precisely; that is, to describe some of the specific mechanisms of group learning that appear to be more successful than others for promoting conceptual understanding.

Coleman's findings are mirrored in a study by King (1990) who did research altering group discourse to determine whether it would affect reading comprehension. The intervention was called "guided reciprocal peer questioning" and involved teaching students question stems (such as "How does...affect...?", "What would happen if...?"). King reported that students who used this procedure generated more critical thinking questions, gave more high-level explanations, and demonstrated higher achievement than students using discussion or an unguided reciprocal questioning approach.

In summary, studies of discourse are generally quite supportive of the benefits of instructional conversation. However, the benefits depend upon the types of talk produced. Specifically, talk that is interpretive (generated in the service of analysis or explanations) is associated with more significant learning gains than talk that is simply descriptive. Furthermore, teachers play an important role in mediating classroom discourse by seeding the conversation with new ideas or alternatives to be considered that push the students' thinking and discussion and prepare them for conversation. Finally, it is important to attend to the structure of group activity so that responsibility is shared, expertise is distributed, and there is an ethos for building preceding ideas.

In the next section, I consider the contributions of social constructivist perspectives to selected contemporary educational issues; namely, acquiring expertise across domains, assessment practices, equity in education, and the transformation of schools.

# THE APPLICATION OF SOCIAL CONSTRUCTIVIST PERSPECTIVES TO CONTEMPORARY EDUCATIONAL ISSUES

## Acquiring Expertise Across Domains

Writing from a traditional psychological perspective, Gallagher, in a 1994 *Annual Review* chapter on teaching and learning, wrote that "[E]ducators are increasingly viewing learners as bundles of knowledge structures that become increasingly sophisticated and hierarchical as they gain experience" (p. 172). In contrast, from social constructivist perspectives, expertise is characterized not in terms of knowledge structures but rather in terms of facility with discourse, norms, and practices associated with particular communities of practice (Lave & Wenger 1991). While from cognitive perspectives knowledge is generally represented in terms of cognitive structures that are acquired and organized in memory, social constructivists generally regard learning as the appropriation of socially derived forms of knowledge that are not simply internalized over time but are also transformed in idiosyncratic ways in the appropriation process. Furthermore, learning is thought to occur through processes of interaction, negotiation, and collaboration (cf Billet 1995, Hicks 1995–1996).

The influence of social constructivist perspectives has led to reexamining what it means to teach and learn across subject matters. From social constructivist perspectives, researchers have asked what it means to "talk science" (Lemke 1990) or to participate in the discourse of mathematics (Cobb & Bauersfeld 1995). For example, Lemke (1990) suggests that talking science means: "observing, describing, comparing, classifying, analyzing, discussing, hypothesizing, theorizing, questioning, challenging, arguing, designing experiments, following procedures, judging, evaluating, deciding, concluding, generalizing, reporting, writing, lecturing, and teaching in and through the language of science" (p. ix). Furthermore, drawing upon anthropological research (e.g. Latour & Woolgar 1986), it is clear that scientific practice in the world is heterogeneous rather than unitary to the extent that practitioners orchestrate a variety of means (tools, discourses) to construct scientific meaning.

In turn, educational researchers have pursued the connection between scientific practice in professional communities and in schools, testing out the implications of this view for curriculum and pedagogy. Illustrative is the research of Rosebery et al (1992) in elementary classrooms where science is organized around students' own questions and inquiries. Students design studies to explore questions that they find compelling; collect, analyze, and interpret data; build and argue theories; establish criteria and evaluate evidence; challenge assumptions; and take action on the basis of their results. Among the many outcomes that Rosebery et al report are: the generative nature of children's thinking in this context and the deepening of scientific thinking (for example, students came to understand that hypotheses are springboards for inquiry rather than explanations). Finally, the researchers report that participants became comfortable identifying with scientific activity and not simply attributing scientific activity to others.

## Assessment

Assessment practices informed by social constructivist perspectives stand in striking contrast with assessment procedures informed by the psychological theory that prevailed in the 1960s, in which testing contexts (e.g. Wisconsin General Test Apparatus) were designed to reduce social influences (Brown 1994). Assessment informed by social constructivist perspectives is frequently referred to as "dynamic assessment" (Feuerstein 1979) and characterizes approaches in which the performance of the individual being assessed is mediated or guided by another individual to determine the individual's potential to profit from assistance or instruction.

Dynamic assessment provides a *prospective* measure of performance, indicating abilities that are developing and is *predictive* of how the child will perform independently in the future. Furthermore, the response of the child to the assistance is intended to inform instruction. In Vygotskian terms, while traditional static measures at best inform us about an individual's actual level of development, dynamic assessment is designed to reveal the child's potential level of development (Vygotsky 1986, pp. 203):

> The state of development is never defined alone by what has matured. If the gardener decides only to evaluate the matured or harvested fruits of the apple tree, he cannot determine the state of his orchard. The maturing trees must also be taken into consideration. Correspondingly, the psychologist must not limit his analysis to functions that have matured; he must consider those that are in the process of maturation…the zone of proximal development.

There are a number of models of dynamic assessment (Lidz 1987, Palincsar et al 1991) that vary in terms of the nature of the task, the type of assistance that is provided, and the outcomes that are reported. For example, the model pioneered by Feuerstein (1980), the Learning Potential Assessment Device (LPAD), is organized around tasks that Feuerstein argues require higher mental processes that are amenable to change, such as matrix problems, digit span tests, and embedded-figures problems. Hence, they bear a strong resemblance to the kinds of tasks used in traditional measures of IQ. However, when administering the LPAD, the examiner interacts in a flexible and individualized manner, anticipating where the child might experience difficulty and noting how the child uses reminders and other prompts. The outcome of the assessment is a cognitive map that is designed to specify the nature of the child's problem in terms of familiarity with content, strategies attempted in problem solving activity, and modifiability of the learner.

Test-train-test is another model of dynamic assessment that has been used in the research of Budoff (1987), Carlson & Wiedl (1979), and Campione & Brown (1984) and colleagues. Some form of guided learning occurs between pre- and posttesting. These programs of research indicate that dynamic assessment procedures do reveal a different picture of competence than do static measures, which typically underestimate many children's abilities to learn in a domain in which they initially performed poorly. The use of transfer tasks in dynamic assessment indicates that learning and transfer scores are better predictors of gain than are static measures.

It has been only recently that the principles of dynamic assessment have been explored within academic contexts. An excellent example is the research reported by Magnusson et al (1997). Magnusson et al were interested in children's conceptual understanding of the flow of electricity and devised a context that would allow the fourth graders in their research to test out their conceptions and then revise their ideas on the basis of the outcomes of their tests. They used the same basic circuit in three tasks, with each circuit differing only in the number of switches, which in turn determined which lightbulbs were lighted as well as the brightness of the bulbs. Hence the students had multiple opportunities to construct, test out, and revise explanations for the flow of electricity. The role of the interviewer in this assessment context was to elicit and probe predictions and explanations that would reveal the conceptions of the student participants. This dynamic science assessment proceeded by engaging the students in (*a*) predicting what they thought would happen, given a specific circuit, along with their reasons for making these predictions; (*b*) describing their observations; (*c*) comparing predictions with observations and discussing differences between them; and (*d*) explaining the result, focusing on underlying causes.

The use and outcomes of microgenetic analysis are illustrated by Schauble's (1996) research in which she examined the development of scientific reasoning as participants completed two experimentation tasks involving the use of fluids and immersed objects. Given recent calls for reexamining the usefulness of high-stakes assessment practices and questioning the extent to which these practices truly inform curriculum and pedagogy, these forms of dynamic and microgenetic assessment offer potentially powerful alternatives to traditional measurement procedures to the extent that they reveal not only what has been learned but also how and why learning has occurred.

## Providing Meaningful Education for All Children

It is hard to imagine a more significant challenge to social constructivism than promoting meaningful learning for all children, especially for those who are linguistically and culturally diverse. Moll (1992) speaks to this possibility when he argues that "[i]n studying human beings dynamically, within their social circumstances, in their full complexity, we gain a more complete and...a much more valid understanding of them. We also gain, particularly in the case of minority children, a more positive view of their capabilities and how our pedagogy often constrains, and just as often distorts, what they do and what they are capable of doing" (p. 239).

A number of sociocultural explanations have been tendered for the failure of schools to serve all children. Examples include: (*a*) discontinuities between the culture (values, attitudes, and beliefs) of the home and school (Gee 1990, McPhail 1996), (*b*) mismatches in the communicative practices between nonmainstream children and mainstream teachers that lead to miscommunication and misjudgment (Heath 1983), (*c*) the internalization of negative stereotypes by minority groups who have been marginalized and may see school as a site for opposition and resistance (Steele 1992), and (*d*) relational issues, such as the failure to attain mutual trust between teachers and students (Moll & Whitmore 1993) and a shared sense of identification between the teacher and the learner (Cazden 1993, Litowitz 1993).

These possibilities have been pursued both in describing the performance of children in schools and in prescribing appropriate instruction. For example, Anderson et al (1997) drew upon these explanations to explore how sixth grade students participated in collaborative problem-solving activities in science. For a prescriptive example, we turn to the research of Needles & Knapp (1994), who conducted a study comparing three approaches to the teaching of writing. The first approach was *skills-based,* as characterized by systematic exposure and mastery of discrete skills (such as spelling and sentence structure). The second approach was *whole language,* which advocates that language is best learned in the context of use, should not be broken into discrete skills, and prescribes a minimal role for the teacher. The third approach reflected a social constructivist perspective, which Needles & Knapp described using the following principles: (*a*) component skills are best learned in the context of the writing task, (*b*) the quality of writing increases when children are writing what is meaningful and authentic, (*c*) fluency and competence are influenced by the extent to which the task connects with the child's background and experience, (*d*) involvement increases when children are encouraged to interact while performing writing tasks, (*e*) children develop competence if they approach the task as a problem solving process, and (*f*) children need ample opportunities to write extended text. They found that writing instruction that reflected these six principles accounted for a substantial proportion of children's improved abilities to write, once initial proficiency was considered.

## Educational Reform

Exciting educational innovations are under way that draw generously upon (and are contributing generously to) the social constructivist perspectives introduced in this review. Perhaps the most striking example is a collection of efforts designed to reconceptualize classrooms—and schools—as learning communities. For example, the Computer Supported Intentional Learning Environments (CSILE), a project led by Scardamalia & Bereiter and their colleagues (Scardamalia et al 1994) places "World 3" knowledge at the center of classroom activity. As described by Popper (1972), World 3 knowledge refers to the public construction of understanding and stands in contrast to "World 2" knowledge, which exists in individual minds. The features of CSILE include a communal data base that students use to generate World 3 knowledge, a curriculum that permits the sustained pursuit of topics of inquiry, a classroom culture that fosters collaboration among peers, and a teacher who engages in instructional design work. The researchers note that the successful implementation of CSILE engages the teacher in moving flexibly between World 2 and

World 3 knowledge, tacking between what is in children's heads and what is taking shape in the public domain.

In the project Guided Discovery in a Community of Learners, Brown & Campione and their colleagues (Brown & Campione 1990, 1994) engage children in the design of their own learning and encourage students to be partially responsible for the design of their own curricula. Working on assigned curricular themes, students form separate research groups to become experts on subtopics of the theme. The students conduct seminars in which they share their expertise so that all members of the group can master the entire theme. Essential characteristics of Community of Learner classrooms include individual responsibility coupled with communal sharing; the use of select participation frameworks that are practiced repeatedly and that are compatible with the work of these communities; classroom discourse that is marked by constructive discussion, questioning, and criticism; conceptions of classrooms as comprised of multiple zones of proximal development (explained above), which include both children and adults at varying levels of expertise, as well as artifacts (such as texts and tools) that support learning; and the expectation that learning occurs as individuals contribute to and appropriate ideas (Brown & Campione 1994). Multifaceted assessments indicate that children in these learning communities retain domain-specific content better than youngsters in control groups, are able to think critically about knowledge, and demonstrate significant progress with an array of literacy skills such as reading comprehension and oral argumentation.

The demands of the types of teaching and classroom organization described throughout this review have special implications for the professional development of teachers. This is an area that has been virtually neglected in earlier educational reform efforts, which may well explain the efforts' demise. An educational innovation of particular importance is the application of the tenets of social constructivism to the design of professional development contexts with teachers. For example, Englert and her colleagues (Englert & Tarrant 1995) have brought teachers together in learning communities to examine their own practices in literacy instruction. This community of teachers works to translate the tenets of a sociocultural perspective into curriculum and pedagogy for students with serious learning difficulties. The teachers, informed by this perspective, systematically try out new practices, conduct their own inquiry regarding the outcomes of these innovations, and share their accumulated wisdom with one another. Additional professional development research, conducted in a similar spirit, has been reported by Grossman & Weinberg (1997; working with secondary literature teachers), Schifter (1996; working with elementary teachers in mathematics), and Palincsar & Magnusson and their colleagues (1997; working with elementary teachers in science).

## Future Directions for Inquiry

The major theoretical contributions to the social constructivist perspective described in this chapter were developed and applied in the 1920s and 1930s by Vygotsky and his collaborators. Based on the notion that human activities take place in cultural contexts, are mediated by language and other symbol systems, and are best understood when investigated in their historical development, this is a complex and multifaceted perspective. Moreover, Vygotsky died at a very young age, with many of his ideas only partially developed. John-Steiner & Mahn (1996) caution that because the theory is complex and breaks radically with traditional educational and psychological theory, there is the tendency to abstract parts of the theory from the whole, which results in distorted understandings and applications. One direction for future inquiry is to continue the development of this theory.

Toward this end, it will be helpful to coordinate constructivist perspectives, informed primarily by cognitive psychology and socioculturalism. How might these perspectives be coordinated? Where constructivists give priority to individual conceptual activity, sociocultural theorists tend to assume that cognitive processes are subsumed by social and cultural processes. Where social constructivists emphasize the homogeneity of thought among the members of the community engaged in shared activity, cognitive constructivists stress heterogeneity of thought as individuals actively interpret social and cultural processes, highlighting the contributions that individuals make to the development of these processes.

It is important that inquiry conducted within this perspective shares a dual orientation to theory and practice (Cole 1996), designed to deepen our understanding of cognitive development as well as to produce change in everyday practice. As the research reviewed above suggests, social constructivist perspectives, which regard schooling as a system rather than as a set of isolated activities, have been extremely useful to understanding and describing the complexities of teaching, learning, and enculturation into schools. However, they have had little influence on the practices of schooling.

The genetic levels of analysis suggested by this perspective, as well as the methodologies that are drawn from this perspective, offer powerful tools for advancing both theory and practice. However, many educational researchers are unfamiliar with these tools. Finally, just as this perspective has been developed through the contributions of many disciplines (psychology, semiotics, linguistics, anthropology, etc), it would seem especially fruitful to promote interdisciplinary collaborations in the quest to advance this scholarship so that it might realize its potential and make a difference for children.

## Literature Cited

Anderson CA, Holland D, Palincsar AS. 1997. Canonical and sociocultural approaches to research and reform in science education: the story of Juan and his group. *Elem. Sch. J.* 97:357–81

Bakhtin M. 1981. Discourse in the novel. In *The Dialogic Imagination,* ed. C Emerson, M Holquist, pp. 259–492. Austin: Univ. Tex. Press

Baumann J. 1988. Direct instruction reconsidered. *J. Read. Behav.* 31:712–18

Bell N, Grossen M, Perret-Clermont AN. 1985. Sociocognitive conflict and intellectual growth. See Berkowitz 1985, pp. 41–54

Berkowitz MW, ed. 1985. *Peer Conflict and Psychological Growth.* San Francisco: Jossey-Bass

Billet S. 1995. Situated learning: bridging sociocultural and cognitive theorizing. *Learn. Instruct.* 6:263–80

Brown AL. 1994. The advancement of learning. *Educ. Res.* 23:4–12

Brown AL, Campione JC. 1990. Communities of learning and thinking, or a context by any other name. *Hum. Dev.* 21:108–25

Brown AL, Campione JC. 1994. Guided discovery in a community of learners. See McGilly 1994, 9:229–72

Brown AL, Palincsar AS. 1989. Guided cooperative learning and individual knowledge acquisition. In *Knowing, Learning, and Instruction: Essays in Honor of Robert Glaser,* ed. L Resnick, pp. 393–451. Hillsdale, NJ: Erlbaum

Bruer J. 1994. Classroom problems, school culture, and cognitive research. See McGilly 1994, 10:273–90

Bruner J. 1990. *Acts of Meaning,* pp. 1–32. Cambridge, MA: Harvard Univ. Press

Budoff M. 1987. Measures for assessing learning potential. See Lidz 1987, pp. 173–95

Campione JC, Brown AL. 1984. Learning ability and transfer propensity as sources of individual differences in intelligence. In *Learning and Cognition in the Mentally Retarded,* ed. PH Brooks, R Sperber, C McCauley, pp. 137–50. Baltimore: Univ. Park Press

Carlson JS, Wiedl KH. 1979. Toward a differential footing approach: testing the limits

employing the Roman matrices. *Intelligence* 3: 323–44

Cazden C. 1993. Vygotksy, Hymes, and Bahktin: from word to utterance and voice. See Forman et al 1993, pp. 197–212

Chan C, Burtis J, Bereiter C. 1997. Knowledge building as a mediator of conflict in conceptual change. *Cogn. Instruct.* 15:1–40

Cobb P, Bauersfeld H. 1995. *Emergence of Mathematical Meaning: Instruction in Classroom Cultures.* Hillsdale, NJ: Erlbaum

Cobb P, Wood T, Yackel E. 1993. Discourse, mathematical thinking, and classroom practice. See Forman et al 1993, pp. 91–119

Cobb P, Wood T, Yackel E. 1991. Analogies from the philosophy and sociology of science for understanding classroom life. *Sci. Educ.* 75: 23–44

Cobb P, Yackel E. 1996. Constructivism, emergent, and sociocultural perspectives in the context of developmental research. *Educ. Psychol.* 31:175–90

Cole M. 1996. *Cultural Psychology.* Cambridge, MA: Harvard Univ. Press

Coleman EB. 1992. *Faciliating conceptual understanding in science: a collaborative explanation based approach.* PhD thesis. Univ. Toronto, Can.

Crook C. 1994. *Computers and the Collaborative Experience of Learning.* London: Routledge

Daiute C, Dalton B. 1993. Collaboration between children learning to write: Can novices be masters? *Cogn. Instruct.* 10: 281–333

Damon W. 1984. Peer education: the untapped potential. *J. Appl. Behav. Psychol.* 5: 331–43

Duffy GG, Roehler L, Meloth MS, Vavrus LG, Book C, et al. 1986. The relationship between explicit verbal explanations during reading skill instruction and student awareness and achievement: a study of reading teacher effects. *Read. Res. Q.* 22: 347–68

Ellis S, Gauvain M. 1992. Social and cultural influences on children's collaborative interactions. In *Children's Development Within Social Context,* ed. LT Winegar, J

Valsiner, pp. 155–80. Hillsdale, NJ: Erlbaum

Englert CS, Tarrant K. 1995. Creating collaborative cultures for educational change. *Rem. Special Educ.* 16:325–36

Feuerstein R. 1979. *The Dynamic Assessment of Retarded Performers: The Learning Potential Assessment Device, Theory, Instruments, and Techniques.* Baltimore: Univ. Park Press

Feuerstein R. 1980. *Instrumental Enrichment: An Intervention Program for Cognitive Modifiability.* Baltimore: Univ. Park Press

Fine GA. 1987. *With the Boys*, pp. 41–57. Chicago: Univ. Chicago Press

Flower L, Schriver KA, Carey L, Haas C, Hayes JR. 1992. Planning in writing: the cognition of a constructive process. In *A Rhetoric of Doing,* ed. S Witte, N Nakadate, R Cherry, pp. 282–311. Carbondale: South. Ill. Univ. Press

Forman EA, Donato R, McCormick D. 1993. *The social and institutional context of learning mathematics: an ethnographic study of classroom discourse.* Presented at Annu. Meet. Am. Educ. Res. Assoc., 75th, New Orleans

Forman EA, Kraker MJ. 1985. The social origins of logic: the contributions of Piaget and Vygotsky. See Berkowitz 1985, pp. 23–39

Forman EA, Minnick N, Stone CA. 1993. *Contexts for Learning: Sociocultural Dynamics in Children's Development.* New York: Oxford Univ. Press

Forman EA, Stein MK, Brown C, Larreamendy-Joerns J. 1995. *The Socialization of Mathematical Thinking: The Role of Institutional, Interpersonal, and Discursive Contexts.* Presented at Annu. Meet. Am. Educ. Res. Assoc., 77th, San Franciso

Gallagher JJ. 1994. Teaching and learning: new models. *Annu. Rev. Psychol.* 45: 171–95

Gee J. 1990. *Social Linguistics and Literacies: Ideology in Discourse.* Bristol, PA: Falmer

Glaser R, Bassok M. 1989. Learning theory and the study of instruction. *Annu. Rev. Psychol.* 40:631–66

Grossman P, Weinberg S. 1997. *Creating a community of learners among high school English and social studies teachers.* Presented at Annu. Meet. Am. Educ. Res. Assoc., 78th, Chicago

Hatano G, Inagaki K. 1991. Sharing cognition through collective comprehension activity. See Resnick et al 1991, pp. 331–48

Heath SB. 1983. *Ways with Words: Language, Life, and Work in Communities and Classrooms.* New York: Cambridge Univ. Press

Hicks D. 1995–1996. Discourse, learning, and teaching. *Rev. Res. Educ.* 21:49–98

John-Steiner V, Mahn H. 1996. Sociocultural approaches to learning and development. *Educ. Psychol.* 31:191–206

King A. 1990. Enhancing peer interaction and learning in the classroom through reciprocal questioning. *Am. Educ. Res. J.* 27: 664–87

Klahr D, Fay A, Dunbar K. 1993. Heuristics for scientific experimentation: a developmental study. *Cogn. Psychol.* 25:111–46

Kuhn D, Amsel E, O'Loughlin M. 1988. *The Development of Scientific Thinking Skills.* New York: Academic

Lampert M. 1990. When the problem is not the question and the solution is not the answer: mathematical knowing and teaching. *Am. Educ. Res. J.* 27:29–63

Latour B, Woolgar S. 1986. *Laboratory Life: The Social Construction of Scientific Facts.* Princeton, NJ: Princeton Univ. Press

Lave J, Wenger E. 1991. *Situated Learning: Legitimate Peripheral Participation.* Cambridge: Cambridge Univ. Press.

Lemke J. 1990. *Talking Science: Language, Learning, and Values.* Norwood, NJ: Ablex

Leontiev AN. 1981. *Problems of the Development of Mind.* Moscow: Progress

Lidz CS, ed. 1987. *Dynamic Assessment: Foundations and Fundamentals.* New York: Guilford

Litowitz B. 1993. Deconstruction in the zone of proximal development. See Forman et al 1993, pp. 184–97

Magnusson SJ, Templin M, Boyle R. 1997. Dynamic science assessment of new approaches for investigating conceptual change. *J. Learn. Sci.* 6:91–142

Matusov EL, Bell N, Rogoff B. 1997. Collaboration and assistance in problem solving by children differing in cooperative schooling backgrounds. Submitted

McGilly K, ed. 1994. *Classroom Lessons: Integrating Cognitive Theory and Classroom Practice.* Cambridge: MIT Press

McPhail J. 1996. *The use of narrative methods to explore failure to succeed in medical school.* Presented at Annu. Meet. Am. Educ. Res. Assoc., 77th, New York

Moll LC. 1992. Literacy research in community and classrooms: a sociocultural approach. In *Multidisciplinary Perspectives on Literacy Research,* ed. R Beach, JL Green, ML Kamil, T Shanahan, pp. 211–44. Urbana, IL: Natl. Counc. Teach. Engl.

Moll LC, Whitmore K. 1993. Vygotsky in

classroom practice: moving from individual transmission to social transaction. See Forman et al 1993, pp. 19–42

Needles MC, Knapp M. 1994. Teaching writing to children who are underserved. *J. Educ. Psychol.* 86:339–49

Newman D, Griffin P, Cole M. 1989. *The Construction Zone: Working for Cognitive Change in Schools.* Cambidge: Cambridge Univ. Press

Nicolopoulou A, Cole M. 1993. Generation and transmission of shared knowledge in the culture of collaborative learning: The Fifth Dimension, its playworld and its institutional contexts. See Forman et al 1993, pp. 283–314

Nystrand M. 1986. *The Structure of Written Communication: Studies in Reciprocity Between Writers and Readers.* Orlando, FL: Academic

O'Connor MC. 1998. Managing the intermental: classroom group discussion and the social context of learning. In *Social Interaction, Social Context, and Language: Essays in Honor of Susan Ervin Tripp*, ed. DI Slobin, J Gerhardt, A Kyratzis, J Guo. Hillsdale, NJ: Erlbaum. In press

Palincsar AS. 1986. The role of dialogue in scaffolded instruction. *Educ. Psychol.* 21:71–98

Palincsar AS, Anderson CA, David YM. 1993a. Pursuing scientific literacy in the middle grades through collaborative problem solving. *Elem. Sch. J.* 93:643–58

Palincsar AS, Brown AL. 1984. Reciprocal teaching of comprehension-fostering and comprehension-monitoring activities. *Cogn. Instruct.* 1:117–75

Palincsar AS, Brown AL. 1989. Classroom dialogues to promote self-regulated comprehension. In *Advances in Research on Teaching*, ed. J Brophy, pp. 35–72. Greenwich: JAI

Palincsar AS, Brown AL, Campione JC. 1993b. First grade dialogues for knowledge acquisition and use. See Forman et al 1993, pp. 43–57

Palincsar AS, Brown AL, Campione JC. 1991. Dynamic assessment. In *Handbook on the Assessment of Learning Disabilities*, ed. L Swanson, 5:75–95. Austin, TX: Pro-Ed.

Palincsar AS, Magnusson SJ. 1997. Design principles informing and emerging from a community of practice. *Teach. Teach. Educ.* In press

Perret-Clermont AN. 1980. Social interaction and cognitive development. *Eur. Monogr. Soc. Psychol. 19.* New York: Academic

Peterson P, Walberg HJ, eds. 1979. *Research in Teaching.* Berkeley, CA: McCutchan

Piaget J. 1985. *The Equilibration of Cognitive Structures: The Central Problem of Intellectual Development,* pp. 36–64. Transl. T Brown, KL Thampy. Chicago: Univ. Chicago Press. (From French)

Popper KR. 1972. *Objective Knowledge: An Evolutionary Approach.* Oxford: Clarendon

Prawat R. 1996. Constructivisms, modern and postmodern. *Educ. Psychol.* 31:215–25

Raphael TE, McMahon SI, Goatley VJ, Bentley JL, Boyd FB, et al. 1992. Research directions: literature and discussion in the reading program. *Lang. Arts* 69:55–61

Resnick LB, Levine JM, Teasely SD, eds. 1991. *Perspectives on Socially Shared Cognition.* Washington, DC: Am. Psychol. Assoc.

Resnick LB, Salmon MH, Zeitz CM, Wathen SH. 1993. The structure of reasoning in conversation. *Cogn. Instruct.* 11:347–64

Rogoff B. 1991. Guidance and participation in spatial planning. See Resnick et al 1991, pp. 349–83

Rogoff B. 1997. Cognition as a collaborative process. In *Cognitive, Language, and Perceptual Development,* ed. RS Siegler, D Kuhn, Vol. 2, *Handbook of Child Psychology,* ed. W Damon. New York: Wiley. In press

Rogoff B, Radziszewska B, Masiello T. 1995. Analysis of developmental processes in sociocultural activity. In *Sociocultural Psychology: Theory and Practice of Doing and Knowing,* ed. L Martin, K Nelson, E Toback, pp. 125–49. Cambridge: Cambridge Univ. Press

Rommetveit R. 1974. *On Message Structure.* London: Wiley

Roschelle J. 1992. Learning by collaborating: convergent conceptual change. *J. Learn. Sci.* 2:235–76

Rosebery A, Warren B, Conant F. 1992. Appropriating scientific discourse: findings from minority classrooms. *J. Learn Sci.* 2:61–94

Roth WM. 1996. *Communities of practice and actor networks: an analysis of the diffusion of knowledge in an elementary classroom in terms of changing resources and practices.* Presented at Annu. Meet. Natl. Assoc. Res. Sci. Teach., Anaheim

Russell J, Mills I, Reiff-Musgrove P. 1990. The role of symmetrical and asymmetrical social conflict in cognitive change. *J. Exp. Child Psychol.* 49:58–78

Sandoval J. 1995. Teaching in subject matter areas: science. *Annu. Rev. Pyschol.* 46:355–74

Scardamalia M, Bereiter C. 1989. Intentional

learning as a goal of instruction. In *Knowing, Learning and Instruction,* ed. LB Resnick, pp. 361–92. Hillsdale, NJ: Erlbaum

Scardamalia M, Bereiter C, Lamon M. 1994. The CSILE project: trying to bring the classroom into world 3. See McGilly 1994, 8:201–28

Schauble L. 1990. Belief revision in children: the role of prior knowledge and strategies for generating evidence. *J. Exp. Child. Psychol.* 49:31–57

Schauble L. 1996. The development of scientific reasoning in knowledge-rich contexts. *Dev. Psychol.* 32:102–19

Schifter D. 1996. *Reconstruction of Professional Identities.* New York: Teacher's College Press

Smagorinsky P, Fly P. 1993. The social environment of the classroom: a Vygotskian perspective on small group processes. *Commun. Educ.* 42:159–71

Snow RE, Swanson J. 1992. Instructional psychology: aptitude, adaptation, and assessment. *Annu. Rev. Psychol.* 43:583–626

Steele C. 1992. Race and the schooling of black Americans. *The Atlantic* 269:68–72

Stodolsky SS. 1988. *The Subject Matters: Classroom Activity in Math and Social Studies.* Chicago, IL: Univ. Chicago Press

Taylor J, Cox BD. 1997. Microgenetic analysis of group-based solution of complex two-step mathematical word problems by fourth graders. *J. Learn. Sci.* 6:183–226

Teasley S. 1995. The role of talk in children's peer collaborations. *Dev. Psychol.* 31: 207–20

Thorndike EL. 1906. *The Principles of Teaching, Based on Psychology.* New York: Seiler

Toulmin S. 1995. Forward. In *Rethinking Knowledge: Reflections Across the Disciplines,* ed. RF Goodman, WR Fisher, pp. ix–xv. Albany: State Univ. NY Press

Valsiner J. 1987. *Culture and the Development of Children's Action.* Cambridge, MA: Harvard Univ. Press

Voss JF, Wiley J, Carretero M. 1995. Acquiring intellectual skills. *Annu. Rev. Psychol.* 46:155–81

Vygotsky L. 1978. *Mind in Society: The Development of Higher Psychological Processes,* ed. M Cole, V John-Steiner, S Scribner, E Souberman. Cambridge, MA: Harvard Univ. Press

Vygotsky L. 1981. The instrumental method in psychology. In *The Concept of Activity in Soviet Psychology,* ed. J Wertsch, pp. 3–35. Armonk, NY: Sharpe.

Vygotsky L. 1986. (1934). *Thought and Language,* ed. A Kozulin. Cambridge, MA: MIT Press

Vygotksy L, Luria A. 1993. (1930). *Studies on the History of Behavior: Ape, Primitive, and Child.* Hillsdale, NJ: Erlbaum

Webb N, Farivar S. 1997. Developing productive group interaction in middle school mathematics. In *Cognitive Perspectives on Peer Learning,* ed. AM O'Donnell, A King. In press

Wertsch J. 1991. *Voices of the Mind: A Sociocultural Approach to Mediated Action.* Cambridge: Harvard Univ. Press

Wertsch J, Bivens J. 1992. The social origins of individual mental functioning: alternatives and perspectives. *Q. Newsl. Lab. Comput. Hum. Cogn.* 14:35–44

Wertsch J, Stone A. 1985. The concept of internalization in Vygotsky's account of the genesis of higher mental functions. In *Culture, Communication, and Cognition: Vygotskian Perspectives,* ed. J Wertsch, pp. 162–79. New York: Cambridge Univ. Press

*Annu. Rev. Psychol. 1998. 49:377–412*

# COMORBIDITY OF ANXIETY AND UNIPOLAR MOOD DISORDERS

## Susan Mineka

Department of Psychology, Northwestern University, Evanston, Illinois 60208;
e-mail: mineka@nwu.edu

## David Watson and Lee Anna Clark

Department of Psychology, The University of Iowa, Iowa City, Iowa 52242-1407

KEY WORDS: depression, anxiety, comorbidity

## ABSTRACT

Research on relationships between anxiety and depression has proceeded at a rapid pace since the 1980s. The similarities and differences between these two conditions, as well as many of the important features of the comorbidity of these disorders, are well understood. The genotypic structure of anxiety and depression is also fairly well documented. Generalized anxiety and major depression share a common genetic diathesis, but the anxiety disorders themselves are genetically hetergeneous. Sophisticated phenotypic models have also emerged, with data converging on an integrative hierarchical model of mood and anxiety disorders in which each individual syndrome contains both a common and a unique component. Finally, considerable progress has been made in understanding cognitive aspects of these disorders. This work has focused on both the cognitive content of anxiety and depression and on the effects that anxiety and depression have on information processing for mood-congruent material.

## CONTENTS

# MEANINGS AND IMPLICATIONS OF ANXIETY-DEPRESSION COMORBIDITY

## Background

Comorbidity is currently one of the "hot" topics in psychopathology research (Kendall & Clarkin 1992). According to Klerman (1990), a neo-Kraeplinian belief in the existence of discrete mental disorders clearly reemerged in the Third Edition of the *Diagnostic and Statistical Manual of Mental Disorders* (*DSM-III*) (American Psychiatric Association 1980), fueled in part by the success of research into diagnostic classification afforded by such developments as the Research Diagnostic Criteria (RDC) (Spitzer et al 1978). Consistent with this belief, the framers of *DSM-III* included extensive exclusionary criteria. However, criticism of these exclusionary rules soon followed on both conceptual and empirical grounds (First et al 1990), and they were largely eliminated in *DSM-III-R* (American Psychiatric Association 1987). Freed from these exclusionary rules, ensuing research documented extensive comorbidity across the entire spectrum of psychopathology (Clark et al 1995, Kendall & Clarkin 1992) and sparked numerous discussions on the meaning and implications of comorbidity in psychopathology.

With regard to anxiety and depression, the modern history of their classification (Clark 1989, Clark & Watson 1991a,b) and the surrounding controversies (Cole et al 1997, Feldman 1993, King et al 1991, Lonigan et al 1994) have been reviewed previously. Throughout the century, the anxiety and depressive disorders have been treated as separate diagnostic classes in official nosologies; many researchers have argued that these disorders are distinct entities (Akiskal 1985, Cox et al 1993). Nonetheless, other researchers have asserted that they represent a single underlying dimension, or that together they form a more general class of mood disorders (Feldman 1993, Hodges 1990). This latter, unitary construct, view has been particularly prominent in Europe where even the term "mood disorders" subsumes both anxiety and depression. In turn, the former, dual construct, view may reflect a more general tendency on the part of American psychiatry toward diagnostic "splitting" rather than "lumping" (Frances et al 1990).

In *DSM-III* exclusion rules limited co-diagnosis both within and across the anxiety and depressive disorders, but as mentioned, early research that ignored these exclusion rules revealed extensive comorbidity. Moreover, research based on the *DSM-III-R* and *DSM-IV* (American Psychiatric Association 1994), in which the exclusion rules were largely eliminated, documented that the anxiety and depressive disorders were among the most notable examples of overlapping disorders (Clark et al 1995). Ironically, insofar as this research is leading some researchers to argue that diagnostic splitting has gone too far and that certain disorders should be recollapsed into a single category, it may serve ultimately to justify the view of the *DSM-III* framers that certain coexisting syndromes actually reflect the same underlying disorder and should not be diagnosed separately.

More generally, researchers gradually have begun to realize that the controversy over the unitary versus dual models is both unnecessary and unproductive. These models increasingly are being replaced by a more nuanced view in which anxiety and depression are posited to have both shared, common components and specific, unique components (Clark & Watson 1991b). We discuss these developments in a subsequent section.

## The Meaning of Comorbidity: Current Controversies

The term *comorbidity* was coined in the context of chronic disease (Feinstein 1970) to refer to "any distinct additional clinical entity that has existed or that may occur during the clinical course of a patient who has the index disease under study" (pp. 456–57). Attempts to extend this definition of comorbidity to psychiatric disorder, however, quickly run into difficulties in delineating the concept of a "distinct clinical entity" (Lilienfeld et al 1994). If the presence of Disorder A significantly increases the likelihood of the occurrence of Disorder B, various reasons may explain this increased co-occurrence. Kaplan & Feinstein (1974) described several types of comorbidity in medical disorders in which the development of Disorder B was specifically related to the presence of Disorder A. For example, Disorder A may be a risk factor for B (prognostic comorbidity), or Disorder B may be a secondary complication of A (pathogenic comorbidity) (for discussions, see Lilienfeld et al 1994, Maser & Cloninger 1990a, Spitzer 1994). But what if Disorder A [(e.g. major depressive disorder (MDD)] is frequently comorbid not only with B [e.g. general anxiety disorder (GAD)] but also with Disorders C, D, E, F, G, and H (e.g. the other anxiety and mood disorders) and further, what if these disorders themselves substantially co-occur? Given these conditions, the concept of a distinct clinical entity is decidedly fuzzy; yet data from the National Comorbidity Survey (NCS) reveal precisely this pattern (e.g. Kessler 1997).

Discussions of this topic have been wide ranging. Frances et al (1990) present a series of methodological issues that affect determination of the degree of comorbidity. For example, they note that higher rates of comorbidity tend to be found in more recent studies using structured interviews. To discount the phenomenon of comorbidity based on this fact, however, would be to blame the messenger for the message. Another issue commonly raised is that the presence of the same symptom in two or more diagnoses (e.g. sleep disturbance in MDD and GAD] artifactually raises the co-occurrence of the disorders (e.g. Caron & Rutter 1991). A key word here is "artifactually." Certainly no one would argue that the presence of fever in the diagnosis of chicken pox and measles artifactually raises their co-occurrence, or that "headaches" should be removed from the list of symptoms of either brain tumors or concussions in order to improve differential diagnosis; nevertheless, similar arguments have been made for overlapping psychological symptoms, perhaps reflecting differential levels of knowledge about the etiology of medical versus mental disorders.

Excessive diagnostic splitting also has been noted as an artifactual "cause" of comorbidity, usually with regard to highly similar disorders (e.g. overanxious disorder and GAD in children; Caron & Rutter 1991). However, the separation of phenotypically diverse syndromes (e.g. MDD and GAD) into distinct categories may reflect the same phenomenon. Thus, the greatest challenge that the extensive comorbidity data pose to the current nosological system concerns the validity of the diagnostic categories themselves—do these disorders constitute distinct clinical entities? Even when one psychological syndrome temporally precedes another (e.g. GAD preceding MDD), the earlier syndrome may represent a prodromal manifestation of the latter.

Lilienfeld et al (1994) advocate avoiding the term "psychiatric comorbidity" because it implies greater knowledge about disorders than currently exists and will lead to reification of the *DSM* syndromes. Others, however, argue that the term is less important than the phenomena it reveals (Robins 1994). Certainly, the challenge is to make sense of surface-descriptive comorbidity data, and to recognize that more extensive information about underlying mechanisms and causal relationships is needed for this purpose (Frances et al 1990).

## *Impact of Comorbidity*

Numerous studies have documented the negative effects of anxiety-depression comorbidity on various aspects of psychopathology, such as course, chronicity, recovery and relapse rates (Brown et al 1996, Rief et al 1995; however, a few studies report no effects, e.g. Hoffart & Martinsen 1993), treatment seeking (Lewinsohn et al 1995, Sartorius et al 1996), and psychosocial functioning (Lewinsohn et al 1995, Reich et al 1993). Insofar as comorbidity rates tend to be substantially higher in individuals with more severe conditions (Kendall et al 1992, Kessler et al 1994), and severity of disorder is also a negative prognostic indicator (Keller et al 1992), it may be impossible at this stage of our knowledge to disentangle the issues of comorbidity and severity of disorder (Clark et al 1995). We next illustrate the negative impact of comorbidity involving anxiety and depression by reviewing evidence related to suicide potential.

SUICIDE POTENTIAL    Multiple studies in a range of settings have found increased rates of suicidal ideation, suicide attempts, and completed suicide in cases with comorbid anxiety and depression compared to those with a single disorder. In general, the risk of suicide is greater in patients with depression than any other single diagnosis (Wilson et al 1996) with the possible exception of substance abuse (Conwell 1996). However, the increased risk associated with comorbidity cannot be attributed simply to the presence of depression (Clark et al 1995). For instance, the co-presence of anxiety in patients with depression, or vice versa, increases the risk of suicide over the risk associated with pure depression (Bronisch & Wittchen 1994, Reich et al 1993). Moreover, the direction of causality is not simply from comorbidity to increased suicide risk: Newly abstinent substance abuse patients were more likely to develop a comorbid anxiety disorder if they had a history of suicidal ideation (Westermeyer et al 1995).

Increased rates of suicide attempts in individuals with comorbid depression and anxiety disorders have been reported in community samples (Angst 1993, Bronisch & Wittchen 1994, Lewinsohn et al 1995, Schneier et al 1992) as well as patient samples (Fawcett et al 1993, Reich et al 1993). Many studies have also examined comorbidity of anxiety and depression with other disorders and found increased suicide risk regardless of the comorbid disorder (e.g. personality disorder, Zisook et al 1994). Similarly, age does not appear to be a factor: Similar findings have been reported in children (Shafii et al 1988), adolescents (Lewinsohn et al 1995), and the elderly (Kunik 1993).

# SYMPTOM CO-OCCURRENCE AND DIAGNOSTIC COMORBIDITY

## Symptom Co-occurrence

The term "comorbidity" probably should be reserved to designate co-occurring disorders (or at least syndromes), but investigation of anxiety-depression comorbidity begins with the observation that key symptoms that define these theoretically distinct syndromes or disorders often co-occur. These symptoms can be divided into those that are unique to each type of disorder (e.g. panic attacks versus feelings of worthlessness) and those that are shared (e.g. difficulty concentrating). However, few of these symptoms clearly differentiate patients with one type of disorder versus the other (Clark 1989). When rated by clinicians, panic attacks, agoraphobic avoidance, and overall autonomic symptoms (but, surprisingly, not anxious mood) tend to be found more frequently in anxiety disorder patients, whereas depressed mood, anhedonia, psychomotor retardation, suicidal behavior, early-morning wakening, and pessimism (but not loss of libido, loss of appetite, feelings of worthlessness, or guilt) are generally found to be more frequent in depressed patients. However, when self-ratings are compared, depressed patients tend to report more symptoms of both types than do those with anxiety disorders (Clark 1989).

A similar picture is obtained at the syndromal level. The psychometric properties of measures assessing syndromal depression and anxiety are generally good in terms of convergent validity for both self- and clinician ratings, but the discriminant validity of self-ratings is poor in both adults (Clark & Watson 1991b) and children (Brady & Kendall 1992). Clinician ratings are notably more discriminating, suggesting that clinicians give more weight to factors that distinguish anxiety from depression than do patients. It is unclear, however, whether this represents (a) sensitivity to subtle cues that patients discount or are unaware of, or (b) rating biases on the part of clinicians. However, ratings of anxiety and depression in children by clinicians, teachers, and parents also show poor discrimination: Analyses of behavioral and observational rating scales typically yield a single anxiety-depression factor in children. It is unclear whether (a) the syndromes are less differentiated in children or (b) the scales used to assess them are less adequate than those available for use with adults (Brady & Kendall 1992).

## Diagnostic Comorbidity

ANXIETY AND DEPRESSION    As noted, lifetime diagnoses of anxiety and depression show extensive comorbidity. In Clark's (1989) meta-analysis, depressed patients had an overall rate of 57% for any anxiety disorder. The NCS found a remarkably similar 58% lifetime prevalence rate (Kessler et al 1996) and an only slightly lower (51.2%) 12-month prevalence rate. In general, the likelihood of a particular anxiety disorder co-occurring with depression mirrors the base-rate prevalence of the anxiety disorder (Kessler et al 1994). That is, social and simple phobias have both higher overall base rates and the highest rates of occurrence in depressed individuals, whereas panic disorder has the lowest rate in both cases. Nonetheless, the odds ratio (OR) in all cases far exceeds co-occurrence due simply to base rates (overall OR = 4.2; Kessler et al 1996). Moras et al (1996) reported a similar phenomenon but at notably lower levels for strictly defined *current* comorbidity across 10 studies.

As for depression comorbid with anxiety, the overall average is the same (e.g. 56% in Clark's 1989 meta-analysis), but with rates widely varying by diagnosis: 67% in panic/agoraphobia, 33% in *DSM-III* GAD, 20% in social and simple phobias. The rates obtained for *DSM-III-R* GAD are considerably higher, however, in both the NCS data (62.4% for MDD, 39.5% for dysthymia; Wittchen et al 1994) and the one study (73% MDD) reported in Clark (1989), which reflects the major changes in GAD criteria between the two versions. Again, Moras et al (1996) reported lower rates for *current* comorbidity of a mood disorder with a principal anxiety disorder (24%, ranging from 15% for simple phobia to 66% for obsessive-compulsive disorder). The various anxiety disorders are also highly comorbid with each other (Brown & Barlow 1992, Brown et al 1997), but anxiety disorders in the NCS were as—or more—comorbid with depression ($M$ OR = 6.6) as among themselves ($M$ OR = 6.2) (Kessler 1997).

The literature on children yields similar results. Angold & Costello's (1993) review reported that comorbidity with anxiety disorders was high, ranging from 30% to 75%. Data from adolescents (e.g. DB Clark et al 1994) and from other countries (King 1990) lead to similar conclusions.

*Anxiety and depression with other disorders*   Our focus is on the comorbidity between anxiety and depressive disorders, but these disorders also show extensive comorbidity with other types of psychopathology. For example, anxiety and/or depressive disorders have been found to be strongly comorbid with substance-use disorders (e.g. Kendler et al 1995, Kessler 1997, Mulder 1991, Westermeyer et al 1995, Wittchen et al 1994), hypochondriasis, somatization and other somatoform disorders (e.g. Rief et al 1995), eating disorders (Braun et al 1994, Castonguay et al 1995, Herpertz-Dahlmann et al 1996), conduct and attention deficit disorders (Angold & Costello 1993, Jensen et al 1993, Loeber & Keenan 1994, Milberger et al 1995), and personality disorder (Farmer & Nelson-Gray 1990, Flick et al 1993, Mulder 1991, Shea et al 1992). This sampling of published research includes both epidemiological and clinic-based studies; draws from populations of children, adolescents, adults, and the elderly; and focuses only on the major classes of disorders for which comorbidity with anxiety and depression have been studied. Throughout this review, therefore, it is important to keep in mind that the data focused on anxiety and depression represent but one piece of a puzzle.

# OTHER IMPORTANT FEATURES OF COMORBIDITY

In 1990, Alloy & Mineka and colleagues identified three "tentative" phenomena that any comprehensive theory of comorbidity in anxiety and depression should ideally be able to explain: (*a*) the sequential relationship between anxiety and depression, (*b*) the differential comorbidity of depression with various anxiety disorders, and (*c*) the relative infrequency of pure depression compared with pure anxiety (Alloy et al 1990). These phenomena were labeled "tentative" because knowledge about comorbidity was relatively sparse at that time. We now examine the current status of these phenomena.

## The Sequential Relationship of Anxiety and Depression Both Within and Across Episodes

The sequential relationship between anxiety and depression has been observed both within episodes and across the lifetime. Within a single episode of illness, anxiety symptoms are more likely to precede depressive symptoms than the reverse (Alloy et al 1990). Such observations stemmed initially from both human and nonhuman primate research examining infants' responses to separation and loss, where there is typically a biphasic response of protest followed by despair or depression (e.g. Bowlby 1973, Mineka & Suomi 1978). Bowlby (1980) later argued that this initial protest response is a prototype for anxiety in adults, whereas the despair response is a prototype for depression. He noted that adults show a similar pattern in response to loss, starting with a brief period of numbness and disbelief, followed by a phase of searching and yearning (cf intense anxiety), and then often by a phase of disorganization and despair (cf severe depression). The experimental literature on response to uncontrollable aversive events also suggests that anxiety symptoms are much more likely to precede depressive symptoms than vice versa (Alloy et al 1990).

Regarding lifetime comorbidity, Alloy et al (1990) also reviewed evidence that an anxiety disorder is significantly more likely to precede a mood disorder than the reverse. This phenomenon is now well established. For example, in the International WHO/ADAMHA CIDI field trials, of the 242 individuals with comorbid anxiety and mood disorders, 59% had had the onset of the first anxiety disorder at least a year before the onset of the first mood disorder, only 15% had experienced the onset of a mood disorder before the onset of the first anxiety disorder, and another 26% experienced the onset of both within the same year (Lepine et al 1993).

Similarly, in the NCS data, Kessler et al (1997) found that all the anxiety disorder diagnoses are associated with an elevated risk of a later diagnosis of minor or major depression. The ORs were especially high for severe major depression (7–9 symptoms), ranging from 2.86 for social phobia to 12.87 for GAD. Kessler (1997) also reported that anxiety disorders were more likely to be temporally primary. For example, nearly 83% of patients with one or more lifetime anxiety disorders reported that one of these was their first disorder; in contrast, only about 44% of those with a mood disorder reported that it was their first disorder. In fact, most cases (roughly 62%) of lifetime major depression are secondary to other *DSM-III-R* disorder(s), with anxiety disorders being the most common primary conditions (about 68% of cases with secondary depression are associated with a temporally primary anxiety disorder) (Kessler et al 1996). The elevated risk of depression in those with a temporally primary anxiety disorder endures for many years without changing in magnitude.

Similarly, recent reanalyses of the ECA study (approximately 18,000 adults) indicated that of the participants with comorbid depression and social phobia, the latter was temporally primary for nearly 71% (Schneier et al 1992). Lewinsohn et al (1997) reported similar findings in a study of over 10,000 high school students. Finally, Kovacs et al (1989) reported that anxiety tends to precede depression in children (reviewed in Brady & Kendall 1992).

## The Differential Comorbidity Between Depression and Different Anxiety Disorders

Alloy et al's (1990) early review also suggested that individuals who received the diagnoses of panic disorder, agoraphobia, obsessive-compulsive disorder, and post-traumatic stress disorder were more likely to experience depression than were those with generalized anxiety disorder, social phobia, or simple phobia. The NCS data generally confirmed this conclusion through the use of OR that take into account the large base-rate differences for the different disorders (Kessler et al 1996). Specifically, lifetime comorbidity data for major depression revealed OR of 2.9 for social phobia, 3.1 for simple phobia, 3.4 for agoraphobia, 4.0 for panic disorder and post-traumatic stress disorder, and 6.0 for GAD (results for obsessive-compulsive disorder are not presented). Thus, the one exception to the pattern observed by Alloy et al (1990) was that GAD was the anxiety disorder *most* likely to co-occur with MDD. Lepine et al (1993) also largely replicated these results, except that social phobia was nearly as highly associated with MDD as were agoraphobia and panic disorder. Finally, Brown & Barlow (1992) reported results from a clinical sample in which obsessive-compulsive disorder and severe agoraphobia were most highly associated with MDD and dysthymia, whereas simple phobia was least associated, and social phobia and GAD were intermediate.

Thus, results seem to confirm that obsessive-compulsive disorder, panic disorder and agoraphobia, and post-traumatic stress disorder are highly associated with MDD and that simple phobia is either less or not associated with it. The results for social phobia and GAD are less consistent, with more recent data suggesting a significantly stronger association with depression. The inconsistent results for GAD likely reflect the major changes in diagnostic criteria made between *DSM-III* and *DSM-III-R*.

## The Relative Infrequency of Pure Depression

Alloy et al (1990) also summarized evidence that cases of pure depression without concomitant anxiety were rarer than cases of pure anxiety without concomitant depression. This pattern can be observed at the purely symptomatic level: Individuals with a diagnosis of MDD typically show levels of anxiety on self-report or clinical rating scales that are as high as—or higher than—those of patients with a diagnosis of GAD or panic disorder (e.g. DiNardo & Barlow 1990). It also occurs at the diagnostic level: The likelihood that someone with a mood disorder also will receive an anxiety-disorder diagnosis (either concurrently or subsequently) appears to be greater than the reverse. In the ECA study, 43% of individuals with a mood disorder also received an anxiety diagnosis at some time in their lives, whereas only 25% of those with an anxiety disorder also received a lifetime mood disorder diagnosis (Regier et al 1990). In the NCS data, 58% of those with a lifetime diagnosis of a depressive disorder also had an anxiety disorder (Kessler et al 1996). Finally, in eight of the nine studies of children and adolescents reviewed by Angold & Costello (1993), the rates of mood disorder in those with an anxiety disorder were substantially lower than vice versa.

## Theoretical Perspectives on These Important Features of Comorbidity

THE HELPLESSNESS/HOPELESSNESS PERSPECTIVE    Alloy, Mineka, and colleagues proposed a helplessness/hopelessness perspective to clarify these important features of anxiety-depression comorbidity (Alloy et al 1990, see also Garber et al 1980). Their model integrates Abramson et al's (1989) hopelessness theory of depression with extensive research documenting the importance of perceived uncontrollability in the etiology of anxiety (e.g. Barlow 1988, Barlow et al 1996, Mineka 1985, Mineka & Kelly 1989, Mineka & Zinbarg 1996). Uncontrollable, stressful life events were originally implicated as playing a central etiological role in depression (e.g. Seligman 1974). However, later reformulations of the helplessness theory of depression deemphasized uncontrollability per se and focused on the central role that key cognitive variables play in determining vulnerability to depression following negative life events (Abramson et al 1978). In a later reformulation, expectations of hopelessness were hypothesized to serve as proximal and sufficient causal factors for the onset of depression (Abramson et al 1989). Concurrently, anxiety researchers—based in large part on animal research—were recognizing the central role that perceptions of uncontrollability play in creating vulnerability to anxiety as well as depression (e.g. Barlow 1988, Mineka 1985, Mineka & Kelly 1989).

Alloy et al (1990) proposed that the interplay of three cognitive components of helplessness and hopelessness may determine, at least in part, whether a person experiences pure anxiety, a mixed anxiety-depression syndrome, or hopelessness depression. Specifically, they proposed that the interplay of helplessness expectancies, negative-outcome expectancies, and the certainty of these expectancies influences which of these states will be experienced. Individuals uncertain about their ability to control important outcomes would be most likely to experience pure anxiety. In contrast, those who are more certain about their helplessness—but still uncertain about whether a negative outcome will actually occur—will experience a mixed anxiety-depressive state. Finally, individuals who are certain of both their helplessness and the occurrence of a negative outcome will experience hopelessness depression, characterized by despair, loss of interest, and suicidality. Thus, anxiety and depression share expectations of helplessness but differ in negative-outcome expectancies (see also Garber et al 1980). Numerous other theorists have also argued that anxiety is characterized by helplessness (e.g. Beck & Emery 1985, Mandler 1972), whereas depression is centered on hopelessness (e.g. Beck 1967, Brown & Harris 1978).

Alloy et al (1990) argued that this perspective is useful in accounting for the three important features of comorbidity discussed. The sequential relationship between anxiety and depressive symptoms is explained by noting that expectancies of helplessness (certain or uncertain) are likely to precede the development of certain negative-outcome expectancies when efforts to exert control may all fail. The across-episode sequential relationship between anxiety and depression may occur because prior experiences with uncertain helplessness (and anxiety) may increase one's vulnerability to more certain helplessness and even hopelessness (and hopelessness depression) in the face of future severe stressors, perhaps especially when an individual has a pessimistic attributional style (i.e. attributing negative outcomes to stable and global causes). This perspective is also consistent with findings that anxiety is associated with anticipated threat or danger, whereas depression is often preceded by a major loss event (e.g. Brown et al 1993, Monroe 1990). Loss events are more likely to lead to hopelessness and depression given that a bad outcome has occurred; threat events have an inherent uncertainty and are more likely to lead to a sense of helplessness and therefore anxiety.

Regarding the differential comorbidity of depression with the different anxiety disorders, Alloy et al (1990) hypothesized that those anxiety disorders characterized by more chronic and pervasive feelings of helplessness would show higher rates of comorbidity with depression. They therefore argued that panic disorder and agoraphobia, obsessive-compulsive disorder, and post-traumatic stress disorder should show a particularly strong degree of overlap with depression, which has been supported by more recent evidence. Alloy et al further argued that the more pervasive feelings of helplessness associated with these disorders might stem, in part, from the intrusive and terrifying nature of many of their symptoms (e.g. panic attacks, obsessions, compulsions, flashbacks, nightmares, etc). To the extent that such symptoms are perceived as uncontrollable, over prolonged periods a state of certain helplessness would be expected to emerge, which would then lead to depression. Individuals with a pessimistic attributional style who have these anxiety disorders (Heimberg et al 1989, Mineka et al 1995) may be particularly prone to developing depression in response to the experience of uncontrollable anxiety symptoms.

Social phobia and simple phobia, by contrast, should be expected to be associated with a more circumscribed sense of helplessness, perhaps accounting for the lower rates of comorbidity of these disorders with depression. Individuals with generalized social phobia, as opposed to specific social phobia, should show higher levels of depression given that their lives are far more restricted in terms of the social situations they fear and avoid. Holt et al (1992) and Turner et al (1992) both reported such findings.

However, Alloy et al (1990) did not predict the recent findings of high rates of comorbidity between GAD and MDD, given that chronic worry and other generalized anxiety symptoms would not generally be expected to lead to as pervasive a sense of uncontrollability as would panic disorder, obsessive-compulsive disorder, and post-traumatic stress disorder. However, below we review evidence for a common genetic diathesis for GAD and MDD that may be the important key to this relationship rather than any factor posited by Alloy et al's perspective.

Finally, the relative infrequency of pure depression is explained by the observation that the cognition of hopelessness is a subset of helplessness cognitions. That is, people who are hopeless also perceive that they are helpless but the reverse is not necessarily true. This could account for why pure anxiety is much more likely to be observed than is pure depression.

BOWLBY'S ATTACHMENT-OBJECT LOSS THEORY   Bowlby wrote extensively about the relationship between anxiety and depression from the vantage point of attachment theory (1973, 1980) and later incorporated ideas from cognitive psychology into his perspective (1980). Attachment theory views attachment behavior in evolutionary/functional terms, with a young infant's attachment behavior serving to create a secure base from which to explore the environment. When separation from the attachment object occurs, a biphasic protest-despair response occurs. Early experiences with separation and loss (as well as the nature of the attachment relationships per se) are postulated to have major effects on adult attachment relationships as well as on response to adulthood stressors. The effects of these early experiences are thought to be mediated through the development of cognitive schemata that later affect an adult's response to disruptions in attachment relationships.

Bowlby's perspective can explain various aspects of comorbidity. First, the sequential relationship between anxiety and depressive symptoms (within episode) is explicitly predicted; indeed, his observations of children and adults in response to separation and loss are key findings documenting this phenomenon (Bowlby 1973). Second, pure depression is infrequent because people first become anxious about the threat of a loss (or as an initial response to an actual loss); however, if the loss does not occur, or does not persist, or if a substitute attachment occurs, then depression may never occur. In this regard, the importance of social support in buffering against depression in the face of major life stressors has received considerable support in the literature (e.g. Brown et al 1993). Bowlby (1980) also noted, however, that once the depression phase occurs, it is usually interspersed with phases of anxiety and longing for the lost attachment object (mixed anxiety-depression). Finally, Bowlby's perspective (1973, 1980) explicitly predicts the high levels of comorbidity between panic disorder/agoraphobia and depression, in that disordered attachment relationships (early in life and/or in adulthood) play a central role in both conditions, and both are often precipitated by a major loss.

## STRUCTURAL MODELS OF ANXIETY AND DEPRESSION

As mentioned, the unitary versus dual construct debate has gradually given way to more sophisticated views of the anxiety-depression relationship. Investigators have used a variety of multivariate techniques to isolate common and unique features of the two constructs and have developed structural models to conceptualize the findings that emerged. We now review the evolution of structural models at both the genotypic and phenotypic levels.

### The Genotypic Structure of Depression and Anxiety

SYMPTOM LEVEL ANALYSES   Beginning in the 1980s, numerous studies have examined the genetic links between anxiety and depression, primarily investigating whether a common genetic diathesis renders certain individuals vulnerable to the development of both types of disorder. The first major analysis investigated self-reported anxious and depressive symptoms in a large, community-based sample of Australian twins (Jardine et al 1984). These analyses indicated that the observed phenotypic covariation between the two types of symptoms was largely due to a single common genetic factor (see also Kendler et al 1987). Moreover, this same genetic factor was shared with neuroticism, a broad personality trait that reflects individual differences in subjective distress and dissatisfaction (see Kendler et al 1993a, Watson et al 1994). Thus, anxiety, depression, and neuroticism could be linked to a single genetic diathesis that apparently represents an underlying vulnerability to subjective distress and negative affectivity.

Subsequent analyses of these same data, however, revealed that symptoms of a panic attack (e.g. breathlessness or heart pounding) reflected unique genetic variance that differentiated them from other symptoms of depression and anxiety (Kendler et al 1987) and from neuroticism (Martin et al 1988). Thus, these symptom-level data revealed an important distinction between the cognitive/affective versus somatic symptoms of anxiety, with the former being more closely related to depression and neuroticism than the latter.

DIAGNOSTIC ANALYSES    More recently, a number of genetic studies have examined the issue at the diagnostic level and again have revealed evidence of both commonality and specificity, with the level of overlap varying systematically across the individual anxiety disorders. At one extreme, analyses consistently have found that major depression and GAD are genetically indistinguishable; that is, the genetic correlation between these disorders is essentially unity, indicating that they reflect a single, common genetic diathesis (Kendler 1996, Kendler et al 1992, Roy et al 1995). Moreover, replicating results at the symptom level, Kendler et al (1993a) found that this common genetic diathesis was also strongly linked to neuroticism, suggesting that this shared genetic factor represents a general tendency to respond poorly to stress and, therefore, to experience frequent and intense episodes of distress and negative affect (Kendler et al 1992, 1995).

In contrast, anxiety disorders other than GAD are more modestly related to depression. Panic disorder, for example, is genetically distinguishable from both GAD and depression (Kendler 1996, Kendler et al 1995, Woodman 1993), a finding that replicates the symptom-level results. Similarly, Kendler et al (1993b) found that major depression shared a moderate amount of genetic variance with agoraphobia, social phobia, and animal phobia but was genetically unrelated to situational phobias (e.g. fears of tunnels, bridges, heights). Other evidence indicates that obsessive-compulsive disorder is genetically distinct from major depression, GAD, panic, and the phobias (Pauls et al 1994); in fact, unlike these other syndromes, obsessive-compulsive disorder appears to have a strong genetic link to Tourette's syndrome (Pauls 1992, Pauls et al 1995).

To date, Kendler et al (1995) have reported the most comprehensive analysis of the genetic architecture of depression and the anxiety disorders, examining the associations among major depression, GAD, panic, and the phobias. They found evidence of two significant genetic factors. One factor was primarily defined by major depression and GAD (loadings of .64 and .47, respectively); panic disorder also had a moderate loading (.35) on this factor, but the phobias were largely unrelated to it (a loading of only .14). In contrast, the second factor was defined primarily by panic disorder and the phobias (loadings of .58 and .57, respectively).

SUMMARY AND IMPLICATIONS    The genetic evidence has important implications for our understanding of the mood and anxiety disorders. First, it is clear that the anxiety disorders themselves are genetically heterogeneous (Kendler 1996, Kendler et al 1995). Thus, one cannot posit a single invariant relation between depression and the anxiety disorders; rather, the nature of the relation necessarily will depend on the type of anxiety that is examined. Consistent with this view, the accumulating data indicate that depression is genetically indistinguishable from GAD, moderately related to panic, and more modestly related to the phobias (which are themselves heterogeneous) (Kendler et al 1993b, 1995). In addition, major depression and GAD both are closely linked to the broad personality trait of neuroticism (LA Clark et al 1994, Jardine et al 1984, Kendler et al 1993a). Taken together, these data suggest that the observed covariation between depression and anxiety is largely attributable to a shared genetic factor that reflects general individual differences in subjective distress and negative affectivity. However, the precise nature of this shared genetic factor remains unclear (for discussions, see Carey & DiLalla 1994, Neale & Kendler 1995, Roy et al 1995).

Finally, these data have potentially important implications for the classification of these disorders within the *DSM*, in that they indicate that GAD is more closely linked to major depression than to the other anxiety disorders (Kendler et al 1995). It is noteworthy, moreover, that comorbidity and structural-modeling data demonstrate this same pattern at the phenotypic level (Brown et al 1995, 1997). Therefore, maximum clarity in this area might be achieved by rearranging the mood and anxiety disorders to place greater emphasis on the close affinity between distress-based disorders such as major depression and GAD.

## The Phenotypic Structure of Depression and Anxiety

TWO-FACTOR AFFECTIVE MODEL    Paralleling the genetic data, phenotypic models increasingly have emphasized that depression and anxiety are characterized by both common and distinctive features. An early example of this approach was a two-factor model based on the seminal work of Tellegen (1985) that emphasized the role of basic dimensions of affect. Extensive research has demonstrated that affective experience is characterized by two general factors:

Negative Affect and Positive Affect (Tellegen 1985, Watson & Clark 1997, Watson & Tellegen 1985). Negative Affect reflects the extent to which a person is experiencing negative mood states such as fear, sadness, anger, and guilt, whereas Positive Affect reflects the extent to which one reports positive feelings such as joy, enthusiasm, energy, and alertness.

These two general dimensions are differentially related to depression and anxiety. Specifically, depression and anxiety both are strongly related to measures of general Negative Affect. In contrast, measures of Positive Affect are consistently negatively correlated with depressed mood and symptomatology but are largely unrelated to anxious mood and symptomatology (Dyck et al 1994, Jolly et al 1994, Tellegen 1985, Watson et al 1988). Thus, in this two-factor model Negative Affect represents a *nonspecific* factor common to depression and anxiety, whereas Positive Affect is a *specific* factor that is related primarily to depression.

TRIPARTITE MODEL    Clark & Watson (1991b) extended this model by proposing a second specific factor—physiological hyperarousal—that is relatively specific to anxiety. They therefore argued that a "tripartite model" offered a more accurate characterization of anxious and depressive phenomena. In this model, symptoms of depression and anxiety can be grouped into three basic subtypes. First, many symptoms are strong indicators of a general distress or Negative Affect factor. This nonspecific group includes both anxious and depressed mood, as well as other symptoms (insomnia, poor concentration, etc) that are prevalent in both types of disorder. However, each syndrome also is characterized by its own cluster of symptoms: somatic tension and hyperarousal (e.g. shortness of breath, dizziness and lightheadedness, dry mouth) are relatively specific to anxiety, whereas manifestations of anhedonia and the absence of Positive Affect (e.g. loss of interest, feeling that nothing is interesting or enjoyable) are relatively specific to depression.

BARLOW'S THREE-FACTOR MODEL    Recently, Barlow and his colleagues have articulated a very similar three-factor model (Barlow et al 1996, Chorpita et al 1997). This model emphasizes that the mood and anxiety disorders are fundamentally disorders of emotion (Barlow 1988, 1991) and so relates these disorders to processes associated with the three basic emotions of anxiety (or "anxious apprehension"), fear, and depression. At the symptom level, Barlow and colleagues argue that (*a*) general distress and Negative Affect are manifestations of *anxiety* (anxious apprehension), (*b*) autonomic arousal is an expression of *fear/panic*, and (*c*) anhedonia, low Positive Affect, and hopelessness are indicators of *depression*. Paralleling the tripartite model of Clark & Watson (1991b), autonomic arousal and anhedonia/low Positive Affect are viewed as unique symptom clusters that are relatively specific to the anxiety and mood disorders, respectively, whereas general distress and Negative Affect are relatively nonspecific symptoms that are strongly characteristic of both types of disorder.

TESTS OF THE THREE-FACTOR MODELS   The formulation of these three-factor models has stimulated a new wave of research into the phenotypic structure of anxious and depressive symptoms. Several early studies subjected existing psychometric instruments to traditional exploratory factor analyses. Consistent with the tripartite model, these studies found clear evidence of three factors: a specific anxiety factor, a specific depression factor, and a general factor that subsumed both types of phenomena (DA Clark et al 1990, Jolly & Dykman 1994, Jolly & Kramer 1994).

One limitation of these studies is that they relied on measures that were laden with items assessing general distress/Negative Affect, and that covered the two hypothesized specific symptom groups (i.e. somatic hyperarousal and anhedonia/low Positive Affect) less satisfactorily. This meant that the nonspecific factor tended to be quite large relative to the two specific factors; moreover, the paucity of good hyperarousal and/or anhedonia items (particularly the latter) made it difficult to identify specific factors that closely matched the predictions generated by the three-factor models. Nevertheless, several investigators obtained structures that offered strong support for these models (DA Clark et al 1994; Steer et al 1994, 1995), with the exception that the third somatic factor was sometimes broader than expected (Dyck et al 1994).

To address these measure-based limitations, Watson & Clark (1991) created the Mood and Anxiety Symptom Questionnaire (MASQ). Watson et al (1995b) tested the prediction that symptoms of somatic arousal and anhedonia offer the best differentiation of anxiety and depression using two specific scales—Anhedonic Depression and Anxious Arousal—composed of items assessing anhedonia/low Positive Affect and somatic arousal, respectively. Consistent with the tripartite model, these specific scales provided the best differentiation of the constructs in each of five samples, with correlations ranging from .25 to .49 ($M = .34$). In contrast, measures of anxious and depressed mood—which, according to the tripartite model, should demonstrate much poorer specificity—consistently showed a much higher level of overlap, with correlations ranging from .61 to .78 ($M = .69$).

Watson et al (1995a) subjected the 90 MASQ items to separate factor analyses in each of five samples (three student, one adult, one patient). Consistent with the model, three large and replicable dimensions could be identified: a nonspecific general distress factor, a bipolar dimension of positive mood versus anhedonia, and a factor defined largely by somatic manifestations of anxiety. However, the specific anxiety factor was somewhat broader than expected and included several somatic symptoms that do not clearly reflect sympathetic arousal (e.g. nausea, diarrhea). Consequently, this third factor is better characterized as "somatic anxiety" rather than the hypothesized dimension of "anxious arousal." Importantly, the same three factors emerged in each of the five data sets, indicating that symptom structure in this domain is reasonably robust across diverse samples.

Several recent studies have broadened the empirical support for the tripartite model in notable ways. For instance, Joiner et al (1996) showed that the three hypothesized factors emerged in a sample of child and adolescent psychiatric inpatients, thereby extending the model to younger respondents. Joiner (1996) explicitly tested the viability of the model in college students using confirmatory factor analysis; he found that the hypothesized three-factor structure provided a good fit to the observed data, whereas one- and two-factor structures did not. Chorpita et al (1997) replicated and extended these findings in a clinical sample of children and adolescents, conducting confirmatory factor analyses on both self- and parent ratings; again, the hypothesized three-factor model best fit the data. Similarly, Brown et al (1997) reported evidence supporting the tripartite model in LISREL analyses using both self-report and interview-based data.

Psychophysiological analyses offer further support for the tripartite model by demonstrating that the three hypothesized symptom groups reflect highly distinctive patterns of brain activity. Specifically, individuals reporting elevated levels of general Negative Affect consistently show augmented base startle reactivity (Cook et al 1991, Lang et al 1993); this exaggerated basal startle response is thought to be mediated by the bed nucleus of the stria terminalis (Cuthbert et al 1996, Davis et al 1997) and can be distinguished from the cue-based reactivity characteristic of phobics (Cuthbert & Melamed 1993, McNeil et al 1993), which appears to be mediated by the base nucleus of the amygdala (Cuthbert et al 1996, Davis et al 1997). Other evidence has linked heightened levels of Negative Affect to increased activity in the right frontal cortex (Bruder et al 1997, Tomarken & Keener 1997).

The two hypothesized specific factors—anhedonia and anxious arousal—show markedly different patterns of psychophysiological activity. Anxious arousal consistently has been linked to *hyper*activation of the right parietotemporal region; in sharp contrast, anhedonia and low Positive Affect are associated with *hypo*activation of this same region (Bruder et al 1997, Heller 1993, Heller et al 1995), as well as hypoactivation of the left prefrontal area (Larsen et al 1995, Tomarken & Keener 1997). It is noteworthy that formerly depressed patients who were currently euthymic also showed left frontal hypoactivation (Henriques & Davidson 1990, see also Allen et al 1993), as did asymptomatic adolescent children of depressed mothers (Tomarken & Keener 1997).

On the basis of these data, Davidson, Tomarken, and their colleagues have argued that left frontal hypoactivation reflects a characterological deficit in a reward-oriented approach system that clinically manifests itself as a loss of interest and motivation (i.e. anhedonia; see Henriques & Davidson 1991, Tomarken et al 1992, Tomarken & Keener 1997). Further evidence links this frontal asymmetry to activity in the mesolimbic dopaminergic system, which also has been related to individual differences in positive emotionality versus anhedonia (Depue et al 1994, Tomarken & Keener 1997).

CLARIFYING THE RELATION AMONG THE THREE FACTORS   Although an impressive array of evidence demonstrates the existence of three separable factors, the nature of the relations among these factors remains an unresolved and somewhat controversial issue. Investigators in some of the earlier studies extracted highly correlated lower order factors corresponding to depression and anxiety, which then gave rise to a second order dimension of general distress or Negative Affect (e.g. DA Clark et al 1994, Steer et al 1995). These results suggest a hierarchical three-factor model in which the traditional syndromes of anxiety and depression represent narrow, lower order constructs that are highly interrelated; in this hierarchical model, the Negative Affect dimension emerges as a broader, more general construct that represents the strong degree of overlap between the lower order syndromes. In other studies, however, general distress, anhedonia/low Positive Affect, and somatic arousal have emerged as three separable first order factors. In some analyses, the somatic anxiety and Negative Affect factors are moderately to strongly interrelated (e.g. Brown et al 1997, Chorpita et al 1997, Joiner 1996), but in other cases all three factors are largely independent of one another (Joiner et al 1996, Watson et al 1995b). These data suggest a nonhierarchical model in which the three hypothesized symptom factors exist at the same basic level of generality.

To a considerable extent, these apparently inconsistent findings reflect the types of variables that were included in these structural analyses. That is, studies using traditional assessment instruments, instruments laden with items tapping general Negative Affect have tended to support a hierarchical model with a dominant higher order factor. In contrast, analyses using carefully selected items that are explicitly linked to the tripartite model have yielded greater support for a nonhierarchical arrangement (see Joiner 1996, Joiner et al 1996). Still, these factors alone cannot account for all of the reported inconsistencies, and further investigations of this issue (e.g. using techniques such as LISREL) are needed. To date, Brown et al (1997) reported the most compelling analysis. They tested various alternative structural models and found evidence of two higher order factors; one of these (Positive Affect) was specifically related to depression, whereas the other (Negative Affect) was nonspecific. The third component of the tripartite model—anxious arousal—emerged as a specific lower order factor.

## An Integrative Hierarchical Model of Anxiety and Depression

HETEROGENEITY OF THE ANXIETY DISORDERS    It has become increasingly apparent that at both the genotypic and phenotypic levels, the anxiety disorders are heterogeneous and subsume a diverse array of symptoms (Brown et al 1997, Kendler 1996, Kendler et al 1995, Zinbarg & Barlow 1996). This heterogeneity has important implications for structural models. First, as reviewed earlier, the individual anxiety disorders clearly are differentially related to depression, with certain types of anxiety showing much greater overlap than others. Second, the individual anxiety disorders are differentially related to one another; for example, panic disorder is much more highly related to GAD than to obsessive-compulsive disorder (Brown et al 1997). Third, it is increasingly clear that a single specific factor—such as the anxious arousal or somatic anxiety component of the tripartite model—is insufficient to account fully for the diversity of symptoms subsumed by the anxiety disorders.

BARLOW'S HIERARCHICAL MODEL OF THE ANXIETY DISORDERS    To address this last problem, Barlow and colleagues have proposed a hierarchical model of the anxiety disorders (Barlow 1991, Brown & Barlow 1992, Zinbarg & Barlow 1996). They assert that each of the individual anxiety disorders contains a shared component that represents the higher order factor in a two-level hierarchical scheme. In earlier treatments of the model, this higher order factor usually was described as "anxious apprehension" (e.g. Barlow 1991, Brown & Barlow 1992); in more recent papers, however, Barlow and colleagues have acknowledged that it essentially represents the general Negative Affect component of the tripartite model (Brown et al 1997, Zinbarg & Barlow 1996). Accordingly, this higher order factor not only is common across the anxiety disorders but is shared with depression; therefore, it primarily is responsible for the observed overlap both among the individual anxiety disorders and between depression and anxiety. In addition to this shared component, however, each of the anxiety disorders also contains a specific, unique component that distinguishes it from all the others (for a parallel analysis of the childhood anxiety disorders, see Spence 1997).

Several recent structural analyses, which use both self-report and interview-based data, have yielded strong support for this hierarchical view (Brown et al 1997, Spence 1997, Zinbarg & Barlow 1996). The results of Brown et al (1997) are especially noteworthy: They found that the anxious arousal component of the tripartite model was not generally characteristic of the anxiety disorders but instead represented the specific, unique component of panic disorder.

AN INTEGRATIVE HIERARCHICAL MODEL OF ANXIETY AND DEPRESSION    We suggest that a more accurate and comprehensive structural model, one that is consistent with both the genotypic and phenotypic data, is one that integrates key features of Clark & Watson's (1991b) tripartite model with Barlow's (1991, Zinbarg & Barlow 1996) hierarchical model of the anxiety disorders. In this integrative, hierarchical model, each individual syndrome can be viewed as containing both a common and a unique component. The shared component represents broad individual differences in general distress and Negative Affect; it is a pervasive higher order factor that is common to both the mood and anxiety disorders and is primarily responsible for the overlap among these disorders. In addition, each disorder also includes a unique component that differentiates it from all the others. For instance, anhedonia, disinterest, and the absence of Positive Affect comprise the specific, unique component of depression.

Thus far, all of these propositions are fully consistent with the original tripartite model. The major change, which is necessitated by the marked heterogeneity of the anxiety disorders, is that anxious arousal no longer is viewed as broadly characteristic of all anxiety disorders; rather, it assumes a more limited role as the specific component of panic disorder (see Brown et al 1997). Note that each of the other anxiety disorders—with the possible exception of GAD, which clearly contains an enormous amount of general distress variance (e.g. Brown & Barlow 1992, Brown et al 1997)—includes its own unique component that is differentiable from anxious arousal. An important task for future research is to specify the nature of these unique components more precisely. In this regard, Brown et al (1997) have demonstrated that one obtains a clearer and more accurate view of these specific components after the influence of the general Negative Affect factor is eliminated.

Both the scope and the precision of this integrative model can be enhanced with three additional considerations. First, the size of the general and specific components differs markedly across the various anxiety disorders. For example, the genetic and phenotypic data both establish that depression and GAD are distress-based disorders containing an enormous amount of variance attributable to general Negative Affect; in contrast, obsessive-compulsive disorder, social phobia, and specific phobia all appear to contain a more modest component of general distress (e.g. Brown et al 1997, Kendler 1996, Kendler et al 1995). Thus, future research must move beyond the simple truism that each disorder is characterized by both a common and a unique component and specify the proportions of general and specific variance that are characteristic of each syndrome.

Second, it now is obvious that this general Negative Affect dimension is not confined solely to the mood and anxiety disorders, but is even more broadly related to psychopathology (e.g. Hinden et al 1997). Significant elevations in Negative Affectivity and neuroticism have been reported in a wide array of syndromes, including substance use disorders, somatoform disorders, eating disorders, personality and conduct disorders, and schizophrenia (e.g. Krueger et al 1996, Trull & Sher 1994, Watson & Clark 1994). Indeed, Widiger & Costa (1994) recently concluded that "neuroticism is an almost ubiquitously elevated trait within clinical populations" (p. 81). Thus, this integrative model clearly need not be confined to the mood and anxiety disorders, and we encourage future investigators to expand its scope to include a broad range of associated phenomena, such as the personality and somatoform disorders.

Third, symptom specificity must be viewed in relative rather than absolute terms. It is highly unlikely that any group of symptoms will be found to be unique to a single disorder across the entire *DSM*, if for no other reason than that the current taxonomic system contains many problematic diagnoses with overlapping symptoms and unclear boundaries (see Clark et al 1995). Moreover, it is clear that symptoms do not conform neatly to existing diagnostic categories but instead tend to characterize clusters of related disorders. For instance, anhedonia and low Positive Affect are not confined solely to depression, but also characterize—to a lesser degree, perhaps—schizophrenia, social phobia, and other disorders (e.g. Brown et al 1997, Watson & Clark 1995, Watson et al 1988). This suggests that we need to move toward more complex, multilevel hierarchical models in which groups of symptoms are classified at varying levels of specificity. Furthermore, it may be best to view individual disorders as representing unique *combinations* of different types of symptoms, with each type showing varying degrees of nonspecificity and with no type being entirely unique to any single disorder.

## COGNITIVE APPROACHES TO ANXIETY AND DEPRESSION

### Beck's Cognitive-Content Specificity Approach

In 1976, Beck expanded his cognitive model of depression into a more general model of psychopathology, focusing especially on similarities and differences between the anxiety and mood disorders. The theory holds that these disorders are characterized by specific kinds of cognitions (Beck 1976, Beck & Emery 1985). The automatic thoughts of depressed people tend to focus on themes of self-depreciation and negative attitudes about the world and the future and are fueled by underlying depressogenic schemas that are organized around themes of loss, personal deficiency, worthlessness, and hopelessness. By contrast, the automatic thoughts of anxious individuals are focused on anticipated future harm or danger and are fueled by schemas organized around themes of danger, uncertainty, and future threat.

Several studies have provided important tests of this cognitive-content specificity approach, as well as of its relationship to the tripartite model of anxiety and depression discussed earlier. An initial test of the theory (Beck et al 1987) involved the development of a Cognition Checklist (CCL) that measured automatic thoughts considered to be relevant to depression (e.g. "I'm worthless," "I don't deserve to be loved") and anxiety (e.g. "I might be trapped," "I am going to have an accident"). The CCL was administered to outpatients at the Center for Cognitive Therapy, together with the Hamilton Rating Scales and structured diagnostic interviews. As predicted, depressed patients had higher scores on the CCL-Depression scale, whereas anxious patients scored more highly on the CCL-Anxiety scale. Moreover, the CCL-Depression scale was significantly correlated with the Hamilton Depression scale, even when controlling for anxiety, and vice versa for the CCL-Anxiety scale.

DA Clark et al (1990) subsequently conducted a similar study of another large outpatient sample, using several additional self-report measures. This study also provided a preliminary test of the extent to which Beck's cognitive-content specificity approach to anxiety and depression was complementary (vs contradictory) to the two-factor affective model discussed previously. An initial factor analysis of the anxiety and depression measures revealed a large general factor, which could be interpreted as negative affectivity, that accounted for roughly 40% of the variance. However, a second analysis in which two factors were extracted, one that clearly represents depression and the other anxiety, provided a better fit to the data. Moreover, depressed patients reported significantly more hopelessness, lower self-worth, and more negative thoughts involving failure and loss; anxious patients had more thoughts of anticipated danger and harm. Not surprisingly, patients with comorbid anxiety-depression diagnoses showed a mixed cognitive profile.

Three recent studies from the same research group (one with 844 outpatients, one with 1000 outpatients, and one with 420 undergraduates) tested the complementarity of the cognitive-content specificity approach with the tripartite model (DA Clark et al 1994, Steer et al 1995). Separate analyses of the three samples yielded a very large second order factor in each case (accounting for approximately 40–50% of the variance), which clearly could be interpreted as the general distress/Negative Affect dimension of the tripartite model. However, each analysis also revealed specific first order factors corresponding to depression and anxiety. Consistent with Beck's model, cognitive content centered on personal loss and failure loaded strongly on the lower order depression factor and more modestly on the higher order Negative Affect factor. Specific motivational and behavioral symptoms of depression (e.g. fatigability, social withdrawal) also were significant markers of the specific depression factor, although they were modestly related to the general distress factor as well. Moreover, consistent with the tripartite model, a measure of positive emotionality was strongly negatively correlated with scores on the specific depression factor (DA Clark et al 1990). Finally, as predicted by the tripartite model, physiological symptoms of anxiety were most strongly related to the first order anxiety factor. Interestingly, the cognitive symptoms of anxiety were more strongly related to the higher order distress factor than to the specific anxiety factor. These results parallel the genetic analyses described earlier, which also revealed cognitive/affective symptoms of anxiety to be more closely related to neuroticism than were somatic symptoms. Overall, analyses of all three samples yielded broad support for both the tripartite and cognitive-content specificity models and clearly establish the compatibility of these approaches.

## Information Processing Approaches: Cognitive Biases for Emotion-Relevant Material

In addition to work comparing the thought *content* of anxious and depressed people, the past decade also has seen much interest in the effects that these disorders have on cognitive *processing*. Researchers have been particularly interested in the role that cognitive biases may play in the etiology and/or maintenance of these disorders. The term "cognitive bias" refers to any selective or nonveridical processing of emotion-relevant information (e.g. Mineka 1992, Mineka & Tomarken 1989). Although the idea that both anxiety and depression can disrupt efficient cognitive processing in a general way has a long history (MacLeod & Mathews 1991), the focus of this research has been to delineate how these disorders often selectively affect processing of *emotion-relevant* material. More than a decade of research has shown that anxiety and depression have prominent effects on different aspects of information processing; most of the research has focused on attentional and memory biases, with a smaller amount addressing judgmental biases. In the current context, it is of particular interest to determine the similarity vs distinctiveness of the biases associated with these disorders.

ATTENTIONAL BIASES    Many studies show that anxiety is associated with an attentional bias for threatening information, such that anxious patients' attention is drawn toward threatening cues when both threatening and nonthreatening cues are available. Nonanxious individuals tend, if anything, to show the opposite bias. These studies have used a number of different paradigms, ranging from the emotional Stroop or interference tasks to various attentional probe tasks. The bias appears to occur preconsciously, that is, without awareness (for reviews, see MacLeod & Mathews 1991, Mathews & MacLeod 1994, Mineka &

Sutton 1992). Many researchers believe that this attentional bias for threat may play a role in the maintenance of anxiety. That is, having one's attention automatically drawn toward threatening information may help to maintain or exacerbate anxiety. Results from at least one experiment suggest that the tendency to exhibit this bias may serve as a risk factor for the development of emotional distress symptoms in response to a major stressor (MacLeod & Hagan 1992).

In sharp contrast to the anxiety data, there is little evidence for a similar attentional bias for negative information in depression. There are a few studies suggesting that depressed individuals may show interference on the emotional Stroop task (e.g. Gotlib & Cane 1987, Williams & Nulty 1986); however, a study that directly compared depression and generalized anxiety failed to find such interference in depression (Mogg et al 1993). Moreover, emotional Stroop interference itself is not generally considered to be a pure measure of attentional bias, and the studies that have reported the bias did not rule out the possibility that the depressed patients' elevated levels of anxiety may be responsible for the effect (Mathews & MacLeod 1994). In contrast, attentional probe tasks provide a purer assessment of attentional bias; studies using this paradigm have sometimes found a relative bias, with depressed patients attending to positive and negative material equally, whereas nondepressed individuals show a bias toward positive material (e.g. Gotlib et al 1988). Again, however, one cannot rule out the possibility that anxiety actually is responsible for any observed effects (see Mogg et al 1991).

There are two recent exceptions to this generally negative pattern. Mathews et al (1996) found evidence for attention to social threat information in depression using an attentional probe task, but primarily when the words were clearly visible, suggesting it was a strategic process rather than the automatic preconscious bias seen with anxiety (see also Mogg et al 1995). At present, it is unclear how these findings can be reconciled with the largely negative results of prior studies; moreover, to clarify their meaning, it will be important to replicate these findings using more of the same paradigms used to study attentional biases in anxiety.

MEMORY BIASES   For the most part, the data on memory biases show a pattern opposite to that attentional biases. That is, a great deal of research demonstrates the presence of mood-congruent memory biases in depression, whereas the evidence for anxiety is relatively sparse and inconsistent (e.g. MacLeod & Mathews 1991, Mathews & MacLeod 1994, Mineka & Nugent 1995). Studies of mood-congruent memory in depression typically compare the performance of depressed and nondepressed participants on various memory tasks (free recall, recognition, autobiographical memory, etc), in which the materials to be remembered vary in affective content (positive vs negative vs neutral). A 1992 meta-analysis indicated that clinically depressed participants consistently show a significant bias to recall negative information, especially when it is self-referential (Matt et al 1992). Nondepressed individuals typically show a trend toward an opposite bias, favoring positive material. Teasdale (1988) argued that this memory bias creates a "vicious cycle of depression": When one is already depressed, having one's memory biased toward remembering negative events can only serve to perpetuate the depression. Results of several studies have demonstrated that such memory biases are indeed significant predictors of greater levels of depression three to seven months later, even when controlling for initial depression (e.g. Brittlebank et al 1993, Dent & Teasdale 1988).

More recent studies have also examined whether depression is associated with implicit or nonconscious memory biases for negative information. Unlike explicit memory tasks in which participants are asked specifically to reflect upon prior experiences, in implicit memory tasks the participants' memory is tested indirectly. Several more recent studies have provided convincing support for the presence of implicit memory biases (e.g. Bradley et al 1995, 1996; Watkins et al 1996). Such findings are of particular interest because they suggest a possible explanation for why depressed individuals so often have negative information entering into their consciousness without any conscious effort to recall such information.

In sharp contrast to the depression data, there is relatively little evidence indicating that similar biases are associated with anxiety (e.g. Mathews & MacLeod 1994, Mineka & Nugent 1995). Moreover, even when significant findings have been reported, they often have failed to replicate. Two studies did suggest the presence of an autobiographical memory bias in anxiety (Burke & Mathews 1992, Richards & Whitaker 1990), but these results are somewhat suspect because of significant methodological problems (Levy & Mineka 1997). Using improved methodology, Levy & Mineka (1997) found no evidence for an autobiographical memory bias in individuals high in trait anxiety.

Furthermore, although an early study suggested the presence of an implicit memory bias for threatening information in anxiety (Mathews et al 1989a), subsequent studies failed to replicate that finding (e.g. Bradley et al 1995, Mathews et al 1995, Nugent & Mineka 1994). One later study did report a significant implicit memory bias using a perceptual identification task, but no attempt was made to determine if the bias was because the anxious participants also had elevated depression levels (MacLeod & McLaughlin 1995). Overall, the pattern of largely negative findings for anxiety—using a wide range of memory bias paradigms—stands in rather striking contrast to the positive findings seen with depression.

Thus, although the results are not entirely consistent, the weight of the evidence suggests that anxiety and depression have different effects on cognitive processing. Interesting theories have emerged to explain these apparent dissociations between the cognitive processes associated with the two syndromes (e.g. Oatley & Johnson-Laird 1987, Williams et al 1988), but none at present can account for all of the findings that have emerged (e.g. Bradley et al 1996, Mineka & Nugent 1995). Nevertheless, the different modes of cognitive operation associated with the different primary emotions may reflect the fact that these emotions evolved to meet different environmental demands (Oatley & Johnson-Laird 1987). Anxiety, like fear, is important for vigilance and preparation for impending danger; it therefore requires a cognitive system that facilitates a quick scanning for—and perception of—cues for danger (Mathews 1993). The attentional biases seen in anxiety seem well suited for this purpose. Depression, by contrast, involves a rather more reflective consideration of events that have led to perceived failure and loss; a cognitive system adept at remembering important information that might have led to such failures or losses certainly would facilitate such reflection. The mood-congruent memory biases we see in depression seem well suited for this purpose as well (Mathews 1993, Mineka 1992). In this context it is noteworthy that over a decade ago, Tellegen (1985) in a broad-ranging article specifically described anxiety as an engaged, "orienting" mode characterized by a focus on the future, and contrasted it with the disengaged, "oriented," past-focusing mode of depression.

JUDGMENTAL OR INTERPRETIVE BIASES    Both anxiety and depression are associated with several forms of judgmental or interpretive biases. For example, relative to normal controls, anxious and depressed subjects show biased judgments of the likelihood that negative events will occur (Butler & Mathews 1983, Krantz & Hammen 1977). More recently, AK MacLeod & Byrne (1996) compared anxious and depressed individuals on their anticipation of both future positive and future negative experiences. Those with relatively pure anxiety showed greater anticipation of future negative experiences than controls, whereas those with depression (who also had elevated anxiety levels) showed both greater anticipation of negative experiences and reduced anticipation of positive experiences. The authors associated the heightened anticipation of future negative experiences with negative affect and the reduced anticipation of future positive experiences with low positive affect (Clark & Watson 1991a,b).

Anxious individuals also show an increased likelihood of interpreting ambiguous information in a negative manner. This occurs both with ambiguous homophones (e.g. die/dye, pain/pane) (Mathews et al 1989b) and with ambiguous sentences ("The doctor examined Little Emma's growth" or "They discussed the priest's convictions") (Eysenck et al 1991). The most elegant study to date involved a text comprehension paradigm; the results demonstrated that these interpretive biases were occurring while the anxious individuals were reading the text rather than afterward (MacLeod & Cohen 1993).

SUMMARY   Depression and anxiety both are associated with cognitive biases for emotion-relevant material. Judgmental and interpretive biases (which have received the least attention) occur with both conditions. Attentional biases for threatening information are more prominent in anxiety than in depression; this conclusion seems especially clear for preconscious automatic biases. Depression, by contrast, is more clearly associated with memory biases for mood-congruent information than is anxiety. From the evolutionary perspective of Oatley & Johnson-Laird (1987), these differences make some sense. However, from the perspective of the structural models and comorbidity viewed earlier, they are somewhat surprising. For example, in nearly all the studies of attentional bias in depression, the depressed individuals show very high levels of anxiety as well as of depression; nevertheless, they do not generally show the patterns of attentional bias seen with anxiety. What is it about the co-occurrence of depressed and anxious mood that seems to mask attentional biases? Future work in this area would profit from using measures with improved discriminant validity, such as the MASQ developed to test the tripartite model (Watson & Clark 1991).

## CONCLUSIONS

Interest in the relationships between anxiety and depression has a long history but only began to receive serious attention from researchers and theoreticians in the mid to late 1980s. Since that time considerable progress has been made in documenting the similarities and differences between these two conditions. In addition, we now have a more sophisticated understanding of many of the important features of both the concurrent and the lifetime comorbidity of these disorders. Major progress also has been made in understanding the genotypic structure of anxiety and depression, with considerable evidence indicating that generalized anxiety and major depression share a common genetic diathesis but that the anxiety disorders themselves are genetically heterogeneous, reflecting multiple genetic diatheses. Phenotypic models also have become quite sophisticated, with data converging on an integrative hierarchical model of mood and anxiety disorders in which each individual syndrome contains both a common and a unique component. The shared component of Negative Affect is common to both the mood and the anxiety disorders. Anxious arousal, one of the components of the tripartite model, seems to be the specific component of panic disorder, whereas the other anxiety disorders have their own unique components that are differentiable from anxious arousal. Finally, considerable progress also has been made in understanding the cognitive components of the anxiety and mood disorders. This work has focused on both the cognitive content of anxiety and depression and the effects that anxiety and depression have on information processing. The majority of evidence suggests that anxiety is associated with automatic attentional biases for emotion-relevant (threatening) material, that depression is associated with memory biases for emotion-relevant (negative) information, and that both anxiety and depression are associated with judgmental or interpretive biases. Much work remains to be done, however, to understand how this pattern of cognitive biases can be related to the hierarchical structural model of the anxiety and mood disorders that has emerged.

Visit the *Annual Reviews home page* at
http://www.AnnualReviews.org.

## Literature Cited

Abramson LY, Metalsky GL, Alloy LB. 1989. Hopelessness depression: a theory based subtype of depression. *Psychol. Rev.* 96: 358–72

Abramson LY, Seligman MEP, Teasdale JD. 1978. Learned helplessness in humans: critique and reformulation. *J. Abnorm. Psychol.* 87:49–74

Akiskal HS. 1985. Anxiety: definition, relationship to depression, and proposal for an integrative model. See Tuma & Maser 1985, pp. 787–97

Allen JL, Iacono WG, Depue RA, Arbisi P. 1993. Regional EEG asymmetries in bipolar seasonal affective disorder before and after phototherapy. *Biol. Psychiatry* 33: 642–46

Alloy L, Kelly K, Mineka S, Clements C. 1990. Comorbidity in anxiety and depressive disorders: a helplessness/hopelessness perspective. See Maser & Cloninger 1990, pp. 499–543

American Psychiatric Association. 1980. *Diagnostic and Statistical Manual of Mental Disorders.* Washington, DC: Am. Psychiatr. Assoc. 3rd ed.

American Psychiatric Association. 1987. *Diagnostic and Statistical Manual of Mental Disorders.* Washington, DC: Am. Psychiatr. Assoc. 3rd ed. Rev.

American Psychiatric Association. 1994. *Diagnostic and Statistical Manual of Mental*

*Disorders.* Washington, DC: Am. Psychiatr. Assoc. 4th ed.

Angold A, Costello EJ. 1993. Depressive comorbidity in children and adolescents: empirical, theoretical, and methodological issues. *Am. J. Psychiatry* 150:1779–91

Angst J. 1993. Comorbidity of anxiety, phobia, compulsion and depression. *Int. Clin. Psychopharmacol.* 8(Suppl.):21–25

Barlow DH. 1988. *Anxiety and Its Disorders: The Nature and Treatment of Anxiety and Panic.* New York: Guilford

Barlow DH. 1991. The nature of anxiety: anxiety, depression, and emotional disorders. In *Chronic Anxiety: Generalized Anxiety Disorder and Mixed Anxiety-Depression,* ed. RM Rapee, DH Barlow, pp. 1–28. New York: Guilford

Barlow DH, Chorpita BF, Turovsky J. 1996. *Fear, panic, anxiety and disorders of emotion. Nebr. Symp. Motiv.* 43:251–328

Beck AT. 1967. *Depression: Clinical, Experimental, and Theoretical Aspects.* New York: Harper & Row

Beck AT. 1976. *Cognitive Therapy and the Emotional Disorders.* New York: Int. Univ. Press

Beck AT, Brown G, Steer RA, Eidelson JI, Riskind JH. 1987. Differentiating anxiety and depression: a test of the cognitive content-specificity hypothesis. *J. Abnorm. Psychol.* 96:179–83

Beck AT, Emery G. 1985. *Anxiety Disorders and Phobias: A Cognitive Perspective.* New York: Basic Books

Bowlby J. 1973. *Attachment and Loss,* Vol. 2: *Separation.* New York: Basic Books

Bowlby J. 1980. *Attachment and Loss,* Vol. 3: *Loss.* New York: Basic Books

Bradley BP, Mogg K, Millar N. 1996. Implicit memory bias in clinical and nonclinical depression. *Behav. Res. Ther.* 34:865–79

Bradley BP, Mogg K, Williams R. 1995. Implicit and explicit memory for emotion-congruent information in clinical depression and anxiety. *Behav. Res. Ther.* 33: 755–70

Brady EU, Kendall PC. 1992. Comorbidity of anxiety and depression in children and adolescents. *J. Consult. Clin. Psychol.* 111:244–55

Braun DL, Sunday SR, Halmi KA. 1994. Psychiatric comorbidity in patients with eating disorders. *Psychol. Med.* 24:859–67

Brittlebank AD, Scott J, Williams JM, Perrier IN. 1993. Autobiographical memory in depression: State or trait marker? *Br. J. Psychiatry* 162:118–21

Bronisch T, Wittchen HU. 1994. Suicidal ideation and suicide attempts: comorbidity with depression, anxiety disorders, and substance abuse disorder. *Eur. Arch. Psychiatry Clin. Neurosci.* 244:93–98

Brown C, Schulberg HC, Madonia MJ, Shear MK. 1996. Treatment outcomes for primary care patients with major depression and lifetime anxiety disorders. *Am. J. Psychiatry* 153:1293–300

Brown GW, Harris TO. 1978. *Social Origins of Depression.* New York: Free

Brown GW, Harris TO, Eales MJ. 1993. Aetiology of anxiety and depressive disorders in an inner-city population. 2. Comorbidity and adversity. *Psychol. Med.* 23: 155–65

Brown TA, Antony MM, Barlow DH. 1995. Diagnostic comorbidity in panic disorder: effect on treatment outcome and course of comorbid diagnoses following treatment. *J. Consult. Clin. Psychol.* 63:408–18

Brown TA, Barlow DH. 1992. Comorbidity among anxiety disorders: implications for treatment and DSM-IV. *J. Consult. Clin. Psychol.* 60:835–44

Brown TA, Chorpita BF, Barlow DH. 1997. Structural relationships among dimensions of the DSM-IV anxiety and mood disorders and dimensions of negative affect, positive affect, and autonomic arousal. *J. Abnorm. Psychol.* In press

Bruder GE, Fong R, Tenke CE, Leite P, Towey JP, et al. 1997. Regional brain asymmetries in major depression with or without an anxiety disorder: a quantitative EEG study. *Biol. Psychiatry.* In press

Burke M, Mathews A. 1992. Autobiographical memory and clinical anxiety. *Cogn. Emot.* 6:23–35

Butler G, Mathews A. 1983. Cognitive processes in anxiety. *Adv. Behav. Res. Ther.* 5:51–62

Carey G, DiLalla DL. 1994. Personality and psychopathology: genetic perspectives. *J. Abnorm. Psychol.* 103:32–43

Caron C, Rutter M. 1991. Comorbidity in child psychopathology: concepts, issues and research strategies. *J. Child. Psychol. Psychiaty* 32:1063–80

Castonguay LG, Eldredge KL, Agras WS. 1995. Binge eating disorder: current state and future directions. *Clin. Psychol. Rev.* 15:865–90

Chorpita BF, Albano AM, Barlow DH. 1997. The structure of negative emotions in a clinical sample of children and adolescents. *J. Abnorm. Psychol.* In press

Clark DA, Beck AT, Stewart B. 1990. Cognitive specificity and positive-negative affectivity: complementary or contradictory views on anxiety and depression? *J. Abnorm. Psychol.* 99:148–55

Clark DA, Steer RA, Beck AT. 1994. Common and specific dimensions of self-reported anxiety and depression: implications for the cognitive and tripartite models. *J. Abnorm. Psychol.* 103:645–54

Clark DB, Smith MG, Neighbors BD, Skerlec LM. 1994. Anxiety disorders in adolescence: characteristics, prevalence, and comorbidities. *Clin. Psychol. Rev.* 14: 113–37

Clark LA. 1989. The anxiety and depressive disorders: descriptive psychopathology and differential diagnosis. In *Anxiety and Depression: Distinctive and Overlapping Features,* ed. PC Kendall, D Watson, pp. 83–129. San Diego: Academic

Clark LA, Watson D. 1991a. Theoretical and empirical issues in differentiating depression from anxiety. In *Psychosocial Aspects of Depression,* ed. J Becker, A Kleinman, pp. 39–65. Hillsdale, NJ: Erlbaum

Clark LA, Watson D. 1991b. Tripartite model of anxiety and depression: evidence and taxonomic implications. *J. Abnorm. Psychol.* 100:316–36

Clark LA, Watson D, Mineka S. 1994. Temperament, personality, and the mood and anxiety disorders. *J. Abnorm. Psychol.* 103:103–16

Clark LA, Watson D, Reynolds S. 1995. Diagnosis and classification of psychopathology: challenges to the current system and future directions. *Annu. Rev. Psychol.* 46: 121–53

Cole DA, Truglio R, Peeke L. 1997. Relation between symptoms of anxiety and depression in children: a multitrait-multimethod-multigroup assessment. *J. Consult. Clin. Psychol.* 65:110–19

Conwell Y. 1996. Relationship of age and Axis I diagnoses in victims of completed suicide: a psychological autopsy study. *Am. J. Psychiatry* 153:1001–8

Cook EW III, Hawk LW Jr, Davis TL, Stevenson VE. 1991. Affective individual differences and startle reflex modulation. *J. Abnorm. Psychol.* 100:5–13

Cox BJ, Swinson PP, Kuch K, Reichman JT. 1993. Self-report differentiation of anxiety and depression in an anxiety disorders sample. *Psychol. Assess.* 5:484–86

Cuthbert BN, Melamed BG. 1993. Anxiety and clinical psychophysiology: three decades of research on three response systems in three anxiety disorders. In *The Structure of Emotion,* ed. N Birbaumer, A Öhman, pp. 93–109. Seattle: Hofgrebe & Huber

Cuthbert BN, Bradley MM, Lang PJ. 1996. Fear and anxiety: theoretical distinction and clinical test. *Psychophysiology* 33 (Suppl. 1):S15

Davis M, Walker DL, Yee Y. 1997. Amygdala and bed nucleus of the stria terminalis: differential roles in fear and anxiety measured with the acoustic startle reflex. In *Biological and Psychological Perspectives on Memory and Memory Disorders,* ed. L Squire, D Schacter. Washington, DC: Am. Psychiatr.

Dent J, Teasdale J. 1988. Negative cognition and the persistence of depression. *J. Abnorm. Psychol.* 97:29–34

Depue R, Luciana M, Arbisi P, Collins P, Leon A. 1994. Dopamine and the structure of personality: relation of agonist-induced dopamine activity to positive emotionality. *J. Pers. Soc. Psychol.* 67:485–98

DiNardo PA, Barlow DH. 1990. Symptom and syndrome co-occurrence in the anxiety disorders. See Maser & Cloninger 1990, pp. 205–30

Dyck MJ, Jolly JB, Kramer T. 1994. An evaluation of positive affectivity, negative affectivity, and hyperarousal as markers for assessing between syndrome relationships. *Pers. Individ. Differ.* 17:637–46

Eysenck M, Mogg K, May J, Richards A, Mathews A. 1991. Bias in interpretation of ambiguous sentences related to threat in anxiety. *J. Abnorm. Psychol.* 100:144–50

Farmer R, Nelson-Gray RO. 1990. Personality

disorders and depression: hypothetical relations, empirical findings, and methodological considerations. *Clin. Psychol. Rev.* 10:453–76

Fawcett J, Clark DC, Busch KA. 1993. Assessing and treating the patient at risk for suicide. *Psychiatr. Ann.* 23:244–55

Feinstein AR. 1970. The pretherapeutic classification of co-morbidity in chronic disease. *J. Chronic Dis.* 23:455–68

Feldman LA. 1993. Distinguishing depression and anxiety in self-report: evidence from confirmatory factor analysis on nonclinical and clinical samples. *J. Consult. Clin. Psychol.* 61:631–38

First MB, Spitzer RL, Williams JBW. 1990. Exclusionary principles and the comorbidity of psychiatric diagnoses: a historical review and implications for the future. See Maser & Cloninger 1990, pp. 83–109

Flick SN, Roy-Byrne PP, Cowley DS, Shores MM, Dunner DL. 1993. DSM-III-R personality disorders in a mood and anxiety disorders clinic: prevalence, comorbidity, and clinical correlates. *J. Affect. Disord.* 27:71–79

Frances A, Widiger TA, Fyer MR. 1990. The influence of classification methods on comorbidity. See Maser & Cloninger 1990, pp. 41–59

Garber J, Miller SM, Abramson LY. 1980. On the distinction between anxiety states and depression: perceived control, certainty, and probability of goal attainment. In *Human Helplessness: Theory and Applications,* ed. J Garber, MEP Seligman. New York: Academic

Gotlib IH, Cane DB. 1987. Construct accessibility and clinical depression: a longitudinal approach. *J. Abnorm. Psychol.* 96: 199–204

Gotlib IH, MacLachlan A, Katz A. 1988. Biases in visual attention in depressed and nondepressed individuals. *Cogn. Emot.* 2: 185–200

Heimberg RG, Klosko JC, Dodge CS, Becker RE, Barlow DH. 1989. Anxiety disorders, depression, and attributional style: a further test of the specificity of depressive attributions. *Cogn. Ther. Res.* 13:21–36

Heller W. 1993. Neuropsychological mechanisms of individual differences in emotion, personality, and arousal. *Neuropsychol.* 7: 476–89

Heller W, Etienne MA, Miller GA. 1995. Patterns of perceptual asymmetry in depression and anxiety: implications for neuropsychological models of emotion and psychopathology. *J. Abnorm. Psychol.* 104: 327–33

Henriques JB, Davidson RJ. 1990. Regional brain electrical asymmetries discriminate between previously depressed subjects and healthy controls. *J. Abnorm. Psychol.* 99: 22–31

Henriques JB, Davidson RJ. 1991. Left frontal hypoactivation in depression. *J. Abnorm. Psychol.* 100:535–45

Herpertz-Dahlmann BM, Wewetzer C, Schulz E, Remschmidt H. 1996. Course and outcome in adolescent anorexia nervosa. *Int. J. Eating Disord.* 19:335–45

Hinden BR, Compas BE, Howell DC, Achenbach TM. 1997. Covariation of the anxious-depressed syndrome during adolescence: separating fact from artifact. *J. Consult. Clin. Psychol.* 65:6–14

Hodges K. 1990. Depression and anxiety in children: a comparison of self-report questionnaires to clinical interview. *Psychol. Assess.* 2:376–81

Hoffart A, Martinsen EW. 1993. The effect of personality disorders and anxious-depressive comorbidity on outcome in patients with unipolar depression and with panic disorder and agoraphobia. *J. Pers. Disord.* 7:304–11

Holt CS, Heimberg RG, Hope DA. 1992. Avoidant personality disorder and the generalized subtype of social phobia. *J. Abnorm. Psychol.* 101:318–25

Jardine R, Martin NG, Henderson AS. 1984. Genetic covariation between neuroticism and the symptoms of anxiety and depression. *Genet. Epidemiol.* 1:89–107

Jensen PS, Shervette RE, Xenakis SN, Richters J. 1993. Anxiety and depressive disorders in attention deficit disorder with hyperactivity: new findings. *Am. J. Psychiatry* 150:1203–9

Joiner TE Jr. 1996. A confirmatory factor-analytic investigation of the tripartite model of depression and anxiety in college students. *Cogn. Ther. Res.* 20:521–39

Joiner TE Jr, Catanzaro SJ, Laurent J. 1996. Tripartite structure of positive and negative affect, depression, and anxiety in child and adolescent psychiatric inpatients. *J. Abnorm. Psychol.* 105:401–9

Jolly JB, Dyck MJ, Kramer TA, Wherry JN. 1994. Integration of positive and negative affectivity and cognitive-content specificity: improved discriminations of anxious and depressive symptoms. *J. Abnorm. Psychol.* 103:544–52

Jolly JB, Dykman RA. 1994. Using self-report data to differentiate anxious and depressive symptoms in adolescents: cognitive content specificity and global distress? *Cogn. Ther. Res.* 18:25–37

Jolly JB, Kramer TA. 1994. The hierarchical arrangement of internalizing cognitions. *Cogn. Ther. Res.* 18:1–14

Kaplan MH, Feinstein AR. 1974. The importance of classifying initial comorbidity in evaluating the outcome of diabetes mellitus. *J. Chronic Dis.* 27:387–404

Keller MB, Lavori PW, Mueller TI, Endicott J, Coryell W, et al. 1992. Time to recovery, chronicity, and levels of psychopathology in major depression: a 5-year prospective follow-up of 431 subjects. *Arch. Gen. Psychiatry* 49:809–16

Kendall PC, Clarkin JF. 1992. Introduction to special section: comorbidity and treatment implications. *J. Consult. Clin. Psychol.* 60: 833–34

Kendall PC, Kortlander E, Chansky TE, Brady EU. 1992. Comorbidity of anxiety and depression in youth: treatment implications. *J. Consult. Clin. Psychol.* 60:869–80

Kendler KS. 1996. Major depression and generalised anxiety disorder: same genes, (partly) different environments—revisited. *Br. J. Psychiatry* 168(Suppl. 30):68–75

Kendler KS, Heath AC, Martin NG, Eaves LJ. 1987. Symptoms of anxiety and symptoms of depression: same genes, different environments? *Arch. Gen. Psychiatry* 44: 451–57

Kendler KS, Neale MC, Kessler RC, Heath AC, Eaves LJ. 1992. Major depression and generalized anxiety disorder: same genes, (partly) different environments? *Arch. Gen. Psychiatry* 49:16–22

Kendler KS, Neale MC, Kessler RC, Heath AC, Eaves LJ. 1993a. A longitudinal twin study of personality and major depression in women. *Arch. Gen. Psychiatry* 50: 853–62

Kendler KS, Neale MC, Kessler RC, Heath AC, Eaves LJ. 1993b. Major depression and phobias: the genetic and environmental sources of comorbidity. *Psychol. Med.* 23:361–71

Kendler KS, Walters EE, Neale MC, Kessler RC, Heath AC, Eaves LJ. 1995. The structure of the genetic and environmental risk factors for six major psychiatric disorders in women: phobia, generalized anxiety disorder, panic disorder, bulimia, major depression, and alcoholism. *Arch. Gen. Psychiatry* 52:374–83

Kessler RC. 1997. The prevalence of psychiatric comorbidity. In *Treatment Strategies for Patients with Psychiatric Comorbidity,* ed. S Wetzler, WC Sanderson, pp. 23–48. New York: Wiley

Kessler RC, McGonagle KA, Zhao S, Nelson CB, Hughes M, et al. 1994. Lifetime and

12-month prevalence of DSM-III-R psychiatric disorders in the United States: results from the National Comorbidity Survey. *Arch. Gen. Psychiatry* 51:8–19

Kessler RC, Nelson CB, McGonagle KA, Liu J, Swartz M, Blazer DG. 1996. Comorbidity of DSM-III-R major depressive disorder in the general population: results from the US National Comorbidity Survey. *Br. J. Psychiatry* 168(Suppl. 30):17–30

Kessler RC, Zhao S, Blazer DG, Swartz MD. 1997. Prevalence, correlates, and course of minor depression and major depression in the National Comorbidity Survey. *J. Affect Disord.* In press

King NJ. 1990. Childhood anxiety disorders and depression: phenomenology, comorbidity, and intervention issues. *Scand. J. Behav. Ther.* 19:59–70

King NJ, Ollendick TH, Gullone E. 1991. Negative affectivity in children and adolescents: relations between anxiety and depression. *Clin. Psychol. Rev.* 11:441–59

Klerman GL. 1990. Approaches to the phenomena of comorbidity. See Maser & Cloninger 1990, pp. 13–37

Kovacs M, Gatsonis C, Paulaskas SL, Richards C. 1989. Depressive disorders in childhood. *Arch. Gen. Psychiatry* 46: 776–82

Krantz S, Hammen C. 1977. Assessment of cognitive bias in depression. *J. Abnorm. Psychol.* 88:611–19

Krueger RF, Caspi A, Moffitt TE, Silva PA, McGee R. 1996. Personality traits are differentially linked to mental disorders: a multitrait-multidiagnosis study of an adolescent birth cohort. *J. Abnorm. Psychol.* 105:299–312

Kunik ME. 1993. Personality disorders in elderly inpatients with major depression. *Am. J. Geriatr. Psychiatry* 1:38–45

Lang PJ, Bradley MM, Cuthbert BN, Patrick CJ. 1993. Emotion and psychopathology: a startle probe analysis. In *Progress in Experimental Personality and Psychopathology Research,* ed. LJ Chapman, JP Chapman, DC Fowles, 16:163–99. New York: Springer

Larsen CL, Davidson RJ, Abercrombie HC. 1995. Prefrontal brain function and depression severity: EEG differences in melancholic and nonmelancholic depressives. *Psychophysiology* 32:S49

Lepine JP, Wittchen H-U, Essau CA. 1993. Lifetime and current comorbidity of anxiety and affective disorders: results from the International WHO/ADAMHA CIDI field trials. *Int. J. Methods Psychiatr. Res.* 3:67–77

Levy E, Mineka S. 1997. *Anxiety and mood-congruent autobiographical memory.* Presented at Midwest. Psychol. Assoc., May

Lewinsohn PM, Rohde P, Seeley JR. 1995. Adolescent psychopathology. III. The clinical consequences of comorbidity. *J. Am. Acad. Child Adolesc. Psychiatry* 34: 510–19

Lewinsohn PM, Zinbarg R, Seeley JR, Lewinsohn M, Sack WH. 1997. Lifetime comorbidity among anxiety disorders and between anxiety disorders and other mental disorders in adolescents. *J. Anxiety Disord.* In press

Lilienfeld SO, Waldman ID, Israel AC. 1994. Critical examination of the use of the term and concept of comorbidity in psychopathology research. *Clin. Psychol. Sci. Pract.* 1:71–83

Loeber R, Keenan K. 1994. Interaction between conduct disorder and its comorbid conditions: effects of age and gender. *Clin. Psychol. Rev.* 14:497–523

Lonigan CJ, Carey MP, Finch AJ Jr. 1994. Anxiety and depression in children and adolescents: negative affectivity and the utility of self-reports. *J. Consult. Clin. Psychol.* 62:1000–8

MacLeod AK, Byrne A. 1996. Anxiety, depression, and the anticipation of future positive and negative experiences. *J. Abnorm. Psychol.* 105:286–89

MacLeod C, Cohen I. 1993. Anxiety and the interpretation of ambiguity: a text comprehension study. *J. Abnorm. Psychol.* 102: 238–47

MacLeod C, Hagan R. 1992. Individual differences in the selective processing of threatening information, and emotional responses to a stressful life event. *Behav. Res. Ther.* 30:151–61

MacLeod C, Mathews AM. 1991. Cognitive-experimental approaches to the emotional disorders. In *Handbook of Behavior Therapy and Psychological Science,* ed. P Martin, pp. 116–50. New York: Pergamon

MacLeod C, McLaughlin K. 1995. Implicit and explicit memory bias in anxiety: a conceptual replication. *Behav. Res. Ther.* 33: 1–14

Mandler G. 1972. Helplessness: theory and research in anxiety. In *Anxiety: Current Trends in Theory and Research,* Vol. 3, ed. CD Spielberger. New York: Academic

Martin NG, Jardine R, Andrews G, Heath AC. 1988. Anxiety disorders and neuroticism: Are there genetic factors specific to panic? *Acta Psychiatr. Scand.* 77:698–706

Maser JD, Cloninger CR. 1990. Comorbidity

of anxiety and mood disorders: introduction and overview. In *Comorbidity of Mood and Anxiety Disorders,* ed. JD Maser, CR Cloninger, pp. 3–12. Washington, DC: Am. Psychiatr. Press

Mathews A. 1993. Anxiety and the processing of emotional information. In *Models and Methods of Psychopathology: Progress in Experimental Personality and Psychopathology Research,* ed. L Chapman, J Chapman, D Fowles, pp. 254–80. New York: Springer

Mathews A, MacLeod C. 1994. Cognitive approaches to emotion and emotional disorders. *Annu. Rev. Psychol.* 45:25–50

Mathews A, Mogg K, Kentish J, Eysenck M. 1995. Effect of psychological treatment on cognitive bias in generalized anxiety disorder. *Behav. Res. Ther.* 33:293–303

Mathews A, Mogg K, May J, Eysenck M. 1989a. Implicit and explicit memory bias in anxiety. *J. Abnorm. Psychol.* 98:236–40

Mathews A, Richards A, Eysenck M. 1989b. Interpretation of homophones related to threat in anxiety states. *J. Abnorm. Psychol.* 98:31–34

Mathews A, Ridgeway V, Williamson D. 1996. Evidence for attention to threatening stimuli in depression. *Behav. Res. Ther.* 34:695–705

Matt G, Vazquez C, Campbell WK. 1992. Mood-congruent recall of affectively toned stimuli: a meta-analytical review. *Clin. Psychol. Rev.* 12:227–55

McNeil DW, Vrana SR, Melamed BG, Cuthbert BN, Lang PJ. 1993. Emotional imagery in simple and social phobia: fear versus anxiety. *J. Abnorm. Psychol.* 102: 212–25

Milberger S, Biederman J, Faraone SV, Murphy J, Tsuang MT. 1995. Attention deficit hyperactivity disorder and comorbid disorder: issues of overlapping symptoms. *Am. J. Psychiatry* 152:1793–99

Mineka S. 1985. Animal models of anxiety-based disorders: their usefulness and limitations. See Tuma & Maser 1985, pp. 199–244

Mineka S. 1992. Evolutionary memories, emotional processing and the emotional disorders. In *The Psychology of Learning and Motivation,* ed. D Medin, 28:161–206. New York: Academic

Mineka S, Kelly K. 1989. The relationship between anxiety, lack of control, and loss of control. In *Stress, Personal Control and Health,* ed. A Steptoe, A Appels, pp. 163–91. New York: Wiley

Mineka S, Nugent K. 1995. Mood-congruent memory biases in anxiety and depression.

In *Memory Distortion: How Minds, Brains, and Societies Reconstruct the Past,* ed. D Schacter, pp. 173–93. Cambridge, MA: Harvard Univ. Press

Mineka S, Pury C, Luten A. 1995. Explanatory style in anxiety versus depression. In *Explanatory Style,* ed. G Buchanan, MEP Seligman, pp. 135–58. Hillsdale, NJ: Erlbaum

Mineka S, Suomi SJ. 1978. Social separation in monkeys. *Psychol. Bull.* 85:1376–400

Mineka S, Sutton S. 1992. Cognitive biases and the emotional disorders. *Psychol. Sci.* 3:65–69

Mineka S, Tomarken A. 1989. The role of cognitive biases in the origins and maintenance of fear and anxiety disorders. In *Aversion, Avoidance, and Anxiety: Perspectives on Aversively Motivated Behavior,* ed. T Archer, L Nilsson, pp. 195–221. Hillsdale, NJ: Erlbaum

Mineka S, Zinbarg R. 1996. Conditioning and ethological models of anxiety disorders: Stress-in-dynamic-context anxiety models. *Perspectives on anxiety, panic, and fear. Nebr. Symp. Motiv.* 43:135–211

Mogg K, Bradley BP, Williams R. 1995. Attentional bias in anxiety and depression: the role of awareness. *Br. J. Clin. Psychol.* 43:17–36

Mogg K, Bradley BP, Williams R, Mathews AM. 1993. Subliminal processing of emotional information in anxiety and depression. *J. Abnorm. Psychol.* 102:304–11

Mogg K, Mathews AM, May J, Grove M, Eysenck M, Weinman J. 1991. Assessment of cognitive bias in anxiety and depression using a colour perception task. *Cogn. Emot.* 5:221–38

Monroe SM. 1990. Psychosocial factors in anxiety and depression. See Maser & Cloninger 1990, pp. 463–98

Moras K, Clark LA, Katon W, Roy-Byrne R, Watson D, Barlow D. 1996. Mixed anxiety-depression. In *DSM-IV Sourcebook,* ed. TA Widiger, AJ Frances, HA Pincus, R Ross, MB First, WW Davis, pp. 623–43. Washington, DC: Am. Psychiatr.

Mulder RT. 1991. The comorbidity of anxiety disorders with personality, depressive, alcohol and drug disorders. *Int. Rev. Psychiatr.* 3:253–63

Neale MC, Kendler KS. 1995. Models of comorbidity for multifactorial disorders. *Am. J. Hum. Genet.* 57:935–53

Nugent K, Mineka S. 1994. The effects of high and low trait anxiety on implicit and explicit memory tasks. *Cogn. Emot.* 8:147–63

Oatley K, Johnson-Laird P. 1987. Towards a

cognitive theory of emotions. *Cogn. Emot.* 1:29–50

Pauls DL. 1992. The genetics of obsessive compulsive disorder and Gilles de la Tourette's syndrome. *Psychiatr. Clin. North Am.* 15:759–66

Pauls DL, Alsobrook JP II, Goodman W, Rasmussen S, Leckman JF. 1995. A family study of obsessive-compulsive disorder. *Am. J. Psychiatry* 152:76–84

Pauls DL, Leckman JF, Cohen DJ. 1994. Evidence against a genetic relationship between Tourette's syndrome and anxiety, depression, panic and phobic disorders. *Br. J. Psychiatry* 164:215–21

Regier DA, Burke JD, Burke KC. 1990. Comorbidity of affective and anxiety disorders in the NIMH Epidemiologic Catchment Area Program. See Maser & Cloninger 1990, pp. 113–22

Reich J, Warshaw M, Peterson LG, White K. 1993. Comorbidity of panic and major depressive disorder. *J. Psychiatr. Res.* 27 (Suppl.):23–33

Richards A, Whitaker TM. 1990. Effects of anxiety and mood manipulation in autobiographical memory. *Br. J. Clin. Psychol.* 29:145–53

Rief W, Hiller W, Geissner E, Fichter MM. 1995. A two-year follow-up study of patients with somatoform disorders. *Psychosomatics* 36:376–86

Robins LN. 1994. How recognizing "comorbidities" in psychopathology may lead to an improved research nosology. *Clin. Psychol. Sci. Pract.* 1:93–95

Roy M-A, Neale MC, Pedersen NL, Mathé AA, Kendler KS. 1995. A twin study of generalized anxiety disorder and major depression. *Psychol. Med.* 25:1037–49

Sartorius N, Ustun TB, Lecrubier Y. 1996. Depression comorbid with anxiety: Results from the WHO study on "Psychological disorders in primary health care." *Br. J. Psychiatry* 168(Suppl. 30):38–43

Schneier FR, Johnson J, Hornig CD, Liebowitz MR. 1992. Social phobia: comorbidity and morbidity in an epidemiologic sample. *Arch. Gen. Psychiatry* 49:282–88

Seligman MEP. 1974. Depression and learned helplessness. In *The Psychology of Depression: Contemporary Theory and Research*, ed. RJ Friedman, MM Katz, pp. 83–113. New York: Winston-Wiley

Shafii M, Steltz-Lenarsky J, Derrick AM, Beckner C. 1988. Comorbidity of mental disorders in the post-mortem diagnosis of completed suicide in children and adolescents. *J. Affect. Disord.* 15:227–33

Shea MT, Widiger TA, Klein MH. 1992.

Comorbidity of personality disorders and depression: implications for treatment. *J. Consult. Clin. Psychol.* 60:857–68

Spence SH. 1997. Structure of anxiety symptoms among children: a confirmatory factor-analytic study. *J. Abnorm. Psychol.* 106:280–97

Spitzer RL. 1994. Psychiatric "co-occurrence"? I'll stick with "comorbidity." *Clin. Psychol. Sci. Pract.* 1:88–92

Spitzer RL, Endicott J, Robins E. 1978. Research Diagnostic Criteria: rationale and reliability. *Arch. Gen. Psychiatry* 35: 773–82

Steer RA, Clark DA, Beck AT, Ranieri WF. 1995. Common and specific dimensions of self-reported anxiety and depression: a replication. *J. Abnorm. Psychol.* 104: 542–45

Steer RA, Clark DA, Ranieri WF. 1994. Symptom dimensions of the SCL-90-R: a test of the tripartite model of anxiety and depression. *J. Pers. Assess.* 62:525–36

Teasdale JD. 1988. Cognitive vulnerability to persistent depression. *Cogn. Emot.* 2: 247–74

Tellegen A. 1985. Structures of mood and personality and their relevance to assessing anxiety, with an emphasis on self-report. See Tuma & Maser 1985, pp. 681–706

Tomarken AJ, Davidson RJ, Wheeler RE, Doss RC. 1992. Individual differences in anterior brain asymmetry and fundamental dimensions of emotion. *J. Pers. Soc. Psychol.* 62:676–87

Tomarken AJ, Keener AD. 1997. Frontal brain asymmetry and depression: a self-regulatory perspective. *Cogn. Emot.* In press

Trull TJ, Sher KJ. 1994. Relationship between the five-factor model of personality and Axis I disorders in a nonclinical sample. *J. Abnorm. Psychol.* 103:350–60

Tuma AH, Maser J, eds. 1985. *Anxiety and the Anxiety Disorders.* Hillsdale, NJ: Erlbaum

Turner SM, Beidel DC, Townsley RM. 1992. Social phobia: a comparison of specific and generalized subtypes and avoidant personality disorder. *J. Abnorm. Psychol.* 101:326–32

Watkins PC, Vache K, Verney SP, Muller S, Mathews A. 1996. Unconscious mood-congruent memory bias in depression. *J. Abnorm. Psychol.* 105:34–41

Watson D, Clark LA. 1991. The mood and anxiety symptom questionnaire. Univ. Iowa, Dep. Psychol. Unpubl. manuscr.

Watson D, Clark LA. 1994. Introduction to the special issue on personality and psychopathology. *J. Abnorm. Psychol.* 103:3–5

Watson D, Clark LA. 1995. Depression and

the melancholic temperament. *Eur. J. Pers.* 9:351–66

Watson D, Clark LA. 1997. Measurement and mismeasurement of mood: recurrent and emergent issues. *J. Pers. Assess.* 68: 267–96

Watson D, Clark LA, Carey G. 1988. Positive and negative affectivity and their relation to anxiety and depressive disorders. *J. Abnorm. Psychol.* 97:346–53

Watson D, Clark LA, Harkness AR. 1994. Structures of personality and their relevance to psychopathology. *J. Abnorm. Psychol.* 103:18–31

Watson D, Clark LA, Weber K, Assenheimer JS, Strauss ME, McCormick RA. 1995a. Testing a tripartite model: II. Exploring the symptom structure of anxiety and depression in student, adult, and patient samples. *J. Abnorm. Psychol.* 104:15–25

Watson D, Tellegen A. 1985. Toward a consensual structure of mood. *Psychol. Bull.* 98:219–35

Watson D, Weber K, Assenheimer JS, Clark LA, Strauss ME, McCormick RA. 1995b. Testing a tripartite model. I. Evaluating the convergent and discriminant validity of anxiety and depression symptom scales. *J. Abnorm. Psychol.* 104:3–14

Westermeyer J, Tucker P, Nugent S. 1995. Comorbid anxiety disorder among patients with substance abuse disorders. *Am. J. Ad-dict.* 4:97–106

Widiger TA, Costa PT Jr. 1994. Personality and the personality disorders. *J. Abnorm. Psychol.* 103:78–91

Williams JMG, Nulty DD. 1986. Construct accessibility, depression and the emotional Stroop task: transient mood or stable structure? *Pers. Individ. Differ.* 7:485–91

Williams JMG, Watts FN, MacLeod C, Mathews AM. 1988. *Cognitive Psychology and the Emotional Disorders,* pp. 1–226. Chichester, NY: Wiley

Wilson GT, Nathan PE, O'Leary KD, Clark LA. 1996. *Abnormal Psychology: Integrating Perspectives,* pp. 1–778. Boston: Allyn & Bacon

Wittchen H-U, Zhao S, Kessler RC, Eaton WW. 1994. DSM-III-R generalized anxiety disorder in the National Comorbidity Survey. *Arch. Gen. Psychiatry* 51:355–64

Woodman CL. 1993. The genetics of panic disorder and generalized anxiety disorder. *Ann. Clin. Psychiatry* 5:231–40

Zinbarg RE, Barlow DH. 1996. Structure of anxiety and the anxiety disorders: a hierarchical model. *J. Abnorm. Psychol.* 105: 181–93

Zisook S, Goff A, Sledge P, Shuchter SR. 1994. Reported suicidal behavior and current suicidal ideation in a psychiatric outpatient clinic. *Ann. Clin. Psychiatry* 6: 27–31

*Annu. Rev. Psychol. 1998. 49:413–46*

# ADOLESCENT DEVELOPMENT:
## Challenges and Opportunities for Research, Programs, and Policies

### Richard M. Lerner

Center for Child, Family, and Community Partnerships, Campion Hall, 140 Commonwealth Avenue, Boston College, Chestnut Hill, Massachusetts 02167; e-mail: Lernerri@bc.edu

### Nancy L. Galambos

University of Victoria, Department of Psychology, Victoria, British Columbia, V8W 3P5, Canada

KEY WORDS: diversity, context, risk, protection, prevention

### ABSTRACT

The basic process of adolescent development involves changing relations between the individual and the multiple levels of the context within which the young person is embedded. Variation in the substance and timing of these relations promotes diversity in adolescence and represents sources of risk or protective factors across this life period. The key risk factors of the contempory American adolescent period are discussed. Behavioral risks involve drug, alcohol, and substance use and abuse; unsafe sex, teenage pregnancy, and teenage parenting; school underachievement, failure, and dropout; and delinquency, crime, and violence. Poverty among youth exacerbates these risks. The features of youth programs effective in preventing the actualization of risk or in promoting positive adolescent development are discussed, as are the characteristics of public policies that may enhance the life chances of the diverse youth of America and the world.

## CONTENTS

413

# INTRODUCTION: CHALLENGES AND OPPORTUNITIES FOR RESEARCH, PROGRAMS, AND POLICIES

Adolescence has been described as a phase of life beginning in biology and ending in society (Petersen 1988). Adolescence may be defined as the period within the life span when most of a person's biological, cognitive, psychological, and social characteristics are changing from what is typically considered childlike to what is considered adult-like (Lerner & Spanier 1980). For the adolescent, this period is a dramatic challenge, one requiring adjustment to changes in the self, in the family, and in the peer group. In contemporary society, adolescents experience institutional changes as well. Among young adolescents, there is a change in school setting, typically involving a transition from elementary school to either junior high school or middle school; and in late adolescence, there is a transition from high school to the worlds of work, university, or childrearing.

Understandably, then, for both adolescents and their parents, adolescence is a time of excitement and of anxiety; of happiness and of troubles; of discovery and of bewilderment; and of breaks with the past and of links with the future. Adolescence can be a confusing time—for the adolescent experiencing this phase of life, for the parents who are nurturing the adolescent during his or her progression through this period, and for other adults charged with enhancing the development of youth during this period.

The hopes, challenges, fears, and successes of adolescence have been romanticized or dramatized in novels, short stories, and news articles. It is commonplace to survey a newsstand and to find a magazine article describing the "stormy years" of adolescence, the new crazes or fads of youth, or the "explosion" of problems with teenagers (e.g. crime or sexuality). Until the past 20–25 years, when medical, biological, and social scientists began to study intensively the adolescent period, there was relatively little sound scientific information available to verify or refute the literary characterizations of adolescence. Today, however, such information does exist, and it is clear that although adolescence presents many challenges, the evidence is not consistent with the frequently reported belief that adolescence is a protracted period of storm and stress for most individuals (Feldman & Elliott 1990; Lerner 1993b, 1995; Lerner et al 1991; Montemayor et al 1990; Petersen 1988).

## KEY FEATURES OF ADOLESCENT DEVELOPMENT

Today, there is an increasingly more voluminous and sophisticated scientific literature about adolescence that allows several generalizations about this period of life and that afford some conclusions about how best to intervene when adolescents are experiencing difficulties. Accordingly, we discuss first key features of adolescent development and then the contemporary sets of problems and risks confronting youth. There are diverse individual and contextual factors that provide bases of these risks or of protection from them. We discuss these respective sets of factors and point to the connections between diverse individual and contextual protective factors and the criteria of intervention programs and the components of policies that are effective in promoting positive youth development.

### Multiple Levels of Context Are Influential During Adolescence

The context or ecology of human development (Bronfenbrenner 1979, Lerner 1995) is composed of multiple, integrated levels of organization, including the biological, individual-psychological, social-interpersonal, institutional, cultural, and historical. There are ubiquitous individual differences in adolescent development, and they involve connections among biological, cognitive, psychological, and sociocultural factors, and no single influence acts either alone or as the "prime mover" of change (Brooks-Gunn & Petersen 1983; Lerner 1993b, 1995; Lerner & Foch 1987; Petersen 1988).

For example, adolescence is a period of rapid physical transitions in such characteristics as height, weight, and body proportions. Hormonal changes are part of this development. Nevertheless, hormones are not primarily responsible for the psychological or social developments of this period (Finkelstein 1993, Petersen & Taylor 1980). In fact, the quality and timing of hormonal or other biological changes influence and are influenced by psychological, social, cultural, and historical contexts (Elder 1980, Gottlieb 1992, Magnusson 1988, Stattin & Magnusson 1990, Susman et al 1987, Tanner 1991). Caspi et al (1993), for example, found that the biological changes of early pubertal maturation were linked to delinquency in adolescent girls, but only among girls who attended mixed-sex schools. Early maturation among girls in single-sex schools was not linked with higher delinquency.

Research on cognitive development suggests that there are integrated, multilevel changes in thinking that occur during adolescence (Graber & Petersen 1991). For instance, there are no global and pervasive effects of puberty on cognitive development, but pubertal changes interact with contextual and experiential factors (e.g. the transition to junior high school) to influence academic achievement (Eccles 1991, Simmons & Blyth 1987). Although a storm-and-stress perspective might lead to the assumption that there are general cognitive disruptions over adolescence because of the presumed upheavals of this period, the evidence does not support this assumption. Rather, cognitive abilities are enhanced in early adolescence as individuals become faster and more efficient at processing information—at least in settings in which they feel comfortable in performing cognitive tasks (Ceci & Bronfenbrenner 1985, Kail 1991).

## Changing Relations Between Adolescents and Their Contexts Produce Development in Adolescence

The period of adolescence is one of continual change and transition between individuals and their contexts (Lerner 1987, 1995). These changing relations constitute the basic process of development in adolescence; they underlie both positive and negative outcomes that occur (Lerner 1984, 1993a,b, 1995).

Accordingly, when the multiple biological, psychological, cognitive, and social changes of adolescence occur simultaneously (e.g. when menarche occurs at the same time as a school transition), there is a greater risk of problems occurring in a youth's development (Eccles et al 1997, Simmons & Blyth 1987). In adolescence, poor decisions (e.g. involving school, sex, drugs) have more negative consequences than in childhood (Dryfoos 1990), and the adolescent is more responsible for those decisions and their consequences than in childhood (Petersen 1988).

Nevertheless, most developmental trajectories across this period involve positive adjustment on the part of the adolescent. Furthermore, for most youth there is a continuation of warm and accepting relations with parents (Guerney & Arthur 1984). The most optimal adjustment occurs among adolescents who are encouraged by their parents to engage in age-appropriate autonomy while maintaining strong ties to their family (Allen et al 1994, Galambos & Ehrenberg 1997).

Adolescence is an opportune time in which to intervene into family processes when necessary. For instance, whereas minor parent-child conflicts (for example, regarding chores and privileges) are normative in adolescence, major conflicts are less frequent; thus, when major conflicts occur often in a family, parents should be concerned (Galambos & Almeida 1992, Smetana 1988). The continued salience of the family in the adolescent period makes such conflicts an appropriate intervention target.

## Individual Differences—Diversity—Characterize Adolescence

There are multiple pathways through adolescence (Offer 1969). Interindividual (between-person) differences and intra-individual (within-person) changes in development are the "rule" in this period of life. Normal adolescent development involves such variability. Temperamental characteristics involving mood and activity level are good examples (Lerner & Lerner 1983). There are differences among adolescents in such characteristics, which may influence adolescent behaviors such as substance use and delinquency (Henry et al 1996, Wills et al 1995). There is also diversity between and within all ethnic, racial, or cultural minority groups. Therefore, generalizations that confound class, race, and/or ethnicity are not useful (Lerner 1991).

Unfortunately, however, there is a major limitation in the status of the contemporary scientific literature about adolescent development. Despite the value of the extant knowledge base about development in adolescence, most studies in the literature have involved the study of European American, middle-class samples (e.g. Fisher & Brennan 1992, Graham 1992, Hagen et al 1990, Lerner 1995). There are, of course, some high-quality investigations that either have studied samples other than European American middle-class ones (e.g. Brookins 1991; Reid 1991; Spencer 1990, 1991; Spencer & Dornbusch 1990; Spencer & Markstrom-Adams 1990; Steinberg et al 1992) or have studied adolescents from national or cultural settings other than the United States (e.g. Arnett & Balle-Jensen 1993, Mead 1928, Silbereisen et al 1994 , Stattin & Magnusson 1990, Whiting & Whiting 1991).

Nevertheless, such studies are relatively few in number. They do not provide a sufficient data base to describe the course of normal development in a manner as detailed as is the case for European American youth. They cannot serve, then, as targets for the design of interventions promoting such development. Interventions that are not devised in light of a group's characteristics of individuality—the specifics of patterns of healthy development within the group—are not likely to promote such development (Lerner 1995). In short, then, all policies and programs, all interventions, must be tailored to the specific target population and, in particular, to a group's developmental and environmental circumstances (Lerner 1995, Lerner & Miller 1993, Lerner & Villarruel 1994). Moreover, because adolescents are so different from one another, one cannot expect any single policy or intervention to reach all of a given target population or to influence everyone in the same way.

## Implications of the Features of Adolescent Development for Research and Application

The breadth and depth of high-quality scientific information currently available about development in adolescence underscores the diversity and dynamics of this period of life. Theoretical interest in studying dynamic person-context relations is a key reason that the changes of this period have garnered increasing scientific attention (Lerner 1987, 1993a,b).

This burgeoning scientific activity devoted to adolescence has occurred synergistically with the recognition within society of the special developmental challenges of this period, involving, for example, pubertal change and the emergence of reproductive capacity, and the development of a self-definition and of roles that will allow youth to become productive and healthy adult members of society. In addition, there has been a recognition in society, also emerging in concert with the growing scientific data base, that the individual differences that occur in adolescent development, and the problems youth encounter in meeting the stressors of this period, represent a special intellectual and professional challenge, especially in contemporary society, which is characterized by a historically unprecedented set of interrelated behavior risks associated with the development of youth (Dryfoos 1990, Lerner 1995). For those who wish not only to understand the nature of adolescence but who desire as well to apply this knowledge to enhance the lives of adolescents, a synthesis of research, policy, and intervention must exist.

Research must be conducted with an appreciation of the individual differences in adolescent development, differences that arise as a consequence of diverse people's development in distinct families, communities, and sociocultural settings (Lerner 1993b, 1995; Lerner & Miller 1993). In turn, policies and programs must be similarly attuned to the diversity of people and context to maximize the chances of meeting the specific needs of particular groups of youth (Lerner et al 1994a,b).

Therefore, such programs and policies must be derived appropriately from research predicated on integrative, multidisciplinary models of human development (Ford & Lerner 1992; Lerner 1986, 1991, 1992, 1995). The need for this dual outcome of the application of theory-based scholarship—that is, of applied developmental science (Fisher et al 1993, Fisher & Lerner 1994)—is brought to the fore by a discussion of the several major problems besetting today's adolescents.

# CONTEMPORARY CRISES OF ADOLESCENT BEHAVIOR AND DEVELOPMENT

Across North America and around the world, many adolescents face the challenges and crises of violence, drug and alcohol use and abuse, unsafe sex, poor nutrition, and the sequelae of persistent and pervasive poverty (Children's Defense Fund 1996; Dryfoos 1990; Hamburg 1992; Hurrelmann 1994; Huston 1991; Lerner 1993a,b, 1995; Little 1993; McKinney et al 1994; Schorr 1988; Wilson 1987; World Health Organization 1993). The life chances of many adolescents are squandered, by school failure, underachievement, and dropout; crime; teenage pregnancy and parenting; lack of job preparedness; challenges to health (e.g. lack of immunizations, insufficient prenatal care); and feelings of despair and hopelessness that pervade the lives of children whose parents have lived in poverty and who see themselves as having little opportunity to do better, that is, to have a life marked by societal respect, achievement, and opportunity (Carnegie Corporation of New York 1995, Children's Defense Fund 1996, Di Mauro 1995, Dryfoos 1990, Huston 1991, Huston et al 1994, Johnston et al 1996, Smith 1994, United States Department of Health and Human Services 1996).

There are numerous manifestations of the severity and breadth of the problems besetting youth, families, and communities. A survey of adolescent behavior in many industrialized and developing nations found that problem behaviors such as delinquency and drug abuse appear to be increasing around the world (Hurrelmann 1994). In the United States, a profile of the quality of life for youth is provided in the 1995 *Kids Count Data Book* (Annie E. Casey Foundation 1995). This analysis compared the quality of life of youth in 1985 and 1992. In several categories, there were trends toward improvement across this seven-year period. Nevertheless, the absolute levels of these indicators remains poor. For instance, despite achieving a 20% improvement in infant mortality rate between 1985 and 1992, the United States ranked eighteenth among all industrialized nations of the world in infant mortality (Children's Defense Fund 1996). Similarly, although there was a 1% improvement in the percentage of children living in poverty, more than 20% of children and youth remain poor.

Given these trends, it is perhaps not surprising to learn that the quality of life provided for children and youth stands in poor comparison to what is provided by other modern industrialized countries (Children's Defense Fund 1996). Although the United States leads other such nations in military and defense expenditures, health technology, and the number of individuals who attain very substantial personal wealth, it falls far behind other nations in indicators of child health and welfare. For instance, the poverty rate for children in the United States is highest among the 18 leading industrial countries.

Moreover, all indicators involving negative trends in the 1995 *Kids Count Data Book* (Annie E. Casey Foundation 1995) between 1985 and 1992 involved problems of adolescence: juvenile violent crime arrest rate, births to unmarried teens, single parent families, percent of low birth-weight babies, and teen violent death rate. Such trends suggest that, relative to other youth age groups in our nation, adolescents may be in particular peril. There are still other indicators that this pessimism is warranted.

To illustrate, consider four major categories of risk behaviors in late childhood and adolescence: (*a*) drug and alcohol use and abuse; (*b*) unsafe sex, teenage pregnancy, and teenage parenting; (*c*) school underachievement, school failure, and drop out; and (*d*) delinquency, crime, and violence (Dryfoos 1990). Clearly, participation in any one of these behaviors would diminish a youth's life chances. Engagement in some of these behaviors would eliminate the young person's chances of even having a life. Such risks to the life chances of children and adolescents are occurring, unfortunately, at historically unprecedented levels.

In the United States, there are approximately 28 million youth between the ages of 10 and 17 years. About 50% of these adolescents engage in two or more of the above-noted categories of risk behaviors. Moreover, 10% of youth engage in all of the four categories of risk behaviors (Dryfoos 1990). These data indicate that risk behaviors are highly interrelated among adolescents. Other research also finds a tendency for diverse risk behaviors such as drug use and unprotected sexual activity to co-occur (Farrell et al 1992, Ketterlinus & Lamb 1994). Adolescents who engage in multiple risk behaviors may be said to evidence a "risk behavior syndrome" (Jessor 1992). To grasp the full magnitude of the problems facing today's youth, and of the challenges society faces in addressing these problems, it is necessary to provide more details about the several types of risk besetting youth.

## ILLUSTRATIONS OF THE RISK BEHAVIORS ENGAGED IN BY YOUTH: THE SAMPLE CASE OF THE UNITED STATES

Within each of the several major categories of risk behavior besetting youth, there are burgeoning indications that problems are getting more extensive. To illustrate the breadth and depth of these problems, we focus on each of the risk behaviors successively. However, we must keep in mind the comorbidity of these problems. Increasingly, researchers are investigating the co-occurrence of several risk behaviors rather than narrowly focusing on a single one (e.g. Ensminger 1990).

## Drug, Alcohol, and Substance Use and Abuse

Adolescents drink and use a wide variety of illegal/illicit drugs and other unhealthy substances (e.g. inhalants such as glues, aerosols, butane, and solvents). Cigarettes and other tobacco products also are used extensively. Recent trends in the United States in the use of all these substances are quite alarming. For instance, although there were declines in the use of a number of these substances across much of the 1980s, since 1992 an increase in the use of marijuana, cocaine, LSD, and other hallucinogens began to be apparent among eighth graders (Johnston et al 1996). By 1993 and again in 1994, eighth graders continued to show increases in the use of these substances and, as well, tenth and twelfth graders joined them in exhibiting an increase in use (Johnston et al 1996). Although earlier surveys of substance use showed that male adolescents engage in more substance use than do females, recent statistics suggest that that there are no gender differences in use of the most common drugs by 12- to 17-year-olds (Ketterlinus et al 1994).

BASES AND IMPLICATIONS OF DRUG, ALCOHOL, AND SUBSTANCE USE AND ABUSE  *Diversity and context*   The growing problems of substance use and abuse are associated with a diverse set of individual and contextual variables. In turn, the use of substances is linked to numerous negative outcomes for youth. For example, alcohol use by adolescents is associated with self-destructive thoughts and behaviors (e.g. suicidal ideation and attempts) and engaging more frequently in risky behaviors (such as taking someone else's medication) (Windle et al 1992). In turn, in research with both Latino and European American youth, drug use is associated with personality problems, lack of adjustment to school, and poor parenting practices (Flannery et al 1996).

Moreover, parents' substance abuse can influence their offspring's abuse of substances (Howard et al 1994). Such parental behavior can also affect adolescent children's cognitive ability. For instance, in one study, the spatial and visual reasoning of 14-year-olds was related to their mother's alcohol use during pregnancy 15 years earlier: The more the mother had drunk, the poorer the adolescent's performance (Hunt et al 1995).

The community context can also influence adolescent substance use. For example, in inner cities both drug use and drug trafficking (termed running, selling, or dealing) is pervasive (Feigelman et al 1993). Among African American youth living in inner-city areas, illicit drug use typically occurs along with cigarette and alcohol use and drug trafficking (Li et al 1994). In turn, however, drug trafficking is just as likely to occur with or without use of such substances.

Most youth, whether they themselves use substances, see such behavior as a matter of personal discretion or personal judgment, rather than as issues of morality or social convention (Nucci et al 1991). Nevertheless, there are personal and social factors that protect youth against their own involvement with such substances. For instance, religious commitments and beliefs are factors that protect African American adolescents against the use of alcohol (Barnes et al 1994). Moreover, although peer substance use is related to substance use by an adolescent, African American youth are less susceptible to such peer influences than are European American youth (Barnes et al 1994). In addition, African American adolescents have higher alcohol abstinence rates and lower rates of alcohol abuse than European American youth. Similarly, among Latino adolescents, both attitudes about alcohol use and positive self-concepts are associated with a decreased likelihood of alcohol use (Alva & Jones 1994). In addition, these youth are less likely to be involved in peer groups that use alcohol. Moreover, low self-efficacy, low conventionality, and drinking simply "to get drunk" were associated with binge drinking among the male adolescents involved in the *Monitoring the Future Study* (Schulenberg et al 1996).

Some groups of youth seem to be at particular risk for substance abuse problems. Research with Native American adolescents (Gfellner 1994, Mitchell et al 1996) suggests that this may be the case with these youth. For instance, with the exception of alcohol, Native American adolescents show higher rates and more frequent use of cigarettes, marijuana, and solvents than European American youth (Gfellner 1994); furthermore, Native American youth have a greater involvement in problem behaviors than do European American adolescents.

CONCLUSIONS ABOUT ADOLESCENT ALCOHOL, DRUG, AND SUBSTANCE USE
There are both individual and contextual differences in the bases and use of alcohol, drugs, and other substances. In turn, there exists also a diverse set of factors that protect youth against involvement with these substances, and thus that act to safeguard adolescents against the problematic behaviors associated with use and abuse of substances.

The presence of factors protective against adolescent problem behavior is quite important. Protective factors decrease the likelihood of an adolescent's engaging in problem behaviors by providing for the youth (*a*) personal controls (e.g. religious beliefs, good self-concepts) and/or (*b*) social controls (e.g. social support, authoritative parenting) against the occurrence of problem behaviors. As the presence of protective factors increases, there are decreases in adolescents' involvement not only in alcohol and drug abuse but in delinquency and sexual precocity (Jessor et al 1995).

## Unsafe Sex, Teenage Pregnancy, and Teenage Parenting

Adolescents have always engaged in sex. Venereal and other sexually transmitted diseases, and pregnancy and childbirth to unmarried teenagers, have occurred throughout history, and there is nothing new about the fact that adolescents of today engage in sex. What is new, however, is the extent and breadth of adolescents' involvement in sex, the younger ages at which this involvement occurs, and the marked increases in the depth and breadth of the problems associated with such sexual behavior.

Illustrations of the magnitude of these problems among contemporary adolescents include the fact that each year one million adolescents in the United States become pregnant (Di Mauro 1995); about half have babies. About every minute, a baby is born to an adolescent (Children's Defense Fund 1995). Moreover, by age 18, 25% of females in the United States have been pregnant at least once (Lerner 1995).

BASES AND IMPLICATIONS OF UNSAFE SEX, TEENAGE PREGNANCY, AND TEEN-AGE PARENTING DIVERSITY AND CONTEXT    The breadth and variation of the above-noted problems pertinent to contemporary adolescent sexual behavior are staggering. The magnitude and diversity of the manifestation of these problems is challenging educational, health care, and social service systems. For example, about $25 billion in federal money is spent annually in the United States to provide social, health, and welfare services to families begun by teenagers (Di Mauro 1995). In 1992, the federal government spent nearly $34 billion on Aid to Families with Dependent Children, Medicaid, and food stamps for families begun by adolescents (Carnegie Corporation of New York 1995). The complexity of these problems is due at least in part to their connection to the other risk behaviors of adolescence and to numerous individual and contextual influences on adolescents (Small & Luster 1994). As we stress again, the multiple influences on adolescents' sexually risky behavior require public policies and intervention programs that are sensitive to the diverse contexts within which youth are embedded (Ensminger 1990).

To illustrate the several individual and contextual levels playing a role in adolescent sexual problems, we note that biological, cognitive, and behavioral variables, as well as peer, family, and community ones, influence adolescent sexual risk behaviors. For example, in regard to individual influences, ambivalent attitudes toward childbearing, contraception, contraceptive efficacy, and abortions are related to adolescent childbearing (Zabin et al 1993). Similarly, possession of attitudes that reject societal norms, when combined with nonconforming behavior, is associated with early initiation of sexual intercourse among both African American and European American adolescents (Costa et al 1995). In addition, among both male and female adolescents, poor psychological adjustment is linked to early initiation of sexual intercourse (Bingham & Crockett 1996).

Pubertal maturation may also be related to adolescents' sexual behaviors. For example, among gay and bisexual male adolescents, pubertal maturation is associated with age of first orgasm and first homosexual activity and with frequency of orgasms during junior high school (Savin-Williams 1995). It should be stressed that gay and heterosexual male adolescents did not differ in their levels of self-esteem.

Other individual variables, however, if shown by gay adolescents, may not bode well for their adjustment. For instance, among African American and Latino gay and bisexual adolescent males, sexually risky attitudes, when coupled with substance abuse, conduct problems, and emotional distress, are associated with the likelihood that this set of problems will remain stable for the youth (Borus et al 1995); in fact, across a two-year period, only about 20–30% of youth change their pattern of problem behaviors.

The peers of adolescents also influence their sexuality. For example, peer rejection in the sixth grade is associated with the number of sexual partners females will have over the next four years. In turn, however, peer acceptance, when it is associated with both a lot of dating and use of alcohol with classmates, is associated as well with the number of sexual partners adolescents have by tenth grade (Feldman et al 1995).

Moreover, the number of sexually active girlfriends that an adolescent female has, as well as the number of her sexually active sisters, and whether she has an adolescent childbearing sister, are linked to her possessing permissive sexual attitudes, having positive intentions for future sex, and being more likely to be a nonvirgin (East et al 1987). Thus, both peer and family contexts can combine to influence adolescent sexuality. This point is underscored by other research. Among African and European Americans, having a girlfriend or a boyfriend and low educational expectations were associated with being sexually active (Scott-Jones & White 1990). Although these associations did not differ across the groups of African Americans and European Americans, it was the case that the former group of youth were less likely to use contraception than the latter group.

Family and peer contexts also influence the likelihood that adolescent girls will experience an incident of unwanted sexual activity (Small & Kerns 1993). About 20% of girls report that unwanted sexual experiences have occurred within the past year. Approximately one third of these encounters involved forced sexual intercourse; the other two thirds of the events involved unwanted touching. Most of these experiences were initiated by boyfriends, dates, friends, or acquaintances (in this order). A girl's history of sexual abuse, a tendency to conform to peers, and having parents whose rearing style was either authoritarian or reflective of low monitoring were predictive of her being a target of an unwanted sexual advance. Similarly, in divorced families, a mother's dating behavior and her possession of sexually permissive attitudes influences both daughters' and sons' sexual activity (Whitbeck et al 1994).

The community context also influences adolescent sexuality. In poor communities, youth have higher rates of abortion and lower rates of marriage (Sullivan 1993). In turn, among both African American and European American female adolescents, living in a socially disorganized, low-income community, one wherein family planning services are not readily available, is associated with the initiation of sexual intercourse and with the young women's subsequent sexual activity. One study of a racially diverse sample of first-time adolescent mothers living in an urban area found that 35% had a repeat pregnancy within 18 months of the first birth (East & Felice 1996).

*Conclusions about problems of adolescent sexuality*   The breadth and depth of the problems associated with the sexual behavior of today's youth exist at historically unprecedented levels. Not only do these problems arise from a diverse set of individual and contextual influences but, in turn, they impact the adolescent's social world (e.g. his or her peers, family of origin, and, with increasing probability, own children). Addressing the problems of adolescent sexuality requires, therefore, an approach that considers the entire system of influences involved in the youth's development.

## School Underachievement, Failure, and Dropout

About 25% of the approximately 40 million children and adolescents enrolled in the 82,000 public elementary and secondary schools in the United States are at risk for school failure (Dryfoos 1994). Each year about 700,000 youth drop out of school, and about 25% of all 18- and 19-year-olds have not graduated from high school (Center for the Study of Social Policy 1992, 1993; Dryfoos 1990; Simons et al 1991). The dropout rate appears to be comparable for males and females (Ketterlinus et al 1994). The costs to society—having large numbers of youth ill-prepared to contribute productively to society—and to youth themselves are enormous.

For instance, remaining in school is the single most important action youth can take to improve their future economic prospects. For example, in 1992, a high school graduate earned almost $6,000 per year more than a high school dropout (Carnegie Corporation of New York 1995). In addition, college graduates in 1992 had a mean annual income of $32,629, whereas high school graduates had a mean annual income of $18,737; earning a professional degree added $40,000 to the average annual income of college graduates (Carnegie Corporation of New York 1995). In turn, each added year of secondary education reduces the probability of public welfare dependency in adulthood by 35% (National Research Council 1993).

BASES AND IMPLICATIONS OF SCHOOL PROBLEMS: DIVERSITY AND CONTEXT
School underachievement, failure, and dropout in adolescence are linked to the sets of individual and contextual variables discussed in regard to substance abuse and sexual risk behaviors. That is, the bases of the influences of schools on a youth's development are associated with (*a*) individual variables, relating to cognitive abilities (Fuligni et al 1995), motivation (Pintrich et al 1994, Wentzel 1993), personality (Guerin et al 1994), and self (Roberts & Petersen 1992); (*b*) peer variables, pertaining to peer reputation or status (East et al 1987, Hartup 1993, Morison & Masten 1991), and to the nature of the social or antisocial behaviors shown by one's peers (Berndt & Keefe 1995, Dishion et al 1995); (*c*) family variables, pertaining to the nature of parenting (i.e. child rearing style) (Baumrind 1983, Lamborn et al 1991), socialization practices (Crystal & Stevenson 1995, Feldman et al 1992, Gjerde & Shimizu 1995, Phinney & Chavira 1995, Weller et al 1995), and types of behavioral interactions between the youth and his or her parents (Brody et al 1996, Ge et al 1996, Lord et al 1994); (*d*) community variables relating to poverty level (Children's Defense Fund 1992, Hernandez 1993), social support for learning (Brooks-Gunn et al 1993, Levitt et al 1991), and programs providing wholesome activities to youth during nonschool hours (Carnegie Corporation of New York 1992); and (*e*) school setting, pertaining to the structure and curriculum of the school (Dryfoos 1994, Epstein & Dauber 1995), and to the sorts of peers and teachers one encounters and to the interactions experienced with them (Gamoran & Nystrand 1991).

As is the case in regard to other problem behaviors of adolescence, the entire system of individual-through-context relations needs to be engaged—not only to understand the source of adolescents' school problems but to design programs effective in keeping youth in schools and, once there, in promoting the positive developments schools can provide: knowledge, abilities and skills, self-esteem, social relationships, and the opportunity to contribute productively to self, family, community, and society (Dryfoos 1994).

CONCLUSIONS ABOUT SCHOOL PROBLEMS IN ADOLESCENCE   The challenges to development faced by youth as they try to attain the knowledge and skills requisite for success in society are many of the same ones adolescents face in trying to build successful personal, family, and community lives. Their personal resources and the social contexts within which they find themselves hold the key to both positive and negative developmental changes.

The role of science is to identify the sets of individual and contextual variables that, when combined, can increase the likelihood that youth will not succumb to the risks they may face. It is to find the factors that protect youth from adversity (Jessor et al 1995) and that can promote their positive development (Pittman 1996). In turn, the issue for application is to translate this knowledge into programs that engage much of the breadth and resources of the system of influences affecting a youth's life, and to design activities that will effectively enable him or her to move forward in a healthy manner (Lerner 1995). Perhaps in no area of youth problem behaviors is the immediacy of this need more apparent than in regard to delinquency, crime, and violence.

## Delinquency, Crime, and Violence

Of all the problems confronting contemporary youth, no set of issues has attracted as much public concern and public fear as youth delinquency and violent crimes. People point to the growth of youth gangs, groups of youth that may or may not (Taylor 1996) be engaged in criminal activity but that, nevertheless, can be found in urban centers as well as in rural communities. In addition, people point in fear to territorial battles and drug trafficking violence and shootings, to random street violence, and to the seemingly younger and younger ages of, often, quite violent criminals.

The breadth and depth of the problems of delinquency, crime, and violence by youth are indeed daunting. For instance, youth, aged 13 to 21 years, accounted for 35.5% of all nontraffic-related arrests in the United States during the 1980s, although this age group was only 14.3% of the population (National Research Council 1993, Simons et al 1991). Moreover, in the mid-1980s, 1.7 million arrests occurred among 10- to 17-year-olds. More than 500,000 of those arrested were 14 years of age or younger, and 46,000 were under age 10 years (National Research Council 1993, Simons et al 1991). In addition, in 1991, 130,000 arrests of youth aged 10 to 17 years were made for rape, robbery, homicide, or aggravated assault. This figure represents an increase of 48% since 1986 (Center for the Study of Social Policy 1993). The societal and economic costs of such behaviors are high. In 1993, for example, the cost of providing emergency transportation, medical care, hospital stays, rehabilitation, and related treatment for firearm victims ages 10 through 19 was $407 million (Carnegie Corporation of New York 1995).

BASES AND IMPLICATIONS OF DELINQUENCY, CRIME, AND VIOLENCE *Diversity and context* As is the case regarding other problems affecting today's adolescents, both individual and contextual variables combine to influence youth engagement in delinquency, crime, and violence. To illustrate what are now familiar themes of adolescent development, we may note that individual influences on the adolescent include variables related to his or her thoughts, behavior characteristics, sense of self, and biological maturation. In turn, peer and family influences are quite salient contextual influences.

For instance, it is not surprising to learn that aggressive conduct is strongly associated with an aggressive personality (Cairns & Cairns 1994, Pakiz et al

1992). However, poor judgment may be associated with the enactment of aggression by delinquent youth (Graham et al 1997). For instance, in situations where negative outcomes of a social interaction are unintentional, aggressive African American male adolescents make more extreme judgments of the other person and of the situation than comparable groups of nonaggressive youth (Graham & Hudley 1994). Other beliefs about aggression may influence youth violence. For instance, African American and Latino urban adolescents believe that their parents would disapprove more if they retaliated aggressively against their siblings than against peers (Herzberger & Hall 1993). Another individual characteristic associated with delinquency is sex of the adolescent. Historically, males have expressed significantly more delinquency than have females, and they still do, but in recent years the violent crime arrest rate among adolescent females has increased (Ketterlinus et al 1994).

Biological variables, *when* they are expressed in a particular context, are also linked to delinquent behavior. In a longitudinal study of Swedish youth, early maturation among girls was related to norm breaking and delinquent behavior when the girls were part of a peer group of older girls (Stattin & Magnusson 1990). However, early maturation was not linked to delinquency among girls who associated with a same-age peer group.

Peer context is, then, an important influence on delinquency; however, it too acts in relation to family variables. For instance, male delinquents who have committed assaultive offenses have family relations characterized by rigidity and low cohesion; as well, they have peers who are highly aggressive (Blaske et al 1989). In addition, these offenders and their mothers show little anxiety or interpersonal discomfort in the face of the youth's offenses. In turn, male delinquents who have committed sexual offenses have high levels of neurotic symptoms, and their mothers show such problems as well (Blaske et al 1989). Sexually offending youth have low-level emotional bonds with their peers. Moreover, multiple family factors (e.g. authoritarian parenting, deviant mother-child interactions, number of parent changes experienced by a child, having a single parent family, quality of family relationships, mother's reading level, and socioeconomic level) are associated with conviction by age 18 for both violent and nonviolent criminal offenses (Henry et al 1996). Violent offenders also show a temperamental style reflective of a lack of control.

CONCLUSIONS ABOUT DELINQUENCY, CRIME, AND VIOLENCE    Many people have argued that the solution to the problems of delinquency and of youth crime and violence is to build more and/or different sorts of prisons, for example, "boot camps" (Taylor 1996). These policy prescriptions are made, however, with little understanding and almost no research evidence about the influence of youth incarceration on youth development (Taylor 1996).

Accordingly, rather than pursue programs untested by systematic research, we believe that a useful approach to the problems of youth crime and violence is one that reflects an attempt to change the interrelated bases of behaviors we have discussed in regard to the other problems of youth development. This approach emphasizes dealing with the multiple problems of youth in an integrative manner. In addition, it points to the use of addressing all facets of the developing person and his or her context with a comparable commitment to integration. These facets of integration, which are discussed below as key features of effective youth intervention programs, underscore the idea that all the people with a stake in the youth's positive development, including the youth himself or herself, can pool their resources to protect the youth and to promote positive outcomes in his or her life. This integrated youth-participatory approach to programming is salient as well when one turns from a consideration of behavioral risks facing youth to an analysis of a key structural problem besetting increasingly greater segments of the adolescent population: poverty.

## Youth Poverty

A key social problem affecting adolescence in the United States is *poverty*. During the 1980s more than 28 million individuals were below the poverty level, and almost half were children or adolescents (Center for the Study of Social Policy 1992). Poverty disproportionately affects the young. As mentioned above, in the United States, about 20% of all youth 18 years of age or less are at or below the poverty level (Huston et al 1994, Simons et al 1991). Poverty also disproportionately affects minority youth. African American, Latino, and Native American youth are more likely than their European American age mates to be among the poor (Center for the Study of Social Policy 1992, Huston 1991, Simons et al 1991). Moreover, race is the most striking and disturbing distinction between youth whose poverty is chronic and youth for whom poverty is transitory (Huston 1991). For example, African Americans spend a significantly larger portion of their childhood years in poverty than do non–African Americans (Duncan 1991). The picture of poverty is worsening. Poverty among children and youth increased dramatically during the 1980s, and these increases were apparent among all racial and ethnic groups. Finally, youth poverty occurs in all geographic regions of the United States. In fact, the rates of poverty in rural areas are as high as those in the inner cities (Huston 1991, Jensen 1988). Poor families in rural areas receive fewer welfare benefits and are less likely to live in states that provide Aid to Families with Dependent Children (AFDC) (Huston 1991, Jensen 1988).

IMPLICATIONS OF YOUTH POVERTY: DIVERSITY AND CONTEXT    Youth poverty exacerbates the risk behaviors of adolescents (Hamburg 1992, Huston 1991,

Lerner 1993a). Schorr (1988) argued that poverty creates several "rotten out-comes" of youth development. For example, poverty is associated with early school failure, unemployability, long-term welfare dependency, violent crime, and feelings of hopelessness and despair (Schorr 1991, Simons et al 1991). Furthermore, poor youth live at high risk for low self-confidence, conduct problems, depression, and peer conflict. In addition, poor youth are at risk for encountering severe health problems (e.g. infant mortality, lack of immuniza-tion against common childhood diseases), physical or mental disabilities, and physical abuse, neglect, and unintended injury (Carnegie Corporation of New York 1994, Klerman 1991, McLoyd & Wilson 1991, Simons et al 1991).

Poverty is also related to disease and undernutrition, civil disturbances, and urban violence. In such a context, many youths, particularly poor youths, are left to "chart their own course" or, much worse, to pick a route from among the often confusing signals put out by the family, peer group, school, and work place (Ianni 1989). With problematic demographic trends, deteriorating local and national economies, and intractably high levels of poverty (both rural and urban), Wilson (1987) has suggested that we are in a self-sustaining chain re-action, one that contributes to a marked increase in levels of crime, addiction, and welfare dependency. These phenomena, unfortunately, are especially brought to our attention by rates of adolescent juvenile delinquency.

The structure of the family is also changing in ways that have placed poor youth and parents at greater risk of problems of family life and individual devel-opment. For instance, during the 1980s, there was a 13% increase in the number of youth living in single-parent families, a trend present in 44 states. Thus, dur-ing the 1987–1991 period, 18, 30, and 57% of European American, Latino, and African American children, respectively, lived in single-parent households (Center for the Study of Social Policy 1992). Overall, approximately 25% of youth in the United States live in single-parent (and, typically, female-headed) families, and poverty rates among female-headed, single-parent or male-headed, single-parent families are much higher (47 and 23%, respectively) than among two-parent families (9%) (Center for the Study of Social Policy 1993, Hernandez 1993). The poverty rates in single-parent households were, by the beginning of the 1990s, 30% for European American families, 51% for African American families, and 53% for Latino families (US Department of Commerce 1991). The fact that increasing numbers of youth live in these fam-ily structures means that the financial resources to support parenting are less likely to be available (Center for the Study of Social Policy 1993).

## Resiliency and Protective Factors Among Poor Adolescents

Despite the challenges of living in poverty, many poor youth overcome the odds (Werner & Smith 1992) and develop in a healthy fashion. Unless one focuses on the protective factors that result in resiliency among poor youth, one may form an inaccurate impression that only risk characterizes these adolescents. Such a "deficit model" is not veridical with the data on development among poor, and particularly minority poor, adolescents. We have much to gain by considering the often creative adaptations to life-course discontinuities required of minority families to survive and thrive amid unacknowledged societal inconsistencies (Chestang 1972). The adaptive modes used by minority parents and their children require insights not available from traditional paradigms (Spencer 1990).

There are both person- and context-protective factors that promote developmental resiliency. For instance, the pioneering work of McAdoo (e.g. 1982) illustrates that satisfying family life exists in minority families having diverse structures (e.g. single- and dual-parent households) and that protective factors, such as faith, play important supportive roles even in families where there is much stress (e.g. in poor, single-parent, female head-of-household families; McAdoo 1995). The strengths that McAdoo (1993) identifies as prototypic in ethnically diverse families have religious institutions as an important, and in fact a key, source. Such sources of resiliency constitute what McAdoo (1982, p. 479) has termed "stress absorbing systems in Black families."

Moreover, in homes where there is an absence of a father, a strong mother-adolescent relation can protect youth from risks (e.g. of having a peer group engaged in problem behaviors) and, in turn, constitutes a source of resiliency and positive development among poor, minority youth (Mason et al 1994). In addition, family social support promotes adjustment in minority youth and, as well, provides resiliency in the face of negative life events (Cauce et al 1982, 1992; Spencer 1983).

Other contextual factors also provide sources of resiliency for poor, minority youth (e.g. Henly 1993). For instance, social support provided within the school setting, for example by teachers, promotes school competence (Cauce et al 1992, Felner et al 1985) and particular school-based programs, such as school-based health service provision programs (Robinson et al 1993), can constitute protective factors for youth. In turn, the work environment of parents and the social support provided by parents combine to reduce externalizing problems among African American adolescents (Mason et al 1994). Similarly, peer emotional support and reciprocal best-friend relationships are linked with school competence and peer competence among young, African American adolescents (Cauce 1986).

Individual-psychological characteristics of poor, minority youth also provide protective factors in their development. For instance, perceived self-competence is a key attribute of positive development among minority youth (Cauce 1986). Other self variables—such as aspirations and future perceptions and self-concept/identity development processes—are also sources of resiliency among minority youth (e.g. Matute-Bianchi 1986; Spencer 1984, 1987).

In essence, then, there are a rich array of individual and contextual protective factors that promote resiliency and successful, healthy development among poor and/or minority youth. We opt, then, to pursue paths of application that emphasize the potential of young people for positive development and healthy lives. Current thinking about public policy and youth-serving programs supports this perspective and underscores the need for a developmental understanding of the nature of risk behavior.

## THE DEVELOPMENTAL COURSE OF RISK BEHAVIOR

Because adolescence, more than any other stage in the life span, is likely to involve experimentation and exploration, it is not surprising that we observe the emergence of risk behaviors during this stage (Hurrelmann 1990). Two trends characterize the nature of risk behavior in adolescence. First, some risk behavior is *normative*. A majority of adolescents, for example, will at least experiment with smoking (Baumrind 1987, Johnston et al 1995, Shedler & Block 1990). Second, risk behaviors *increase* in adolescence, although the developmental course that a particular behavior follows (when it reaches its height) is unique to the specific behavior (Arnett 1992, Maggs et al 1995). Delinquency, for instance, rises and falls in adolescence, but alcohol use and sexual intercourse continue to increase into adulthood (Bachman et al 1997, Gottfredson & Hirschi 1994, Petersen et al 1993).

Given that the majority of adolescents will engage at one time or another in one or more risk behaviors, how do we know when the behavior is likely to pose significant threats to the adolescent's health and well-being in the long term? First, risk behavior is most likely to turn out to be a real problem when it begins early. Young people who begin engaging in delinquent acts at the age of 9 or 10, for instance, are more likely than those with a later onset to be headed for trouble. Second, *continued engagement* in risk behavior, rather than experimentation, is likely to signal future difficulties. Third, the adolescent may already be in significant trouble when he or she becomes immersed in a *risk-behavior lifestyle* to the exclusion of a constructive, positive lifestyle. A risk-behavior lifestyle may be indicated by continuing engagement in multiple or very serious problem behaviors and a set of close friends who engage in these same activities (Elliott et al 1989, Petersen et al 1993, Shedler & Block 1990).

There has been some suggestion to date that some risk behaviors may lead to others (i.e. there may be a sequential process in which diverse risk behaviors accumulate in an orderly and predictable fashion). For example, adolescents who drink beer may then proceed to use marijuana, which finally leads to hard drug use (Kandel 1989). The co-occurrence of many risk behaviors naturally leads to the question of whether there is a causal sequence in which risk behaviors emerge cumulatively. Although the idea of a causal sequence in risk behaviors is attractive because it would help to identify, early on, adolescents who are most at risk for immersion in a risk behavior lifestyle, there is currently too little research available to support the existence of a stagelike sequence. Some scientists have argued against the notion of such a causal sequence (Gottfredson & Hirschi 1994, Udry 1994). Until there is more research examining the development and co-occurrence of multiple and diverse risk behaviors over time, however, the question of whether there is a causal sequence remains unanswered.

When do adolescents stop engaging in risk behaviors? In other words, is risk behavior a pattern that is so stable that adolescents may have trouble extricating themselves from it? Certainly, adolescents who are engaged early on and frequently in a variety of serious risk behaviors will be less likely to discontinue this behavior. There is little research, however, examining the correlates of stability in risk behaviors from adolescence into adulthood. One exception is the *Monitoring the Future Study,* which charted the substance use risk behaviors of multiple cohorts of high school seniors as they moved through early adulthood (Bachman et al 1997). One-year stability rates in substance use are high as the individual moves from adolescence to adulthood, and become even more stable with each passing year. (Cigarette use is especially stable.) The 14-year stability rate (from high school to approximately age 32) for cigarettes is 0.65; for alcohol and marijuana use it is 0.45, and the 14-year stability for cocaine is 0.25. This research also found that decreases in the use of tobacco, alcohol, and other drugs occurred when individuals became engaged, married, or pregnant—decreases that were reversed among individuals who became divorced. Thus, this research suggests that the responsibilities of early adulthood have an inhibitory effect on drug use (Bachman et al 1997). Whether other risk behaviors also decrease with initiation into the responsibilities of adulthood is open to question.

CONCLUSIONS ABOUT THE DEVELOPMENTAL COURSE OF RISK BEHAVIORS
Across the diverse sets of individual and contextual factors that are associated with the actualization of risk behaviors in adolescence—that is, with substance use and abuse; unsafe sex, adolescent pregnancy, and childbearing; school failure and dropping out; and crime and delinquency—or with the prevention of these risk behaviors, respectively, there are six common characteristics that are involved in the occurrence during adolescence of one or more of these risk behaviors (Dryfoos 1990). Consistent with the stress on the system of relations involving individuals and contexts as integral in human development, three in-

dividual and three contextual factors appear central in the genesis of risk behaviors or their prevention:

1. *Age.* The earlier the initiation of any of the risk behaviors of adolescence, the more likely it is that the youth will engage in the behavior to a great extent and that he or she will suffer negative consequences.
2. *Expectations for education and school grades.* Youth who do not expect to do well in school, and who do not in fact do well, are at risk for all the problem behaviors reviewed.
3. *General behavior.* Inappropriate behaviors and inadequate conduct (e.g. acting out, truancy, and conduct disorders) are related to the appearance of risk behaviors.
4. *Peer influences.* An individual's likelihood of engaging in problem behaviors is not due just to individual factors (such as early pubertal maturation) but to contextual factors as well, for instance, having peers who engage in risk behaviors.
5. *Parental influences.* Particular styles of parenting—that is, authoritarian or permissive styles, as compared with an authoritative one (Baumrind 1983)—place a youth at risk for problem behaviors. Similarly, if parents do not monitor their children, or do not supervise, guide, or communicate with them effectively, there is a strong likelihood that an at-risk status will be actualized (Crouter et al 1990). In addition, if adolescents are not positively affectively tied to their parents, risk behaviors are also likely to occur.
6. *Neighborhood influences.* The community context also plays a role in the actualization of risk. A neighborhood characterized by poverty, or by urban, high-density living, is involved with risk actualization. Not surprisingly, race and minority status are also associated with higher likelihoods of risk behaviors, as particular minority groups (African American and Latino ones) are likely to be the people living in such communities in the United States.

In short, then, a particular set of integrations among individual, familial, peer, and community levels is involved in the actualization of risk behaviors among adolescents (Dryfoos 1990). In turn, however, there are other integrations, involving these very same levels, that are involved in the design and delivery of successful prevention programs for "at-risk" youth.

# RISK, PROTECTION, AND PREVENTION IN ADOLESCENCE: POLICY AND PROGRAM OPTIONS FOR PROMOTING POSITIVE YOUTH DEVELOPMENT

If programs are to be successful in addressing the combined individual and contextual influences on youth problems, they must engage these same levels in ways that promote the positive development of young people (Schulenberg et al 1997, Pittman 1996). That is, whether aimed at alcohol or drug use (Rohrbach et al 1994, Wagenaar & Perry 1994), aggression and delinquency (Guerra & Slaby 1990), unsafe and unprotected sexual practices (Alan Guttmacher Institute 1994), school problems (Switzer et al 1995), or socioeconomic disadvantage (Furstenberg & Hughes 1995), effective programs engage the system of individual and contextual variables affecting youth development.

By involving multiple characteristics of the young person—for instance, his or her developmental level, knowledge of risk taking, intrapersonal resources (e.g. self-esteem, self-competence, beliefs, and values), interpersonal management skills (e.g. being able to engage useful social support and prosocial behaviors from peers)—successful risk prevention programs may be developed (Levitt et al 1991, Petersen et al 1997). However, these programs are more than ones focusing on diminishing risk. The most effective programs emphasize the strengths and assets of young people, that is, their capacities for positive development, their possession of attributes—protective factors—that keep them moving forward in a positive developmental path. Protective factors—individual attributes, such as self-esteem, religious values, and knowledge, skills, and motivation to do well; and contextual attributes, such as the experience of having authoritative parents and a socially supportive, prosocial peer group—have been identified as integral in the healthy development of young people (Feldman 1995, Jessor et al 1995, Schulenberg et al 1997, Stiffman et al 1992).

A multiplicity of needs must be met for adolescents to develop into healthy and productive adults. These needs include: feeling valued as a person, forming close and lasting human relationships, establishing a place in a productive group, being useful to others, making use of support systems, making informed choices, and believing in a future with real opportunities (Carnegie Corporation of New York 1995). Moreover, in a technologically advanced democratic society—one that places an increasingly high premium on competence in many domains—adolescents must master social skills, engage in inquiring and problem-solving strategies that enhance lifelong learning, acquire technical and analytic abilities necessary in a world-class economy, and become ethical, responsible citizens with a healthy respect and tolerance for diversity among individuals (Carnegie Corporation of New York 1995).

## Features of Effective Programs for Youth

What sorts of programs meet these needs? The scholarship of Dryfoos (1990) is especially helpful in providing some answers. Based on the evaluation of 100 programs, Dryfoos (1990) identified 11 features that should be integrated into successful programs for adolescents. These features—many of which are also advocated by the Carnegie Council on Adolescent Development (Carnegie Corporation of New York 1995)—involve coordinated attention to the youth's characteristics of individuality and to the specifics of his or her social context. These features are found in youth-service programs that have been evaluated as effective (Carnegie Corporation of New York 1995; Dryfoos 1990, 1994; Hamburg 1992; Schorr 1988).

1. *Intensive individualized attention.* Successful programs involve having a youth attached to a responsible adult who is attuned to the adolescent's characteristics of individuality and his or her specific needs.

2. *Communitywide, multiagency collaboration.* To address all the different needs, issues, and actual or potential problems of youth, the different programs and services that exist need to work together collaboratively.

3. *Early identification and intervention.* Given the association between age of onset of risk behaviors and eventual negative outcomes, successful programs are ones that begin at the earliest period within the course of development.

4. *Locus in schools.* Given the important role of scholastic expectations and school performance in adolescent risk behaviors, successful prevention programs are often located in schools.

5. *Administration of school programs by agencies outside of schools.* Given the importance of community-wide, multiagency collaboration, the successful programs that are located in schools are often ones that are administered by nonschool community agencies.

6. *Location of programs outside of schools.* Moreover, consistent with the importance of multiagency coordination and collaboration, a successful overall program involves nonschool-based (community) interventions as well.

7. *Arrangements for training.* Successful programs include an orientation to the program, in-service training, supervision, and often multidisciplinary support staffs.

8. *Social skills training.* Many successful programs include the training of personal and social skills among youth. Such training enables adolescents to cope with and/or resist the potentially negative influences of features of the social context, e.g. antisocial peers.

9. *Engagement of peers in interventions.* However, given the salience of the peer group in the adolescent period, many successful programs have included the peer group.

10. *Involvement of parents.* Similarly, given the central role of the family in adolescent behavior, programs have been successful when they have in-

volved parents, for instance, as classroom aides or, have included parent education and support through home visits.

11. *Link to the world of work.* Given the centrality of work in the identity development of adolescents, successful prevention programs afford the adolescent the opportunity to have work experiences and to prepare to enter the labor force (Dryfoos 1990).

In essence, then, there are multiple features of person and context that should be combined to design and deliver a successful program preventing the actualization of risk in adolescence. Building on the general developmental characteristics of the period—involving identity, family, peer, and institutional (e.g. school and work) contextual levels—these programs, when attuned as well to the specific characteristics and needs of the youth and his or her setting, will help the adolescent not just avoid the development of risk behaviors. In addition, positive youth development may be promoted.

Optimism about the likely success of programs is warranted if they are designed and delivered in the context of keeping in mind that no one, single or isolated effort is apt to succeed, given that risk behaviors are interrelated and influenced by a host of individual and contextual factors. Thus, a coordinated set of community-based programs, aimed at both individuals and their contexts, is required for success; these programs should begin as early as possible and should be maintained for as much of the adolescent years as feasible. No one effort, even a comprehensive one, can continue to prevent the appearance of risk across all this period. As a consequence, collaboration across programs is a necessary strategy to pursue. Whereas it may not be feasible for any one effort (e.g. one aimed at reducing drug abuse) to address all the interrelated problems faced by youth, community-wide, integrated efforts can have mutually positive influences on adolescent development.

Clearly, then, means may be found to design and deliver programs that will help prevent, among the proportion of youth at risk for the development of major instances of problem behaviors, the development of such an undesirable status. Perhaps more significant, means exist for not just keeping youth from following a course of negative behaviors. Knowledge of design criteria for effective youth programs serves also as a guide for devising means to capitalize on the potentials and strengths of all youth, their families, and communities and, through meeting their developmental needs, promote their positive development.

However, if this knowledge about how to promote positive development is to reach the maximum number of youth possible, the resources of society must be marshaled in the service of designing effective programs. To this end, scholars of youth development must engage public policy and policymakers in the support of comprehensive programs for youth (Lerner 1995, Lipsitz 1991, Hamburg & Takanishi 1996). These ideas about building effective youth programs have clear implications for public policy.

## Public Policy for Youth Development Programs

Public policies represent standards, or rules, for the conduct of individuals, organizations, and institutions (Lerner 1995). Simply, policies indicate a society's level of investment in and care for its members. If we value our youth, we will promote public policies that enable effective programs to be designed and sustained for all youth that need them. We know how to design effective programs. The task now is to formulate a set of social rules—policies—that will enable the value placed on youth to be translated into effective actions.

The Carnegie Council offers five policy directions that, if followed, will marshal the resources needed to enhance the lives of today's youth. Their recommendations are (Carnegie Corporation of New York 1995, pp. 13–14):

1. Reengage families with their adolescent children;
2. Create developmentally appropriate schools for adolescents;
3. Develop health promotion strategies for young adolescents;
4. Strengthen communities with young adolescents; and
5. Promote the constructive potential of the media.

The first four recommendations noted in the Carnegie Report are consistent with the features of effective programs noted above. The last recommendation is crucial to add, however. The media is needed to disseminate information about the constructive potential of integrated youth programming. If society's resources are to be devoted to the needs of youth, fellow citizens must be convinced that these resources will be well spent and beneficial. The media has a responsibility and can be encouraged to help tell this story—which is one, on balance, of hope and potential—to all segments of society.

## CONCLUSIONS

Adolescence today presents a contradictory picture. About 50% of youth in the United States may be at moderate or greater levels of risk for engaging in unhealthy, unproductive, and even life-threatening behaviors. Yet most individuals pass through adolescence resolving the challenges they face to become competent, productive adult members of society. Most adolescents will go on to lead fulfilled lives; they will manage the dissatisfactions and crises they experience. We cannot, however, ignore those individuals—and in sheer numbers, there are many of them—who are at risk for long-term poor physical and mental health—in many cases, adolescents who because of an unfortunate confluence of sets of individual and contextual factors (e.g. poverty) find themselves in situations that are difficult to escape. Our knowledge of these individual and contextual influences, however, can be used integratively to design and deliver programs preventing the actualization of risk among adolescents.

Adolescence is, then, a "double-edged sword." It is a period wherein myriad risk behaviors may exist. Yet, the scientific evidence indicates that conditions *can be created* to allow at-risk youth to pass through this period by successfully meeting its challenges. Comprehensive intervention programs can help at-risk youth integrate in a coherent way the biological, cognitive, emotional, and social changes they are experiencing, and to form a useful self-definition. This sense of self, or identity, will allow most youth to make decisions and commitments—first to educational paths, and then to careers and to other people. These decisions and commitments eventuate in the adoption of social roles (e.g. worker, spouse, and parent) that keep society moving forward effectively into the future.

Insofar as the limits of scientific generalization permit, most youth have the personal, emotional, and social context resources necessary to meet successfully the biological, psychological, and social challenges of this period of life. For those who do not, social scientists, educators, caregivers, parents, and public policymakers can pool their resources and knowledge to create conditions that maximize the opportunities for these youth to leave the period of adolescence with a developmentally new, but nevertheless, useful sense of themselves. With a supportive social context attuned to the developmental changes and individuality of youth, healthy and successful people will emerge from the period of adolescence.

> **Visit the *Annual Reviews home page* at http://www.AnnualReviews.org.**

## Literature Cited

Alan Guttmacher Inst. 1994. *Sex and America's Teenagers*. New York: Alan Guttmacher Inst.

Allen JP, Hauser ST, Bell KL, O'Connor TG. 1994. Longitudinal assessment of autonomy and relatedness in adolescent family interactions as predictors of adolescent ego development and self-esteem. *Child Dev.* 65:179–94

Alva SA, Jones M. 1994. Psychosocial adjustment and self-reported patterns of alcohol use among Hispanic adolescents. *J. Early Adolesc.* 14:432–48

Annie E. Casey Found. 1995. *Kids Count Data*

*Book: State Profiles of Child Well-Being.* Baltimore: Annie E. Casey Found.

Arnett J. 1992. Reckless behavior in adolescence: a developmental perspective. *Dev. Rev.* 12:339–73

Arnett J, Balle-Jensen L. 1993. Cultural bases of risk behavior: Danish adolescents. *Child Dev.* 64:1842–59

Bachman JG, Wadsworth KN, O'Malley PM, Johnston LD, Schulenberg JE. 1997. *Smoking, Drinking, and Drug Use in Young Adulthood: The Impacts of New Freedoms and New Responsibilities.* Hillsdale, NJ: Erlbaum. 241 pp.

Barnes GM, Farrell MP, Banerjee S. 1994. Family influences on alcohol abuse and other problem behaviors among black and white adolescents in a general population sample. *J. Res. Adolesc.* 4:183–202

Baumrind D. 1983. Rejoinder to Lewis's reinterpretation of parental firm control effects: Are authoritative families really harmonious? *Psychol. Bull.* 94:132–42

Baumrind D. 1987. A developmental perspective on adolescent risk taking in contemporary America. In *Adolescent Social Behavior and Health: New Directions for Child Development,* ed. CE Irwin, 37:93–125. San Francisco: Jossey-Bass

Berndt TJ, Keefe K. 1995. Adolescents' perceptions of the transition to junior high school. *J. Res. Adolesc.* 5(1):123–24

Bingham CR, Crockett LJ. 1996. Longitudinal adjustment patterns of boys and girls experiencing early, middle, and late sexual intercourse. *Dev. Psychol.* 32(4):647–58

Blaske DM, Borduin CM, Henggeler SW, Mann BJ. 1989. Individual, family, and peer characteristics of adolescent sex offenders and assaultive offenders. *Dev. Psychol.* 25(5):846–55

Borus M, Rosario M, Van Rossem R, Reid H. 1995. Prevalence, course, and predictors of multiple problem behaviors among gay and bisexual male adolescents. *Dev. Psychol.* 1:75–85

Boyer CB, Hein K. 1991. AIDS and the HIV infection in adolescents: The role of education and antibody testing. See Lerner et al 1991, 2:1028–41

Brody GH, Stoneman Z, Flor D. 1996. Parental religiosity, family processes, and youth competence in rural, two-parent African American families. *Dev. Psychol.* 32(4): 696–706

Bronfenbrenner U. 1979. *The Ecology of Human Development: Experiments by Nature and Design.* Cambridge, MA: Harvard Univ. Press. 330 pp.

Brookins GK. 1991. Socialization of African-American adolescents. See Lerner et al 1991, 2:1072–76

Brooks-Gunn J, Gus G, Furstenberg FF. 1993. Who drops out of and who continues beyond high school? A 20-year follow-up of black urban youth. *J. Res. Adolesc.* 3(3): 271–94

Brooks-Gunn J, Petersen AC. 1983. *Girls at Puberty: Biological and Psychosocial Perspectives.* New York: Plenum. 341 pp.

Cairns RB, Cairns BD. 1994. Lifelines and risks: Pathways of youth in our time. New York: Cambridge Univ. Press. 315 pp.

Carnegie Corporation of New York. 1992. *A Matter of Time: Risk and Opportunity in the Nonschool Hours.* New York: Carnegie Corp. NY. 152 pp.

Carnegie Corporation of New York. 1994. *Starting Points: Meeting the Needs of Our Youngest Children.* New York: Carnegie Corp. NY. 132 pp.

Carnegie Corporation of New York. 1995. *Great Transitions: Preparing Adolescents for a New Century.* New York: Carnegie Corp. NY. 55 pp.

Caspi A, Lynam D, Moffitt TE, Silva PA. 1993. Unraveling girls' delinquency: biological, dispositional, and contextual contributions to adolescent misbehavior. *Dev. Psychol.* 29:19–30

Cauce AM. 1986. Social networks and social competence: exploring the effects of early adolescent friendships. *Am. J. Community Psychol.* 14:607–28

Cauce AM, Felner RD, Primavera J. 1982. Social support in high-risk adolescents: structural components and adaptive impact. *Am. J. Community Psychol.* 10: 417–28

Cauce AM, Hannon K, Sargeant M. 1992. Life stress, social support, and locus control during early adolescence: interactive effects. *Am. J. Community Psychol.* 20: 787–98

Ceci SJ, Bronfenbrenner U. 1985. "Don't forget to take the cupcakes out of the oven": prospective memory, strategic time monitoring, and context. *Child Dev.* 56: 152–64

Center for the Study of Social Policy. 1992. *1992 KIDS COUNT Data Book: State Profiles of Child Well-Being.* Washington, DC: Cent. Stud. Soc. Policy

Center for the Study of Social Policy. 1993. *Kids Count Data Book.* Washington, DC: Cent. Stud. Soc. Policy. 166 pp.

Chestang LW. 1972. *Character development in a hostile environment. Occas. Pap.* No. 3, pp. 1–12. Chicago: Univ. Chicago

Children's Defense Fund. 1992. *Child Poverty*

*Data from 1990 Census.* Washington, DC: Child. Defense Fund. 11 pp.

Children's Defense Fund. 1995. *The State of America's Children Yearbook.* Washington, DC: Child. Defense Fund. 136 pp.

Children's Defense Fund. 1996. *The State of America's Children Yearbook.* Washington, DC: Children's Defense Fund. 110 pp.

Costa FM, Jessor R, Donovan JE, Fortenberry JD. 1995. Early initiation of sexual intercourse: the influence of psychosocial unconventionality. *J. Res. Adolesc.* 5:93–122

Crouter AC, MacDermid SM, McHale SM, Perry-Jenkins M. 1990. Parental monitoring and perceptions of children's school performance and conduct in dual- and single-earner families. *Dev. Psychol.* 26: 649–57

Crystal DS, Stevenson HW. 1995. What is a bad kid? Answers of adolescents and their mothers in three cultures. *J. Res. Adolesc.* 5(1):71–91

Di Mauro D. 1995. *Sexuality Research in the United States: An Assessment of Social and Behavioral Sciences.* New York: Soc. Sci. Res. Counc. 100 pp.

Dishion TJ, Andrews DW, Crosby L. 1995. Antisocial boys and their friends in early adolescence: relationship characteristics, quality, and interactional process. *Child Dev.* 66:139–51

Dryfoos JG. 1990. *Adolescents at Risk: Prevalence and Prevention.* New York: Oxford Univ. 280 pp.

Dryfoos JG. 1994. *Full Service Schools: A Revolution in Health and Social Services for Children, Youth and Families.* San Francisco: Jossey-Bass. 310 pp.

Duncan GJ. 1991. The economic environment of childhood. See Huston 1991, pp. 23–50

East PL, Felice ME. 1996. *Adolescent Pregnancy and Parenting: Findings from a Racially Diverse Sample.* Mahwah, NJ: Erlbaum. 168 pp.

East PL, Hess LE, Lerner RM. 1987. Peer social support and adjustment of early adolescent peer groups. *J. Early Adolesc.* 7(2): 153–63

Eccles JS. 1991. Academic achievement. See Lerner et al 1991, 1:1–9

Eccles JS, Lord SE, Roeser RW, Barber BL, Jozefowicz DMH. 1997. The association of school transitions in early adolescence with developmental trajectories through high school. See Schulenberg et al 1997, pp. 283–320

Elder GH Jr. 1980. Adolescence in historical perspective. In *Handbooks of Adolescent Psychology,* ed. J Adelson, pp. 3–46. New York: Wiley. 624 pp.

Elliott DS, Huizinga D, Menard S. 1989. *Multiple-Problem Youth: Delinquency, Substance Use, and Mental Health Problems.* New York: Springer-Verlag. 266 pp.

Ensminger ME. 1990. Sexual activity and problem behaviors among black, urban adolescents. *Child Dev.* 61:2032–46

Epstein JL, Dauber SL. 1995. Effects on students of an interdisciplinary program linking social studies, arts, and family volunteers in the middle grades. *J. Early Adolesc.* 15(1):114–44

Farrell AD, Danish SJ, Howard CW. 1992. Relationship between drug use and other problem behaviors in urban adolescents. *J. Consult. Clin. Psychol.* 60:705–12

Feigelman S, Stanton BF, Ricardo I. 1993. Perceptions of drug selling and drug use among urban youth. *J. Early Adolesc.* 13(3):267–84

Feldman B. 1995. The search for identity in late adolescence. In *Incest Fantasies & Self-Destructive Acts: Jungian and Post-Jungian Psychotherapy in Adolescence,* ed. M Sidoli, G Bovensiepen, pp. 153–66. New Brunswick, NJ: Transaction Books. 328 pp.

Feldman SS, Elliott GE. 1990. *At the Threshold: The Developing Adolescent.* Cambridge, MA: Harvard Univ. Press. 641 pp.

Feldman SS, Mont-Reynaud R, Rosenthal DA. 1992. When east moves west: the acculturations of values of Chinese adolescents in the U.S. and Australia. *J. Res. Adolesc.* 2(2):147–73

Feldman SS, Rosenthal DR, Brown NL, Canning RD. 1995. Predicting sexual experience in adolescent boys from peer rejection and acceptance during childhood. *J. Res. Adolesc.* 5(4):387–412

Felner RD, Aber MS, Primavera J, Cauce AM. 1985. Adaptation and vulnerability in high-risk adolescents: an examination of environmental mediators. *Am. J. Community Psychol.* 13:365–79

Finkelstein JW. 1993. Familial influences on adolescent health. See Lerner 1993b, pp. 111–26

Fisher CB, Brennan M. 1992. Application and ethics in developmental psychology. In *Life-Span Development and Behavior,* ed. DL Featherman, RM Lerner, M Perlmutter, 11:189–219. Hillsdale, NJ: Erlbaum. 238 pp.

Fisher CB, Lerner RM. 1994. Foundations of applied developmental psychology. In *Applied Developmental Psychology,* ed. CB Fisher, RM Lerner, pp. 3–20. New York: McGraw-Hill. 555 pp.

Fisher CB, Murray JP, Dill JR, Hagen JW, Hogan MJ, et al. 1993. The national conference on graduate education in the applications of developmental science across the life span. *J. Appl. Dev. Psychol.* 14:1–10

Flannery DJ, Vazsonyi AT, Rowe DC. 1996. Caucasian and Hispanic early adolescent substance use: parenting, personality, and school adjustment. *J. Early Adolesc.* 16(1):71–89

Ford DL, Lerner RM. 1992. *Developmental Systems Theory: An Integrative Approach.* Newbury Park, CA: Sage. 259 pp.

Fuligni AJ, Eccles JS, Barber BL. 1995. The long-term effects of seventh-grade ability grouping in mathematics. *J. Early Adolesc.* 15(1):58–89

Furstenberg FF, Hughes ME. 1995. Social capital and successful development among at-risk youth. *J. Marriage Fam.* 57:580–92

Galambos NL, Almeida DM. 1992. Does parent-adolescent conflict increase in early adolescence? *J. Marriage Fam.* 54: 737–47

Galambos NL, Ehrenberg MF. 1997. The family as health risk and opportunity: a focus on divorce and working families. See Schulenberg et al 1997, pp. 139–60

Gamoran A, Nystrand M. 1991. Background and instructional effects on achievement in eighth-grade English and Social Studies. *J. Res. Adolesc.* 1(3):277–300

Ge X, Best KM, Conger RD, Simons RL. 1996. Parenting behaviors and the occurrence and co-occurrence of adolescent depressive symptoms and conduct problems. *Dev. Psychol.* 32(4):717–31

Gfellner BB. 1994. A matched group comparison of drug use and problem behavior among Canadian Indian and White adolescents. *J. Early Adolesc.* 14(1):24–28

Gjerde PF, Shimizu H. 1995. Family relationships and adolescent development in Japan: a family-systems perspective on the Japanese family. *J. Res. Adolesc.* 5(3): 281–318

Gottfredson MR, Hirschi T. 1994. A general theory of adolescent problem behavior: Problems and prospects. See Ketterlinus & Lamb 1994, pp. 41–56

Gottlieb G. 1992. *Individual Development and Evolution: The Genesis of Novel Behavior.* New York: Oxford Univ. Press. 231 pp.

Graber JA, Petersen AC. 1991. Cognitive changes at adolescence: biological perspectives. In *Brain Maturation and Cognitive Development: Comparative and Cross-Cultural Perspectives,* ed. KR Gibson, AC Petersen, pp. 253–79. New York: Aldine de Gruyter. 390 pp.

Graham S. 1992. "Most of the subjects were white and middle class": trends in published research on African Americans in selected APA journals, 1970–1989. *Am Psychol.* 5:629–39

Graham S, Hudley C. 1994. Attributions of aggressive and nonaggressive African American male early adolescents: a study of construct accessibility. *Dev. Psychol.* 30(3):365–73

Graham S, Hudley C, Williams E. 1997. Attributional and emotional determinants of aggression among African American and Latino young adolescents. *Dev. Psychol.* 28: 731–40

Guerin DW, Gottfried AW, Oliver PH, Thomas CW. 1994. Temperament and school functioning during early adolescence. *J. Early Adolesc.* 14(2):200–25

Guerney L, Arthur J. 1984. Adolescent social relationships. In *Experiencing Adolescence: A Sourcebook for Parents, Teachers, and Teens,* ed. RM Lerner, NL Galambos, pp. 87–118. New York: Garland. 422 pp.

Guerra NG, Slaby RG. 1990. Cognitive mediators of aggression in adolescent offenders: Intervention. *Dev. Psychol.* 26(2): 269–77

Hagen JW, Paul B, Gibb S, Wolters C. 1990. Trends in research as reflected by publications in *Child Development:* 1930–1989. Bienn. Meet. Soc. Res. Adolesc., Atlanta, GA

Hamburg DA. 1992. *Today's Children: Creating a Future for a Generation in Crisis.* New York: Time Books. 376 pp.

Hamburg DA, Takanishi R. 1996. Great transitions: preparing American youth for the 21st century—the role of research. *J. Res. Adolesc.* 6(4):379–96

Hartup WW. 1993. Adolescents and their friends. *New Dir. Child Dev.* 60:3–22

Henly J. 1993. The significance of social context: the case of adolescent childbearing in the African American community. *J. Black Psychol.* 19:461–77

Henry B, Caspi A, Moffitt TE, Silva PA. 1996. Temperamental and familial predictors of violent and nonviolent criminal convictions: age 3 to age 18. *Dev. Psychol.* 32: 614–23

Hernandez DJ. 1993. *America's Children: Resources from Family, Government, and the Economy.* New York: Russell Sage Found. 482 pp.

Herzberger SD, Hall JA. 1993. Children's evaluations of retaliatory aggression against siblings and friends. *J. Interpers. Viol.* 8(1):77–89

Howard J, Boyd GM, Zucker RA. 1994. Overview of issues. *J. Res. Adolesc.* 4(2): 175–82

Hunt E, Streissguth AP, Kerr B, Olson HC. 1995. Mothers' alcohol consumption during pregnancy: effects on spatial-visual reasoning in 14-year-old children. *Psychol. Soc.* 6:339–42

Hurrelmann K. 1990. Health promotion for adolescents: preventive and corrective strategies against problem behavior. *J. Adolesc.* 13:231–50

Hurrelmann K, ed. 1994. *International Handbook of Adolescence.* Westport, CT: Greenwood. 470 pp.

Huston AC, ed. 1991. *Children in Poverty: Child Development and Public Policy.* Cambridge: Cambridge Univ. Press. 331 pp.

Huston AC, McLoyd VC, Coll CG. 1994. Children and poverty: issues in contemporary research. *Child Dev.* 65:275–82

Ianni F. 1989. *The Search for Structure: A Report on American Youth Today.* New York: The Free Press. 336 pp.

Jensen L. 1988. Rural-urban differences in the utilization of ameliorative effects of welfare programs. *Policy Stud. Rev.* 7: 782–94

Jessor R. 1992. Risk behavior in adolescence: a psychosocial framework for understanding and action. *Dev. Rev.* 12:374–90

Jessor R, Van Den Bos J, Vanderryn J, Costa FM, Turbin MS. 1995. Protective factors in adolescent problem behavior: moderator effects and developmental change. *Dev. Psychol.* 31:923–33

Johnston LD, O'Malley PM, Bachman JG. 1995. *National Survey Results on Drug Use from the Monitoring the Future Study, 1975–1995,* Vol. 1: *Secondary School Students.* Washington, DC: Natl. Inst. Drug Abuse. 327 pp.

Johnston LD, O'Malley PM, Bachman JG. 1996. *National Survey Results on Drug Use from The Monitoring the Future Study, 1975-1994.* Washington, DC: US Dep. Health Hum. Serv. 189 pp.

Kail R. 1991. Processing time declines exponentially during childhood and adolescence. *Dev. Psychol.* 27:259–66

Kandel DB. 1989. Issues of sequencing of adolescent drug use and other problem behaviors. *Drugs Soc.* 35:55–76

Ketterlinus RD, Lamb ME, eds. 1994. *Adolescent Problem Behaviors: Issues and Research.* Hillsdale, NJ: Erlbaum. 238 pp.

Ketterlinus RD, Lamb ME, Nitz KA. 1994. Adolescent nonsexual and sex-related problem behaviors: their prevalence, consequences, and co-occurrence. See Ketterlinus & Lamb 1994, pp. 17–39

Klerman LV. 1991. The health of poor children: problems and programs. See Huston 1991, pp. 1–22

Lamborn SD, Mounts NS, Steinberg L, Dornbusch SM. 1991. Patterns of competence and adjustment among adolescents from authoritative, authoritarian, indulgent, and neglectful families. *Child Dev.* 62: 1049–65

Lerner JV, Lerner RM. 1983. Temperament and adaptation across life: theoretical and empirical issues. In *Life-Span Development and Behavior,* ed. PB Baltes, OG Brim Jr, 5:197–230. New York: Academic. 411 pp.

Lerner RM. 1984. *On the Nature of Human Plasticity.* New York: Cambridge Univ. Press. 208 pp.

Lerner RM. 1986. *Concepts and Theories of Human Development.* New York: Random House. 324 pp. 2nd ed.

Lerner RM. 1987. A life-span perspective for early adolescence. See Lerner & Foch 1987, pp. 9–34

Lerner RM. 1991. Changing organism-context relations as the basic process of development: a developmental-contextual perspective. *Dev. Psychol.* 27:27–32

Lerner RM. 1992. *Final Solutions: Biology, Prejudice, and Genocide.* University Park, PA: Pa. State Press. 238 pp.

Lerner RM. 1993a. Investment in youth: the role of home economics in enhancing the life chances of America's children. *AHEA Monogr. Ser.* 1:5–34

Lerner RM. 1993b. Early adolescence: toward an agenda for the integration of research, policy, and intervention. In *Early Adolescence: Perspectives on Research, Policy, and Intervention,* ed. RM Lerner, pp. 1–13. Hillsdale, NJ: Erlbaum. 535 pp.

Lerner RM. 1995. *America's Youth in Crisis: Challenges and Options for Programs and Policies.* Thousand Oaks, CA: Sage. 147 pp.

Lerner RM, Foch TT, eds. 1987. *Biological--Psychosocial Interactions in Early Adolescence.* Hillsdale, NJ: Erlbaum. 394 pp.

Lerner RM, Miller JR. 1993. Integrating human development research and intervention for America's children: the Michigan State University model. *J. Appl. Dev. Psychol.* 14:347–64

Lerner RM, Miller JR, Knott JH, Corey KE, Bynum TS, et al. 1994a. Integrating scholarship and outreach in human development research, policy, and service: a developmental perspective. In *Life-Span Develop-*

*ment and Behavior,* ed. DL Featherman, RM Lerner, M Perlmutter, 12:249–73. Hillsdale, NJ: Erlbaum. 294 pp.

Lerner RM, Petersen AC, Brooks-Gunn J, eds. 1991. *Encyclopedia of Adolescence,* Vols. 1, 2. New York: Garland. 1222 pp.

Lerner RM, Spanier GB. 1980. A dynamic interactional view of child and family development. In *Child Influences on Marital and Family Interaction: A Life-Span Perspective,* ed. RM Lerner, GB Spanier, pp. 1–20. New York: Academic. 360 pp.

Lerner RM, Terry PA, McKinney MH, Abrams LA. 1994b. Addressing child poverty within the context of a community-collaborative university: comments on Faber, Martin, and Smith (1994) and McLoyd (1994). *Fam. Consum. Sci. Res. J.* 23:67–75

Lerner RM, Villarruel FA. 1994. Adolescence. In *International Encyclopedia of Education,* ed. T Husen, N Postlethwaite, 1:83–89. Oxford: Pergamon. 607 pp. 2nd ed.

Levitt MZ, Selman RL, Richmond JB. 1991. The psychosocial foundations of early adolescents' high-risk behavior: implications for research and practice. *J. Res. Adolesc.* 1(4):349–78

Li X, Stanton B, Feigelman S, Black MM. 1994. Drug trafficking and drug use among urban African American early adolescents. *J. Early Adolesc.* 14(4):491–508

Lipsitz J. 1991. Public policy and young adolescents: a 1990s context for researchers. *J. Early Adolesc.* 11:20–37

Little RR. 1993. *What's working for today's youth: the issues, the programs, and the learnings.* Presented at ICYF Fellows Coll., Mich. State Univ., East Lansing

Lord SE, Eccles JS, McCarthy KA. 1994. Surviving the junior high school transition: family processes and self-perceptions as protective and risk factors. *J. Early Adolesc.* 14:162–99

Maggs JL, Almeida DM, Galambos NL. 1995. Risky business: the paradoxical meaning of problem behavior for young adolescents. *J. Early Adolesc.* 15:339–57

Magnusson D. 1988. Individual development from an interactional perspective. In *Paths Through Life,* ed. D Magnusson, 1:3–31. Hillsdale, NJ: Erlbaum. 226 pp.

Mason CA, Cauce AM, Gonzales N, Hiraga Y. 1994. Adolescent problem behavior: the effects of peers on the moderating role of father absence and the mother-child relationship. *Am. J. Community Psychol.* 22: 723–43

Matute-Bianchi ME. 1986. Ethnic identities and patterns of school success and failures among Mexican descent and Japanese American students in a California high school: an ethnographic analysis. *Am. J. Educ.* 95:233–55

McAdoo HP. 1982. Stress absorbing systems in Black families. *Fam. Relat.* 31:479–88

McAdoo HP, ed. 1993. *Family Ethnicity: Strength in Diversity.* Newbury Park, CA: Sage. 397 pp.

McAdoo HP. 1995. Stress levels, family help patterns, and religiosity in middle- and working-class African American single mothers. *J. Black Psychol.* 21:424–49

McKinney M, Abrams LA, Terry PA, Lerner RM. 1994. Child development research and the poor children of America: a call for a developmental contextual approach to research and outreach. *Fam. Consult. Sci. Res. J.* 23:26–42

McLoyd VC, Wilson L. 1991. The strain of living poor: parenting, social support, and child mental health. See Huston 1991, pp. 105–35

Mead M. 1928. *Coming of Age in Samoa: A Psychological Study of Primitive Youth for Western Civilization.* New York: Morrow. 297 pp.

Mitchell CM, O'Nell TD, Beals J, Dick RW, Keane E, Manson SM. 1996. Dimensionality of alcohol use among American Indian adolescents: latent structure, construct validity, and implication for developmental research. *J. Res. Adolesc.* 6(2): 151–80

Montemayor R, Adams GR, Gullotta TP, eds. 1990. *From Childhood to Adolescence: A Transitional Period?* Newbury Park, CA: Sage. 308 pp.

Morison P, Masten AS. 1991. Peer reputation in middle childhood as a predictor of adaptation in adolescence: a seven-year follow-up. *Child Dev.* 62:991–1007

National Research Council. 1993. *Losing Generations: Adolescents in High-Risk Settings.* Washington, DC: Natl. Acad. Press. 276 pp.

Nucci L, Guerra N, Lee J. 1991. Adolescent judgment of the personal, prudential, and normative aspects of drug usage. *Dev. Psychol.* 27(5):841–48

Offer D. 1969. *The Psychological World of the Teen-Ager.* New York: Basic Books. 286 pp.

Pakiz B, Reinherz HZ, Frost AK. 1992. Antisocial behavior in adolescence: A community study. *J. Early Adolesc.* 12(3): 300–13

Petersen AC. 1988. Adolescent development. *Annu. Rev. Psychol.* 39:583–607

Petersen AC, Leffert N, Graham B, Alwin J, Ding S. 1997. Promoting mental health during the transition into adolescence. See Schulenberg et al 1997, pp. 471–97

Petersen AC, Richmond JB, Leffert N. 1993. Social changes among youth: the United States experience. *J. Adolesc. Health* 14: 632–37

Petersen AC, Taylor B. 1980. The biological approach to adolescence: biological change and psychological adaptation. In *Handbook of Adolescent Psychology,* ed. J Adelson, pp. 117–55. New York: Wiley. 624 pp.

Phinney JS, Chavira V. 1995. Parental ethic socialization and adolescent coping with problems related to ethnicity. *J. Res. Adolesc.* 5(1):31–54

Pintrich PR, Roeser RW, De Groot E. 1994. Classroom and individual differences in early adolescents' motivation and self-regulated learning. *J. Early Adolesc.* 14(2): 139–61

Pittman K. 1996. Community, youth, development: three goals in search of connection. *New Des. Youth Dev.* Winter:4–8

Reid PT. 1991. Black female adolescents, socialization of. See Lerner et al 1991, 1: 85–87

Roberts LR, Petersen AC. 1992. The relationship between academic achievement and social self-image during early adolescence. *J. Early Adolesc.* 12(2):197–219

Robinson W, Ruch-Ross HS, Watkins-Ferrell P, Lightfoot SL. 1993. Risk behavior in adolescents: methodological challenges in school-based research. *Sch. Psychol. Q.* 8: 241–54

Rohrbach LA, Hodgson CS, Broder BI, Montgomery SB, Flay BR, et al. 1994. Parental participation in drug abuse prevention: results from the midwestern prevention project. *J. Res. Adolesc.* 4(2):295–318

Savin-Williams RC. 1995. An exploratory study of pubertal maturation timing and self-esteem among gay and bisexual male youths. *Dev. Psychol.* 31(1):56–64

Schorr LB. 1988. *Within our Reach: Breaking the Cycle of Disadvantage.* New York: Doubleday. 398 pp.

Schorr LB. 1991. Effective programs for children growing up in concentrated poverty. See Huston 1991, pp. 260–81

Schulenberg J, Maggs JL, Hurrelmann K, eds. 1997. *Health Risks and Developmental Transitions During Adolescence.* Cambridge: Cambridge Univ. Press. 580 pp.

Schulenberg J, Wadsworth KN, O'Malley PM, Bachman JG, Johnston LD. 1996. Adolescent risk factors for binge drinking during the transition to young adulthood: variable and pattern centered approaches to change. *Dev. Psychol.* 32(4):659–74

Scott-Jones D, White AB. 1990. Correlates of sexual activity in early adolescence. *J. Early Adolesc.* 10(2):221–38

Shedler J, Block J. 1990. Adolescent drug use and psychological health. *Am. Psychol.* 45: 612–30

Silbereisen R, Noack P, Schönpflug U. 1994. Comparative analyses of beliefs, leisure contexts, and substance abuse in West Berlin and Warsaw. In *Adolescence in Context: The Interplay of Family, School, Peers, and Work in Adjustment,* ed. R Silbereisen, E Todt, pp. 176–94. New York: Springer-Verlag. 431 pp.

Simmons RG, Blyth DA. 1987. *Moving into Adolescence: The Impact of Pubertal Change and School Context.* Hawthorne, NJ: Aldine. 441 pp.

Simons JM, Finlay B, Yang A. 1991. *The Adolescent and Young Adult Fact Book.* Washington, DC: Children's Defense Fund. 150 pp.

Small SA, Kerns D. 1993. Unwanted sexual activity among peers during early and middle adolescence: incidence and risk factors. *J. Marriage Fam.* 55:941–52

Small SA, Luster T. 1994. An ecological risk-factor approach to adolescent sexual activity. *J. Marriage Fam.* 56:181–92

Smetana JG. 1988. Concepts of self and social convention: adolescents' and parents' reasoning about hypothetical and actual family conflicts. *Development During the Transition to Adolescence. Minn. Symp. Child Psychol.,* ed. MR Gunnar, WA Collins, 21:79–122. Hillsdale, NJ: Erlbaum. 220 pp.

Smith TM. 1994. Adolescent pregnancy. In *Risk, Resilience and Prevention, Promoting the Well-Being of All Children,* ed. RJ Simeonsson, pp. 125–49. Baltimore: Brookes. 356 pp.

Spencer H. 1990. *The Principles of Sociobiology.* New York: Appleton

Spencer MB. 1983. Children's cultural values and parental child-rearing strategies. *Dev. Rev.* 3:351–70

Spencer MB. 1984. Black children's race awareness, racial attitudes, and self-concept: a reinterpretation. *J. Child Psychol. Psychiatry Allied Discip.* 25:433–41

Spencer MB. 1987. Black children's ethnic identity formation: risk and resilience of castelike minorities. In *Children's Ethnic Socialization: Pluralism and Development,* ed. JS Phinney, MJ Rotheram, pp. 103–16. Newbury Park, CA: Sage. 328 pp.

Spencer MB. 1991. Identity, minority development of. See Lerner et al 1991, 1:111–30

Spencer MB, Dornbusch S. 1990. Challenges in studying minority adolescents. In *At the Threshold: The Developing Adolescent,* ed. S Feldman, G Elliott, pp. 123–46. Cambridge, MA: Harvard Univ. Press. 641 pp.

Spencer MB, Markstrom-Adams C. 1990. Identity process among racial and ethic minority children in America. *Child Dev.* 61: 290–310

Stattin H, Magnusson D. 1990. *Pubertal Maturation in Female Development.* Hillsdale, NJ: Erlbaum. 402 pp.

Steinberg L, Dornbusch SM, Brown BB. 1992. Ethnic differences in adolescent achievement: an ecological perspective. *Am. Psychol.* 47:723–29

Stiffman AR, Chueh H, Earls F. 1992. Predictive modeling of change in depressive disorder and counts of depressive symptoms in urban youth. *J. Res. Adolesc.* 2(4): 295–316

Sullivan ML. 1993. Culture and class as determinants of out-of-wedlock childbearing and poverty during late adolescence. *J. Res. Adolesc.* 3(3):295–316

Susman EJ, Inoff-Germain G, Nottelmann ED, Loriaux DL, Cutler GB Jr, Chrousos GP. 1987. Hormones, emotional dispositions, and aggressive attributes in young adolescents. *Child Dev.* 58:1114–34

Switzer GE, Simmons RG, Dew MA, Regalski JM. 1995. The effect of a school based helper program on adolescent self-image, attitudes, and behavior. *J. Early Adolesc.* 15(4):429–55

Tanner J. 1991. Menarche, secular trend in age of. See Lerner et al 1991, 1:637–41

Taylor CS. 1996. *The unintended consequences of incarceration: youth development, the juvenile corrections systems, and crime.* Presented at Conf. Vera Inst., Harriman, NY

Udry JR. 1994. Integrating biological and sociological models of adolescent problem behaviors. See Ketterlinus & Lamb 1994, pp. 93–107

US Dep. Commerce, Aug. 1991. *Poverty in the United States: 1990.* Washington, DC: US Dep. Commer. 221 pp.

US States Dep. Health and Human Services. 1996. *Trends in the Well-Being of America's Children and Youth: 1996.* Washington, DC: US Dep. Health Hum. Serv. 342 pp.

Wagenaar AC, Perry CL. 1994. Community strategies for the reduction of youth drinking: theory and application. *J. Res. Adolesc.* 4(2):319–47

Weller A, Florian V, Mikulincer M. 1995. Adolescents' reports on parental division of power in a multicultural society. *J. Res. Adolesc.* 5(4):413–29

Wentzel KR. 1993. Motivation and achievement in early adolescence: the role of multiple classroom goals. *J. Early Adolesc.* 13(1):4–20

Werner EE, Smith RS. 1992. *Overcoming the Odds: High Risk Children from Birth to Adulthood.* Ithaca, NY: Cornell Univ. Press. 280 pp.

Whitbeck LB, Simons RL, Kao M. 1994. The effects of divorced mothers' dating behaviors and sexual attitudes on the sexual attitudes and behaviors of their adolescent children. *J. Marriage Fam.* 56:615–21

Whiting BB, Whiting JWM. 1991. Preindustrial world, adolescence in. See Lerner et al 1991, 2:814–29

Wills TA, DuHamel K, Vaccaro D. 1995. Activity and mood temperament as predictors of adolescent substance use: test of a self-regulation mediational model. *J. Pers. Soc. Psychol.* 68:901–16

Wilson WJ. 1987. *The Truly Disadvantaged: The Inner City, the Underclass, and Public Policy.* Chicago: Univ. Chicago Press. 254 pp.

Windle M, Miller-Tutzauer C, Domenico D. 1992. Alcohol use, suicidal behavior, and risky activities among adolescents. *J. Res. Adolesc.* 2(4):317–30

World Health Organization. 1993. *The Health of Young People: A Challenge and a Promise.* Geneva: WHO. 109 pp.

Zabin LS, Astone NM, Emerson MR. 1993. Do adolescents want babies? The relationship between attitudes and behavior. *J. Res. Adolesc.* 3:67

Annu. Rev. Psychol. 1998. 49:447–77

# JUDGMENT AND DECISION MAKING

## B. A. Mellers[1], A. Schwartz[2], and A. D. J. Cooke[3]

[1]Department of Psychology, Ohio State University, Columbus, Ohio 43210, e-mail:
mellers.1@osu.edu; [2]Department of Medical Education, University of Illinois,
Chicago, Illinois 60612-7309; [3]Marketing Department, University of Florida,
Gainesville, Florida 32611

KEY WORDS: risk, emotions, choices, beliefs, utilities

## ABSTRACT

For many decades, research in judgment and decision making has examined
behavioral violations of rational choice theory. In that framework, rationality
is expressed as a single correct decision shared by experimenters and subjects that satisfies internal coherence within a set of preferences and beliefs.
Outside of psychology, social scientists are now debating the need to modify
rational choice theory with behavioral assumptions. Within psychology, researchers are debating assumptions about errors for many different definitions of rationality. Alternative frameworks are being proposed. These
frameworks view decisions as more reasonable and adaptive than previously
thought. For example, "rule following." Rule following, which occurs when
a rule or norm is applied to a situation, often minimizes effort and provides
satisfying solutions that are "good enough," though not necessarily the best.
When rules are ambiguous, people look for reasons to guide their decisions.
They may also let their emotions take charge. This chapter presents recent research on judgment and decision making from traditional and alternative
frameworks.

## CONTENTS

0066-4308/98/0201-0447$08.00

# INTRODUCTION

This chapter, the ninth in a series of annual reviews on judgment and decision making, presents research from 1992 to 1996. Edwards (1961) set the stage in the first review of behavioral decision theory by presenting psychological and economic theories of riskless choice, risky choice, and games. Becker & McClintock (1967) followed with a discussion of utilities and values—topics that link behavioral decision theory to philosophy and other social sciences. Rapoport & Wallsten (1972) presented experimental tests of normative and descriptive theories with an emphasis on measurement. Slovic et al (1977) both reflected and anticipated the emerging interest in judgmental heuristics and biases. Einhorn & Hogarth (1981) attempted to reconcile judgmental biases with functional arguments that imply decisions must be sensible and intelligent. Pitz & Sachs (1984) discussed judgment and decision making in the context of human information processing. Payne et al (1992) stressed use of multiple decision strategies in the construction of preferences. Finally, in a special-topic chapter, Lopes (1994) compared philosophical and methodological views of psychologists and economists on risk, cooperation, and the marketplace.

This review examines assumptions about rationality and alternative frameworks. For many years, rational choice theory has been the dominant framework in economics, political science, finance, marketing, and other fields. Many scholars believed that failures of rationality could not survive competitive market forces. Violations were viewed as relatively trivial or artifactual; decision makers either learn quickly or they are eliminated from the game. Research in judgment and decision making has demonstrated increasingly more violations of rational choice theory, and the importance of behavioral assumptions is now a lively topic of debate among social scientists. Behavioral assumptions are showing up in new subdisciplines. In addition to behavioral decision theory (Edwards 1961), we now have behavioral game theory (Camerer 1990), behavioral finance theory (Thaler 1993), and behavioral accounts of law (Sunstein 1997). These areas have identified both real-world and laboratory situations in which people violate fundamental precepts of rational choice.

In the meantime, psychologists in judgment and decision making have learned a great deal about errors and biases. Unlike economists, psychologists never questioned the need for behavioral assumptions. Instead, they have been questioning definitions of errors and biases within rational choice theory and are examining alternative frameworks. Errors are always defined relative to a normative framework that makes assumptions about human goals. Within the rational choice theory, definitions of errors are usually based on three faulty assumptions. First, there is a single correct response. Second, correct responses can be expressed as coherence within a system of preferences and beliefs. Third, the subject and the experimenter agree on what constitutes a correct response. Below we examine each assumption in detail.

## Rationality is a Single Correct Response

During the last several years, researchers have pointed out that laboratory tasks often have many correct answers. Why? Tasks are inadequately specified, and different normative frameworks can apply. For example, if a Bayesian and a frequentist were asked, "What is the probability of discovering extraterrestrial life somewhere in the solar system in the next twenty years?" they would give very different, albeit "correct," answers. The frequentist would balk at the question, while the Bayesian would provide a number between 0 and 1 that expresses a degree of belief. Even when theoretical positions are recognized, problems may lack sufficient detail for a single correct response. Birnbaum (1983) shows that the famous cab problem has many correct answers, depending on one's theory of the witness. The Monty Hall problem—should a contestant on The Monty Hall show change doors after one door has been opened—has multiple solutions, depending on one's assumptions about Monty. Even insensitivity to regression may be appropriate if people are neither taught nor told to minimize the sum of squared errors when making intuitive predictions.

## Rationality is Internal Coherence and Logical Consistency

In the rational choice framework, rationality is expressed as internal coherence and logical consistency within a system of beliefs and preferences. This assumption has been widely criticized. Gigerenzer (1991, 1996) points out that we are really interested in good judgment, and good judgment requires an analysis of content, in addition to laws, principles, and axioms. Gigerenzer (1996) and Cosmides & Tooby (1996) argue that good judgment is domain specific and should reflect basic principles of survival and adaptation. Kahneman (1994) suggests that logical analyses should be supplemented with substantive evaluations that assess the quality of decision outcomes. Are the person's beliefs grossly out of kilter with available evidence? Does the decision damage the person's interest? Finally, Hammond (1996) believes that people struggle with both coherence, or internal consistency of decisions, and correspondence, or empirical accuracy of decisions based on multiple fallible indicators. He argues for the integration of these perspectives in views of rationality.

## Rationality is the Same for Subjects and Experimenters

Subjects and experimenters are typically assumed to agree on what constitutes rationality. This assumption has also been questioned (e.g. see Frisch & Clemen 1994). Many tasks have flat maxima or multiple good solutions (von Winterfeldt & Edwards 1986). Furthermore, thinking about one decision takes energy away from another. Subjects often have other concerns, not known to the experimenter.

Early metaphors for decision makers posited human beings as intuitive scientists, statisticians, and economists. Researchers investigated how well people sized up against professional standards of competence based on expected utility theory, Bayesian inference, and least squares regression. Some have argued that decision errors associated with these metaphors may not necessarily be errors within other ontological frameworks. Depending on the situation, people may be better understood as intuitive politicians who balance pressures from competing constituencies, intuitive prosecutors who demand accountability, or intuitive theologians who protect sacred values from contamination (Tetlock 1992).

## Alternatives to Rational Choice Theory

One of the most interesting developments in the last five years has been a movement away from normative frameworks. March (1994) offers a dichotomy between preference-based choices and rule following. The traditional view is preference based; choices are consequential, and options are evaluated using prior assessments of beliefs and values. Rule following involves the application of rules or principles to situations. Elster (1989) refers to these decisions as norms or conventions. Although rule following has not received the same formal treatment as preference-based decisions, it appears to describe many automatic decisions that do not involve tradeoffs.

This review discusses both rule-based choices and preference-based choices involving tradeoffs between beliefs and values. The first and second sections begin with research on the decision maker and the decision task, respectively. The third and fourth sections discuss rule following and preference-based choices, respectively. The last section concludes with a few thoughts about the state of the field and future directions. The review is selective, not exhaustive. The reader is urged to read Camerer (1995) for a more extensive review of experimental economics and Dawes (1997) for more extensive coverage of judgmental errors and biases.

## THE DECISION MAKER

There are many dimensions along which decision makers vary; this section focuses on two: risk and emotions. Several books and reviews have appeared on risk (Fischhoff et al 1997, Schoemaker 1993, Shapira 1995, Yates 1992) and emotions (Landman 1993, Parducci 1995, Roese & Olson 1995). We begin with the distinction between risk perceptions—how risky we view objects, hazards, or technologies—and risk attitudes—how willing we are to accept risk.

### Risk Perceptions

Two approaches have been used to study individual differences in risk perceptions. In the first, risk is a multidimensional construct with dimensions labeled as dread, lack of familiarity, and lack of controllability (Fischhoff et al 1981). Slovic (1996) argues that those who have less trust in governments, institutions, and authorities perceive risks of hazards or technologies as greater than those with more trust. For example, environmental hazards are perceived as riskier by women than by men. Environmental disasters are perceived as riskier by blacks than by whites. Well-educated, conservative, white men perceive environmental hazards as least risky (Flynn et al 1994, Slovic et al 1993). Finally, experts and nonexperts differ in their estimates of environmental disasters, particularly for low-probability risks (Gregory et al 1996, Peters & Slovic 1997). Experts are less willing than the public to generalize from animal studies to human beings about chemical causes of cancer (Kraus et al 1992). Furthermore, experts show large affiliation effects; chemical risks are often perceived as lower by toxicologists in industry than by toxicologists in academia (Kraus et al 1992).

How accurate are the perceptions of these groups? Slovic (1996) argues that this question is impossible to answer because there is no single, objective definition of risk. Risk is a social construct invented to cope with the dangers and uncertainties of life. For example, between 1950 and 1970, coal mines became less risky in terms of deaths from accidents per ton of coal, but riskier in terms of accidents per employee (Wilson & Crouch 1982). Was coal mining riskier in 1950 or 1970? There is no right answer. Likewise, there is no single, objective definition of safety. For example, airline safety can be measured on many dimensions, including the percentage of flights ending in accidents relative to total number of flights and the percentage of traveler deaths relative to total number of travelers. But there is no single definition of safety.

The second approach to risk, reviewed by Yates & Stone (1992), examines the perceived riskiness of monetary gambles. Over a decade ago, Coombs & Lehner (1984) found that losses have greater impact than gains, an asymmetry well known in choice behavior (Kahneman & Tversky 1979). Coombs & Lehner described this asymmetry in risk judgments with a bilinear model, similar to subjective expected utility theory with sign-dependent utilities and probabilities. Luce & Weber (1986) proposed a theory of risk judgments called conjoint expected risk. Risk perceptions were described as a weighted combination of three probabilities (winning, losing, and receiving nothing), expected gains (each gain raised to a power) conditional on winning, and expected losses (each loss raised to a different power) conditional on losing.

More recently, Weber et al (1992) find that, holding probability constant, the effect of a given outcome on risk judgments decreases as the number of other outcomes in the gamble increases. This averaging effect cannot be explained by the previous models. Weber et al propose a relative weight averaging model with sign-dependent utilities and probabilities. Although each of the models describes risk judgments in some contexts, none of them gives a complete account, because changes in the stimulus context can alter decision strategies used to form risk perceptions (Mellers & Chang 1994). Simply by including certain gambles within the stimulus set, experimenters can get subjects to change their strategies for judging risk.

This approach to risk perception has identified some cultural differences. Bontempo et al (1997) asked students in Hong Kong, Taiwan, the Netherlands, and the United States to rate the riskiness of monetary gambles. Responses are well-described by the conjoint expected risk model. Parameters of the model differ for subjects from Western countries and those from Asian countries. Western subjects place greater weight on the probabilities of losses, and Asians place greater emphasis on the magnitudes of losses. For Westerners, perceived risk decreases as some of the outcomes in a gamble improve and become positive. For Asians, perceived risk is less influenced by whether any of the outcomes are positive. Risk is clearly a cultural construct.

## Risk Attitudes

In economic theories, risk attitudes are measured by revealed preferences. Consider a choice between a gamble and a sure thing equal to the expected value of the gamble. People who choose the sure thing are said to have risk-averse preferences, and those who choose the gamble have risk-seeking preferences. Preferences are often risk averse in the domain of gains. Kahneman & Lovallo (1993) point out that risk premiums (differences between the expected value of a gamble and its certainty equivalent) can be substantially reduced if risks are aggregated over time. Thaler et al (1997) provide additional support for this claim.

Although preferences are typically risk averse in the gain domain, they are frequently risk seeking in the loss domain, a result known as the reflection effect (Kahneman & Tversky 1979). In earlier research, the effect has been attributed to utility functions that differ for gains and losses. More recently, different weighting functions for gains and losses have been proposed instead of, or in addition to, changes in utilities. March (1996) examines whether preferences for risk can be described from experienced outcomes. Consider a two-alternative, forced-choice task with variable reinforcement. Reinforcement learning theories assume that choice depends only on the outcomes experienced. March defines a set of simple stochastic models that describe trial-by-trial learning and shows what happens when a learner is confronted with options of variable risk over many trials. When experienced outcomes are positive, learners favor less risky alternatives. When experienced outcomes are negative, learners favor riskier alternatives in the short run and risk neutrality in the long run. In short, the tendency for greater risk aversion with gains than with losses is predicted by simple theories of accumulated learning.

Do decision makers believe their own risk attitudes change across gain and loss domains? Weber & Milliman (1997) hypothesize that when risk preferences are defined by the decision maker, not by economic theory, perceived-risk attitudes will show greater consistency across domains. Weber & Milliman present subjects with pairs of gambles and measure both preferences for gambles and risk perceptions. The majority of subjects choose gambles perceived as less risky in both domains. Perceptions of risk vary across domains, but perceived-risk attitudes are more stable and consistent than risk attitudes defined by economic theory. Mellers et al (1997b) find similar results.

## Emotions

Emotions have powerful effects on decisions. Moreover, the outcomes of decisions have powerful effects on emotions. This section reviews research on both predecision and postdecision affect.

PREDECISION AFFECT    Isen (1993) argues that positive emotions increase creative problem solving and facilitate the integration of information. Estrada et al (1994) find that doctors in whom positive affect has been induced integrate information more efficiently than do controls, show less anchoring on earlier diagnoses, and display more creativity in their thinking. Positive feelings can promote variety seeking (Kahn & Isen 1993), overestimation of the likelihood of favorable events, and underestimation of the likelihood of unfavorable events (Nygren et al 1996, Wright & Bower 1992). In contrast, Bodenhausen et al (1994) find that people in positive moods are likely to engage in more stereotyped thinking than people in neutral moods. However, the effect vanishes when people are held accountable for their judgments.

Negative affect can produce a narrowing of attention and a failure to search for new alternatives (Fiedler 1988). People in negative moods make more attribute-based comparisons than alternative-based comparisons (Luce et al 1997). In addition, they make faster and less discriminate use of information that can increase choice accuracy in easier tasks and decrease it in harder tasks.

Research in this domain often treats emotions as a unidimensional construct, ranging from positive to negative. Lewinsohn & Mano (1993) propose a two-dimensional model of affect, based on pleasantness and arousal. People in pleasant moods deliberate longer, use more information, and reexamine more information than others. People in aroused states tend to take more risks. Those who are aroused and in unpleasant moods employ simpler decision strategies and form more polarized judgments (Mano 1992, 1994).

Even a two-dimensional model seems inadequate for describing emotional experiences. Anger, sadness, and disgust are all forms of negative affect, and arousal does not capture all of the differences among them. Furthermore, many emotions, such as parental love, are domain specific. A more detailed approach is required to understand relationships between emotions and decisions.

POSTDECISION AFFECT    Most of us know all too well the feeling of regret that can follow a decision. Gilovich & Medvec (1994, 1995) show that in the short term, people feel greater regret about actions than inactions, but in the long term, people feel greater regret about inactions than actions. Gilovich & Medvec suggest that time reduces the sting of regrettable actions and increases the sadness of regrettable inactions. In contrast, Kahneman (1995) believes people regret actions more than inactions throughout their lives. He contends that Gilovich & Medvec are measuring two distinct emotions, one being an intense, "hot" feeling that accompanies action and the other being a reflective, "wistful" feeling that captures the sadness of missed opportunities.

Mellers et al (1997a) devised a paradigm for measuring both choices and affective responses to monetary outcomes of gambles. After a choice, subjects learn the outcome of the chosen gamble and describe their emotional response to it on a scale ranging from very elated to very disappointed. This paradigm allows the estimation of decision utilities from choices and experienced utilities from emotions. Decision utilities differ from hedonic responses in two important respects. First, unlike decision utilities, experienced utilities are influenced by subjective probabilities. Surprising wins are more pleasurable than expected wins, and surprising losses are more disappointing. Second, unlike decision utilities, experienced utilities depend on counterfactual possibilities. Obtained outcomes are evaluated relative to what might have happened under different states of the world and different choices. These comparisons can make larger losses feel less painful than smaller losses and smaller gains feel more pleasurable than larger gains, a result also found by Boles & Messick (1995). Mellers et al provide an account of emotional responses that they call decision affect theory. With some additional assumptions, this theory can predict choices from emotions.

Memories of hedonic experiences can be important guides to future choice. Kahneman and his colleagues show that when we make global evaluations of past experiences, we are often insensitive to the duration of the experience (Fredrickson & Kahneman 1993, Varey & Kahneman 1992). In one study, Redelmeier & Kahneman (1996) examined moment-to-moment and retrospective evaluations of the pain experienced by patients undergoing diagnostic colonoscopy. Patients indicated their discomfort every 60 s during the procedure and their overall discomfort at the end. The duration of the procedure, which ranged from 4 min to 69 min, does not predict retrospective evaluations. Instead, a peak-end rule, representing an average of the worst moments and the final moments of the experience, predicts global hedonic responses. In other experiments, Kahneman and his colleagues show that by adding diminishing pain to the end of a painful experience, global evaluations can be made more positive (Kahneman et al 1993a). These results have both humane and Orwellian implications and suggest enormous possibilities for decision engineering.

## THE DECISION TASK

Framing effects, stimulus contexts, environments, and response modes might seem innocuous, but they can profoundly shape decisions (Payne et al 1992). Preferences can reverse depending on each of these factors. These effects have important implications for policy making, market decisions, and pollsters.

### Framing Effects

One of the most basic findings in decision making is what Slovic (1972) called the "concreteness principle"; people often accept and use information in the form in which they receive it. When this principle holds, preferences for identical options with different reference points can reverse (Tversky & Kahneman 1981). These effects have been widely investigated (de Dreu et al 1994, Kashima & Maher 1995, Paese et al 1993, Ritov et al 1993, Schweitzer 1995, Sullivan & Kida 1995). For example, Johnson et al (1993) show that preferences for insurance coverage can vary, depending on whether premiums are described as rebates or deductibles. At the time they were conducting their experiments, New Jersey and Pennsylvania offered lower insurance rates if drivers would give up the right to sue other drivers in a collision. In New Jersey, the default option did not include the right to sue, although the driver could purchase it at additional cost. In Pennsylvania, the default option included the right to sue, although the driver could decline it and receive a cost reduction. Prices for comparable coverage were roughly the same. When offered a choice between the two policies, only 20% of New Jersey drivers bought the right to sue, but 75% of Pennsylvania drivers purchased it. Johnson et al estimated that if limited tort had been the default in Pennsylvania, drivers would have saved approximately $200 million in insurance costs.

Not everyone who looks for framing effects finds them, and there are undoubtedly many reasons (Christensen et al 1995, Fagley & Miller 1990). First, framing effects are often examined with verbal scenarios, and small changes in wording can have big effects on preferences (Schneider 1992). In the Asian disease problem (Tversky & Kahneman 1981), one group of subjects choose between two programs designed to combat a disease that is expected to kill 600 people. If one program is adopted, 200 people will be saved, and if the other program is adopted, there is one third probability that 600 people will be saved and two thirds probability that no people will be saved. Another group of subjects choose between the programs described in terms of lives lost. If one program is adopted, 400 people will die, and if the other program is adopted, there is one third probability that nobody will die, and two thirds probability that 600 people will die. Kühberger (1995) notes that outcomes in the Asian disease problem are inadequately specified; knowing that 200 people will be saved does not tell us explicitly what will happen to the other 400 people. When he makes outcomes explicit, preference reversals vanish.

A second reason for the absence of framing effects is because researchers have manipulated the salience of the good or bad features of the outcomes rather than the reference point (van Schie & van der Pligt 1995). For example, descriptions of beef as 90% lean or 10% fat emphasize either the positive or negative features of the beef, respectively, but do not alter the reference point. van Schie & van der Pligt show that emphasis on positive features promotes greater risk-seeking preferences in both the gain and loss domains, and emphasis on negative features promotes greater risk aversion in both domains.

Third, the magnitude of framing effects may depend on the content domain. Frisch (1993) asked subjects to compare identical problems framed differently and decide whether the problems should be treated the same. Subjects tend to think that problems with well-specified monetary gains and losses are equivalent, but other problems, such as those involving sunk costs, seem different. When asked why, they say those problems have different emotional consequences.

## Stimulus Contexts and Environments

Preferences are not created in a vacuum; they depend on the stimulus context. This context might include the environment or the local stimulus context in the world. It might also include a larger context based on the decision maker's past and present experiences.

In inference tasks, people might be asked to consider which of two cities, San Francisco, California, or Columbus, Ohio, has a larger population. They search through their memories to make a response by recalling cues of varying validity. Gigerenzer (1997) and Gigerenzer & Goldstein (1996) examine a simple, lexicographic rule called "take the best, ignore the rest." Cues are represented in memory as binary variables. The first cue is recognition (i.e. does the decision maker recognize the cities?). If only one city is recognized, that city is assumed to be larger. If neither city is recognized, a guess is made. If both cities are recognized, the search continues and the cue with the highest perceived validity is assessed. If one city has a value on that cue, that city is assumed to be larger. If neither city has a cue, the search continues. Likewise, if both cities have cues, the search continues. With relatively few cues, "take the best" can actually outperform linear regression. As the number of cues increases, linear regression outperforms "take the best" (Gigerenzer 1997). Predicted performance based on this simple, satisfying rule varies, depending on the number and validity of the cues in the environment.

In choice tasks, there is a local stimulus context created by the choice set and a global stimulus context provided by all of the choice sets presented for judgment. Asymmetric dominance is a well-known local context effect (Huber et al 1982). Suppose a decision maker chooses between two options, A and B. Later, the decision maker chooses among three options, A, B, and C. The new option, C, is dominated by B but not A. Huber et al find that the relative preference for B over A increases in the larger choice set, a violation of the property of independence of irrelevant alternatives. Several authors have suggested theories of this effect in which weights and/or utilities of the attributes change with the addition of new options (Ariely & Wallsten 1995, Simonson & Tversky 1992, Tversky & Simonson 1993, Wedell 1991, Wedell & Pettibone 1996).

The range and spacing of the attributes presented for choice determine the global stimulus context. Mellers & Cooke (1996) and Simonson & Tversky (1992) find that a given attribute difference has a greater effect on choice when the global range is narrow than when it is wide, and preferences between identical pairs of options can reverse in different global contexts. Such effects cannot be explained as response biases, because response transformations are typically assumed to be monotonic functions that could not produce ordinal changes in preferences.

What psychological processes are affected by the global stimulus context? Mellers & Cooke (1994) and Cooke & Mellers (1997) propose that changes in range and spacing influence the utilities of the attributes in a manner consistent with range-frequency theory (Parducci 1995). In contrast, Tversky & Simonson (1993) propose that changes in the global context affect attribute weights. An earlier account, proposed by Simonson (1989), posits that contextual effects influence the relative justifiability of response options. These theories are not mutually exclusive, and Wedell & Pettibone (1996) find support for both the range-frequency and justification accounts.

WEIGHT ELICITATION    Weights are important in applied contexts. In decision analysis, options are typically decomposed into weights and scales, and information is combined by means of normative rules (Keeney & Raiffa 1976, von Winterfeldt & Edwards 1986). Weights should be sensitive to scale changes: If the range of an attribute presented for judgment is reduced by one half, the effective weight of that attribute should be doubled to compensate. Researchers have tested the sensitivity of different procedures to the range of attributes presented within an experiment. Direct weight assessments do not vary greatly with changes in attribute range (Fischer 1995, Mellers & Cooke 1994, von Nitzsch & Weber 1993). Comparative weight elicitation procedures, such as swing weights, ratio weights, and tradeoff weights, show greater range sensitivity, although less than what is required to compensate for the change in range (Fischer 1995, von Nitzsch & Weber 1993, Weber & Borcherding 1993).

Edwards & Barron (1994) suggest that by eliciting rank orders of importance over all attributes and using rank-ordered centroid weights, one has nearly the same accuracy as is found with more complex methods. Barron & Barrett (1996a) compare three methods for aggregating rank order weights: (a) divide each rank by the sum of the ranks, (b) divide the reciprocal of each rank by the sum of the reciprocals, and (c) average the vertices in the weight space to produce rank-ordered centroid weights. All three procedures work well, although rank-ordered centroid weights consistently outperform the others. Procedures are also given for sensitivity analyses (Barron & Barrett 1996b).

## *Response Mode Effects*

Preferences have been shown to vary with the method of assessment. Consider two gambles, A and B, having equal expected values and different variances. People may assign a higher value to A than B in a pricing task but choose B over A in a choice task. Preference reversals are robust; they have been demonstrated with prices and choices, ratings and choices, and other pairs of response modes. Furthermore, when confronted with the reversals, most subjects adamantly defend them (Ordóñez et al 1995). This simple fact makes it extremely difficult to call preference reversals forms of decision errors.

Tversky et al (1988) propose a compatibility hypothesis to explain reversals: When attributes are compatible with the response scale, they are assigned greater weight. This hypothesis is offered for preference reversals between gambles using price and rating tasks. Mellers et al (1992a) propose an alternative account of preference reversals between gambles with the same two tasks called change-of-process theory. Decision strategies depend on the task, but utilities remain constant. They provide a test between change-of-process and contingent weighting and find evidence supporting the change-of-process theory.

There are undoubtedly multiple causes for preference reversals, depending on the options and the tasks. Fischer & Hawkins (1993) contrast compatibility of attributes and responses with compatibility of tasks and strategies. The latter type of compatibility implies that qualitative tasks, such as choice, induce qualitative strategies (e.g. lexicographic orders) favoring the more prominent attribute, and quantitative tasks, such as matching, evoke quantitative strategies (e.g. averaging) with more uniform weighting of attributes. Fischer & Hawkins find that preference reversals between riskless options using choices and ratings are better described by strategy compatibility than scale compatibility. That is, the more important attribute is weighted more heavily in choices than ratings, a result also found by Mellers et al (1995) and Mellers & Cooke (1996).

Others have speculated that it is not strategy compatibility but rather the salience of comparisons in choices versus ratings that produces preference reversals (Hsee 1996, Markman & Medin 1995). Nowlis & Simonson (1997) note that comparable attributes have greater influence in choice tasks. They ask subjects to evaluate products described by comparable attributes (e.g. price) and less-comparable attributes (e.g. brand name) and find that comparable attributes have greater effects in choices than ratings.

## RULE FOLLOWING

We base many of our decisions on rules or heuristics that convey information about who we are and how we interact with others. These decisions may have involved tradeoffs at one point, but they have become "generic" applications of rules to situations. They may express habits, such as when we wake up in the morning or which foods we purchase at the grocery store. They may convey a personal or moral identity, such as kindness or honesty. They may also convey a social identity, including professional or family ties. Regardless of the function of the rule, this procedure minimizes effort and allows us to turn our attention to other matters.

This section begins with a discussion of rule following for individual and social decisions. Sometimes rules do not apply, either because the rules are poorly defined or because they conflict with other rules. In these cases, decision makers may search for reasons or emotions to guide their choices.

## Individual and Social Decisions

Prelec & Herrnstein (1991) discuss cases in which people avoid cost-benefit analysis and use prudential rules for moral considerations and matters of self-control. For example, what is the cost of eating one piece of chocolate cake or taking one car trip without a seat belt? Adopting a rule is especially useful for controlling one's behavior when the impact of the act is felt only with repetition (e.g. smoking a cigarette), with a delay between costs and benefits (e.g. dieting), or with benefits that are hard to imagine (e.g. spending versus saving). Following a rule minimizes effort and allows people to avoid difficult tradeoffs.

Fiske (1992) maintains that social decisions can be described by four basic rules: communal sharing, authority ranking, equality matching, and market pricing. Communal sharing stresses common bonds among group members, as found with families, lovers, and nations. Authority ranking focuses on inherent asymmetries in relationships; some people have higher rank, privilege, or prestige than others. Equality matching stresses reciprocity. Examples include babysitting cooperatives or car pooling, where one should get back whatever one puts in. In market pricing, decisions are governed by supply and demand, expected utilities, or tradeoffs between costs and benefits.

What happens when the decision maker applies the wrong rule? Fiske & Tetlock (1997) examine such cases and, following Tetlock et al (1996), label them taboo tradeoffs. Proposals to place monetary values on things we think of as priceless, such as children, body organs, or votes, do not just trigger cognitive confusion—they activate moral outrage. Most people respond with contempt and wish to punish norm violators; taboo tradeoffs are threats to both personal identities and the social order.

## Reason-Based Choice

When rules don't single out one best action (Tversky & Shafir 1992a), people may look for reasons to make choices. Reasons may be lists of pros and cons, or they may take the form of stories. Pennington & Hastie (1992, 1993) argue that jurors construct stories to explain the facts. Pennington & Hastie present evidence to subjects either as stories or issues and find that story organizations result in stronger and more confident jury decisions than issue organizations.

Reasons allow us to justify decisions to ourselves (Hogarth & Kunreuther 1995). Shafir et al (1993) create decisions in which people have reasons to choose an act $X$ if an event $A$ occurs, and different reasons to choose $X$ if $A$ does not occur. But if $A$ is unknown, there are no reasons to choose $X$, so it is rejected. This pattern violates Savage's sure-thing principle. For example, Tversky & Shafir (1992b) ask subjects to assume they just took a tough qualifying exam. One group is told they passed, another group is told they failed, and a third group is told they will learn the results tomorrow. Each group is offered a choice among buying a vacation to Hawaii on sale today only, not buying the vacation, or paying $5 to retain the right to buy the vacation package tomorrow. The majority of those who think they passed or failed the exam select the vacation, but the majority of those who don't know the results want to retain the right to buy the vacation tomorrow, presumably because they have no reason to purchase the package today.

Reasons also allow us to justify decisions to others. Justifiability can increase certain decision errors and decrease others (Simonson & Nye 1992, Tetlock & Kim 1987). Tetlock & Boettger (1994) examine situations in which people make choices between the status quo and options that provide gains for society as a whole, but impose losses on an identifiable minority. In these cases, accountability to others can enhance both loss aversion and decision avoidance. People who must justify past acts or expenses to others also get locked into decisions, a finding known as commitment to sunk costs. Arkes (1996) examines how people who are motivated to avoid the appearance of wastefulness compromise their self-interests and attend to sunk costs. Commitment to sunk costs has received much attention (Garland & Newport 1991, Larrick et al 1993, McCarthy et al 1993), and some have found methods for attenuating it (Simonson & Staw 1992, Tan & Yates 1995).

## Emotion-Based Choice

Since the work of Bell (1982, 1985) and Loomes & Sugden (1982, 1986), there has been growing interest in the role of anticipated emotions in choice. Anticipated regret influences choices between gambles (Bar-Hillel & Neter 1996), medical decisions (Ritov & Baron 1990), consumer products (Simonson 1992), and sexual practices (Richard et al 1996). Baron and his colleagues demonstrate that anticipated regret can also produce an omission bias—a preference inaction over action (Baron 1994, Baron & Ritov 1994, Spranca et al 1991). For example, Ritov & Baron (1990) find that people prefer not to vaccinate their child when the vaccine has potentially fatal side effects, even if the death rate from the vaccine is a fraction of the death rate from the disease. People anticipate regret about causing their child's death, but by avoiding the vaccine, they actually increase their child's risk of dying.

Outcome feedback also influences anticipated regret. When people know they will learn the outcomes of unchosen options, they often make choices that minimize chances of feeling regret (Josephs et al 1992, Ritov & Baron 1995, Ritov 1996, Zeelenberg et al 1996). Tests of this theory have been done with pairs of gambles having equal expected values, and results have been consistent with the theory. However, support declines with pairs of gambles that differ in expected value (BA Mellers, A Schwartz & I Ritov, working paper).

## PREFERENCE-BASED DECISIONS

Preference-based choices are consequential because actions depend on beliefs about the value of future outcomes. This section begins with a discussion of beliefs and values and then presents theories of choices and certainty equivalents. See Edwards (1992) for a more extensive review of utility theories.

### Beliefs

Decisions are based on beliefs about the likelihood of future events. Those beliefs are expressed as probability judgments, judgments under uncertainty, and confidence judgments.

PROBABILITY JUDGMENTS   Koehler (1996) examines research on base-rate neglect and argues that base rates are frequently used in decision making. The degree of use depends on task structure and representation. Within-subject designs, direct experience, frequentistic problems, unambiguous sample spaces, and random sampling promote base-rate usage (Cosmides & Tooby 1996, Gigerenzer & Hoffrage 1995, Tversky & Kahneman 1974, Weber et al 1993). Kruschke (1996) examines base rates in category learning tasks. He proposes that when subjects receive feedback, they quickly learn base rates. Common categories are encoded first, and rare categories are encoded later. As a result, people learn typical features of common categories and unusual features of rare categories. This theory predicts base-rate neglect (Gluck & Bower 1988) and the inverse base-rate effect in which people judge higher base-rate events as less likely than lower base-rate events (Medin & Edelson 1988, Nelson 1996).

Tversky & Koehler's (1994) support theory offers an account of explicit and implicit disjunctive probability judgments. In support theory, subjective probability is assigned to hypotheses. Subjective probability increases as hypotheses are "unpacked" into more explicit disjunctions. Judged probabilities are complementary in the binary case but subadditive in the general case. When people are asked, "What is the probability that a given person selected at random from a population will die from an accident?", judgments are less than the sum of the judgments of the components (e.g. car crashes, plane crashes, fire, drowning, and other accidents). Support theory explains conjunction fallacies, hypothesis generation, decisions under uncertainty, and fault-tree errors (Russo & Kolzow 1994). It has also been used to describe choice under uncertainty (Fox & Tversky 1997).

JUDGMENTS UNDER UNCERTAINTY   Decisions about financial investments, litigation, environmental disasters, and insurance are usually based on a lack of knowledge about relevant probabilities. In these situations, people are often ambiguity averse—they prefer known probability distributions over uncertain probability distributions. Actuaries suggest higher warranty prices for ambiguous probabilities than for well-specified probabilities (Hogarth & Kunreuther 1992), and underwriters set higher insurance premiums for ambiguous probabilities and losses than for well-specified probabilities and losses (Kunreuther et al 1995). See Camerer & Weber (1992) for a review of the literature on ambiguity.

Heath & Tversky (1990) note an exception to ambiguity aversion. People often prefer to bet on their own (ambiguous) beliefs over matched chance events when they feel competent about a knowledge domain. What makes them feel competent? Fox & Tversky (1995) suggest that feelings of competence occur when people have clear versus ambiguous knowledge. Fox & Tversky argue that the contrast between differential knowledge states occurs in all previous tests of ambiguity aversion. Subjects typically make choices between clear and ambiguous urns. In these comparative contexts, subjects will pay more for gambles based on clear than ambiguous probabilities. But in non-comparative contexts, subjects value the gambles equally. These results highlight the importance of local contexts in theories of ambiguity.

CONFIDENCE JUDGMENTS   Many studies have examined internal uncertainty, such as the confidence that people place in their own abilities. Typical tasks involve one's belief in one's performance on general knowledge tests. Lack of calibration based on comparisons of confidence judgments against percentages of correct items have led researchers to argue that people are often overconfident. Recently, this conclusion has been criticized on two grounds.

First, some authors argue that overconfidence is simply regression to the mean. Erev et al (1994), Dawes & Mulford (1996), and Pfeifer (1994) show that when relative frequencies (or percentages of correct items) are averaged over confidence ratings, people are often overconfident. But when confidence ratings are averaged over relative frequencies, people are often underconfident or conservative. In short, the same set of data can show overconfidence and underconfidence, depending on the analysis. Furthermore, the "hard-easy" effect—the fact that hard tests are often associated with overconfidence and easy tests with underconfidence —is also expected from a regression interpretation.

To avoid this criticism, some studies compare means, or average confidence ratings, with overall percentage correct. Average confidence ratings are sometimes greater than the average number of correct items, consistent with overconfidence (Brenner et al 1996, Griffin & Tversky 1992, Schneider 1995). Other studies report no average difference (Juslin 1994). Reasons for the discrepancies are unclear.

Second, Gigerenzer et al (1991) and Gigerenzer (1993) argue that overconfidence is not the result of judgment errors, because it only occurs when test items are sampled in nonrandom ways. When questions are selected randomly, overconfidence disappears (Juslin 1994). Using over 25 studies, Juslin et al (1997) demonstrate that overconfidence is only mildly related to the hard-easy effect. However, Griffin & Tversky (1992) find that even with random sampling, overconfidence remains. Reasons for the discrepancies are unclear.

Gigerenzer et al (1991) give another reason why overconfidence may not be a judgment error. They point out that if overconfidence is a general phenomena, it should appear regardless of whether it is measured with single test items or overall number of items. Results often show greater overconfidence with single items than judgments of percentage correct (Gigerenzer et al 1991, Sniezek et al 1990). Once again, there are conflicting results (Griffin & Tversky 1992), and reasons for the discrepancies remain unclear.

BAYESIAN BELIEF NETWORKS    Inference, a process of deriving a conclusion from initial information and a set of rules, plays a key role in expert systems. The most common form of inference comes from Boolean logic in which statements are either true or false. Sometimes, however, evidence is neither true nor false; it is uncertain. In these cases, Bayesian belief networks can be extremely useful (Pearl 1988). Bayesian belief networks consist of nodes, representing probabilistic variables, and links, representing relations between nodes. Networks provide mechanisms for combining uncertain information and making probabilistic inferences. Decision problems that, in the past, were hopelessly complex and unmanageable, are made both visually simple and intuitively obvious largely due to assumptions about conditional independence.

Influence diagrams are used for making decisions. They contain value nodes, decision nodes, and Bayesian belief networks. Influence diagrams also provide power and visual simplicity (Howard & Matheson 1984). Much of the material published on Bayesian belief networks and influence diagrams is fairly technical. For introductory material on Bayesian belief networks, see Shafer (1996) and Morawski (1989). Edwards (1991) provides a paper on applications in legal domains. More information on both theory and applications is available on the World Wide Web.

## *Values*

The endowment effect refers to the observation that people value objects they own more than objects that are not part of their subjective endowment (Kahneman et al 1990). Not only current ownership but history of ownership affects value (M Strahilevitz & GF Loewenstein, manuscript in preparation). For objects in one's possession, value increases with the duration of ownership. For objects that are currently not in one's possession but were at one time, value increases with the duration of past ownership.

Loewenstein & Issacharoff (1994) further demonstrate that value is influenced by how the object was obtained. People who obtain an object due to exemplary performance value that object more highly than people who obtain the same object due either to chance or to poor performance. Their results have implications for public policies, such as housing programs. Policies that give homes away to lower income families may be less effective at improving neighborhoods than policies requiring families to purchase homes, even at extremely low prices. These results converge with those of Arkes et al (1994) who find that windfall gains are spent more readily than other types of assets, presumably because they are valued less. Similarly, unexpected tax rebates, lottery winnings, and inheritances may have less value than earned income.

DELAYED VALUES   When the outcomes of decisions are delayed in time, people often discount the value of the delayed outcome. Discounting functions are often assumed to be exponential, although many experiments suggest they follow a hyperbolic rather than exponential form. Hyperbolic functions imply that when faced with an inferior option now or a superior option later, people want the option now. However, their preferences reverse when the same two options are offered with a constant delay added to each. Loewenstein & Elster (1992) provide a review of this literature.

Discount rates depend on many factors. Chapman (1996a) shows that discount rates differ for health and money. Shelley (1994) finds that discount rates differ for losses and gains, and Stevenson (1992, 1993) demonstrates that discount rates differ for risky and riskless outcomes, as well as for single and multiple outcomes. Discounting behavior can change dramatically when outcomes are embedded in sequences. Loewenstein & Prelec (1993) find that people often prefer improving sequences or uniform sequences over declining sequences. Stevenson (1992) shows no discounting in sequences, and Chapman (1996b) demonstrates that discounting rates vary across domains; people prefer increasing sequences of money, but decreasing sequences of health.

## Risky and Uncertain Choice

Standard economic theories are based on the assumption that utilities and beliefs are separable, but there is growing evidence against this notion. Rank-dependent utility theories relax this assumption by allowing decision weights to depend on the rank of an outcome among the set of all possible outcomes.

Luce (1991) and Luce & Fishburn (1991, 1995) propose and axiomatize a rank- and sign-dependent utility theory using an operation of joint receipt, or the simultaneous receipt of two or more objects. The utility of a risky or uncertain option is a weighted sum of the utilities of its component outcomes, where the weight of an outcome depends in a particular fashion on the rank order of the outcome and the sign of the outcome relative to the status quo. The utility function is assumed to be a negative exponential. Luce and his colleagues test the theory by studying individual axioms, and results have generally supported the theory (Cho et al 1994, Cho & Luce 1995).

In one test, Chung et al (1994) examine a property called event commutativity; the order of events should not matter to a decision maker as long as the outcomes arise under the same conditions (except for ordering). Violations would be problematic for the entire class of rank-dependent theories. Chung et al find solid evidence of event commutativity, consistent with both subjective expected utility and rank-dependent theories.

Tversky & Kahneman's (1992) cumulative prospect theory is another rank- and sign-dependent representation that is identical to rank- and sign-dependent theory in all but two respects. First, it is based on a different axiomatization (Wakker & Tversky 1993), and second, it makes different assumptions about the utility function and the weighting function. In cumulative prospect theory, the utility function is a concave power function for gains, and a convex power function with a steeper slope for losses. The weighting function has an inverse-S form, first concave then convex.

These assumptions have not gone without criticism. Luce (1996) takes issue with the assumption of a power function for utilities; he shows that assumptions of cumulative prospect theory imply a negative exponential rather than a power function. The inverse-S shape of the weighting function has found support in some studies (Wu & Gonzales 1996, Tversky & Fox 1995, Fox et al 1996), but in a more general test, Birnbaum & McIntoch (1996) provide evidence against the inverse-S shaped form.

Lopes (1990, 1995, 1996) develops another rank-dependent theory called security-potential/aspiration (SP/A) theory. She argues that when subjects make risky choices, they are concerned with both security mindedness (avoiding the worst outcome) and potential mindedness (achieving the best outcome). Changes in attention to these goals influence the weighting function.

SP/A theory assumes that the weighting function is both "optimistic" for smaller probabilities and "pessimistic" for larger ones, a function she calls "cautiously hopeful." The theory maximizes both a rank-dependent weighted average of the utilities and the probability of achieving an aspiration level.

Birnbaum and his colleagues have tested rank-dependent theories by examining branch independence: If two gambles have a common outcome for an event of known probability, the value of that common outcome should have no effect on the preference order induced by the other probability-outcome branches. This property must hold under expected utility theory, but not necessarily under rank-dependent theories. Birnbaum & McIntosh (1996) find violations of branch independence. Furthermore, the pattern is the opposite of that implied by cumulative prospect theory.

To account for these results, Birnbaum and others advance configural weight theory (Birnbaum et al 1992, 1997; Birnbaum & Beeghley 1997; Birnbaum & McIntosh 1996; Birnbaum & Viera 1997). Decision weights can vary with the rank and sign of the outcome as in the other theories, but also with the value of the outcome, the number of outcomes, the spacing of the outcomes, and the decision maker's point of view. Testability comes from the assumption that utilities are invariant across all of these factors. Configural weight theory does not assume cumulative weighting. Cumulative weighting implies consequence monotonicity—if people prefer $X$ to $Y$ in one gamble, that preference should be in the same direction in the context of another gamble (Birnbaum & McIntosh 1996). Systematic violations of this property have also been found (Birnbaum & Sutton 1992, Mellers et al 1992b).

Some evidence suggests that the entire class of generic utility theories (Miyamoto 1988, 1992), including rank- and sign-dependent theories, does not capture preferences for gambles. Chechile & Cooke (1996) presented people with a reference gamble and two outcomes of a comparison gamble. Subjects were asked to adjust the probability of winning in the comparison gamble until the overall worth of the two gambles was perceived to be identical. In this task, special cases of generic utility theory could be represented as linear functions with an invariant slope across all reference gambles and a changing intercept. However, both the slope and the intercept systematically varied. The overall worth of a gamble depends not only on the properties that gamble, but also on the comparison gamble. Mellers & Biagini (1994) also show that the utility of an option systematically depends on the other option with which it is compared. Rank- and sign-dependent theories are insensitive to this dependency.

In summary, there is widespread agreement that risky and uncertain choices are rank dependent. But specific issues about the utility function and the weighting function—including shape, form (cumulative vs noncumulative), and factors that influence it—are still points of controversy.

## Dynamic Decision Processes

Busemeyer & Townsend (1993) propose decision field theory to capture the deliberation process that occurs with conflicting values. The theory predicts the feeling of pleasure we may have about an important decision when the action is far away, and the later dread we feel when the action is imminent. Decision field theory also predicts preference reversals as a function of time pressure, violations of stochastic dominance, and the inverse relationship between decision time and choice proportions. This theory of decision making is similar to other accounts of cognitive processing, such as Link's (1992) theory of perceptual discrimination and Ratcliff's (1978) theory of memory retrieval. Diederich (1997) provides a generalization to the multiattribute case.

## Certainty Equivalents

The certainty equivalent of a gamble is the amount of money for which a decision maker is indifferent between receiving the money for sure or playing the gamble. With judgment-based certainty equivalents, subjects state the worth of a risky option, often as buying prices or selling prices. With choice-based certainty equivalents, the point of indifference is inferred from a series of choices between a gamble and sure things.

Certainty equivalents differ from choices in two ways. First, they can produce different preference orders. Second, they can violate consequence monotonicity (Birnbaum et al 1992, Mellers et al 1992b). For example, Birnbaum et al (1992) found that subjects assign higher prices to a gamble with a 95% chance of $96, otherwise $0, than to a gamble with a 95% chance of $96, otherwise $24. This result has also been found with simple choice-based certainty equivalents (Birnbaum 1992) but not with direct choices (Birnbaum & Sutton 1992) or more complex choice-based certainty equivalents, such as those based on the PEST procedure (von Winterfeldt et al 1997). Differences between measures are important enough that any general account of preference should not assume they are equivalent; attempts should be made to describe similarities and differences among measures.

CONTINGENT VALUATION METHODS    In the past two decades, contingent valuation (CV) methods have been used to measure the value of goods for which markets do not exist. People are often asked to state the maximum amount they would be willing to pay (WTP or buying price) to maintain a resource or return a damaged resource to the status quo. If CV responses represent economic values, they should vary with relevant factors and remain constant in the face of irrelevant factors (Baron 1997). However, CV responses are typically insensitive to the economic factors, such as the quantity of the good

(Baron & Greene 1996, Jones-Lee & Loomes 1995, Kahneman & Knetsch 1992, Kahneman et al 1993b) and sensitive to irrelevant factors such as normatively equivalent response modes (Green et al 1994, Irwin 1994, Irwin et al 1993).

Some researchers argue that CV methods measure attitudes (Kahneman & Ritov 1994, Schkade & Payne 1994), moral sentiments (Kahneman & Knetsch 1992), or inferences about missing information (Fischhoff & Furby 1988). Occasionally, respondents are unwilling to answer questions. Baron & Spranca (1997) propose that these responses are evidence of protected values, a notion resembling taboo tradeoffs, that should not occur in economic theory. In sum, CV measures do not appear to be good measures of economic values, and better methods are desperately needed given the size of the monetary stakes.

## CONCLUSION

Research on judgment and decision making has identified important limitations in cognitive and, more recently, emotional processing. The message of decisions errors and biases has had widespread effects. Confronted with real-world violations of rational choice theory, many economists and other social scientists now recognize the need for behavioral assumptions in the marketplace.

Within psychology, the concept of rationality is being reexamined. Errors are always defined relative to a normative framework, and within rational choice theory, definitions of errors have often rested on faulty assumptions. Researchers are now more circumspect about labeling behavior as irrational. Psychologists are examining alternative frameworks, and some theorists are moving away from rational choice theory to explore ways in which people find efficient, adaptive, satisfying decisions. For example, March (1994) proposes the notion of rule following. Rules have a generic form and can reduce the effort of tradeoffs. Many if not most of our decisions are of this type.

In sum, events occurring inside and outside of psychology are raising the level of debate about rational choice theory. Some social scientists now recognize the need for behavioral assumptions within their framework. Furthermore, psychologists, who have provided most of the behavioral violations, are more careful about what they call irrational.

The future of judgment and decision making research within psychology lies in its ability to develop other frameworks that make connections with research on emotions (Landman 1993) and cognition (Busemeyer et al 1995, Dougherty et al 1997), as well as on social and institutional factors (Kagel & Roth 1995). Such connections will undoubtedly influence our views of rationality and adaptiveness and provide fertile ground for research in the years ahead.

ACKNOWLEDGMENTS

Preparation of this chapter was supported by NSF grants SBR-94-09818 and SBR-96-15993. We are extremely grateful for the comments of Jerry Busemeyer, Ward Edwards, Gerd Gigerenzer, Duncan Luce, Lisa Ordóñez, Philip Tetlock, and Elke Weber during the preparation of this manuscript.

## POSTSCRIPT

A tragic event that occurred during the period of our review was the death of Amos Tversky. Amos shaped the field in profound ways and made the field of judgment and decision making a much more exciting enterprise than it otherwise would have been. Ward Edwards, one of Amos's graduate advisors, wrote an obituary in the Decision Analysis Society newsletter. Ward speaks for us when he says, "Certainly the care and depth of thought that shines through every paper on which Amos Tversky's name appears, regardless of order of authorship, more than explains his overwhelming impact. The broad outlines of contemporary cognitive science show his fingerprints everywhere. We who will do the missing will continue to work in an intellectual environment of which he was a major designer. This is our good fortune, and his lasting achievement."

> Visit the *Annual Reviews home page* at
> http://www.AnnualReviews.org.

## *Literature Cited*

Ariely D, Wallsten TS. 1995. Seeking subjective dominance in multidimensional space: an explanation of asymmetric dominance effect. *Org. Behav. Hum. Decis. Process.* 63:223–32

Arkes HR. 1996. The psychology of waste. *J. Behav. Decis. Mak.* 9:213–24

Arkes HR, Joyner CA, Pezzo MV, Nash JG, Seigel-Jacobs K, Stone E. 1994. The psychology of windfall gains. *Org. Behav. Hum. Decis. Process.* 59:331–47

Bar-Hillel M, Neter E. 1996. Why are people reluctant to exchange lottery tickets? *J. Pers. Soc. Psychol.* 70:17–27

Baron J. 1994. Nonconsequentalist decisions. *Behav. Brain Sci.* 17:1–42

Baron J. 1997. Biases in the quantitative measurement of values for public decisions. *Psychol. Bull.* 122:72–88

Baron J, Greene J. 1996. Determinants of insensitivity to quantity in valuation of public goods: contribution, warm glow, budget constraints, availability, and prominence. *J. Exp. Psychol. Appl.* 2:107–25

Baron J, Ritov I. 1994. Reference points and omission bias. *Org. Behav. Hum. Decis. Process.* 59:475–98

Baron J, Spranca M. 1997. Protected values. *Org. Behav. Hum. Decis. Process.* 70:1–16

Barron FH, Barrett BE. 1996a. The efficacy of SMARTER-Simple Multiattribute Rating Technique Extended to Ranking. *Acta Psychol.* 93:23–36

Barron HF, Barrett BE. 1996b. Decision quality using ranked attribute weights. *Manage. Sci.* 42:1515–23

Becker GM, McClintock CG. 1967. Value: behavioral decision theory. *Annu. Rev. Psychol.* 18:239–86

Bell D. 1982. Regret in decision making under uncertainty. *Opin. Res.* 20:961–81

Bell D. 1985. Disappointment in decision making under uncertainty. *Opin. Res.* 33:1–27

Birnbaum MH. 1983. Base rates in Bayesian inference: signal detection analysis of the cab problem. *Am. J. Psychol.* 96:85–94

Birnbaum MH. 1992. Issues in utility measurement. *Org. Behav. Hum. Decis. Process.* 52:319–30

Birnbaum MH, Beeghley D. 1997. Violations of branch independence in judgments of the value of gambles. *Psychol. Sci.* 8:87–94

Birnbaum MH, Coffey G, Mellers BA, Weiss R. 1992. Utility measurement: configural-weight theory and the judge's point of view. *J. Exp. Psychol. Hum. Percept. Perform.* 18:331–46

Birnbaum MH, McIntosh WR. 1996. Violations of branch independence in choices between gambles. *Org. Behav. Hum. Decis. Process.* 67:91–110

Birnbaum MH, Sutton SE. 1992. Scale convergence and utility measurement. *Org. Behav. Hum. Decis. Process.* 52:183–215

Birnbaum MH, Thompson LA, Bean DJ. 1997. Tests of interval independence vs. configural weighting using judgments of strength of preference. *J. Exp. Psychol.: Hum. Percept. Perform.* In press

Birnbaum MH, Viera R. 1997. Configural weighting in two- and four-outcome gambles. *J. Exp. Psychol.: Hum. Percept. Perform.* 23:939–47

Bodenhausen GV, Kramer GP, Susser K. 1994. Happiness and stereotypic thinking in social judgment. *J. Pers. Soc. Psychol.* 66:621–32

Boles TL, Messick DM. 1995. A reverse outcome bias: the influence of multiple reference points on the evaluation of outcomes and decisions. *Org. Behav. Hum. Decis. Process.* 61:262–75

Bontempo RN, Bottom WP, Weber EU. 1997. Cross-cultural differences in risk perception: a model-based approach. *Risk Anal.* 17:479–88

Brenner LA, Koehler DJ, Liberman V, Tversky A. 1996. Overconfidence in probability and frequency judgments: a critical examination. *Org. Behav. Hum. Decis. Process.* 65:212–19

Busemeyer JR, Medin DL, Hastie R, eds. 1995. *Decision Making from a Cognitive Perspective.* San Diego: Academic

Busemeyer JR, Townsend JT. 1993. Decision field theory: a dynamic-cognitive approach to decision making in an uncertain environment. *Psychol. Rev.* 100:432–59

Camerer C. 1995. Individual decision making. See Kagel & Roth 1995, pp. 587–703

Camerer C. 1990. Behavioral game theory. In *Insights in Decision Making,* ed. RM Hogarth, pp. 311–36. Chicago: Univ Chicago Press

Camerer C. 1995. Individual decision making. In *The Handbook of Experimental Economics,* ed. JH Kagel, AE Roth, pp. 587–703. Princeton, NJ: Princeton Univ. Press

Camerer C, Weber M. 1992. Recent developments in modeling preferences: uncertainty and ambiguity. *J. Risk Uncertain.* 5:325–70

Chapman GB. 1996a. Temporal discounting and utility for health and money. *J. Exp. Psychol. Learn. Mem. Cogn.* 22:771–91

Chapman GB. 1996b. Expectations and preferences for sequences of health and money. *Org. Behav. Hum. Decis. Process.* 67:59–75

Chechile R, Cooke AC. 1996. An experimental test of a general class of utility models: evidence for context dependency. *J. Risk Uncertain.* 14:75–93

Cho Y, Luce RD. 1995. Tests of hypotheses about certainty equivalents and joint receipt of gambles. *Org. Behav. Hum. Decis. Process.* 64:229–48

Cho Y, Luce RD, von Winterfeldt D. 1994. Tests of assumptions about the joint receipt of gambles in rank- and sign-dependent utility theory. *J. Exp. Psychol.: Hum. Percept. Perform.* 20:931–43

Christensen C, Heckerling P, Mackesy-Amiti ME, Bernstein LM, Elstein AS. 1995. Pervasiveness of framing effects among physicians and medical students. *J. Behav. Decis. Mak.* 8:169–80

Chung N, von Winterfeldt D, Luce RD. 1994. An experimental test of event commutativity in decision making under uncertainty. *Psychol. Sci.* 5:394–400

Cooke ADJ, Mellers BA. 1997. Multiattribute judgment: context effects in single attributes. *J. Exp. Psychol.: Hum. Percept. Perform.* In press

Coombs CH, Lehner PE. 1984. Conjoint design and analysis of the bilinear model: an application to judgments of risk. *J. Math. Psychol.* 28:1–42

Cosmides L, Tooby J. 1996. Are humans good intuitive statisticians after all? Rethinking some conclusions from the literature on judgment under uncertainty. *Cognition* 58:1–73

Dawes RM. 1997. Judgment, decision making,

and interference. In *The Handbook of Social Psychology,* ed. D Gilbert, S Fiske, G Lindzey. Boston, MA: McGraw-Hill. pp. 497–548

Dawes RM, Mulford M. 1996. The false consensus effect and overconfidence: flaws in judgment or flaws in how we study judgment? *Org. Behav. Hum. Decis. Process.* 65:201–11

de Dreu CKW, Carnevale PJD, Emans BJM, van de Vliert E. 1994. Effects of gain-loss frames in negotiation: loss aversion, mismatching, and frame adoption. *Org. Behav. Hum. Decis. Process.* 60:90–107

Diederich A. 1997. Dynamic stochastic models for decision making under time constraints. *J. Math. Psychol.* 41:260–74

Dougherty MRP, Gettys CF, Oden EE. 1997. MINERVA-DM: a memory processes model for judgments of likelihood. *Psychol. Rev.* In press

Edwards W. 1961. Behavioral decision theory. *Annu. Rev. Psychol.* 12:473–98

Edwards W. 1991. Influence diagrams, Bayesian imperialism, and the *Collins* case: an appeal to reason. *Cardozo Law Rev.* 13: 1025–74

Edwards W. 1992. *Utility Theories: Measurements and Applications.* Boston: Kluwer

Edwards W, Barron FH. 1994. SMARTS and SMARTER: improved simple methods for multiattribute utility measurement. *Org. Behav. Hum. Decis. Process.* 60:306–25

Einhorn HJ, Hogarth RM. 1981. Behavioral decision theory: processes of judgment and choice. *Annu. Rev. Psychol.* 32:53–88

Elster J. 1989. Social norms and economic theory. *J Econ. Per.* 3:99–117

Erev I, Wallsten TS, Budescu DV. 1994. Simultaneous over- and underconfidence: the role of error in judgment processes. *Psychol. Rev.* 101:519–27

Estrada CA, Isen AM, Young MJ. 1994. Positive affect improves creative problem solving and influences reported source of practice satisfaction in physicians. *Motiv. Emot.* 18:285–99

Fagley NS, Miller PM. 1990. The effect of framing on choice: interactions with risk taking propensity, cognitive style, and sex. *Person. Soc. Psychol. Bull.* 16:496–510

Fiedler K. 1988. Emotional mood, cognitive style, and behavioral regulation. In *Affect, Cognition, and Social Behavior,* ed. K Fielder, J Forgas, pp. 100–19. Toronto: Hogrefe Int.

Fischer GW. 1995. Range sensitivity of attribute weights in multiattribute value models. *Org. Behav. Hum. Decis. Process.* 62: 252–66

Fischer GW, Hawkins SA. 1993. Strategy compatibility, scale compatibility, and the prominence effect. *J. Exp. Psychol.: Hum. Percept. Perform.* 19:580–97

Fischhoff B, Bostrom A, Quadrel MJ. 1997. Risk perception and communication. In *Oxford Textbook of Public Health,* ed. R Detels, W Holland, J McEwen, GS Omenn, pp. 987–1002. Oxford, UK: Oxford Univ. Press

Fischhoff B, Furby L. 1988. Measuring values: a conceptual framework for interpreting transactions. *J. Risk Uncertain.* 1: 147–84

Fischhoff B, Lichtenstein S, Slovic P, Derby SC, Keeney RL. 1981. *Acceptable Risk.* Cambridge: Cambridge Univ. Press

Fiske AP. 1992. The four elementary forms of sociality: framework for a unified theory of social relations. *Psychol. Rev.* 99: 689–723

Fiske AP, Tetlock PE. 1997. Taboo tradeoffs: reactions to transactions that transgress the domains of relationships. *Polit. Psychol.* 18:255–97

Flynn J, Slovic P, Mertz CK. 1994. Gender, race, and perception of environmental health risks. *Risk Anal.* 14:1101–8

Fox CR, Rogers BA, Tversky A. 1996. Options traders exhibit subaddititve decision weights. *J. Risk Uncertain.* 13:5–17

Fox CR, Tversky A. 1995. Ambiguity aversion and comparative ignorance. *Q. J. Econ.* 110:585–603

Fox CR, Tversky A. 1997. A belief-based account of decision under uncertainty. *Manage. Sci.* In press

Fredrickson BL, Kahneman D. 1993. Duration neglect in retrospective evaluations of affective episodes. *J. Pers. Soc. Psychol.* 65: 45–55

Frisch D. 1993. Reasons for framing effects. *Org. Behav. Hum. Decis. Process.* 54: 399–429

Frisch D, Clemen RT. 1994. Beyond expected utility: rethinking behavioral decision research. *Psychol. Bull.* 116:46–54

Garland H, Newport S. 1991. Effects of absolute and relative sunk costs on the decision to persist with a course of action. *Org. Behav. Hum. Decis. Process.* 48:55–69

Gigerenzer G. 1991. How to make cognitive illusions disappear: beyond "heuristics and biases." *Eur. Rev. Soc. Psychol.* 2: 83–115

Gigerenzer G. 1993. The bounded rationality of probabilistic mental models. In *Rationality: Psychological, and Philosophical Perspectives,* ed. KI Manktelow, DE Over, pp. 243–313. London: Routledge

Gigerenzer G. 1996. Rationality: why social context matters. In *Interactive Minds: Life-span Perspectives on the Social Foundation of Cognition,* ed. P Baltes, UM Staudinger, pp. 319–46. Cambridge: Cambridge Univ. Press

Gigerenzer G. 1997. Bounded rationality: models of fast and frugal inference. *Swiss J. Econ. Stat.* 133:201–18

Gigerenzer G, Goldstein D. 1996. Reasoning the fast and frugal way: models of bounded rationality. *Psychol. Rev.* 103:650–69

Gigerenzer G, Hoffrage U. 1995. How to improve Bayesian reasoning without instruction: frequency formats. *Psychol. Rev.* 102:684–704

Gigerenzer G, Hoffrage U, Kleinbolting H. 1991. Probabilistic mental models: a Brunswikian theory of confidence. *Psychol. Rev.* 98:506–28

Gilovich T, Medvec VH. 1994. The temporal pattern to the experience of regret. *J. Pers. Soc. Psychol.* 67:357–65

Gilovich T, Medvec VH. 1995. The experience of regret: what, why, and when. *Psychol. Rev.* 102:379–95

Gluck MA, Bower GH. 1988. From conditioning to category learning: an adaptive network model. *J. Exp. Psychol.* 117:227–47

Green DP, Kahneman D, Kunreuther H. 1994. How the scope and method of public funding affect willingness to pay for public goods. *Public Opin. Q.* 58:49–67

Gregory R, Brown TC, Knetsch JL. 1996. Valuing risks to the environment. *Ann. Am. Acad. Polit. Soc. Sci.* 545:54–63

Griffin D, Tversky A. 1992. The weighing of evidence and the determinants of confidence. *Cogn. Psychol.* 24:411–35

Hammond K. 1996. *Human Judgment and Social Policy.* New York: Oxford Univ. Press

Heath C, Tversky A. 1990. Preference and belief: ambiguity and competence in choice under uncertainty. In *Contemporary Issues in Decision Making,* ed. K Borcherding, OI Larichev, DM Messick, pp. 93–123. Amsterdam: North-Holland

Hogarth RM, Kunreuther H. 1992. Pricing insurance and warranties: ambiguity and correlated risks. *Geneva Pap. Risk Insur. Theory* 17(1):35–60

Hogarth RM, Kunreuther H. 1995. Decision making under ignorance: arguing with yourself. *J. Risk Uncertain.* 10:15–36

Howard R, Matheson J. 1984. Influence diagrams. In *II Readings on the Principles and Applications of Decision Analysis,* ed. R Howard, J Matheson, pp. 721–62. Menlo Park, CA: Strat. Decis.

Hsee C. 1996. The evaluability hypothesis: an explanation for preference reversals between joint and separate evaluations of alternatives. *Org. Behav. Hum. Decis. Process.* 67:247–57

Huber J, Payne JW, Puto C. 1982. Adding asymmetrically dominated alternatives: violations of regularity and the similarity hypothesis. *J. Consum. Res.* 9:90–98

Irwin JR. 1994. Buying/selling price preference reversals: preference for environmental changes in buying versus selling modes. *Org. Behav. Hum. Decis. Process.* 60:431–57

Irwin JR, Slovic P, Lichtenstein S, McClelland GH. 1993. Preference reversals and the measurement of environmental values. *J. Risk Uncertain.* 6:5–18

Isen AM. 1993. Positive affect and decision making. In *Handbook of Emotions,* ed. M Lewis, JM Haviland, pp. 261–77. New York: Guilford

Johnson EJ, Hershey J, Meszaros J, Kunreuther H. 1993. Framing, probability distortions, and insurance decisions. *J. Risk Uncertain.* 7:35–51

Jones-Lee MW, Loomes G. 1995. Scale and context effects in the valuation of transportation safety. *J. Risk Uncertain.* 11: 183–203

Josephs RA, Larrick RP, Steele CM, Nisbett RE. 1992. Protecting the self from the negative consequences of risky decisions. *J. Pers. Soc. Psychol.* 62:26–37

Juslin P. 1994. The overconfidence phenomenon as a consequence of informal experimenter-guided selection of almanac items. *Org. Behav. Hum. Decis. Process.* 57:226–46

Juslin P, Olsson H, Bjorkman M. 1997. Brunswikian and Thurstonian origins of bias in probability assessment: on the interpretation of stochastic components of judgment. *J. Behav. Decis. Mak.* In press

Kagel JH, Roth AE, eds. 1995. *The Handbook of Experimental Economics.* Princeton, NJ: Princeton Univ. Press

Kahn BE, Isen AM. 1993. The influence of positive affect on variety seeking among safe, enjoyable products. *J. Consum. Res.* 20:257–70

Kahneman D. 1994. New challenges to the rationality assumption. *J. Inst. Theor. Econ.* 150:18–36

Kahneman D. 1995. Varieties of counterfactual thinking. See Roese & Olson 1995. pp. 375–96

Kahneman D, Fredrickson BL, Schreiber CA, Redelmeier DA. 1993a. When more pain is preferred to less: adding a better end. *Psychol. Sci.* 4:401–5

Kahneman D, Knetsch JL. 1992. Valuing public goods: the purchase of moral satisfaction. *J. Environ. Econ. Manage.* 22:55–70

Kahneman D, Knetsch JL, Thaler RH. 1990. Experimental tests of the endowment effect and the Coase theorem. *J. Polit. Econ.* 98:1325–48

Kahneman D, Lovallo D. 1993. Timid choices and bold forecasts: a cognitive perspective on risk taking. *Manage. Sci.* 39:17–31

Kahneman D, Ritov I. 1994. Determinants of stated willingness to pay for public goods: a study in the headline method. *J. Risk Uncertain.* 9:5–38

Kahneman D, Ritov I, Jacowitz JE, Grant P. 1993b. Stated willingness to pay for public goods: a psychological perspective. *Psychol. Sci.* 4:310–15

Kahneman D, Tversky A. 1979. Prospect theory: an analysis of decision under risk. *Econometrica* 47:263–91

Kashima Y, Maher P. 1995. Framing of decisions under ambiguity. *J. Behav. Decis. Mak.* 8:33–49

Keeney RL, Raiffa H. 1976. *Decisions with Multiple Objectives: Preferences and Value Tradeoffs.* New York: Wiley

Koehler JJ. 1996. The base rate fallacy reconsidered: descriptive, normative, and methodological challenges. *Behav. Brain Sci.* 19:1–53

Kraus N, Malmfors T, Slovic P. 1992. Intuitive toxicology: expert and lay judgments of chemical risks. *Risk Anal.* 12:215–32

Kruschke JK. 1996. Base rates in category learning. *J. Exp. Psychol. Learn. Mem. Cogn.* 22:3–26

Kühberger A. 1995. The framing of decisions: a new look at old problems. *Org. Behav. Hum. Decis. Process.* 62:230–40

Kunreuther H, Meszaros J, Hogarth RM, Spranca M. 1995. Ambiguity and underwriter decision processes. *J. Econ. Behav. Org.* 26:337–52

Landman J. 1993. *Regret: The Persistence of the Possible.* Oxford: Oxford Univ. Press

Larrick RP, Nisbett RE, Morgan JN. 1993. Who uses the cost-benefit rules of choice? Implications for the normative status of microeconomic theory. *Org. Behav. Hum. Decis. Process.* 56:331–47

Lewinsohn S, Mano H. 1993. Multiattribute choice and affect: the influence of naturally occurring and manipulated moods on choice processes. *J. Behav. Decis. Mak.* 6:33–51

Link SW. 1992. *The Wave Theory of Difference and Similarity.* Hillsdale, NJ: Erlbaum

Loewenstein GF, Elster J, eds. 1992. *Choice Over Time.* New York: Russell Sage Found.

Loewenstein GF, Issacharoff S. 1994. Source dependence in the valuation of objects. *J. Behav. Decis. Mak.* 7:157–68

Loewenstein GF, Prelec D. 1993. Preferences for sequences of outcomes. *Psychol. Rev.* 100:91–108

Loomes G, Sugden R. 1982. Regret theory: an alternative theory of rational choice under uncertainty. *Econ. J.* 92:805–24

Loomes G, Sugden R. 1986. Disappointment and dynamic consistency in choice under uncertainty. *Rev. Econ. Stud.* 53:271–82

Lopes LL. 1990. Re-modeling risk aversion: a comparison of Bernoullian and rank dependent value approaches. In *Acting Under Uncertainty: Multidisciplinary Conceptions,* ed. GM von Furstenberg, pp. 267–99. Boston: Kluwer

Lopes LL. 1994. Psychology and economics: perspectives on risk, cooperation, and the marketplace. *Annu. Rev. Psychol.* 45:197–227

Lopes LL. 1995. Algebra and process in the modeling of risky choice. In *The Psychology of Learning and Motivation,* ed. JR Busemeyer, DL Medin, R Hastie, 32:177–219. San Diego: Academic

Lopes LL. 1996. When time is of the essence: averaging, aspiration, and the short run. *Org. Behav. Hum. Decis. Process.* 65:179–89

Luce M, Bettman J, Payne JW. 1997. Choice processing in emotionally difficult decisions. *J. Exp. Psychol. Learn. Mem. Cogn.* 23:384–405

Luce RD. 1991. Rank- and sign-dependent linear utility models for binary gambles. *J. Econ. Theory* 53:75–100

Luce RD. 1996. When four distinct ways to measure utility are the same. *J. Math. Psychol.* 40:297–317

Luce RD, Fishburn PC. 1991. Rank- and sign-dependent linear utility models for finite first-order gambles. *J. Risk Uncertain.* 4:29–59

Luce RD, Fishburn PC. 1995. A note on deriving rank-dependent utility using additive joint receipts. *J. Risk Uncertain.* 11:5–16

Luce RD, Weber EU. 1986. An axiomatic theory of conjoint, expected risk. *J. Math. Psychol.* 30:188–205

Mano H. 1992. Judgments under distress: assessing the role of unpleasantness and arousal in judgment formation. *Org. Behav. Hum. Decis. Process.* 52:216–45

Mano H. 1994. Risk taking, framing effects, and affect. *Org. Behav. Hum. Decis. Process.* 57:38–58

March JG. 1994. *A Primer of Decision Making.* New York: Free

March JG. 1996. Learning to be risk averse. *Psychol. Rev.* 103:309–19

Markman AB, Medin DL. 1995. Similarity and alignment in choice. *Org. Behav. Hum. Decis. Process.* 63:117–30

McCarthy AM, Schoorman FD, Cooper AC. 1993. Reinvestment decisions by entrepreneurs: rational decision-making or escalation of commitment? *J. Bus. Vent.* 8: 9–24

Medin DL, Edelson SM. 1988. Problem structure and the use of base-rate information from experience. *J. Exp. Psychol.* 117: 68–85

Mellers BA, Biagini K. 1994. Similarity and choice. *Psychol. Rev.* 101:505–18

Mellers BA, Chang S. 1994. Representations of risk judgments. *Org. Behav. Hum. Decis. Process.* 57:167–84

Mellers BA, Chang S, Birnbaum MH, Ordóñez LD. 1992a. Preferences, prices, and ratings in risky decision making. *J. Exp. Psychol.: Hum. Percept. Perform.* 18: 347–61

Mellers BA, Cooke ADJ. 1994. Trade-offs depend on attribute range. *J. Exp. Psychol.: Hum. Percept. Perform.* 20:1055–67

Mellers BA, Cooke ADJ. 1996. The role of task and context in preference measurement. *Psychol. Sci.* 7:76–82

Mellers BA, Schwartz A, Ho K, Ritov I. 1997a. Decision affect theory: emotional reactions to the outcomes of risky options. *Psychol. Sci.* In press

Mellers BA, Schwartz A, Weber EU. 1997b. Another look at the reflection effect. In *Choices, Decisions, and Measurement: Essays in Honor of R. Duncan Luce,* ed. AA Marley, pp. 57–72. Mahwah, NJ: Erlbaum

Mellers BA, Weber EU, Ordóñez LD, Cooke ADJ. 1995. Utility invariance despite labile preferences. See Busemeyer et al 1995, pp. 221–46

Mellers BA, Weiss R, Birnbaum MH. 1992b. Violations of dominance in pricing judgments. *J. Risk Uncertain.* 5:73–90

Miyamoto JM. 1988. Generic utility theory: measurement foundations and applications in multiattribute utility theory. *J. Mark. Res.* 54:174–205

Miyamoto JM. 1992. Generic analysis of utility models. In *Utility Theories: Measurements and Applications,* ed. W Edwards, pp. 73–108. Boston: Kluwer

Morawski P. 1989. Understanding Bayesian belief networks. *AI Expert.* 4:44–48

Nelson MW. 1996. Context and the inverse base rate effect. *J. Behav. Decis. Mak.* 9: 23–40

Nowlis SM, Simonson I. 1997. Attribute-task compatibility as a determinant of consumer preference reversals. *J. Mark. Res.* 34:205–18

Nygren TE, Isen AM, Taylor PJ, Dulin J. 1996. The influence of positive affect on the decision rule in risk situations: Focus on outcome (and especially avoidance of loss) rather than probability. *Org. Behav. Hum. Decis. Process.* 66:59–72

Ordóñez LD, Mellers BA, Chang S, Roberts J. 1995. Are preference reversals reduced when made explicit? *J. Behav. Decis. Mak.* 8:265–77

Paese PW, Bieser M, Tubbs ME. 1993. Framing effects and choice shifts in group decision making. *Org. Behav. Hum. Decis. Process.* 56:149–65

Parducci A. 1995. *Happiness, Pleasure, and Judgment: The Contextual Theory and Its Applications.* Mahwah, NJ: Lawrence Erlbaum

Payne JW, Bettman JR, Johnson EJ. 1992. Behavioral decision research: a constructive processing perspective. *Annu. Rev. Psychol.* 43:87–131

Pearl J. 1988. *Probabilistic Reasoning in Intelligent Systems: Networks of Plausible Inference.* San Mateo, CA: Morgan Kaufman

Pennington N, Hastie R. 1992. Explaining the evidence: tests of the story model for juror decision making. *J. Pers. Soc. Psychol.* 62:189–206

Pennington N, Hastie R. 1993. Reasoning in explanation-based decision making. *Cognition* 49:123–63

Peters E, Slovic P. 1997. The role of affect and world views as orienting dispositions in the perception and acceptance of nuclear power. *J. Appl. Soc. Psychol.* 26:1427–53

Pfeifer PE. 1994. Are we overconfident in the belief that probability forecasters are overconfident? *Org. Behav. Hum. Decis. Process.* 58:203–13

Pitz GF, Sachs NJ. 1984. Judgment and decision: theory and application. *Annu. Rev. Psychol.* 35:139–63

Prelec D, Herrnstein RJ. 1991. In *Strategy and Choice,* ed. RJ Zeckhauser, pp. 319–40. Cambridge, MA: MIT Press

Rapoport A, Wallsten TS. 1972. Individual decision behavior. *Annu. Rev. Psychol.* 23: 131–76

Ratcliff R. 1978. A theory of memory retrieval. *Psychol. Rev.* 85:59–108

Redelmeier DA, Kahneman D. 1996. Patients' memories of painful medical treatments:

real-time and retrospective evaluations of two minimally invasive procedures. *Pain* 66(1):3–8

Richard R, van der Pligt J, de Vries N. 1996. Anticipated regret and time perspective: changing sexual risk-taking behavior. *J. Behav. Decis. Mak.* 9:185–99

Ritov I. 1996. Probability of regret: anticipation of uncertainty resolution in choice. *Org. Behav. Hum. Decis. Process.* 66: 228–36

Ritov I, Baron J. 1990. Reluctance to vaccinate: omission bias and ambiguity. *J. Behav. Decis. Mak.* 3:263–77

Ritov I, Baron J. 1995. Outcome knowledge, regret, and omission bias. *Org. Behav. Hum. Decis. Process.* 64:119–27

Ritov I, Baron J, Hershey JC. 1993. Framing effects in the evaluation of multiple risk reduction. *J. Risk Uncertain.* 6:145–59

Roese NJ, Olson JM, eds. 1995. *What Might Have Been: The Social Psychology of Counterfactual Thinking.* Mahwah, NJ: Erlbaum

Russo JE, Kolzow KJ. 1994. Where is the fault in fault trees? *J. Exp. Psychol.: Hum. Percept. Perform.* 20:17–32

Schkade DA, Payne JW. 1994. How people respond to contingent valuation questions: a verbal protocol analysis of willingness to pay for an environmental regulation. *J. Environ. Econ.* 26:88–109

Schneider SL. 1992. Framing and conflict: aspiration level, contingency, the status quo, and current theories of risky choice. *J. Exp. Psychol. Learn. Mem. Cogn.* 18:1040–57

Schneider SL. 1995. Item difficulty, discrimination, and the confidence-frequency effect in a categorical judgment task. *Org. Behav. Hum. Decis. Process.* 61:148–67

Schoemaker PJH. 1993. Determinants of risk-taking: behavioral and economic views. *J. Risk Uncertain.* 6:49–73

Schweitzer M. 1995. Multiple reference points, framing, and the status quo bias in health care financing decisions. *Org. Behav. Hum. Decis. Process.* 63:69–72

Shafer G. 1996. *Probabilistic Expert Systems.* Philadelphia, PA: SIAM

Shafir E, Simonson I, Tversky A. 1993. Reason-based choice. *Cognition* 49:11–36

Shapira Z. 1995. *Risk Taking: A Managerial Perspective.* New York: Russell Sage Found.

Shelley MK. 1994. Gain/loss asymmetry in risky intertemporal choice. *Org. Behav. Hum. Decis. Process.* 59:124–59

Simonson I. 1989. Choice based on reasons: the case of attraction and compromise effects. *J. Consum. Res.* 16:158–74

Simonson I. 1992. The influence of anticipating regret and responsibility on purchase decisions. *J. Consum. Res.* 19:105–18

Simonson I, Nye P. 1992. The effect of accountability on susceptibility to decision errors. *Org. Behav. Hum. Decis. Process.* 51:416–46

Simonson I, Staw BM. 1992. Deescalation strategies: a comparison of techniques for reducing commitment to losing courses of action. *J. Appl. Psychol.* 77:419–26

Simonson I, Tversky A. 1992. Choice in context: tradeoff contrast and extremeness aversion. *J. Mark. Res.* 29:281–95

Slovic P. 1972. From Shakespeare to Simon: speculations—and some evidence—about man's ability to process information. *Res. Bull. Ore. Res. Inst.* 12:1–29

Slovic P. 1996. Trust, emotion, sex, politics, and science: surveying the risk-assessment battlefield. In *Psychological Perspectives to Environment and Ethics in Management,* ed. M Bazerman, D Messick, A Tenbrunsel, K Wade-Benzoni, pp. 277–313. San Francisco: Jossey-Bass

Slovic P, Fischhoff B, Lichtenstein S. 1977. Behavioral decision theory. *Annu. Rev. Psychol.* 28:1–39

Slovic P, Flynn J, Mertz CW, Mullican L. 1993. *Health Risk Perception in Canada. Rep. No. 93-EHD-170.* Ottawa: Dep. Natl. Health Welf.

Sniezek JA, Paese PW, Switzer FS. 1990. The effect of choosing on confidence in choice. *Org. Behav. Hum. Decis. Process.* 46: 264–82

Spranca M, Minsk E, Baron J. 1991. Omission and commission in judgment and choice. *J. Exp. Soc. Psychol.* 27:76–105

Stevenson MK. 1992. The impact of temporal context and risk on the judged value of future outcomes. *Org. Behav. Hum. Decis. Process.* 52:455–91

Stevenson MK. 1993. Decision making with long-term consequences: temporal discounting for single and multiple outcomes in the future. *J. Exp. Psychol.* 122:3–22

Sullivan K, Kida T. 1995. The effect of multiple reference points and prior gains and losses on managers' risky decision making. *Org. Behav. Hum. Decis. Process.* 64: 76–83

Sunstein CR. 1997. *Which Risks First? Univ. Chicago Legal Forum.* Chicago: Univ. Chicago Press. In press

Tan H, Yates JF. 1995. Sunk cost effects: the influences of instruction and future return estimates. *Org. Behav. Hum. Decis. Process.* 63:311–19

Tetlock PE. 1992. The impact of accountability on judgment and choice: toward a social contingency model. *Adv. Exp. Soc. Psychol.* 25:331–76

Tetlock PE, Boettger R. 1994. Accountability amplifies the status quo effect when change creates victims. *J. Behav. Decis. Mak.* 7:1–23

Tetlock PE, Kim JI. 1987. Accountability and judgment processes in a personality prediction task. *J. Pers. Soc. Psychol.* 52: 700–9

Tetlock PE, Peterson RS, Lerner JS. 1996. Revising the value pluralism model: incorporating social content and context postulates. In *The Psychology of Values,* ed. C Seligman, JM Olson, MP Zanna, pp. 25–51. Mahwah, NJ: Erlbaum

Thaler R. 1993. *Advances in Behavioral Fianance.* New York: Russell Sage

Thaler RH, Tversky A, Kahneman D, Schwartz A. 1997. An experimental test of myopic loss aversion. *Q. J. Econ.* 112: 647–61

Tversky A, Fox CR. 1995. Weighing risk and uncertainty. *Psychol. Rev.* 102:269–83

Tversky A, Kahneman D. 1974. Judgment under uncertainty: heuristics and biases. *Science* 185:1124–31

Tversky A, Kahneman D. 1981. The framing of decisions and the psychology of choice. *Science* 211:453–58

Tversky A, Kahneman D. 1992. Advances in prospect theory: cumulative representation of uncertainty. *J. Risk Uncertain.* 5: 297–323

Tversky A, Koehler DJ. 1994. Support theory: a nonextensional representation of subjective probability. *Psychol. Rev.* 101:547–67

Tversky A, Sattath S, Slovic P. 1988. Contingent weighting in judgment and choice. *Psychol. Rev.* 95:371–84

Tversky A, Shafir E. 1992a. Choice under conflict: the dynamics of deferred decision. *Psychol. Sci.* 3:358–61

Tversky A, Shafir E. 1992b. The disjunction effect in choice under uncertainty. *Psychol. Sci.* 3:305–9

Tversky A, Simonson I. 1993. Context-dependent preferences. *Manage. Sci.* 39: 1179–89

van Schie ECM, van der Pligt J. 1995. Influencing risk preference in decision making: the effects of framing and salience. *Org. Behav. Hum. Decis. Process.* 63:264–75

Varey C, Kahneman D. 1992. Experiences extended across time: evaluation of moments and episodes. *J. Behav. Decis. Mak.* 5: 169–85

von Nitzsch R, Weber M. 1993. The effect of attribute ranges on weights in multiattribute utility measurements. *Manage. Sci.* 39: 937–43

von Winterfeldt D, Chung N, Luce RD, Cho Y. 1997. Tests of consequence monotoncity in decision making under uncertainty. *J. Exp. Psychol. Learn. Mem. Cogn.* 23: 406–26

von Winterfeldt D, Edwards W. 1986. *Decision Analysis and Behavioral Research.* New York: Cambridge Univ. Press

Wakker P, Tversky A. 1993. An axiomatization of cumulative prosect theory. *J. Risk Uncertain.* 7:147–56

Weber EU, Anderson CJ, Birnbaum MH. 1992. A theory of perceived risk and attractiveness. *Org. Behav. Hum. Decis. Process.* 52:492–523

Weber EU, Böckenholt U, Hilton DJ, Wallace B. 1993. Determinants of diagnostic hypothesis generation: effects of information, base rates, and experience. *J. Exp. Psychol. Learn. Mem. Cogn.* 19:1151–64

Weber EU, Milliman RA. 1997. Perceived risk attitudes: relating risk perception to risky choice. *Manage. Sci.* 43:123–44

Weber M, Borcherding K. 1993. Behavioral influences on weight judgments in multiattribute decision making. *Eur. J. Opin. Res.* 67:1–12

Wedell DH. 1991. Distinguishing among models of contextually induced preference reversals. *J. Exp. Psychol. Learn. Mem. Cogn.* 17:767–78

Wedell DH, Pettibone JC. 1996. Using judgments to understand decoy effects in choice. *Org. Behav. Hum. Decis. Process.* 67:326–44

Wilson R, Crouch E. 1982. *Risk/Benefit Analysis.* Cambridge, MA: Balllinger

Wright WF, Bower GH. 1992. Mood effects on subjective probability assessment. *Org. Behav. Hum. Decis. Process.* 52:276–91

Wu G, Gonzales R. 1996. Curvature of the probability weighting function. *Manage. Sci.* 42:1676–90

Yates JF, ed. 1992. *Risk-Taking Behavior.* New York: Wiley

Yates JF, Stone ER. 1992. The risk construct. In *Risk-Taking Behavior,* ed. JF Yates, pp. 1–25. New York: Wiley

Zeelenberg M, Beattie J, van der Pligt J, de Vries NK. 1996. Consequences of regret aversion: effects of expected feedback on risky decision making. *Org. Behav. Hum. Decis. Process.* 65:148–58

Annu. Rev. Psychol. 1998. 49:479–502

# HUMAN ABILITIES

*Robert J. Sternberg and James C. Kaufman*

Department of Psychology, Yale University, Box 208205, New Haven, Connecticut 06520-8205; e-mail: robert.sternberg@yale.edu; e-mail: james.kaufman@yale.edu

KEY WORDS: intelligence, biological approaches, psychometric approaches, cultural approaches, cognitive approaches

### ABSTRACT

This chapter reviews recent literature, primarily from the 1990s, on human abilities. The review opens with a consideration of the question of what intelligence is, and then considers some of the major definitions of intelligence, as well as implicit theories of intelligence around the world. Next, the chapter considers cognitive approaches to intelligence, and then biological approaches. It proceeds to psychometric or traditional approaches to intelligence, and then to broad, recent approaches.

The different approaches raise somewhat different questions, and hence produce somewhat different answers. They have in common, however, the attempt to understand what kinds of mechanisms lead some people to adapt to, select, and shape environments in ways that match particularly well the demands of those environments.

## CONTENTS

0066-4308/98/0201-0479$08.00

# INTRODUCTION

The study of intelligence is like a real-world *Jeopardy* game. Curiously, there is more agreement regarding answers than there is regarding what questions these answers answer. For example, it is uncontroversial that on conventional tests of intelligence, members of certain socially identified racial and ethnic groups differ on average. But what does such a difference show? What question does it answer? Does it answer the question of whether there are differences across groups in intelligence, whether the tests are differentially biased for members of different groups, whether different groups have had different educational opportunities, or whether different groups differ on a narrow subset of skills that constitutes only a small part of intelligence, or some other question still? To understand the field of human abilities and intelligence, one must consider questions at least as much as answers.

The goal of this chapter is to consider some of the main questions being asked and answers being offered today in the field of human abilities, in general, and of human intelligence, in particular, and to consider the match between them. What are the important questions, and what are the questions that available data answer?

We organize our review around some of the main paradigms in the study of human abilities, because the paradigm one uses generates, to a large extent, the questions that are viewed as important or not important. Before we consider these theories, however, we first consider even what intelligence is, going back in history and up to the present.

# DEFINITIONS OF INTELLIGENCE

What is intelligence? It turns out that the answer depends on whom you ask, and that the answer differs widely across disciplines, time, and places. We discuss the diversity of views about what intelligence is because empirical studies often assume rather than explore the nature of the construct they are investigating—in this case, intelligence.

## Western Psychological Views

How have Western psychologists conceived of intelligence? Almost none of these views is adequately expressed by Boring's (1923) operationistic view of intelligence as whatever it is that intelligence tests test. This empty and circular definition is still used by some investigators in the field.

For example, in a 1921 symposium (Intelligence and Its Measurement: A Symposium) on experts' definitions of intelligence, researchers emphasized the importance of the ability to learn and the ability to adapt to the environment. Sixty-five years later, Sternberg & Detterman (1986) conducted a similar symposium, again asking experts their views on intelligence. Learning and adaptive abilities retained their importance, and a new emphasis crept in: metacognition, or the ability to understand and control oneself. Of course, the name is new, but the idea is not, because Aristotle emphasized long before the importance for intelligence of knowing oneself.

## Cross-Cultural Views

In some cases, Western notions about intelligence are not shared by other cultures. For example, at the mental level, the Western emphasis on speed of mental processing (Sternberg et al 1981) is not shared by many cultures. Other cultures may even be suspicious of the quality of work done very quickly and may emphasize depth rather than speed of processing. They are not alone: Some prominent Western theorists have pointed out the importance of depth of processing for full command of material (e.g. Craik & Lockhart 1972).

Yang & Sternberg (1997a) have reviewed Chinese philosophical conceptions of intelligence. The Confucian perspective emphasizes the characteristic of benevolence and of doing what is right. As in the Western notion, the intelligent person spends much effort in learning, enjoys learning, and persists in life-long learning with enthusiasm. The Taoist tradition, in contrast, emphasizes the importance of humility, freedom from conventional standards of judgment, and full knowledge of oneself and of external conditions.

The difference between Eastern and Western conceptions of intelligence may persist even today. Yang & Sternberg (1997b) studied contemporary Taiwanese Chinese conceptions of intelligence and found five factors underlying these conceptions: (a) a general cognitive factor, much like the g factor in conventional Western tests; (b) interpersonal intelligence; (c) intrapersonal intelligence; (d) intellectual self-assertion; and (e) intellectual self-effacement. In a related study but with different results, Chen (1994) found three factors underlying Chinese conceptualizations of intelligence: nonverbal reasoning ability, verbal reasoning ability, and rote memory. The difference may be due to different subpopulations of Chinese, to differences in methodology, or to differences in when the studies were done.

The factors uncovered in both studies differ substantially from those identified in US people's conceptions of intelligence by Sternberg et al (1981)—(a) practical problem solving, (b) verbal ability, and (c) social competence—although in both cases, people's implicit theories of intelligence seem to go quite far beyond what conventional psychometric intelligence tests measure. Of course, comparing the Chen (1994) study to the Sternberg et al (1981) study simultaneously varies both language and culture.

Chen & Chen (1988) varied only language. They explicitly compared the concepts of intelligence of Chinese graduates from Chinese-language versus English-language schools in Hong Kong. They found that both groups considered nonverbal reasoning skills as the most relevant skills for measuring intelligence. Verbal reasoning and social skills came next, and then numerical skills. Memory was seen as least important. The Chinese-language-schooled group, however, tended to rate verbal skills as less important than did the English--language-schooled group. Moreover, in an earlier study, Chen et al (1982) found that Chinese students viewed memory for facts as important for intelligence, whereas Australian students viewed these skills as of only trivial importance.

Das (1994), also reviewing Eastern notions of intelligence, has suggested that in Buddhist and Hindu philosophies, intelligence involves waking up, noticing, recognizing, understanding, and comprehending but also includes such things as determination, mental effort, and even feelings and opinions in addition to more intellectual elements.

Differences between cultures in conceptions of intelligence have been recognized for some time. Gill & Keats (1980) noted that Australian University students value academic skills and the ability to adapt to new events as critical to intelligence, whereas Malay students value practical skills, as well as speed and creativity. Dasen (1984) found that Malay students emphasize both social and cognitive attributes in their conceptions of intelligence.

The differences between East and West may be due to differences in the kinds of skills valued by the two kinds of cultures (Srivastava & Misra 1996). Western cultures and their schools emphasize what might be called "technological intelligence" (Mundy-Castle 1974), and so things like artificial intelligence and so-called smart bombs are viewed, in some sense, as intelligent, or smart. According to this view, intelligence ends up being oriented toward the development and improvement of technology.

Western schooling also emphasizes other things (Srivastava & Misra 1996), such as generalization, or going beyond the information given (Connolly & Bruner 1974, Goodnow 1976), speed (Sternberg 1985a), minimal moves to a solution (Newell & Simon 1972), and creative thinking (Goodnow 1976). Moreover, silence is interpreted as a lack of knowledge (Irvine 1978). In contrast, the Wolof tribe in Africa views people of higher social class and distinction as speaking less (Irvine 1978). This difference between the Wolof and Western notions suggests the usefulness of looking at African notions of intelligence and its manifestations in behavior as a possible contrast to US notions.

Studies in Africa, in fact, provide yet another window on the substantial differences. Ruzgis & Grigorenko (1994) have argued that, in Africa, conceptions of intelligence revolve largely around skills that help to facilitate and maintain harmonious and stable intergroup relations; intragroup relations are probably equally important and at times more important. For example, Serpell (1974, 1977, 1982) found that Chewa adults in Zambia emphasize social responsibilities, cooperativeness, and obedience as important to intelligence; intelligent children are expected to be respectful of adults. Kenyan parents also emphasize responsible participation in family and social life as important aspects of intelligence (Super & Harkness 1982; CM Super & S Harkness, unpublished manuscript). In Zimbabwe, the word for intelligence, *ngware,* actually means to be prudent and cautious, particularly in social relationships. Among the Baoule, service to the family and community and politeness toward and respect for elders are seen as key to intelligence (Dasen 1984).

Similar emphasis on social aspects of intelligence has been found as well among two other African groups—the Songhay of Mali and the Samia of Kenya (Putnam & Kilbride 1980). The Yoruba, another African tribe, emphasize the importance of depth—of listening rather than just talking—to intelligence, and of being able to see all aspects of an issue and to place the issue in its proper overall context (Durojaiye 1993).

The emphasis on the social aspects of intelligence is not limited to African cultures. Notions of intelligence in many Asian cultures also emphasize the social aspect of intelligence more than does the conventional Western or IQ--based notion (Azuma & Kashiwagi 1987, Lutz 1985, Poole 1985, White 1985).

It should be noted that neither African nor Asian notions emphasize exclusively social notions of intelligence. In a collaborative study with a number of investigators, Sternberg & Grigorenko (1997b) are currently studying conceptions of intelligence in rural Kenya. In one village (Kissumu), many and probably most of the children are at least moderately infected with a variety of parasitic infections. Consequently, they experience stomachaches quite frequently. Traditional medicine suggests the usefulness of a large variety (actually hundreds) of natural herbal medicines that can be used to treat such infections. It appears that at least some of these—although perhaps a small percentage—actually work. More important for our purposes, however, is that children who learn how to self-medicate with these natural herbal medicines are viewed as being at an adaptive advantage over those who do not have this kind of informal knowledge. Clearly, the kind of adaptive advantage that is relevant in this culture would be viewed as totally irrelevant in the West, and vice versa.

Although these conceptions of intelligence much more emphasize social skills than do conventional US conceptions of intelligence, they simultaneously recognize the importance of cognitive aspects of intelligence. Note, however, that there is no one overall US conception of intelligence. Okagaki & Sternberg (1993) found that different ethnic groups in San Jose, California, had rather different conceptions of what it means to be intelligent. For example, Latino parents of schoolchildren tended to emphasize the importance of social-competence skills in their conceptions of intelligence, whereas Asian parents tended rather heavily to emphasize the importance of cognitive skills. Anglo parents also more emphasized cognitive skills. Teachers, representing the dominant culture, more emphasized cognitive- rather than social-competence skills. The rank order of children of various groups' performance (including subgroups within the Latino and Asian groups) could be perfectly predicted by the extent to which their parents shared the teachers' conception of intelligence. That is, teachers tended to reward those children who were socialized into a view of intelligence that happened to correspond to the teachers' own. Yet, as we argue below, social aspects of intelligence, broadly defined, may be as important as or even more important than cognitive aspects of intelligence in later life. For example, a team that needs to complete a cognitive task may not be able to do so if the members are unable to work together. Some, however, prefer to study intelligence not in its social aspect but in its cognitive one.

## COGNITIVE APPROACHES TO INTELLIGENCE

Cronbach (1957) called for a merging of the two disciplines of scientific psychology—the differential and the experimental approaches. Serious responses to Cronbach came in the 1970s, with cognitive approaches to intelligence attempting this merger. Hunt et al (1973) introduced the cognitive-correlates approach, whereby scores on laboratory cognitive tests were correlated with scores on psychometric intelligence tests. Sternberg (1977) introduced the cognitive-components approach, whereby performance on complex psychometric tasks was decomposed into elementary information-processing components. Cronbach & Snow (1977; see also Snow 1994) have summarized and synthesized a large literature on aptitude-treatment interaction approaches, whereby instruction and assessment would be tailored to patterns of abilities.

In the 1990s, cognitive and biological approaches (discussed next) have begun to merge. A prototypical example is the inspection-time task (Nettlebeck 1982; see review by Deary & Stough 1996). In this task, two adjacent vertical lines are presented tachistoscopically or by computer, followed by a visual mask (to destroy the image in visual iconic memory). The two lines differ in length, as do the lengths of time for which the two lines are presented. The subject's task is to say which line is longer. Instead of using raw response time as the dependent variable, however, investigators typically use measures derived from a psychophysical function estimated after many trials. For example, the measure might be the mean duration of a single inspection trial at which 50% accuracy is achieved. Correlations between this task and measures of IQ appear to be about 0.4, a bit higher than is typical in psychometric tasks. There are differing theories about why such correlations are obtained, but such theories generally attempt to relate the cognitive function of visual inspection time to some kind of biological function, such as speed of neuronal conduction. Let us consider, then, some of the biological functions that may underlie intelligence.

# BIOLOGICAL APPROACHES TO INTELLIGENCE

An important approach to studying intelligence is to understand it in terms of the functioning of the brain, in particular, and of the nervous system, in general. Earlier theories relating the brain to intelligence tended to be global in nature, although not necessarily backed by strong empirical evidence.

## Early Biological Theories

Halstead (1951) suggested that there are four biologically based abilities, which he called (*a*) the integrative field factor, (*b*) the abstraction factor, (*c*) the power factor, and (*d*) the directional factor. Halstead attributed all four of these abilities primarily to the functioning of the cortex of the frontal lobes.

More influential than Halstead has been Hebb (1949), who distinguished between two basic types of intelligence: Intelligence A and Intelligence B. Hebb's distinction is still used by some theorists today. According to Hebb, Intelligence A is innate potential; Intelligence B is the functioning of the brain as a result of the actual development that has occurred. These two basic types of intelligence should be distinguished from Intelligence C, or intelligence as measured by conventional psychometric tests of intelligence. Hebb also suggested that learning, an important basis of intelligence, is built up through cell assemblies, by which successively more and more complex connections among neurons are constructed as learning takes place.

A third biologically based theory is that of Luria (1973, 1980), which has had a major impact on tests of intelligence (Kaufman & Kaufman 1983, Naglieri & Das 1997). According to Luria, the brain comprises three main units with respect to intelligence: (*a*) a unit of arousal in the brain stem and midbrain structures; (*b*) a sensory-input unit in the temporal, parietal, and occipital lobes; and (*c*) an organization and planning unit in the frontal cortex.

## Modern Biological Views and Research

SPEED OF NEURONAL CONDUCTION    More recent theories have dealt with more specific aspects of brain or neural functioning. For example, one view has suggested that individual differences in nerve-conduction velocity are a basis for individual differences in intelligence. Two procedures have been used to measure conduction velocity, either centrally (in the brain) or peripherally (e.g. in the arm).

Reed & Jensen (1992) tested brain nerve conduction velocities via two medium-latency potentials, N70 and P100, which were evoked by pattern-reversal stimulation. Subjects saw a black and white checkerboard pattern in which the black squares would change to white and the white squares to black. Over many trials, responses to these changes were analyzed via electrodes attached to the scalp in four places. Correlations of derived latency measures with IQ were small (generally in the 0.1–0.2 range of absolute value), but were significant in some cases, suggesting at least a modest relation between the two kinds of measures.

Vernon & Mori (1992) reported on two studies investigating the relation between nerve-conduction velocity in the arm and IQ. In both studies, nerve-conduction velocity was measured in the median nerve of the arm by attaching electrodes to the arm. In the second study, conduction velocity from the wrist to the tip of the finger was also measured. Vernon & Mori found significant correlations with IQ in the 0.4 range, as well as somewhat smaller correlations (around −0.2) with response-time measures. They interpreted their results as supporting the hypothesis of a relation between speed of information transmission in the peripheral nerves and intelligence. However, these results must be interpreted cautiously, as Wickett & Vernon (1994) later tried unsuccessfully to replicate these earlier results.

GLUCOSE METABOLISM    Some of the most interesting recent work under the biological approach has been done by Richard Haier and his colleagues. For example, Haier et al (1988) showed that cortical glucose metabolic rates as revealed by positron emission tomography (PET) scan analysis of subjects solving Raven Matrix problems were lower for more-intelligent than for less-intelligent subjects, suggesting that the more intelligent subjects needed to expend less effort than the less intelligent ones to solve the reasoning problems. A later study (Haier et al 1992) showed a similar result for more- versus less-practiced performers playing the computer game of Tetris. That is, smart people or intellectually expert people do not have to work as hard as less-smart or intellectually expert people at a given problem.

What remains to be shown, however, is the causal direction of this finding. One could sensibly argue that the smart people expend less glucose (as a proxy for effort) because they are smart, rather than that people are smart because they expend less glucose. Or both high IQ and low glucose metabolism may be related to a third causal variable. In other words, we cannot always assume that the biological event is a cause (in the reductionistic sense). It may be, instead, an effect.

BRAIN SIZE    Another approach considers brain size. Willerman et al (1991) correlated brain size with Wechsler Adult Intelligence Scale (WAIS-R) IQs, controlling for body size. They found that IQ correlated 0.65 in men and 0.35 in women, with a correlation of 0.51 for both sexes combined. A follow-up analysis of the same 40 subjects suggested that, in men, a relatively larger left hemisphere better predicted WAIS-R verbal than it predicted nonverbal ability, whereas in women a larger left hemisphere predicted nonverbal ability better than it predicted verbal ability (Willerman et al 1992). These brain-size correlations are suggestive, but it is difficult to say what they mean at this point.

BEHAVIOR GENETICS    Another approach that is at least partially biologically based is that of behavior genetics. A fairly complete review of this extensive literature is found in Sternberg & Grigorenko (1997a). The literature is complex, but it appears that about half the total variance in IQ scores is accounted for by genetic factors (Loehlin 1989, Plomin 1997). This figure may be an underestimate, because the variance includes error variance and because most studies of heritability have been with children, but we know that heritability of IQ is higher for adults than for children (Plomin 1997). In addition, some studies, such as the Texas Adoption Project (Loehlin et al 1997), suggest higher estimates: 0.78 in the Texas Adoption Project, 0.75 in the Minnesota Study of Twins Reared Apart (Bouchard 1997, Bouchard et al 1990), and 0.78 in the Swedish Adoption Study of Aging (Pedersen et al 1992).

At the same time, some researchers argue that effects of heredity and environment cannot be clearly and validly separated (Bronfenbrenner & Ceci 1994, Wahlsten & Gottlieb 1997). Perhaps, the direction for future research is better to figure out how heredity and environment work together to produce phenotypic intelligence (Scarr 1997), concentrating especially on within-family environmental variation, which appears to be more important than between-family variation (Jensen 1997). Such research requires, at the very least, very carefully prepared tests of intelligence—perhaps some of the newer tests described in the next section.

## THE PSYCHOMETRIC APPROACH TO INTELLIGENCE

The psychometric approach to intelligence is among the oldest of approaches, and dates back to Galton's (1883) psychophysical account of intelligence and attempts to measure intelligence in terms of psychophysical abilities (such as strength of hand grip or visual acuity) and later to Binet & Simon's (1916) account of intelligence as judgment, involving adaptation to the environment, direction of one's efforts, and self-criticism.

### Theoretical Developments: Carroll's and Horn's Theories

Two of the major new theories proposed during the past decade have been Carroll's (1993) and Horn's (1994) theories. The two theories are both hierarchical, suggesting more nearly general abilities higher up in the hierarchy and more nearly specific abilities lower in the hierarchy. Carroll's theory will be described briefly as representative of these new developments.

Carroll (1993) proposed his hierarchical model of intelligence, based on the factor analysis of more than 460 data sets obtained between 1927 and 1987.

His analysis encompasses more than 130,000 people from diverse walks of life and even countries of origin (although non-English-speaking countries are poorly represented among his data sets). The model Carroll proposed, based on his monumental undertaking, is a hierarchy comprising three strata: Stratum I, which includes many narrow, specific abilities (e.g. spelling ability, speed of reasoning); Stratum II, which includes various group-factor abilities (e.g. fluid intelligence, involved in flexible thinking and seeing things in novel ways; and crystallized intelligence, the accumulated knowledge base); and Stratum III, which is just a single general intelligence, much like Spearman's (1904) general intelligence factor.

Of these strata, the most interesting is perhaps the middle stratum, which includes, in addition to fluid and crystallized abilities, learning and memory processes, visual perception, auditory perception, facile production of ideas (similar to verbal fluency), and speed (which includes both sheer speed of response and speed of accurate responding). Although Carroll does not break much new ground, in that many of the abilities in his model have been mentioned in other theories, he does masterfully integrate a large and diverse factor-analytic literature, thereby giving great authority to his model.

## An Empirical Curiosity: The Flynn Effect

We know that the environment has powerful effects on cognitive abilities. Perhaps the simplest and most potent demonstration of this effect is the "Flynn effect" (Flynn 1984, 1987, 1994). The basic phenomenon is that IQ has increased over successive generations around the world through most of the century—at least since 1930. The effect must be environmental, because obviously a successive stream of genetic mutations could not have taken hold and exerted such an effect over such a short period. The effect is powerful—at least 15 points of IQ per generation for tests of fluid intelligence. And it occurs all over the world. The effect has been greater for tests of fluid intelligence than for tests of crystallized intelligence. The difference, if linearly extrapolated (a hazardous procedure, obviously), would suggest that a person who in 1892 fell at the 90th percentile on the Raven Progressive Matrices, a test of fluid intelligence, would, in 1992, score at the 5th percentile.

There have been many potential explanations of the Flynn effect, and in 1996 a conference was organized by Ulric Neisser and held at Emory University to try to explain the effect. Some of the possible explanations includes increased schooling, greater educational attainment of parents, better nutrition, and less childhood disease. A particularly interesting explanation is that of more and better parental attention to children (see Bronfenbrenner & Ceci 1994). Whatever the answer, the Flynn effect suggests we need to think carefully about the view that IQ is fixed. It probably is not fixed within individuals (Campbell & Ramey 1994, Ramey 1994), and it is certainly not across generations.

## Psychometric Tests

STATIC TESTS    Static tests are the conventional kind where people are given problems to solve, and are expected to solve them without feedback. Their final score is typically the number of items answered correctly, sometimes with a penalty for guessing.

Psychometric testing of intelligence and related abilities has generally advanced evolutionarily rather than revolutionarily. Sometimes what are touted as advances seem cosmetic or almost beside the point, as in the case of newer versions of the SAT, which are touted to have not only multiple-choice but fill-in-the-blank math problems. Perhaps the most notable trend is a movement toward multifactorial theories—often hierarchical ones—and away from the notion that intelligence can be adequately understood only in terms of a single general, or $g$, factor (e.g. Gustafsson 1988). For example, the third edition of the Wechsler Intelligence Scales for Children (WISC-III; Wechsler 1991) offers scores for four factors (verbal comprehension, perceptual organization, processing speed, and freedom from distractibility), but the main scores remain the verbal, performance, and total scores that have traditionally dominated interpretation of the test. The Fourth Edition of the Stanford-Binet Intelligence Scale (Thorndike et al 1986) also escapes from the orientation toward general ability that characterized earlier editions, yielding scores for crystallized intelligence, abstract-visual reasoning, quantitative reasoning, and short-term memory.

Two new tests also are constructed on the edifice of the theory of fluid and crystallized intelligence (Cattell 1971, Horn 1994): the Kaufman Adolescent and Adult Intelligence Test (KAIT; Kaufman & Kaufman 1993; see also Kaufman & Kaufman 1996) and the Woodcock-Johnson Tests of Cognitive Ability–Revised (Woodcock & Johnson 1989; see also Woodcock 1996) (for a review of these and other tests, see Daniel 1997). Although the theory is not new, the tendency to base psychometric tests closely on theories of intelligence is a welcome development.

The new Das-Naglieri Cognitive Assessment System (Naglieri & Das 1997) is based not on fluid-crystallized theory but rather on the theory of Luria (1973, 1976; see also Das et al 1994), mentioned above. It yields scores for attention, planning, simultaneous processing, and successive processing.

DYNAMIC ASSESSMENT    In dynamic assessment, individuals learn at the time of test. If they answer an item incorrectly, they are given guided feedback to help them solve the item, until they either get it correct or until the examiner has run out of clues to give them.

The notion of dynamic testing appears to have originated with Vygotsky (1962, 1978) and was developed independently by Feuerstein et al (1985). Dynamic assessment is generally based on the notion that cognitive abilities are modifiable, and that there is some kind of zone of proximal development (Vygotsky 1978), which represents the difference between actually developed ability and latent capacity. Dynamic assessments attempt to measure this zone of proximal development, or an analogue to it.

Dynamic assessment is cause both for celebration and for caution (EL Grigorenko & RJ Sternberg, unpublished manuscript). On the one hand, it represents a break from conventional psychometric notions of a more or less fixed level of intelligence. On the other hand, it is more a promissory note than a realized success. The Feuerstein test, The Learning Potential Assessment Device (Feuerstein et al 1985), is of clinical use but is not psychometrically normed or validated. There is only one formally normed test available in the United States (Swanson 1996), which yields scores for working memory before and at various points during and after training, as well as scores for amount of improvement with intervention, number of hints that have been given, and a subjective evaluation by the examiner of the examinee's use of strategies. Other tests are perhaps on the horizon (Guthke & Stein 1996), but their potential for standardization and validity, too, remains to be shown.

TYPICAL PERFORMANCE TESTS    Traditionally, tests of intelligence have been maximum-performance tests, requiring examinees to work the hardest they can to maximize their scores. Ackerman (1994, Ackerman & Heggestad 1997, Goff & Ackerman 1992) has recently argued that typical-performance tests—which, like personality tests, do not require extensive intellectual effort—should supplement maximal-performance ones. On such tests, subjects might be asked to what extent they are characterized by statements like "I prefer my life to be filled with puzzles I must solve" or "I enjoy work that requires conscientious, exacting skills." A factor analysis of such tests yielded five factors: intellectual engagement, openness, conscientiousness, directed activity, and science/technology interest.

Although the trend has been toward multifaceted views of intelligence and away from reliance on general ability, some have bucked this trend. Among those who have are Herrnstein & Murray (1994).

## The Bell Curve Phenomenon

A somewhat momentous event in the perception of the role of intelligence in society came with the publication of *The Bell Curve* (Herrnstein & Murray 1994). The impact of the book is shown by the rapid publication of a number of responses. A whole issue of *The New Republic* was devoted to the book, and two edited books of responses (Fraser 1995, Jacoby & Glauberman 1995) quickly appeared. Some of the responses were largely political or emotional in character, but others attacked the book on scientific grounds. A closely reasoned attack appeared a year after these collections (Fischer et al 1996). The American Psychological Association also sponsored a report that, although not directly a response to *The Bell Curve,* was largely motivated by it (Neisser et al 1996).

Some of the main arguments of the book are that (*a*) conventional IQ tests measure intelligence, at least to a good first approximation; (*b*) IQ is an important predictor of many measures of success in life, including school success but also including economic success, work success, success in parenting, avoidance of criminality, and avoidance of welfare dependence; (*c*) as a result of this prediction, people who are high in IQ are forming a cognitive elite, meaning that they are reaching the upper levels of society, whereas those who are low in IQ are falling toward the bottom; (*d*) tests can and should be used as a gating mechanism, given their predictive success; (*e*) IQ is fairly highly heritable, and hence is passed on through the genes from one generation to the next, with the heritability of IQ probably in the .5–.8 range; (*f*) there are racial and ethnic differences in intelligence, with blacks in the United States, for example, scoring about one standard deviation below whites; (*g*) it is likely, although not certain, that at least some of this difference between groups is due to genetic factors.

Herrnstein & Murray attempted to document their claims, using available literature and also their own analysis of the NLSY (National Longitudinal Study of Youth) data that were available to them. Although their book was written for a trade (popular) audience, the book was unusual among books for such an audience in its use of fairly sophisticated statistical techniques.

It is not possible here to review the full range of responses to Herrnstein & Murray (1994). Among psychologists, there seems to be fairly widespread agreement that the social-policy recommendations of Herrnstein & Murray—which call for greater isolation of and paternalism toward those with lower IQs—do not follow from their data, but rather represent a separate ideological statement (Neisser et al 1996). Beyond that, there is a great deal of disagreement regarding the claims made by these authors.

Our own view (Sternberg 1995) is that it would be easy to draw much stronger inferences from the Herrnstein-Murray analysis than the data warrant, and perhaps even than Herrnstein & Murray themselves would support.

First, Herrnstein & Murray (1994) acknowledge that, in the United States, IQ typically accounts only for roughly 10% of the variation, on average, in individual differences across the domains of success they survey. Put another way, about 90% of the variation, and sometimes quite a bit more, remains unexplained.

Second, even the 10% figure may be inflated by the fact that US society uses IQ-like tests to select, place, and ultimately, to stratify students, so that some of the outcomes that Herrnstein & Murray mention may actually be results of the use of IQ-like tests rather than results of individual differences in intelligence per se. For example, admission to selective colleges in the US typically requires students to take either the Scholastic Assessment Test (SAT) or the American College Test (ACT), both of which, for whatever they may be named, are similar (although not identical) in kind to conventional tests of IQ. Admission to graduate and professional programs requires similar kinds of tests. The result is that those who do not test well may be denied access to these programs, and to the routes that would lead them to job, economic, and other socially sanctioned forms of success in our society.

It is thus not surprising, in a sense, that test scores would be highly correlated with, say, job status. People who do not test well have difficulty gaining access to high-status jobs, which in turn pay better than other jobs to which they might be able to gain access. If we were to use some other index instead of test scores—for example, social class or economic class—then different people would be selected for the access routes to societal success. In fact, we do use these alternative measures to some degree, although less so than in the past.

Finally, although group differences in IQ are acknowledge by virtually all psychologists to be real, the cause of them remains very much in dispute. What is clear is that the evidence in favor of genetic causes is weak and equivocal (Nisbett 1995; Scarr et al 1977; Scarr & Weinberg 1976, 1983). We are certainly in no position to assign causes at this time. Understanding of group differences requires further analysis and probably requires looking at these differences through the lens of broader theories of intelligence.

## BROAD THEORIES OF INTELLIGENCE AND OF KINDS OF INTELLIGENCE

During recent years, there has been a trend toward broad theories of intelligence. We consider some of the main such theories next.

### Multiple Intelligences

Gardner (1983) proposed that there is no single, unified intelligence but rather a set of relatively distinct, independent, and modular multiple intelligence. His theory of multiple intelligences (MI theory) originally proposed seven multiple intelligences: (*a*) linguistic, as used in reading a book or writing a poem; (*b*) logical-mathematical, as used in deriving a logical proof or solving a mathematical problem; (*c*) spatial, as used in fitting suitcases into the trunk of a car; (*d*) musical, as used in singing a song or composing a symphony; (*e*) bodily-kinesthetic, as used in dancing or playing football; (*f*) interpersonal, as used in understanding and interacting with other people; and (*g*) intrapersonal, as used in understanding oneself.

Recently, Gardner 1998 has proposed one additional intelligence as a confirmed part of his theory—naturalist intelligence—the kind shown by people who are able to discern patterns in nature. Charles Darwin would be a notable example. Gardner has also suggested that there may be two other "candidate" intelligences: spiritual intelligence and existential intelligence. Spiritual intelligence involves a concern with cosmic or existential issues and the recognition of the spiritual as the achievement of a state of being. Existential intelligence involves a concern with ultimate issues. Gardner believes the evidence for these latter two intelligences to be less powerful than the evidence for the other eight intelligences. Whatever the evidence may be for the other eight, we agree that the evidence for these two new intelligences is speculative at this point. As of 1997, there have been no empirical investigations directly testing the validity of Gardner's theory as a whole.

In the past, factor analysis served as the major criterion for identifying abilities. Gardner (1983) proposed a new set of criteria, including but not limited to factor analysis, for identifying the existence of a discrete kind of intelligence: (*a*) potential isolation by brain damage, in that the destruction or sparing of a discrete area of the brain may destroy or spare a particular kind of intelligent behavior; (*b*) the existence of exceptional individuals who demonstrate an extraordinary ability (or deficit) in a particular kind of intelligent behavior; (*c*) an identifiable core operation or set of operations that are essential to performance of a particular kind of intelligent behavior; (*d*) a distinctive developmental history leading from novice to master, along with disparate levels of expert performance; (*e*) a distinctive evolutionary history, in which increases in intelligence may be plausibly associated with enhanced adaptation to the environment; (*f*) supportive evidence from cognitive-experimental research; (*g*) supportive evidence from psychometric tests; and (*h*) susceptibility to encoding in a symbol system.

Since the theory was first proposed, many educational interventions have arisen that are based on the theory, sometimes closely and other times less so (Gardner 1993). Many of the programs are unevaluated, and evaluations of others of these programs seem still to be ongoing, so it is difficult to say at this point what the results will be. In one particularly careful evaluation of a well-conceived program in a large southern city, there were no significant gains in student achievement or changes in student self-concept as a result of an intervention program based on Gardner's (1983) theory (Callahan et al 1997). There is no way of knowing whether these results are representative of such intervention programs, however.

## Successful Intelligence

Sternberg (1996) has suggested that we may wish to pay less attention to conventional notions of intelligence and more to what he terms *successful intelli-*

*gence,* or the ability to adapt to, shape, and select environments to accomplish one's goals and those of one's society and culture. A successfully intelligent person balances adaptation, shaping, and selection, doing each as necessary. The theory is motivated in part by repeated findings that conventional tests of intelligence and related tests do not predict meaningful criteria of success as well as they predict scores on other similar tests and school grades (e.g. Sternberg & Williams 1997).

Successful intelligence involves an individual's discerning his or her pattern of strengths and weaknesses, and then figuring out ways to capitalize upon the strengths and at the same time to compensate for or correct the weaknesses. People attain success, in part, in idiosyncratic ways that involve their finding how best to exploit their own patterns of strengths and weaknesses.

Three broad abilities are important to successful intelligence: analytical, creative, and practical abilities.

Analytical abilities are required to analyze and evaluate the options available to oneself in life. They include things such as identifying the existence of a problem, defining the nature of the problem, setting up a strategy for solving the problem, and monitoring one's solution processes.

Creative abilities are required to generate problem-solving options in the first place. Creative individuals are ones who "buy low and sell high" in the world of ideas (Sternberg & Lubart 1995, 1996): They are willing to generate ideas that, like stocks with low price-earnings ratios, are unpopular and perhaps even depreciated. Having convinced at least some people of the value of these ideas, they then sell high, meaning that they move on to the next unpopular idea. Research shows that these abilities are at least partially distinct from conventional IQ, and that they are moderately domain-specific, meaning that creativity in one domain (such as art) does not necessarily imply creativity in another (such as writing) (Sternberg & Lubart 1995).

Practical abilities are required to implement options and to make them work. Practical abilities are involved when intelligence is applied to real-world contexts. A key aspect of practical intelligence is the acquisition and use of tacit knowledge, which is knowledge of what one needs to know to succeed in a given environment that is not explicitly taught and that usually is not verbalized. Research shows that tacit knowledge is acquired through mindful utilization of experience, that it is relatively domain specific, that its possession is relatively independent of conventional abilities, that it predicts criteria of job success about as well as and sometimes better than does IQ (McClelland 1973, Sternberg & Wagner 1993, Sternberg et al 1995).

The separation of practical intelligence from IQ has been shown in a number of different ways in a number of different studies. Scribner (1984, 1986) showed that experienced assemblers in a milk-processing plant used complex strategies for combining partially filled cases in a manner that minimized the number of moves required to complete an order. Although the assemblers were the least educated workers in the plant, they were able to calculate in their heads quantities expressed in different base number systems, and they routinely outperformed the more highly educated white collar workers who substituted when the assemblers were absent. Scribner found that the order-filling performance of the assemblers was unrelated to measures of academic skills, including intelligence test scores, arithmetic test scores, and grades.

Ceci & Liker (1986) carried out a study of expert racetrack handicappers and found that expert handicappers used a highly complex algorithm for predicting post time odds that involved interactions among seven kinds of information. Use of a complex interaction term in their implicit equation was unrelated to the handicappers' IQ.

In a series of studies, it has been shown that shoppers in California grocery stores were able to choose which of several products represented the best buy for them (Lave et al 1984, Murtaugh 1985), even though they did very poorly on the same kinds of problems when they were presented in the form of a paper-and-pencil arithmetic computation test. The same principle that applies to adults appears to apply to children as well: Carraher et al (1985) found that Brazilian street children who could apply sophisticated mathematical strategies in their street vending were unable to do the same in a classroom setting (see also Ceci & Roazzi 1994, Nunes 1994).

One more example of a study of practical intelligence was provided by individuals asked to play the role of city managers for the computer-simulated city of Lohhausen (Dorner & Kreuzig 1983, Dorner et al 1983). A variety of problems were presented to these individuals, such as how best to raise revenue to build roads. The simulation involved more than one thousand variables. No relation was found between IQ and complexity of strategies used.

There is also evidence that practical intelligence can be taught (Gardner et al 1994), at least in some degree. For example, middle-school children given a program for developing their practical intelligence for school (strategies for effective reading, writing, execution of homework, and taking of tests) improved more from pretest to posttest than did control students who received an alternative but irrelevant treatment.

None of these studies suggests that IQ is unimportant for school or job performance or other kinds of performance, and indeed, the evidence suggests to the contrary (Barrett & Depinet 1991, Hunt 1995, Hunter & Hunter 1984, Schmidt & Hunter 1981, Wigdor & Garner 1982). What the studies do suggest, however, is that there are other aspects of intelligence that are relatively independent of IQ and that are important as well. A multiple-abilities prediction model of school or job performance would probably be most satisfactory.

According to the theory of successful intelligence, children's multiple abilities are underused in educational institutions because teaching tends to value analytical (as well as memory) abilities at the expense of creative and practical abilities. Sternberg et al (1996) designed an experiment to illustrate this point. They identified 199 high school students from around the United States who were strong in either analytical, creative, or practical abilities; all three kinds of abilities; or none of the kinds of abilities. Students were then brought to Yale University to take a college-level psychology course that was taught in a way that emphasized either memory, analytical, creative, or practical abilities. Some students were matched, and others were mismatched, to their own strength(s). All students were evaluated for memory-based, analytical, creative, and practical achievements.

Sternberg et al found that students whose instruction matched their pattern of abilities performed significantly better than did students who were mismatched. They also found that prediction of course performance was improved by taking into account creative and practical as well as analytical abilities.

## True Intelligence

Perkins (1995) has proposed the theory of *true intelligence,* which he believes synthesizes classic views as well as new ones. According to Perkins, there are three basic aspects to intelligence: neural, experiential, and reflective.

According to Perkins, neural intelligence is in the functioning of people's neurological systems, with some people's systems running faster and with more precision than do the neurological systems of others. He mentions "more finely tuned voltages" and "more exquisitely adapted chemical catalysts" as well as a "better pattern of connectivity in the labyrinth of neurons" (Perkins 1995, p. 97), although it is not entirely clear what any of these terms mean. Perkins believes this aspect of intelligence to be largely genetically determined and unlearnable. This kind of intelligence seems to be somewhat similar to Cattell's (1971) idea of fluid intelligence.

The experiential aspect of intelligence is what has been learned from experience. It is the extent and organization of the knowledge base, and thus is similar to Cattell's (1971) notion of crystallized intelligence.

The reflective aspect of intelligence refers to the role of strategies in memory and problem solving and appears to be similar to the construct of metacognition or cognitive monitoring (Brown & DeLoache 1978, Flavell 1981). Ceci (1996) also believes that reflection is important in intelligence.

## The Bioecological Model of Intelligence

Ceci (1996) has proposed a bioecological model of intelligence, according to which multiple cognitive potentials, context, and knowledge are all essential bases of individual differences in performance. Each of the multiple cognitive potentials enables relationships to be discovered, thoughts to be monitored, and knowledge to be acquired within a given domain. Although these potentials are biologically based, their development is closely linked to environmental context, and hence it is difficult if not impossible to separate cleanly biological from environmental contributions to intelligence. Moreover, abilities may express themselves very differently in different contexts. For example, children given essentially the same task in the context of a video game and in the context of a laboratory cognitive task performed much better when the task was presented in the context of the video game. Part of this superiority may have been a result of differences in emotional response, which brings us to the last broader conception we consider.

## Emotional Intelligence

Emotional intelligence is the ability to perceive accurately, appraise, and express emotion; the ability to access and/or generate feelings when they facilitate thought; the ability to understand emotion and emotional knowledge; and the ability to regulate emotions to promote emotional and intellectual growth (Mayer & Salovey 1997). The concept was introduced by Salovey & Mayer (Mayer & Salovey 1993, Salovey & Mayer 1990) and popularized and expanded upon by Goleman (1995).

There is some, though still tentative, evidence for the existence of emotional intelligence. For example, Mayer & Gehr (1996) found that emotional perception of characters in a variety of situations correlates with SAT scores, with empathy, and with emotional openness. Full convergent-discriminant validation of the construct, however, appears to be needed.

## CONCLUSION

Cultures designate as "intelligent" the cognitive, social, and behavioral attributes that they value as adaptive to the requirements of living in those cultures. To the extent that there is overlap in these attributes across cultures, there will be overlap in the cultures' conceptions of intelligence. Although conceptions of intelligence may vary across cultures, the underlying cognitive attributes probably do not. There may be some variation in social and behavioral attributes. As a result, there is probably a common core of cognitive skills that underlies intelligence in all cultures, with the cognitive skills having different manifestations across the cultures.

A variety of paradigms has been used to study intelligence. These paradigms are largely complementary rather than contradictory, looking at different aspects of and questions about intelligence. Many active research programs are pursuing answers to these questions. Although there is no one right approach, we believe that the field particularly needs research that expands our notions about what intelligence is. At the same time, we must be cautious about theories that are advanced without direct empirical support. We also must be cautious about how to interpret behavior-genetic studies, which deal with correlations, not means. The Flynn effect shows that whatever the heritability of IQ, IQ is highly modifiable, at least across generations. Perhaps the increases in IQ that have been observed across generations will one day start to manifest themselves in people's behavior. To date, signs that increases in IQ are reflected in more intelligent everyday behavior have been conspicuous by their absence.

## ACKNOWLEDGMENTS

Preparation of this chapter was supported in part under the Javits Act Program (Grant R206R50001) as administered by the Office of Educational Research and Improvement, US Department of Education. The opinions expressed in this chapter do not necessarily reflect the positions or policies of the Office of Educational Research and Improvement or the US Department of Education.

> Visit the *Annual Reviews home page* at http://www.AnnualReviews.org.

## Literature Cited

Ackerman P. 1994. Intelligence, attention, and learning: maximal and typical performance. In *Current Topics in Human Intelligence: Theories of Intelligence,* ed. DK Detterman, 4:1–27. Norwood, NJ: Ablex

Ackerman PL, Heggestad ED. 1997. Intelligence, personality, and interests: evidence for overlapping traits. *Psychol. Bull.* 121: 219–45

Azuma H, Kashiwagi K. 1987. Descriptions for an intelligent person: a Japanese study. *Jpn. Psychol. Res.* 29:17–26

Barrett GV, Depinet RL. 1991. A reconsideration of testing for competence rather than for intelligence. *Am. Psychol.* 46:1012–24

Binet A, Simon T. 1916. *The Development of Intelligence in Children.* Transl. ES Kite. Baltimore: Williams Wilkins

Boring GG. 1923. Intelligence as the tests test it. *New Republic,* June 6, pp. 35–37

Bouchard TJ Jr. 1997. IQ similarity in twins reared apart: findings and responses to critics. *Intelligence, Heredity, and Envi-*ronment, ed. RJ Sternberg, EL Grigorenko, pp. 126–60. New York: Cambridge Univ. Press

Bouchard TJ Jr, Lykken DT, McGue M, Segal NL, Tellegen A. 1990. Sources of human psychological differences: the Minnesota study of twins reared apart. *Science* 250: 223–28

Bronfenbrenner U, Ceci SJ. 1994. Nature-nurture reconceptualized in developmental perspective: a bioecological model. *Psychol. Rev.* 101:568–86

Brown AL, DeLoache JS. 1978. Skills, plans, and self-regulation. In *Children's Thinking: What Develops?,* ed. R Siegler, pp. 3–35. Hillsdale, NJ: Erlbaum

Callahan CM, Tomlinson CA, Plucker J. 1997. *Project START using a multiple intelligences model in identifying and promoting talent in high-risk students.* Storrs, CT: Natl. Res. Cent. Gift. Talent., Univ. Conn. Tech. Rep.

Campbell FA, Ramey CT. 1994. Effects of

early intervention on intellectual and academic achievement: a follow-up study of children from low-income families. *Child Dev.* 65:684–98

Carraher TN, Carraher D, Schliemann AD. 1985. Mathematics in the streets and in schools. *Br. J. Dev. Psychol.* 3:21–29

Carroll JB. 1993. *Human Cognitive Abilities: A Survey of Factor-Analytic Studies.* New York: Cambridge Univ. Press

Cattell RB. 1971. *Abilities: Their Structure, Growth, and Action.* Boston: Houghton-Mifflin

Ceci SJ. 1996. *On Intelligence: A Bioecological Treatise on Intellectual Development.* Cambridge, MA: Harvard Univ. Press. Expanded ed.

Ceci SJ, Liker J. 1986. Academic and nonacademic intelligence: an experimental separation. In *Practical Intelligence: Nature and Origins of Competence in the Everyday World,* ed. RJ Sternberg, RK Wagner, pp. 119–42. New York: Cambridge Univ. Press

Ceci SJ, Roazzi A. 1994. The effect of context on cognition: postcards from Brazil. *Mind in Context: Interactionist Perspectives on Human Intelligence,* ed. RJ Sternberg, RK Wagner, pp. 74–101. New York: Cambridge Univ. Press

Chen MJ. 1994. Chinese and Australian concepts of intelligence. *Psychol. Dev. Soc.* 6:101–17

Chen MJ, Braithwaite V, Huang JT. 1982. Attributes of intelligent behaviour: perceived relevance and difficulty by Australian and Chinese students. *J. Cross-Cult. Psychol.* 13:139–56

Chen MJ, Chen HC. 1988. Concepts of intelligence: a comparison of Chinese graduates from Chinese and English schools in Hong Kong. *Int. J. Psychol.* 223:471–87

Connolly H, Bruner J. 1974. Competence: its nature and nurture. In *The growth of Competence,* ed. K Connolly, J Bruner. New York: Academic

Craik FIM, Lockhart RS. 1972. Levels of processing: a framework for memory research. *J. Verbal Learn. Verbal Behav.* 11: 671–84

Cronbach LJ. 1957. The two disciplines of scientific psychology. *Am. Psychol.* 12: 671–84

Cronbach LJ, Snow RE. 1977. *Aptitudes and Instructional Methods.* New York: Irvington

Daniel MH. 1997. . Intelligence testing: status and trends. *Am. Psychol.* In press

Das JP. 1994. Eastern views of intelligence. See Sternberg 1994, p. 391

Das JP, Naglieri JA, Kirby JR. 1994. *Assessment of Cognitive Processes: The PASS Theory of Intelligence.* Needham Heights, MA: Allyn Bacon

Dasen P. 1984. The cross-cultural study of intelligence: Piaget and the Baoule. *Int. J. Psychol.* 19:407–34

Deary I, Stough C. 1996. Intelligence and inspection time: achievements, prospects, and problems. *Am. Psychol.* 51:599–608

Dorner D, Kreuzig H. 1983. Problemlosefahigkeit und intelligenz [Problem solving and intelligence]. *Psychol. Rundsch.* 34: 185–92

Dorner D, Kreuzig H, Reither F, Staudel T. 1983. *Lohhausen: Vom Umgang mit Unbestimmtheir und Komplexitat.* Bern: Huber

Durojaiye MOA. 1993. Indigenous psychology in Africa. In *Indigenous Psychologies: Research and Experience in Cultural Context,* ed. U Kim, JW Berry. Newbury Park, CA: Sage

Feuerstein R, Rand Y, Haywood HC, Hoffman M, Jensen M. 1985. *The Learning Potential Assessment Device (LPAD): Examiner's Manual.* Jerusalem: Hadassah-Wizo-Canada Res. Inst.

Fischer CS, Hout M, Sanchez Janowski M, Lucas SR, Swidler A, Voss K. 1996. *Inequality by Design: Cracking the Bell Curve Myth.* Princeton, NJ: Princeton Univ. Press

Flanagan DP, Genshaft JL, Harrison PL, eds. 1996. *Beyond Traditional Intellectual Assessment: Contemporary and Emerging Theories, Tests, and Issues.* New York: Guilford

Flavell JH. 1981. Cognitive monitoring. In *Children's Oral Communication Skills,* ed. WP Dickson, pp. 35–60. New York: Academic

Flynn JR. 1984. The mean IQ of Americans: massive gains 1932 to 1978. *Psychol. Bull.* 95:29–51

Flynn JR. 1987. Massive IQ gains in 14 nations: What IQ tests really measure. *Psychol. Bull.* 101:171–91

Flynn JR. 1994. IQ gains over time. See Sternberg 1994, pp. 617–23

Fraser S, ed. 1995. *The Bell Curve Wars.* New York: Basic Books

Galton F. 1883. *Inquiry into Human Faculty and Its Development.* London: Macmillan

Gardner H. 1983. *Frames of Mind: The Theory of Multiple Intelligences.* New York: Basic Books

Gardner H. 1993. *Multiple Intelligences: The Theory in Practice.* New York: Basic Books

Gardner H. 1998. Are there additional intelligences? The case for naturalist, spiritual, and existential intelligences. In *Education, Information, and Transformation,* ed. J Kane. Englewood Cliffs, NJ: Prentice-Hall

Gardner H, Krechevsky M, Sternberg RJ, Okagaki L. 1994. Intelligence in context: enhancing students' practical intelligences for school. In *Classroom Lessons: Integrating Cognitive Theory and Classroom Practice,* ed. K McGilly, pp. 105–27. Cambridge, MA: MIT Press

Gill R, Keats DM. 1980. Elements of intellectual competence: judgments by Australian and Malay university students. *J. Cross-Cult. Psychol.* 11:233–43

Goff M, Ackerman PL. 1992. Personality-intelligence relations: assessment of typical intellectual engagement. *J. Educ. Psychol.* 84:537–52

Goleman D. 1995. *Emotional Intelligence.* New York: Bantam Books

Goodnow JJ. 1976. The nature of intelligent behavior: questions raised by cross-cultural studies. In *The Nature of Intelligence,* ed. L Resnick, pp. 169–88. Hillsdale, NJ: Erlbaum

Gustafsson J-E. 1988. Hierarchical models of individual differences in cognitive abilities. In *Advances in the Psychology of Human Intelligence,* ed. RJ Sternberg, 1: 35–71. Hillsdale, NJ: Erlbaum

Guthke J, Stein H. 1996. Are learning tests the better version of intelligence tests? *Eur. J. Psychol. Assess.* 12:1–13

Haier RJ, Nuechterlein KH, Hazlett E, Wu JC, Paek J. 1988. Cortical glucose metabolic rate correlates of abstract reasoning and attention studied with positron emission tomography. *Intelligence* 12:199–217

Haier RJ, Siegel B, Tang C, Abel L, Buchsbaum MS. 1992. Intelligence and changes in regional cerebral glucose metabolic rate following learning. *Intelligence* 16:415–26

Halstead WC. 1951. Biological intelligence. *J. Pers.* 20:118–30

Hebb DO. 1949. *The Organization of Behavior.* New York: Wiley

Herrnstein RJ, Murray C. 1994. *The Bell Curve: Intelligence and Class Structure in American Life.* New York: Free Press

Horn JL. 1994. Fluid and crystallized intelligence, theory of. See Sternberg 1994, pp. 443–51

Hunt EB. 1995. *Will We Be Smart Enough?* New York: Russell Sage Found.

Hunt EB, Frost N, Lunneborg C. 1973. Individual differences in cognition: a new approach to intelligence. In *The Psychology of Learning and Motivation,* ed. G Bower, pp. 87–122. New York: Academic

Hunter HE, Hunter RF. 1984. Validity and utility of alternative predictors of job performance. *Psychol. Bull.* 96:72–98

Intelligence and Its Measurement: A Symposium. *J. Educ. Psychol.* 12:123–47, 195–216, 271–75

Irvine JT. 1978. "Wolof magical thinking": culture and conservation revisited. *J. Cross-Cult. Psychol.* 9:300–10

Jacoby R, Glauberman N, eds. 1995. *The Bell Curve Debate: History, Documents, Opinions.* New York: Times Books

Jensen AR. 1997. The puzzle of nongenetic variance. In *Intelligence, Heredity, and Environment,* ed. RJ Sternberg, EL Grigorenko, pp. 42–88. New York: Cambridge Univ. Press

Kaufman AS, Kaufman NL. 1983. *Kaufman Assessment Battery for Children (K-ABC).* Circle Pines, MN: Am. Guid. Serv.

Kaufman AS, Kaufman NL. 1993. *Kaufman Adolescent and Adult Intelligence Test.* Circle Pines, MN: Am. Guid. Serv.

Kaufman AS, Kaufman NL. 1996. The Kaufman adolescent and adult intelligence test (KAIT). See Flanagan et al 1996, pp. 209–29

Lave J, Murtaugh M, de la Roche O. 1984. The dialectic of arithmetic in grocery shopping. See Rogoff & Lave 1984, pp. 67–94

Loehlin JC. 1989. Partitioning environmental and genetic contributions to behavioral development. *Am. Psychol.* 44:1285–92

Loehlin JC, Horn JM, Willerman L. 1997. Heredity, environment, and IQ in the Texas Adoption Project. See Sternberg & Grigorenko 1997a, pp. 105–25

Luria AR. 1973. *The Working Brain.* New York: Basic Books

Luria AR. 1976. *Cognitive Development: Its Cultural and Social Foundations.* Cambridge, MA: Harvard Univ. Press

Luria AR. 1980. *Higher Cortical Functions in Man.* New York: Basic Books. 2nd ed.

Lutz C. 1985. Ethnopsychology compared to what? Explaining behaviour and consciousness among the Ifaluk. See White & Kirkpatrick 1985, pp. 35–79

Mayer JD, Gehr G. 1996. Emotional intelligence and the identification of emotion. *Intelligence* 22:89–114

Mayer JD, Salovey P. 1993. The intelligence of emotional intelligence. *Intelligence* 17: 433–42

Mayer JD, Salovey P. 1997. What is emotional intelligence? See Salovey & Sluyter 1997, pp. 3–31

McClelland DC. 1973. Testing for competence rather than for "intelligence." *Am. Psychol.* 28:1–14

Mundy-Castle AC. 1974. Social and Technological Intelligence in Western or Non-western Cultures. *Universitas* 4:46–52

Murtaugh M. 1985. The practice of arithmetic by American grocery shoppers. *Anthropol. Educ. Q.* Fall

Naglieri J, Das JP. 1997. *Das-Naglieri Cognitive Assessment System (CAS).* Itasca, IL: Riverside

Neisser U, Boodoo G, Bouchard TJ, Boykin AW, Brody N, et al. 1996. Intelligence: knowns and unknowns. *Am. Psychol.* 51: 77–101

Nettlebeck T. 1982. Inspection time: an index for intelligence? *Q. Exp. Psychol.* 34A: 299–312

Newell A, Simon HA. 1972. *Human Problem Solving.* Englewood Cliffs, NJ: Prentice-Hall

Nisbett R. 1995. Race, IQ, and scientism. In *The Bell Curve Wars: Race, Intelligence and the Future of America,* ed. S Fraser, pp. 36–57. New York: Basic Books

Nunes T. 1994. Street intelligence. See Sternberg 1994, 2:1045–49

Okagaki L, Sternberg RJ. 1993. Parental beliefs and children's school performance. *Child Dev.* 64:36–56

Pedersen NL, Plomin R, Nesselroade JR, McClearn GE. 1992. A quantitative genetic analysis of cognitive abilities during the second half of the life span. *Psychol. Sci.* 3:346–53

Perkins DN. 1995. *Outsmarting IQ: The Emerging Science of Learnable Intelligence.* New York: Free Press

Plomin R. 1997. Identifying genes for cognitive abilities and disabilities. See Sternberg & Grigorenko 1997a, pp. 89–104

Poole FJP. 1985. Coming into social being: cultural images of infants in Bimin-Kuskusmin folk psychology. See White & Kirkpatrick 1985, pp. 183–244

Putnam DB, Kilbride PL. 1980. *A relativistic understanding of social intelligence among the Songhay of Mali and Smaia of Kenya.* Presented at Meet. Soc. Cross-Cult. Res., Philadelphia, PA

Ramey CT. 1994. Abecedarian project. See Sternberg 1994, pp. 1–3

Reed TE, Jensen AR. 1992. Conduction velocity in a brain nerve pathway of normal adults correlates with intelligence level. *Intelligence* 16:259–72

Rogoff B, Lave J, eds. 1984. *Everyday Cognition: Its Development in Social Context.* Cambridge, MA: Harvard Univ. Press

Ruzgis P, Grigorenko EL. 1994. Cultural

meaning systems, intelligence, and personality. In *Personality and Intelligence,* ed. RJ Sternberg, P Ruzgis, pp. 248–70. New York: Cambridge Univ. Press

Salovey P, Mayer JD. 1990. Emotional intelligence. *Imagin. Cogn. Pers.* 9:185–211

Salovey P, Sluyter D. 1997. *Emotional Development and Emotional Intelligence: Educational Implications.* New York: Basic Books

Scarr S. 1997. Behavior-genetic and socialization theories of intelligence: truce and reconciliation. See Sternberg & Grigorenko, 1997a, pp. 3–41

Scarr S, Pakstis AJ, Katz SH, Barker WB. 1977. Absence of a relationship between degree of white ancestry and intellectual skill in a black population. *Hum. Genet.* 39:69–86

Scarr S, Weinberg RA. 1976. IQ test performance of black children adopted by white families. *Am. Psychol.* 31:726–39

Scarr S, Weinberg RA. 1983. The Minnesota adoption studies: genetic differences and malleability. *Child Dev.* 54:260–67

Schmidt FL, Hunter JE. 1981. Employment testing: old theories and new research findings. *Am. Psychol.* 36:1128–37

Scribner S. 1984. Studying working intelligence. See Rogoff & Lave 1984, pp. 9–40

Scribner S. 1986. Thinking in action: some characteristics of practical thought. In *Practical Intelligence: Nature and Origins of Competence in the Everyday World,* ed. RJ Sternberg, RK Wagner, pp. 13–30. New York: Cambridge Univ. Press

Serpell R. 1974. Aspects of intelligence in a developing country. *Afr. Soc. Res.* 17: 578–96

Serpell R. 1977. Strategies for investigating intelligence in its cultural context. *Q. Newsl. Inst. Compar. Hum. Dev.* 1:11–15

Serpell R. 1982. Measures of perception, skills, and intelligence. In *Review of Child Development Research,* ed. WW Hartup, 6:392–440. Chicago: Univ. Chicago Press

Snow RE. 1994. A person-situation interaction theory of intelligence in outline. In *Intelligence, Mind, and Reasoning: Structure and Development,* ed. A Demetriou, A Efklides, pp. 11–28. Amsterdam: Elsevier

Spearman C. 1904. General intelligence, objectively determined and measured. *Am. J. Psychol.* 15:201–93

Srivastava AK, Misra G. 1996. Changing perspectives on understanding intelligence: an appraisal. *Indian Psychol. Abstr. Rev.* 3:1–34

Sternberg RJ. 1977. *Intelligence, Information Processing, and Analogical Reasoning:*

*The Componential Analysis of Human Abilities.* Hillsdale, NJ: Erlbaum

Sternberg RJ. 1985a. *Beyond IQ: A Triarchic Theory of Human Intelligence.* New York: Cambridge Univ. Press

Sternberg RJ. 1985b. Implicit theories of intelligence, creativity, and wisdom. *J. Pers. Soc. Psychol.* 49:607–27

Sternberg RJ. 1990. *Metaphors of Mind: Conceptions of the Nature of Intelligence.* New York: Cambridge Univ. Press

Sternberg RJ, ed. 1994. *Encyclopedia of Human Intelligence.* New York: Macmillan

Sternberg RJ. 1995. For whom the Bell Curve tolls: a review of *The Bell Curve. Psychol. Sci.* 6:257–61

Sternberg RJ. 1996. *Successful Intelligence.* New York: Simon Schuster

Sternberg RJ, Conway BE, Ketron JL, Bernstein M. 1981. People's conceptions of intelligence. *J. Pers. Soc. Psychol.* 41:37–55

Sternberg RJ, Detterman DK, eds. 1986. *What Is Intelligence? Contemporary Viewpoints on Its Nature and Definition.* Norwood, NJ: Ablex

Sternberg RJ, Ferrari M, Clinkenbeard PR, Grigorenko EL. 1996. Identification, instruction, and assessment of gifted children: a construct validation of a triarchic model. *Gifted Child Q.* 40:129–37

Sternberg RJ, Grigorenko EL, eds. 1997a. *Intelligence, Heredity, and Environment.* New York: Cambridge Univ. Press

Sternberg RJ, Grigorenko EL. 1997b. The cognitive costs of physical and mental ill health: Applying the psychology of the developed world to the problems of the developing world. *Eye on Psi Chi.* In press

Sternberg RJ, Lubart TI. 1995. *Defying the Crowd: Cultivating Creativity in a Culture of Conformity.* New York: Free Press

Sternberg RJ, Lubart TI. 1996. Investing in creativity. *Am. Psychol.* 51:677–88

Sternberg RJ, Wagner RK. 1993. The *g*-ocentric view of intelligence and job performance is wrong. *Curr. Dir. Psychol. Sci.* 2:1–4

Sternberg RJ, Wagner RK, Williams WM, Horvath J. 1995. Testing common sense. *Am. Psychol.* 50:912–27

Sternberg RJ, Williams WM. 1997. Does the Graduate Record Examination predict meaningful success in the graduate training of psychologists?: A Case Study. *Am. Psychol.* 52:630–41

Super CM, Harkness S. 1982. The infants' niche in rural Kenya and metropolitan America. In *Cross-Cultural Research at Issue,* ed. LL Adler, pp. 47–55. New York: Academic

Swanson HL. 1996. *Swanson Cognitive Processing Test.* Austin, TX: PRO-ED

Thorndike RL, Hagen EP, Sattler JM. 1986. *Stanford-Binet Intelligence Scale: Fourth Edition.* Itasca, IL: Riverside

Vernon PA, Mori M. 1992. Intelligence, reaction times, and peripheral nerve conduction velocity. *Intelligence* 8:273–88

Vygotsky LS. 1962. (1934). *Thought and Language.* Cambridge, MA: MIT Press

Vygotsky LS. 1978. *Mind in Society.* Cambridge, MA: Harvard Univ. Press

Wahlsten D, Gottlieb G. 1997. The invalid separation of effects of nature and nurture: lessons from animal experimentation. See Sternberg & Grigorenko 1997a, pp. 163–92

Wechsler D. 1991. *Wechsler Intelligence Scale for Children—Third Edition.* San Antonio, TX: Psychological Corp.

White GM. 1985. Premises and purposes in a Solomon Islands ethnopsychology. See White & Kirkpatrick 1985, pp. 328–66

White GM, Kirkpatrick J, eds. 1985. *Person, Self, and Experience: Exploring Pacific Ethnopsychologies.* Berkeley: Univ. Calif. Press

Wickett JC, Vernon PA. 1994. Peripheral nerve conduction velocity, reaction time, and intelligence: an attempt to replicate Vernon and Mori. *Intelligence* 18:127–32

Wigdor AK, Garner WR, eds. 1982. *Ability Testing: Uses, Consequences, and Controversies.* Washington, DC: Nat. Acad. Press

Willerman L, Schultz R, Rutledge JN, Bigler ED. 1991. In vivo brain size and intelligence. *Intelligence* 15:223–28

Willerman L, Schultz R, Rutledge JN, Bigler ED. 1992. Hemispheric size asymmetry predicts relative verbal and nonverbal intelligence differently in the sexes: an MRI study of structure-function relations. *Intelligence* 16:315–28

Woodcock RW. 1996. The Woodcock-Johnson tests of cognitive ability—Revised. See Flanagan et al 1996, pp. 230–46

Woodcock RW, Johnson MB. 1989. *Woodcock-Johnson Tests of Cognitive Ability—Revised.* Itasca, IL: Riverside

Yang S-Y, Sternberg RJ. 1997a. Conceptions of intelligence in ancient Chinese philosophy. *J. Theor. Philos. Psychol.* In press

Yang S-Y, Sternberg RJ. 1997b. Taiwanese conceptions of intelligence. Submitted

*Annu. Rev. Psychol. 1998. 49:503–35*

# LOWER-LEVEL VISUAL PROCESSING AND MODELS OF LIGHT ADAPTATION

## D. C. Hood

Department of Psychology, Columbia University, New York, New York 10027;
e-mail: don@psych.columbia.edu

KEY WORDS: vision, visual sensitivity, retina, psychophysics, ganglion cell

---

### ABSTRACT

Before there was a formal discipline of psychology, there were attempts to understand the relationship between visual perception and retinal physiology. Today, there is still uncertainty about the extent to which even very basic behavioral data (called here candidates for lower-level processing) can be predicted based upon retinal processing. Here, a general framework is proposed for developing models of lower-level processing. It is argued that our knowledge of ganglion cell function and retinal mechanisms has advanced to the point where a model of lower-level processing should include a testable model of ganglion cell function. This model of ganglion cell function, combined with minimal assumptions about the role of the visual cortex, forms a model of lower-level processing. Basic behavioral and physiological descriptions of light adaptation are reviewed, and recent attempts to model lower-level processing are discussed.

---

## CONTENTS

0066-4308/98/0201-0503$08.00

# INTRODUCTION

## Background: The Need for a Model of Adaptation

For years, certainly since the work of Helmholtz, Hering, and Mach, the role played by the retina in human vision has been a concern of both physiologist and psychologist. Today, many speak of a psychophysical result as "having a retinal basis" or "being mediated by the retina" or "having a neural substrate in the retina" or being an example of "lower-level processing." Since the retina cannot "see," what do these terms mean to convey? In general, they try to convey the notion that when retinal function is understood, then these psychophysical data will be understood, or, more precisely, that the data in question will be predicted with very few assumptions about what the brain is doing. In the terminology used here, the behavioral data would be "explained by lower-level processing" when they are predicted from the retinal output with few additional assumptions.

Over the past 40 years or more, behavioral phenomena thought to have a simple retinal explanation by one cohort of visual scientists have been shown by the next cohort of physiologists and psychophysicists to be inconsistent with a retinal explanation. Today, a full range of opinions exists concerning the role of the retina. This range reflects the inadequacies of our models. Many attempts to relate basic behavioral phenomena to retinal physiology have been flawed because of a failure to separate a model of retinal physiology from a model relating the physiology to behavior. The fact that we lack a good understanding of the human retina has contributed to this state of affairs. In this chapter, I review the status of our understanding of the retinal basis of light adaptation and suggest a framework for deciding which behavioral data can be understood based upon retinal function, that is, predicted by a model of lower-level processing.

Light adaptation refers to the changes in our sensitivity to light that allow us to adapt to a wide range of light levels. Our visual system can adjust to ambient light levels that vary by a factor of $10^8$ or more. These adjustments do not simply modify our sensitivity to light; they change the way our visual system processes the spatial and temporal variations in light that make up our visual world. Hundreds of hypotheses about the role of the retina have been generated based upon extensive behavioral measures of these changes in sensitivity (see reviews by Shapley & Enroth-Cugell 1984, Graham 1989, Hood & Finkelstein 1986). In spite of the advances made in our understanding of the retinal mechanisms involved, we still cannot answer basic questions about the extent to which these behavioral measures depend upon retinal processing.

How close are we to a model of light adaptation that predicts behavioral sensitivity based upon lower-level processing? In addition to seeking an answer to this question, the goal here is to review some of the behavioral, physiological, and theoretical results concerning the basic mechanisms of light adaptation controlling ganglion cell and/or behavioral function. This review is organized within a general framework for a model of lower-level processing.

## Characteristics of a Model of Lower-Level Processing

A schematic of a model of lower-level processing is shown in Figure 1. The input $E(\lambda,x,t)$ is the energy distribution (the number of quanta of a particular wavelength, $\lambda$) falling on the retina at point $x$, as a function of time $t$. As this is a model of behavior, the final output $\psi$ is a behavioral response such as "yes I

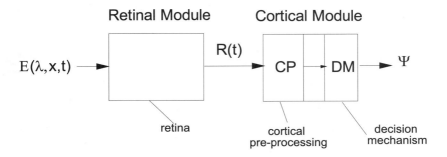

*Figure 1*   A schematic of a model of lower-level processing.

see it" or "yes it is different." The model has a retinal and a cortical module. There are three key features of the class of models proposed here.

First, the retinal module is explicitly specified and is therefore testable with data from primate ganglion cells. The term $R(t)$ is the output of the retina; it is the array of responses of the ganglion cells. There is currently available a variety of data from primate ganglion cells collected with paradigms similar to those used by the psychophysicists. Some of these data are summarized below in the section entitled "Basic Ganglion Cell Data: Candidates for Retinal Modeling." The model of lower-level processing is formulated such that these data can be predicted. Ideally, the functional units of the retinal module would be retinal cells (e.g. receptors, horizontals, bipolars, etc), and the model would be substantiated in such a way that data from these cells could be predicted. Although the pace of new discoveries suggests that this may be a viable goal in the near future, the current state of knowledge suggests a more modest goal. The suggestion here is that the hypothesized retinal mechanisms should be informed by current information about the physiology and anatomy of the primate retina and should not contradict any of this information that is well established. In the section on "Lessons from Inside the Retina," a summary of some of this information is provided. However, regardless of the retinal mechanisms hypothesized, the retinal module must predict the "basic ganglion cell data." Without the ability to predict the response of the ganglion cells, it is difficult to avoid the confusing, and occasionally circular, arguments that accompany attempts to explain psychophysical data in terms of retinal processing. In particular, when behavioral data fail to confirm a hypothesized role for retinal processing, some modify their view of the retina, while others change the assumptions linking the retinal output to behavior. Thus, the role of the cortex must also be stated explicitly in a model of lower-level processing.

This is the second feature of the model in Figure 1: There is an explicit set of assumptions about the role of the cortex, and these assumptions comprise the cortical module. These assumptions allow us to determine whether a candidate model can predict the data from a particular psychophysical paradigm. The section on "Basic Behavioral Data: Candidates for Lower-Level Processing" reviews some basic psychophysical data that have been attributed by some to lower-level (retinal) functioning, and the section entitled "The Cortical Module" reviews some of the assumptions that have been made about the cortical module. The assumptions that comprise the cortical module are divided into those about a decision mechanism (DM) and those about the cortical processing (CP) before the decision mechanism. The DM assumptions are the traditional detection assumptions or criteria (e.g. peak detector or a constant signal-to-noise criterion). The CP assumptions are required for the model to predict $\psi$ from the retinal output $R(t)$ given a particular DM.

We can now operationally define what is meant by stating that a psycho-physical phenomenon "has a retinal basis," "is mediated by the retina," "has a neural substrate in the retina," or is an example of "lower-level processing." By definition, these phrases mean a very simple set of CP assumptions followed by a traditional DM. This is an example of what Teller (1984) referred to as a "nothing mucks it up" theory. (See Teller 1984 for an analysis, as well as history, of attempts to relate perceptual and physiological states.)

As its third feature, the model in Figure 1 is computational. By computational, it is meant that the model will produce values for $R(t)$ and $\psi$, for any arbitrary retinal input $E(\lambda,x,t)$. As discussed in the next section, the models considered here have more modest goals in terms of what is considered computational. However, they all compute outputs as a function of time for any variation in light intensity including changes in ambient light levels. There are a number of other models that successfully predict a variety of psychophysical or physiological data for a fixed level of ambient light. To predict data at a different ambient light level, however, a new set of parameters must be estimated. While these models have made enormous contributions, and while they have informed and constrained computational models, they will not substitute for a computational model. The reasons are quite simple. First, it is more difficult to hide our lack of knowledge of the adaptation process in a model that is fully computational. Second, a computational model is of more general use.

Finally, though it should be possible in the relatively near term to describe the retinal output ($R$ in Figure 1) with a model that computes the response of the ganglion cells to any light distribution, the same cannot be said for a model designed to predict behavior ($\psi$ in Figure 1). We restrict our attention here to psychophysical data that are, in principle, predictable with relatively simple assumptions about cortical processing. This excludes arbitrary variations in the spatial distribution, as it is clear that in such cases the cortical module would need to include multiple spatial-frequency and orientation-selective channels (Graham 1989). Multiple temporal-frequency channels have also been identified by the psychophysicist. Including these in the cortical module seems more tractable because there are at most three for any spatial-frequency range. Further, when their relation to the P and M cells of the physiologist is clarified, it may be possible to incorporate these temporal-frequency channels into the CP with relatively simple assumptions. In any case, this review largely discusses models that are computational in time, not space. In particular, the focus is on computational models of the dynamics of light adaptation of foveal vision under conditons where spatial parameters are held constant. Some recent attempts at computational modeling are reviewed in the section on "Computational Models of Light Adaptation."

## BASIC BEHAVIORAL DATA: CANDIDATES FOR LOWER-LEVEL PROCESSING

Various aspects of light adaptation have been studied with psychophysical paradigms, and many of these aspects have been hypothesized to have a retinal basis. In this section, the data from some of these psychophysical paradigms are reviewed. These data are among the candidates to be predicted by a model of lower-level processing. Although reviewing these data is the primary purpose of this section, psychophysical experiments have long been a source of information about the physiological mechanisms involved in lower-level processing, including those in the retina. While care is needed to avoid building mechanisms into the retinal module that belong in the cortex, there is a long history of psychophysical experiments correctly predicting retinal physiology. For example, nineteenth-century behavioral observations by Helmholtz and Hering correctly anticipated the underlying retinal mechanisms of color vision. Further, models based strictly on psychophysics, such as Hurvich & Jameson's model, did not merely correctly anticipate the role of receptor and postreceptoral retinal mechanisms in color vision but also influenced the design of and interpretation of the data from physiological experiments. This fertile interaction is likely to continue.

### The tvi Function: Sensitivity Changes Induced by Ambient Light

With increases in ambient light level, mechanisms of adaptation come into play, and both the rod and cone systems become less sensitive to incremental lights. Background or field adaptation refers to the change in sensitivity that takes place with changes in the intensity of a steady background. A fundamental measure of field adaptation is the tvi (threshold versus intensity) function that is a plot of the intensity needed to detect a test light as a function of the intensity of the background upon which it is presented. For the cone system, there is a wide range of data on tvi functions (see Hood & Finkelstein 1986 for a review). A summary statistic of these curves is the background upon which threshold is raised by a factor of 2. This value, called $I_0$ here, is about 10 trolands (td) for foveal detection of a relatively large test flash. For fields greater than about 100 td (2 log td), the tvi curve plotted as log threshold ($\delta I$) versus log field intensity ($I_A$) has a slope of 1.0. Over this range, $\delta I/I_A$ is approximately constant, and Weber's law holds. With small foveal test flashes, $I_0$ and the value of $I_A$ first yielding Weber's law are about a factor of 10 higher. These data are among the most fundamental that a model of lower-level processing should attempt to predict. (The recent revision of the book "Color Vision" by Kaiser & Boynton 1996 provides a good tutorial on the basics of visual science, including adaptation, as well as a more extensive discussion of the tvi paradigm.)

TWO-COLOR TVI FUNCTIONS   There is a large and quantitatively rich literature using what has been called the Stiles' two-color threshold technique (Stiles 1978). In this paradigm, the spectral composition of the test and/or adapting field is changed. This technique was introduced by Stiles to determine the spectral properties of independent color mechanisms (called $\pi$ mechanisms). There was considerable elaboration of this work in the 1970s and 1980s [see the review by Pugh & Kirk 1986 and other articles in *Perception,* Vol. 16]. Although the initial idea was to identify the spectral sensitivities of the three cone mechanisms, it soon became apparent that more—eventually seven—$\pi$ mechanisms could be identified based upon their sensitivity to spectral backgrounds. The data from these experiments have not been given sufficient attention by either the physiologist studying ganglion cell responses or the model builder seeking a computational model of light adaptation. The nature of the paradigm, combined with the precision of measurement by both Stiles and the neo-Stilesians, makes the psychophysical experiments easy to replicate and comparable physiological experiments easy to design. Further, the conceptual framework is well developed and specified in terms that allow tests of retinal mechanisms of adaptation. As an example, take the hypothesis that adaptation takes place within a single cone, or within groups of cones of the same spectral type. In the Stilesian framework, the "field and test sensitivities" (i.e. the spectral effectiveness of both the test and the field) should be identical, "test and field displacement laws" should be satisfied, and "test and field additivity" should hold (see Pugh & Kirk 1986 for a definition of these terms). Only $\pi$-3 and $\pi$-5 satisfy all these requirements (Pugh & Kirk 1986). In addition, only the field sensitivities of $\pi$-4' and $\pi$-3 match the spectral sensitivity of the human cone pigments derived from color matching and from the sensitivity of dichromats (Stockman & Mollon 1986, Stockman et al 1993). Thus only $\pi$-3 (the S-cone mechanism) meets all criteria and, of course, only under the restricted conditions where this mechanism controls sensitivity.

Some have used the psychophysical two-color tvi data to argue against pooling of signals across cone types on the grounds that adaptation is restricted to a single cone type. Strictly speaking, the data do not support this argument. However, it is striking how closely the field sensitivities of the $\pi$ mechanisms approximate the absorption spectra of single classes of cones over a wide range of conditions. Although these $\pi$ mechanisms do not meet the exacting standards of the psychophysically defined cone fundamentals, where one tenth of a log unit can disqualify a candidate mechanism, from the perspective of adaptation, it is impressive how little other cone types appear to be involved under most conditions. This is not to say that strong influences of more than one cone type cannot be found under some conditions. In fact, cancellation of an adapting signal because of an opponent interaction of cone types occurs under a variety of conditions where thresholds are raised by one log unit or more (e.g. for $\pi$-5 see Wandell & Pugh 1980; for $\pi$-1 see Pugh & Mollon 1979).

## The Probe-Flash Paradigm: Measures of the Dynamic Range

To obtain a measure of the dynamic range of the human visual system, a paradigm has been employed in which a brief light (the probe) is presented at the onset of an adapting flash (Geisler 1978, Hood et al 1978). By adding a steady adapting field, this probe-flash paradigm was modified to test alternative mechanisms of adaptation phrased in terms of the nonlinear, response-intensity functions measured by the physiologist. These data have been fitted by models with a nonlinear response-intensity function that is static in time and a decision rule that states that threshold is reached when the incremental response to the probe reaches a constant value (Geisler 1979, Hood et al 1979). Two classes of adaptation mechanisms have been identified by this work. One mechanism modifies sensitivity as a function of increased ambient light by scaling the intensity of all lights by a common factor. This has been called von Kries adaptation, the dark glasses hypothesis (MacLeod 1978), and multiplicative (or divisive) gain change. The second mechanism, called subtractive or additive, acts to remove signal due to the steady background but not due to the test (Adelson 1982, Geisler 1981). Subsequent work with the probe-flash paradigm has identified properties of these mechanisms that should help guide our computational models. In particular, much of the multiplicative gain change occurs very quickly, within 50 ms, after the onset of an adapting field and decays more slowly at offset (Hayhoe et al 1987). While some of the subtractive changes also occur rapidly (Hayhoe et al 1987), slower subtractive changes are observed when the probe and flash are of the same size (Hayhoe et al 1992). Center-surround antagonism has been hypothesized to be the cause of the fast subtractive changes (Hayhoe et al 1992). (Reviews of this work can be found in Graham & Hood 1992b, Hayhoe et al 1987, Hood & Finkelstein 1986, and Kortum & Geisler 1995. See Tyler & Liu 1996 for a different paradigmatic approach to estimating the dynamic range psychophysically. See Makous 1997 for a discussion of difficulties involved in distinguishing alternative mechanisms.)

Models of the probe-flash data have, in general, dealt with achromatic stimuli. When monochromatic lights are used, the probe-flash curves can develop multiple branches. These branches and the accompanying changes in the appearance of the probe's color suggest that multiple pathways are involved

(Finkelstein & Hood 1981). To explain these data, two nonlinear sites are needed, one before and one after an opponent interaction. Unlike the steady field data, it is easy to demonstrate in the probe-flash data a prominent contribution of a second site with an opponent input. For example, the effect of a red (640 nm) flash in elevating the threshold of a red probe can be nearly canceled by adding a green flash to the red flash. To put this in Stiles's terms, the field sensitivity for a small, brief probe can show signs of a spectrally opponent input even under conditions where the probe's test sensitivity is clearly nonopponent. Below, a possible retinal mechanism for this observation is discussed in the section on "Site of Spectrally Opponent Inputs." The first site implied by these experiments may well be the receptor (Finkelstein et al 1990). Saturating this site requires very intense flashes (Hood et al 1978, King-Smith & Webb 1974) in the range of those needed to saturate single cones (Schnapf et al 1990). These results are consistent with retinal physiology in suggesting that more than one static, nonlinear site will be needed in our retinal module with saturation occurring at lower flash energies as we move from the receptor to the ganglion cell.

By measuring probe-flash curves with different sinusoidal grating targets as probes, Kortum & Geisler (1995) provided a particularly interesting bridge to the work using sinusoidal spatial gratings. The static nonlinearity in the model fitted to these data depended upon spatial frequency. However, the multiplicative and subtractive mechanisms of the model were essentially the same for all spatial frequencies, suggesting that these mechanisms exist at or before the cone-bipolar synapse.

## The Temporal Contrast Sensitivity Function: Changes in Temporal Dynamics

The application of linear systems theory to vision was pioneered by DeVries, deLange, and Kelly, who measured thresholds for lights sinusoidally varying with time and who started to define the conditions under which the human visual system could be considered a linear system. The temporal contrast sensitivity function (TCSF) refers to the sensitivity (the reciprocal of threshold contrast) plotted against the temporal frequency of the stimulus. The popularity of sine wave stimuli in vision research attests to the success of this approach. This quantitatively and theoretically rich literature has been reviewed in books by Graham (1989) and DeValois & DeValois (1988) (see also the book by Wandell 1995 for a more general coverage of this and related issues). Although our focus is more on the nonlinear processes implied by light adaptation, this work is of fundamental importance for three reasons. First, the spatial and temporal sensitivity functions change as mean luminance is changed, and these changes provide basic data to be predicted by a model of adaptation. Second, these paradigms are easily transferable to physiological recording (see next section). Third, to the extent that a linear theory describes the results for aperiodic stimuli, this reduces the number of paradigms needed to test a model of light adaptation.

Although a variety of stimulus parameters affect the shape of the spatial and temporal contrast sensitivity functions, the basic changes with mean luminance are easy to describe. Consider the foveal TCSF for a relatively large test light (e.g. Kelly 1972). For low mean luminance, it resembles a low-pass filter. As mean luminance is increased, the TCSF becomes more band-pass (i.e. there is a more pronounced low frequency fall-off), and the peak of the function moves to higher frequencies. For a mean luminance above about 10 td and a low temporal frequency, the data obey Weber's law. For high temporal frequencies, sensitivity is relatively unaffected by the change in mean luminance. For chromatic variations of equal luminance, the function (called the chromatic TCSF) differs from the luminance TCSF (Kelly & von Norren 1977, Swanson et al 1987, Swanson 1994). For example, there is a lower high-frequency cut-off.

The temporal frequency-dependent adaptation described by these studies is considered by many to be largely determined by retinal mechanisms, and thus these data are candidates for explanations based upon models of lower-level processing (Figure 1). Consequently, such models will need a temporal frequency-dependent gain change such as the feedback filter used by Sperling & Sondhi (1968) (see reviews by Shapley & Enroth-Cugell 1984 and Graham & Hood 1992b).

## Other Adaptation Paradigms

CRAWFORD PARADIGM: THE TIME COURSE OF CHANGES IN SENSITIVITY    The Crawford paradigm refers to one in which thresholds are measured for a range of times before, during, and after the presentation of an adapting field that is typically 0.5–2 s in duration. Some of the basic data obtained with this paradigm have been summarized elsewhere (Hood & Finkelstein 1986). The time course of threshold variations after the onset of the field differs from the time course after the offset, and these data may be particularly useful in testing models with ON and OFF channels. Battersby & Wagman (1962) demonstrated that some threshold elevations occurred even when the test was presented to one eye and the adapting field to the other. Although this transfer may suggest binocular cortical processing in this simple paradigm, the demonstration of binocular transfer is not sufficient to conclude that when stimuli are presented monocularly, the mechanisms elevating threshold are beyond the retina. Conversely, of course, the failure to demonstrate binocular effects does not mean the effect is retinal. In any case, these data require an explanation. It is of interest that the binocular effect was relatively large when the test probe and adapting flash were the same size and relatively small when the adapting flash was considerably larger than the test flash.

INCREMENTS VERSUS DECREMENTS    Models of adaptation will need to predict data from paradigms employing decrements as well as increments. Earlier studies often found that thresholds for decrements were lower than for increments by about 0.1–0.2 log unit (e.g. Boynton et al 1964, Krauskopf 1980). With sawtooth stimuli that have an abrupt onset (rapid-on) or an abrupt offset (rapid-off), the difference between rapid-on and rapid-off thresholds diminishes with decreases in mean luminance or increases in temporal frequency (Bowen et al 1989, 1992; Kremers et al 1993). These data have been taken as evidence for separate ON and OFF pathways with different sensitivities. The ganglion cell data summarized below provide a retinal basis for two pathways but not for differential sensitivity.

PROBED-SINEWAVE PARADIGM: TEMPORAL DYNAMICS OF ADAPTATION    To study the temporal properties of adaptation mechanisms, Boynton et al (1961) measured the detection threshold for a brief light presented at various phases of a modulated background. The variations in threshold tracked a 30-Hz flickering background, providing evidence for a very fast adjustment of sensitivity (see also Wu et al 1997). Subsequent work has found that the threshold variations with low rates of modulation are not as simple (e.g. Hood et al 1997, Maruyama & Takahashi 1977). This paradigm, which combines an aperiodic test with a periodic adapting field, provides a challenge for computational models of adaptation (Hood et al 1997). Although Hood & Graham (1997) have recently offered an explanation of the original finding by Boynton et al (1961), a full theoretical account of the probed-sinewave data has yet to be given.

MODULATIONS IN CONE SPACE: ADAPTATION AND HABITUATION    A variety of paradigms have made use of advances in computer-controlled color monitors and LEDs in order to specify stimuli as some linear transformation of cone absorption spectra (MacLeod & Boynton 1979). For example, if the quantal absorption in the S-cones is held constant and L- and M-cone stimulation is varied in such a way that the sum of their quantal catch is constant, then this produces stimulation along an axis that is particularly effective for an L/M-cone opponent site. This work cannot be adequately addressed here, but summaries can be found in four recent articles (Chaparro et al 1995, Krauskopf 1997, Swanson 1994, Zaidi & Shapiro 1993). For the purposes of this review, it is important to distinguish at least two different classes of paradigms. In one, an adapting field is turned off when the test is presented. This is called habituation in this literature, although the term habituation is used differently in other literature. Krauskopf et al (1982) argued that habituation took place along unique directions in color space and that these directions represented stimulation of a second stage, a stage after opponent interaction of cone signals. However, the mechanisms identified with this habituation paradigm are unlikely to be retinal. The response of LGN cells to test lights show little or no change in sensitivity under the same conditions that produce changes in human psychophysical thresholds (Derrington et al 1984, Krauskopf 1997).

A second class of paradigms, in which the test is presented upon a steady or flashed adapting field, resembles the tvi and probe-flash paradigms discussed above but with the lights specified in terms of stimulation along various cone axes (Boynton & Kambe 1980). To account for the results of these experiments, adaptation mechanisms have been proposed to operate both before and after opponent interaction of cone signals (Chaparro et al 1995, Shapiro & Zaidi 1992, Yeh et al 1993, Zaidi et al 1992; see also earlier work cited by Chaparro et al 1995). The data from these experiments may be candidates for lower-level processing.

SPATIAL SPREAD OF ADAPTATION   A few paradigms have been designed to measure the spatial extent of light adaptation. Normally, light cannot be restricted to a single receptor because of diffraction and other optical sources of image blurring. The most elegant measures of the spatial spread of adaptation use interference fringe patterns to bypass the optics of the eye. In a number of studies, independent regulation of sensitivity was shown to take place over a spatial region of 12′ to 21.5′ (Chen et al 1993, He & MacLeod 1997, MacLeod et al 1992). This region is, in fact, smaller than the light-collecting diameter of the inner segment of central cones. A similar conclusion was reached using conventional optics (Burr et al 1985, Cicerone et al 1990). Substantial adaptation appears to take place before the signals of individual cones are spatially combined. The extent to which behavioral as well as physiological data argue for receptor-based adaptation is considered below in the section entitled "Evidence for 'Private Cone Pathways.'"

# BASIC GANGLION CELL DATA: CANDIDATES FOR RETINAL MODELING

The retinal module in Figure 1 is a computational model of light adaptation expressed in terms of the retinal output, the ganglion cell response. This section reviews some of the basic data that such a model might predict. Because our ultimate interest is in a model of lower-level processing in the human visual system, this review is restricted largely to two species, humans and macaque monkeys. Although there are undoubtedly differences between species starting at the retina (Goodchild et al 1996), many studies implicitly accept macaque ganglion cell data as if "they were our own," even for paradigms that have not been tested in behavioral studies with macaques. I too make this assumption knowing that it is yet to be tested under many conditions. Further, the recordings of S-potentials in the LGN are treated here as ganglion cell recordings (Kaplan & Shapley 1984). In some cases, data from studies of LGN-cells are also included. Although in general the LGN-cells are expected to mirror the ganglion cell responses (Kaplan & Shapley 1984), the conditions under which this is not true have yet to be fully established.

Extensive work has been done on anatomical and functional typing of the macaque ganglion cell, but there is no generally accepted terminology. Here M-GC denotes the parasol ganglion cells projecting to the magnocellular layers of the LGN, and M-LGN denotes the cells in those layers. Likewise, P-GC denotes the midget ganglion cells projecting to the parvocellular layers of the LGN, and P-LGN the cells in those layers. About 10% of primate ganglion cells are M-GC, and 75–80% are P-GC. Thus there are seven to eight times more P- than M-GC; this is a fundamental fact of retinal anatomy that must be considered. This ratio of about 8:1 holds from fovea to the near periphery beyond which the relative number of M-GC increases somewhat. There are two general types of M-GC, ON and OFF. In addition, there are six types of P-GC. There are three ON P-GC and three OFF P-GC, each receiving one predominate input, excitatory in the case of the ON-cells and inhibitory in the case of the OFF-cells, coming from one of the three cone types. Thus, the retinal output function, $R(t)$ in Figure 1, is not a single function but is at least eight functions, one for each ganglion cell type, although for many tasks the role of the two types of P-GC with S-cone input will be relatively minor. (See the review of macaque retinal anatomy and physiology by Lee 1996 for references.)

## Steady Fields: tvi and Response Versus Intensity Functions

Surprisingly few studies have obtained response-intensity data for flashes presented upon steady fields; most studies have used sinusoidally modulated stimuli (see next section). Virsu & Lee (1983) measured response versus intensity functions for P- and M-LGN cells and derived tvi functions that resemble behavioral tvi data. These data support the general position that substantial light adaptation takes place in the retina. Further, the response functions were shifted along the log flash intensity axis consistent with the psychophysical models that are based upon the probe-flash data discussed above. Surrounds outside the traditionally defined receptive field also shift the response functions of the P-LGN, but not M-LGN, cells (Valberg et al 1991).

## Temporal Contrast Sensitivity Function

For the ganglion cell, the equivalent of the psychophysical temporal contrast sensitivity function (TCSF) can be obtained by determining the contrast needed to obtain a small, constant response. The reciprocal of this contrast threshold plotted against temporal frequency is called here the ganglion cell's TCSF. (In practice, a variety of techniques and terms have been used.) A number of studies have obtained both spatial and temporal contrast sensitivity functions of ganglion and LGN cells. Like their psychophysical counterparts, these functions change with mean luminance. Two studies, in particular, have reported TCSFs for a wide range of mean luminances (Lee et al 1990, Purpura et al 1990). These studies are in essential agreement. With achromatic lights, both M- and P-GC become more band-pass as mean luminance is increased. The peak of the TCSF shifts to higher temporal frequencies, as do the psychophysical data discussed above. However, while the TCSF for M- and P-GC are band-pass for achromatic stimulation, the response of P-GC to chromatic stimulation is low-pass (Lee et al 1990).

Another important difference between M- and P-GC is the greater sensitivity shown by M-GC for achromatic stimuli. This difference presents a challenge for models of lower-level processing (see the section on "Cortical Preprocessing" below). The median peak sensitivity of the M-GC is about six to eight times higher than that of the P-GC (Croner & Kaplan 1995, Kaplan & Shapley 1986, Lee et al 1990, Purpura et al 1988). However, the range of sensitivities for both cell types is quite large. Although sensitivity depends somewhat on retinal location, the ratio of M- to P-GC sensitivity stays approximately constant with retinal eccentricity (Croner & Kaplan 1995).

## Response Versus Contrast and Retinal Contrast Gain Control

The M- and P-GC show markedly different response versus contrast functions (Kaplan & Shapley 1986, Lee et al 1990, Purpura et al 1988). At any fixed mean luminance, the response of the P-GC increases approximately linearly with contrast. Although the response versus contrast functions of P-GC are often fitted with a nonlinear function, the deviation from linearity is minor, especially below 50% contrast. In addition, responses to aperiodic stimuli and complex periodic stimuli (e.g. sawtooth changes) can be predicted from the responses to sinusoidal stimuli by assuming linearity (Kremers et al 1993, Lee et al 1994). Compared to the P-GC, the response versus contrast function for the M-GC is markedly nonlinear, and this nonlinearity depends upon the temporal frequency of the stimulus (Benardete et al 1992, Lee et al 1994). As a consequence, the TCSF for the M-GC depends upon the contrast of the stimulus to a far greater extent than it does for the P-GC. As contrast is increased, the TCSF for the M-GC peaks at higher temporal frequencies and shows a larger low-frequency fall-off. This change in the shape of the TCSF has been called "contrast gain control" by Shapley & Victor (1978) and is called "retinal contrast gain control" here, as there are clearly additional mechanisms at the cortex that adjust gain as contrast is changed. Although the mechanisms involved in retinal contrast gain control may be different from those produced by mean luminance changes, it is not yet clear the extent to which the same retinal circuits are involved.

## Other Selected Data

INCREMENTAL VERSUS DECREMENTAL STIMULI    Given the psychophysical interest in rapid-on and rapid-off sawtooth stimuli, it is of interest to know how ganglion cells respond to these stimuli. Kremers et al (1993) showed that ON and OFF M-GC have a 10-fold higher sensitivity to the preferred sawtooth polarity than to the opposite polarity. Although this study provides strong evidence that, for achromatic lights, psychophysical detection of rapid-on stimuli are mediated by ON M-GC and rapid-off by OFF M-GC, the lower threshold for off- as opposed to on-stimuli does not appear to have a basis at the ganglion cell level.

OTHER PARADIGMS WITH CHROMATIC MODULATION    Derrington et al (1984) studied macaque LGN cells with stimuli specified in terms of cone excitations (see the section on "Modulations in Cone Space" above). The data were analyzed to provide a measure of the relative weights of inputs from the three cone types into M- and P-LGN cells. In a more recent study of macaque ganglion cells, Smith et al (1992) used sinusoidally modulated red and green lights that were varied in phase, and they developed a model that accounted for the phase and amplitude of the responses in terms of the timing of the cone inputs. These studies should prove useful in developing computational models of the ganglion cell responses to chromatic lights.

Many psychophysical experiments, some discussed above, determine thresholds for chromatic (equi-luminance) or luminance modulations of test lights. Employing a paradigm similar to that used by the psychophysicist, Lee et al (1993) suggested that although the shape of the psychophysicist's detection curves for chromatic modulation may bear a simple relation to the curves for the P-GC, the same will probably not hold for luminance modulation and the M-GC.

TIME COURSE OF ADAPTATION    Given the attention to the time course of adaptation in behavioral studies, surprisingly little has been done at the level of the macaque ganglion cell. Yeh et al (1996) followed the time course of adaptation of both P- and M-GC following changes in luminance or chromaticity. Their results show a general agreement with behavioral data. For example, the time course is fast after luminance changes and slower after chromatic changes.

Also of interest for models of adaptation is the suggestion that some of the slow recovery of the P-GC following chromatic adaptation is taking place after the opponent combination of cone signals.

## LESSONS FROM INSIDE THE RETINA

The variety of retinal cells should give pause to anyone attempting to model the retina. For the primate, the anatomist has distinguished at least 2 horizontal-cell, 10 bipolar-cell, 20–25 ganglion-cell, and 20–40 amacrine-cell types (as reviewed by Dacey 1996). Further, intracellular recording from the cells of the primate retina is still in its infancy. Thus, although it is possible to model M- and P-GC activity, it is probably premature to identify the mechanisms in the retinal module with particular cell types. In constructing a retinal model, it does seem prudent, however, to avoid assumptions that violate basic accepted findings. At the same time, there is much that we know about the primate retina that should inform these models. Here, selective topics that might be helpful in constructing computational models of lower-level processing are reviewed. This information comes from two sources. First, a number of direct studies of single cell physiology and anatomy in human and macaque retinas have been performed during the past 10 years. (See reviews by Dacey 1996, Kolb 1994, Lee 1996, Sterling 1997, Wassle & Boycott 1991.) Second, the human ERG is beginning to supply quantitative information about the response properties of single classes of cells in the human retina. (See reviews of the physiology of human rods, cones, and rod ON-bipolars by Hood & Birch 1993a,b, 1996; Pepperberg et al 1997.)

### Adaptation at the Cone Receptor

Considerable confusion still exists about the extent to which primate cones adapt. Part, but by no means all, of the uncertainty can be resolved by examining the level of analysis. We start with the cone outer segment. The best guess based upon the current evidence is that there is relatively little adaptation in the primate cone outer segment. Schnapf et al (1990) recorded from single cone outer segments in the macaque retina and found that, on average, a background ($I_O$) of about 2000 td was needed to decrease the sensitivity by a factor of 2. (Makous 1997 estimates that the value is closer to 8000 td. Makous also has a valuable discussion of the assumptions involved in calculating quanta absorbed by the receptors in humans and macaques.) In any case, this value of $I_O$ for the receptor is considerably above the value for human tvi curves. Because this value of $I_O$ is also higher than other physiological estimates (discussed below), some have questioned whether this finding was due to the ionic environment inside the suction electrode used for recording. However, human ERG techniques also assumed to measure outer segment current show excellent quantitative agreement with the Schnapf et al (1990) study (Hood & Birch 1993b, Hood et al 1996). Some adaptation takes place in the rod receptor, and this adaptation is time dependent (Hood & Birch 1993a, Kraft et al 1993, Pepperberg et al 1997). Interestingly, the adaptation-dependent gain change in the cone outer segment studies is similar in magnitude to that seen for the rod outer segment. However, unlike the case of the rods, the relatively small changes in cone sensitivity are important. These sensitivity changes are sufficient to protect the cones from saturating upon ambient lights below the levels where pigment bleaching serves the purpose.

There are two older studies that argue for more adaptation at the primate cone than is suggested by the outer segment results. Using techniques to isolate a receptor component of the ERG called the late receptor potential (LRP), Boynton & Whitten (1970) and Valeton & van Norren (1983) concluded that there was considerable adaptation in the macaque cone receptor. A background ($I_O$) of about 100 td decreased sensitivity by a factor of 2. One way to reconcile these findings with the outer segment studies discussed above is to assume that postreceptoral potentials contribute to the LRP. It is also possible that substantial adaptation is taking place between outer segment activity and synaptic release by the cone pedicle or that there are problems with the outer segment studies that we do not understand. In either case, there is a large quantitative discrepancy between the different views concerning the extent of adaptation in the primate receptor. Thus, we are not ready to specify with certainty the cone receptor in the retinal module of Figure 1.

Although we do not know how much adaptation is taking place in the receptor, there is clear evidence for some adaptation beyond the receptor. First, although the LRP studies suggest sensitivity changes are occurring at relatively low adapting fields, the value of $I_O$ is still a factor of 10 higher than those in the psychophysical tvi function obtained under most conditons. (Virsu & Lee 1983 point out that, when small brief test lights are used, the psychophysical tvi function is in approximate agreement with the LRP data.) Second, there is little evidence for Weber's law at the receptor level except for very high adapting fields. The slope of the tvi function in the Valeton & van Norren (1983) study is 0.7 over a range of adapting fields for which some behavioral data show a slope of 1.0. This is a fact often overlooked by psychophysicists seeking to compare their data to a measure of receptor function.

## Outer Plexiform Layer and Temporal Frequency-Dependent Adaptation

Horizontal cells, including those in the macaque (Lee et al 1997), show gain changes that are dependent upon both the temporal frequency and the level of mean luminance. These gain changes have been adequately described with models in the case of the turtle (e.g. Tranchina et al 1984) and cat (e.g. van de Grind et al 1996). It is not clear, however, the extent to which these changes reflect changes in the cone receptors per se. Further, the manner in which the horizontal cells modulate the cone-horizontal cell synapse and ultimately affect bipolar activity is still incompletely understood. These unresolved issues are of fundamental importance for a complete retinal model.

However, a number of conclusions can be reached concerning adaptation in the outer retina. In the case of the rod system, while little adaptation takes place at the rod receptor, substantial adaptation occurs by the time the bipolars have responded. Studies of human rod ON-bipolar activity using the ERG indicate that most, but not all, of the sensitivity change seen in the rod psychophysical tvi curve takes place by the time the bipolars respond (Hood & Birch 1996). For the rods, it is equally clear that some adaptation to steady fields occurs beyond the bipolar (Frishman et al 1996), although it appears complete by the time the early components of the VEP are generated (Shady et al 1997).

In the case of the cone system, evidence from cone-ERG studies suggests that much of the temporal frequency-dependent adaptation measured at the ganglion cell level is already present by the time the bipolars have responded (e.g. Seiple et al 1992).

## Evidence for "Private Cone Pathways"

The psychophysical evidence discussed above suggests that either substantial adaptation takes place in the cone receptor or else within a pathway that is relatively unaffected by other cone types (see sections TWO-COLOR TVI FUNCTIONS and SPATIAL SPREAD OF ADAPTATION above). Pointing to the evidence for "cross-talk at the cone receptor" and for lateral connections via horizontal and amacrine cells, many interpret the psychophysical data as strong evidence that adaptation is taking place almost entirely within the receptor. A close look at this evidence suggests that it does not rule out postreceptor adaptation within pathways driven by single cones.

CROSS-TALK AT THE CONE RECEPTOR    The terminals of the foveal cones of the macaque are connected via gap junctions (Tsukamoto et al 1992). Thus, there is evidence for electrical coupling of adjacent foveal receptors, as has been demonstrated for a variety of lower vertebrates. Based upon behavioral evidence (see section on "Spatial Spread of Adaptation"), Tsukamoto et al (1992) suggested that the cones are functionally uncoupled at higher luminances. It is also possible that the effect of these gap junctions is relatively minor under all conditions and that the behavioral effects are entirely postreceptoral. By recording the photovoltage response from single macaque cones, Schneeweis & Schnapf (1995) showed that the cones received an input from the rods. However, this input is relatively small even for dark-adapted conditions.

PRIVATE CONE PATHWAYS AND THE INFLUENCE OF LATERAL CONNECTIONS    If we temporarily ignore the gap junctions just discussed as well as the lateral connections made by horizontal and amacrine cells, then there is anatomical evidence for a "private cone pathway." At least out to 7° from the central fovea, each midget bipolar receives a direct synaptic connection from a single cone. In fact, each L- or M-cone supplies the only direct synapse onto two midget bipolars (one ON and one OFF). Further, each midget bipolar contacts only a single P-GC (Calkins et al 1994). Thus, each midget bipolar and each P-GC center is served by a single cone receptor. In the far periphery, the midget bipolar still receives input from one cone, but the P-GC gets input from both L-center and M-center bipolars (Dacey 1996). The S-cones appear to have a distinct type of ganglion cell, the bistratified ganglion cell, which receives excitatory input from both S-cone driven ON-bipolar and an L/M-cone driven OFF-bipolar (Dacey & Lee 1994). In the case of the M-GC, it is clear that the parasol bipolar gets input from more than one cone type and that the M-GC receives input from more than one bipolar. Thus, the best evidence for private cone pathways is the P-GC in the central retina.

The lateral connections supplied by the horizontal and amacrine cells are not cone-specific and would appear to provide evidence against totally private pathways. Both large (H1) and small (H2) horizontal cells receive input from more than one cone type (Wassle et al 1989). Dacey et al (1996) recorded from macaque horizontal cells and found that H1-cells receive input from L- and M-cones and that H2-cells receive strong input from S-cones and weaker input from L- and M-cones. There is a similar situation in the inner plexiform layer, where amacrine cells receive excitatory input from bipolars and provide nonselective inhibitory input to bipolar and midget ganglion cells (Calkins & Sterling 1996).

How do we reconcile the lateral connections just described with the psychophysical evidence of substantial adaptation before pooling of cone signals? It is still possible that there is substantial adaptation in the cone receptor, as discussed above. Another possibility is that the gain changes measured in the psychophysical paradigms are largely determined by direct, private synaptic contacts at the cone-bipolar synapse. We say largely because the psychophysical data reviewed above suggest that some pooling of cone receptor signals takes place even with foveal lights. There is evidence for more pooling in behavioral tvi data when parafoveal instead of foveal lights are used (Haegerstrom-Portnoy et al 1988). One would also expect, however, that when detection is mediated by the M-GC, postreceptor gain changes would show the effects of pooling across cone types.

## Site of Spectrally Opponent Inputs

The retinal site of spectrally opponent inputs is of interest to psychophysicists. Psychophysical data for both steady and flashed fields show that, under some conditions, desensitization occurs after the opponent inputs from two cone types have been combined. We know such opponent interactions occur before the P-GC responds. The so-called L+/M- P-GC, for example, gives a spectrally opponent response because quanta absorbed in one type of cone (L) result in increased activity, whereas quanta absorbed in the other type of cone (M) result in decreased activity. Since each midget bipolar and each P-GC is served by a single cone receptor, possible sites of an opponent signal include the horizontal cells and amacrine cells. However, recent anatomical and electrophysiological evidence suggests that the horizontal cell receives input from more than one cone type but that these inputs are not spectrally opponent (see above). Since the center of the midget bipolar field will be a single cone that dominates the response, it is possible that a horizontal cell fed from a mixture of L- and M-cones could provide the basis for a spectrally opponent response (Dacey 1996). An equivalent mechanism is possible in the inner plexiform layer with amacrine feedback onto bipolars, since amacrine cells also appear to get mixed cone signals (see above). In any case, the evidence indicates that the opponent interaction in the L/M-cone driven P-GC comes via lateral interactions, although the relative importance of the horizontal and amacrine cells has yet to be determined. As larger lights should be more effective in stimulating horizontal and amacrine cells, the involvment of these cells in opponent interaction provides a possible physiological basis for the increased influence of opponent interactions in behavioral experiments with large test spots.

## ON and OFF Pathways Without a Push-Pull Input

Some of the models of lower-level function discussed below hypothesize push-pull mechanisms at the ganglion cell. If an ON-center ganglion cell received an excitatory input from an ON-bipolar and an inhibitory input from an OFF-bipolar, then this would be an example of a push-pull input. However, there is little anatomical or physiological support for such an input. In fact, the ON and OFF pathways appear to be completely segregated in the retina (Schiller 1992, Sterling 1997). Freed & Nelson (1994) explicitly looked for evidence of a push-pull mechanism at the cat ON-ganglion cell and found little or none. Further, intraretinal blocking of the ON-bipolar synapse with APB eliminates responses of ON-center cells in the LGN with little effect on the responses of the OFF-center cells (Schiller 1982).

## Forms of the Static Nonlinearity

Both receptor and ganglion cell recordings show nonlinear response-intensity functions, with the receptors saturating at much higher flash intensities (cf Schnapf et al 1990, Virsu & Lee 1983). These differences in saturating intensities have potential counterparts in the first and second sites of static nonlinearity identified by the probe-flash experiments reviewed above. At least four functions have been used to describe the data from physiological and psychophysical experiments. Two of these, the saturating exponential and the Michaelis-Menton equations, have two parameters: One is the maximum response, and the other can be related to a semisaturation intensity, the intensity needed to reach half of the maximum. The third equation (the Naka-Rushton) is a general form of the Michaelis-Menton with a third parameter, an exponent $n$. This equation, with $n$ both less than and greater than 1.0, has been fitted to a variety of psychophysical and physiological data. However, this equation is nonlinear for small values of input, while much of the data fitted are not. A fourth nonlinear function was fitted to dogfish bipolar responses by Ashmore & Falk (1980). Their function is a better choice than the Naka-Rushton because it is linear for small signals and will do as well as the Naka-Rushton in most cases for larger signals (e.g. Hood & Birch 1996).

## THE CORTICAL MODULE

### Decision Mechanism

Predicting behavior from the output of the retinal module requires assumptions. At a minimum, a detector must be specified. There are no clear rules for deciding what is part of the decision mechanism (DM) and what is part of cortical preprocessing (CP). Here we assume the DM is one of the generally accepted decision rules. There is a substantial body of literature on this topic, so little will be said here (see reviews by Green & Swets 1988 and Graham 1989). Most attempts to model lower-level processing or to make quantitative comparisons between behavior and M- and P-GC activity have included a relatively simple DM, for example, a peak detector or a peak-to-trough detector. Although under many conditions there will be little difference between the two, the peak-to-trough detector may do better under some conditions (Graham & Hood 1992b, Kremers et al 1993). The most obvious omission in the models reviewed below is a consideration of noise. Many detection models have some form of noise as the limiting factor for determining threshold (see reviews in Cohn & Lasley 1986, Geisler 1989, Graham 1989). Of course, quantal noise exists in the physical stimulus, but its role in limiting foveal detection is debated. A review by Graham & Hood (1992a) concluded that quantal noise is rarely a limiting factor for foveal vision (see also the discussions in Geisler 1989, Hayhoe 1990, Pelli 1990). In the models discussed here, the most common assumption, often implicit, is that biological noise is constant. The variance of the responses in the cortex appears to increase in proportion to the mean of the response (see review in Geisler & Albrecht 1995). It is relatively easy to incorporate this type of noise into a computational model (Arnow & Geisler 1996) and under many conditions it would produce only marginally different conclusions (Kortum & Geisler 1995).

## Cortical Preprocessing

Within the conceptual framework of Figure 1, a psychophysical finding is said "to have a retinal basis" or "to be based upon lower-level processing" only if the assumptions embedded in the CP are relatively simple. If the assumptions become complex, then we have entered the realm of cortical models. The recent literature provides some clues about the types of assumptions that might be necessary to predict some of the behavioral data reviewed above.

COMPARING HUMAN PSYCHOPHYSICS TO MACAQUE GANGLION CELL PHYSIOLOGY   One source of information comes from studies comparing macaque M- and P-GC activity to human psychophysical data. The most useful experiments are those in which macaque physiological and human psychophysical data were collected with the same equipment using the same paradigms. Comparing temporal contrast sensitivity functions (TCSF) for humans with those for ganglion cells, Lee et al (1990) concluded that there was strong support for M- and P-GC being the "physiological substrate" for detection of luminance and chromatic variations, respectively. They reported, however, that the M-GC can contribute to the behaviorally measured chromatic sensitivity under restricted conditions. In addition, there were other differences between the shapes of the behavioral and physiological functions and between the way they changed with mean luminance. It is not yet clear how complicated the CP must be to predict these differences. On the other hand, there is one difference between the physiology and behavior that can be predicted with a relatively simple CP. The TCSF for the ganglion cell has a higher high-frequency cutoff than does the behaviorally determined TCSF. It appears as if the limit for temporal resolution is set beyond the retina, and this can be represented by assuming a CP with a linear low-pass filter (Lee et al 1990). This is a plausible assumption given the filtering expected by subsequent synaptic transfer. (See also Lee et al 1993, Smith et al 1992, Swanson 1994, and Yeh et al 1996 for additional discussion of where behavioral and physiological functions do and do not agree.)

   Simply because a physiological function looks like a behavioral function does not mean we have a physiological explanation (see discussion of the analogy proposition in Teller 1984). A discussion of the physiological substrate of the luminosity function by Lennie et al (1993) nicely illustrates this general point. They argue that, while M-GC probably underlie many behavioral tasks (e.g. flicker photometry) that produce the $V\lambda$ psychophysical function, other behavioral tasks yielding a $V\lambda$ function are undoubtedly not mediated by M-GC. For example, although the $V\lambda$ function describes the spectral sensitivity obtained with small test spots, these tasks probably involve the P-GC (Crook et al 1987, Hood & Finkelstein 1983). A computational model, as described here, helps to remove such comparisons from the realm of simple analogy.

The ON and OFF M-GC are thought to underlie psychophysical detection of achromatic, rapid-on and rapid-off stimuli. However, the question of which data can or cannot be predicted based upon a model of lower-level processing has only begun to be explored (Kremers et al 1993). In addition, we do not have an explanation for the lower sensitivity to incremental as opposed to decremental stimuli (see above). In particular, the ON- and OFF-ganglion cells appear to have equal sensitivity under conditions where behavioral sensitivity is greater for decrements (Kremers et al 1993). It is possible that the small differences measured in the behavioral experiments are not easy to see in the ganglion cell data. A second possibility is that the ON-ganglion cell is noisier and thus the DM needs a larger signal for detection (Kremers et al 1993). However, the evidence suggests that the OFF, not the ON, M-GC is slightly noisier (Troy & Lee 1994). A third way to handle the increment-decrement difference is to assume independent detectors for increments and decrements with different inputs (Krauskopf 1980). In the current framework, these detectors would examine the peak of either the positive going response of the ON-cells or the negative going response of the OFF-cells. To account for the asymmetry in thresholds, the gain of the ON and OFF cell input would differ. That is, the CP would change equal responses from the retina to unequal responses before sending them to the detector. Interestingly, Kelly & Savoie (1978) came to a similar conclusion when trying to model data from an entirely different task (i.e. a comparison of TCSFs for a uniform field and a spatial grating). (See Chichilnisky & Wandell 1996 for evidence, based upon color appearance, for different adaptation mechanisms in ON and OFF pathways.)

Nonlinear assumptions about the CP can be mimicked with assumptions in the DM. For example, to explain the increment-decrement asymmetry, instead of assuming a difference in cortical gain, one can assume that the DM is more sensitive to negative going responses than to positive going responses. As another example, Kremers et al (1993) point out that the low-pass filter of the CP assumed by Lee et al (1990) could be removed if the DM is assumed to integrate over a fixed time. [See also Graham & Hood (1992b) for a similar point concerning the low-pass filter in Geisler's (1979) model.] In some cases, single cortical cell recordings or VEP data may help us decide among these alternatives. For example, in this case, to account for the VEPs evoked by increments or decrements in contrast, Zemon et al (1988) argued for a greater sensitivity of OFF-cells at the level of the visual cortex.

Finally, it should go without saying that there is a wide range of psychophysical data that will require an elaborate CP and are thus not candidates for explanations based upon lower-level processing. While some of these (e.g. binocular effects, orientation-selective adaptation) are obvious, some may not be. An example of the latter group is the habituation paradigm discussed above that has been used to study, for example, ON and OFF pathways (Krauskopf 1980). Although some have thought of the behavioral data in terms of retinal mechanisms, conditions producing relatively large sensitivity changes measured behaviorally cause little, if any, sensitivity changes at the LGN. Under such conditions, a candidate for lower-level processing is disqualified if complicated and nonlinear CP assumptions are needed.

MONKEY PSYCHOPHYSICS AND LESIONS OF M AND P CELLS   A second line of information about possible CP assumptions comes from psychophysical experiments on macaques with lesions. (See the recent review by Merigan & Maunsell 1993 and Lennie 1993.) Recent advances have allowed selective chemical lesions of M and P pathways at the ganglion cell and LGN levels. A variety of behaviors have been measured following selective destruction of M- or P-cells. While some of the behaviorally measured deficits are consistent with relatively simple schemes relating M- and P-cells to behavior, many are not. Much of this work is beyond our scope here. However, in a particularly relevant set of experiments, TCSFs were behaviorally measured following M or P lesions (reviewed in Merigan & Maunsell 1993). The destruction of P-cells affects the detection of stimuli of low temporal and spatial frequencies to a far greater extent than expected based upon the sensitivity of M- and P-GC. In particular, the mean peak sensitivity of P-GC is far lower than these behavioral measures suggest. Similarly, Lennie (1993) points out that a single P-GC is seven times less sensitive in discriminating chromaticity than human psychophysics would suggest and warns that we do not know what significance to place on a difference in sensitivity until we know how signals are combined. In other words, we need to specify the assumptions of the CP. There are about eight times more P- than M-GC and a greater cortical pooling of P-cells has been offered as one possible explanation for the greater estimate of P-cell sensitivity in behavioral as opposed to single cell experiments. Watson (1992), as part of a more general framework for comparing TCSFs from behavioral and physiological experiments, demonstrates how spatial pooling can account in part for the relatively greater influence by P-cells on behavioral sensitivity. Although I do not mean to draw a tight parallel, one is reminded here that the sensitivities of individual rod and cone receptors measured physiologically are far closer to one another than are the rod-mediated and cone-mediated behavioral thresholds. There are about 20 times more rods than cones, and substantial spatial summation takes place at the rod bipolar and ganglion cell levels. In addition to spatial pooling, other explanations have been offered for why the contribution of P-cells to behavior is greater than expected based upon the sensitivity of single P-GC. Among these are: 1. The P-GC for the central fovea, for which we have relatively little information, may be more sensitive than the parafoveal P-GC. 2. M-cells may be differentially routed to V5 and be less involved than we think in detection tasks. 3. Probability summation across cells may help increase P-cell effectiveness (Lennie 1993, Merigan & Maunsell 1993). In terms of Figure 1, the first of these would require a modification of the retinal module, while the later two would require modification of the cortical module.

Behavioral measures have been obtained from macaques following intraretinal injection to selectively block the activity of the ON-bipolars (Schiller 1992). Behavioral sensitivity to incremental lights is markedly decreased, leaving thresholds for decrements largely unaffected (Dolan & Schiller 1994). These results are qualitatively consistent with the effective elimination of ON-cells that, in fact, are blocked by this procedure. However, the paradigms of the behavioral and physiological experiments are different enough that it is not clear whether a simple CP will suffice.

## Comparison Across Channels

Channels segregated by psychophysical paradigms often suggest clearer functional boundaries than their analogous cell types. For example, using flicker photometry, two monochromatic lights can be equated for luminance, and an equiluminous pair of lights can be defined that vary only chromatically. While it is likely that the flicker photometric task is mediated by M-GC, it is unlikely that the chromatic stimuli thus defined silence all M-GC (see discussion in Lennie et al 1993). Further, so-called luminance variations will elicit activity in many P-GC. This raises the question of whether our cortical module should focus on the most sensitive cell or on some comparison across cells. It is clear that in the case of the appearance of a light, a comparison across cells is likely to be involved. To illustrate this point, consider unique yellow, an indisputable psychophysical measure implying no neural coding for red or green. However, no single monochromatic light will silence the four P-GC with L- and M-cone input. The yellow sensation is likely computed as some ratio of activity among these cells and the cells with S-cone input (see discussion in Hood & Finkelstein 1983). Likewise, comparisons across ON- and OFF-cells or between M- and P-GC may underlie other tasks. Although in principle such comparisons could be made across cells as part of the DM, comparison at the single cell level cannot be ruled out, because cortical cells, even as early as area 17, can receive inputs from both ON- and OFF-cells as well as M- and P-cells (e.g. Nealey & Maunsell 1994, Schiller 1982).

## COMPUTATIONAL MODELS OF LIGHT ADAPTATION

There is a considerable literature on models of light adaptation that are not computational in the sense used here. Psychophysicists and physiologists have successfully predicted a wide range of data by resetting the parameters of their models for different mean luminances (see reviews in Shapley & Enroth-Cugell & Shapley 1984, Graham 1989, Watson 1986. See also Donner & Hemila 1996 for a recent attempt to model the dynamics of the ganglion cell and to predict responses to both periodic and aperiodic stimuli). It is not possible to review this work here, but the serious model builder should examine this literature in detail because many of the proposed mechanisms are relevant. Here we summarize attempts to develop computational models of the dynamics of light adaptation; these are models designed to predict psychophysical data and/or ganglion cell responses.

### Models of Ganglion Cell Response

There have been at least five recent attempts to produce computational models of the dynamics of light adaptation of the ganglion cell. Interestingly, all consider only achromatic lights, omitting the detection of chromatic variations. Two of these models describe the responses of the cat's X- and Y-GC (Dahari & Spitzer 1996, Gaudiano 1994). Although X- and Y-GC are not the same as P- and M-GC (Kaplan & Shapley 1982), these models with appropriate adjustments could, in principle, serve as the retinal module for the primate. However, for our purposes, neither of these models has been tested against a wide enough range of the basic ganglion cell data reviewed above, although the Dahari & Spitzer model produces a qualitative description of a range of data from aperiodic paradigms. The same can be said of one of the models of primate ganglion cells. Purpura et al (1990) fitted their TCSF data with a linear negative feedback model adapted from a model used to describe responses from turtle horizontal cells (Tranchina et al 1984). Although this model can function like a computational retinal module (Tranchina & Peskin 1988), it is not clear which of the ganglion cell data it will predict.

There are two ambitious and reasonably successful attempts to predict a range of data from primate ganglion cells (Shah & Levine 1996a,b, Wilson

1997). Both computational models restrict themselves to achromatic, foveal cone vision; both attempt to capture the response of P- and M-GC for a range of spatiotemporal stimuli; and both explicitly describe the role played by each of the major classes of retinal cells. In terms of the basic paradigms presented above, both describe the TCSFs of P- and M-GC. Further, the predicted TCSFs for both models show the change in shape from low-pass to band-pass with increased mean luminance. However, the Shah & Levine model does not predict the large shift in the peak frequency of the TCSF, as mean luminance is changed. In addition, although Wilson's model captures this shift, it does not, unlike the Shah & Levine model, show retinal contrast gain control as defined by the change in the TCSF with contrast level (Hood & Graham 1997).

Finally, both models are too ambitious in ascribing specific functions to individual cell types in the retina given what we know about retinal physiology. In fact, there are two aspects of these models that provide a signature of the current state of our knowledge. First, both clearly violate some accepted retinal findings. For example, both models make different assumptions about the receptors, and in both models these assumptions are, in part, at odds with the physiology summarized above. In addition, Shah & Levine do not have a role for amacrine cells in their model, whereas Wilson's model, following Gaudiano (1994), has a push-pull input into the ganglion cell, a type of input for which there is little evidence (see section above on "ON and OFF Pathways Without a Push-Pull Input" above). Second, both models are reasonably successful in predicting ganglion cell activity, but they differ substantially in the nature of the retinal processes suggested. For example, the horizontal cells provide a fast subtractive feedback to the cones in Wilson's model but a fast multiplicative feedback in the Shah & Levine model.

## Psychophysical Models of Lower-Level Processing

In principle, all the models of the ganglion cell just described can be turned into models of lower-level processing by adding a cortical module (e.g. the CP and DM in Figure 1). In practice, only one of these retinal models has been so modified to predict psychophysical data (Wilson 1997). In fact, there have been relatively few attempts to predict data from basic psychophysical paradigms with computational models of light adaptation. A number of studies have attempted to describe steady-state and flashed tvi data with models, but these were not computational in time. However, central to our concerns here, these static models were assumed, at least in part, to describe retinal mechanisms. Thus, they supply possible mechanisms to include in the retinal module of a computational model (e.g. see the section above on "The Probe-Flash Paradigm: Measures of the Dynamic Range"). Graham & Hood (1992b) modified a class of these models to be computational and showed that it could not adequately predict the change in the TCSF with mean luminance. One of the earliest and most successful computational models was that of Sperling & Sondhi (1968), which incorporated feedback and feedforward mechanisms to predict changes in the TCSF with mean luminance as well as some limited data from aperiodic paradigms (e.g. tvi paradigm). Graham & Hood (1992b) argued that this model and others from the periodic tradition could not predict data from the aperiodic tradition, in particular probe-flash data. They suggested that a model of the dynamics of light adaptation needed to incorporate elements of each class of models and that candidate models should meet the challenge of predicting data from both periodic and aperiodic traditions. Two recent studies attempted to meet this challenge and successfully predicted data from both periodic and aperiodic paradigms (von Wiegand et al 1996, Wilson 1997). However, the von Wiegand et al model cannot predict the data from the probed-sinewave paradigm (Hood at al 1997). Wilson's model can, at least under limited conditions, predict these data (Hood & Graham 1997), and, as discussed above, it is also a model of the ganglion cell response.

In fact, to my knowledge, Wilson's model is the only current model that fits the general form of Figure 1. The retinal module was discussed above. The DM is a simple peak detector, and the CP is a simple low-pass filter as proposed by Lee et al (1990). It remains to be seen which classes of psychophysical data this model will fail to predict.

## SUMMARY AND FUTURE DIRECTIONS

How close are we to a computational model of light adaptation that predicts behavioral sensitivity based upon lower-level processing? The answer is: reasonably close. Although we are some distance from an accurate model of the inner workings of the retina, we are reasonably close to an adequate retinal module. An adequate retinal module is one that will predict the outputs of M- and P-ganglion cells for a wide range of temporal variations of both achromatic and chromatic lights. The current models do not allow for chromatic variations in light. However, it should be possible to incorporate what is known about cone absorption spectra and cone influence on ganglion cell responses into a computational model. How well these models will predict the data associated with lower-level processing by the psychophysicist remains to be seen. It is entirely possible that these models will account for the data from only a few behavioral paradigms. If so, by definition there would be a very small set of lower-level behaviors. However, even if this is the case, it should prove possible to make simplifying assumptions about cortical processing and to extend the predictions of a model to a larger range of spatiotemporal stimuli.

In any case, a model of lower-level processing will prove useful, if not necessary, if we are to develop computational models of higher-level processing. An adequate model of lower-level processing appears within our reach.

ACKNOWLEDGMENTS

The preparation of this chapter was supported by National Eye Institute grants EY-02115 and EY-09076. As always, conversations with N Graham clarified my thinking and helped me to avoid errors. She is to be held harmless for any remaining inaccuracies; the size of the literature involved and my own limitations are to blame. I am also grateful to S Shady and W Swanson for their help and to the numerous colleagues who responded to my many questions by phone, fax, and e-mail.

> **Visit the *Annual Reviews* home page at**
> **http://www.AnnualReviews.org.**

## Literature Cited

Adelson EH. 1982. The delayed rod afterimage. *Vis. Res.* 22:1313–28

Arnow T, Geisler W. 1996. Visual detection following retinal damage: predictions of an inhomogeneous retino-cortical model. *Proc. Int. Soc. Opt. Engr.* 2674:119–30

Ashmore J, Falk G. 1980. Responses of rod bipolar cells in the dark-adapted retina of the dogfish, *Scyliorhinus canicula. J. Physiol.* 300:115–50

Battersby WS, Wagman IH. 1962. Neural limitations of visual excitability. IV: spatial determinants of retrochiasmal interaction. *Am. J. Physiol.* 203:359–65

Benardete EA, Kaplan E, Knight BW. 1992. Contrast gain control in the primate retina: P-cells are not X-like, some M-cells are. *Vis. Neurosci.* 8:483–86

Boff KR, Kaufman L, Thomas JP, eds. 1986. *Handbook of Perception and Human Performance,* Vol. 1: *Sensory Processes and Perception.* New York: Wiley

Bowen RW, Pokorny J, Smith VC. 1989. Sawtooth contrast sensitivity: decrements have the edge. *Vis. Res.* 29:1501–9

Bowen RW, Pokorny J, Smith VC, Fowler MA. 1992. Sawtooth contrast sensitivity: effects of mean illuminance and low temporal frequencies. *Vis. Res.* 32:1239–47

Boynton RM, Ikeda M, Stiles WS. 1964. Interactions among chromatic mechanisms as inferred from positive and negative increment thresholds. *Vis. Res.* 4:87–117

Boynton RM, Kambe N. 1980. Chromatic difference steps of moderate size measured along theoretically critical axes. *Color Res. Appl.* 5:13–23

Boynton RM, Sturr JF, Ikeda M. 1961. Study of flicker by increment threshold technique. *J. Opt. Soc. Am.* 51:196–201

Boynton RM, Whitten DN. 1970. Visual adaptation in monkey cones: recordings of late receptor potentials. *Science* 170:1423–26

Burr DC, Ross J, Morrone MC. 1985. Local regulation of luminance gain. *Vis. Res.* 25: 717–27

Calkins DJ, Schein SJ, Tsukamoto Y, Sterling P. 1994. M and L cones in macaque fovea connect to midget ganglion cells by different numbers of excitatory synapses. *Nature* 371:70–72

Calkins DJ, Sterling P. 1996. Absence of spectrally specific lateral inputs to midget ganglion cells in primate retina. *Nature* 381: 613–15

Chaparro A, Stromeyer CF, Chen G, Kronauer RE. 1995. Human cones appear to adapt at low light levels: measurements on the red-green detection mechanism. *Vis. Res.* 35: 3103–18

Chen B, Makous W, Williams DR. 1993. Serial spatial filters in vision. *Vis. Res.* 33: 413–27

Chichilnisky EJ, Wandell BA. 1996. Seeing gray through the ON and OFF pathways. *Vis. Neurosci.* 13:591–96

Cicerone CM, Hayhoe MM, MacLeod DI. 1990. The spread of adaptation in human foveal and parafoveal cone vision. *Vis. Res.* 30:1603–15

Cohn TE, Lasley DJ. 1986. Visual sensitivity. *Annu. Rev. Psychol.* 37:495–21

Croner LJ, Kaplan E. 1995. Receptive fields of P and M ganglion cells across the primate retina. *Vis. Res.* 35:7–24

Crook JM, Lee BB, Tigwell DA, Valberg A. 1987. Thresholds to chromatic spots of cells in the macaque geniculate nucleus. *J. Physiol.* 392:193–211

Dacey DM. 1996. Circuitry for color coding in the primate retina. *Proc. Natl. Acad. Sci. USA* 93:582–88

Dacey DM, Lee BB. 1994. The 'blue-on' opponent pathway in primate retina originates from a distinct bistratified ganglion cell type. *Nature* 367:731–35

Dacey DM, Lee BB, Stafford DK, Pokorny J, Smith VC. 1996. Horizontal cells of the primate retina: cone specificity without spectral opponency. *Science* 271:656–59

Dahari R, Spitzer H. 1996. Spatiotemporal adaptation model for retinal ganglion cells. *J. Opt. Soc. Am.* 13:419–35

Derrington AM, Krauskopf J, Lennie P. 1984. Chromatic mechanisms in lateral geniculate nucleus of macaque. *J. Physiol.* 357: 241–65

DeValois R, DeValois K. 1988. *Spatial Vision.* New York: Oxford Univ. Press

Dolan RP, Schiller PH. 1994. Effects of ON channel blockade with 2-amino-4-phosphonobutyrate (APB) on brightness and contrast perception in monkeys. *Vis. Neurosci.* 11:23–32

Donner K, Hemila S. 1996. Modelling the spatio-temporal modulation response of ganglion cells with difference-of-Gaussians receptive fields: relation to photoreceptor response kinetics. *Vis. Neurosci.* 13:173–86

Finkelstein MA, Harrison M, Hood DC. 1990. Sites of sensitivity control within a long-wavelength cone pathway. *Vis. Res.* 30: 1145–58

Finkelstein MA, Hood DC. 1981. Cone system saturation: more than one stage of sensitivity loss. *Vis. Res.* 21:319–28

Freed MA, Nelson R. 1994. Conductances evoked by light in the ON-ß ganglion-cell of cat retina. *Vis. Neurosci.* 11:261–69

Frishman LJ, Reddy MG, Robson JG. 1996. Effects of background light on the human dark-adapted electroretinogram and physchophysical threshold. *J. Opt. Soc. Am.* 13:601–12

Gaudiano P. 1994. Simulations of X and Y retinal ganglion cell behavior with a non-linear push-pull model of spatiotemporal retinal processing. *Vis. Res.* 34:1767–84

Geisler WS. 1978. Adaptation, afterimage and cone saturation. *Vis. Res.* 18:279–89

Geisler WS. 1979. Initial-image and afterimage discrimination in the rod and cone system. *J. Physiol.* 294:165–79

Geisler WS. 1981. Effect of bleaching and backgrounds on the flash response of the cone system. *J. Physiol.* 312:413–34

Geisler WS. 1989. Sequential ideal-observer analysis of visual discriminations. *Psychol. Rev.* 96:267–314

Geisler WS, Albrecht DG. 1995. Bayesian analysis of identification performance in monkey visual cortex: nonlinear mechanisms and stimulus certainty. *Vis. Res.* 35: 2723–30

Goodchild AK, Ghosh KK, Martin PR. 1996. Comparison of photoreceptor spatial density and ganglion cell morphology in the retina of human, macaque monkey, cat, and the marmoset *Callithrix jacchus. J. Comp. Neurol.* 366:55–75

Graham N, Hood DC. 1992a. Quantal noise and decision rules in dynamic models of light adaptation. *Vis. Res.* 32:779–87

Graham N, Hood DC. 1992b. Modeling the dynamics of light adaptation: the merging of two traditions. *Vis. Res.* 32:1373–93

Graham NV. 1989. *Visual Pattern Analyzers.* New York: Oxford Univ. Press

Green DM, Swets JA. 1988. *Signal Detection Theory and Psychophysics.* New York: Wiley

Haegerstrom-Portnoy G, Verdon W, Adams AJ. 1988. Cone interaction occurs in the parafovea under p-4 stimulus conditions. *Vis. Res.* 28:397–406

Hayhoe MM. 1990. Spatial interactions and models of adaptation. *Vis. Res.* 30:957–65

Hayhoe MM, Benimoff NI, Hood DC. 1987. The time-course of multiplicative and subtractive adaptation processes. *Vis. Res.* 27: 1981–96

Hayhoe MM, Levin ME, Koshel RJ. 1992. Subtractive processes in light adaptation. *Vis. Res.* 32:323–33

He S, MacLeod DIA. 1997. Contrast-modulation flicker: dynamics and spatial resolution of the light adaptation process. *Vis. Res.* 37: In press

Hood DC, Birch DG. 1993a. Light adaptation

of human rod receptors: the leading edge of the human a-wave and models of rod receptor activity. *Vis. Res.* 33:1605–18

Hood DC, Birch DG. 1993b. Human cone receptor activity: the leading edge of the a-wave and models of receptor activity. *Vis. Neurosci.* 10:857–71

Hood DC, Birch DG. 1996. The b-wave of the scotopic (rod) ERG as a measure of the activity of human ON-bipolar cells. *J. Opt. Soc. Am.* 13:623–33

Hood DC, Birch DG, Pepperberg D. 1996. The trailing edge of the photoresponse from human cones derived using a two-flash ERG paradigm. *Vis. Sci. Appl. 1996 Opt. Soc. Am. Dig. Ser.* 1:64–67

Hood DC, Finkelstein MA. 1983. A case for the revision of textbook models of color vision: the detection and appearance of small brief lights. In *Colour Vision: Physiology and Psychophysics,* ed. JD Mollon, LT Sharpe, pp. 385–98. London: Academic

Hood DC, Finkelstein MA. 1986. Sensitivity to light. See Boff et al 1986, pp. 5:1–66

Hood DC, Finkelstein MA, Buckingham E. 1979. Psychophysical tests of models of the response-intensity function. *Vis. Res.* 19:401–6

Hood DC, Graham N. 1997. Threshold fluctuations on temporally modulated backgrounds: a complex physiological explanation of a simple psychophysical finding. *Suppl. Optics Photonics News* 8:(Abstr.)

Hood DC, Graham N, von Wiegand T, Chase VM. 1997. Probed-sinewave paradigm: a test of models of light-adaptation dynamics. *Vis. Res.* 37:1177–91

Hood DC, Ilves T, Maurer E, Wandell B, Buckingham E. 1978. Human cone saturation as a function of ambient intensity: a test of models of shifts in the dynamic range. *Vis. Res.* 18:983–93

Kaiser PK, Boynton RM. 1996. *Human Color Vision.* Washington, DC: Opt. Soc. Am. 2nd ed.

Kaplan E, Shapley R. 1982. X and Y cells in the lateral geniculate nucleus of macaque monkeys. *J. Physiol.* 330:125–43

Kaplan E, Shapley R. 1984. The origin of the S (slow) potential in the mammalian lateral geniculate nucleus. *Exp. Brain Res.* 55:111–16

Kaplan E, Shapley RM. 1986. The primate retina contains two types of ganglion cells, with high and low contrast sensitivity. *Proc. Natl. Acad. Sci. USA* 83:2755–57

Kelly DH. 1972. Adaptation effects on spatiotemporal sine-wave thresholds. *Vis. Res.* 12:89–101

Kelly DH, Savoie RE. 1978. Theory of flicker and transient responses. III. An essential nonlinearity. *J. Opt. Soc. Am.* 68:1481–90

Kelly DH, von Norren D. 1977. Two-band model of heterochromatic flicker. *J. Opt. Soc. Am.* 67:1081–91

King-Smith PE, Webb JR. 1974. The use of photopic saturation in determining the fundamental spectral sensitivity curves. *Vis. Res.* 14:421–29

Kolb H. 1994. The architecture of functional neural circuits in the vertebrate retina. *Invest. Ophthal. Vis. Sci.* 35:2385–404

Kortum PT, Geisler WS. 1995. Adaptation mechanisms in spatial vision—II. Flash thresholds and background adaptation. *Vis. Res.* 35:1595–609

Kraft TW, Schneeweis DM, Schnapf JL. 1993. Visual transduction in human rod photoreceptors. *J. Physiol.* 464:747–65

Krauskopf J. 1980. Discrimination and detection of changes in luminance. *Vis. Res.* 20:671–77

Krauskopf J. 1997. Higher order color mechanism. In *Color Vision: from Molecular Genetics to Perception,* ed. KR Gegenfortner, LT Sharpe. Cambridge: Cambridge Univ. Press. In press

Krauskopf J, Williams DR, Heeley DW. 1982. Cardinal directions of color space. *Vis. Res.* 22:1123–31

Kremers J, Lee BB, Pokorny J, Smith VC. 1993. Responses of macaque ganglion cells and human observers to compound periodic waveforms. *Vis. Res.* 33:1997–2011

Lee BB. 1996. Receptive field structure in the primate retina. *Vis. Res.* 36:631–44

Lee BB, Dacey D, Smith V, Pokorny J. 1997. Tme course and cone specificity of adaptation in the primate outer retina. *Invest. Ophthal. Vis. Sci.* S1163 (Abstr.)

Lee BB, Martin PR, Valberg A, Kremers J. 1993. Physiological mechanisms underlying psychophysical sensitivity to combined luminance and chromatic modulation. *J. Opt. Soc. Am.* 10:1403–12

Lee BB, Pokorny J, Smith VC, Kremers J. 1994. Responses to pulses and sinusoids in macaque ganglion cells. *Vis. Res.* 34:3081–96

Lee BB, Pokorny J, Smith VC, Martin PR, Valberg A. 1990. Luminance and chromatic modulation sensitivity of macaque ganglion cells and human observers. *J. Opt. Soc. Am.* 7:2223–36

Lennie P. 1993. Roles of M and P pathways. In *Contrast Sensitivity,* ed. R Shapley, DMK Lam, pp. 201–13. Cambridge, MA: MIT Press

Lennie P, Pokorny J, Smith VC. 1993. Luminance. *J. Opt. Soc. Am.* 10:1283–93

MacLeod DIA. 1978. Visual sensitivity. *Annu. Rev. Psychol.* 29:613–45

MacLeod DIA, Boynton RM. 1979. Chromaticity diagram showing cone excitation by stimuli of equal luminance. *J. Opt. Soc. Am.* 69:1183–85

MacLeod DIA, Williams DR, Makous W. 1992. A visual nonlinearity fed by single cones. *Vis. Res.* 32:347–63

Makous WL. 1997. Fourier models and the loci of adaptation. *J. Opt. Soc. Am.* 14: 2323–45

Maruyama K, Takahashi M. 1977. Wave form of flickering stimulus and visual masking function. *Tohoku Psychol. Folia* 36:120–33

Merigan WH, Maunsell JHR. 1993. How parallel are the primate visual pathways? *Annu. Rev. Neurosci.* 16:369–402

Nealey TA, Maunsell JHR. 1994. Magnocellular and parvocellular contributions to the responses of neurons in macaque striate cortex. *J. Neurosci.* 14:2069–79

Pelli DG. 1990. The quantum efficiency of vision. In *Vision: Coding and Efficiency of Vision,* ed. C Blakemore, pp. 3–24. Cambridge: Cambridge Univ. Press

Pepperberg D, Birch DG, Hood DC. 1997. Photoresponses of human rods *in vivo* derived from paired-flash electroretinograms. *Vis. Neurosci.* 14:73–82

Pugh ENJ, Kirk DB. 1986. The pi mechanisms of W S Stiles: an historical review. *Perception* 15:705–28

Pugh ENJ, Mollon JD. 1979. A theory of the pl and p3 color mechanisms of Stiles. *Vis. Res.* 19:293–312

Purpura K, Kaplan E, Shapley RM. 1988. Background light and the contrast gain of primate P and M retinal ganglion cells. *Proc. Natl. Acad. Sci. USA* 85:4534–37

Purpura K, Tranchina D, Kaplan E, Shapley RM. 1990. Light adaptation in the primate retina: analysis of changes in gain and dynamics of monkey retinal ganglion cells. *Vis. Neurosci.* 4:75–93

Schiller PH. 1982. Central connections of the retinal ON and OFF pathways. *Nature* 297: 580–83

Schiller PH. 1992. The ON and OFF channels of the visual system. *Trends Neurosci.* 15: 86–92

Schnapf JL, Nunn BJ, Meister M, Baylor DA. 1990. Visual transduction in cones of the monkey *Macaca fascicularis. J. Physiol.* 427:681–713

Schneeweis D, Schnapf J. 1995. Photovoltage of rods and cones in the macaque retina. *Science* 268:1053–56

Seiple WH, Holopigian K, Greenstein V, Hood DC. 1992. Temporal frequency dependent adaptation at the level of the outer retina in humans. *Vis. Res.* 32:2043–48

Shady S, Firoz BF, Wladis EJ, Bauer RM, Li J, Hood DC. 1997. The full-field scotopic VEP provides evidence for post retinal adaptation. *Invest. Ophthalmol. Vis. Sci.* 38(Suppl.):S991 (Abstr.)

Shah S, Levine MD. 1996a. Visual information processing in primate cone pathways—part I: a model. *IEEE Trans. Syst. Man Cybern.* 26:259–74

Shah S, Levine MD. 1996b. Visual information processing in primate cone pathways—part II: experiments. *IEEE Trans. Syst. Man Cybern.* 26:275–89

Shapiro A, Zaidi Q. 1992. The effects of prolonged temporal modulation on the differential response of color mechanisms. *Vis. Res.* 32:2065–75

Shapley RM, Enroth-Cugell C. 1984. Visual adaptation and retinal gain controls. *Progress Retin. Res.* 3:263–346

Shapley RM, Victor JD. 1978. The effect of contrast on the transfer properties of cat ganglion cells. *J. Physiol.* 285:275–98

Smith VC, Lee BB, Pokorny J, Martin PR, Valberg A. 1992. Responses of macaque ganglion cells to the relative phase of heterochromatically modulated lights. *J. Physiol.* 458:191–221

Sperling G, Sondhi MM. 1968. Model for visual luminance discrimination and flicker detection. *J. Opt. Soc. Am.* 58:1133–45

Sterling P. 1997. Retina. In *Synaptic Organization of the Brain,* ed. GM Shepherd. New York: Oxford Univ. Press. 4th ed. In press

Stiles WS. 1978. *Mechanisms of Colour Vision.* London: Academic

Stockman A, MacLeod DIA, Johnson NE. 1993. Spectral sensitivities of the human cones. *J. Opt. Soc. Am.* 10:2491–521

Stockman A, Mollon J. 1986. The spectral sensitivities of the middle- and long-wavelength cones: an extension of the two-colour threshold technique of W S Stiles. *Perception* 15:729–54

Swanson WH. 1994. Time, color, and phase. In *Visual Science and Engineering,* ed. DH Kelly, pp. 191–225. New York: Dekker

Swanson WH, Ueno T, Smith VC, Pokorny J. 1987. Temporal modulation sensitivity and pulse detection thresholds for chromatic and luminance perturbations. *J. Opt. Soc. Am.* 4:1992–2005

Teller DY. 1984. Linking propositions. *Vis. Res.* 24:1233–46

Tranchina D, Gordon J, Shapley R. 1984. Retinal light adaptation-evidence for a feedback mechanism. *Nature* 310:314–16

Tranchina D, Peskin C. 1988. Light adaptation in the turtle retina: embedding a parametric family of linear models in a single nonlinear model. *Vis. Neurosci.* 1:339–48

Troy JB, Lee BB. 1994. Steady discharges of macaque retinal ganglion cells. *Vis. Neurosci.* 11:111–18

Tsukamoto Y, Masarachia P, Schein SJ, Sterling P. 1992. Gap junctions between the pedicles of macaque foveal cones. *Vis. Res.* 32:1809–15

Tyler CW, Liu L. 1996. Saturation revealed by clamping the gain of the retinal light response. *Vis. Res.* 36:2553–62

Valberg A, Lee BB, Creutzfeldt OD. 1991. Remote surrounds and the sensitivity of primate p-cells. In *From Pigments to Perception: Advances in Understanding Visual Processes,* ed. A Valberg, BB Lee, pp. 177–80. New York: Plenum

Valeton JM, van Norren D. 1983. Light adaptation of primate cones: an analysis based upon extracellular data. *Vis. Res.* 23: 1539–47

van de Grind WA, Lankheet MJM, van Wezel RJA, Rowe MH, Hulleman J. 1996. Gain control and hyperpolarization level in cat horizontal cells as a function of light and dark adaptation. *Vis. Res.* 36:3969–85

Virsu V, Lee BB. 1983. Light adaptation in cells of macaque lateral geniculate nucleus and its relation to human light adaptation. *J. Neurophys.* 50:864–77

von Wiegand T, Hood DC, Graham N. 1996. Testing a computational model of light-adaptation dynamics. *Vis. Res.* 35: 3037–51

Wandell BA. 1995. *Foundations of Vision.* Sunderland, MA: Sinauer

Wandell BA, Pugh ENJ. 1980. Detection of long-duration, long-wavelength incremental flashes by a chromatically coded pathway. *Vis. Res.* 20:625–36

Wassle H, Boycott BB. 1991. Functional architecture of the mammalian retina. *Physiol. Rev.* 71:447–80

Wassle H, Boycott BB, Rohrenbeck J. 1989. Horizontal cells in the monkey retina: cone connections and dendritic network. *Eur. J. Neurosci.* 1:421–35

Watson AB. 1986. Temporal Sensitivity. See Boff et al 1986, pp. 6-1/6-43

Watson AB. 1992. Transfer of contrast sensitivity in linear visual networks. *Vis. Neurosci.* 8:65–76

Wilson HR. 1997. A neural model of foveal light adaptation and afterimage formation. *Vis. Neurosci.* 14:403–23

Wu S, Burns SA, Elsner AE, Eskew RT, He J. 1997. Rapid sensitivity changes on flickering backgrounds: tests of models of light adpatation. *J. Opt. Soc. Am.* 14:2367–78

Yeh T, Lee BB, Kremers J. 1996. Time course of adaptation in Macaque retinal ganglion cells. *Vis. Res.* 36:913–31

Yeh T, Pokorny J, Smith VC. 1993. Chromatic discrimination with variation in chromaticity and luminance: data and theory. *Vis. Res.* 33:1835–45

Zaidi Q, Shapiro AG. 1993. Adaptive orthogonalization of opponent-color signals. *Biol. Cybern.* 69:415–28

Zaidi Q, Shapiro AG, Hood DC. 1992. The effect of adaptation on the differential sensitivity of the S-cone color system. *Vis. Res.* 32:1297–318

Zemon V, Gordon J, Welch J. 1988. Asymmetries in ON and OFF visual pathways of humans revealed using contrast-evoked cortical potentials. *Vis. Neurosci.* 1:145–50

*Annu. Rev. Psychol. 1998. 48:537–58*

# CATEGORICAL DATA ANALYSIS

## Thomas D. Wickens

Department of Psychology, University of California, Los Angeles, California 90095;
e-mail: twickens@psych.ucla.edu

KEY WORDS:    contingency tables, frequency tables, statistical models

### ABSTRACT

This chapter reviews recent developments in the analysis of categorical and contingency-table data. The first portion examines developments in model testing and selection. The second portion examines work on models for the structure of dependence. These include log-linear parameter models, models for latent classes, models for missing observations, numerical-scale-based association and correlation models (such as correspondence analysis), the treatment of ordered categories, and models for marginal distributions.

## CONTENTS

Over the past quarter century, the range of procedures for the analysis of categorical data has increased enormously, fueled partly by increases in computer power—see the influential books by Bishop, Fienberg & Holland (1975), Haberman (1978, 1979), and such texts as Agresti (1990, 1996), Clogg & Shihadeh (1994), Wickens (1989). The expansion continues, both in statistics and allied fields. Computing power remains central to the expansion—new methods become available as their computational basis is worked out. Along

0084-6570/98/0201-0537$08.00

with these advances has come consolidation, as the relationship between apparently dissimilar representations has been discovered. This chapter begins with a brief review of some background results, then examines some of these advances. Citations (whose number could easily be increased several-fold) are selective, emphasizing reviews and general or recent articles. In particular, historical development is not reflected.

## BACKGROUND

First, some notation. In this chapter, $n_i$ denotes the observed frequency of the category indexed by the multivariate subscript $\mathbf{i}$ (the frequency in a two-way table is $n_{ij}$) and $p_i$ the comparable proportion. The probability of an observation in cell $\mathbf{i}$ under a theoretical model is $\pi_i$, and the expected number of observations in that cell is $\mu_i$. Estimates of $\mu_i$ obtained by fitting a model are $\widehat{\mu}_i$. Uppercase letters denote the categorizations by which the observations are classified.

Much of the current work with frequency data derives from one of three overlapping traditions. One approach originates in the conventional "chi-square" test for independence in a two-way table, and emphasizes the data as a table of frequencies. The second approach extends the linear models from normally distributed statistics to nonlinear models with other distributions. This approach is most strongly represented by the *generalized linear models* (McCullagh & Nelder, 1989). The third approach derives from the measurement of association through correlation and the construction of factor-analytic or structural-equation models (Muthén, 1984; Lee, Poon & Bentler, 1990, 1992). This review treats only the first two approaches.

The starting point is unrelatedness. With design classification $D$ (e.g., groups) and response classification $A$, unrelatedness is the hypothesis of homogeneity of the distribution of $A$ over the levels of $D$; with two measured classifications $A$ and $B$, it is the hypothesis of independence. Denote these relationships by $D \perp\!\!\!\perp A$ and $A \perp\!\!\!\perp B$ (sometimes, particularly in Goodman's work, $\otimes$ is used instead of $\perp\!\!\!\perp$). As is well known, the relationship $A \perp\!\!\!\perp B$ implies that the data fit the log-linear model $\log \mu_{ij} = \lambda + \lambda_i^A + \lambda_j^B$ (the logarithms are natural; some treatments use $u$ instead of $\lambda$, and the location of the variable and instance indicators varies). To identify the parameters, the $\lambda_i^A$ and $\lambda_j^B$ are constrained, typically by making each set sum to zero or by fixing the coefficients of a reference category. When unrelatedness fails, i.e., $A \not\perp\!\!\!\perp B$, then the term $\lambda_{ij}^{AB}$ must be added to the model. The log-linear models are essential, both because they express the notion of probabilistic unrelatedness and because they are concordant with the Poisson or multinomial distributions that describe the sampling process. When one classification is treated as an outcome, an equivalent, but more compact treatment models the *logit*, which is the logarithm of the odds ratio $\log(\pi_i/1 - \pi_i)$.

The log-linear representation is more general than simple independence. In many sets of data, certain combinations of categories are excluded, either because they are impossible or because they are blocked out as part of a model. Although these voids or "structural zeros" create dependencies, a log-linear model of unrelatedness may still fit. Such data show *quasi-independence*. The estimation algorithms for most models readily accommodate these voids (although degrees of freedom can be altered; see Clogg & Eliason, 1987).

Multifactor configurations can show more complex forms of unrelatedness, either complete probabilistic unrelatedness of one set of dimensions to another or the unrelatedness of two sets conditional on the level of the classifications in a third set. For example, the assertion that classifications $B$ and $C$ are unrelated to $A$ is $A \perp\!\!\!\perp BC$, and the assertion that response classifications $A$ and $B$ are independent at each level of design classifications $D$ and $E$ is $A \perp\!\!\!\perp B \mid DE$. These are *graphical* models and are illustrated by a graph in which nodes are variables and lines denote potential association; for example, the assertions $A \perp\!\!\!\perp BC$ and $A \perp\!\!\!\perp B \mid DE$ are

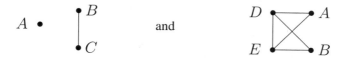

Conditional independence models are good null hypotheses to use when searching for a connection between classifications and good base models on which to build a description of this connection; so, the model $A \perp\!\!\!\perp B \mid DE$ introduces a study of *A-B* relationships. If this model is rejected, then various forms of *A-B* connection must be added. Whittaker (1990) develops the analysis in these terms, and Cox & Wermuth (1993) extend the notation.

A description that asserts the unrelatedness of several classifications can usually be decomposed into the conjunction of independence or conditional-independence assertions, often in simpler tables (Goodman, 1970). For example, the complete dissociation of three classifications is equivalent to the unrelatedness of $A$ to each of the $B$ and $C$, combined with the conditional independence of $B$ and $C$ at the levels of $A$:

$$(\text{Unrelatedness of } A, \ B \text{ and } C) \equiv (A \perp\!\!\!\perp B) \cap (A \perp\!\!\!\perp C) \cap (B \perp\!\!\!\perp C \mid A).$$

Note that complete independence is not equivalent to two-factor independence in the three marginal tables: a three-term assertion is required. The likelihood-ratio test statistics $G^2$ for these individual assertions sum to the omnibus test statistic and can be presented in an analysis-of-variance-like table.

An important characteristic of the log-linear models is that, under Poisson or multinomial sampling, sufficient statistics for the parameters exist. This fact greatly simplifies the fitting of the model, which can be done by straightforward iterative schemes. In a multiway table, the most familiar log-linear models are *hierarchical*, where the presence of a term indexed by some combination of factors implies the presence of all terms indexed with subsets of those factors, and the absence of a term implies the absence of all terms indexed with supersets of those factors. These models are identified by their maximal factors (e.g., $[A][BC]$ or $[ADE][BDE]$ for the models above; notation varies). Their expected frequencies are determined by these marginal distributions and can be found by the familiar iterative proportional fitting algorithm.

More generally, a matrix representation of the log-linear models is useful. Write the $n_i$ in a vector $\mathbf{n}$, and let $\mu_y$ denote the expected value of $\log \mathbf{n}$. A log-linear model is $\mu_y = \mathbf{X}\lambda$, where $\mathbf{X}$ is a design matrix and $\lambda$ is a vector containing the $\lambda$ parameters. The matrix notation is flexible and allows non-hierarchical (sometimes called *nonstandard*) log-linear models to be written easily (for simple examples, see Rindskof, 1990; von Eye & Spiel, 1996).

The generalized linear model approach emphasizes the individual responses instead of the cell frequencies. Let $Y_s$ be the value of the $s$th observation (for binomial events, $Y_s$ is 0 or 1). Assume that this random variable has a distribution that is a member of the exponential family (a collection that includes both the binomial and the Poisson distributions). The mean value $\mu_s$ of $Y_s$ is described by a transformation, known as the *link function*, and a linear combination of parameters: $g(\mu_s) = \mathbf{X}_s\beta$. The design matrix $\mathbf{X}_s$ includes such observation-specific information as group membership or other covariates. Each distribution has associated with it a natural link function, known as the *canonical link*, for which the analysis is particularly simple. Of most relevance to categorical data, the natural links for the binomial and Poisson distributions produce logit and log-linear models, respectively. Because the generalized linear model allows individual response processes to be described, it extends more easily than the cell-frequency models.

## MODEL FITTING AND TESTING

Much of the analysis of frequency data involves the fitting of a statistical description or *model* to a set of data. This process has two functions. A model that fits satisfactorily describes the data and is the basis for an interpretation of their effects. A model that does not fit shows where this picture must be extended. The counterpart of these applications is a pair of hypothesis tests. One test uses a simple null hypothesis and the model as the alternative. Rejection shows that the model represents an appreciable portion of the variability of the data. The other test uses the model as a null hypothesis and a more general, usually saturated, alternative. Rejection shows that the model is insufficient (although it can still be a component of a better model).

## Test Statistics

When a model has been fitted, the quality of that fit must be evaluated. The most familiar approach is to obtain a collective measure of the difference between the observed data $n_i$ and the expected values $\widehat{\mu}_i$ for these cells under the fitted model, using the *Pearson statistic* $X^2$ or the *likelihood-ratio statistic* $G^2$ (sometimes denoted $L^2$):

$$X^2 = \sum (n_i - \widehat{\mu}_i)^2 / \widehat{\mu}_i \quad \text{and} \quad G^2 = 2 \sum n_i \log(n_i / \widehat{\mu}_i).$$

The sum is over all cells except structural voids. These (and many other) test statistics are special cases of a family of test statistics known as *power divergence statistics* (Cressie & Read, 1984; Read & Cressie, 1988), all of which have the same large-sample chi-square distribution under the null hypothesis. Cressie & Read propose a third member of the power-divergence family as a compromise between $X^2$ and $G^2$, but presently this statistic is more acknowledged than used.

The power-divergence formulation unifies a study of the properties of the individual statistics (Cressie & Read, 1989). There is evidence that as a test of overall fit, the $X^2$ statistic is preferable to $G^2$ in its convergence to a chi-square distribution when the categories are fixed. When the number of categories increases with the sample size, such as when a researcher collapses categories or restricts the dimension of the examined models to keep cell sizes above some limit, the situation is more complicated, and the most appropriate strategies are not yet established (e.g., Koehler, 1986).

Exact tests are alternatives to the asymptotic power-divergence tests. With small tables and simple hypotheses, the configurations that are consistent with a model and the data can be enumerated. The exact probabilities of these configurations under a sampling model (binomial, multinomial, etc) are summed over all tables that are at least as deviant from the null hypothesis as the data, according to some measure (e.g., the probability of occurrence, the value of $X^2$, etc). The most familiar of these tests is *Fisher's exact test* for $2 \times 2$ table. Extensions of this test apply to both two-way $I \times J$ tables and simple multidimensional tables (Agresti, 1992; Zelterman, Chan & Mielke, 1995). Continuing development (e.g., Fourier methods; Baglivo, Olivier & Pagano, 1992) and expanding computer power will make these methods increasingly important. The exact methods are computationally infeasible in tables with many marginal categories, large cell counts, and approximately equal marginal frequencies. They would be particularly useful in large tables with sparse data, where the asymptotic approximations are bad (Monte Carlo methods may be alternatives; e.g., Agresti, Wackerly & Boyett, 1979).

Some controversial issues arise with the exact tests (particularly Fisher's test). First, their discrete nature makes them conservative. When only a few configurations are consistent with the constraints, the cumulated sum of probabilities may be much less than the nominal significance level. Second, the tests are usually conditioned on all marginal distributions of the table, which is more restricted than the sampling models for most common designs. The two issues are related; the calculations would be less quantized could the sampling variation of the marginal distributions be included. There is a large and contentious literature on this topic (reviewed in Agresti, 1992; see Camilli, 1990; Haber, 1990, for two positions). The arguments also involve opinions about the appropriateness of null hypothesis testing and of the relative merits of Bayesian and frequentist methods, and so—the point on which all agree—will not be resolved easily, if ever. In multiway tables, the number of alternatives is larger and the problems are less severe (see also Kim & Agresti, 1995).

## Model Comparison and Selection

Many different models can be fitted to a multiway or large two-way table. No single rule can select the best of these, as the choice is influenced by the size and complexity of the pool of candidate models, concerns about multiple tests, the tradeoff between accurate fit and parsimony, and the compatibility of the representation with theoretical and practical properties of the data. A good start is to plot their goodness-of-fit statistics ($X^2$ or $G^2$) against their degrees of freedom (Fowlkes, Freeny & Landwehr, 1988). Simple models, with many degrees of freedom to their tests, appear on the right and more complex models on the left. Among models with the same horizontal coordinate, those lowest on the vertical axis are superior.

The choice among models with different degrees of complexity is more difficult. Where the models are related hierarchically, differences in $G^2$ statistics give comparative likelihood-ratio tests. A helpful illustration is a diagram in which nodes representing models are placed at a height roughly determined by their degrees of freedom, with lines between nodes showing hierarchical relationships.

Nonhierarchical models are harder to compare. Sometimes useful information is obtained by treating them as submodels of a single combined model, but this structure is often unrealistic, particularly when both models explain the same effects in related ways (e.g., the CA(1) and RC(1) models described below). The choice must balance a model's goodness of fit against its parameters. This tradeoff is influenced by the state of theorizing in an area, with simpler models usually being better in less mature areas.

A criterion of model goodness that carries across models with differing degrees of freedom is useful. Contours of this criterion can be drawn on the goodness-of-fit plot for $G^2$ mentioned above. The most obvious possibility is the criterion for a conventional test—that is, the value of the chi-square statistic that corresponds to rejection of the model at some level of significance. Although they are useful, conventional significance tests have several limitations, including their insensitivity to the size of the model pool (their "$p$ values" cannot be taken seriously), the number of parameters fitted (they favor complex models), and the amount of data available for fitting. Two other criteria avoid some of these problems.

The *Akaike information criterion* (Akaike, 1973; see Sakamoto, Ishiguro & Kitagawa, 1986; Sakamoto, 1991) introduces a penalty for excess parameters. Based on information-theoretic considerations, it adds twice the number of parameters fitted in the model to the likelihood-ratio statistic:

$$\text{AIC} = G^2 + 2(\text{number of parameters}).$$

A model has a low value of the AIC either when it fits well or when it has few parameters. Between two models, hierarchical or nonhierarchical, the one with the smaller AIC is the better choice. Its contours can also be drawn on the $G^2$ plot.

The second form of penalty is based on Bayesian decision theory (Kass & Raftery, 1995; Raftery, 1995). A pure Bayesian choice between models would be based on their posterior probabilities (i.e., those given the data), but that analysis is limited by the need to find appropriate prior probabilities for the models. However, when only very weak prior information that does not favor any model is available, so that the decision depends almost completely on the data at hand (Spiegelhalter & Smith, 1982), the logarithm of the *Bayes factor*, i.e., the ratio of posterior to prior odds in favor of a model, is approximated by the *Bayesian information criterion*:

$$\text{BIC} = G^2 + (\log N)(\text{number of parameters}),$$

where $N$ is the total sample size (see Weakliem, 1992 for application examples). Unless the sample is very small (and unrealistic for model fitting), the BIC penalizes excess parameters more than the AIC and selects a more parsimonious model with less good fit. Differences in the BIC for a pair of models give evidence in favor of one model or the other. An important property of the BIC is that it can support the more restricted member of a pair of hierarchical models, even though that model constitutes a null hypothesis from a conventional testing point of view.

## *Variability Effects*

Statistical inference for categorical data has a particular point of vulnerability. Under the standard sampling distributions (Poisson, multinomial, etc), the variability of the observations is not measured directly but is inferred from the model for the expected frequencies. In this respect, the techniques differ from tests in multiple regression or the analysis of variance that use separate estimates of the variability. However, because the parameters of the underlying model can differ from one observation to the next, real data are often overdispersed relative to those sampling models. With single observations, excess variability is absorbed in the category probabilities, but when the observations are clustered (e.g., when several come from the same subject), this overdispersion is important. As has long been recognized, naïvely ignoring clustering underestimates the variability and overestimates the precision and statistical significance of the results. There is a vast literature concerning these cluster effects in biomedical statistics (for reviews, see Agresti, 1989b; Ashby et al, 1992; Diggle, Liang & Zeger, 1994; Pendergast et al, 1996). The field is very active but has not yet produced a set of easily applied techniques.

The most direct approach uses generalized linear models. These models contain a dispersion parameter on top of the standard multinomial or Poisson sampling distributions, which can be estimated in a variety of ways (Collett, 1991; McCullagh & Nelder, 1989; for examples, see Liang & McCullagh, 1993). The goodness of fit of an overdispersed model cannot be tested, but one can still compare hierarchically related models.

Another approach is to posit a distribution of cluster effects as a random factor in the design. For example, a model for binomial outcomes could express the logit for each observation as the sum of a normally distributed base value and a fixed effect distinguishing the different measures. Estimation of the parameters for this simple model is feasible, but parameter estimation for the random-effect models with structures of much greater complexity is conceptually and computationally difficult. One way to avoid these problems is to model the effects of the random variability instead of the variables themselves. Both conditional (given the cluster) and marginal (collapsed over clusters) parameters are used, measuring either association or correlation. These approaches yield tests of both between- and within-cluster parameters, but again without overall goodness-of-fit tests.

In some circumstances the random-effect models reduce to simpler forms. Suppose that the logit for the $j$th response in cluster $i$ is the sum of a cluster-specific random parameter $\alpha_j$ and a response-specific parameter $\beta_j$. In a test-theory context, this representation is a Rasch model ($\alpha_i$ corresponds to individual ability and $\beta_j$ to item difficulty), which places both cluster and response on a single unidimensional scale. The number of responses in cluster $i$ in a consistent direction is a sufficient statistic for $\alpha_i$, and a conditional likelihood for $\beta_j$ can be constructed. The result has the simple aggregate log-linear form of the symmetry and quasi-symmetry models discussed below (Agresti, 1993b, 1995, 1997). This work contacts the literature on item response theory, although it emphasizes item properties, not individual abilities.

Sometimes the relevant data from each cluster can be reduced to a small set of scores. Simulations by Wickens (1993) suggest that then conventional parametric techniques, such as the analysis of variance, give good estimates of subject heterogeneity and are as powerful as methods specifically based on categorical assumptions.

## MODELS FOR STRUCTURE

The balance of this chapter reviews models that represent various forms of association. It emphasizes two-dimensional tables, both because they are common and because they are the base on which multiway models are built.

Many models are built from measures of local association, which can be described in three ways. First are the *standardized residuals*, such as the *components of the Pearson chi-square*, $(n_i - \widehat{\mu}_i)/\sqrt{\widehat{\mu}_i}$. The sums of squares of these residuals equal the Pearson statistic $X^2$. Comparable residuals exist for all the power divergence statistics (Cressie & Read, 1989). In particular, the likelihood-ratio statistic is also the sum of positive deviations:

$$G^2 = \sum 2[n_i \log(n_i/\widehat{\mu}_i) + (\widehat{\mu}_i - n_i)].$$

The denominator term in the Pearson residuals gives them roughly unit variance. Better estimates of the variance take into account the parameters estimated in fitting the model but are computationally more difficult (Haberman, 1978). However, one should not treat the standardized residuals as test statistics, both because of multiple comparison problems and because they are not independent. They are best used to spot patterns. Friendly (1994) describes several ways to plot them as blocks of varying width.

A second approach to dependence uses the log-linear model. In a two-way table, the term $\lambda_{ij}^{AB}$ of the saturated model indicates how the cells deviate from independence. With an estimation procedure that generates standard errors, these terms can be standardized, although, as with the deviations, they are better examined for patterns.

The third approach focuses on measures of association. An $I \times J$ table can be considered as an $(I - 1) \times (J - 1)$ collection of $2 \times 2$ tables relating adjacent pairs of rows and columns. Each of these tables has one association degree of freedom, which can be summarized by any of a dozen or so association coefficients. The measure most compatible with log-linear modeling is the logarithm of the ratio of frequencies on the two diagonals, known as the *local odds ratio* or *cross-product ratio*: $\log[(n_{ij}n_{i+1,j+1})/(n_{i,j+1}n_{i+1,j})]$. A table of local association coefficients can be plotted in the same way as a table of residuals.

## Models for Log-Linear Parameters

One way to write a model intermediate between independence and complete dependence is to include constrained parameters $\lambda_{ij}^{AB}$ in the log-linear model. To do so, partition the cells of the table into subsets $C_1, C_2, \ldots, C_K$, within each of which $\lambda_{ij}^{AB}$ is constant. The quasi-independence model that expresses this condition in a two-way table is $\log \mu_{ij} = \lambda + \lambda_i^A + \lambda_j^B + \lambda_{k(i,j)}^C$, where the subscript $k(i, j)$ specifies the subset to which cell $i, j$ belongs. With the new classification, $A \perp\!\!\!\perp B \mid C$, although $A \not\!\perp\!\!\!\perp B$. This model adds $K - 1$ parameters to the independence model (when the categories are not redundant with the marginals), so that a test of whether the model improves on the independence model has $K - 1$ degrees of freedom and a goodness-of-fit test has $(I - 1)(J - 1) - K + 1$ degrees of freedom.

Specification of the subsets depends on the substance of the situation, and there are many versions of these models (e.g., Goodman, 1972). In one standard group of models, the row and column categorizations are identical, so that the entries can be treated as transitions from row to column categorization. (Many of these were first applied to social mobility tables, reviewed by Goodman & Clogg, 1992.) For example, the *band diagonal model* takes as subsets the cells at a fixed distance from the major diagonal, with constant values of $i - j$.

Probably the most widely used set of these models contains those that concern symmetry relationships. A table with symmetrical interchange has transitions from row category $i$ to column category $j$ balanced by those in the other direction, so that $n_{ij} \approx n_{ji}$. In each of the $I(I - 1)/2$ diagonal pairs, this *symmetry model* has $\widehat{\mu}_{ij} = \widehat{\mu}_{ji} = \frac{1}{2}(n_{ij} + n_{ji})$. The diagonal cells play no role in this analysis and are excluded as structural voids. In log-linear form, symmetry implies that $\log \mu_{ij} = \lambda + \lambda_{ij}^S$, where $\lambda_{ij}^S + \lambda_{ji}^S$. This model does not lie between independence and complete dependence, as it enforces homogeneity of the marginal distributions (a symmetric matrix is its own transpose). The *quasi-symmetry* model adds row and column terms, combining symmetrical association with potentially differing marginals: $\widehat{\mu}_{ij} = \lambda + \lambda_i^A + \lambda_j^B + \lambda_{ij}^S$. These models play an important role in the analysis of marginal distributions, as discussed below.

In a multiway table, symmetry relationships connect cells with like index patterns. For example, a symmetry-like model for $K$ directional binary items groups cells with equal numbers of items in the same direction (e.g., all yes, all but one yes, etc, as in the Rasch representation mentioned above). A model in which the items are conditionally independent, given their total, implies that the data have a unidimensional character (Goodman, 1990).

The quasi-symmetry model becomes saturated when combined with an anti-symmetric or skew-symmetric term $\lambda_{ij}^D$ for which $\lambda_{ij}^D = -\lambda_{ji}^D$ (each symmetrical pair of cells is controlled by two parameters $\lambda_{ij}^C$ and $\lambda_{ij}^D$). van der Heijden & Mooijaart (1995) and Yamaguchi (1990) treat quasi-symmetry as a base model and interpret the departures from it using a series of restricted models for the skew-symmetric terms.

## Latent Class and Latent Structure Models

In quasi-independence models, the ancillary classifications are completely defined by the classification in the original table. Latent class models are similar in that an additional dimension of classification is created, but differ in that this dimension is only inferred. The population is viewed as inhomogeneous, with individuals arising from two or more latent classes. The observed association results from the mixing of these classes (reviewed by Clogg, 1995).

The assignment of individuals to latent classes cannot be done without assuming structure for the individual classes. The usual assumption is that the responses are independent in the latent classes. The original table of probabilities $\mathbf{P}$ is written as a mixture of $K$ tables $\mathbf{\Pi}_1, \ldots, \mathbf{\Pi}_K$ with mixing proportions $\pi_1, \ldots, \pi_K$. The two-way $AB$ table is the marginal sum of a three-way $ABC$ table in which the two manifest classifications are conditionally independent given the latent class: $A \perp\!\!\!\perp B \mid C$. This structure extends directly to multiway tables. The most commonly used model has two latent classes: $\widehat{\mathbf{\Pi}} = \pi\mathbf{\Pi}_1 + (1-\pi)\mathbf{\Pi}_2$. This model implies that the table $\widehat{\mathbf{\Pi}}$ has rank two (de Leeuw & van der Heijden, 1991; this result does not apply to more than two classes). It can be fitted by any procedure that extracts a two-dimensional representation of $\mathbf{P}$, such as the CA(1) model discussed below.

A different approach was proposed by Rudas, Clogg & Lindsay (1994; see Clogg, Rudas & Xi, 1995, for a less technical treatment and Xi & Lindsay, 1996, for estimation). Instead of two classes with independent categorizations, they considered $\mathbf{P}$ to be a mixture of a table $\mathbf{\Pi}_I$ with independent categories and a table $\mathbf{\Pi}_D$ with unspecified dependence: $\mathbf{P} = \pi\mathbf{\Pi}_I + (1-\pi)\mathbf{\Pi}_D$. From among the many such representations, they select the one that combines the largest possible sample from a population in which the categories are independent with the smallest possible sample from a population in which they are associated. The maximum value of $\pi$ is an index of the degree of association in the table, and the table $\mathbf{\Pi}_D$ is another form of cell deviate.

An approach to inferring a latent structure to categorical data from another tradition was proposed by Batchelder & Riefer (1986, 1990; Riefer & Batchelder,

1988; see Hu & Batchelder, 1994, for estimation). Their model applies to situations in which the row categorization refers to distinct treatments and the column categorization to observable responses. A set of latent *cognitive states* is proposed, with different response distributions associated with each state. Models based on probabilistic tree structures relate the populations to the cognitive states and the cognitive states to the responses, linking row and column categorizations. For example, Riefer & Batchelder (1988) considered a task in which subjects had to both recognize particular sentences and recall the language in which they had been learned. They hypothesized separate learning parameters for the sentence and for its representation in a particular language (the cognitive states), then mapped these states onto the observable responses.

## Incomplete Observations

Incomplete data are a serious problem in any study with multivariate responses. Simply ignoring the data from individuals who do not provide a response in every category is both inefficient and potentially biasing. Techniques for treating incomplete categorical data are beginning to be developed.

One approach is through an ancillary categorization. Suppose a two-way $DA$ table is observed, with $D$ a design categorization (or combination of classifications) and $A$ an outcome categorization. Some observations omit classification $A$. Define a new binary categorization $R$ to equal 1 when $A$ is observed and 0 when it is not (Little & Rubin, 1987), so that the observations come from an incompletely observed three-way $RDA$ table. When $R = 1$, the complete $DA$ subtable is recorded; when $R = 0$, only the $D$ marginal is recorded. The extent to which the missing observations affect inference about the relationship of $D$ to $A$ depends on how the observations are missing. If $DA \perp\!\!\!\perp R$ in the hypothetical three-way table, then the observations are *missing completely at random*, and inference based on the observed table is valid. If $A \perp\!\!\!\perp R \mid D$ in the three-way table, then the data are *missing at random*. Inferences about the relationship of $D$ and $A$ are valid, although the characteristics of categorization $D$ can be biased. If $A \not\!\perp\!\!\!\perp R \mid D$, then the missing observations are *nonignorable*, and inference about the $D$-$A$ relationship may be biased.

Because there are so many possible missing-data mechanisms, the missing portion of the $RDA$ table cannot be estimated in general. However, because nonignorable nonresponse is a serious problem, restricted analyses are valuable (Baker & Laird, 1988; Fitzmaurice, Laird & Zahner, 1996; Williamson & Haber, 1994; Winship & Mare, 1989). With an appropriate model for nonresponse (e.g., $D \perp\!\!\!\perp R \mid D$), estimates of the missing observations can be made and unbiased inference obtained. Conaway (1992) considers a nonignorable nonresponse model that includes individual differences in the subject parameters. A substantial problem with these models is their instability, and Park & Brown (1994) use empirical Bayes methods to stabilize the estimates.

## Models with Scale Values

In an important class of partial dependence models, numerical scores are assigned to the categories to represent the pattern of association. Either correlation or association measures can be modeled. The correlation approach has by far the longer history, with many antecedents and several independent discoveries. It is currently best expressed as *correspondence analysis*, as described in many books (Benzécri, 1992; Gifi, 1990; Greenacre, 1984, 1993b; Lebart, Morineau & Warwick, 1984; Nishisato, 1980, 1994; van de Geer, 1993a, 1993b). The approach through association modeling derives directly from the log-linear association modeling tradition (Goodman, 1979, and papers collected in Goodman, 1984; also Goodman, 1984; for summary, see Clogg & Shihadeh, 1994). Recent work has clarified the relationship between these approaches.

The simplest scaling models express the association as a single term. Both models express the deviation from independence. The *correlation models* use the deviation of the observed frequencies $n_{ij}$ from the expected frequencies $\widehat{\mu}_{ij} = n_{i+}n_{+j}/n_{++}$. The single-term correlation model CA(1) writes this deviate as the product of a correlation, a row score, and a column score: $(n_{ij} - \widehat{\mu}_{ij})/\widehat{\mu}_{ij} \approx \rho\alpha_i\beta_j$. The parameters conventionally are identified by fixing their weighted sum and sum of squares: $\sum p_{i+}\alpha_i = \sum p_{+j}\beta_j = 0$ and $\sum p_{i+}\alpha_i^2 = \sum p_{+j}\beta_j^2 = 1$ (other standardizations are possible; e.g., Goodman, 1991, 1996). The scores $\alpha_i$ and $\beta_j$ give association-based scale values to the rows and columns, and $\rho = \sum \alpha_i\beta_j n_{ij}$ is the Pearson product-moment correlation coefficient obtained when each observation is given the scores $\alpha_i$ and $\beta_j$.

The *association models* measure the deviations from independence by the log-linear term $\lambda_{ij}^{AB}$. In the single-term *row and column association model* RC(1), these terms are written as products: $\lambda_{ij}^{AB} = \phi\zeta_i\eta_i$. The parameters are conventionally constrained absolutely: $\sum \zeta_i = \sum \eta_j = 0$ and $\sum \zeta_i^2 = \sum \eta_j^2 = 1$. This model also expresses the odds ratio for the association between any two rows $i$ and $k$ and any two columns $j$ and $l$,

$$\log[(n_{ij}n_{kl})/(n_{il}n_{kj})] \approx \phi(\zeta_i - \zeta_k)(\eta_j - \eta_l).$$

Both models also determine the cell frequencies. The CA(1) model extends the product representation for independence:

$$\widehat{\mu}_{ij} = p_{i+}p_{+j}[1 + \rho\alpha_i\beta_j],$$

and the RC(1) model extends the log-linear model:

$$\log \widehat{\mu}_{ij} = \lambda + \lambda_i^A + \lambda_j^B + \phi\zeta_i\eta_j.$$

The scale values in these models may either be manifest or latent, i.e., either given a priori or estimated. In the former case, all the association is measured by the single estimated parameter $\rho$ or $\phi$, giving a very compact description. The *uniform correlation* and *uniform association models* arise when the scale values are equally spaced. When the rows or columns have no intrinsic numerical values, or where their spacing is unknown, their parameters are estimated. Depending on the situation, estimates can be made either freely or under order constraints (i.e., with $\alpha_i \leq \alpha_{i+1}$, etc; see Ritov & Gilula, 1991, 1993). With unconstrained estimates, an association-based ordering of the categories is produced.

The CA(1) and RC(1) models have a variety of interpretations. Generally, the properties of the CA(1) model are more closely related to the probabilities and those of the RC(1) model to the association elements. A perfect fit of the CA(1) model implies that the data have rank two, so that it is equivalent to the latent class model with two classes (de Leeuw & van der Heijden, 1991; Goodman, 1987). The association model is a remarkably good representation of an underlying bivariate normal distribution cut by a series of criteria (Goodman, 1981), while the correlation model requires two association terms (Baccini, Caussinus & de Falguerolles, 1993). For data with ordered categories, the RC(1) model minimizes the entropy of the resulting configuration and the CA(1) model expresses the stochastic order of the distributions by maximizing the gap between cumulative distribution functions (Gilula, Krieger & Ritov, 1988; Gilula & Ritov, 1990).

When the smaller dimension of the table has three or more levels, neither the CA(1) model nor the RC(1) model is saturated. Both models are extended by adding multiplicative terms. The CA($M$) model is

$$n_{ij} = p_{i+}p_{+j} \left[ 1 + \sum_{m=1}^{M} \rho_m \alpha_{im} \beta_{jm} \right]$$

and the RC(M) model is

$$\log n_{ij} = \lambda + \lambda_i^A + \lambda_j^B + \sum_{m=1}^{M} \phi_m \zeta_{im} \eta_{jm}.$$

A perfect fit requires $M^* = \min (I, J) - 1$ terms. To identify these models, the extracted dimensions are ordered in terms of their associations or correlations (i.e., $\rho_1 \geq \ldots \geq \rho_M$ or $\phi_1 \geq \ldots \geq \phi_M$), and some form of orthogonality is imposed on the coefficients. The parameters of the multiple-term models are almost always estimated (although see Eliason, 1995), using procedures that characteristically differ for the two approaches. The saturated CA($M^*$) and RC($M^*$) models are singular-value decompositions of the residuals or log-linear parameters. As implemented in most statistical packages, the CA($M$) model with $M < M^*$ is fitted by dropping the least important dimensions from the CA($M^*$) solution (see Gilula & Haberman, 1986 for an alternative). The RC($M$) model is usually fitted by maximum-likelihood methods (Haberman, 1995; for a Bayesian approach, Evans, Gulula & Guttman, 1993).

Usually a representation with $M < M^*$ terms suffices to express the important characteristics of a set of data. The two-dimensional CA(2) or RC(2) models are easily plotted and aid in visualizing the structure of the association. The interpretation of these plots can be subtle, particularly with *biplots* that contain both row and column information on the same chart. Distance and configural relationships are discussed in the correspondence books (especially Benzécri, 1992; Gower & Hand, 1996; Greenacre, 1984; see also Greenacre & Hastie, 1987; Greenacre, 1993a). Goodman (1986, 1991, 1993) discusses issues related to both CA($M$) and RC($M$) models.

Neither the correlation nor the association approach is uniformly preferable, and whether a CA($M$) or RC($M$) fits better depends on the data under consideration. Beyond the particulars of their representation, the greatest differences between them arise from their history and the philosophy of data analysis that underlies them. Correspondence analysis grew from essentially descriptive techniques that deemphasized statistical tests. The models are generally fitted by dropping the least important dimensions from the CA($M^*$) model without refitting. They are often applied to very large tables with dependent observations. In contrast, the association models grew out of an inferential context and are linked to the hierarchical fitting and testing procedures of log-linear models. Likelihood-based estimates and model comparisons play a larger role. It is more usual to start by fitting the RC(1) model, then work upwards, fitting separate models for each $M$.

Both the correspondence and association models depend on a breakdown of association components into bilinear terms. There is no single way to generalize the singular-value decomposition above two dimensions, so applications to multiway tables have used several approaches. In the exploratory tradition of correspondence analysis, multiway tables are often reduced to two-way tables by factorially combining dimensions, by abutting all two-way tables in a *Burt table*, or by reinterpreting the data as an indicator table of response classifications by subjects. The two-way models, now known as *multiple correspondence analysis*, are fitted (see references above and Greenacre, 1993c). An exception is Carlier & Kroonenberg (1996), who apply several representations directly to a three-way table.

A reduction to a two-way table is less often used with association models (although see Gilula & Haberman, 1988). More attention has been paid to extending the two-way models to three dimensions. For example, in the *conditional association models*, the RC(*M*) model is applied to the two-way tables obtained by fixing the third category, then the parameters of these models are modeled across tables (Becker & Clogg, 1989; Clogg & Shihadeh, 1994; Goodman, 1986). Various three-way parameterizations are also used (e.g., Anderson, 1996).

The association and correlation approaches are sometimes combined. Graphical models were used by de Falguerolles, Jamel & Whittaker (1995) to simplify the structure and parameters of a correlation model. As a descriptive device, correspondence analysis can express the residuals of any two-way log-linear models, not just independence (de Leeuw & van der Heijden, 1988; van der Heijden & de Leeuw, 1985; van der Heijden & Worsley, 1988; van der Heijden, de Falguerolles & de Leeuw, 1989).

## Ordered Categories

Many categorizations have an intrinsic order. Models fitted to such a table should respect this ordering. Such models abound (Agresti, 1984, 1989a). Many of these models build on the unordered models by using the ordering to provide structure. Mentioned above were the band diagonal quasi-independence models developed for mobility tables and the order-constrained versions of the RC(1) and CA(1) models. The use of manifest scores in these models also implies ordering. For example, the *uniform row-association model* assigns equally spaced scores to the rows and estimates the column scores. When both categorizations are ordered and uniformly spaced, the *uniform association model* results.

Ordinal relationships are embodied in several forms of logits. The *local logits* express the ordering by relating adjacent categories; when the column categorization is ordered, these logits in row $i$ are $\log[\pi_{i,j+1}/\pi_{ij}]$. The *cumulative logits* use the total probability to either side of a category; again in row $i$, $\log[(\pi_{i,j+1} + \cdots + \pi_{ij})/(\pi_{i1} + \cdots + \pi_{ij})]$. The cumulative logits mix linear and logarithmic parts and must ascend over the course of a row (see Agresti, 1989a for fitting procedures). Comparable odds ratios can be formed when both categories are ordered. A model for these logits is a model for the ordered table. How these models are interpreted depends on which type of logit was used. For example, a two-term model in which the logits depend separately on row and column parameters is logit $= \alpha_i + \beta_j$. With the local logits, this model is a constrained version of RC(1); with the cumulative logits it has the structure of a Rasch model.

## Marginal Distributions

The models described above are representations of the association between categorizations. Another class of models focuses on the marginal relationship in the multiway table created when several responses are recorded from each unit (e.g., subject). The analysis of a marginal model encounters difficulties of three types: first, the observations are not independent, so a measure-by-response table cannot be used; second, individuals usually vary, so the marginal distributions are overdispersed; third, marginal hypotheses do not determine the expected frequencies, making goodness-of-fit measures problematic (in fact, hypotheses about joint and marginal distributions are asymptotically separable; see Lang & Agresti, 1994). Special approaches are needed.

One approach uses the symmetry and quasi-symmetry models mentioned above. The former model implies identical marginal distributions and the latter does not. As the analysis of random effects shows, this comparison is appropriate when the observations vary on the same dimension and their characteristics do not interact with the observed units, in the manner of the Rasch model (Agresti, 1993a; Tjur, 1982).

When the categories do not have a unidimensional structure (i.e., quasi-symmetry does not hold), marginal homogeneity is still possible. Other techniques are needed. Three approaches are used. The older and more established procedure fits models by least-squares and tests them with Wald tests (Grizzle, Stamer & Koch, 1969; Koch et al, 1977; PROC CATMOD of SAS). However, although readily available, this methodology is less satisfactory than maximum-likelihood methods, particularly in small samples. The second approach models both joint and marginal distributions by fitting mixed linear and logarithmic models. A very broad class of models, including those for both joint and marginal effects, are subsumed in the general matrix form $\mathbf{C} \log \mathbf{A}\mu_y = \mathbf{X}\beta$ (Lang & Agresti, 1994; see Haber, 1985; Haber & Brown, 1986 for fitting methodology and Becker, 1994 for an application). The third approach derives from the biomedical work on variability effects discussed above. In much of this work, the important hypotheses refer to the margins (e.g., the status before and after a treatment), and the associations among the longitudinal measures are nuisance parameters.

---

Visit the *Annual Reviews home page* at
http://www.AnnualReviews.org.

---

*Literature Cited*

Agresti A. 1984. *Analysis of ordinal categorical data.* New York: Wiley

Agresti A. 1989a. Tutorial on modeling ordered categorical response data. *Psychol. Bull. 105,* 290–301

Agresti A. 1989b. A survey of models for repeated ordered categorical response data. *Statist. Med. 8,* 1209–24

Agresti A. 1990. *Categorical data analysis.* New York: Wiley

Agresti A. 1992. A survey of exact inference for contingency tables. *Statist. Sci. 7,* 131–177 (Includes discussion.)

Agresti A. 1993a. Computing conditional maximum likelihood estimates for generalized Rasch models using simple loglinear models with diagonals parameters. *Scand. J. Statist.,* 20, 63–71

Agresti A. 1993b. Distribution-free fitting of logit models with random effects for repeated categorical responses. *Statist. Med. 12*, 1969–87

Agresti A. 1995. Logit models and related quasi-symmetric log-linear models for comparing responses to similar items in a survey. *Sociol. Methods Res. 24*:68–95

Agresti A. 1996. *An Introduction to Categorical Data Analysis.* New York: Wiley

Agresti A. 1997. A model for repeated measurements of a multivariate binary response. *J. Am. Statist. Assoc. 92*:315–21

Agresti A, Wackerly D, Boyett, JM. 1979. Exact conditional tests for cross-classifications: approximations of attained significance levels. *Psychometrika 44*:75–83

Akaike H. 1973. Information theory and an extension of the maximum likelihood principle. In BN Petrov & F Csaki (Eds), *2nd International Symposium on Information Theory.* Budapest: Akademiai Kiado

Anderson CJ. 1996. The analysis of three-way contingency tables by three-mode association models. *Psychometrika 61*, 465–83

Ashby M, Neuhaus JM, Hauck WW, Bacchetti P, Heilbron DC, Jewell NP, Segal MR, Fusaro RE. 1992. An annotated bibliography of methods for analyzing correlated categorical data. *Statist. Med. 11*, 67–99

Baccini A, Caussinus H, de Falguerolles A. 1993. Analyzing dependence in large contingency tables: Dimensionality and patterns in scatter-plots. In CM Cuadras & CR Rao (Eds.), *Multivariate analysis: Future directions 2* (pp. 245–63). Amsterdam: North Holland

Baglivo J, Olivier D, Pagano M. 1992. Methods for exact goodness-of-fit tests. *J. Am. Statist. Assoc. 87*, 464–69

Baker SG, Laird NM. 1988. Regression analysis for categorical variables with outcome subject to nonignorable nonresponse. *J. Am. Statist. Assoc. 83*, 62–69

Batchelder WH, Riefer DM. 1986. Statistical analysis of a model for storage and retrieval processes in human memory. *Br. J. Math. Statist. Psychol. 39*, 129–49

Batchelder WH, Riefer DM. 1990. Multinomial processing models of source monitoring. *Psychol. Rev. 97*, 548–64

Becker MP. 1994. Analysis of cross-classifications of counts using models for marginal distributions: An application to trends in attitudes on legalized abortion. In PV Marsden ed., *Sociol. methodol.* (Vol. 24, pp. 229–65). Washington, DC: Am. Sociol. Assoc.

Becker MP, Clogg CC. 1989. Analysis of sets of two-way contingency tables using association models. *J. Am. Statist. Assoc. 84*, 142–51

Benzécri JP. 1992. *Correspondence analysis handbook* (TK Gopalan, Trans.). New York: Marcel Dekker

Bishop YMM, Fienberg SE, Holland PW. 1975. *Discrete multivariate analysis: Theory and practice.* Cambridge, MA: MIT Press

Camilli G. 1990. The test of homogeneity for $2 \times 2$ contingency tables: a review of and some personal opinions on the controversy. *Psychol. Bull., 108*, 135–45

Carlier A, Kroonenberg PM. 1996. Decompositions and biplots in three-way correspondence analysis. *Psychometrika, 61*, 355–73

Clogg CC. 1995. Latent class models. In G Arminger, CC Clogg & ME Sobel (Eds.), *Handbook of statistical modeling for the social and behavioral sciences* (pp. 311–59). New York: Plenum

Clogg CC, Eliason SR. 1987. Some common problems in log-linear analysis. *Sociol. Methods Res. 16*, 8–44

Clogg CC, Rudas T, Xi L. 1995. A new index of structure for the analysis of models for mobility tables and other cross-classifications. In PV Marsden (Ed.), *Sociol. methodol.* (Vol. 25, pp. 197–222). Washington, DC: Am. Sociol. Assoc

Clogg CC, Shihadeh ES. 1994. *Statistical models for ordinal variables.* Thousand Oaks, CA: SAGE Publications

Collett D. 1991. *Modelling binary data.* London: Chapman & Hall

Conaway MR. 1992. The analysis of repeated categorical measurements subject to nonignorable nonresponse. *J. Am. Statist. Assoc. 87*, 817–24

Cox DR, Wermuth N. 1993. Linear dependencies represented by chain graphs. *Statist. Sci. 8*, 204–18,269–77 (Includes discussion)

Cressie NAC, Read TRC. 1994. Multinomial goodness-of-fit tests. *J. Roy. Statist. Soc. B 46*, 440–64

Cressie NAC, Read TRC. 1989. Pearson's $X^2$ and the loglikelihood ratio statistic $G^2$: a comparative review. *Int. Statist. Rev. 57*, 19–43

de Falguerolles A, Jamel S, Whittaker J. 1995. Correspondence analysis and association models constrained by a conditional independence graph. *Psychometrika 60*, 161–80

de Leeuw J, van der Heijden PGM. 1988. Correspondence analysis of incomplete contingency tables. *Psychometrika 53*, 223–33

de Leeuw J, van der Heijden PGM. 1991 Reduced rank models for contingency tables. *Biometrika 78*, 229–32

Diggle PJ, Liang KY, Zeger SL. 1994. *Analysis*

*of longitudinal data.* Oxford: Clarendon

Eliason SR. 1995. Modeling manifest and latent dimensions of association in two-way cross-classifications. *Sociol. Methods Res. 24*, 30–67

Evans M, Gulula Z, Guttman I. 1993. Computational issues in the Bayesian analysis of categorical data: Log-linear and Goodman's RC model. *Statist. Sinica 3*, 391–406

Fitzmaurice GM, Laird NM, Zahner GEP. 1996. Multivariate logistic models for incomplete binary responses. *J. Am. Statist. Assoc. 91*, 99–108

Fowlkes EB, Freeny AE, Landwehr JM. 1988. Evaluating logistic models for large contingency tables. *J. Am. Statist. Assoc. 83*, 611–22

Friendly M. 1994. Mosaic displays for multiway contingency tables. *J. Am. Statist. Assoc. 89*, 190–200

Gifi A. 1990. *Non-linear multivariate analysis.* New York: Wiley

Gilula Z, Haberman SJ. 1986. Canonical analysis of contingency tables by maximum likelihood. *J. Am. Statist. Assoc. 81*, 780–88

Gilula Z, Haberman SJ. 1988. The analysis of multivariate contingency tables by restricted canonical and restricted association models. *J. Am. Statist. Assoc. 83*, 760–71

Gilula Z, Krieger AM, Ritov Y. 1988. Ordinal association in contingency tables: some interpretative aspects. *J. Am. Statist. Assoc. 83*, 540–45

Gilula Z, Ritov Y. 1990. Inferential ordinal correspondence analysis: motivation, derivation and limitations. *Int. Statist. Rev. 58*, 99–108

Goodman LA. 1970. The multivariate analysis of qualitative data: interactions among multiple classifications. *J. Am. Statist. Assoc. 65*, 226–56 (Included in Goodman, 1978.)

Goodman LA. 1972. Some multiplicative models for the analysis of cross-classified data. In L LeCam (Ed.), *Proceedings of the sixth Berkeley symposium on mathematical statistics and probability* (pp. 649–96). Berkeley, CA: University of California Press (Included in Goodman, 1984.)

Goodman LA. 1978. *Analyzing qualitative/categorical data: log-linear models and latent structure analysis.* Cambridge, MA: Abt Books (Contains contributions by James A. Davis and Jay Magidson)

Goodman LA. 1979. Simple models for the analysis of association in cross-classifications having ordered categories. *J. Am. Statist. Assoc. 74*, 537–52 (Included in Goodman, 1984.)

Goodman LA. 1981. Association models and the bivariate normal for contingency tables with ordered categories. *Biometrika 68*, 347–

55 (Included in Goodman, 1984.)

Goodman LA. 1984. *The analysis of cross-classified data having ordered categories.* Cambridge, MA: Harvard Univ. Press. (Includes contributions by Clifford C. Clogg.)

Goodman LA. 1986. Some useful extensions of the usual correspondence analysis approach and the usual log-linear models approach in the analysis of contingency tables. *Int. Statist. Rev. 54*, 243–309 (Includes discussion)

Goodman LA. 1987. New methods for analyzing the intrinsic character of qualitative variables using cross-classified data. *Am. J. Sociol. 93*, 529–83

Goodman LA. 1990. Total-score models and Rasch-type models for the analysis of a multidimensional contingency table, or a set of multidimensional contingency tables, with specified and/or unspecified order for response categories. In CC Clogg (Ed.), *Sociol. methodol.* (Vol. 20, pp. 249–94). Washington, DC: Am. Sociol. Assoc.

Goodman LA. 1991. Measures, models, and graphical displays in the analysis of cross-classified data. *J. Am. Statist. Assoc. 86*, 1085–1138 (Includes discussion)

Goodman LA. 1993. Correspondence analysis, association analysis, and generalized nonindependence analysis of contingency tables: saturated and unsaturated models, and appropriate graphical displays. In CM Cuadras & CR Rao (Eds.), *Multivariate analysis: Future directions 2* (pp. 265–94). Amsterdam: North Holland

Goodman LA. 1996. A single general method for the analysis of cross-classified data: recognition and synthesis of some methods of Pearson, Yule, and Fisher, and also some methods of correspondence analysis and association analysis. *J. Am. Statist. Assoc. 91*, 408–28

Goodman LA, Clogg CC. 1992. New methods for the analysis of occupational mobility tables and other kinds of cross-classifications. *Contemp. Sociol. 21*, 609–22

Gower JC, Hand DJ. 1996. *Biplots.* London: Chapman & Hall

Greenacre MJ. 1984. *Theory and applications of correspondence analysis.* London: Academic

Greenacre MJ. 1993a. Biplots in correspondence analysis. *J. Appl. Statist. 20*, 251–69

Greenacre MJ. 1993b. *Correspondence analysis in practice.* London: Academic

Greenacre MJ. 1993c. Multivariate generalizations of correspondence analysis. In CM Cuadras & CR Rao (Eds.), *Multivariate analysis: Future directions 2* (pp. 327–40). Amsterdam: North Holland

Greenacre MJ, Hastie T. 1987. The geometric interpretation of correspondence analysis. *J.*

*Am. Statist. Assoc. 82*, 437–47

Grizzle JE, Starmer CF, Koch GG. 1969. Analysis of categorical data by linear models. *Biometrics 25*, 489–504

Haber M. 1985. Maximum likelihood methods for linear and log-linear models in categorical data. *Comput. Statist. Data Anal. 3*, 1–10

Haber M. 1990. Comments on "the test of homogeneity for $2 \times 2$ contingency tables: a review of and some personal opinions on the controversy" by G. Camilli. *Psychol. Bull. 108*, 146–49

Haber M, Brown MB. 1986. Maximum likelihood methods for log-linear models when expected frequencies are subject to linear constraints. *J. Am. Statist. Assoc. 81*, 477–82

Haberman SJ. 1978. *Analysis of quantitative data, Vol. 1: introductory topics.* New York: Academic

Haberman SJ. 1979. *Analysis of quantitative data, Vol. 2: new developments.* New York: Academic

Haberman SJ. 1995. Computation of maximum likelihood estimates in association models. *J. Am. Statist. Assoc. 90*, 1438–46

Hu X, Batchelder WH. 1994. The statistical analysis of general processing tree models with the EM algorithm. *Psychometrika 59*, 21–47

Kass RE, Raftery AE. 1995. Bayes factors. *J. Am. Statist. Assoc. 90*, 773–95

Kim D, Agresti A. 1995. Improved exact inference about conditional association in three-way contingency tables. *J. Am. Statist. Assoc. 90*, 632–39

Koch GG, Landis JR, Freeman JL, Freeman DH, Jr., Lehnen RG. 1977. A general methodology for the analysis of experiments with repeated measurement of categorical data. *Biometrics 33*, 133–58

Koehler KJ. 1986. Goodness-of-fit tests for log-linear models in sparse contingency tables. *J. Am. Statist. Assoc. 81*, 483–93

Lang JB, Agresti A. 1994. Simultaneous modeling joint and marginal distributions of multivariate categorical responses. *J. Am. Statist. Assoc. 89*, 625–32

Lebart L, Morineau A, Warwick KM. 1984. *Multivariate descriptive statistical analysis: Correspondence analysis and related techniques for large matrices* (EM Berry, Trans.). New York: Wiley

Lee SY, Poon WY, Bentler PM. 1990. Full maximum-likelihood analysis of structural equation models with polytomous variables. *Statist. Probability Lett. 9*, 91–97

Lee SY, Poon WY, Bentler PM. 1992. Structural equation models with continuous and polytomous variables. *Psychometrika 57*, 89–105

Liang KY, McCullagh P. 1993. Case studies in binary dispersion. *Biometrics 49*, 623–30

Little RJA, Rubin DB. 1987. *Statistical analysis with missing data.* New York: Wiley

McCullagh P, Nelder JA. 1989. *Generalized linear models* (2 ed.). London: Chapman, Hall

Muthéen B. 1984. A general structural equation model with dichotomous, ordered categorical, and continuous latent variables. *Psychometrika 49*, 115–32

Nishisato S. 1980. *Analysis of categorical data: dual scaling and its applications.* Toronto: Univ. Toronto Press

Nishisato S. 1994. *Elements of dual scaling: An introduction to practical data analysis.* Hillsdale, NJ: Erlbaum

Park T, Brown MB. 1994. Models for categorical data with nonignorable nonresponse. *J. Am. Statist. Assoc. 89*, 44–52

Pendergast JF, Gange SJ, Newton MA, Lindstrom MJ, Palta M, Fisher MR. 1996. A survey of methods for analyzing clustered binary response data. *Int. Statist. Rev. 64*, 89–118

Raftery AE. 1995. Bayesian model selection in social research. In PV Marsden (Ed.), *Sociol. methodol.* (Vol. 25, pp. 111–95). Washington, DC: Am. Sociol. Assoc. (Includes discussion.)

Read TRC, Cressie NAC. 1988. *Goodness-of-fit statistics for discrete multivariate data.* New York: Springer-Verlag

Riefer DM, Batchelder WH. 1988. Multinomial modeling and the measurement of cognitive processes. *Psychol. Rev. 95*, 318–39

Rindskof D. 1990. Nonstandard log-linear models. *Psychol. Bull. 108*, 150–62

Ritov Y, Gilula Z. 1991. The order-restricted RC model for ordered contingency tables: estimation and testing for fit. *Ann. Statist. 19*, 2090–2101

Ritov Y, Gilula Z. 1993. Analysis of contingency tables by correspondence models subject to order constraints. *J. Am. Statist. Assoc. 88*, 1380–87

Rudas T, Clogg CC, Lindsay BG. 1994. A new index of fit based on mixture methods for the analysis of contingency tables. *J. Roy. Statist. Soc. B 56*, 623–39

Sakamoto Y. 1991. *Categorical data analysis by AIC.* Tokyo: KTK Scientific Publishers

Sakamoto Y, Ishiguro M, Kitagawa G. 1986. *Akaike information criterion statistics.* Tokyo: KTK Scientific Publishers

Spiegelhalter DJ, Smith AFM. 1982. Bayes factors for linear and log-linear models with vague prior information. *J. Roy. Statist. Soc. B 44*, 377–87

Tjur T. 1982. A connection between Rasch's item analysis model and a multiplicative Poisson model. *Scand. J. Statist. 9*, 23–30 van de Geer JP. 1993a. *Multivariate analysis of categorical data: theory.* Thousand Oaks, CA: SAGE Publications

van de Geer JP. 1993b. *Multivariate analysis of categorical data: applications.* Thousand Oaks, CA: SAGE Publications

van der Heijden PGM, de Falguerolles A, de Leeuw J. 1989. A combined approach to contingency table analysis using correspondence analysis and log-linear analysis. *Appl. Statist. 38,* 249–92 (Includes discussion.)

van der Heijden PGM, de Leeuw J. 1985. Correspondence analysis used complementary to loglinear analysis. *Psychometrika 50,* 429–47

van der Heijden PGM, Mooijaart A. 1995. Some new log-bilinear models for the analysis of asymmetry in a square contingency table. In PV Marsden (Ed.), *Sociol. methodol.* (Vol. 24, pp. 7–29). Washington, DC: Am. Sociol. Assoc

van der Heijden PGM, Worsley KJ. 1988. Comment on "correspondence analysis used complementary to loglinear analysis". *Psychometrika 53,* 287–91

von Eye A, Spiel C. 1996. Standard and nonstandard log-linear symmetry models for measuring changes in categorical variables. *Am. Statist. 50,* 300–5

Weakliem DL. 1992. Comparing non-nested models for contingency tables. In PV Marsden (Ed.), *Sociol. methodol.* (Vol. 22, pp. 147–78). Washington, DC: Am. Sociol. Assoc

Whittaker J. 1990. *Graphical models in applied multivariate statistics.* Chichester: Wiley

Wickens TD. 1989. *Multiway contingency tables analysis for the social sciences.* Hillsdale, NJ: Erlbaum

Wickens TD. 1993. Analysis of contingency tables with between-subject variability. *Psychol. Bull. 113,* 191–204

Williamson GD, Haber M. 1994. Models for three-dimensional contingency tables with completely and partially cross-classified data. *Biometrics 49,* 194–203

Winship C, Mare RD. 1989. Loglinear models with missing data: a latent class approach. In CC Clogg (Ed.), *Sociol. methodol.* (Vol. 19, pp. 331–67). Washington, DC: Am. Sociol. Assoc.

Xi L, Lindsay BG. 1996. A note on calculating the $\pi^*$ index of fit for the analysis of contingency tables. *Sociol. Methods Res. 25,* 248–59

Yamaguchi K. 1990. Some models for the analysis of asymmetric association in square contingency tables with ordered categories. In CC Clogg (Ed.), *Sociol. methodol.* (Vol. 20, 181–212). Washington, DC: Am. Sociol. Assoc.

Zelterman D, Chan ISF, Mielke PJ, Jr. 1995. Exact tests of significance in higher dimensional tables. *Am. Statist. 49,* 357–61

*Annu. Rev. Psychol. 1998. 49:559–84*

# THEORIES LINKING CULTURE AND PSYCHOLOGY: Universal and Community-Specific Processes

*Catherine R. Cooper and Jill Denner*

Department of Psychology, University of California at Santa Cruz, Santa Cruz, California 95064; e-mail: ccooper@cats.ucsc.edu

KEY WORDS: culture, theory, identity, education, immigration, diversity

## ABSTRACT

Psychological theories and research often assume nations are culturally homogeneous and stable. But global demographic, political, and economic changes and massive immigration have sparked new scholarly and policy interest in cultural diversity and change within nations. This chapter reviews interdisciplinary advances linking culture and psychological development. These challenge and strengthen the external and ecological validity of psychological theories and their applications. Seven theoretical perspectives are reviewed: individualism-collectivism; ecological systems; cultural-ecological; social identity; ecocultural and sociocultural; structure-agency; and multiple worlds. Reviews of each theory summarize key constructs and evidence, recent advances, links between universal and community-specific research and applications, and strengths and limitations. The chapter traces complementarities across theories for the case of personal and social identity. It concludes by discussing implications for science and policy. By viewing theories as distinct yet complementary, researchers and policy makers can forge interdisciplinary, international, and intergenerational collaborations on behalf of the culturally diverse communities of which we are a part.

# CONTENTS

0066-4308/98/0201-0559$08.00

# INTRODUCTION

The concept of culture has come to the forefront of social science and social policy to address issues of human diversity in psychological processes and performance. Debates about the role of culture in psychological processes have sparked a movement towards research that is directly applicable to social problems. A key challenge lies in how to reconcile community-specific applications with broader theories that guide research.

This is a timely debate for reasons both within and outside the field of psychology. In anthropology, definitions of culture have long been disputed. Although themes of shared values, beliefs, and behaviors that are transmitted through generations are common, some scholars emphasize cognitive orientations to ideas, beliefs, and knowledge; others focus on materialist orientations to technological and environmental features; and others concentrate on behavioral orientations or on moral themes. Anthropologists also increasingly probe the disputed aspects of culture between ethnic groups or nation-states rather than values held in common.

Demographers have since ancient times mapped variation within nation-states by asking adults to identify the country of birth, race, ethnicity, language, income, gender, age, education, and occupation of each member of their household. These responses, analyzed according to political and geographical units such as census tracts, cities, states, or provinces, form the basis for policy decisions regarding the allocation of resources; practical decisions about what is done in daily life in families, schools, and workplaces; and scientific decisions involving the generality or representativeness of studies based, inevitably, on samples rather than entire populations. Historical studies of changing census categories and current debates on a "multiracial" category for the US census illustrate the changing and interacting links among political, practical, and scientific bases of demographic indicators of variation within multicultural societies.

Although psychologists typically conceptualize diversity within nations in terms of demographic variables, they often treat such variables categorically as quasi-independent variables to assess differences between groups. Problems can then arise when scholars view any one variable as a superordinate "package" of other dimensions and interpret that variable as not only descriptive but also explanatory (Whiting 1976). Interpreting racial or ethnic-group differences as minority-group deficits is an inherent risk of such designs, particularly when only two groups are compared (Cooper et al 1998, García Coll et al 1997, McLoyd 1991).

Views of cultures as static and/or stable have been disrupted by global demographic, economic, and political changes and growing economic disparities between rich and poor. These massive changes have sparked fresh debate about cultural change, diversity, and equity among intellectual and political leaders who once viewed their nations as stable, homogeneous, and just. Policies such as the US Civil Rights Act of 1964 and the Japanese Equal Employment Opportunity Law of 1985 are examples of changes that acknowledge diversity by increasing access to educational and occupational mobility.

Recent waves of immigration, however, now pose a fresh challenge to the democratic ideals of tolerating diversity while enhancing equal access to education. In many nations, immigrant families—both relatively impoverished families and families from relatively impoverished countries (Daniels 1990; Hurrelman 1994)—have arrived in great numbers, seeking better lives for their children. For these families, free public schools are the "hills of gold." Yet despite their dreams, as immigrant youth move through schools, their numbers shrink, making them expensive social dilemmas rather than economic and social assets. Educational disparity, once seen as an issue between Black and "white" populations, is now understood as one of cultural pluralism and inclusion, involving in some communities over 100 different linguistic groups. Their sheer numbers challenge local practices and government policies stating that schools should provide acculturation for immigrants, liberal education, and preparation for work and citizenship in democracies.

Consequently, worldwide social changes are stimulating psychologists, demographers, sociologists, anthropologists, and other social scientists to rethink issues of cultural diversity both within and across national boundaries. Of course, there is precedent for social scientists to consider as valid what appear to be incompatible models of the same phenomena. Globalization has led to increased awareness of differences and similarities both within and across cultures and a search for new models of culture. In the physical sciences, compelling empirical evidence supports the validity of viewing electrons as both particles and waves. Similarly, social scientists in multicultural nations increasingly view culture as both stable and dynamic, shared by groups and disputed within and across borders, and operating at multiple levels of analysis.

Nonetheless, enduring tensions between cultural diversity and national unity fuel ongoing debate among scientists as well as politicians, families, educators, and youth (Cooper et al 1995, Spindler 1990). To address these issues of linking culture and psychology, this chapter examines development in multicultural nations. For example, identity development involves personal exploration in domains such as ethnicity, occupation, gender role, political ideology, and religious beliefs (Erikson 1968, Grotevant & Cooper 1985, 1998); social negotiations in close relationships with families, peers, and others (Archer 1992, Heath & McLaughlin 1993); and collective processes of categorization and recategorization of group memberships (Brewer 1991, Root 1992). In addition, societal, institutional, and intergenerational changes point to mechanisms affecting individual development. Societal changes, such as new laws regulating eligibility for citizenship or university entrance, can affect how youth develop national or international identities (Denner et al 1997, Goodman 1990). Institutional changes, such as schools' offering new bilingual algebra classes, can foster occupational development (Chisholm et al 1990, Kroger 1993). Intergenerational changes, such as when elders tell old stories while youth learn to ask about them, can foster academic, family, religious, or ethnic identity development (Cooper 1994; Mehan et al 1994, 1996). Presentation of these theories in one place may help us find new ways of linking universal and community-specific perspectives on culture and psychology.

## Two Dilemmas in Linking Cultural-Universal and Community-Specific Perspectives

The resurgence of scholarly and policy debates regarding cultural diversity has also renewed the classic universalism-relativism debate: how to build scientific generalizations while trying to understand diversity, variation, and change in human beliefs and behaviors. Variations across cultural communities are rooted in complex histories and interpretations of intergroup relations and varying access to education, employment, and other opportunities. Yet, attending to the unique histories within each community challenges fundamental goals of science to build theories that describe and predict human development as well as explain and enhance life conditions across a range of communities.

Thus scholars and policy makers seeking to link universal and community-specific perspectives face the classic dilemma of scientific goals conflicting with research application. A traditional scientific goal is to challenge and strengthen existing theoretical models, both their assumptions of universality and their claims of descriptive, predictive, and explanatory adequacy. A second goal is to understand and explain existing variation in performance or responses to opportunities among individuals who vary in country of origin, race, ethnicity, gender, and other characteristics. In the application of research findings, the goal is often to be context- or community-specific, incorporating the history and current issues of each social group, thereby regarding generalization beyond that community as less relevant or even inappropriate (Phinney & Landin 1998).

This chapter traces classic dilemmas in linking cultural-universal and community-specific goals across seven models of culture and psychological processes. In doing so, we make two arguments. We argue, first, that bringing concepts of culture into psychological theories is an abstract, disputed, and inherently unresolvable process, yet that doing so is crucial to both social science and policy in multicultural societies, particularly democracies. Second, we argue that explicit interdisciplinary, international, and intergenerational discussions of culture and psychological processes—addressing issues of theories and application—advance global, national, and local goals.

This chapter is written to promote such a discussion of these issues. By showing how bringing concepts of culture into psychology enhances the underlying goals of the field, it seeks to challenge and strengthen the validity of theories and their application. The seven theoretical models of psychological functioning in culturally diverse societies we discuss are: individualism-collectivism theories (Markus & Kitayama 1991; Triandis et al 1995, Triandis 1996); ecological systems theories (Bronfenbrenner 1979, Sameroff 1995); cultural-ecological theory (Gibson & Bhachu 1991, Ogbu 1991); social identity theories (Berry 1993, Brewer 1995, Tajfel 1978); ecocultural and sociocultural theories (Rogoff 1990, 1991; Shweder 1996; Tharp & Gallimore 1988); theories of structure and agency (Bourdieu & Passeron 1977, Coleman 1988, Mehan 1992); and multiple-worlds theories (Cooper et al 1995, Cooper 1998, Phelan et al 1991).

The review of each model addresses its research goals and philosophies of application by summarizing key theoretical constructs and evidence, recent conceptual and empirical advances, emerging links between cultural-universal and community-specific theories and applications, and the strengths and limitations of the theory. For each model, the examples cited are chosen to represent cultural, interdisciplinary, international, and intergenerational breadth and collaboration. The chapter summary considers potential complementarities across models and concludes by discussing implications of these advances for science and policy in culturally diverse nations. We caution readers that the seven theoretical perspectives are actually sets of theories that combine divergent and sometimes disputed viewpoints keenly felt by insiders.

# SEVEN THEORIES OF CULTURE AND PSYCHOLOGICAL PROCESSES WITHIN NATIONS

## Culture as Core Societal Values: Individualism-Collectivism Theories

THEORY AND EVIDENCE    Harry Triandis, Hazel Markus, and Shinobo Kita-yama, all social psychologists, bring culture into psychology by arguing that shared values of social groups play key roles in individuals' cognitive, emotional, and social functioning. Triandis and his colleagues distinguish groups on the basis of individualist and collectivist values and distinguish individuals on the basis of allocentrism and idiocentrism (1988, 1996). Triandis defined these as multidimensional "cultural syndromes," seen in "shared attitudes, beliefs, norms, role and self definitions, and values of members of each culture organized around a theme" (1996, p. 407). To assess these syndromes, Triandis (1996) developed questionnaires composed of items "to which 90% of each sample responded on the same side of a neutral point and those to which 90% of triads agreed, with shorter times to reach agreement interpreted as reflecting a greater likelihood that an item reflects a cultural syndrome" (1996, p. 407). This method illustrates the focus of individualism-collectivism theories on locating shared beliefs within groups and differences in beliefs between groups.

In a related effort to build a universal theory to explain community-specific differences, Markus & Kitayama (1991, Kitayama & Markus 1995) proposed a "collective constructionist" model of independence-interdependence. They argue that "core cultural ideas" can be seen in "key ideological and philosophical texts and institutions at the collective level." These foster "cultural shaping of psychological reality" thereby affecting "customs, norms, practices and institutions" (Kitayama et al 1993, p. 4). Markus & Kitayama argued that American culture emphasizes the core cultural idea of independence by valuing attending to oneself and discovering and expressing individual qualities "while neither assuming nor valuing overt connectedness." These values are reflected in educational and legal systems, employment and caretaking practices, and individual cognition, emotion, and motivation. In contrast, they argue that Asian cultures emphasize interdependence by valuing the self and individuality as part of social context, connections among persons, and attending to and harmoniously coordinating with others. When Kitayama et al (1993) asked 65 middle-class Caucasian American and 90 Japanese students (whose social class and race/ethnicity were reported) attending the same Oregon university to list situations in which their feelings of self-esteem (*jisonshin* in Japanese, meaning a feeling of self-respect) would either increase or decrease, the American students focused more on self-enhancement than the Japanese students, who showed more self-deprecation.

RECENT ADVANCES    Recent scholarly work traces both continuity and change within cultural groups in the values of interdependence and independence, particularly in Japan, China, Mexico, and other countries with collectivist traditions. For example, traditional developmental goals in Japan portray the ideal adolescent as *otonashi*—reserved, modest, and reflective—and *omoiyari*—understanding others' needs without needing to communicate verbally (Gjerde et al 1995). Research on the socialization of these qualities often focuses on mother-child relationships and portrays ties between fathers and children as more remote, because of fathers' great involvement in work (Azuma 1994; Gjerde et al 1995). Recent research, however, documents social change in Japanese norms of independence and interdependence. Fathers in urban families are becoming increasingly involved in child care and joint family decision making, especially when wives are employed, as 60% of Japanese women are (Gjerde et al 1995). Thus, scientific work based on ideals of culture as core societal values can reflect both continuity and change in community-specific expectations for men, women, and children.

LINKING UNIVERSAL AND COMMUNITY-SPECIFIC RESEARCH AND APPLICATIONS    How do universal theories apply to specific groups? When scholars use universal theories and norms of health, success, and competence, differences across diverse groups can be interpreted as deficits. For example, some scholars hold that individual achievement by children and adults is hampered by collectivist or agrarian values of immigrant or ethnic minority families. However, psychological evidence does not support this view. Valenzuela & Dornbusch (1994) assessed the relation between familistic values and school achievement in a questionnaire study of 2666 Northern California high school students of Anglo origin and 492 students of Mexican origin. Behavioral, attitudinal, and structural dimensions of familism were positively related to grades in the Mexican-origin sample, provided parents had completed at least 12 years of schooling. These findings challenge the view that school achievement is hampered by collectivist values; if anything, they indicate that collectivism may enhance school performance. This research points to the need for more intensive study of the interplay of values, parental education, and family process.

Greenfield & Cocking (1993, 1994) convened an international and interdisciplinary group of scholars to assess the descriptive and explanatory adequacy of individualism-collectivism theories, originally developed to describe ancestral traditions of Africa, Asia, and indigenous America, for their relevance to the experiences of immigrant families (see Harrison et al 1990). Scholars traced variation and change in collectivist values in "sending" and "receiving" countries. For example, while Ho (1994) analyzed variation in patterns of socialization among "Confucian heritage" cultures, and Uribe et al (1994) traced change in a Mexican community, Schneider et al (1994) and Delgado-Gaitan (1994) revealed continuities and changes among Japanese American and Mexican American immigrant families. This work illuminates diversity in cultural values within nations in terms of competence rather than deviance.

Studies of variation in individualism and collectivism within cultural communities have also contributed to moving beyond deficit interpretations of either quality. Recent examples address strengths as well as challenges for families of African descent (Gibbs 1996, McAdoo 1988), Chinese descent (Chao 1997, Lin & Fu 1990), Latino or Hispanic descent (Hurtado et al 1993, Zambrana 1995), and European descent (Eckert 1989). Examining variation within groups can be combined with tracing both similarities and differences across groups, in what Sue & Sue (1987) have called "parallel designs." These combine the benefits of external and ecological validity (Azmitia et al 1996; Cooper et al 1993, 1998).

Thus, the strengths of individualism-collectivism theories lie in their challenge to psychological theories of individuals and groups that assume universality and their evidence of culture-specific meanings in universal processes involving the self, emotion, and cognition. Their limitations stem from their emphasizing differences between societies, thus portraying cultural communities as holding mutually exclusive, stable, and uniform views. However, recent work with this model examines variation and change among individuals within each group and similarities across groups, particularly in culturally diverse societies experiencing high rates of immigration. Although the United States may be unusual in its focus on individualism and the size of its continuing waves of immigrants from traditionally collectivist societies, social scientists from many nations are rethinking individuality and community.

## Culture as Context: Ecological Systems Theories

THEORY AND EVIDENCE    The developmental psychologist Urie Bronfenbrenner proposed what he called an "ecological systems model" of psychological development: an evolving systemic process of interaction between the human organism and the environment. Persons are nested within their immediate social and material setting or microsystem, within linkages across settings or mesosystems, and interacting with more distal exosystems and macrosystems, all seen across historical time (chronosystems) (1989, 1993, 1995). In this model, culture is defined as societal customs and values and lies among the distal properties of the exosystem (for other developmental systems perspectives, see Sameroff 1995).

RECENT ADVANCES    Although ecological systems researchers do not locate culture as an explicit property of the individual person, some see culture in the meanings people derive or construct from their experiences across contexts—how they make sense of their worlds. Social and physical contexts can be seen as settings of safety or violence and of opportunity or risk for children's development. Garbarino et al (1991), arguing that all children and adults try to make sense of their lives and need love and acceptance, advocate respect for a range of strategies parents may use to raise competent children, but say general standards are part of universal explanations for behavior and coping. Gabarino et al (1991) interviewed children and families in several countries and found that adult support for dealing with stress and offering positive options was key to helping children cope with war trauma.

Transitions across contexts are an expanding area of work in ecological systems theory. As children and youth move beyond their families into the worlds of peers and communities, their life choices and identities may differ as a function of their perceptions of opportunities and risks. For example, in Burton et al's (1996) ethnographic and intergenerational studies of low-income African American youth living in urban neighborhoods, a sense of high risk of early death was linked to teenage childbearing.

Newman (1996) reported how competent African American youth living in Harlem (New York City), where unemployment is high, commuted between local friendships (with their alienated peers) and jobs in distal neighborhoods. Similarly, Allen et al (1996) examined the links between neighborhoods, families, and schools and adolescents' ethnic and racial identity; and Eccles et al (1993) probed how transitions between experiences in elementary and middle school often undermine a sense of "fit" in adolescents' family- and school-based expectations for autonomy and control.

LINKING UNIVERSAL AND COMMUNITY-SPECIFIC RESEARCH AND APPLICATIONS    Ecological systems research has contributed to both theory and application based on understanding how children and adults create meaning in their lives. For example, Garbarino & Stott (1989) detail the use of interviews in child abuse cases, custody disputes, and medical settings to help them communicate about stressful experiences and help adults interpret what children say. To conduct such culturally sensitive inquiry, children's drawings are also used in both research and clinical settings and in communities experiencing violence (Lewis & Osofsky 1997).

Bronfenbrenner developed his model to address the lack of attention to context in psychological theories, and argued against the false dichotomy between basic and applied research. While setting "social address" or demographic categories in the background, Bronfenbrenner differentiated societal, institutional, social, and physical levels of analysis, all viewed across time. The strength of this work lies in its revealing how perceptions and interactions in relationships and in settings such as poverty neighborhoods or child care can make a difference for children's well-being (Duncan 1991). Limitations of ecological systems theories were addressed by Goodnow (1994), who observed that metaphors of nested contexts do not foster analyses of children's interactions with peers, schools, communities, or cultures that do not come through their parents (increasingly likely as adolescence begins) or how families, schools, or cultures themselves change. These remarks are echoed in Taylor &Wang's (1997) call for bringing ecological theory and culture together.

## Culture as Caste: Cultural-Ecological Theories of Adaptation in Stratified Societies

THEORY AND EVIDENCE    The cultural anthropologist John Ogbu (1990, 1993, 1995) developed a theoretical alternative to universal models of child rearing and competence based on studies of European American middle-class children. Such models, Ogbu argued, tend to explain the widespread school failure of minority children in terms either of cultural deficiencies in their early family experiences or of their genetic inferiority. In response to such deficit-oriented accounts, Ogbu proposed his cultural-ecological theory, in which individual competence is defined not in universal terms but within the cultural and historical contexts in which children develop. For example, according to Ogbu, inner-city Black children have had academic difficulties not because of their oral ancestral culture (as opposed to traditions of literacy) but because they typically live in conditions of inequitable access to educational opportunities. This can be seen in urban areas, where schools often lack classes required for university entrance, while schools in upper-income suburbs of the same city offer ample college-preparatory classes. Ogbu argued that under such historical, cultural, and ecological conditions, a sequence of events occurs: Inner-city families initially aspire toward school success for their children, but as they become aware of barriers to educational and occupational opportunities they develop bleak perceptions of their children's future opportunities. The children themselves can develop oppositional identities, which affirm peer group solidarity while defending against failure in mainstream schools and jobs.

Ogbu drew his original evidence for this model from an ethnographic study combining participant observation; interviews of children, parents, and teachers; and analyses of school records and other documents (1990). Ogbu traced the history of racial stratification in the school system of Stockton, California. The original public school system (1863–1869) had barred Black and American Indian children from attending school with "white" children. Later patterns of residential segregation reinforced the prior patterns of school segregation. Ogbu documented that among a sample of 17 Black and Mexican American children who received the average grade of C (where A is the top grade and

F is failing) at the end of first grade in 1964–1965, all but one continued receiving Cs through grade six. Ogbu interpreted this pattern as not differentiating children's performance over time, thereby denying them opportunities to experience rewards for their educational accomplishments. In an extension of this model, Fordham (1988, Fordham & Ogbu 1986) conducted an ethnographic study of African American high school youth in Washington, DC. To cope with the stresses of being successful amid a peer group facing limited opportunities, some Black high school students reported downplaying their racial identity or hiding their academic success by acting as "class clown."

RECENT ADVANCES   Key advances in cultural-ecological theory involve tracing variation within ethnic minority groups, and similarity across groups, in stress and in coping with barriers to educational mobility, and probing under what conditions youth develop school identities or oppositional identities. Ford & Harris (1996) compared the views of 148 fifth and sixth grade Black youth programs for gifted, above-average, and average students in Virginia, measuring their support for achievement ideology, the importance they placed on school, and their level of effort in school. Students in the gifted program were most supportive of the achievement ideology and students in the average program were least supportive.

In related ethnographic work, Gibson investigated "accommodation without assimilation" in northern California among academically successful Punjabi Sikh (1988) and Mexican immigrant youth (1995). Many students who were optimistic about their own prospects were found to be aware of their peers' limited opportunities. Similarly, Matute-Bianchi (1991) studied how students' peer affiliations, including their involvement in school student organizations, revealed patterns of "situational ethnicity" and links to school performance among immigrant and nonimmigrant students of Mexican descent in central California.

LINKING UNIVERSAL AND COMMUNITY-SPECIFIC RESEARCH AND APPLICATIONS   Gibson & Ogbu (1991) edited a volume of comparative case studies of immigrant and indigenous minority youth and schooling. Examples include a paper by Inglis & Manderson on Turkish immigrants in Australia; Shimahara's analysis of the Burakumin, a stigmatized ethnic minority group in Japan; Barrington's account of the experiences of the indigenous Maori community in New Zealand; and Kramer's work on the Ute Indian tribe in the United States. In addition, Gibson & Ogbu's volume allows for the comparison of the experiences of immigrants from the same sending country in different receiving countries, as illustrated by Gibson's comparison of Sikh communities in the United States and Great Britain. These comparative case studies link "emic" or community-specific meanings, based on ethnographic interviews and observations, with "etic" or universal perspectives, including survey, achievement, and demographic data. This classic anthropological approach holds promise for psychological research.

In sum, the cultural anthropologists Ogbu, Gibson, and their colleagues have examined the psychological consequences of differences in social position and in children's and families' adaptations to inequalities in access to education and employment in and across a range of nations. The strength of their work stems from its explicitly addressing inequalities in access or performance and speaking to the experiences of specific communities. Cultural-ecological theorists view as universal the psychological processes of setting educational aspirations and goals, assessing future prospects for attaining these goals, and seeking group identity. However, they view minority families' development of pessimism and hopelessness and their children's development of oppositional identity in reaction to racial and class stratification as community specific. The limitation of this approach appears in its placing less emphasis on variation and change within communities, particularly the experiences of upwardly mobile ethnic minority families and children.

## Culture as Intergroup Relations: Social Identity Theories

THEORY AND EVIDENCE    According to social identity theorists John Berry (1993), Marilynn Brewer (1995), and Henri Tajfel (1978), members of all societies engage in social categorization and recategorization. Tajfel stated that social identity is constructed in the context of attitudes toward one's group, and is related to prejudice, intergroup conflict, culture, and acculturation. Brewer (1991) demonstrated that individuals' motivation to claim and express their social identities "depends on the competing needs for inclusiveness and uniqueness, whereby people seek an optimal level of distinctiveness" (Ethier & Deaux 1994, p. 243) in choosing a group. Situational cues can shift the salience of an identity, but individuals also see themselves and others in consistent terms and create situations that support these views. Although studies of social identity have typically used artificial social groups such as college students brought together in short-term laboratory situations, normal transitions through the life that affect social identities and self definition can, in turn, affect how individuals adapt to changing environmental opportunities and threats (Ruble 1994).

RECENT ADVANCES    Ethnic identity is one domain of personal and group identity that changes across context through the life span (Rumbaut 1994, Waters 1994). To test the social identity perspective regarding how individuals maintain their social identities across transitions and in response to threat, Ethier & Deaux (1994) conducted a longitudinal study of ethnic identity among Hispanic college students, who were interviewed three times during their first year at universities with predominantly European American student bodies. Combining qualitative and quantitative methods, Ethier & Deaux asked students to name their important identities, providing examples such as age, gender, relationships, and race or ethnicity, as well as to complete standardized survey measures of collective self-esteem. Two developmental pathways emerged that supported social identity theory: Students who began college with a strong Hispanic identity, as indicated by their language, generation of immigration, and ties to family and peers, were more likely to affiliate with ethnic student organizations and to report a positive personal and group identity. In contrast, students who came to college with a weak sense of ethnic identity were less likely to affiliate with ethnic student organizations and more likely to respond to threat with negative emotions and negative self-esteem. In a related vein, Hurtado & García (1994) and Banks (1988, 1989) have conducted work linking social identity to achievement and feelings of efficacy.

LINKING UNIVERSAL AND COMMUNITY-SPECIFIC RESEARCH AND APPLICATIONS   Research designs that compare members of majority or mainstream groups can create norms based on mainstream middle-class experience (McLoyd 1991). These can lead to interpreting differences between groups in terms of deficits from the referent group or mainstream and to viewing minority youth and families in terms of negative stereotypes. In the United States, for example, Spindler (1990) has argued that the referent group consists of upper-middle-class Protestant males of Northern European origins—as reflected in the membership of legislative, executive, and judicial systems. He also argues that members of a referent group may not view themselves as having ethnicity; only other groups are marked by ethnicity. The focus of government funding on research and policies involving ethnic minority youth and problems of crime, drug use, and pregnancy reinforce the links from ethnicity or cultural diversity to high-risk status rather than to competence (Spencer & Dornbusch 1990).

Phinney (1996) criticized using demographic categories pertaining to ethnicity as causal explanations of psychological functioning and argued for using psychological dimensions such as cultural norms and values; the strength, salience, and meaning of ethnic identity; and the experiences and attitudes associated with minority status within and between groups. In such a study of the meanings of ethnic identity, Berry (1993) built on Tajfel's (1978) distinction between *criterial attributes*, which are based on discrete categories or define boundaries for inclusion or exclusion, and *correlated (dimensional) attributes*, which are continuous and indicate how much of a certain quality is present. Berry asked 661 English Canadian and 398 French Canadien respondents to sort cards bearing names of ethnocultural groups. Multidimensional scaling analysis revealed that identity based on criterial attributes was unstable while identity based on dimensional attributes was stable.

In sum, social-identity theorists have linked group- and individual-level definitions of self and context and have made important contributions with laboratory and field studies. Their more recent work points to an important new direction: toward tracing the mechanisms of change and stability over time and place. The work of Ruble (1994) and Tropp (1996) is also building promising bridges between social and developmental psychology.

## Culture as Universally Adaptive Tools: Ecocultural and Sociocultural Theories

THEORY AND EVIDENCE    Ecocultural theory, an integration of ecological and cultural perspectives, is based on the universalist assumption that all families seek to make meaningful accommodations to their ecological niches through sustainable routines of daily living (Gallimore et al 1993, Tharp & Gallimore 1988, Weisner et al 1988). These routines, known as activity settings, have been examined in terms of interdependent dimensions, including who participates in daily activities, known as personnel; the salient goals, values, and beliefs that underlie and organize these activities; and the recurring patterns of social interaction, or scripts. Beatrice Whiting (1976) first challenged scholars to "unpackage" static categories related to culture in order to understand their multiple dimensions and to separate child-rearing practices and behaviors from material aspects of culture. She saw "ecology, economics, and social and political organizations as setting the parameters for the behavior of the agents of child rearing [and] child behavior as an index of child personality and adult behavior and beliefs and values as indices of adult personality" (Whiting 1963, p. 5).

From this perspective, Harkness et al (1992) developed the concept of the *developmental niche* to examine cultural structuring of child development through the everyday physical and social settings in which children live, community customs of child care and child rearing, and the psychology of caretakers. Harkness et al drew their evidence from ethnographic work in a range of communities, including a farming community in Kenya and a suburban community near Boston, Massachusetts. They examined questions of universality and cultural variation in mothers' and children's expression of emotion and began to delineate the interrelationships among culture, parental behavior, and children's developmental outcomes.

RECENT ADVANCES    Rogoff et al (1993) investigated young children's experiences in *guided participation* in four cultural communities: San Pedro, a Mayan Indian town in Guatemala; Salt Lake City, Utah, a middle-class urban community in the United States; Dhol-Ki-Patti, a tribal village in India; and Keçiören, a middle-class urban neighborhood in Turkey. Studying 14 toddlers and their families in each community, Rogoff et al combined ethnographic description of everyday activities and more conventional procedures taken into everyday contexts—e.g. presenting a novel toy and videotaping in the homes and later coding and comparing across groups. Commonalities across the four communities emerged in that adults structured teaching, but in Salt Lake City and Keçiören, toddlers were more segregated from adult activities, and in Dhol-ki-Patti and San Pedro, how toddlers learned by watching and participating in adult activities with caregivers' support.

LINKING UNIVERSAL AND COMMUNITY-SPECIFIC RESEARCH AND APPLICATIONS  Ecocultural researchers move beyond demographic categories in defining cultural groups as communities. For example, Shweder (1996) has argued for the use of ethnographic methods to identify moral communities, whose members share values; such moral communities are embedded in all complex societies. Shweder et al drew from their study of moral, emotional, and personality functioning and development in the Hindu temple town of Orissa, India (1995). In their work on what they term cultural psychology, Shweder et al have sought to build a universal psychological theory consistent with evidence from diverse cultural communities by reconceptualizing fundamental problems in psychology so cultural variability is central. To allow for "universalism without the uniformity," in which basic constructs encompass both universality and cultural variability, Shweder et al contend that each person holds a similarly heterogeneous collection of concept and psychological processes, which are activated differentially across history and culture, thereby enabling humans to understand one another.

Jessor et al (1996) convened an interdisciplinary group, including sociocultural researchers, to consider the relationships between ethnography and human development. Participating scholars reported investigations of individual meaning systems over time, including contradictions and differences as well as convergences in meanings. Ethnographic approaches, including observing behavior and interactions in their immediate and historical contexts, are relevant to particular communities and allow investigators "to make sure ideas and concepts exhibited when informants talk to researchers also occur spontaneously with one another" (Shweder 1996, p. 40). Analysis of field notes based on observations allows integrating personal, relational, and institutional aspects of what are typically thought of as constructs found in the individual.

Thus, the strength of ecocultural and sociocultural theories lies in their having linked universal and community-specific research goals; they focus on individual, interpersonal, and institutional processes considered universal (Cole 1996, Goodnow et al 1995, Penuel & Wertsch 1995). Culture-specific content, including values, practices, roles, and modes of communication as well as the material circumstances of living, presume potential relativism in defining valued qualities of group members as well as community-specific adaptations to particular ecological niches. A potential limitation of this approach was articulated by Damon (1996), who challenged the moral relativism of ethnographic and community-specific theorists to define not only communities but also moral outcomes.

## Culture as Capital: Theories of Structure, Agency, and Social Capital

THEORY AND EVIDENCE   Social capital refers to the relationships and networks from which individuals are able to derive institutional support. According to sociologist Pierre Bourdieu (Bourdieu & Passeron 1977), social capital is cumulative, leads to benefits in the social world, can be converted into other forms of capital, and can be reproduced in the same or expanded form (Stanton-Salazar et al 1996). Both Bourdieu and John Coleman, also a sociologist, saw social capital as rooted in the family, with networks among elite families benefiting their children through links to college and occupational status (Coleman 1988).

What role does schooling play in creating social capital? Mehan (1992) critiqued the "cultural reproduction" theory outlined above as overly deterministic, asserting that it emphasizes structural constraints while ignoring the potential roles played by the social organization of school practices and by individual actions. According to Mehan, ethnographic studies in the interpretive tradition help account for social inequality: Cultural elements, human agency, and schooling have revealed "reflexive relations between institutional practices and students' careers. Schools are composed of processes and practices that respond to competing demands and often unwittingly contribute to inequality, while social actors become active sense-makers choosing among alternatives in often contradictory circumstances" (Mehan 1992, p. 1).

RECENT ADVANCES   The structure-agency theories of Bourdieu and of Coleman have sparked research on creating cultural and social capital. Work has been done toward developing interventions among culturally diverse youth that enhance their access to educational opportunities (Heath & McLaughlin 1993) and that trace change within nations in youth's experiences of agency, communion, and academic mobililty (Gándara 1995, Gándara & Osugi 1994).

Can low-income families be sources of cultural capital? Moll & Gonzalez (1994) described how children from low-income Mexican immigrant families bring to school the cultural knowledge and information from their households and neighborhoods used by community members to succeed in everyday life, as well as community-based knowledge that can be used by teachers and other agents. This validates the importance of such knowledge and builds respect for diversity. It also enhances institutionally based skills such as how to operate in bureaucracies and engage the help of adults. Immigrant, working-class, and minority children may come to school with cultural resources and as competent decoders in cultural domains that do not necessarily include the school (Moll et al 1991).

LINKING UNIVERSAL AND COMMUNITY-SPECIFIC RESEARCH AND APPLICATIONS    Like upper-class families, low-income youth and families negotiate access to schooling by using family members' experiences and social networks; in addition, when they are unfamiliar with US institutions, they make use of brokers and advocates in schools or community-based organizations. Through these relationships, youth learn how and when to shift dialects or languages and how to access the help of mentoring, advocacy, and institutional bridging. Stanton-Salazar et al (1996) described interventions in how institutional agents and community mentors enhanced the development and schooling of youth from economically marginalized communities. Their access to institutional resources depended on their embeddedness in social networks that provide attachments to institutional agents who were able and willing to broker opportunities. These brokers' positions in schools, government agencies, programs, colleges, and community-based organizations allowed them to provide knowledge and place youth in resource-rich social networks.

The structure-agency theories bring concepts of power and access to the analysis of cultural change while highlighting an active role for individuals. The concepts of social capital are useful for understanding the role of culture in the academic performance of diverse youth within nations. Recent work has illuminated the role of attitudes and behavior of youth and low-income families in accessing educational resources (Denner et al 1997). The limitations of this area stem from the relatively small amount of empirical work that has been conducted so far.

## Culture as Navigating and Negotiating Borders: Multiple Worlds Theories

THEORY AND EVIDENCE    The educational anthropologists Patricia Phelan, Ann Locke Davidson, and Hanh Cao Yu (Phelan et al 1991) proposed that all youth in diverse societies are challenged as they attempt to move across their multiple worlds, which are defined in terms of the "cultural knowledge and behavior found within the boundaries of students' particular families, peer groups, and schools.... [E]ach world contains values and beliefs, expectations, actions, and emotional responses familiar to insiders" (1991, p. 53). Phelan et al conducted a two-year longitudinal ethnographic study of 54 African American, Filipino, Vietnamese American, Mexican American, and European American adolescents attending large urban desegregated high schools in Northern California. On the basis of case studies of how these adolescents migrated across borders between their worlds of family, peers, and school, Phelan et al (1991) described four prototypic patterns. Some crossed borders smoothly, with a sense that their parents, friends, and teachers held compatible goals and expectations for them. However, even though they seemed on track for their future occupational plans, they were often isolated from students who were not part of their smoothly connected worlds. A second group occupied different worlds from their school peers in terms of culture, social class, ethnicity, or religion but still found crossing between school and home worlds manageable. They could adapt to mainstream patterns yet return to community patterns when with friends in their neighborhoods, even though they risked criticism from people in each world who expected unwavering adherence to their expectations. A third group occupied different worlds but found border crossing difficult. They were able to do well in classrooms where teachers showed personal interest in them, but they "teetered between engagement and withdrawal, whether with family, school, or friends" (1991, p. 84). Finally, students in the fourth group found the borders impenetrable. They found moving between worlds so difficult that they had become alienated—from school, family, or peers. Even so, many still hoped to move successfully into the world of school. Phelan et al concluded that students' abilities to move between worlds affect their chances of using educational institutions as steppingstones to further their education, work experiences, and meaningful adult lives but that success in managing these transitions varies widely (p. 85). Key assets were people who also moved across these boundaries, such as parents who were involved in school or teachers who knew parents and friends; but many students were left to navigate across their worlds without help.

RECENT ADVANCES   In industrialized countries, the student's pathway through school to work has been described as a smooth *academic pipeline,* with access by choice and advancement through merit; families support the school while fostering their children's autonomous achievement. Cooper et al (1995) have argued that this idealized view is particularly inappropriate for youth who encounter ethnic, gender, linguistic, or economic barriers in schooling and employment (Chisholm et al 1990, Hurrelman 1994). As each wave of students moves through elementary and secondary school toward college in the United States, the numbers of ethnic minority youth shrink (O'Brien 1993). Simultaneously, youth who leave school can become alienated and are overrepresented in unemployed and prison populations (Vigil & Yun 1996).

Cultural mismatch models consider ethnic minority youth at risk for dropping out of school and engaging in criminal activity that leads to prison. Scholars in several countries have mapped how youth navigate their multiple worlds, persist in school, and attain occupational success (Azmitia et al 1996, Grotevant & Cooper 1998, Hurtado & García 1994). For example, Cooper et al (1995) built on the multiple worlds model (Phelan et al 1991), the ecocultural model (Gallimore et al 1993), and the individuality-connectedness model (Grotevant & Cooper 1985, 1986) to examine how 60 African American and 60 Latino adolescents in Northern California bridged their multiple worlds of family, peers, neighborhoods, and schools while participating in university academic outreach programs. Students reported that their worlds included families, countries of origin, friends' homes, churches, mosques, academic outreach programs, shopping malls, video arcades, school clubs, and sports. Most worlds—including schools—were sources of positive expectations, but neighborhoods were the greatest source of expectations that students would fail, become pregnant and leave school, or engage in delinquent activities. Both African American and Latino students reported benefit from "brokering": Their families, program staff, teachers, siblings, and friends had provided support or had spoken up for them at school, at home, or in the neighborhood. Students also reported "gatekeeping": School counselors, for example, had discouraged them from taking classes required for university admission (Erickson & Shultz 1982). Students named parents and teachers most frequently as resources but saw peers and themselves as both resources and difficulties. Students making higher math grades were more likely to name mothers, fathers, teachers, and sisters as resources, while those making lower grades were more likely to report providing their own resources and having difficulties with peers.

LINKING UNIVERSAL AND COMMUNITY-SPECIFIC RESEARCH AND APPLICATIONS    Combining ethnographic and survey methods, Cooper et al (1995) conducted interviews with program founders and staff about the histories of their programs, reported participant observations, and initiated focus groups with male and female students at junior high, high school, and college levels. They developed a survey with both open- and closed-ended questions to assess adolescents' challenges and resources in navigating across their multiple worlds. Similarly, Davidson (1996) linked ethnographic studies in the interpretive tradition, by using focus groups as collaborative participation in research with students and in-service training for teachers. Davidson addresses a key need of multiple world theories: explaining variation in school performance in societies among youth who share similar worlds.

## SUMMARY AND IMPLICATIONS

The seven theoretical perspectives reviewed in this chapter provide complementary views of culture and psychological processes. By defining culture as core societal values, *individualism-collectivism theories* trace variation in behavior across cultures explained by core values that exist outside the individual. The model is relevant across countries (universal) and is used to look at community-specific values. By defining culture as contexts, *ecological system theories* hold the potential to address diversity in psychological processes by looking at the interrelationships of individuals and contexts. The theory is applicable to differences in school performance by addressing how children make sense of their environments. By defining culture as caste, *cultural-ecological theories* move beyond deficit models of cultural differences to explain cultural variations in behavior as a function of psychological processes, particularly perceptions of opportunity and efficacy. By defining culture as capital, *structure-agency theories* interface the concept of culture as core values with those of context and caste. By defining culture as a set of universally adaptive tools, *ecocultural and sociocultural theories* posit universal concepts to understand similarities and differences across cultures and variations within cultures as a function of dynamic interactions. By defining culture as intergroup relations, *social identity theories* see culture in psychological terms and link individual with social-group processes. By defining culture as a dynamic psychological construct, *multiple-worlds theories* link individuals with contexts and conceptualize people as agentic in negotiating cultural boundaries.

Of course, some critics assert that psychologists should omit cultural processes from consideration in their theoretical or empirical work. Psychology, they argue, is primarily about understanding the behavior of individuals, not of groups; the most important psychological processes and mechanisms are universal, while environmental variation helps little to explain individual functioning. Some take an alternative position, arguing that historical and societal processes are so powerful in creating distinctive communities, institutional systems, and situations that individual meanings become trivial and that meaningful comparisons across cultural communities become impossible. It may seem easier to take either of these positions—cultural-universal or community-specific—than to try to understand what makes humans similar and what makes them different, particularly when we do not know beforehand for which domain the first or second position might be more true.

Another approach to understanding individual and cultural systems is based on tracing individuals moving from one system to another or within a system (RG Cooper, personal communication). If change occurs in a social structure, such as when public schools in a low-income neighborhood add college preparatory classes, then one should see change in individuals within the structure, such as more students planning to attend college. If relatively stable qualities of individuals, such as their future orientation (Nurmi et al 1995), influence the effects of structural qualities, then individual theoretical constructs are necessary. Thus we need psychological constructs, not only demographic categories, to integrate cultural processes in both psychological and structural terms (García Coll et al 1997). Meanwhile psychologists continue to generalize beyond their samples; while studying only their own countries, for example, they assume that psychological phenomena are universal enough to make such studies representative.

Finally, scholars are also moving beyond "giving science away." Consideration of the role of cultural diversity in psychological theory and methods has begun to cause a shift in how research is done. This has resulted in more integration of scholarly and policy debates on issues of application and ethics, as seen in the US Human Capital Initiative emerging from a coalition of government agencies and professional organizations. Policy regarding children and youth in many nations focuses on the relative authority and fiscal responsibility of central governments, states, and localities. Similarly, debates on the universal applicability of the United Nations Convention for the Rights of the Child have compared individualistic—often industrialized—versus collectivist societies, noting that the influence of policy depends on these culture-specific values (Limber & Flekkoy 1995). Issues of equity and access to resources bring issues of universality beyond scholarship to those of policy and practice in which scholarship is entwined (Werner 1997).

Social scientists will continue to debate models of cultural-universal and community-specific research and application within and across nations (Seginer et al 1993). But the international scholarly community is finding new ways to understand the role of culture in human development without overemphasizing or ignoring either psychological ("micro") or structural ("macro") processes. Psychologists are coming to understand cultures as developing systems of individuals, relationships, material and social contexts, and institutions. By viewing theories linking culture and psychological processes as distinct yet complementary, researchers and policy makers can forge interdisciplinary, international, and intergenerational collaborations on behalf of the culturally diverse communities of which we are a part.

ACKNOWLEDGMENTS

The authors thank Renee Ferigo Marshall for preparing references for this chapter. We also thank the following reviewers for their helpful comments on drafts of this chapter: Margarita Azmitia, Cynthia García Coll, Robert G Cooper, Barbara Rogoff, Linda Tropp, Tom Weisner, and Chaim Richman. Partial support in preparing this review was provided to Catherine Cooper by the John D and Catherine T MacArthur Foundation Research Network on Successful Transitions through Middle Childhood, to Margarita Azmitia and Catherine Cooper from the US Department of Education Office of Educational Research Institute (National Center for Research on Education, Diversity, and Excellence), and to Catherine Cooper, Francisco Hernandez, and Jill Denner from the University of California Regents' Diversity Initiative. Support for Jill Denner was provided by a grant to Barrie Thorne and Catherine Cooper from the John D and Catherine T MacArthur Foundation Research Network on Successful Transitions through Middle Childhood.

---

Visit the *Annual Reviews home page* at
http://www.AnnualReviews.org.

---

## Literature Cited

Allen L, Denner J, Yoshikawa H, Seidman E, Aber JL. 1996. Acculturation and depression among Latina urban girls. See Leadbeater & Way 1996, pp. 337–45

Archer SL. 1992. A feminist's approach to identity research. In *Adolescent Identity Formation,* ed. GR Adams, TP Gullotta, R Montemayor, pp. 25–49. Newbury Park, CA: Sage

Azmitia M, Cooper CR, García EE, Dunbar N. 1996. The ecology of family guidance in low-income Mexican-American and European-American families. *Soc. Dev.* 5:1–23

Azuma H. 1994. Two modes of cognitive socialization in Japan and the United States. See Greenfield & Cocking 1994, pp. 275–84

Banks JA. 1988. Ethnicity, class, cognitive, and motivational styles: research and teaching implications. *J. Negro Educ.* 57: 452–66

Banks JA. 1989. Black youth in predominately White suburbs. In *Black Adolescents,* ed. RL Jones, pp. 65–77. Berkeley, CA: Cobb & Henry

Bernal ME, Knight GP, eds. 1993. *Ethnic Identity: Formation and Transmission Among Hispanics and Other Minorities.* New York: SUNY Press

Berry JW. 1993. Ethnic identity in plural societies. See Bernal & Knight 1993, pp. 65–77

Bourdieu P, Passeron C. 1977. *Reproduction in Education, Society and Culture.* London: Sage

Brewer MB. 1991. The social self: on being the same and different at the same time. *Pers. and Soc. Psych. Bulletin* 17:475–82

Bronfenbrenner U. 1979. *The Ecology of Human Development: Experiments by Nature and Design.* Cambridge, MA: Harvard Univ. Press

Bronfenbrenner U. 1989. Ecological systems theory. *Ann. Child Dev.* 6:185–246

Bronfenbrenner U. 1993. The ecology of cognitive development: research models and fugitive findings. In *Development in Context: Acting and Thinking in Scientific Environments,* ed. RH Wozniak, KW Fischer, pp. 3–44. Hillsdale, NJ: Erlbaum

Bronfenbrenner U. 1995. The bioecological model from a life course perspective: reflections of a participant observer. In *Examining Lives in Context: Perspectives on the Ecology of Human Development*, ed. P Moen, H Elder Jr, K Luscher, pp. 599–618. Washington, DC: Am. Psychol. Assoc.

Burton LM, Obeidallah DA, Allison K. 1996. Ethnographic insights on social context and adolescent development among inner-city African-American teens. See Jessor et al 1996, pp. 395–418

Chao RK. 1997. *The 'meaningfulness' of our most familiar constructs: Research on parenting for ethnically diverse populations*. Presented at Bienn. Meet. Soc. Res. Child Dev., Washington, DC

Chisholm L, Büchner P, Krüger H, Brown P. 1990. *Childhood, Youth, and Social Change: A Comparative Perspective*. London: Falmer

Cole M. 1996. *Cultural Psychology: A Once and Future Discipline*. Cambridge, MA: Harvard Univ. Press

Coleman JS. 1988. Social capital in the creation of human capital. *Am. J. Sociol. Suppl.* 94:95–120

Cooper CR. 1994. Cultural perspectives on continuity and change in adolescents' relationships. In *Advances in Adolescent Development. Personal Relationships During Adolescence*, ed. R Montemayor, GR Adams, TP Gulotta, 6:78–100. Newbury Park, CA: Sage

Cooper CR. 1998. Multiple selves, multiple worlds: cultural perspectives on individuality and connectedness in adolescent development. In *Minnesota Symposium on Child Psychology: Culture and Development*, ed. C Nelson, A Masten. Hillsdale, NJ: Erlbaum. In press

Cooper CR, Baker H, Polichar D, Welsh M. 1993. Values and communication of Chinese, European, Filipino, Mexican, and Vietnamese American adolescents with their families and friends. In *The Role of Fathers in Adolescent Development: New Directions in Child Development*, ed. S Shulman, WA Collins, pp. 73–89. San Francisco: Jossey-Bass

Cooper CR, Jackson JF, Azmitia M, Lopez E, Dunbar N. 1995. Bridging students' multiple worlds: African American and Latino youth in academic outreach programs. In *Changing Schools for Changing Students: An Anthology of Research on Language Minorities*, ed. RF Macías, RG Ramos, pp. 211–34. Santa Barbara: Univ. Calif.

Cooper CR, Jackson JF, Azmitia M, Lopez EM. 1998. Multiple selves, multiple worlds: three useful strategies for research with ethnic minority youth. See McLoyd & Steinberg 1998. In press

Damon W. 1996. Nature, second nature, and individual development: an ethnographic opportunity. See Jessor et al 1996, pp. 459–75

Daniels R. 1990. *Coming to America: A History of Immigration and Ethnicity in American Life*. New York: Harper Collins

Davidson AL. 1996. *Making and Molding Identity in Schools: Student Narratives on Race, Gender, and Academic Engagement*. Albany: SUNY Press

Delgado-Gaitan C. 1994. Socializing young children in Mexican-American families: an intergenerational perspective. See Greenfield & Cocking 1994, pp. 55–86

Denner J, Cooper CR, Dunbar N, Lopez EM. 1997. *Strategies children use to negotiate access to resources for education*. Presented at the Am. Educ. Res. Assoc. Meet., Chicago

Duncan GJ. 1991. The economic environment of childhood. In *Children in Poverty*, ed. AC Huston, pp. 23–50. New York: Cambridge Univ. Press

Eccles J, Midgley C, Wigfield A, Buchanan CM, Reuman D, et al. 1993. Development during adolescence: the impact of stage-environment fit on young adolescents' experiences in schools and in families. *Am. Psychol.* 48:90–101

Eckert P. 1989. *Jocks and Burnouts: Social Categories and Identity in the High School*. New York: Teachers College Press

Erickson F, Shultz J. 1982. *The Counselor as Gatekeeper: Social Interaction in Interviews*. New York: Academic

Erikson EH. 1968. *Identity: Youth and Crisis*. New York: Norton

Ethier KA, Deaux K. 1994. Negotiating social identity when contexts change: maintaining identification and responding to threat. *J. Per. Soc. Psychol.* 67:243–51

Ford DY, Harris JJ. 1996. Perceptions and attitudes of Black students toward school, achievement and other educational variables. *Child Dev.* 67:1141–52

Fordham S. 1988. Racelessness as a factor in Black students' school success: pragmatic strategy or Pyrrhic victory? *Harvard Educ. Rev.* 58:54–84

Fordham S, Ogbu JU. 1986. Black students' school success: coping with the "burden of acting white." *Urban Rev.* 18:176–206

Gallimore R, Goldenberg CN, Weisner TS. 1993. The social construction and subjective reality of activity settings: implications for community psychology. *Am. J. Community Psychol.* 21:537–59

582    COOPER & DENNER

Gándara P. 1995. *Over the Ivy Walls: The Educational Mobility of Low-Income Chicanos.* New York: SUNY Press

Gándara P, Osugi L. 1994. Educationally ambitious Chicanas. *NEA High. Educ. J.* 10: 7–35

Garbarino J, Kostelny K, Dubrow N. 1991. What children can tell us about living in danger. *Am. Psychol.* 46:376–83

Garbarino J, Stott FM. 1989. *What Children Can Tell Us: Eliciting, Interpreting, and Evaluating Information from Children.* San Francisco: Jossey-Bass

García Coll CT, Thorne B, Cooper CR, Scott-Jones D, Eccles J, Nakashima C. 1997. *Beyond social categories: "race," ethnicity, social class, gender, and developmental research.* Presented at the Soc. Res. Child Dev. Meet., Washington, DC

Gibbs JT. 1996. Health-compromising behaviors in urban early adolescent females: ethnic and socioeconomic variations. See Leadbeater & Way 1996, pp. 309–27

Gibson M, Ogbu J, eds. 1991. *Minority Status and Schooling: A Comparative Study of Immigrant and Involuntary Minorities.* New York: Garland

Gibson MA. 1988. *Accommodation Without Assimilation: Sikh Immigrants in an American High School.* Ithaca, NY: Cornell Univ. Press

Gibson MA. 1995. Patterns of acculturation and high school performance. *Linguist. Minor. Res. Inst. News* 4:1–3

Gibson MA, Bhachu PK. 1991. Ethnicity, gender, and social class: the school adaptation patterns of West Indian youths. See Gibson & Ogbu 1991, pp. 169–204

Gjerde PF, Cooper CR, Azuma H, Kashiwagi K, Kosawa Y, et al. 1995. *An ecocultural analysis of adolescent development in Japan and the U.S.: Between-and within-cultural analyses.* Presented at the Soc. Res. Child Dev. Meet., Indianapolis

Goldberger NR, Veroff J. 1995. *The Culture and Psychology Reader.* New York: NY Univ. Press

Goodman R. 1990. *Japan's 'International Youth': The Emergence of a New Class of Schoolchildren.* Oxford, NY: Clarendon

Goodnow J. 1994. *What's new in perspectives on development-in-context?* Presented at the Int. Soc. Study Behav. Dev. Meet., Amsterdam

Goodnow JJ, Miller PJ, Kessel F. 1995. *Cultural Practices as Contexts for Development.* San Francisco: Jossey-Bass

Greenfield PM. 1993. International roots of minority child development: introduction

to the special issue. *Int. J. Behav. Dev.* 16:385–94

Greenfield PM, Cocking RR, eds. 1994. *Cross Cultural Roots of Minority Child Development.* Hillsdale, NJ: Erlbaum

Grotevant HD, Cooper CR. 1985. Patterns of interaction in family relationships and the development of identity formation in adolescence. *Child Dev.* 56:415–28

Grotevant HD, Cooper CR. 1986. Individuation in family relationships: a perspective on individual differences in the development of identity and role taking in adolescence. *Hum. Dev.* 29:82–100

Grotevant HD, Cooper CR. 1998. Individuality and connectedness in adolescent development: review and prospects for research on identity, relationships and context. In *Personality Development in Adolescence: A Cross National and Life Span Perspective,* ed. E Skoe, A von der Lippe. London: Routledge. In press

Harkness S, Super C, Keefer S. 1992. Learning to be an American parent: how cultural models gain directive force. In *Human Motives and Cultural Models: Publications for Psychological Anthropology,* ed. RG D'Andrade, C Strauss, pp. 163–78. Cambridge: Cambridge Univ. Press

Harrison AO, Wilson MN, Pine CJ, Chan SQ, Buriel R. 1990. Family ecologies of ethnic minority children. *Child Dev.* 61: 347–62

Heath SB, McLaughlin MW. 1993. *Identity and Inner-City Youth: Beyond Ethnicity and Gender.* New York: Teachers College

Ho DYF. 1994. Cognitive socialization in Confucian heritage cultures. See Greenfield & Cocking 1994, pp. 285–313

Hurrelmann K, ed. 1994. *International Handbook of Adolescence.* Westport, CT: Greenwood

Hurtado A, García EE, eds. 1994. *The Educational Achievement of Latinos: Barriers and Successes.* Santa Cruz: Regents Univ. Calif

Hurtado A, Rodriguez J, Guri P, Beals JL. 1993. The impact of Mexican descendants' social identity on the ethnic socialization of children. See Bernal & Knight 1993, pp. 131–62

Jessor R, Colby A, Shweder RA, eds. 1996. *Ethnography and Human Development: Context and Meaning in Social Inquiry.* Chicago: Univ. Chicago Press

Kitayama S, Markus HR. 1995. Culture and self: implications for internationalizing psychology. See Goldberger & Veroff 1995, pp. 366–83

Kitayama S, Markus HR, Lieberman C. 1993.

The collective construction of self esteem: implications for culture, self, and emotion. In *Everyday Concepts of Emotions,* ed. J Russell, J Wellenkamp, T Manstead, JMF Dols, pp. 1–15. Dordrecht: Kluwer

Kroger J. 1993. The role of historical context in the identity formation process of late adolescence. *Youth Soc.* 24:363–76

Leadbeater BJR, Way N, eds. 1996. *Urban Girls: Resisting Stereotypes, Creating Identities.* New York: NY Univ. Press

Lewis ML, Osofsky JD. 1997. Violent cities, violent streets: children draw their neighborhoods. In *Children in a Violent Society,* ed. JD Osofsky, pp. 277–99. New York: Guilford

Limber SP, Flekkoy MG. 1995. The U.N. Convention on the Rights of the Child: its relevance for social scientists. *Soc. for Res. in Child Dev. Social Policy Reports* 9:1–15

Lin C-YC, Fu VR. 1990. A comparison of child-rearing practices among Chinese, immigrant Chinese, and Caucasian-American parents. *Child Dev.* 61: 429–33

Markus HR, Kitayama S. 1991. Culture and the self: implications for cognition, emotion, and motivation. *Psychol. Rev.* 98: 224–53

Matute-Bianchi ME. 1991. Situational ethnicity and patterns of school performance among immigrant and non-immigrant Mexican descent students. See Gibson & Ogbu 1991, pp. 205–48

McAdoo HP. 1988. Transgenerational patterns of upward mobility in African-American families. In *Black Families,* pp. 148–68. Newbury Park, CA: Sage. 2nd ed.

McLoyd V, Steinberg L, eds. 1998. *Conceptual and Methodological Issues in the Study of Minority Adolescents and Their Families.* Hillsdale, NJ: Erlbaum. In press

McLoyd VC. 1991. What is the study of African-American children the study of? In *Black Psychology,* ed. RJ Jones, pp. 419–40. Berkeley, CA: Cobb & Henry

Mehan H. 1992. Understanding inequality in schools: the contribution of interpretive studies. *Soc. Educ.* 65:1–20

Mehan H, Hubbard L, Villanueva I. 1994. Forming academic identities: accommodation without assimilation among involuntary minorities. *Anthropol. Educ. Q.* 25: 91–117

Mehan H, Villanueva I, Hubbard L, Lintz A. 1996. *Constructing School Success: The Consequences of Untracking Low Achieving Students.* Cambridge, UK: Cambridge Univ. Press

Moll LC, Gonzalez N. 1994. Lessons from research with language-minority children. *J. Read. Behav.* 26:439–56

Moll LC, Velez-Ibanez C, Gonzalez N. 1991. *Funds of Knowledge.* Santa Cruz: Nat. Cent. Res. Cult. Divers. Second Lang. Learn., Univ. Calif., Santa Cruz

Newman KS. 1996. Working poor: low wage employment in the lives of Harlem youth. In *Transitions through Adolescence: Interpersonal Domains and Context,* ed. JA Graber, J Brooks-Gunn, AC Petersen, pp. 141–65. Mahwah, NJ: Erlbaum

Nurmi JE, Poole ME, Seigner R. 1995. Tracks and transitions: a comparison of adolescent future-oriented goals, explorations, and commitments in Australia, Israel and Finland. *Int. J. Psychol.* 30:355–75

O'Brien EM. 1993. *Latinos in Higher Education.* Washington, DC: Am. Coun. Educ. Res. Brief Ser.

Ogbu JU. 1990. Cultural model, identity and literacy. In *Cultural Psychology: Essays on Comparative Human Development,* ed. JW Stigler, RA Shweder, G Herdt, pp. 520–41. New York: Cambridge Univ. Press

Ogbu JU. 1991. Minority coping responses and school experience. *J. Psychohist.* 18:433–56

Ogbu JU. 1993. Differences in cultural frame of reference. *Int. J. Behav. Dev.* 16: 483–506

Ogbu JU. 1995. Origins of human competence: a cultural-ecological perspective. See Goldberger & Veroff 1995, pp. 245–75

Penuel WR, Wertsch JV. 1995. Vygotsky and identity formation: a sociocultural approach. *Educ. Psychol.* 30:83–92

Phelan P, Davidson AL, Yu HC. 1991. Students' multiple worlds: navigating the borders of family, peer, and school cultures. In *Cultural Diversity: Implications for Education,* ed. P Phelan, AL Davidson, pp. 52–88. New York: Teachers College Press

Phinney JS. 1996. When we talk about American ethnic groups, what do we mean? *Am. Psychol.* 51:918–27

Phinney JS, Landin J. 1998. Research paradigms for studying ethnic minority families within and across groups. See McLoyd & Steinberg 1998. In press

Rogoff B. 1990. *Apprenticeship in Thinking: Cognitive Development in Social Context.* New York: Oxford Univ. Press

Rogoff B, Minstry J, Goncu A, Mosier C. 1993. Guided participation in cultural activity by toddlers and caregivers. *Monogr. Soc. Res. Child Dev.* 58 pp.

Root MPP, ed. 1992. *Racially Mixed People in America.* Newbury Park: Sage

Ruble DN. 1994. A phase model of transitions: cognitive and motivational consequences. *Adv. Exp. Soc. Psychol.* 26:163–214

Rumbaut RG. 1994. The crucible within: ethnic identity, self-esteem, and segmented assimilation among children of immigrants. *Int. Migr. Rev.* 28:748–94

Sameroff AJ. 1995. General systems theories and developmental psychopathology. In *Developmental Psychopathology. Theory and Methods,* ed. D Cicchetti, DJ Cohen, 1:659–95. New York: Wiley

Schneider B, Hieshima JA, Lee S, Plank S. 1994. East-Asian academic success in the United States: family, school, and community explanations. See Greenfield & Cocking 1994, pp. 323–50

Seginer R, Trommsdorff G, Essau C. 1993. Adolescent control beliefs: cross-cultural variations of primary and secondary orientations. *Int. J. Behav. Dev.* 16:243–60

Shweder RA. 1996. True ethnography: the lore, the law, and the lure. See Jessor et al 1996, pp. 175–82

Shweder RA, Jensen L, Goldstein WM. 1995. Who sleeps by whom revisited: a method for extracting the moral goods implicit in practice. In *Cultural Practices as Contexts for Development. New Directions for Child Development,* ed. JJ Goodnow, PJ Miller, F Kessel, 67:21–39. San Francisco: Jossey-Bass

Spencer MB, Dornbusch SM. 1990. Challenges in studying minority youth. In *At the Threshold: The Developing Adolescent,* ed. SS Feldman, GR Eliot, pp. 123–46. Cambridge, MA: Harvard Univ. Press

Spindler GD. 1990. *The American Cultural Dialogue and Its Transmission.* London: Falmer

Stanton-Salazar RD, Vasquez OA, Mehan H. 1996. Engineering success through institutional support. In *The Latino Pipeline,* ed. A Hurtado, R Figueroa, EE García, pp. 100–36. Santa Cruz: Regents Univ. Calif.

Sue D, Sue S. 1987. Cultural factors in the clinical assessment of Asian Americans. *J. Consult. Clin. Psychol.* 55:479–87

Tajfel H, ed. 1978. *Differentiation Between Social Groups: Studies in the Social Psychology of Intergroup Relations.* New York: Academic

Taylor RD, Wang MC, eds. 1997. *Social and Emotional Adjustment and Family Relations in Ethnic Minority Families.* Mahwah, NJ: Erlbaum

Tharp RG, Gallimore R. 1988. *Rousing Minds to Life: Teaching, Learning and Schooling in Social Context.* Cambridge, UK: Cambridge Univ. Press

Triandis HC. 1988. The future of pluralism revisited. In *Eliminating Racism: Profiles in Controversy,* ed. PA Katz, DA Taylor, pp. 31–50. New York: Plenum

Triandis HC. 1996. The psychological measurement of cultural syndromes. *Am. Psychol.* 51:407–15

Triandis HC, Chan DK, Bhawuk DP, Iwao S, et al. 1995. Multimethod probes of allocentrism and idiocentrism. *Int. J. Psychol.* 30:461–80

Tropp L. 1996. *Viewing the Self in Social Context: The Interpretation and Integration of Contributions from Developmental and Social Psychology.* Santa Cruz: Univ. Calif.

Uribe FMT, LeVine RA, LeVine SE. 1994. Maternal behavior in a Mexican community: the changing environments of children. See Greenfield & Cocking 1994, pp. 41–54

Valenzuela A, Dornbusch SM. 1994. Familism and social capital in the academic achievement of Mexican origin and Anglo adolescents. *Soc. Sci. Q.* 75:18–36

Vigil JD, Yun SC. 1996. Southern California gangs: comparative ethnicity and social control. In *Gangs in America,* ed. CR Huff, pp. 139–56. Thousand Oaks, CA: Sage. 2nd ed.

Waters MC. 1994. Ethnic and racial identities of second-generation black immigrants in New York City. *Int. Migr. Rev.* 28:795–820

Weisner TS, Gallimore R, Jordan C. 1988. Unpackaging cultural effects on classroom learning: native Hawaiian peer assistance and child-generated activity. *Anthropol. Educ. Q.* 19:327–51

Werner EE. 1997. *Conditions that facilitate the well being of minority children around the world.* Presented at the Soc. Res. Child Dev. Meet., Indianapolis

Whiting BB, ed. 1963. *Six Cultures: Studies of Child Rearing.* New York: Wiley

Whiting BB. 1976. The problem of the packaged variable. In *The Developing Individual in a Changing World: Historical and Cultural Issues,* ed. K Reigel, J Meacham. Chicago: Aldine

Zambrana RE. 1995. *Understanding Latino Families: Scholarship, Policy and Practice.* Thousand Oaks, CA: Sage

*Annu. Rev. Psychol. 1998. 49:585–612*

# PERCEPTUAL LEARNING

*Robert L. Goldstone*

Psychology Building, Indiana University, Bloomington, Indiana 47405;
e-mail: rgoldstone@indiana.edu

KEY WORDS: perception, cognition, discrimination, training, expertise

## ABSTRACT

Perceptual learning involves relatively long-lasting changes to an organism's perceptual system that improve its ability to respond to its environment. Four mechanisms of perceptual learning are discussed: attention weighting, imprinting, differentiation, and unitization. By attention weighting, perception becomes adapted to tasks and environments by increasing the attention paid to important dimensions and features. By imprinting, receptors are developed that are specialized for stimuli or parts of stimuli. By differentiation, stimuli that were once indistinguishable become psychologically separated. By unitization, tasks that originally required detection of several parts are accomplished by detecting a single constructed unit representing a complex configuration. Research from cognitive psychology, psychophysics, neuroscience, expert/novice differences, development, computer science, and cross-cultural differences is described that relates to these mechanisms. The locus, limits, and applications of perceptual learning are also discussed.

## CONTENTS

0066-4308/98/0201-0585$08.00

# INTRODUCTION

The field of perceptual learning has changed significantly since the last *Annual Review of Psychology* chapter—Eleanor Gibson's 1963 review entitled "Perceptual Learning" [reprinted and reappraised by Gibson (1991)]—appeared. Eleanor and James Gibson's ecological approach to perception, with its emphasis on the direct perception of information from the world, has had a profound influence on the direction of the entire field. By this approach, perceptual learning consists of extracting previously unused information (Gibson & Gibson 1955). Identifying what external properties are available to be picked up by people is one of the major research goals. The ecological approach to perceptual learning continues to offer a fertile research program in developmental psychology (Pick 1992) and event perception (Bingham et al 1995, Reed 1996). The focus of the current review will be quite different from a direct perception perspective. The research reviewed here will be predominantly concerned with the internal mechanisms that drive perceptual learning and mediate between the external world and cognition. The bulk of this review will be organized around proposals for specific mechanisms of perceptual adaptation.

Perceptual learning involves relatively long-lasting changes to an organism's perceptual system that improve its ability to respond to its environment and are caused by this environment. As perceptual changes become more ephemeral, the inclination is to speak of adaptation (Helson 1948), attentional processes (Nosofsky 1986), or strategy shifts rather than perceptual learning. If the changes are not due to environmental inputs, then maturation rather than learning is implicated. Perceptual learning may occasionally result in worse performance in perceptual tasks, as is the case with Samuel's (1981) finding that experience with spoken words hinders subjects' decisions about whether they heard white noise or noise combined with speech sounds. Even in this case, experience with words probably increases people's ability to decipher noisy speech, the task with which they are most often confronted. The premise of this definition is that perceptual learning benefits an organism by tailoring the processes that gather information to the organism's uses of the information.

One of the theoretical and empirical challenges underlying the above definition is to distinguish between perceptual and higher-level, cognitive learning. In fact, Hall (1991) has persuasively argued that many results that have been explained in terms of perceptual learning are more parsimoniously described by changes involving the strengthening and weakening of associations. Several strategies have been proposed for identifying perceptual, rather than higher-level, changes. Under the assumption that perception involves the early stages of information processing, one can look for evidence that experience influences early processes. For example, subjective experience not only alters the perceived colors of familiar objects (Goldstone 1995) but apparently also exerts an influence on color perception before the perceptual stage that creates color after-images has completed its processing (Moscovici & Personnaz 1991). Likewise, experience with the silhouettes of familiar objects exerts an influence before figure/ground segregation is completed (Peterson & Gibson 1994). A second approach to identifying perceptual changes is to observe the time course of the use of particular types of information. For example, on the basis of priming evidence, Sekuler et al (1994) argue that knowledge about what an occluded object would look like if it were completed influences processing after as little as 150 ms. This influence is sufficiently early to typically be counted as perceptual processing. Neurological evidence can provide convergent support to timing studies. For example, practice in discriminating small motions in different directions significantly alters electrical brain potentials that occur within 100 ms of the stimulus onset (Fahle & Morgan 1996). These electrical changes are centered over the primary visual cortex, suggesting plasticity in early visual processing. Karni & Sagi (1991) find evidence, based on the specificity of training to eye (interocular transfer does not occur) and retinal location, that is consistent with early, primary visual cortex adaptation in simple discrimination tasks. Similarly, classical conditioning leads to shifts of neuronal receptive fields in primary auditory cortex toward the frequency of the rewarded tone (Weinberger 1993). In fact, training in a selective attention task may produce differential responses as early as the cochlea, the neural structure that is connected directly to the eardrum via three small bones (Hillyard & Kutas 1983). In short, there is an impressive amount of converging evidence that experimental training leads to changes to very early stages of information processing.

Of the many interesting questions regarding perceptual learning ("What is learned?," "How long does learning take and last?," and "How widely does learning transfer?"), this review is organized around "How does learning occur?" Consequently, a wide range of fields that investigate mechanisms underlying perceptual learning will be surveyed. Evidence from developmental psychology is very important because many of the most dramatic changes to human perceptual systems occur within the first seven years of life (Aslin & Smith 1988). Neuroscience provides concrete mechanisms of adaptation, and the field of neural plasticity has recently experienced tremendous growth (Kolb 1995, McGaugh et al 1995). Analyses of expertise and cross-cultural comparisons assess the perceptual impact of extended environmental influences. Researchers in computer science have made valuable contributions to our understanding of human psychology by describing functional algorithms for adaptation in networks involving many interacting units. In many cases, perceptual changes that have been empirically observed through studies of experts, laboratory training studies, and different cultures are given concrete accounts by computational and neural models.

## MECHANISMS OF PERCEPTUAL LEARNING

Perceptual learning is not achieved by a unitary process. Psychophysicists have distinguished between relatively peripheral, specific adaptations and more general, strategic ones (Doane et al 1996, Sagi & Tanne 1994), and between quick and slow perceptual learning processes (Karni & Sagi 1993). Cognitive scientists have distinguished between training mechanisms driven by feedback (supervised training) and those that require no feedback, instead operating on the statistical structure inherent in the environmentally supplied stimuli (unsupervised training). Organizing perceptual learning in terms of mechanisms rather than domains results in some odd couplings (linking, for example, neuroscientific and cross-cultural studies bearing on perceptual differentiation), but has the advantage of connecting phenomena that are deeply related and may inform each other.

### Attentional Weighting

One way in which perception becomes adapted to tasks and environments is by increasing the attention paid to perceptual dimensions and features that are important, and/or by decreasing attention to irrelevant dimensions and features. A feature is a unitary stimulus element, whereas a dimension is a set of linearly ordered features. "3 centimeters" and "red" are features; length and color are dimensions.

Attention can be selectively directed toward important stimulus aspects at several different stages in information processing. Researchers in animal learning and human categorization have described shifts toward the use of dimensions that are useful for tasks (Nosofsky 1986) or have previously been useful (Lawrence 1949). Lawrence describes these situations as examples of stimulus dimensions "acquiring distinctiveness" if they have been diagnostic in predicting rewards. Nosofsky describes attention shifts in terms of psychologically "stretching" dimensions that are relevant for categorizations. During category learning, people show a trend toward deemphasizing preexperimentally salient features, and emphasizing features that reliably predict experimental categories (Livingston & Andrews 1995). The stimulus aspects that are selectively attended may be quite complex; even pigeons can learn to selectively attend to the feature "contains human" in photographs (Herrnstein 1990). In addition to important dimensions acquiring distinctiveness, irrelevant dimensions also acquire equivalence, becoming less distinguishable (Honey & Hall 1989). For example, in a phenomenon called "latent inhibition," stimuli that are originally varied independently of reward are harder to later associate with reward than those that are not initially presented at all (Lubow & Kaplan 1997, Pearce 1987). Haider & Frensch (1996) find that improvements in performance are frequently due to reduced processing of irrelevant dimensions.

The above studies illustrate shifts in the use of dimensions as a function of their task relevance, but these shifts may be strategic choices rather than perceptual in nature. One source of evidence that they are not completely voluntary is that attentional highlighting of information occurs even if it is to the detriment of the observer. When a letter consistently serves as the target in a detection task and then later becomes a distractor—a stimulus to be ignored—it still automatically captures attention (Shiffrin & Schneider 1977). The converse of this effect, negative priming, also occurs: targets that were once distractors are responded to more slowly than never-before-seen items (Tipper 1992). In the negative priming paradigm, the effect of previous exposures of an item can last upward of two weeks (Fox 1995), suggesting that a relatively permanent change has taken place.

CATEGORICAL PERCEPTION   A phenomenon of particular interest for attentional accounts of perceptual adaptation is categorical perception. According to this phenomenon, people are better able to distinguish between physically different stimuli when the stimuli come from different categories than when they come from the same category (Calder et al 1996; see Harnad 1987 for several reviews of research). The effect has been best documented for speech phoneme categories. For example, Liberman et al (1957) generated a continuum of equally spaced consonant-vowel syllables going from /be/ to /de/. Observers listened to three sounds—A followed by B followed by X—and indicated whether X was identical to A or B. Subjects performed the task more accurately when syllables A and B belonged to different phonemic categories than when they were variants of the same phoneme, even when physical differences were equated.

There is evidence that some categorical perception effects are not learned but are either innate or a property of the acoustical signal itself. Infants as young as 4 months showed categorical perception for speech sounds (Eimas et al 1971), and even chinchillas (Kuhl & Miller 1978) and crickets (Wyttenbach et al 1996) show categorical perception effects for sound.

Still, recent evidence has indicated that sound categories, and categorical perception more generally, are subject to learning (Lively et al 1993). Whether categorical perception effects are found at particular physical boundaries depends on the listener's native language. In general, a sound difference that crosses the boundary between phonemes in a language will be more discriminable to speakers of that language than to speakers of a language in which the sound difference does not cross a phonemic boundary (Repp & Liberman 1987, Strange & Jenkins 1978). The laboratory training on the sound categories of a language can produce categorical perception among speakers of a language that does not have these categories (Pisoni et al 1982). Expert musicians, but not novices, show a pronounced categorical perception effect for relative pitch differences, suggesting that training was instrumental in sensitizing boundaries between semitones (Burns & Ward 1978, Zatorre & Halpern 1979). A visual analog exists: faces for which subjects are "experts," familiar faces, show categorical perception (increased sensitivity to differences at the half-way point between the faces) as one familiar face is transformed into another familiar face; however, no categorical perception is found for unfamiliar faces (Beale & Keil 1995).

There are several ways that physical differences between categories might become emphasized relative to within-category differences. In support of the possibility that people lose their ability to make within-category discriminations, very young infants (2 months old) show sensitivity to differences between speech sounds that they lose by the age of 10 months (Werker & Lalonde 1988, Werker & Tees 1984). This desensitization only occurs if the different sounds come from the same phonetic category of their native language. However, given the difficulty in explicitly instructing infants to respond to physical rather than phonetic differences between sounds, these results should be conservatively interpreted as showing that physical differences that do not make a functional difference to children become perceptually or judgmentally deemphasized. Laboratory experiments by Goldstone (1994) have suggested that physical differences between categories become emphasized with training. After learning a categorization in which one dimension was relevant and a second dimension was irrelevant, subjects were transferred to same/different judgments ("Are these two squares physically identical?"). Ability to discriminate between stimuli in the same/different judgment task was greater when they varied along dimensions that were relevant during categorization training, and was particularly elevated at the boundary between the categories. Further research showed that category learning systematically distorts the perception of category members by shifting their perceived dimension values away from members of opposing categories (Goldstone 1995). In sum, there is evidence for three influences of categories on perception: (*a*) category-relevant dimensions are sensitized, (*b*) irrelevant variation is deemphasized, and (*c*) relevant dimensions are selectively sensitized at the category boundary.

Computational efforts at explaining categorical perception have mainly centered on neural networks. In two such models, equally spaced stimuli along a continuum are associated with category labels, and the networks adapt their input-to-category connections so that the stimuli come to evoke their correct category assignment (Anderson et al 1977, Harnad et al 1995). In effect, the category feedback establishes attractor states that pull the different members of a category to a common point, thereby reducing their distinctiveness.

## Stimulus Imprinting

A second way that perception can adapt to an environment is by directly imprinting to it. Through imprinting, detectors (also called receptors) are developed that are specialized for stimuli or parts of stimuli. The term imprinting captures the idea that the form of the detector is shaped by the impinging stimulus. Internalized detectors develop for repeated stimuli, and these detectors increase the speed, accuracy, and general fluency with which the stimuli are processed. Although evidence for neural implementations of acquired detectors will be considered, more generally the reviewed studies support functional detectors—any abstract device or process that explains the selective benefit to important, repeated patterns.

WHOLE STIMULUS STORAGE   Imprinting may occur for entire stimuli, in which case a receptor develops that internalizes specific instances. Models that preserve stimuli in their entirety are called exemplar (Nosofsky 1986) or instance-based (Logan 1988) models. For example, in Logan's model, every exposure to a stimulus leads to an internalized trace of that stimulus. As more instances are stored, performance improves because more relevant instances can be retrieved, and the time required to retrieve them decreases. Instance-based models are supported by results showing that people's performance in perceptual tasks is closely tied to their amount of experience with a particular stimulus. Consistent with this claim, people can identify spoken words more accurately when they are spoken by familiar voices (Palmeri et al 1993). Doctors' diagnoses of skin disorders are facilitated when they are similar to previously presented cases, even when the similarity is based on attributes that are irrelevant for the diagnosis (Brooks et al 1991). Increasing the frequency of a cartoon face in an experiment increases its classification accuracy (Nosofsky 1991). After several hours of training in a numerosity judgment task ("How many dots are there?"), people's response times are the same for all levels of numerosity between 6 and 11 dots, but only for dots that are arranged as they were during training (Palmeri 1997), consistent with the notion that slow counting processes can be circumvented by storing specific arrangements of dots. Even when people know a simple, clear-cut rule for a perceptual classification, performance is better on frequently presented items than rare items (Allen & Brooks 1991). Thus, even in situations where one might think abstract or rule-based processes are used, there is good evidence that observers become tuned to the particular instances to which they are exposed.

People are better able to perceptually identify unclear or quickly presented stimuli when they have been previously exposed to them. Although this effect is traditionally discussed in terms of implicit memory for exposed items, it also provides a robust example of perceptual learning. The identification advantage for familiarized instances lasts at least three weeks, requires as few as one previous presentation of an item, and is often tied to the specific physical properties of the initial exposure of the item (Schacter 1987). In brief, instance memories that are strong and quickly developed facilitate subsequent perceptual tasks involving highly similar items.

The power of instance-based models has not been ignored by object recognition researchers. This has led to a renewed interest in the recently dismissed class of "template" models. According to these models, objects are recognized by comparing them to stored, photograph-like images (templates) of known objects. Objects are placed into the same category as the template to which they are most similar. In some cases, preprocessing operations rotate and distort templates to maximize their overlap with the presented object (Hinton et al 1992). Ullman (1989) has shown that template models can be highly effective, and that preprocessing operations can find good matches between an object and template without knowing ahead of time what the object is, as long as at least three points of alignment between the object and template can be found on the basis of local physical cues. Poggio & Edelman (1990) present a neural network model that learns to recognize three-dimensional objects by developing units specialized for presented two-dimensional views, associating them with their correct three-dimensional interpretation, and interpolating between stored views for recognizing novel objects. Consistent with this model's assumption that receptors become tuned to particular viewpoints, humans can learn to identify three-dimensional objects by seeing two-dimensional views that have been arbitrarily paired with the three-dimensional object (Sinha & Poggio 1996). Tarr (1995) provides support for the storage of multiple views to aid recognition by showing that the time to recognize rotated objects is a function of their rotational distance to the nearest stored viewpoint.

FEATURE IMPRINTING    Rather than imprinting on entire stimuli, there is also evidence that people imprint on parts or features of a stimulus. If a stimulus part is important, varies independently of other parts, or occurs frequently, people may develop a specialized detector for that part. This is a valuable process because it leads to the development of new "building blocks" for describing stimuli (Schyns et al 1998, Schyns & Murphy 1994). Parts that are developed in one context can be used to efficiently describe subsequent objects. Efficient representations are promoted because the parts have been extracted because of their prevalence in an environment, and thus are tailored to the environment.

Schyns & Rodet (1997) find that unfamiliar parts (arbitrary curved shapes within an object) that are important in one task are more likely to be used to represent subsequent categories. Their subjects were more likely to represent a conjunction of two parts, X and Y, in terms of these two components (rather than as a whole unit, or a unit broken down into different parts) when they received previous experience with X as a defining part for a different category. Configurations of dots are more likely to be circled as coherent components of patterns if they were previously important for a categorization (Hock et al 1987). Likewise, Hofstadter (1995) and his colleagues describe how learning to interpret an object as possessing certain parts creates a bias to see other objects in terms of those parts.

Several computational models have been recently devised that create perceptual building blocks during the course of being exposed to, or categorizing, objects. Neural networks have been particularly popular because they often possess hidden units that intervene between inputs and outputs and can be interpreted as developing internal representations of presented inputs (Rumelhart et al 1986). These internal representations can function as acquired feature detectors, built up through environmental exposure. For example, simple exposure to photographs of natural scenes suffices to allow neural networks to create a repertoire of oriented line segments to be used to describe the scenes (Miikkulainen et al 1997, Schmidhuber et al 1996). These feature detectors bear a strong resemblance to neural detectors found in the primary visual cortex and are created by learning algorithms that develop units that respond to independent sources of regularity across photographs. Networks with detectors that adapt by competing for the privilege to accommodate inputs can generate specialized detectors resembling ocular dominance and orientation columns found in the visual cortex (Obermayer et al 1995). These networks do not require feedback labels or categorizations; the stimuli themselves contain sufficient regularities and redundancies that can be exploited to generate efficient vocabularies (Grossberg 1991). However, if neural networks do receive feedback about stimulus categorizations, then the features that they develop can be tailored to these categories (Intrator 1994, Rumelhart et al 1986). The simplicity, predictive power, and value of neural networks that create their own featural descriptions make these systems exciting and fruitful avenues for exploration.

There is also neurological evidence for perceptual learning via imprinting on specific features within a stimulus. Weinberger (1993) reviews evidence that cells in the auditory cortex become tuned to the frequency of often-repeated tones. Ascending in complexity, cells in the inferior temporal cortex can be tuned by extended experience (about 600,000 trials) with 3D objects (Logothetis et al 1995); these cells also show heightened response to novel views of the trained object. Cells in this same area can be highly selective for particular faces, and this specificity is at least partially acquired given that it is especially pronounced for familiar faces (Perrett et al 1984).

The cognitive, computational, and neurophysiological results indicate that the "building blocks" used to describe objects are adapted to environmental inputs. In many of the cases considered thus far, feature and part detectors are devised that capture the regularities implicit in the set of input stimuli. However, the detectors that develop are also influenced by task requirements and strategies. For example, altering the color of target objects from training to transfer does not influence performance unless the training task requires encoding of color (Logan et al 1996). In general, whether a functional detector is developed will depend on both the objective frequency and subjective importance of the physical feature (Sagi & Tanne 1994, Shiu & Pashler 1992). Systems that can acquire new feature detectors have functional advantages over systems that employ a hard-wired set of detectors. One difficulty with fixed sets of features is that it is hard to choose exactly the right set of elements that will suffice to accommodate all possible future entities. On the one hand, if a small set of primitive elements is chosen, then it is likely that two entities will eventually arise that must be distinguished, but cannot with any combination of available primitives. On the other hand, if a set of primitives is sufficiently large to construct all entities that might occur, then it will likely include many elements that lie unused, waiting for their moment of need to possibly arise (Schyns et al 1998). However, by developing new elements as needed, newly important discriminations can cause the construction of detectors that are tailored for the discrimination.

TOPOLOGICAL IMPRINTING   A third type of imprinting occurs at a more abstract level. Rather than developing detectors for particular stimuli or features, environmental regularities that span across a set of stimuli can also be internalized. The patterns impinging upon an organism will have certain similarities to one another. These similarities can be represented by plotting each pattern in a multidimensional space. Topological imprinting occurs when the space and the positions of patterns within the space are learned as a result of training with patterns. Rather than simply developing independent detectors, topological imprinting implies that a spatially organized network of detectors is created.

The simplest form of topological imprinting is to create a set of feature values ordered along a single dimension. Developmental evidence suggests that dimensional organizations are learned. On the basis of evidence from a "Which is more?" task, children and adults agree that large objects are "more" than small objects, but three-year-old children treat dark objects as more than light objects, unlike adults (Smith & Sera 1992). Loudness is originally disorganized for children, but comes to be dimensionally organized with loud sounds being perceived as more than soft sounds. The importance of dimensionally organized percepts is apparent from Bedford's (1993, 1995) work on learning the relations between dimensions. She argues that perceptual learning involves adaptively mapping from one dimension to another. For example, upon wearing prism eyeglasses that distort the relation between visual information and proprioceptive feedback, learning is much easier when the entire visual dimension can be shifted or warped to map onto the proprioceptive dimension than when unrelated visual-motor associations must be acquired. Both experiments point to people's natural tendency to draw associations between dimensions. One of the most striking examples of this phenomenon continues to be Howells' (1944) experiment in which people learn to associate a particular tone with the color red after several thousand trials, and then are transferred to a task where they try to identify a neutral color white. When the tone is present, people systematically choose as white a color that is slightly green, suggesting that the tone has come to substitute for redness to some extent. Perceptual learning involves developing dimensional structures and also mappings across these dimensions.

Quite a bit is known about the neural and computational mechanisms underlying the acquisition of topologically structured representations of the environment. Sensory maps in the cortex preserve topological structures of the peripheral sensory system; for example, the primary sensory area responsible for the middle finger (digit 3) of the Macaque monkey lies between the areas responsible for digits 2 and 4. Several types of adaptive cortical change, all of which preserve topological mapping, are observed when environmental or cortical changes occur (Garraghty & Kaas 1992). When cortical areas are lesioned, neighboring areas newly respond to sensory information formerly controlled by the lesioned area; when external sensory organs are disabled, cortical areas formerly activated by the organ become sensitive to sensory stimulation formerly controlled by its neighboring areas (Kaas 1991). When two fingers are surgically fused, creating highly correlated inputs, a large number of cortical areas develop that respond to both fingers (Allard et al 1991). Kohonen (1995) has developed a framework for describing neural networks that develop topological structures with learning. These networks are composed of detectors that compete for the opportunity to learn to respond to inputs more strongly, and are arranged in topologies (typically, two-dimensional lattices). These topologies influence learning—not only does the unit that is best adapted to an input learn to respond more vigorously to the input, but so do its neighbors. Variants of Kohonen's networks can acquire topologies similar to those found in the cortex, and can adapt in similar ways to network lesions and alterations in the environment (Miikkulainen et al 1997). Other neural networks capture more abstract spatial dimensions, learning dimensions that optimally describe the similarities between a set of objects (Edelman & Intrator 1997). In general, these networks develop detectors that are locally tailored to particular inputs, and also arrange their detectors in a global configuration that represents similarities and dimensions across inputs.

## Differentiation

A major mechanism of perceptual learning is for percepts to become increasingly differentiated from each other. By differentiation, stimuli that were once psychologically fused together become separated. Once separated, discriminations can be made between percepts that were originally indistinguishable. As with imprinting, differentiation occurs at the level of whole stimuli and features within stimuli.

DIFFERENTIATION OF WHOLE STIMULI   In the classic examples of wine experts learning to distinguish the upper and lower halves of a bottle of Madeira by taste, poultry sorters learning to distinguish male from female chicks, and parents learning to uniquely identify their identical twin children, perceptual adaptation involves developing increasingly differentiated object representations. In many cases, simple preexposure to the stimuli to be distinguished promotes their differentiation. Rats who have cutout shapes visible from their cages are better able to learn subsequent discriminations involving these shapes than rats who are exposed to other shapes (Gibson & Walk 1956). Practice in identifying visual "scribbles" increases their discriminability, even when no feedback is provided (Gibson & Gibson 1955). However, learning to differentiate between objects is typically accelerated by training in which the objects are associated with different labels or responses (Gibson 1969, Hall 1991).

*Psychophysical differentiation*   Laboratory studies have extensively studied training effects involving simple discriminations. In vernier discrimination tasks, subjects respond whether one line is displaced above or below a second line. Training in this task can produce impressive improvements, to the point that subjects exhibit resolution finer than the spacing between individual photoreceptors (Poggio et al 1992). Such hyperacuity is possible because receptive fields of cells overlap considerably, and thus points that fall within the receptive field of one cell can be discriminated by differential impacts on other cells. Discrimination training is often highly specific to the task. Trained performance on a horizontal discrimination task frequently does not transfer to a vertical version of the same task (Fahle & Edelman 1993, Poggio et al 1992), does not transfer to new retinal locations (Fahle et al 1995, Shiu & Pashler 1992), and does not completely transfer from the trained eye to the untrained eye (Fahle et al 1995).

The surprising specificity of simple discrimination learning has led some researchers to posit an early cortical locus of adaptation, perhaps as early as the primary visual cortex (Gilbert 1996, Karni & Sagi 1991). Improvement in the discrimination of motion of a random dot field has been shown to be associated with a change in the response characteristics of individual cells in area MT in the parietal cortex (Zohary et al 1994). Computational models have explained improvements in discrimination training in terms of changes in weights between cells and output units that control judgments (Poggio et al 1992). Each cell has a limited receptive field and specific orientation, and cells that predict vernier discriminations become more influential over time. Thus, the proposed mechanism for differentiation is selective emphasis of discriminating receptive cells.

A related method for implementing differentiation is to develop expanded representations for receptive cells that permit discrimination of objects that should receive different responses. Monkeys trained to make discriminations between slightly different sound frequencies develop larger cortical representations for the presented frequencies than control monkeys (Recanzone et al 1993). Similarly, monkeys learning to make a tactile discrimination with one hand develop a larger cortical representation for that hand than for the other hand (Recanzone et al 1992). Elbert et al (1995) measured brain activity in the somatosensory cortex of violinists as their fingers are lightly touched. There was greater activity in the sensory cortex for the left hand than the right hand, consistent with the observation that violinists require fine movements of their left-hand fingers considerably more than their right-hand fingers.

A third neural mechanism for stimulus differentiation is to narrow the tuning of critical receptors. Receptors that are originally broadly tuned (large receptive fields) often become responsive to an increasingly limited range of stimuli with training. Recanzone et al (1993) observe a narrowing of frequency-sensitive receptors following auditory discrimination. Saarinen & Levi (1995) also find evidence that training in a vernier discrimination task results in receptors that are more narrowly tuned to diagnostic orientations. A mechanism for differentiation explored by Luce et al (1976) is that a roving attentional band can be selectively placed on critical regions of a perceptual dimension, and that signals falling within the band are given a sensory representation about an order of magnitude greater than signals falling outside of the band. These four mechanisms—selective weighting of discriminating cells, expanding regions dedicated to discriminating cells, narrowing tuning of discriminating cells, and shifting attentional "magnifiers" to critical regions—all serve to differentiate stimuli by psychologically warping local regions of stimulus space.

*Differentiation of complex stimuli*   Differentiation of more complex stimuli that differ across many dimensions has also been studied. Lively et al (1993) report training procedures that allow Japanese speakers to acquire a discrimination between the phonemes /r/ and /l/ that is not present in their native language. The methodological innovations apparently needed to assure general transfer performance are to provide the phonemes in natural words, to give listeners words spoken by many different speakers, and to give immediate feedback as to the correct word. A general finding has been that increasing the variability of instances within the categories to be discriminated increases the amount of training time needed to reach a criterion level of accuracy, but also yields better transfer to novel stimuli (Posner & Keele 1968). Another result of practical interest is that discrimination performance can be improved by an "easy-to-hard" procedure in which subjects are first exposed to easy, highly separated discriminations along a dimension (such as black versus white stimuli on the dimension of brightness), and then are given successively more difficult discriminations along the same dimension (Mackintosh 1974). Apparently, first presenting the easy discrimination allows organisms to allocate attention to the relevant dimension.

A major subfield within stimulus differentiation has explored expertise in face perception. People are better able to identify faces belonging to races with which they are familiar (Shapiro & Penrod 1986). For example, in general, Caucasian participants in the United States are better able to identify Caucasian faces than African-American faces. This is another example of familiar objects becoming increasingly differentiated. A common account for the difficulty in recognizing cross-race faces is that people become adept at detecting the features that are most useful in distinguishing among faces we commonly see (O'Toole et al 1996). Interestingly, people are faster at categorizing those faces that are more difficult to identify. For example, in an African-American/Caucasian discrimination task, Caucasian participants are faster at categorizing African-Americans (as African-Americans) than Caucasians (Valentine 1991). Valentine explains this effect in terms of greater perceived distances between familiar faces, which slows tasks such as a two-category discrimination that require treating familiar faces as equivalent. In contrast, Levin (1996) obtains evidence that African-American categorizations are facilitated for Caucasians because of a quickly coded race feature that marks cross-race but not same-race faces. This later possibility suggests that object differentiation may be achieved by developing features that uniquely pick out less common objects from familiar objects (Goldstone 1996), and is consistent with results showing that perceptual retention of abnormal chest X-rays increases with radiological expertise, whereas retention of normal X-rays actually decreases with expertise (Myles-Worsley et al 1988). Levin's account is not necessarily incompatible with the standard account; features may become salient if they serve to either discriminate among familiar objects or to distinguish rare objects from familiar ones.

The results are somewhat mixed with respect to the benefit of instructional mediation in learning to differentiate stimuli. For learning to discriminate between beers (Peron & Allen 1988), experience with tasting beers improved performance, but increased experience with beer-flavor terminology did not. However, in learning to sort day-old chickens by gender, college students with no experience were able to categorize photographs of chickens nearly as well as were expert chicken sorters if they were given a short page of instructions describing shape-based differences between male and female chickens (Biederman & Shiffrar 1987). It is an open question whether genuinely perceptual changes can be produced after simply reading a brief set of instructions. Those who argue that perceptual phenomena are generally not highly malleable to instructions and strategies (Rock 1985) might consider Biederman & Shiffrar's results to merely show that perceptual features that have previously been learned can become linked to categories by instructions. On the other hand, strategic intentions and labels can produce phenomenologically different percepts of ambiguous objects, and the linguistic labels chosen to describe an object can radically reorganize its perception (Wisniewski & Medin 1994). The possibility that perceptual processes are altered by instructional or strategic manipulations cannot be dismissed.

*Differentiation of categories*   Ascending even further in terms of the complexity of stimuli to be differentiated, not only do simple and complex objects become differentiated with experience, but entire categories do as well. Category learning often involves dividing a large, general category into subcategories. Intuition tells us that experts in a field have several differentiated categories where the novice has only a single category. Empirical support for this notion comes from Tanaka & Taylor's (1991) study of speeded classification by dog and bird experts. Categories can be ordered in terms of specificity, from highly general superordinate categories (e.g. "animal"), to moderately specific basic-level categories ("dog"), to highly specific subordinate categories ("German shepherd"). When shown photographs of objects and asked to verify whether they belong to a particular category, experts are able to categorize at basic and subordinate levels equally quickly, but only for the objects within their domain of expertise. In contrast, novices (e.g. bird experts shown dog photographs) show a pronounced advantage for basic-level categorizations. Extending the previously described identification advantage for same-race faces, O'Toole et al (1996) find that Caucasians and Japanese are faster at classifying faces of their own race into "male" and "female" categories than faces of the other race. Categories, not just objects, are more differentiated within familiar domains.

Cross-cultural differences provide additional evidence that categories that are important become highly differentiated (Malt 1995). For example, the Tzletal Indians group all butterflies together in one category, but have 16 different categories for their larvae, which are culturally important as food sources and crop pests (Hunn 1982). The observer-relative terms "Left" and "Right" are important spatial concepts in some cultures, whereas other cultures (e.g. speakers of Guugu Yimithrr) much more frequently describe space in terms of absolute directions such as "North" and "South." Levinson (1996) argues that this cultural difference has an influence on perceptual tasks such as completing paths and discriminating between events that differ as to their relative or absolute spatial relations. Generally, the degree of differentiation among the categories of a culture is a joint function of the importance of the categories for the culture and the objective number and frequency of the categories in the environment (Geoghegan 1976).

There is also developmental evidence that categories become more differentiated with age. Infants tend to successively touch objects that are perceptually similar. Using successive touching as an indicator of subjective groupings, Mandler et al (1991) show that 18-month-old infants group objects at the superordinate level (e.g. successively touching toy goats and cats more frequently than dogs and planes) before they show evidence of basic-level categories (e.g. by successively touching two cats more frequently than a cat and a dog). In sum, evidence from expert/novice differences, cross-cultural differences, development, and neuroscience (Farah 1990) provide converging evidence that broader levels of categorization are deeply entrenched and perhaps primary, and that experience yields more subtly differentiated categories.

DIFFERENTIATION OF DIMENSIONS    Just as experience can lead to the psychological separation of stimuli or categories, it can also lead to the separation of perceptual dimensions that comprise a single stimulus. Dimensions that are originally treated as fused often become segregated with development or training. People often shift from perceiving stimuli in terms of holistic, overall aspects to analytically decomposing objects into separate dimensions.

This trend has received substantial support from developmental psychology. Evidence suggests that dimensions that are easily isolated by adults, such as the brightness and size of a square, are treated as fused together for children (Smith 1989a). It is relatively difficult for young children to say whether two objects are identical on a particular property, but relatively easy for them to say whether they are similar across many dimensions (Smith 1989a). Children have difficulty identifying whether two objects differ on their brightness or size even though they can easily see that they differ in some way (Kemler 1983). Children also show considerable difficulty in tasks that require selective attention to one dimension while ignoring another (Smith & Evans 1989). When given the choice of sorting objects by their overall similarity or by selecting a single criterial dimension, children tend to use overall similarity, whereas adults use the single dimension (Smith 1989b). Perceptual dimensions seem to be more tightly integrated for children than adults, such that children cannot easily access the individual dimensions that compose an object.

The developmental trend toward differentiated dimensions is echoed by adult training studies. In certain circumstances, color experts (art students and vision scientists) are better able to selectively attend to dimensions (e.g. hue, chroma, and value) that comprise color than are nonexperts (Burns & Shepp 1988). People who learn a categorization in which color saturation is relevant and color brightness is irrelevant develop selectively heightened sensitivity at making saturation discriminations (Goldstone 1994), even though prior to training it is difficult for adults to selectively attend to brightness without attending to saturation. Melcher & Schooler (1996) provide suggestive evidence that expert, but not nonexpert, wine tasters isolate independent perceptual features in wines that closely correspond to the terminology used to describe wines.

Several computational models have been proposed for differentiation. Competitive learning networks differentiate inputs into categories by specializing detectors to respond to classes of inputs. Random detectors that are slightly more similar to an input than other detectors will learn to adapt themselves toward the input and will inhibit other detectors from doing so (Rumelhart & Zipser 1985). The end result is that originally similar detectors that respond almost equally to all inputs become increasingly specialized and differentiated over training. Detectors develop that respond selectively to particular classes of input patterns or dimensions within the input. Smith et al (1997) present a neural network simulation of the development of separated dimensions in children. In the network, dimensions become separated by detectors developing strong connections to specific dimensions while weakening their connections to all other dimensions. The model captures the empirical phenomenon that dimension differentiation is greatly facilitated by providing comparisons of the sort "this red square and this red triangle have the same color."

## Unitization

Unitization is a perceptual learning mechanism that seemingly operates in a direction opposite to differentiation. Unitization involves the construction of single functional units that can be triggered when a complex configuration arises. Via unitization, a task that originally required detection of several parts can be accomplished by detecting a single unit. Whereas differentiation divides wholes into cleanly separated parts, unitization integrates parts into single wholes.

In exploring unitization, LaBerge (1973) found that when stimuli were unexpected, participants were faster at responding to actual letters than to letter-like controls. Furthermore, this difference was attenuated as the unfamiliar letter-like stimuli became more familiar with practice. He argued that the components of often-presented stimuli become processed as a single functional unit when they consistently occur together. More recently, Czerwinski et al (1992) have described a process in which conjunctions of stimulus features are "chunked" together so that they become perceived as a single unit. Shiffrin & Lightfoot (1997) argued that even separated line segments can become unitized following prolonged practice with the materials. Their evidence comes from the slopes relating the number of distractor elements to response time in a feature search task. When participants learned a conjunctive search task in which three line segments were needed to distinguish the target from distractors, impressive and prolonged decreases in search slopes were observed over 20 sessions.

Other evidence for unitization comes from word perception. Researchers have argued that words are perceived as single units because of people's lifelong experience with them. These word units can be processed automatically and interfere with other processes less than do nonwords (O'Hara 1980, Smith & Haviland 1972). Results have shown that the advantages attributable to words over nonwords cannot be explained by the greater informational redundancy of letters within words (Smith & Haviland 1972). Instead, these researchers argue for recognition processes that respond to information at levels higher than the individual letters. Salasoo et al (1985) find that the advantage of words over nonwords in perceptual identification tasks can be eliminated by repetitively exposing participants to the stimuli. They explain their results in terms of developing single, unitized codes for repeated nonwords.

Evidence for unitization also comes from researchers exploring configural perception. For example, researchers have argued that faces are processed in a holistic or configural manner that does not involve analyzing faces into specific features (Farah 1992). According to the "inversion effect" in object recognition, the recognition cost of rotating a stimulus 180 degrees in the picture plane is much greater for specialized, highly practiced stimuli than for less specialized stimuli (Diamond & Carey 1986, Tanaka & Gauthier 1997). For example, recognition of faces is substantially less fast and accurate when the faces are inverted. This large difference between upright and inverted recognition efficiency is not found for other objects and is not found to the same degree for less familiar cross-race faces. Diamond & Carey (1986) report a large inversion cost for dog breed recognition, but only for dog experts. Similarly, Gauthier & Tarr (1997) report that large inversion costs for a nonsense object can be created in the laboratory by giving participants prolonged exposure to the object. They conclude that repeated experience with an object leads to developing a configural representation of it that combines all of its parts into a single, viewpoint-specific, functional unit.

There is also evidence that children develop increasingly integrated representations of visual objects as they mature. Whereas three-year-old children tend to break objects into simple, spatially independent parts, five-year-olds use more complicated spatial relations to connect the parts together (Stiles & Tada 1996). It has even been claimed that configural association systems require about 4.5 years to develop, and before this time, children can solve perceptual problems requiring elements but not configurations of elements (Rudy et al 1993).

Computer and neural sciences have provided insights into methods for implementing unitization. Grossberg's self-organizing ART systems (Grossberg 1984, 1991) create units by building bidirectional links between several perceptual features and a single unit in a deeper layer of the neural network. Triggering the single unit suffices to reproduce the entire pattern of perceptual features. Mozer et al (1992) develop a neural network that creates configural units by synchronizing neurons responsible for visual parts to be bound together. Visual parts that co-occur in a set of patterns will tend to be bound together, consistent with the evidence above indicating that units are created for often-repeated stimuli. Neural mechanisms for developing configural units with experience are located in the superior colliculus and inferior temporal regions. Cells in the superior colliculus of several species receive inputs from many sensory modalities (e.g. visual, auditory, and somatosensory), and differences in their activities reflect learned associations across these modalities (Stein &

Wallace 1996). Within the visual modality, single cells of the inferior temporal cortex become selectively responsive to complex objects that have been repetitively presented (Logothetis et al 1995).

Unitization may seem at odds with dimension differentiation. There is an apparent contradiction between experience creating larger "chunks" via unitization and dividing an object into more clearly delineated parts via differentiation. This incongruity can be transformed into a commonality at a more abstract level. Both mechanisms depend on the requirements established by tasks and stimuli. Objects will tend to be decomposed into their parts if the parts reflect independent sources of variation, or if the parts differ in their relevancy (Schyns & Murphy 1994). Parts will tend to be unitized if they co-occur frequently, with all parts indicating a similar response. Thus, unitization and differentiation are both processes that build appropriate-sized representations for the tasks at hand. Both phenomena could be incorporated in a model that begins with a specific featural description of objects, and creates units for conjunctions of features if the features frequently occur together, and divides features into subfeatures if independent sources of variation within the original features are detected.

## THE LIMITATIONS AND POTENTIAL OF PERCEPTUAL LEARNING

Thus far, the reviewed evidence has focused on positive instances of perceptual learning—situations where training produces changes, oftentimes strikingly large, to our perceptual systems. However, a consideration of the limits on perceptual learning leads to a better understanding of the constraints on learning, and hence of the mechanisms that are at work when learning is achieved.

Previously reviewed evidence suggests strong limits on the generality of perceptual learning. Training on simple visual discriminations often does not transfer to different eyes, to different spatial locations, or to different tasks involving the same stimuli (Fahle & Morgan 1996, Shiu & Pashler 1992). As suggested by the strong role played by imprinting, perceptual learning often does not transfer extensively to new stimuli or tasks different from those used during training. Several researchers have argued that generalization between tasks is only found to the extent that the tasks share procedural elements in common (Anderson 1987, Kolers & Roediger 1984). At the same time, perceptual training does often transfer not just within a sensory modality, but across sensory modalities. Training on a visual discrimination involving certain shapes improves performance on a later tactile discrimination involving the same shapes (Hughes et al 1990). Not only does cross-modality transfer occur, but it has also been shown computationally that two modalities that are trained at the same time and provide feedback for each other can reach a level of performance that would not be possible if they remained independent (Becker 1996, de Sa & Ballard 1997, Edelman 1987). Consistent with these arguments for mutually facilitating modalities, children with auditory deficits but normal IQs also tend to show later deficits in visual selective attention tasks (Quittner et al 1994). One principle for unifying some of the evidence for and against generalization of training seems to be that when perceptual learning involves changes to early perceptual processes, then there will be less generalization of that learning to other tasks (Sagi & Tanne 1994, Sireteanu & Rettenbach 1995).

In addition to constraints on generalization, there are limits on whether perceptual learning occurs at all. To take unitization as an example, many studies indicate a surprising inability of people to build single chunks out of separated dimensions. In Treisman & Gelade's (1980) classic research on feature search, the influence of distractor letters in a conjunctive search remained essentially unchanged over 1664 trials, suggesting that new functional units cannot be formed for conjunctions of color and shape. Although these results are replicable, they depend on the particular features to be joined together. Shiffrin & Lightfoot (1997) report five-fold improvements in response times in a similar, conjunctive search paradigm in which the conjunctions are defined not by color and shape but by different line segments. Searching for conjunctions of shape parts that are formed by life-long experience with letters (Wang et al 1994), or brief laboratory experience (Lubow & Kaplan 1997), is quite different from searching for unfamiliar conjunctions. The influence of distractors on a conjunctive task involving relations such as "dash above plus" is not modulated by practice if the dash and plus are disconnected, but if they are connected, then pronounced practice effects are observed (Logan 1994). People are much more adept at learning conjunctions between shape and position than between shape and color, even when position and color are equally salient (Saiki & Hummel 1996). Thus, logically equivalent conjunctive search tasks can produce very widely different perceptual learning patterns depending on the conjoined features. Features or dimensions that are similar to each other are easy to join together and difficult to isolate (Melara & Marks 1990), and perceptual learning is constrained by these relations.

Perceptual learning at any given time is always constrained by the existing structure of the organism. As such, it is misguided to view perceptual learning as the opposite of innate disposition. Although apparently paradoxical, it is the constraints of systems that allow for their adaptation. Eimas (1994, 1997) provides convincing evidence that infants come into the world with techniques for segmenting speech into parts, and it is these constraints that allow them later to learn the meaning-bearing units of language. Many models of perception are shifting away from generic, general-purpose neural networks and toward highly structured, constrained networks that have greater learning and generalization potential because of their preexisting organization (Regier 1996). Early constraints on perception serve to bootstrap the development of more sophisticated percepts. For example, infants seem to be constrained to treat parts that move together as coming from the same object, but this constraint allows them to learn about the color and shape regularities found within objects (Spelke 1990). The preexisting structures that provide the basis of perceptual learning may be innate, but also may be the result of earlier learning processes (Elman et al 1996). At any given time, what can be learned depends on what has already been learned; the constraints on perceptual change may themselves evolve with experience.

Despite limits on the generalization, speed, and occurrence of perceptual learning, it remains an important source of human flexibility. Human learning is often divided into perceptual, cognitive, and procedural varieties. These divisions are regrettable, causing fruitful links to be neglected. There are deep similarities between perceptual unitization and chunking in memory, and between perceptual differentiation and association-building (Hall 1991). In many cases, perceptual learning involves acquiring new procedures for actively probing one's environment (Gibson 1969), such as learning procedures for efficiently scanning the edges of an object (Hochberg 1997, Salapatek & Kessen 1973). Perhaps the only reason to selectively highlight perceptual learning is to stress that flexible and consistent responses often involve adjusting initial representations of stimuli. Perceptual learning exerts a profound influence on behavior precisely because it occurs early during information processing and thus shifts the foundation for all subsequent processes.

In her 1991 preface to her 1963 *Annual Review of Psychology* article, Gibson laments, "I wound up pointing out the need for a theory and the prediction that 'more specific theories of perceptual learning are on the way.' I was wrong there—the cognitive psychologists have seldom concerned themselves with perceptual learning" (Gibson 1991, p. 322). The reviewed research suggests that this quote is too pessimistic; there has been much progress on theories of the sort predicted by Gibson in 1963. These theories are receiving convergent support from several disciplines. Many of the concrete proposals for implementing mechanisms of perceptual learning come from neural and computer sciences. Traditional disciplinary boundaries will have to be crossed for a complete account, and considering the field in terms of underlying mechanisms of adaptation (e.g. attention weighting, imprinting, differentiation, and unitization) rather than domains (e.g. expertise, psychophysics, development, and cross-cultural comparison) will perhaps result in more unified and principled accounts of perceptual learning.

Note: Further information about the topic and author can be accessed via http://cognitrn.psych.indiana.edu/

> Visit the *Annual Reviews home page* at
> http://www.AnnualReviews.org.

## Literature Cited

Allard T, Clark SA, Jenkins WM, Merzenich MM. 1991. Reorganization of somatosensory area 3b representation in adult Owl Monkeys after digital syndactyly. *J. Neurophysiol.* 66:1048–58

Allen SW, Brooks LR. 1991. Specializing the operation of an explicit rule. *J. Exp. Psychol. Gen.* 120:3–19

Anderson JA, Silverstein JW, Ritz SA, Jones RS. 1977. Distinctive features, categorical perception, and probability learning: some applications of a neural model. *Psychol. Rev.* 84:413–51

Anderson JR. 1987. Skill acquisition: compilation of weak-method problem solutions. *Psychol. Rev.* 94:192–210

Aslin RN, Smith LB. 1988. Perceptual development. *Annu. Rev. Psychol.* 39:435–73

Beale JM, Keil FC. 1995. Categorical effects in the perception of faces. *Cognition* 57:217–39

Becker S. 1996. Mutual information maximization: models of cortical self-organization. *Netw. Comput. Neural Syst.* 7:7–31

Bedford FL. 1993. Perceptual learning. In *The Psychology of Learning and Motivation,* ed. DL Medin, pp. 1–60. San Diego: Academic

Bedford FL. 1995. Constraints on perceptual learning: objects and dimensions. *Cognition* 54:253–97

Biederman I, Shiffrar MM. 1987. Sexing day-old chicks: a case study and expert systems analysis of a difficult perceptual-learning task. *J. Exp. Psychol.: Learn. Mem. Cogn.* 13:640–45

Bingham GP, Schmidt RC, Rosenblum LD. 1995. Dynamics and the orientation of kinematic forms in visual event recognition. *J. Exp. Psychol.: Hum. Percept. Perform.* 21:1473–93

Brooks LR, Norman GR, Allen SW. 1991. Role of specific similarity in a medical diagnostic task. *J. Exp. Psychol. Gen.* 120:278–87

Burns B, Shepp BE. 1988. Dimensional interactions and the structure of psychological space: the representation of hue, saturation, and brightness. *Percept. Psychophys.* 43:494–507

Burns EM, Ward WD. 1978. Categorical perception—phenomenon or epiphenomenon: evidence from experiments in the perception of melodic musical intervals. *J. Acoust. Soc. Am.* 63:456–68

Calder AJ, Young AW, Perrett DI, Etcoff NL, Rowland D. 1996. Categorical perception of morphed facial expressions. *Vis. Cogn.* 3:81–117

Czerwinski M, Lightfoot N, Shiffrin RM. 1992. Automatization and training in visual search. *Am. J. Psychol.* 105:271–315

de Sa VR, Ballard DH. 1997. Perceptual learning from cross-modal feedback. See Goldstone et al 1997, pp. 309–52

Diamond R, Carey S. 1986. Why faces are and are not special: an effect of expertise. *J. Exp. Psychol. Gen.* 115:107–17

Doane SM, Alderton DL, Sohn YW, Pellegrino JW. 1996. Acquisition and transfer of skilled performance: Are visual discrimination skills stimulus specific? *J. Exp. Psychol. Gen.* 22:1218–48

Edelman GM. 1987. *Neural Darwinism: The Theory of Neuronal Group Selection.* New York: Basic Books

Edelman S, Intrator N. 1997. Learning as extraction of low-dimensional representations. See Goldstone et al 1997, pp. 353–80

Eimas PD. 1994. Categorization in early infancy and the continuity of development. *Cognition* 50:83–93

Eimas PD. 1997. Infant speech perception: processing characteristics, representational units, and the learning of words. See Goldstone et al 1997, pp. 127–70

Eimas PD, Siqueland ER, Jusczyk PW, Vigorito J. 1971. Speech perception in infants. *Science* 171:303–6

Elbert T, Pantev C, Wienbruch C, Rockstroh B, Taub E. 1995. Increased cortical reprentation of the fingers of the left hand in string players. *Science.* 270:305–7

Elman JL, Bates EA, Johnson MH, Karmiloff-Smith A, Parisi D, Plunkett K. 1996. *Rethinking Innateness.* Cambridge, MA: MIT Press

Fahle M, Edelman S. 1993. Long-term learning in vernier acuity: effects of stimulus orientation, range and of feedback. *Vis. Res.* 33:397–412

Fahle M, Edelman S, Poggio T. 1995. Fast perceptual learning in hyperacuity. *Vis. Res.* 35:3003–13

Fahle M, Morgan M. 1996. No transfer of perceptual learning between similar stimuli in the same retinal position. *Curr. Biol.* 6: 292–97

Farah MJ. 1990. *Visual Agnosia: Disorders of Object Recognition and What They Tell Us About Normal Vision.* Cambridge, MA: MIT Press

Farah MJ. 1992. Is an object an object an object? Cognitive and neuropsychological investigations of domain-specificity in visual object recognition. *Curr. Dir. Psychol. Sci.* 1:164–69

Fox E. 1995. Negative priming from ignored distractors in visual selection: a review. *Psychonom. Bull. Rev.* 2:145–73

Garraghty PE, Kaas JH. 1992. Dynamic features of sensory and motor maps. *Curr. Opin. Neurobiol.* 2:522–27

Gauthier I, Tarr MJ. 1997. Becoming a "Greeble" expert: exploring mechanisms for face recognition. *Vis. Res.* 37:1673–82

Geoghegan WH. 1976. Polytypy in folk biological taxonomies. *Am. Ethnol.* 3:469–80

Gibson EJ. 1969. *Principles of perceptual learning and development.* New York: Appleton-Century-Crofts

Gibson EJ. 1991. *An Odyssey in Learning and Perception.* Cambridge, MA: MIT Press

Gibson EJ, Walk RD. 1956. The effect of prolonged exposure to visually presented patterns on learning to discriminate them. *J. Compar. Physiol. Psychol.* 49:239–42

Gibson JJ, Gibson EJ. 1955. Perceptual learning: differentiation or enrichment? *Psychol. Rev.* 62:32–41

Gilbert CD. 1996. Plasticity in visual perception and physiology. *Curr. Opin. Neurobiol.* 6:269–74

Goldstone RL. 1994. Influences of categorization on perceptual discrimination. *J. Exp. Psychol. Gen.* 123:178–200

Goldstone RL. 1995. Effects of categorization on color perception. *Psychol. Sci.* 6: 298–304

Goldstone RL. 1996. Isolated and interrelated concepts. *Mem. Cogn.* 24:608–28

Goldstone RL, Schyns PG, Medin DL, eds. 1997. *The Psychology of Learning and Motivation.* San Diego: Academic

Grossberg S. 1984. Unitization, automaticity, temporal order, and word recognition. *Cogn. Brain Theory* 7:263–83

Grossberg S. 1991. Nonlinear neural networks: principles, mechanisms, and architectures. In *Pattern Recognition by Self-Organizing Neural Networks,* ed. GA Carpenter, S Grossberg, pp. 36–109. Cambridge, MA: MIT Press

Haider H, Frensch PA. 1996. The role of information reduction in skill acquisition. *Cogn. Psychol.* 30:304–37

Hall G. 1991. *Perceptual and Associative Learning.* Oxford: Clarendon

Harnad S, ed. 1987. *Categorical Perception.* Cambridge: Cambridge Univ. Press

Harnad S, Hanson SJ, Lubin J. 1995. Learned categorical perception in neural nets: Implications for symbol grounding. In *Symbolic Processors and Connectionist Network Models in Artificial Intelligence and Cognitive Modelling: Steps Toward Principled Integration,* ed. V Honavar, L Uhr, pp. 191–206. Boston: Academic

Helson H. 1948. Adaptation-level as a basis for a quantitative theory of frames of reference. *Psychol. Rev.* 55:297–313

Herrnstein RJ. 1990. Levels of stimulus control: a functional approach. *Cognition* 37: 133–66

Hillyard HC, Kutas M. 1983. Electrophysiology of cognitive processes. *Annu. Rev. Psychol.* 34:33–61

Hinton G, Williams K, Revow M. 1992. Adaptive elastic models for handprinted character recognition. In *Advances in Neural Information Processing Systems, IV,* ed. J Moody, S Hanson, R Lippmann, pp. 341–76. San Mateo, CA: Morgan Kaufmann

Hochberg J. 1997. The affordances of perceptual inquiry: pictures are learned from the world, and what that fact might mean about perception quite generally. See Goldstone et al 1997, pp. 15–44

Hock HS, Webb E, Cavedo LC. 1987. Perceptual learning in visual category acquisition. *Mem. Cogn.* 15:544–56

Hofstadter D. 1995. *Fluid Concepts and Creative Analogies.* New York: Basic Books

Honey RC, Hall G. 1989. Acquired equivalence and distinctiveness of cues. *J. Exp. Psychol. Anim. Behav. Proc.* 15:338–46

Howells TH. 1944. The experimental development of color-tone synesthesia. *J. Exp. Psychol.* 34:87–103

Hughes B, Epstein W, Schneider S, Dudock A.

1990. An asymmetry in transmodal perceptual learning. *Percept. Psychophys.* 48: 143–50

Hunn ES. 1982. The utilitarian factor in folk biological classification. *Am. Anthropol.* 84:830–47

Intrator N. 1994. Feature extraction using an unsupervised neural network. *Neural Comput.* 4:98–107

Kaas JH. 1991. Plasticity of sensory and motor maps in adult mammals. *Annu. Rev. Neurosci.* 14:137–67

Karni A, Sagi D. 1991. Where practice makes perfect in texture discrimination: evidence for primary visual cortex plasticity. *Proc. Natl. Acad. Sci. USA* 88:4966–70

Karni A, Sagi D. 1993. The time course of learning a visual skill. *Nature* 365:250–52

Kemler DG. 1983. Holistic and analytic modes in perceptual and cognitive development. In *Perception, Cognition, and Development: Interactional Analyses,* ed. TJ Tighe, BE Shepp, pp. 77–101. Hillsdale, NJ: Erlbaum

Kolb B. 1995. *Brain Plasticity and Behavior.* NJ: LEA

Kohonen T. 1995. *Self-Organizing Maps.* Berlin: Springer-Verlag

Kolers PA, Roediger HL. 1984. Procedures of mind. *J. Verbal Learn. Verbal Behav.* 23: 425–49

Kuhl PK, Miller JD. 1978. Speech perception by the chinchilla: identification functions for synthetic VOT stimuli. *J. Acoust. Soc. Am.* 63:905–17

LaBerge D. 1973. Attention and the measurement of perceptual learning. *Mem. Cogn.* 1:268–76

Lawrence DH. 1949. Acquired distinctiveness of cue. I. Transfer between discriminations on the basis of familiarity with the stimulus. *J. Exp. Psychol.* 39:770–84

Levin DT. 1996. Classifying faces by race: the structure of face categories. *J. Exp. Psychol.: Learn. Mem. Cogn.* 22:1364–82

Levinson SC. 1996. Relativity in spatial conception and description. In *Rethinking Linguistic Relativity,* ed. J Gumperz, SC Levinson, pp. 177–202. Cambridge: Cambridge Univ. Press

Liberman AM, Harris KS, Eimas PD, Lisker L, Bastian J. 1957. The discrimination of speech sounds within and across phoneme boundaries. *J. Exp. Psychol.* 61: 379–88

Lively SE, Logan JS, Pisoni DB. 1993. Training Japanese listeners to identify English /r/ and /l/. II. The role of phonetic environment and talker variability in learning new perceptual categories. *J. Acoust. Soc. Am.* 94:1242–55

Livingston KR, Andrews JK. 1995. On the interaction of prior knowledge and stimulus structure in category learning. *Q. J. Exp. Psychol. Hum. Exp. Psychol.* 48A:208–36

Logan GD. 1988. Toward an instance theory of automatization. *Psychol. Rev.* 95: 492–527

Logan GD. 1994. Spatial attention and the apprehension of spatial relations. *J. Exp. Psychol.: Hum. Percept. Perform.* 20: 1015–36

Logan GD, Taylor SE, Etherton JL. 1996. Attention in the acquisition and expression of automaticity. *J. Exp. Psychol.: Learn. Mem. Cogn.* 22:620–38

Logothetis NK, Pauls J, Poggio T. 1995. Shape representation in the inferior temporal cortex of monkeys. *Curr. Biol.* 5: 552–63

Lubow RE, Kaplan O. 1997. Visual search as a function of type of prior experience with target and distractor. *J. Exp. Psychol.: Hum. Percept. Perform.* 23:14–24

Luce RD, Green DM, Weber DL. 1976. Attention bands in absolute identification. *Percept. Psychophys.* 20:49–54

Mackintosh NJ. 1974. *The Psychology of Animal Learning.* London: Academic

Malt BC. 1995. Category coherence in cross-cultural perspective. *Cogn. Psychol.* 29: 85–148

Mandler JM, Bauer PJ, McDonough L. 1991. Separating the sheep from the goats: differentiating global categories. *Cogn. Psychol.* 23:263–98

McGaugh JL, Bermudez-Rattoni F, Prado-Alcala RA. 1995. *Plasticity in the Central Nervous System.* Mahwah, NJ: LEA

Melara RD, Marks LE. 1990. Dimensional interactions in language processing: investigating directions and levels of crosstalk. *J. Exp. Psychol.: Learn. Mem. Cogn.* 16: 539–54

Melcher JM, Schooler JW. 1996. The misremembrance of wines past: verbal and perceptual expertise differentially mediate verbal overshadowing of taste memory. *J. Mem. Lang.* 35:231–45

Miikkulainen R, Bednar JA, Choe Y, Sirosh J. 1997. Self-organization, plasticity, and low-level visual phenomena in a laterally connected map model of primary visual cortex. See Goldstone et al 1997, pp. 257–308

Moscovici S, Personnaz B. 1991. Studies in social influence. VI. Is Lenin orange or red? Imagery and social influence. *Eur. J. Soc. Psychol.* 21:101–18

Mozer MC, Zemel RS, Behrmann M, Williams CKI. 1992. Learning to segment images using dynamic feature binding. *Neural Comput.* 4:650–66

Myles-Worsley M, Johnston WA, Simons MA. 1988. The influence of expertise on X-ray image processing. *J. Exp. Psychol.: Learn. Mem. Cogn.* 14:553–57

Nosofsky RM. 1986. Attention, similarity, and the identification-categorization relationship. *J. Exp. Psychol. Gen.* 115:39–57

Nosofsky RM. 1991. Tests of an exemplar model for relating perceptual classification and recognition memory. *J. Exp. Psychol.: Hum. Percept. Perform.* 17:3–27

Obermayer K, Sejnowski T, Blasdel GG. 1995. Neural pattern formation via a competitive Hebbian mechanism. *Behav. Brain Res.* 66:161–67

O'Hara W. 1980. Evidence in support of word unitization. *Percept. Psychophys.* 27:390–402

O'Toole AJ, Peterson J, Deffenbacher KA. 1996. An 'other-race effect' for categorizing faces by sex. *Perception* 25:669–76

Palmeri TJ. 1997. Exemplar similarity and the development of automaticity. *J. Exp. Psychol.: Learn. Mem. Cogn.* 23:324–54

Palmeri TJ, Goldinger SD, Pisoni DB. 1993. Episodic encoding of voice attributes and recognition memory for spoken words. *J. Exp. Psychol.: Learn. Mem. Cogn.* 19:309–28

Pearce JM. 1987. A model for stimulus generalization in Pavlovian conditioning. *Psychol. Rev.* 94:61–73

Peron RM, Allen GL. 1988. Attempts to train novices for beer flavor discrimination: a matter of taste. *J. Gen. Psychol.* 115:403–18

Perrett DI, Smith PAJ, Potter DD, Mistlin AJ, Head AD, Jeeves MA. 1984. Neurones responsive to faces in the temporal cortex: studies of functional organization, sensitivity to identity and relation to perception. *Hum. Neurobiol.* 3:197–208

Peterson MA, Gibson BS. 1994. Must figure-ground organization precede object recognition? An assumption in peril. *Psychol. Sci.* 5:253–59

Pick HL. 1992. Eleanor J. Gibson: learning to perceive and perceiving to learn. *Dev. Psychol.* 28:787–94

Pisoni DB, Aslin RN, Perey AJ, Hennessy BL. 1982. Some effects of laboratory training on identification and discrimination of voicing contrasts in stop consonants. *J. Exp. Psychol.: Hum. Percept. Perform.* 8:297–314

Poggio T, Edelman S. 1990. A network that learns to recognize three-dimensional objects. *Nature* 343:263–66

Poggio T, Fahle M, Edelman S. 1992. Fast perceptual learning in visual hyperacuity. *Science* 256:1018–21

Posner MI, Keele SW. 1968. On the genesis of abstract ideas. *J. Exp. Psychol.* 77:353–63

Quittner AL, Smith LB, Osberger MJ, Mitchell TV, Katz DB. 1994. The impact of audition on the development of visual attention. *Psychol. Sci.* 5:347–53

Recanzone GH, Merzenich MM, Jenkins WM. 1992. Frequency discrimination training engaging a restricted skin surface results in an emergence of a cutaneous response zone in cortical area 3a. *J. Neurophysiol.* 67:1057–70

Recanzone GH, Schreiner CE, Merzenich MM. 1993. Plasticity in the frequency representation of primary auditory cortex following discrimination training in adult owl monkeys. *J. Neurosci.* 13:87–103

Reed E. 1996. *Encountering the World: Toward an Ecological Psychology.* New York: Oxford Univ. Press

Regier T. 1996. *The Human Semantic Potential.* Cambridge, MA: MIT Press

Repp BH, Liberman AM. 1987. Phonetic category boundaries are flexible. See Harnad 1987, pp. 89–112

Rock I. 1985. Perception and knowledge. *Acta Psychol.* 59:3–22

Rudy JW, Keither JR, Georgen K. 1993. The effect of age on children's learning of problems that require a configural association solution. *Dev. Psychobiol.* 26:171–84

Rumelhart DE, Hinton GE, Williams RJ. 1986. Learning internal representations by back-propagating errors. *Nature* 323:533–36

Rumelhart DE, Zipser D. 1985. Feature discovery by competitive learning. *Cogn. Sci.* 9:75–112

Saarinen J, Levi DM. 1995. Perceptual learning in vernier acuity: What is learned? *Vis. Res.* 35:519–27

Sagi D, Tanne D. 1994. Perceptual learning: learning to see. *Curr. Opin. Neurobiol.* 4:195–99

Saiki J, Hummel JE. 1996. Attribute conjunctions and the part configuration advantage in object category learning. *J. Exp. Psychol.: Learn. Mem. Cogn.* 22:1002–19

Salapatek P, Kessen W. 1973. Prolonged investigation of a plane geometric triangle by the human newborn. *J. Exp. Child Psychol.* 15:22–29

Salasoo A, Shiffrin RM, Feustel TC. 1985. Building permanent memory codes: codification and repetition effects in word identification. *J. Exp. Psychol. Gen.* 114: 50–77

Samuel AG. 1981. Phonemic restoration: insights from a new methodology. *J. Exp. Psychol. Gen.* 110:474–94

Schacter DL. 1987. Implicit memory: history and current status. *J. Exp. Psychol.: Learn. Mem. Cogn.* 13:501–18

Schmidhuber J, Eldracher M, Foltin B. 1996. Semilinear predictability minimization produces well-known feature detectors. *Neural Comput.* 8:773–86

Schyns PG, Goldstone RL, Thibaut J. 1998. Development of features in object concepts. *Behav. Brain Sci.* In press

Schyns PG, Murphy GL. 1994. The ontogeny of part representation in object concepts. In *The Psychology of Learning and Motivation,* ed. DL Medin, 31:305–54. San Diego: Academic

Schyns PG, Rodet L. 1997. Categorization creates functional features. *J. Exp. Psychol.: Learn. Mem. Cogn.* 23:681–96

Sekuler AB, Palmer SE, Flynn C. 1994. Local and global processes in visual completion. *Psychol. Sci.* 5:260–67

Shapiro PN, Penrod SD. 1986. Meta-analysis of face identification studies. *Psychol. Bull.* 100:139–56

Shiffrin RM, Lightfoot N. 1997. Perceptual learning of alphanumeric-like characters. See Goldstone et al 1997, pp. 45–82

Shiffrin RM, Schneider W. 1977. Controlled and automatic human information processing. II. Perceptual Learning, automatic attending and a general theory. *Psychol. Rev.* 84:127–90

Shiu L, Pashler H. 1992. Improvement in line orientation discrimination is retinally local but dependent on cognitive set. *Percept. Psychophys.* 52:582–88

Sinha P, Poggio T. 1996. Role of learning in three-dimensional form perception. *Nature* 384:460–63

Sireteanu R, Rettenbach R. 1995. Perceptual learning in visual search: fast, enduring, but nonspecific. *Vis. Res.* 35:2037–43

Smith EE, Haviland SE. 1972. Why words are perceived more accurately than nonwords: inference versus unitization. *J. Exp. Psychol.* 92:59–64

Smith LB. 1989a. From global similarity to kinds of similarity: the construction of dimensions in development. In *Similarity and Analogical Reasoning,* ed. S Vosniadu, A Ortony, pp. 146–78. Cambridge: Cambridge Univ. Press

Smith LB. 1989b. A model of perceptual classification in children and adults. *Psychol. Rev.* 96:125–44

Smith LB, Evans P. 1989. Similarity, identity, and dimensions: perceptual classification in children and adults. In *Object Perception: Structure and Process,* ed. BE Shepp, S Ballesteros, pp. 325–56. Hillsdale, NJ: Erlbaum

Smith LB, Gasser M, Sandhofer C. 1997. Learning to talk about the properties of objects: a network model of the development of dimensions. See Goldstone et al 1997, pp. 219–56

Smith LB, Sera M. 1992. A developmental analysis of the polar structure of dimensions. *Cogn. Psychol.* 24:99–142

Spelke ES. 1990. Principles of object perception. *Cogn. Sci.* 14:29–56

Stein BE, Wallace MT. 1996. Comparisons of cross-modality integration in midbrain and cortex. *Prog. Brain Res.* 112:289–99

Stiles J, Tada WL. 1996. Developmental change in children's analysis of spatial patterns. *Dev. Psychol.* 32:951–70

Strange W, Jenkins JJ. 1978. Role of linguistic experience in the perception of speech. In *Perception and Experience,* ed. RD Walk, HL Pick Jr, pp. 125–69. New York: Plenum

Tanaka J, Gauthier I. 1997. Expertise in object and face recognition. See Goldstone et al 1997, pp. 83–126

Tanaka J, Taylor M. 1991. Object categories and expertise: Is the basic level in the eye of the beholder? *Cogn. Psychol.* 23:457–82

Tarr MJ. 1995. Rotating objects to recognize them: a case study on the role of viewpoint dependency in the recognition of three-dimensional objects. *Psychon. Bull. Rev.* 2:55–82

Tipper SP. 1992. Selection for action: the role of inhibitory mechanisms. *Curr. Dir. Psychol. Sci.* 1:105–9

Treisman AM, Gelade G. 1980. A feature-integration theory of attention. *Cogn. Psychol.* 12:97–136

Ullman S. 1989. Aligning pictorial descriptions: an approach to object recognition. *Cognition* 32:193–254

Valentine T. 1991. A unified account of the effects of distinctiveness, inversion, and race in face recognition. *Q. J. Exp. Psychol.: Hum. Exp. Psychol.* 43:161–204

Wang Q, Cavanagh P, Green M. 1994. Familiarity and pop-out in visual search. *Percept. Psychophys.* 56:495–500

Weinberger NM. 1993. Learning-induced changes of auditory receptive fields. *Curr. Opin. Neurobiol.* 3:570–77

Werker JF, Lalonde CE. 1988. Cross-language speech perception: initial capabilities and developmental change. *Dev. Psychol.* 24: 672–83

Werker JF, Tees RC. 1984. Cross-language speech perception: evidence for perceptual reorganization during the first year of life. *Infant Behav. Dev.* 7:49–63

Wisniewski EJ, Medin DL. 1994. On the interaction of theory and data in concept learning. *Cogn. Sci.* 18:221–81

Wyttenbach RA, May ML, Hoy RR. 1996. Categorical perception of sound frequency by crickets. *Science* 273:1542–44

Zatorre RJ, Halpern AR. 1979. Identification, discrimination, and selective adaptation of simultaneous musical intervals. *Percept. Psychophys.* 26:384–95

Zohary E, Celebrini S, Britten KH, Newsome WT. 1994. Plasticity that underlies improvement in perceptual performance. *Science* 263:1289–92

# AUTHOR INDEX

## N

Patnoe S, 67, 71
Patrick CJ, 394
Patrick JR, 67
Patterson GR, 7, 13, 18, 19, 126, 171, 172, 175
Patterson MJ, 321
Paul B, 417
Paulaskas SL, 385
Pauls DL, 390
Pauls J, 594, 604
Paulsen C, 135
Paulsen JS, 100
Paunonen SV, 148
Pavia TM, 324
Payne DG, 296, 305
Payne JW, 448, 454, 455, 457, 469
Payne M, 99
Peake PK, 234, 245, 248
Pearce JM, 589
Pearl D, 187
Pearl J, 464
Pearlman K, 148
Pearlmutter NJ, 34, 36
Pechmann C, 323, 324, 329
Pedersen NL, 390, 391, 486
Pedrick JH, 323
Peeke L, 378
Pehling G, 52
Pellegrino JW, 588
Pelli DG, 524
Pendergast JF, 544
Penke M, 215
Pennington N, 274, 275, 461
Penrod SD, 598
Pentland J, 307
Penuel WR, 574
Pepler D, 16, 18
Pepperberg D, 518, 519
Peracchio LA, 323, 325, 326, 329
Perdue CW, 75
Perdue S, 55
Perey AJ, 590
Perez–Granados DR, 16
Perfetti CA, 35
Perkins DN, 496
Perlman M, 8, 14
Perlstein WM, 89, 96
Peron RM, 599
Perret–Clermont AN, 350
Perrett DI, 93, 589, 594
Perrier IN, 402
Perry CL, 435
Perry–Jenkins M, 434
Personnaz B, 587
Pervin LA, 231, 234, 236, 250
Peskin C, 528
Peter JP, 320, 322

Peters DP, 277
Peters E, 451
Peters LH, 151, 152
Petersen AC, 414–16, 426, 432, 435
Petersen SE, 89, 91, 95, 96, 105, 293, 303
Peterson DR, 250
Peterson EW, 98
Peterson JL, 170, 598
Peterson LG, 381
Peterson MA, 587
Peterson P, 347
Peterson RA, 322
Peterson RS, 460
Petrides M, 95, 96, 99
Pettibone JC, 457, 458
PETTIGREW TF, 65–85; 66, 68, 69, 72, 75, 77, 79
Petty RE, 272, 325
Peyrefitte J, 157
Pezdek K, 261
Pezzo MV, 465
Pfeifer PE, 463
Pham TM, 325
Phelan P, 563, 575
Phelps EA, 92, 107, 299
Phelps ME, 55, 99
Phinney JS, 426, 563, 571, 579
Piaget J, 210, 350
Pick HL, 586
Pickrell JE, 306
Piette MJ, 277
Pinching AJ, 51
Pincus AL, 231, 250
Pine CJ, 565
Pinker S, 215–17, 219
Pinsof WM, 188
Pintrich PR, 426
Pinuelas A, 14
Pisoni D, 203
Pisoni DB, 589–91, 598
Pitman J, 68
Pittman K, 426, 435
Pitz GF, 448
Plank S, 566
Platt JR, 276
Plomin R, 3, 4, 7, 8, 238, 252, 486
Plous S, 266
Plucker J, 493
Plunkett K, 206, 216, 606
Pluzinski C, 332
Podsakoff PM, 149
Poggio T, 592, 594, 597, 604
Pokorny J, 512–14, 516, 517, 519, 521, 523–25, 527, 530
Poldrack RA, 99, 103

Polichar D, 566
Polinsky M, 49
Polka L, 202
Pollay RW, 334
Pollins LD, 132
Polster MR, 91, 96, 293, 301
Polycarpou MP, 72
Poole FJP, 482
Poole ME, 579
Poon WY, 538
Pope LK, 233
Popper KR, 271, 276, 369
Port RF, 201
Porter B, 170
Porter TM, 261
Posner MI, 13, 28, 95, 235, 238, 252, 598
Potter DD, 594
Potter J, 38
Powers DA, 69, 72
Powers S, 17
Pozzilli C, 104
Prabhakaran V, 95
Pradere D, 300, 307
Prado–Alcala RA, 587
Prasada S, 216
Pratkanis AR, 276, 277
Prawat R, 347
Prelec D, 460, 465
Prendergast C, 142
Press GA, 91
Preston E, 266, 271, 275, 277
Preston IL, 334
Preston JD, 66
Presty S, 99
Price C, 94
Price LL, 328
Primavera J, 431
Prince SE, 188
Pritchard RD, 160
Prusky G, 46
Pugh ENJ, 509, 510
Pulakos ED, 155–57
Purbhoo M, 71, 75
Purpura DP, 55, 58
Purpura K, 516, 528
Pury C, 388
Putnam DB, 482
Puto C, 457
Putsis WP, 324
Pylyshyn Z, 219
Pyryt MC, 127
Pyszczynski T, 272, 276

**Q**

Quadrel MJ, 451
Qualls WJ, 334
Quera V, 176

# SUBJECT INDEX

# CUMULATIVE INDEXES

## CONTRIBUTING AUTHORS, VOLUMES 39–49

# CHAPTER TITLES, VOLUMES 39–49